WELCOME TO MY HOME
One Family, Four Countries

Roy E. Blackwood

Welcome To My Home, *One Family, Four Countries* © *Roy E. Blackwood*

ISBN: 978-0-578-47302-4

Dedication

For Wang Tei Zhu and his family, Zhao Xian and his family, Chob and Oy Petpichetchian and their sons, Natalia Himmirska, and Kalinka Georgeva. Because of them, they were experiences we will always treasure.

Acknowledgments

I didn't intend to write this book. While we were in China, I recorded about 15 hours of audio journals, which I sent back to Curt Peterson, news director at KCRB—Minnesota Public Radio. Curt did a sensitive job of choosing and editing 5-minute segments, which he aired each week. When we returned, many people told me how much they had enjoyed listening to "China Journal," and asked me if I intended to write a book based on the material. So many people asked, that I began to consider it.

I just couldn't see why I should write a book about China when so many others knew so much more about the country, the people, and the customs. I put the question to a friend and writer, Will Weaver, and he answered (as he often does) with another question: "What's the worst thing that could happen?" I said I could spend hundreds of hours writing; then not be able to find a publisher. "Then what?" he asked. I said then I would publish it myself, printing enough copies for my family and friends. He said if I only made two copies—one for each of my sons to remember the experience—that might be enough to warrant the effort. He was right. I just kept reminding myself that I was writing for Cooper and Jesse.

Then Sandra Robinson, enough of a friend to edit my first draft, reminded me that people who hadn't been to China might need to hear it differently. She was perceptive enough to know what I should keep, what I should change, and what I should get rid of. She was kind enough to tell me about the parts that were really good, and sensitive enough to know how to tell me about the parts that weren't.

I hope the book will at least make up for some of the evenings and the Saturday mornings I stole from Cooper and Jesse—and from Laurie. How do I make them up for her? All I can do is ask her, as so many times before, to understand. And (as so many times before) she will.

Fifteen years after I wrote the words above, we had spent three more years in other countries and the book on China remained an unpublished manuscript. In addition, I had copies of extensive e-mails that I had sent from Thailand, Bulgaria, and Kyrgyzstan to a short list of friends. Off and on, for another eighteen years, I toyed with the idea of putting those e-mail accounts into some sort of order to match the China manuscript, cobbling it all together, and having a few copies printed at a local print shop. When I finally searched for them in my computer storage, however, I found that because of the format in which they were written so many years ago, many of the e-mails were unintelligible to my current computer.

When I told Laurie that too much of the material was unavailable to make it work, she disappeared into deep storage in the attic, and returned with a thick, dusty manilla folder. I had completely forgotten that when she died, a sweet old lady from our church had bequeathed us printed copies of the e-mails I had sent her. For her graciousness, I hereby add Mikky McCullough's name as well-deserving of acknowledgement. Her copies, combined with the electronic material I could salvage, left few holes in the accounts of highlights from our years in Thailand, Bulgaria, and Kyrgyzstan.

Then Galen Garwood, a friend with whom I travelled around Southeast Asia fifty years ago, and who is now an author and artist who lives in Thailand, informed me by e-mail that he was going to be in the United States for a couple of months. He would be doing a promotional tour for an autobiography he had just published with the compelling title "Sell the Monkey." I invited him to visit us in Northern Minnesota, if he could fit it into his schedule. He could, and did. I had just finished compiling the material from our years abroad, and made him a computer copy to listen to when he got back to Thailand. A couple of months later, he e-mailed to say I should publish it as a book, and that he would help me through the process. I'm sure my computer illiteracy made the process more trying than he expected, but he prevailed. A fact for which I am grateful.

CONTENTS

I — CHINA

Introduction *i*
Chapter One   August 1
Chapter Two   September 21
Chapter Three   October 45
Chapter Four   November 69
Chapter Five   December 95
Chapter Six   January 117
Chapter Seven   February 141
Chapter Eight   March/April 163
Chapter Nine   April/May 173
Chapter Ten   Week of June 4 187
Epilogue 199

II — THAILAND

Introduction 203
Chapter One   June 205
Chapter Two   July 211
Chapter Three   August 221
Chapter Four   September 233
Chapter Five   October 241
Chapter Six   November 261
Chapter Seven   December 275
Chapter Eight   February 287
Chapter Nine   March 291

III — BULGARIA

Introduction 297
Chapter One   August   299
Chapter Two   September 313
Chapter Three   October   327
Chapter Four   November   337
Chapter Five   December   351
Chapter Six   January   365
Chapter Seven   February   389
Chapter Eight   March   399
Chapter Nine   April   405
Chapter Ten   May   415

IV — KYRGYZSTAN

Introduction 421
Chapter One   August and September   423
Chapter Two   October   437
Chapter Three   November   461
Chapter Four   December   481
Chapter Five   End of December and January   493
Chapter Six   March   523
Chapter Seven   April   539
Chapter Eight   May   543

AFTERWORD 545

I
CHINA

Introduction

By June of 1987, I had been teaching journalism at Bemidji State University for five years. I didn't teach summer school, but I did come in a couple of times a week to check my mail. So it was that one Friday I found in my mail a letter from the chairman of the journalism department at the Brooklyn campus of Long Island University. He wondered if I would like to be included in the first ever tour of the Chinese media by American academics. It was a project that had been arranged in conjunction with China News Service, and was being partially subsidized by them.

I called him and said I would love to go, as my research for several years had concentrated on the international media. For three weeks that August, 16 of us visited about 20 university journalism programs, newspapers, and television stations throughout eastern China. In addition to wanting to learn about the Chinese media, I had a secondary objective. I was eligible for a sabbatical leave during the 1988-89 school year, and thought it would be great to spend it teaching journalism at a Chinese university. I took every opportunity during the 3-weeks to explore that possibility with people I met.

One of those contacts developed into an agreement for an on-going faculty exchange between my university and Liaoning (Lee oh' ning) University in Shenyang (Shen yung'), the largest city in northern China. The administration of Liaoning University requested that I be their first visiting professor—a request that I welcomed.

I wasn't the only one involved, however. My wife, Laurie, and our sons, Cooper, six, and Jesse, two, also had to be considered. I had spent several years in other countries, but Laurie's only international travel had been a couple of short trips to Canada. She and Cooper, however, were both excited about spending a year in China. Jesse was too young, of course, to know what was going on, but we figured the experience couldn't hurt him.

None of us spoke any Chinese, and we expected that to be a problem, but as it turned out, knowing we didn't understand was less of a problem than thinking we did. There were many people at Liaoning University who were able, and very willing, to translate for us, so we were seldom in situations where we didn't understand what people were saying. The problem that we continually encountered, however, was understanding what was said, and assuming that we also understood what was meant.

Shortly after we arrived, my assistant introduced me to a professor who greeted me in Chinese. Obviously, as I did not speak Chinese, I had no idea what he had said, so my assistant translated, saying, "Welcome to my home." Well, that I understood, so I responded with, "We'd love to come—when would be good for you?" The man looked surprised, and there was a long pause before he said, "How about if you and your family come to dinner Friday?" I said that would be fine, and we said goodbye.

After we left, I asked my assistant what had been wrong, why the man had been so surprised when I accepted his invitation. My assistant paused, then said, "Oh, nothing, he was just thinking about when the best time would be." I wasn't entirely convinced, but I accepted his explanation. Months later, I learned that, "Welcome to my home," was a standard greeting to people visiting China, and meant something like, "I hope you are enjoying China." It wasn't an invitation to his home any more than my saying, "Hello, how are you doing?" would have been an invitation for him to catalogue his ailments and personal problems in detail.

Similar situations-in which we assumed we understood meanings just because we understood the meanings of words-plagued us throughout our year in China. We adjusted quickly, however, to most of the cultural differences, and learned to accept even those customs we didn't like, but there always remained the inherent possibility that, although we acted in good faith, we acted incorrectly. We could never be sure that our understanding of what people said to us—even in English—was cultural, as well as linguistic. Little did we know this situation would haunt us three more years in other countries.

Our experiences in China left us with a strong desire to experience other cultures—not just as tourists, but to spend enough time living among the people to begin to understand them and be accepted by them. We realized that a year wouldn't be long enough to gain a truly deep grasp of any culture, but we didn't want to become expats. We decided five years at home and one in another country would be a good compromise. Thus, we spent a year in Thailand in 1993-94, and Bulgaria in 1999-2000. I retired in the spring of 2005, but had an offer to teach in Kyrgyzstan starting that September. Cooper had just graduated from college and gotten married, Jesse had just graduated from high school and was looking to start college, and we had just sold our house. Laurie and I were discussing whether it was realistic to even consider a year abroad, when I said, "Any time we start a sentence with 'Do you remember when...', it inevitably concludes with 'China', 'Thailand', or 'Bulgaria' in there somewhere." We decided to take the offer in Kyrgyzstan. We assumed the boys would pass on it, but that we should offer to have them go with us. The five of us left that August.

Chapter One
AUGUST

We were to leave Bemidji at 6:00 a.m. and connect with a Northwest Airlines flight from Minneapolis to San Francisco. There we would transfer to CAAC (Civil Aviation Authority of China, or as it was affectionately referred to by our Chinese friends, China Air Always Cancels). There were to be stopovers in Shanghai (Shawng' hi) and Beijing (Bay zhing') before our destination of Shenyang. We left Bemidji two hours late because of a lightning storm; consequently we missed our connecting flight in Minneapolis. No problem—we caught the next available flight, and were assured we would have about an hour and five minutes to get our luggage from the Northwest baggage claim, check it onto our CAAC flight, and get on the plane. That was according to a computer print-out we were going by, but it seems the airplane wasn't.

When we got to San Francisco, I stopped at the baggage claim to pick up our eleven pieces and take them, with our carry-on luggage, to CAAC in the next building—about a 5-minute walk. Laurie went with the boys to get in line, so if it was crowded, we would be sure to have a space on the flight. I secured the services of a sky cap and cart, and had been waiting about five minutes when I heard my name being called on the paging system. I picked up a courtesy phone, and Cooper said, "Dad, Mom says the plane is leaving right now, get over here or they'll leave without us." It seems we had a choice of going to China without luggage or not going to China with luggage.

I set out immediately to "get over there," sky cap in tow with six pieces of carry-on luggage on a large cart. The metal detectors beeped frantically, and a heated discussion ensued that included the sky cap, a CAAC representative, and airport security. Meanwhile, another CAAC person hustled us, bags still unchecked, onto the plane, which I swear (although in the interest of objectivity I must admit Laurie disagrees) was making low, growling noises of impatience.

So we spent our first three weeks in China without luggage. What happened was it sat in San Francisco. As far as Northwest was concerned, that's where it was supposed to be. That's where we'd checked it—to San Francisco. As far as CAAC was concerned, it had never been checked in with them, so to them it may as well not have existed. Okay, so it was my fault—I was supposed to pick it up at the Northwest baggage claim and take it over to CAAC, but I couldn't do it. So for that we deserved three weeks with an un-toilet-trained two-year-old and no diapers?

The Chinese didn't use diapers, so we couldn't get any. What they did was dress their children in pants with slits in the crotches—the younger the child, the wider the slit. In fact, with the youngest, their little buns hung right out. The idea was that when the children had to go, they just squatted (causing the slit pants to spread open) and went. That was one of several Chinese customs we weren't willing to adopt, which left us with dish towels.

The best thing we could find to use as diapers for Jesse during those three weeks were dish towels. He didn't like it any better than we did. Of course there were no plastic pants available, so we used plastic bags, cutting the corners out of the bottoms for his legs, and tucking the tops in. Needless to say, they didn't work nearly as well as real plastic pants; especially in a situation in which Jesse's system was becoming accustomed to a different cuisine (if you get what I mean).

After almost three weeks of attempts initiated from China to do something about getting our luggage, we gave up and contacted friends in the United States. Two days later we got it. Laurie said she understood how people in developing nations must feel on receipt of care packages. We reveled in our very much missed equipment. Things like a tape recorder and tapes. Things like lecture notes and books that I needed in preparing to teach. Things like diapers.

That first night we had arrived and entered our, what they called "flat," at about midnight—having spent the past 29 hours with two small boys either in airports or on airplanes. We walked into our home for the next year: two bedrooms, a short hall, and a very small combination kitchen/bathroom. Nothing in our experience had prepared us for that.

Along one wall were a sink, a small table with two of what they called "fire rings" (basically gas hotplates), and a tiny refrigerator (about two and half feet square and nose high). Along the opposite wall were a toilet and a large bathtub. The toilet was what, in China, they called "Western style," in other words, the kind we had back home. It was the exception rather than the rule. Everywhere except in the foreign faculty and foreign student housing, they had "Asian style" toilets. They were oblong, porcelain-lined holes in the floor—maybe a foot and a half wide by two and a half feet long. The idea was to put one foot on either side and squat over them. Cooper and Jesse (after he started using them) had no problem. Laurie and I, however, seemed to have lost our squatting ability at some time in our youth, and had to have something to grab hold of to keep from falling in.

The tub had a faucet with a diverter; the kind that can be used to either fill the tub or send water to a hand-held shower. There was no shower curtain, but that didn't really matter, because the walls and floor were tile, and there was a floor drain in the low point of the floor that any overspray drained into—along with water from the tub, which emptied onto the floor near the drain. We agreed that when the door was open, the room would be the kitchen, and when the door was closed it would be the bathroom, with the latter having priority in questionable cases.

Opposite the door sat the Chinese version of a washer and drier. It was an automatic washer about the size of a trash compactor—and about as gentle with our clothes. Jesse's diapers, being of much softer material than the rest of our clothes, were especially vulnerable. They shredded a bit more each time we washed them, and we began to worry whether they would last through toilet training. It was a race with time and nature. Even when things looked their darkest, however, we couldn't bring ourselves to go with the slit

Our kitchen/bathroom in one of its tidier moments.

pants. It was close. We were down to using triple layers for even minimal effectiveness when Jesse finally decided he'd had enough of that nonsense, and toilet trained himself, literally overnight. It wasn't the most momentous day of our stay, but it ranked right up there.

The drier wasn't really a drier. We called it a "damper" because what it did was spin the clothes very fast, forcing some of the water out with centrifugal force. The clothes weren't really dry, however, and we still had to hang them somewhere—anywhere we could find. We had clothes strung all over the apartment most of the time. The first few days we were there were extremely humid, and we ended up wearing damp clothes most of the time.

Laurie's and my bedroom was about nine by twelve feet, and served as Laurie's office, as well. With a large double bed and a desk and chair, there was just enough room left to get into bed. The other room, which was about ten by twelve feet, served as our living room and dining room, as well as the boy's bedroom. When we arrived, the two single beds extended from one wall into the center of the room, in the typical hotel room setup, leaving very little room for anything else. We moved them into one corner against the walls and used them as couches during the day, which gave us a bit more room. Two easy chairs, two straight-backed chairs, a small folding table, and a large color television completed the furnishings.

All but the bathroom had off-white, plastic, drop ceilings. The walls were covered with off-white, flocked, plasticized wallpaper, which because of moisture problems in the concrete behind it, tended to come loose in many places. The floor in our bedroom/office was covered with brightly patterned, yellow/green linoleum (not glued down, but the bed and desk held it pretty much in place). The boys' room/living room/dining room sported a bright red indoor/outdoor carpet (also not glued down).

Our quarters seemed quite small for a family of four, but we adapted quickly—after all, the smaller the apartment, the less to clean. We found, as we visited Chinese friends, that our apartment was about average in size for senior faculty, and larger than most people's. It was certainly nicer than most homes we visited, in that they almost all had bare concrete floors, and nothing but whitewash on the walls and ceilings.

For example, the dean of my department was one of the most highly-respected scholars in Northern China. He lived with his wife, their daughter, their son-in-law, and their infant grandson in an apartment that had two bedrooms of about ten by twelve feet (one which doubled as the dean's office), a living room about the same size, an even smaller kitchen, a bathroom just large enough for a tub and toilet, and a kind of open area that doubled as a hallway and eating area. They had a folding table they put up at dinnertime, and moved chairs in from the other rooms. They had only cold running water, so had to heat water for bathing.

Whatever our apartment lacked was made up for by my office. It was an absolutely gorgeous office, by Chinese standards. They adapted a meeting room that had couches, easy chairs and coffee tables in it. They took out most of them, but left a couple of couches and chairs for me. They put in a couple of desks, some bookcases, a reading table and chairs, a coat tree, and a wash stand complete with soap and towel. It was wonderful—very comfortable. It smelled a bit musty in the morning when I first came in, and I realized why when I touched the wall—it was damp.

Workers had spent all summer renovating the building—it was of Soviet design and about 35 years old, from the time when relations between Beijing and Moscow were much more cordial. They must not have included the roof in the renovation plan, because it leaked—badly. During the year, I watched the finish work they had done just before I moved in deteriorate in one corner of the room. By the time I left, I had to sweep fallen plaster from that corner daily. Despite that small inconvenience, the office was wonderful, and the members of my host department were much more bothered by its

Cooper and Jesse in front of one of the couch
beds in our living room/dining room/boys' bedroom.

shortcoming than I. One or more of them would come by every week or two to cluck their tongues and apologize to me for the inconvenience. At least that's what I think they were saying—I tried to make them understand that it didn't matter, but they were such impeccable hosts, that I'm sure it bothered them for years.

Shenyang was big, dirty, and polluted. Coal dust sifted everywhere, even in August, when most of it resulted from their shoveling it around into piles, getting ready to burn it during the winter. The little bit of burning they did in the summer (other than in the manufacturing districts) was in the small boilers they kept going to boil water. We couldn't drink the water unless it had been boiled. That took a bit of getting used to.

We kept a bottle of boiled water in the refrigerator that lasted us about a day. Laurie boiled a large kettle each evening. We let it cool overnight; then in the morning, along with washing, shaving, and brushing my teeth, I would pour it into the nearly-empty bottle in the refrigerator. It's funny how quickly things like that fit into a routine. It wasn't long before we didn't even think about it (much) anymore, we just did it.

The Chinese also boiled their water, but they didn't wait for it to get cold. In addition to using hot water for tea and occasionally a vile Chinese version of instant coffee, they drank their water hot. The milk wasn't pasteurized, so it had to be boiled, as well. The Chinese drank it hot, usually with a teaspoon or two of sugar. We just couldn't get used to hot water or hot milk—especially hot, sweet milk—although it was great for making cocoa for the boys.

Every morning at breakfast we bought a liter of hot milk in the dining room, took it up to our apartment, and put it in the refrigerator. The next morning we took it down cold, poured it into glasses for breakfast, and got the container refilled with hot milk. We did the same sort of thing for beer. They sold returnable bottles of warm beer in the dining room, so we bought a few warm beers and put them in the refrigerator. As we drank our cold beers, we returned the bottles for the deposit, and bought more warm beer. It was a quite workable system—we just had to keep track of which end of the row was the cold beer, and which end was the getting-cold beer.

The Chinese couldn't accept the fact that they were host to people so barbaric as to drink cold water, so our housekeeper also brought us freshly boiled water each morning and each afternoon. We had two very large, very efficient thermos bottles. U.S. manufacturers could take some lessons from the Chinese in making thermos bottles. Those Chinese bottles kept water hot enough for a couple of days to make instant coffee or tea.

Our housekeeper brought in a huge kettle of freshly boiled water, uncorked (yep, they used real corks) our thermoses, clucked disapprovingly at how little water we had used, and spoke sternly in what we had to assume constituted a scolding for not drinking enough hot water and a warning that we would surely get sick if we didn't do better. She then poured the old, hot water into the bathtub and replaced it with new, hotter water. After a couple of months, we had a brainstorm.

We paid careful attention to her schedule—not very difficult, for it seldom varied by more than a matter of minutes—then began pouring most of the old, hot water into the sink to use for washing dishes before she came to replace it with the new, hotter water. It saved us having to heat water to do the dishes, but more importantly, it gained our housekeeper's approval and convinced her we were much healthier for our increased intake of hot water.

The process of day-to-day living was much more time-consuming for us in China than it was in the States, because we lacked many of the labor-saving devices we were used to. Most of the Chinese had at least one retired grandparent in their home who took care of preschool children, cleaned, cooked, and did the laundry. Neither Laurie nor I could see our parents thriving in that situation, so we didn't proffer the invitation. Therefore, we were without the benefit of extended family, and when both of us began teaching, were hard-pressed to get everything done and still have time to spend with the boys.

To alleviate the situation, we hired our housekeeper to do our laundry. For about $10 a month, which probably doubled her salary, she collected our dirty clothes on Mondays, Wednesdays and Friday. She washed them and returned them the next day. At first, she was unwilling to do the job, which surprised us, because of the amount of money she stood to make. After some awkward discussion with the interpreter from the Foreign Affairs Office, we understood the problem: she refused to have anything to do with the clearly barbaric custom of washing Jesse's dirty diapers (an attitude that I must admit didn't diminish her a bit in my mind). After we explained that we did that little task separately, she agreed. A couple of the other apartments were usually unoccupied, so she used the washers in them and hung our laundry in them to dry.

Now, our housekeeper was a wonderful woman—very conscientious. She did a great job with our laundry. She was very friendly and paid a lot of attention to the boys. She even tried to teach Cooper some of the positions of the traditional Chinese exercise—without overwhelming success, it just moved too slowly for him. But she had one unforgivable shortcoming.

Every time she came into the apartment—whether to bring hot water, pick up our laundry, vacuum the rug, hose down the bathroom, or take out the trash—she left the door wide open. We had screens on the windows, but no screen door, so when the door was open, mosquitoes came in. Then they hid until the middle of the night.

American mosquitoes are bad enough, but Chinese mosquitoes didn't sound the same—their wings were different or something, and the resulting whine was at a different pitch. Even if they didn't bite—which they did— just their sound drove me crazy. I would wake up at 3:00 a.m., leap out of bed like someone possessed, turn on the lights, and start throwing pillows at mosquitoes. It wasn't Laurie's favorite thing for me to do, but she's a good woman, and an understanding wife—she was in touch with the sorts of things that could have tipped the scales of sanity for me during that year.

We assumed that with the advent of cold weather we would see the last of my midnight tussles, but Chinese mosquitoes were also hardy. One night in mid-November I was awakened by one of them chewing ardently on my ear. I whopped him so hard my ear rang for about 15 minutes, but it was worth it, "knowing" he was the last one of the season. A couple of weeks later, however, we were set upon by another.

I don't know where he came from, or where he hid during the day, but we saw him every couple of days. He was cunning. I spent weeks tracking him. I was reminded of the northern Minnesota legend of Lobo the Wolf: hundreds of farmers and hunters after him for years, but unable to get him because he was old, wise, and experienced. I thought maybe I had discovered "Lobo the Mosquito," with wisdom beyond his years. I couldn't get him. He kept eluding my grasp. The funny thing is, he didn't bite anybody, so we couldn't complain too much. Just when we had decided to tame him and keep him as a pet—were discussing what tricks we might teach him—he disappeared. We all missed him.

One thing that took a lot of getting used to was the sheer number of people. There were more than a billion people in China, and about 4 1/2 million of them were in Shenyang. As in all Chinese cities, there were not very many cars, quite a few heavy trucks, but mostly bicycles.

It didn't take us long to learn our way around. As with many large cities, Shenyang is really just a collection of small neighborhoods crammed together in one space. We found most of the things we needed day by day in stores on or near the campus. They were very haphazard sorts of little stores that seemed to have the strangest assortment of things. They may have had soap, meat, fruit, candy, cigarettes, wine, and toys, but only a few of any one thing, and it didn't seem to make a whole lot of sense. They might have bath soap, but not laundry soap; or they might have chicken, but not pork; then a store a block away would have pork, but not chicken. It seemed to us a very strange way of doing things, and it was difficult for us at first, because we didn't know which stores had which things, so it was a matter of trial and error. Eventually, however, we began to find which store had the kind of soap that seemed to work best, and which had eggs, and which had fresh vegetables.

Right outside the gates of the university compound there was a relatively large general store that had—among other things—bicycles, mattresses, electrical equipment, fruit, vegetables, and bread. The impression we got was that they carried whatever they could get, so they didn't always have the same things. We would buy something in a store; then go back a week later deciding we'd like another one, and that store wouldn't have them any longer. The store across the street might have them, whereas the week before it hadn't. It was a hide 'n seek process, trying to find the things we needed.

These stores were government-owned, and until a couple of years before our visit, they were the only alternative. That had changed—a couple of blocks away, on the corner, were two yogurt ladies, a fry bread lady, and a bicycle repair man. Turn the corner, and there were about two blocks of what we used to call "free market." We were told, however, that was no longer acceptable terminology. They must have figured if those were free markets, then nothing else in China was free, so they requested that we call them "agricultural produce stands." Never mind the fact that they might also sell very non-agricultural items such as toys or clothes. Anyway, there were about two blocks of agricultural produce stands. They were very orderly—all of the fruits first and then all of the vegetables. We found the reason for the order was that it was a government sanctioned area, so each stand was licensed.

First came a stretch of stands that were semi-permanent, metal structures, obviously assigned to a person or family. There followed a series of homemade wooden stands that were not permanent, but either wheeled in or constructed anew each day. Finally, there were positions that were no more than spots of ground on which a person or family had the right to spread produce. It was clear that the original intent of the government, to provide limited opportunity for free commerce, had been over-run and the process had lagged far behind expansion. Evidence of this was the fact that many non-government markets existed.

Anywhere space permitted, entrepreneurs had set up shop on the sidewalks and streets. In fact, efforts were often made where space did not permit, resulting in sometimes awesome traffic jams and police intervention. As nearly as we could tell, such interference with the flow of traffic was the only situation that brought about official repercussions. Otherwise the sellers seemed free to operate when, where, and as they pleased. The resulting situation was one in which buyers might save money at non-sanctioned markets, but they had no recourse if their purchase did not meet their expectations. We saw many arguments that resulted from disagreements about whether buyers had been ill-served, some escalating to physical blows.

About eight blocks from the university was one of the biggest markets in the city—the equivalent of most major supermarkets in the United States. Creatively named the North Market, to distinguish it from a similar facility on the south side of town, it was situated in an X-shaped alley, two blocks along each axis. The market contained half-block long counters of seafood, pork, fowl, grain, and eggs; and block-long counters of vegetables and fruit. It also offered counters of clothes, watches, toys, kitchen utensils, bike parts, and numerous other commodities. Stories of a China deprived of food and other basic goods were obviously outdated.

On the counters of the North Market were just about anything we could find in a Western supermarket—rather the Chinese version of anything we could find. One of the challenges we faced was trying to cook Western meals. We had access to a dining room, but it offered a very limited menu, and being used to more variety, it didn't take long for us to weary of their selection.

The dining room, which was immediately adjacent to our apartment building, served breakfast from 7:15 to 7:40 a.m., lunch from 12:00 to 12:40 p.m., and dinner from 6:00 to 6:40 p.m. If we wanted to eat, those were the times we ate—the doors were unlocked and locked on time—no exceptions. This rigid scheduling was one of many examples of lack of flexibility compared to what we were used to in the States, but we worked it into our routine and it became part of our everyday expectations.

There was only one menu for lunch and dinner, and we had to order during breakfast what we thought we would want for lunch, and at lunch for dinner. The menu was less than varied—it contained 30 items, but only ten were available at a time. It was in three columns of ten items each. We could order from column one for three days, column two for three days, column three for three days, and then back to column one. Of course the whole thing was in Chinese, so we had to get someone from the Foreign Affairs Office to make us an English translation, which we carried with us to meals. It consisted of the Chinese, the English translation, and—as we ordered in neither English or Chinese—the number of each item on the menu.

After breakfast I would go to a little pad they had on the counter and write my name (the one thing I learned to write in Chinese), and the numbers of three or four items I thought we might like for lunch. The problem was that every few days they changed some of the items on the menu. It was on a chalkboard, so it was easy for them to erase an item and write in a new one. The new item, then, would have the same number the old one had, with the result that I sometimes thought I was ordering one thing, and ended up with something entirely different.

Another problem was getting the boys, who had just finished eating their breakfast, to decide what they wanted for lunch. Good luck—preschool boys don't know if they want the food on their plates, let alone what they'll want in four or five hours. We also didn't have a clue how much they would eat. Some days they ate everything we put in front of them, plus part of our food; others, it was, "But I'm just not hungry, Dad," and we ended up with more material for "leftover soup" than we could use. Anyway, it was the rule, so each morning I would test my clairvoyance, and would choose about four items I thought we might like—or at least be willing to eat—for lunch. Items ranged from "salt horse" (which we never did try, but were told was a very salty beef dish) to what they called "salad," which was sliced cucumbers and tomatoes. They had noodles, and they had rice—plain rice, fried rice, boiled rice—rice just about any way we might want it.

Most of the dishes, however, were primarily vegetables: scrambled eggs with peppers, scrambled eggs with onions, and scrambled eggs with what the boys called "skinny beans"—a long, thin, crunchy green bean that tasted somewhat like what, in the States are called "pole beans." We had scrambled eggs with pork, pork with peppers, pork with onions, and pork with "skinny beans." We ate lots of pork, eggs, onions, and beans, in just about any combination of two imaginable, but almost never more than two in combination. And had they been held to truth in labelling laws, they would have had to name the dishes with the vegetables first, because they had very little pork and a lot of vegetables. Consequently, it was difficult for us to maintain the variety we were used to, and we decided to cook our evening meals in our apartment.

Our first attempt was as close as we could get to bratwurst on buns, with corn on the cob and salad. The bratwurst was actually some kind of Chinese sausage. We never did figure out quite what, but it was sort of halfway between hot dogs and bratwurst. The salad was chunks of cabbage, tomato, and cucumber with a kind of oil and vinegar dressing we were able to put together. It was a very poor approximation, frankly, of the real thing. The longer we were there, however, the more ingredients we were able to track down that bore passable resemblance to those we used back home. Also, Laurie is a very good cook and I'm pretty good, so, as with most things, we got better as we gained experience. Either that, or the longer we were there, the more our memory of the real thing faded.

By the time we left, though, we were having dinners such as meatballs, mashed potatoes and gravy, toast, and wilted Chinese cabbage; or steak, baked potatoes, and tossed salad. We made things that closely resembled pizza, chili, and New England boiled dinner. Our favorite dinner to serve Chinese friends was hamburgers and French fries.

One cultural difference between China and the U.S. we learned as a result of something that happened in the dining room. In the States, we had learned to expect that rules would be clearly posted or provided in some written form. In China, the attitude seemed to be that there was no sense messing with all that. Only if a particular rule applied would it be brought to someone's attention. This situation was difficult for us to accept. The Chinese seemed willing to trust the rule makers, and didn't give it a second thought, but to us it seemed like playing a game with a child who makes up new rules as the game progresses.

The dining room was set up with a counter where, at exactly noon, a young woman began handing out the dishes we had ordered at breakfast. Everybody came right at noon, because the later we came, the longer our food sat, and the colder it got. So, there were often 35 or 40 foreign faculty and students competing for service. The students had several advantages: first, they were there studying Chinese, so they could make themselves understood much better than we could. Second, as faculty, we could hardly be expected to take part in the shouting matches that sometimes evolved when hungry young people were impatient for their food. Third, the students were fending only for themselves. They had ordered one dish apiece, so when they got that dish, they could sit down and eat.

As a family of four, even when we got our dishes, we still had to have plates and bowls to eat from. Although the chopsticks were out where each person could get her or his own, the plates and bowls were behind the counter, because the dining room workers said too many of them had been taken away by students and never returned. So, we had to ask for them, a difficult process with many hungry students trying to get food at the same time.

In an effort to help alleviate the problem, Cooper had started going behind the counter to get the bowls and plates we needed. It seemed to work well: the woman behind the counter had one less thing to worry about, and Cooper felt good about being helpful. Unfortunately, as sometimes happens with six-year-olds, Cooper dropped three bowls one day. The consternation was great among the staff, and they charged us the equivalent of 15 cents apiece for them. That wasn't much money, but I balked on principle. It

Daily collection of leftovers dumped out of cafeteria window.

seemed capricious and arbitrary that we should be charged for those bowls when Cooper was only trying to help.

I said that we had often seen people go behind the counter when they needed something and couldn't get the attendant's attention, and argued that it's pretty difficult to tell a six-year-old he shouldn't do something when it is clearly helpful, and besides grownups are doing it. I was told that the rules of the dining room were: 1) people other than staff weren't allowed behind the counter, and 2) if you broke anything, you had to pay for it. I asked who wrote those rules and where were they—I hadn't seen them anywhere. They said they weren't written down. I asked if anybody had ever told us those rules. They said maybe not. I said it's pretty hard to abide by the rules if you don't know what they are. They gave up and gave us our money back.

Although I didn't really care about the money, I considered its return tacit admission of the fact that things were not as they should have been. After all, I reasoned, if there were going to be rules, then everybody should know what those rules were, and everybody should obey them equally. I saw the return of the money as their capitulation in the face of my overwhelming logic. It wasn't until much later that I realized it was nothing of the kind. They had given our money back as a practical measure to get me to go away and stop being obnoxious—and it had worked. The fact was that the Chinese did not feel comfortable with written rules—they lacked flexibility.

Chinese breakfast was a kind of rice gruel—a watery porridge of hot rice—accompanied by several small saucers of salty, chopped vegetables. The idea was to mix some of the salty vegetables with each mouthful of rice gruel. It just wasn't the kind of thing we particularly wanted for breakfast, so we learned to substitute. Chinese yogurt was very cheap, and much better, to our taste, than what we got in the States. We could buy it on many street corners, except in the winter. Fruit was readily available all year—although it was significantly more expensive in the winter—so most mornings Laurie and I had fruit and yogurt.

The boys didn't eat the yogurt, but liked the rice porridge with a spoonful of sugar and some milk. They said it was just like hot cereal back home. I couldn't taste even a vague resemblance. Laurie agreed with them, but I didn't see her eating it very often, so I assume her support was to humor them in case we couldn't find anything else they would eat. If so, her fears were groundless. After we had been there a while, we found a cold cereal they liked even better.

On many of the street corners, they sold what they called "exploded corn." When we first heard the phrase, Laurie and I smiled smugly at each other; amused at the quaint mistranslation of "popcorn." Then we saw it made. They poured field corn (with or without a pinch of sugar for sweetening) into containers that were basically pressure cookers rigged on spits over charcoal fires. The vendor turned a crank with each hand—one operating a bellows to keep the charcoal fire very hot; the other turning the pressure cooker to keep the corn from lying on the bottom and burning.

When the corn inside the pressure cooker reached a very high temperature and pressure, the vendor put one end inside a big wire basket, yanked back on a release lever popping the end open, and the corn—with a sound like a cannon—literally exploded into the wire container. It was so loud that when we were walking or riding bike, and Jesse saw a vendor ahead, he made us take a detour because he said the sound hurt his ears. The corn puffs that resulted were pretty good immediately, but quickly got too stale to eat. From the first time we saw it made, we too, referred to it as "exploded corn."

One day, when Laurie and Jesse were out walking, she noticed a vendor loading rice into his container instead of corn. Intrigued, she stopped to watch. Her reaction when the puffed rice exploded into the basket was, "Why didn't we think of that?" A quick trip to the market for a pound of rice (about 30 cents), a few minutes wait while he puffed it (about 10 cents), and we had three week's worth of breakfast cereal for the boys.

We all supplemented our breakfasts with the Chinese version of toast.

Steamed buns were a staple in northern China, and when the cooks sliced them in half and tossed them into boiling oil, the result was a deep-fried toast. It was delicious, and we ate it in vast quantities with peanut butter and jelly. Jelly, although scarce when we first got there, became readily available before we left. We thought at first we would not be able to get peanut butter, but after a diligent search, found it in one store and bought all they had.

It was in little containers, about the size of individual servings of coleslaw slaw or baked beans at Kentucky Fried Chicken. Our Chinese friends told us the reason they were so little was that they use peanut butter only to season cold dishes. The store had six of those little containers in stock, so we bought them all. My interpreter was with us that day, so we had him inform them we would be willing to buy that much every week if they could get it. They said they would check and see if they could start ordering that much, but we didn't really hold much hope—it was a government store, so for them to make any changes in their ordering system would probably have required approval at the highest levels of bureaucracy. We were right—they never got any more before we left—nor could we find it anywhere else. So, peanut butter was not available—but it doesn't take a chemist to figure out how to make it.

We found a small meat grinder, and became one peanut vendor's favorite family. Peanuts, by Chinese standards, were a bit expensive—about 60 cents a pound—so they don't buy much at a time, using them mostly as a snack, or as a garnish on some dishes. Try to tell that to young American boys, for whom peanut butter has been the elixir of life. We went through at least a pound a week.

The meat grinder produced a consistency about halfway between creamy and chunky, and with a couple tablespoons of soybean oil and a pinch of salt, it was every bit as good as any we had eaten back home. It took about an hour to make a decent-sized batch of peanut butter, and that only lasted us about a week. We had a list of repetitive things to do, such as boiling water every evening, so we just added a weekly stint of peanut butter making to the list.

We were told that butter was unavailable in northern China, but found that was not true. Butter was available, it just wasn't in stock at any of the stores. We became friends with a young Australian named Peter, who worked for his embassy in Beijing. He had studied Chinese at Liaoning University for several years, and returned often to visit his fiancee, a young Chinese woman who was an English teacher there.

One morning when we were eating breakfast with him, Laurie mentioned she missed butter for her toast. To our surprise, he said, "Oh, they have butter in Shenyang." When we fell all over ourselves asking where, he said, "Number two dairy—about six blocks from here." He said it was rather difficult to find, because it didn't look anything like the dairies we were used to, but he gave us directions, and wrote the characters for "dairy" on a piece of paper for us.

Thus equipped, we set off at our first opportunity in search of the elusive butter. After following his directions as best we could, we found ourselves in a residential neighborhood that clearly could not house a dairy. Before giving up, however, we showed the paper to the bicycle repairman on the corner. He grinned and pointed down the alley behind him. Clearly he had misunderstood what we wanted—that minuscule track obviously did not lead to one of the biggest dairies in a town of almost five million. We didn't want to make the old guy feel bad, however, so we humored him and pedaled down the alley. All there was were little houses behind the ubiquitous brick wall. Then there was a break in the wall. We looked in and saw thousands of bottles in cases.

They were empty, but looked very much like the little glass pint bottles we used to get before plastic jugs and cardboard cartons. Laurie said, "That looks more dairy-like than anything we've seen so far," so we went through the gate. Inside was a loading dock with people transferring bottles onto trucks and donkey carts. Some looked to be full of milk, so we went around the building to the only door we could find. It looked like the employees' entrance, and there were employee-looking people sitting on the steps. We parked our bikes and showed them the characters that Peter had written for us. They smiled, nodded vigorously, and said what I assumed was, "Yes, yes, this is a dairy." I mentally kicked myself for not having Peter write the characters for "butter" on the same piece of paper, and launched into an impromptu game of charades. Maybe they play charades in China too, or I'm just good at nonverbal communication, but they didn't seem to have much difficulty recognizing my spreading motions as applying butter to bread and not a sudden itch in my palm. They said the Chinese words for "yes, yes" (The Chinese never said "yes" or "no" any less than twice, and often several times, in response to questions.), so I took my wallet out and made questioning noises like, "Can I buy some?" They replied—twice—in the affirmative.

They took us upstairs, down a dingy, dimly-lit hall into a dingy, dimly-lit room—the inspection standards for Chinese dairies were clearly from a different manual that those in the States. There, they presented us to a person who, judging from her dexterity with an abacus, must have been their accountant. We spent the next 15 minutes with her and an ever-increasing number of others—peaking at about 20—in the room, all talking in Chinese at the same time to Laurie and me, to the boys, and to each other. My ability at charades had been established, but I defy the best to quickly work out how much butter is being purchased, and for what cost—especially when both the units of measure and the units of payment—not to mention the language of discourse—are unfamiliar.

After about a half hour we had agreed to buy an amount of butter that I understood to be equivalent to about a double handful, for what, by Chinese standards, seemed a pretty steep price. We filled out some forms in triplicate—standard procedure at government-run facilities. One of the workers went down the hall and returned with a glob of something that looked reassuringly like butter. He asked what we had brought to carry it in, and didn't seem thrilled when we said "nothing."

The forms were already completed, however, and the money stowed in their safe, so they set out to find something for us. We were a bit surprised when the result was a large plastic bag, similar to those we got bread in back home, but of a consistency more like that we got on clothes coming back from dry-cleaning. It looked pretty well used, but we didn't argue.

We found out later that the measure of weight they were using was a standard one equivalent to half a kilogram, so it was close enough to a pound that we just thought of it as such. We figured out that we had paid the equivalent of about $1.50 a pound for the butter—placing it among the more expensive Chinese commodities—but it was delicious. It was sweet butter, which we were not used to, but the taste was great. Although it was a bit of a hassle to spend an hour at the dairy just to buy butter, we considered it well worth it. By the next spring, when we found the dairy stopped producing butter during the summer, it had become more available, and we could get it in one-pound packages in a few stores.

During a subsequent trip to the dairy, I asked for cheese, and was told it was available only in Beijing. We found that although it was available in Beijing, it was only at stores for Westerners, and at prices way beyond our means. Where we missed cheese most was for pizza. Pizza is just not the same without cheese. The boys were crazy about pizza and, not surprisingly, we couldn't get it in China. We found reasonable substitutes for all the other ingredients, and we ran down several leads about where to get cheese while we were in China, but we never did find any we could afford, so it became our favorite article in packages from home.

We did find a way to make a sort of cheese curd. Interestingly, the recipe was in a book of creative play activities for children. Laurie's background is in early childhood education, so she's never without such great resources. The recipe was very easy: heat milk until just before it boils and stir in a tablespoon of vinegar. When it begins to curdle, pour it into a clean handkerchief or dish towel and squeeze all the whey out of it. After refrigeration, the result is a ball like one big cottage cheese curd. With a little salt, it was very tasty, but didn't melt worth a darn, creating some of the strangest pizza we'd ever eaten.

Finding the necessary ingredients for chili was an interesting process. We put more ingredients in our chili than most people: onions, green peppers, mushrooms, tomatoes, tomato sauce, beans, and spices. The first five were no problem—we eventually found all of them in nearby markets—but we never did find dry beans—at least not the kidney or pinto beans we were used to. What they did have was something called "mung beans." They were a bit like pinto beans, only about the size of the dried peas we used for split pea soup back home. They tasted similar to kidney beans, only we never could get them soft enough. Even after soaking them for two days, and boiling them for several hours, they lent a noticeable crunch to chili or baked beans. For several months, that was the best we could do, though. Then we found sprouted soybeans. They made chili and baked beans that tasted a bit different than we were used to, but they were much easier to use, and the texture was so much better, we switched to them.

We enjoy split pea soup, so were pleased when we found what we thought were dried peas. When we tried to use them to make pea soup, however, they didn't work at all. They were just as hard after being soaked for three days and boiled for another, so we gave up. I'm not sure what they were, but green pebbles might be a good guess.

A common Chinese dish, which we enjoyed, was stir-fried peas in the pod. One day I found some peas at the market that were about half the usual price, and being a smart shopper, I snatched up just short of a ton of them. Imagine my dismay when the boys, who usually gobbled up peas, wouldn't eat them. Imagine my further dismay when I tried to eat mine and realized why. Not only were the pods tough and fibrous, but the peas inside were very starchy and semi-dry. Having a large supply of these fossilized peas, and being the kind of person who will not waste food, I was left with only one alternative—to be creative. There was no hope for the pods, but I found that the shelled peas made (you guessed it) something very like pea soup. It wasn't the real thing, but in the absence of the real thing, it was certainly acceptable.

Sundays were the only time we cooked breakfast. Both Laurie and I taught classes on Saturday morning, so Sundays were the only days we could sleep in—that is, of course, if we were willing to either do without a morning shower, take it in cold water, or move it to the night before. Generally, we took it the night before and slept in until about 7:00. Then we got up and Laurie played with the boys while I made Western-style breakfasts. They always included fruit salad, accompanied at various times by eggs Benedict, pancakes, French toast, American fries, hash browns, fried eggs, scrambled eggs, and omelets.

Something we couldn't find when we first got there were breakfast meats, such as ham, bacon, or sausage. We found a pre-cooked lunch meat, however, that the Chinese called sausage, but that resembled a cross between ham and salami. They generally used small pieces of it chopped up in soup for flavor. It was pretty greasy cold, but sliced and fried, it made very good sand-

Grinding peanut butter on our dining room.

wiches, and was pretty good as a breakfast meat. A couple of months before we left, they began to stock a very high quality—and by Chinese standards, very expensive—canned ham. At the equivalent of about $2.25 a pound, it was some of the most expensive food we bought in Shenyang.

We couldn't find any maple syrup for our pancakes and French toast, but we could get plenty of haw apples, which were like small, sweet crab apples. By boiling them down and mixing them with sugar, we created a very tasty syrup. One concession we made to our Western desires was to have "real" coffee sent from home. We found an orange drink, which, although not exactly the same as fresh-squeezed orange juice, at least wasn't carbonated and sweetened.

We often invited Chinese friends for Sunday brunch (try cooking an omelet for six in a round-bottomed wok), and after we got to know them well enough, we asked them to rate the various Western dishes. As fruit is a common food for them, we assumed they would rank the fruit salad first, but to our surprise, it was usually third or fourth. We asked why, and they said it was strange for them to have fruit with, rather than before or after their meal, and it was unheard of to cut several kinds of fruit into pieces and mix them together. They most often named omelets, pancakes and French toast as favorites. Eggs Benedict—which, of course, were by far the most difficult to prepare—were always at the bottom of their lists.

The Chinese were very gracious hosts, and loved to entertain; especially when a meal was involved. Often, the guests came hours before the meal, and everyone took part in the preparation. A couple of weeks after we arrived at the university, my assistant invited us to his home for dinner. He and his wife lived with her parents, and her father was the dean of my department. My dean and his wife didn't speak English, nor did my assistant's wife, so he served as interpreter for that and many subsequent family get-togethers.

For our first visit, they wanted to teach us to make jiao zi (jow' dza)—a half-moon-shaped dumpling filled with a very finely-chopped mixture of seafood, meat, and vegetables. They were usually steamed or boiled, but sometimes fried. A traditional Chinese food, they were often used as an integral part of the celebration of holidays and special events. We said we'd be please to come to his house for dinner, but please not to do anything extravagant. We knew the Chinese were very proud people who put a lot of store in ceremony and gift giving. We had heard that usually when they invited people to their home for the first time, they prepared a full-scale banquet and probably spent a month's salary on the preparations. We asked him not to do that, and said that we'd rather just share an ordinary meal with them. He said okay they wouldn't, but we asked the impossible.

We went over, and they showed us how to make the jiao zi. It seemed the preparation of the filling was boring and time-consuming, so it wasn't considered part of the shared ritual. They had it already prepared, and the dough mixed when we arrived. After we thoroughly washed our hands, the participatory part began with one person making little balls of dough, and another using a small, handleless, rolling pin—about six inches long and two inches in diameter—to roll the balls into thin, circular, crepe-like cakes.

A third person put little globs of the filling on the center of the crepes, folded them in half over the filling, and pinched the edges together. The results looked much like tiny apple turnovers. We were slow, but our hosts assured us we did well—with one exception. Usually, after we pinched the edges together, one of them would patiently show us how they should be pinched. We tried every pinching method known to humanity, and invented some of our own, but to no avail. I'm sure it was just our unpracticed eyes, but I asked Laurie, and she agreed she could see no difference whatsoever between the edges of the ones we had pinched and those pinched by our friends. Several times, however, out of the corner of my eye, I saw them surreptitiously re-pinching ones I thought I had snuck onto the tray unnoticed. They said Cooper was the only one of us foreigners who really pinched correctly.

When they started setting the table, we couldn't believe the food they had: sweet and sour prawns, an expensive whole fish in sauce, and all sorts of other very fancy, very expensive dishes. I said to my assistant, "I thought you promised you wouldn't do this." He said, "Well, I promised I wouldn't, but my father-in-law insisted, and as he is both the head of my household and your dean, we're having a banquet." It was an extravagant affair—absolutely delicious—and we couldn't possibly eat all of the food they set before us.

It was that evening we learned another Chinese custom that was very different from ours. At a dinner in the States, if guests fail to finish the food on their plates, their hosts are likely to assume they didn't like it. In China, if we cleaned our plates, they immediately refilled them. Custom dictated that if they didn't, it was because they didn't have enough food for their guests, and they would be shamed. That was no problem for Cooper and Jesse, boys that age seldom clean their plates. For Laurie and me, however, it was a different story.

Chinese hosts often serve their guests, at least for the first plate full, so we didn't always get the most of what we liked most and the least of what we liked least, as in family-style, "pass the mashed potatoes, please" dinners in the States. We ate every scrap, though—even of the things, such as sea slugs, that weren't our favorite. After all, they had clearly gone to a lot of effort and expense for that meal, and we didn't want to seem ungrateful.

Because we were eating from dishes only about three inches in diameter, it was no problem the first few times they rushed to refill them. Imagine our consternation, though, when over our most vocal protests, they were refilled for the eighth and ninth times. As serving dishes were emptied they were rushed from the room. After delays—during which sounds of cooking emanated from the kitchen—they were returned, brimming. Despite our resolve to triumph as good guests, we eventually succumbed to the onslaught of food, and were unable to clean our plates. We apologized for our inability to eat another bite, and they assured us, with what we later realized were looks of profound relief, that it was quite alright.

As we prepared to leave, I told my assistant we'd never come to their home again if every time we came they spent that much money. He said, "No, just the first time," in a way that led me to believe he had not been forced by his father-in-law at all, and promised that next time we came it would be for a "simple Chinese family-style meal." Of course they sent half the food home with us—another Chinese custom.

In addition to containers filled with various of the dishes, Laurie counted 30 jiao zi. Well, for a Chinese family that's not many, but for us that was enough jiao zi for a month, so we reheated them and took them down to the dining room for lunch the next day. Jiao zi is a traditional food of the Japanese, as well, so the Japanese students snatched them up pretty quickly. My assistant and his family were impressed by how soon we returned the empty dishes. We didn't have the heart to tell him we shared them with the students, so to this day they probably think our family can eat jiao zi with the best of them.

Chapter Two
September

The boys adjusted very quickly; especially Jesse. The apartment was a bit cramped for them, but for the first couple of months the weather was nice enough for them to play outside, and by the time it got too nasty, they had forgotten the more ample space of what Jesse called "our Bemidji home." We were able to find Cooper a bike, and that went a long way toward keeping him occupied. It was a little big for him, and he crashed quite a bit at first, but it didn't seem to bother him too much. He had learned to ride a bike before we left home, but most of his problem was that he wanted to get on and off the way the Chinese did.

Chinese bikes were pretty well built except for two things: the valves stems and the brakes. The valve stems just didn't hold air completely. We always had to leave an extra five minutes when going anywhere to allow time to pump up our tires, which had become half-flat overnight. Each building had a pump stored inside the door for just that purpose. As with many problems in China, it was one that was not a high enough priority to be fixed, so people—including us—learned to live with it.

Inadequate brakes were something a bit harder for us to accept. The problem was that they would not stay adjusted. We chose to spend the few cents necessary to have them readjusted every few days, but most of the Chinese chose to do without. The result was that if it looked as though they were in danger of colliding with something, they would hop off, holding onto the handlebars, and run alongside the bike until they could bring it to a standstill. Keep in mind that their bike would, as often as not, be loaded with many pounds of some unwieldy load—one or two other people, for instance. This process reminded us somewhat of the bulldogging event at a Western rodeo.

If they were just taking part in a planned stop, they would stand with their weight on the left pedal, the bike leaning a bit to the right to compensate, and swing their right leg over the back of the bike to a position immediately behind their left leg. They would then coast, sometimes as much as a block, to their chosen stopping place, where they would hop off. By this time, they would be going slowly enough that a couple of short steps would be enough to bring everything to a stop.

Most of them, from years of practice, had gotten quite good at this running dismount, and they really did quite well without brakes—provided, of course, that the space between them and imminent collision was adequate. Cooper, on the other hand, lacked the prerequisite experience, and was much less successful, with the result (staying with the rodeo image) that the bull was often the victor.

The Chinese also mounted their bikes differently than we did. We never found out why—perhaps just for the sake of consistency—but they mounted much in the reverse of their dismount. Holding onto the handlebars, they took a couple of running steps, put their left foot onto the left pedal, swung their right foot over the back of the bike onto the right pedal, and took off. Incidentally, when some students saw Cooper trying to learn that process, they pointed out to him that he was doing it all wrong because he was starting with his right foot, and everyone knew the process must begin with the left. I doubt that there was any inherent political statement—simply another example of the (to us) amazing lack of individuality; the propensity for everyone in China to do things the same way.

Getting Cooper into kindergarten made a real difference for him. He started September 1, the day after he turned six. He was the only Westerner in the school, which had separate classes for children from one to six years old. We took him to the school, which was about two blocks from our living quarters, at 8:00 a.m. He had classes until 11:30, then lunch. They played all afternoon, until 4:30, when we picked him up and brought him home. That was Monday through Friday—Saturday we picked him up at noon. The Chinese children go six days a week from about 7:30 a.m. to 5:30 p.m., and have all three meals there, but they made allowances for the Westerners, and let us have him for breakfast and dinner, and Saturday afternoon.

It did not go well at first. Cooper would run away from the school and come home, saying he couldn't stand it. We assumed the problem was that he couldn't understand anyone, and that he was having trouble adjusting to a new cultural situation. Thinking the only way to overcome the problem was for him to stick it out, we took a hard line and kept sending him right back. That didn't seem to be working, so Laurie went with him for a day to see if she could figure out what the problem was.

All went well until after lunch—in fact, she was amazed at how well he had adjusted to the quite different cultural situation, and especially how much of the language he had learned in such a short time. It was after lunch, when the children were put to bed for a 3-hour nap that she understood the problem. Cooper, as with most American school children, had not been taking naps for years. Nonetheless he was expected to lie in his bed for three hours, and if he couldn't sleep, he would at least lie still with his eyes closed. That's quite a bit to ask of any normal Western 6-year-old. We arranged to begin picking him up before lunch and bringing him back after the children had finished their naps. From then on, he loved school, and went each morning with anticipation.

We learned that it wasn't just kindergarten children who took naps. Almost everything in China stopped each day from noon until 2:00 p.m., while the Chinese took their naps. I can't count the times I pedaled my bike across town after lunch to do some business, only to find the office closed until later in the afternoon. The exceptions were the free enterprises; if there was money to be made, the new entrepreneurs didn't sleep. Such enterprise forced some of the government stores to stay open to compete, and we may have seen the beginning of the end for the traditional Chinese nap.

I started teaching September 1—a single class on the theories of Western journalism, from 8:00-10:00 a.m., Thursday and Saturday. They ran things a bit differently than in the United States. The students had no choice—if they were sophomore or junior journalism majors, they were assigned to my class by the administration of the department. That's how it was with all of their classes: they were offered certain classes, and those were the ones they took. Therefore, every member of a graduating class within a particular major had taken exactly the same courses as all others of that class with the same major.

Although I didn't have to teach very many hours, it was exhausting. When they first told me that because I was a respected foreign expert I would teach only four hours a week, I thought I would be bored after the 12 hours a week I was used to at Bemidji State. In fact, that was not the case, because I taught at a much different level. All of the material I used back home had to be rewritten, because it presupposed basic cultural knowledge that my Chinese students did not have.

For example, discussion of the newsworthiness of an item with my students in the States included elements of timeliness and local impact, whereas these elements are not taken for granted by Chinese editors. They are much more likely to consider benefit to the State a criteria for newsworthiness. Until I learned to take this and countless other differences into account, I drew many puzzled looks from both my students and my interpreter.

Teaching through an interpreter was also difficult—I had to try to make sure he understood what I meant and was conveying it the way I intended. If my theory is correct—that one of the most difficult elements to convey is humor—my interpreter was very good. I use a lot of humor in my teaching, and the students laughed at the right times. I suppose he could have been making snide remarks about me ("How about this guy—what a turkey, huh?"), and they were laughing at those, but I don't think that was the case. I think he did a good job of conveying not just the information, but the tone of my lectures, as well.

During the year, my classes ranged in size from a graduate-level class of 20 to one of 145 that combined all the junior and senior journalism majors. If I had eight there for the graduate class, or 75 for the other, though, I considered it a good day. Of those who did show up, many sat in the back and talked, smoked, read magazines, or slept. Three times during the term, however, I was startled to find the classroom full. When I asked my assistant, he said that the department administration had chosen those days to conduct "surprise" roll calls, to make sure everyone was attending class. I'm sure they were gratified to find, at the end of the term, that all of their students had perfect attendance records. The biggest disappointment of my year in China was the students. I knew that only the very best were admitted to college, so I expected a challenging and rewarding teaching experience—such was not the case. With very few exceptions, the students were coasting through college.

The reason, I learned, was that they worked incredibly hard throughout their middle and high school years to be admitted to university study. The universities were unofficially ranked, and the higher the rank of the university to which students were admitted, the better the position to which they were assigned after graduation. Their performance during college had nothing to do with anything, and it was nearly impossible for them to fail.

I wrote an exam for my fall-term class that incorporated material from my lectures, constructing it so that a thorough knowledge of the material would be necessary to do well. As with the exams I construct for my students in the States, I set a grading scale with 90-100 percent correct an A, 80-89 a B, 70-79 a C, 60-69 a D, and anything below 60 failing. My interpreter translated it into Chinese. As was usual with exams at that university, the department faculty graded it cooperatively. Clearly, it would have been too much to expect anyone to translate all the answers back into English so I could take part in the grading. After the grading was complete, my interpreter happily informed me that everyone in the class—including those who, to my knowledge, had attended only on the three days attendance was taken—had passed. Scores had ranged from 62 to 96, with the curve decidedly skewed toward the top end.

It occurred to me that I would have more control over grading second term, when I would be teaching some of my classes to English majors. I would then be able to administer and grade my own tests. When I mentioned this to an American who had done so first term, he told me not to count on it making any difference. I was puzzled by his cynical response, and he explained. After writing, administering, and grading his own exams, he took the grades to the "office teacher." The closest to this position we had in American universities was office manager, but office teachers had more power. It was as though the position of department chair or dean were split into academic and administrative responsibilities, with the office teacher responsible for administration, including grading.

My friend said the office teacher for his department took his list of grades, began to look it over, and stopped at the third person on the list, who had earned a C. "Oh no," said the office teacher, taking out a pen and changing the grade, "this person didn't get a C, he is a B student." My friend replied that he might be a B student in other classes, but that he had earned a C in his. "But that can't be," replied the office teacher, nonchalantly, "he is a B student." Holding his temper, my friend realized that if he insisted, the woman would change the grade back, but that it would only last until he left the room. Having been in China long enough to understand the concept of saving face, my friend said, "Okay," and left. "As I went out the door," he said, "I looked back to see her busily changing the grades I had worked so hard to establish, bringing them in line with what must have been already established guidelines."

College students in China attended classes six days a week, but usually only in the morning. There were two exceptions: many English language classes were in the afternoon, and Wednesday afternoons were set aside for political indoctrination. These sessions were compulsory, not only for students, but for everyone. Many of our faculty friends said that although for years they seldom were subjected to political indoctrination, they still had to show up, so they used the time for faculty meetings, reading, or grading papers.

Two classes were scheduled each morning--from 8:00 to 10:00 and 10:00 to 12:00. The faculty generally allowed fifteen minutes for the students to arrive before they began, however, and released the first class about fifteen minutes early so students had more of a break between

Our primary mode of transportation.

classes. They generally dismissed the second class about 11:15, because the dining room workers put the hot food out at 11:30, and if students got there late, it was gone. Essentially, then, teaching time was an hour and a half for the first class, and an hour for the second.

Following lunch, most students napped from noon until 2:00 p.m.; then played games such as soccer, volleyball, badminton, basketball, or tennis until time for dinner at 5:00 p.m. Most summer evenings they spent walking, or talking in small groups outside. When the weather drove them into their dorms, they read, or gathered in someone's room to play cards or chat. Once or twice during the week, and usually at least once on the weekend, the administration of the university brought a movie or live show to campus, and they were well-attended by students.

We never figured out how the beginning and end of the terms were determined. It seemed various teachers began and ended their classes at different times. Some of them began teaching near the middle of August, and continued until the middle of February; others didn't start until the first of September, or didn't teach past the first of February. They had two terms, which seemed to be about 18 to 20 weeks each, with a break of about a month between. As a special consideration for the foreign expert, I was allowed to end my classes January first, so we had plenty of time to travel between terms.

Classification of foreign scholars in China was confusing. There were foreign experts and foreign teachers. Few people came to China as official foreign experts, and only by invitation of the Chinese government—everyone else was, officially, a foreign teacher. There were national, provincial, and municipal level universities, however, and they all wanted foreign experts, because they brought more prestige to the institutions. As there just weren't enough official foreign experts to go around, many of the universities created their own by unofficially relabeling foreign teacher positions.

There was, therefore, an unofficial set of criteria for judging who was a foreign expert and who was a foreign teacher. Basically, foreign experts were those people with advanced degrees who had been invited to a university to teach a discipline-based subject. Foreign teachers were those who had come to teach language, and were paid by the hour. Foreign experts were paid more, or expected to teach less, or both. They were also given more respect, had better living quarters, are were generally treated better than foreign teachers.

The foreign teachers were still treated with respect, and certainly made more money than their Chinese counterparts. Chinese professors made the equivalent of about $40-$50 a month. Foreign teachers, depending on their teaching load, made $100-$300 a month, and foreign experts made about the same, but with about half the teaching load.

However, much more was expected of foreign experts outside the classroom. For example, in addition to teaching, I was expected to do research and serve as a consultant to my department in everything from curriculum to editing English language documents. I was often asked to serve in ceremonial functions as well, displayed as a sort of prize by my department—not an unpleasant task, given that such functions almost always included food and drink of the highest caliber.

Cooper trying out the playground in front of his school.

Laurie was hired by the administration to teach conversational English to non-English majors, graduate students, and faculty from throughout the university. As such, she was officially a foreign teacher, but generally, her treatment seemed tied more to her capacity as wife of a foreign expert. This diminished capacity was sometimes frustrating for her, but she accepted it with equanimity. She realized that, despite official protestations to the contrary, women in China were not treated with the equality she had come to expect in the States.

For the purpose of teaching English, the administration of the university had purchased copies of a text called Living and Learning in the West. It was written from the perspective of a Chinese graduate student planning to go to the United States to study. Such a context was unrealistic for nearly all of Laurie's students, so she used the book as a springboard for conversations about China, rather than having the students repeat canned dialog. The hours of discussion that resulted often centered on the lives of the people in her classes. Consequently, Laurie not only learned much about daily life in China, she also became quite close to her students.

As the students returned to campus, I began to notice, and was surprised by, their attire. This was true for the population of Shenyang in general, but for the students in particular. I expected very modest clothing in Shenyang. I knew, having been to places like Shanghai and Beijing the year before, that clothes in China were much more Western than most people realized. The concept of everyone dressed in monochromatic Mao suits had been outdated for years—at least in the major cities. Shenyang, although it is the major city in northeast China, however, is a much more parochial area than Shanghai or Beijing, so I expected the clothing there to be very conservative.

I couldn't have been more wrong. Many of the young people especially, both men and women, looked as though they had just parked their motorcycles around the corner. They wore tight black pants, high black boots, and black leather, aviator-style jackets with fur collars. Many were relatively poor people, but they seemed to spend a lot of money on clothes. When I asked Chinese friends about that, they said yes, the students did spend a lot of money on each article of clothing, but they probably had one, or at most two, changes of clothing.

I started watching, and noticed that many students wore the same thing every time they came to class. There were some students that I never saw in any but that one set of clothes. They all had running suits, provided by their work units, to wear while taking part in university sporting events. They wore those for informal situations, and while they washed their other clothes.

Standard summer attire for the well-dressed female student was either a short, colorful skirt or the tightest pants she could get into, and a quite daring—by Chinese standards at least--blouse or sweater, with only a light cotton tee-shirt under it. The blouses and sweaters were very colorful. The pants, usually black, were silk or acrylic fiber. Most of the young men wore tight clothes as well: short-sleeved, silk shirts, unbuttoned to the navel, and silk or acrylic fiber slacks or short-shorts.

Both men and women wore high-heeled sandals and black, net, knee-high stockings, often with something like a paisley pattern woven into them. Although most older people dressed much more conservatively, they didn't seem to mind the more radical outfits of the young. Occasionally I saw an older woman look askance at a young woman dressed in tight clothing, but as a rule, they didn't seem to notice.

In the States, such attire would have sent some kind of sexual message, but that did not seem to be the case in China. Almost all the young people, as a result of relatively fat-free diets and a lot of exercise, had very good bodies, but took little overt notice of each other. To see

29

young people holding hands, or standing with their arms around each other was common, but almost never mixed couples. Boys held hands or put their arms around each other, as did girls, but it was rare to see boys holding hands with, or embracing, girls. This was true even of married couples. Some of Laurie's graduate students were married, but the university had no married student housing, so they lived apart. When they walked together in the evening, they did not hold hands or kiss.

About the middle of September, patterns of dress began to change radically. People began to don their winter clothes, beginning with their first layer of long johns. By the end of January, my assistant told us, some people had on 14 or 15 layers of clothing, including as many as four layers of long underwear. We could never figure out a way of verifying that information, but he was an honest young man, and we could think of no reason he would have been exaggerating. We did see normally very thin people who, in the middle of the winter, looked remarkably like the Pillsbury Dough Boy, and whose body movements seemed quite constrained.

Two of the first Chinese words we learned were those for boy and girl. Jesse was so pretty to the Chinese they insisted he must be a girl, and we were sometimes hard-pressed to convince them he was a boy. The words for boy and girl are quite similar, and they assumed that we must have gotten them mixed up. There were a few times we got into big—but friendly—arguments, and were afraid we would have to take down his pants so they would let us go.

They knew Cooper was a boy, but they thought he was a very pretty boy. They probably considered his finer Caucasian features attractive. After Cooper started to kindergarten, and we began showing up at the market with just Jesse, everyone would ask, "Cooper, where's Cooper?" We learned to explain that he was in kindergarten. After a while, I think they continued to ask just to be friendly, and because they wanted us to speak Chinese and realized that was something we knew how to say.

One question we learned to understand quickly from sheer repetition was whether both boys were ours. "It must be wonderful," they would say, "to have two children." Because of their "one child" policy, they considered us lucky to have two. The Chinese government encouraged each family to have only one child. There were exceptions concerning minorities, and twins, and they didn't have to go to Siberia or anything if they had more than one, but there were certain positive and negative incentives.

If couples signed an agreement to have only one child, they were awarded cash and certain privileges. If they reneged on the agreement and had a second child, those privileges were taken away and they had to pay back the money. If they had additional children, strong negative incentives, such as taxes and other financial penalties, came into play. For example, couples had to pay all the medical and school expenses for additional children. As a socialist country, China normally provided those things free for people, but not if they had a third child.

Boys were highly valued by Chinese couples, so the fact that both our children were boys made us, in their eyes, especially fortunate. We couldn't go anywhere without people stopping to collect around us. They liked to touch the boys, and even Cooper, as much as he liked attention and to be around people, withdrew a bit after several minutes of being pawed by exuberant Chinese women. They wanted to touch his light skin, and feel his hair. They were especially enthralled with his combination of dark hair and blue eyes. They wanted to pick him up and hold him, and they thought he was so big for being only six years old. The Chinese children, as a result of their mostly rice and vegetable diets, were quite a bit smaller than our boys. Cooper often had problems because children tend to choose playmates based at least partly on size, and the ten- or eleven- year-old boys he tried to play with weren't very interested in his six-year-old's games.

There were many similarities between the postal service in China and the United States. The process was essentially the same, in that they had a main post office downtown, branch offices throughout the city, and delivery to major institutions, although very little delivery to homes. Facilities in the post offices were similar to those in the States, as were hours and services. There were some noticeable differences, however. Even in the main post office, they still had only one person cancelling all the stamps by hand, which created a bottleneck as the quantity of mail in the system increased.

The Chinese, for example, had increasingly adopted the tradition of sending greeting cards, and their postal system was ill-equipped to handle that growing load of mail. Reassigning someone temporarily to help with the overload during holidays wasn't feasible, as people did only the job assigned to them by the government. Often, we saw several other postal clerks sitting around drinking tea and chatting, while the person responsible for hand cancellation was nearly buried under a load of greeting cards.

Another basic difference caused me no end of consternation. When I first entered a Chinese post office, I couldn't figure why so many people were gathered around a counter in the middle of the room. It seemed nobody mailed anything, however, before first pushing up to that crowded counter. I dislike crowds, so I was glad that whatever they were after I didn't need. My happiness lasted until I bought my stamps, licked them, stuck them to my envelopes, and watched them flutter to the floor.

I spent the next fifteen minutes at that counter, which had in its center a large well. Each morning one of the workers mixed up a batch of slimy paste and ladled it into that well. Patrons of the post office had at their disposal two chopsticks (or, if they chose to forego the niceties, any one of ten fingers) with which to spread the stuff onto the back of their stamps. The success of that operation depended a great deal on the consistency of the paste, which I am convinced depended on the mood of the mixer that day and how much grief she wanted to bestow on her patrons. My personal success rate ranged from poor to adequate. Sometimes the paste was thick and gummy and we didn't need much at all. Other times it was thin and watery. then we had to use a lot, and it wrinkled the envelope, slid the stamps around, and was generally a mess.

On top of everything else, they seldom had stamps in the larger denominations, so when we mailed things overseas we generally had to use several stamps. One morning I sent a manuscript of an article to a professional organization in Canada. It was a pretty bulky envelope, and I had to virtually cover the back with stamps. At least the fact that they used hand cancellation meant the stamps could go anywhere on the envelope they would fit. I vowed never to complain about the taste of American stamps again.

We didn't have to learn a new way of addressing our mail, though. Before we arrived, the Chinese had changed their format for addressing envelopes to that used by the U.S. Post Office, with the address centered on the front of the envelope and the return address in the upper left hand corner. Although that was fine for us, it often made life difficult for the Chinese. Once when I was standing in line at the central post office, a man came in with hundreds of envelopes. He spoke English, and, as was often the case, took advantage of my captivity in line to practice on me.

He told me he worked for an import business, and had used his knowledge of Westerners to engineer a public relations coup. He had convinced his boss that it would be great for relations with their Western customers to send them greeting cards. They had spent a significant amount of money on cards, envelopes, and stamps, and he had spent many hours addressing each of the envelopes by hand—in the old format. He stood in line for about half an hour, only to find that the clerk would not accept them until they had been addressed properly. Stamps in China, and especially international stamps, are quite expensive compared to the cost of other things—about 40 cents for a regular letter to the States—so he certainly couldn't afford to throw all of those stamped envelopes away.

I was astounded by the equanimity with which he accepted the news, listened while she explained the new way of addressing envelopes, and retired to a corner of the room. I stopped to wish him luck as I left fifteen minutes later—he had about 20 of the addresses crossed out and rewritten in the new format on the back. He assured me that it was a minor problem; he should be able to finish them in no more than three or four hours, and that because they were hand cancelled it didn't matter that the stamps and addresses were on opposite sides of the envelopes. I believe his cheerful smile was sincere as he returned to his task.

One evening Laurie and I were reading and the boys were getting ready for bed when there was a knock at the door. It was the woman from the university mail room. She had a sealed envelope with my name on it, and something for me to sign. She didn't speak any English, but I got the idea: it was a registered letter or something. So, I signed in the box where she pointed and took the sealed envelope, and she left. The envelope contained a sheet of paper with Chinese writing on it. I had absolutely no idea what it was.

Fortuitously, there was another knock, and it was one of Laurie's graduate students who spoke very good English. She asked him to interpret for us. He said it was a notice of a package at the downtown post office, and that we had seven days to pick it up or we would be fined. She said, "Seven days from now?" He said, "No, seven days from when it's dated." It was dated five days earlier, so we had two days to find time for the 45-minute bike ride to the main post office. Laurie asked if it said anything else, and he said, "Oh, it says you'll have to pay 160 yuan for it." That was about $40--a lot of money to us back home, and a heck of a lot of money on our Chinese salary.

I said, "160 yuan?" He said, "That's what it says." I said, "Who's it from?" He said, "It doesn't say that." I said, "Well, what is it?" He said, "It doesn't say that, either."

We didn't know what to do. This was before we had learned not to worry so much about things, so we worried. We couldn't afford to pay $40 to get a package unless it was something really good, and we had no way of knowing. That was more than we had paid for Laurie's bike; more than we spent on groceries in a month.

We took 160 yuan along, just in case they would tell us what was in the package; just in case it was something we were willing to pay that much for. we couldn't imagine what that would be. A box of goodies from home? Forget it. We wondered what they would do if we didn't pay the money. Would the fines just keep accumulating until they came to get us, like they do for parking tickets in New York City? What if it was an early Christmas present from somebody? Maybe we could refuse it. Maybe we could send it back unopened—write to whomever had sent it and tell them we'd get it from them in July.

It was with trepidation that we approached the international desk at the post office. A very nice young man got the package for us and informed us in flawless English that we owed the Chinese government 1.60 yuan for delivering it. Not 160 yuan—not $40. One point six zero yuan—40 cents. It was a package of candy, cookies, and cheese from friends in the States, and it was great—worth every penny.

We were right about one thing: if we hadn't picked it up, the fines would have kept accumulating. We had friends who were traveling between terms at their school, and were gone about three weeks. They returned to find that one of those cards had arrived the day after they left. They ended up paying about $65 for a small box containing $8-worth of candy bars from a friend back home. They savored each bite of those $4 candy bars.

September 15 was the 30th anniversary of the founding of the University, and I received an official invitation to attend the ceremonies as an honored guest. According to the invitation, it was "formal attire," so I wore the only suit I had taken with me--a khaki number—and I looked quite sharp, although somewhat short of formal. "Formal attire" obviously meant different things to different people, however, because there were some people in Mao suits, some in light autumn jackets, some in polo shirts, and some in sports jackets and ties. I felt slightly over-dressed for the occasion. By our standards, the Chinese were not exactly formal dressers. In the summer, the men often attended what seemed to be at least semi-formal functions in Bermuda shorts and short-sleeved shirts.

The invitation said I would be seated at the head table for the celebration. It took place in a huge auditorium that must have seated 700 or 800 people. The "head table" was on stage, and consisted of five rows of tables that stretched from one side of the stage to the other. I was seated with the other foreign scholars in the third row back, which put us somewhere between the provincial bureaucrats and the city bureaucrats. The Chinese didn't take seating arrangements at all lightly, so I'm sure it was more precise than that, but the meaning was lost on me.

When we arrived, we were asked to sign our names in a very fancy guest book. That created a problem. The Chinese signed their names vertically, so their guest book had vertical spaces in it. Undaunted, I simply turned the book on its side and signed my name from bottom to top in very large letters. Nobody made a fuss, so I guess that must have been okay.

We received a program and a name tag, both in Chinese, and were ushered onto the stage and left to find our seats. As the markers on our seats were also in Chinese, it left those of us who didn't read Chinese in a surrealistic game of musical chairs. We wandered around trying to match our name tags with the place markers. I considered it grounds for measurable pride when I found mine without too much trouble. I suppose I shouldn't have been too smug, however, as all of the foreign scholars were seated together, and I wasn't the first (nor, in my defense, the last) to sit.

For the next hour and a half, we were numbed by numerous speeches and ceremonial doings—all in Chinese. Suddenly we realized they were introducing everybody on stage. There were about six English-speaking people there, and a couple of them understood a bit of Chinese. One of them recognized the Chinese word for "American," so we knew they were talking about one of us, but we didn't know which one. One of the men who spoke some Chinese thought he recognized his name, so he stood up. Everyone applauded. The second introduction came and he hissed, "Roy, that's you—stand up." I stood up and bestowed my most gracious smile on the audience. They roared with laughter.

Later a Chinese friend who had been in the crowd explained what had happened. Mine had been the first introduction, but few people realized that I was not the man who stood. It was pretty clear to everybody, however, that I was not the Michelle LaRouch who was introduced when I stood up. Festivities for the 30th anniversary continued throughout the day, but everyone assured me that I had been the highlight.

The anniversary celebration including an alumni track meet that was great fun. Jesse and I went over one morning while Cooper was in kindergarten and Laurie was teaching. The events were much the same as those in an American meet: javelin, discus, shot-put, pole vault, high jump, long jump, triple jump, and 100-yard dash. In addition, there were 220-, 440-, and 880-yard runs and 220-, 440-, and 880-yard relays.

There were two major differences in this meet, however. First, the field on which the events took place, as was the case with every such field we saw, was composed entirely of dirt. It was laid out the same as a Western field for track and field events, with the track around a soccer field, but the whole thing was of very hard, very gritty dirt—as though whoever had constructed it had gotten the directions wrong, and spread the track surfacing material over the whole area.

The second difference was the contestants. Now, we have alumni meets each year at my university, but none of the contestants fall into the geriatric range. The contestants in this meet were divided into age categories, and some of the largest categories were those with the 60- to 70-year-olds. I mean, those people--about the same number of women as men—were clearly 60 and 70 years old, and they were out there putting the shot, throwing the discus, running relays, and doing broad jumps—it was truly a sight to see.

As the crowning event of the anniversary, they had a big party one night. There was a large, white-tiled building on campus near the main gate. In front of the building was a big fountain and a huge paved quadrangle that held thousands of people. In preparation for the party, they had decorated that building and the quad with about half a dozen huge balloons towing red banners that must have been 20 feet long and three feet wide. Each banner had messages painted on it in gold calligraphy. There were continuous fireworks for hours, and music. All of the lights were on—many of them with colored bulbs for the occasion, and the fountain was going full force.

The fountain wasn't on all the time—even on the hottest days of summer. We never did figure out for sure when they turned it on. We thought at first it was on a timer, but then realized it wasn't that regular. It seemed they started it up on hot windy days so people could stand in the spray, when somebody important was going to be on campus, or any time they had a celebration. There were times, however, when it came on with none of these criteria seemingly met.

The climate in Shenyang was much like we were used to in Minnesota, but a bit milder, so, with the exception of the daily wind, autumn was really beautiful. Most September evenings were cool and mild, and it seemed as though everyone on campus liked to get out and walk around. One Thursday evening our whole family was out walking, and we ended up at the fountain in the quad in front of the main building. As we sauntered around the fountain, Cooper and Jesse, as usual, acted like magnets to the Chinese, and we were gradually surrounded. We noticed something different, however—we could understand them.

We had happened on the university's "English corner," where people could go to practice speaking English with each other. If native English speakers showed up, the Chinese would crowd around enthusiastically, all speaking at once, sometimes causing the objects of their attention to fear inadvertent trampling. The English corner at Liaoning University was from 6:30-9:30 Thursday evenings on the front steps of the main building, and we were there. They were very pleased to have four of us with which to interact, but Cooper was especially popular—those who weren't as confident of their abilities felt less threatened talking with him.

They elicited a promise from us to come every Thursday evening we could. We left feeling very good, being there and being exposed to those delightful young people—they were so curious, dynamic, and full of life. They wanted so much to improve themselves, because they saw China changing so quickly and they wanted to keep up. It was a delight to be part of that dynamic.

One of the young people that evening approached me and said, "Excuse me, I am from TV university, and I wonder if it might be possible for you to come over and lecture to our university?" Well, I didn't know what "TV university" was, but I said if their dean would get in touch with me we could talk about it. The next Tuesday, they sent a car to pick me up. Their university was all the way across town—about a half hour ride. When we got there, the president of the university was waiting to welcome me. She told me they were desperate to have a native English speaker come and talk with their English majors, to give them a chance to converse with someone in "real English." She said these students would be expected to teach English in middle and high schools when they graduated, but some of them had never talked to a native English speaker.

Most students in China learned English from English-speaking Chinese, so although their reading and writing was good, their speaking and comprehension was generally poor. There were many programs on television to teach English, but the people on them were Chinese, as well. Many of Laurie's and my students told us they had studied English for six or eight years, but the first time they heard it spoken by a native English speaker, they had no idea what was being said.

I agreed to go to TV University two hours a week. They said they would send a car for me every Thursday afternoon at 1:00 and take me back at 4:00. The president asked how much I wanted for this. I said they need not pay me, that I was making more money than I needed at

Liaoning University. She said, "You must be paid for your work. Will 200 yuan a month be alright?" I said that was very generous, and went away feeling guilty. I found out later that they were paying me more each month for talking two hours a week than her monthly salary as president.

TV universities were originally just that—universities at which students gathered to receive their lectures by television. Teachers from major universities were televised at a central studio, and the lectures were carried to thousands of students at TV universities by satellite and microwave. They were three-year, non-degree granting institutions. Many were trying to legitimize their schools and become degree-granting universities, but they were finding the bureaucratic process very difficult.

While I was there, they conducted almost all their classes in standard, face-to-face format. In fact, I never saw a televised class on campus. It was, however, practically impossible to change their name, which was one of their biggest problems. They were viewed as bottom of the heap, so students only went there if they couldn't qualify for any other university. Consequently, they did not get the best students. Discussing the quality of their students, one of the teachers said, "The reason most of these students are here, rather than at more highly-rated schools, is that they are more well-rounded, outgoing people. They were more social in high school, and didn't spend all their time glued to their books, so they didn't do as well on the entrance exams." The result was that many of the students at TV University were the most dynamic, active learners I encountered in China.

About the middle of September, the staff of the university's Foreign Affairs Office started arranging almost weekly visits for the foreign students, and foreign scholars and their families, to interesting sites throughout Liaoning Province. Each time representatives of the Foreign Affairs Office proudly announced that they had arranged a trip for us, we would attempt to get more details from them. Our questioning their plans was very perplexing for them.

Whereas we were only curious and meant no criticism, questioning bureaucratic decisions was just not something the Chinese did, and they assumed we were finding fault.

We had noticed a decided reticence on the part of most Chinese to offer more information about anything than absolutely compelled to. Once a personal friendship was established, this tendency dissipated, but it was always an annoying inconvenience in dealing with the bureaucracy. At first we didn't understand why they were so reluctant to disclose facts.

After several months, we began to realize that a complex set of disincentives existed that created a general wariness about conveying any kind of information. Basically, people knew they were unlikely to get into trouble if they did not talk. The feeling was that the more they said, the more likely they were to say something they shouldn't. This attitude had been prevalent for so long that it permeated all aspects of society. We were bemused by the seemingly obsessive way the Chinese exchanged business cards, until we realized that it was almost impossible to find telephone books. As with most other information, telephone numbers were treated as confidential information. Unless we had met people and received their cards, they were almost impossible to get in touch with.

One Sunday people from the Foreign Affairs Office took us to the East Tombs, the burial ground for one of the emperors who ruled during the time when Shenyang was the capitol city. It was an absolutely gorgeous, park-like setting, about an hour's drive from the university. The areas around Chinese cities were densely populated and farm land was precious, so there were few urban parks. Instead, people used the areas surrounding tombs—of which there were many—for recreational activities. On weekends the tombs were over-run with people of all ages—eating picnics; playing games, cards, and musical instruments; exercising; walking; chatting; napping; riding bikes; and jogging or speed walking.

In the recently-condoned entrepreneurial spirit of China, these parks drew a staggering variety of money-making schemes. People sold toys, clothes (including tee-shirts with computer-generated photos printed on the front), books, postcards, food, and patent medicines. They told fortunes from cards, palms, tea leaves, bones, and (honest) blood samples. They furnished rides on toy trains, bumper cars, bumper boats, toy animals, go carts, Ferris wheels, merry-go-rounds, space ships, airplanes, roller skates, and rowboats. They offered activities such as darts, Ping-pong, bowling, ring toss, slides, teeter-totters, swings, video games, haircuts, shoe repair, fun houses, and photos. They provided for viewing musical concerts, dance concerts, plays, puppet shows, trained animals, thrill shows, and circus acts. It warmed our hearts to see the finest elements of capitalism at work.

About six blocks from the university was Beiling Park, site of the

An afternoon at Beiling Park.

North Tombs. We took the boys there often, to walk or ride bikes in the park, and to enjoy the games and rides at the amusement park. One ride they had added the year we were there (the first of its kind in northern China) was a go-cart track. It was an absolute hoot to watch the Chinese drive go-carts. Very few of them had driven cars—or anything powered by an engine, for that matter. About the only people in the northern part of China who had were truck drivers and taxi drivers.

It was a sight to behold: they'd take off and immediately run off the track into the field. One of the attendants would hop into a spare cart and roar out there to show them how to turn the steering wheel to the right to go to the right and turn it to the left to go to the left. They were by far the most expensive ride--the equivalent of about a dollar for one lap of the track. That was at least three times as much as anything else, but people lined up for a block to get in there.

We had go-carts back home, and Cooper, Jesse, and I liked to ride them occasionally. The boys weren't allowed to drive them there, so they just sat on my lap. At six, Cooper was old enough that he kept at me until I let him steer while I pushed on the gas, but he was never allowed to go on one by himself. Well, that same kind of rule was in effect in China, but nobody paid any attention to it. When Cooper found out he was allowed to drive one himself, he just had to do it. I hate to stand in line, but in the interest of family harmony, I succumbed.

When we finally got there, Cooper got in one cart, I got in another with Jesse, and we took off. Cooper looked like A. J. Foyt or some big-time race driver compared to the Chinese. They all stopped to watch him and he weaved in and around them. I almost lost control myself, I was laughing so hard.

Cooper had completed his lap before he realized it, and was concentrating so hard on driving that he was still going full speed when he got back to the starting line. He slammed on his brakes, skidded to a stop at the feet of the attendant in the finest four-wheel drift ever witnessed in that part of China, hopped out, and was shouting, "Let's go again! Let's go again!" before I even got there. The Chinese were stupefied. He had literally run circles around some of the young men, who had spent much hard-earned cash in an effort to impress their lady friends with their driving skill. I dismounted, looked around at the stunned expressions, and decided the Chinese, if not Cooper, had had enough daredevil driving for that day. We left amid scattered applause.

When the Chinese women saw Cooper and Jesse running around in shorts and short-sleeved shirts, they let us know in no uncertain terms that we were terrible parents for letting them freeze to death like that. The problem was compounded by the fact that when their Chinese playmates saw our boys dressed like that, they began shrugging out of some of the four layers of clothing their mothers had put on them. Now, if there was anything that aroused the ire of Chinese mothers and grandmothers faster than seeing us let our children freeze, it was seeing us as the instruments (albeit indirect) of destruction for theirs.

For some reason, they seemed to get cold a lot easier than we did—perhaps it was the fact that their diet of mostly rice and vegetables just didn't build up a layer of body fat like we had for insulation. At any rate, we didn't start wearing sweatshirts, let alone jackets, until well into October.

The temperature during the last couple of weeks in September was commonly in the mid-70's; yet the Chinese had been wearing their long-johns since the first of the month. We learned from a Chinese friend that everyone in Shenyang began to wear long underwear September first, and the decision had nothing to do with the weather. He assured me there was no rule, but that it was "the way it had always been done."

This friend was very intelligent and, for a Chinese, quite an independent thinker, so I asked him why he wore his long-johns when there was clearly no need. "The weather in Shenyang is very changeable," he said, "and we never know when it might get cold." I pointed out that first, the temperature would have to take a drop of historic magnitude to go from 75 degrees to something that required long underwear.

Second, he never got more than a 45-minute bike ride from the university. Try as I might, I couldn't picture him caught downtown in a freak blizzard, freezing to death on his bike in a valiant effort to make it home to the saving warmth of the long underwear he had spuriously discarded that very morning, in the face of a deceptively temporary 85-degree heat wave. At least, I pointed out, his death would have served as an object lesson in the wisdom of the elders, who had decreed August 31 safe, and not a moment later. He thought my story hilarious, but I noticed a couple of days later, when we were playing tennis, that he had sweated completely through both layers.

Until the weather started getting really nasty, we could count on one daily event. At 6 a.m. a whistle would blow; then from a loud speaker somewhere (and the operative word here is "loud") would come the strains of something we assumed was a kind of reveille. One difference between it and the traditional reveille in the States was that it lasted half an hour. The initial bugle call was followed by a very long, complicated rendition of "Auld Lang Syne"—sort of a "Variations on the Theme of Auld Lang Syne."

After about 15 minutes, they segued into a snappy rendition of the Chinese national anthem, which, incidentally, doesn't sound at all Chinese. After another 15 minutes, and several more whistle blasts, silence descended once more on the university. It was actually rather nice, to lie in bed and listen to the music—like a collective clock radio—although we would have preferred a bit of variety.

We asked a Chinese friend what it was all about and he said, "It's just the way they get everybody up and going." He said the students got up immediately when the bugle started, and the reason it went on for half an hour was that they jumped into sweatsuits and ran outside for exercises. Although Laurie and I kept telling ourselves we were going to, we never mustered the nerve to join them. A couple of foreign students who got up and went out to watch said it was a sight to behold—thousands of people out on the playing field doing exercises in time to "Auld Lang Syne."

One morning in late September, we got up at 6:30 a.m. as we always did, invigorated by the thought of all those students out there exercising to the strains of their national anthem. We got dressed and ready by 7:00 to go down to breakfast at 7:15. The doors were locked. The lights were out. There wasn't a soul around. We couldn't figure out why in the world there was no breakfast. By 7:30 we assumed there was some national catastrophe we hadn't been told about. Nothing less would have swayed our cooks and waitresses from their appointed rounds.

We found an old man who, as nearly as we could determine, was a "fix-it man" for the Foreign Affairs Office. He must have been on night duty, because he would not have been there that early otherwise. Anyway, he seemed to know what the problem was, but his Chinese was so bad that neither Laurie nor I could understand him. By the time a German student who was there studying Chinese arrived, the fix-it man's Chinese must have improved, because she seemed to understand most of what he was saying. She said that as nearly as she could determine, it was something about a time change. Maybe they don't have daylight savings time in Germany, because she didn't seem to know what that meant. We put it all together, and figured out the Chinese must have daylight savings time the same as we do.

Sure enough, at 8:15 on the button (or 7:15 for the previously-informed) the dining room opened. What had happened, of course, was we had gone off daylight savings time, but nobody had told us it was going to happen. Maybe they thought we wouldn't be interested. I had paranoid delusions of a plot against us until I realized they must have neglected to inform the guy that started "Auld Lang Syne" as well, as we had gotten up at 6:30 (alias 5:30) because of him.

Chapter Three
October

October was a time of many festivals in Shenyang, so the last week in September they began decorating the city. Somewhere they must have had some incredible greenhouses, because for about a week they trucked out flatbed trailers full of an amazing variety of foliage. They placed shrubs, flowers, and even small, flowering trees along all the streets, in the tree lawns and medians, as well as creating ornate displays at all the parks and plazas. The transformation was absolute—the city became a veritable hotbed of flowers and greenery for a month.

To water all those potted plants, they drove what appeared to be tank trucks from the fire department around every couple of days and hosed them down. The only problem was that the water pressure, after a few weeks, began to take its toll in the form of overturned and broken pots, and uprooted plants. Some of the displays began to look a bit bedraggled by the end of the month, when they were gathered up and taken back to the greenhouses for rejuvenation.

We celebrated National Day the first week of October by a three-day weekend with no classes or work. It was like our Fourth of July, and marked the 39th anniversary of the founding of the People's Republic of China. The staff of our Foreign Affairs Office scheduled a two-day trip for the foreign students and foreign scholars to a mountain about 150 kilometers south of Shenyang. They told us we would go by bus, leaving at 11:30 Saturday morning. It seemed strange to us to be leaving so late, but as always, we could get no explanation—that was just how it was.

We were told we would have box lunches on the bus, arrive early evening, have dinner, go to bed, and as they put it, "climb the mountain to watch the sunrise" the next morning. We didn't know exactly what that meant, but as we were off daylight savings time, sunrise was pretty early. If it was much of a mountain at all, we'd have to start about four or five in the morning. Besides, assuming it was any kind of mountain to speak of, how were we supposed to see to climb it in the dark? We were looking forward to the trip, however, because we had seen a promotional brochure that described it, in the Chinese' own inimitable way, as being very beautiful in the autumn because you could "look around you and see things turning red all over the place." Now, who could resist a phrase like that?

Saturday morning went pretty much as planned, except that the trip took much less time than we expected. To our great surprise, there was a brand-new, four-lane, limited-access, super highway that connected Shenyang with a city near the mountain. The toll booths weren't finished, so we drove around them, as did the rest of the traffic. It was a nearly surreal experience to see cars and trucks moving faster than any we had seen before in China; sharing the highway with donkey carts and pedestrians moving slowly along the berm, past digital electronic speed signs.

When we got there, they told us we had two hours before dinner to "walk around the trails" on the mountain. We expected something like the well-maintained trails (with guard rails on the narrow spots) that we had encountered in parks throughout the United States and Canada. Oh no—the Chinese seemed to have this inherent desire to commit suicide by falling off a mountain. They had almost no safety features. We literally just climbed the mountain.

It was thronging with people, many of the younger ones competing to see who could get to the top fastest. It was a real mountain, with places where we had to take Jesse around and find safer ways, because there was no way we were going to take him up the "trail" others were using: handholds cut in the side of sheer rock ledges. It was no Mount Everest, but it certainly offered some pretty rugged rock climbing in spots. And the Chinese looked like they were dressed for a Sunday stroll in the park: the men in dress slacks, sport shirts, and leather-soled dress shoes; the women in dresses, or skirts and sweaters. Some of them were even wearing high-heeled shoes.

Sure it was inherently racist of me, but I couldn't help thinking that maybe because there were so many of them they didn't hold life as sacred as we did. I don't know, but we were struck on numerous other occasions during trips we took in which we climbed mountains, chugged around on lakes and rivers, or explored caves, that the Chinese seemed to have little regard for their personal safety. They were allowed—in fact, encouraged—by officials to do things that would have turned any self-respecting park ranger in the States several shades of green.

We made it to the top, and it was absolutely gorgeous—surrounded by other mountains. They were the first real mountains we had been to in China, and they were truly beautiful. Then we noticed at our feet a wide assortment of plastic wrappers, film cartridges, bottles, cans, and various other refuse left by the Chinese. As with all the scenic spots in China that we saw, we were inevitably dismayed when their beauty was marred by the garbage from thousands of Chinese visitors.

The Chinese had a terrible propensity to litter—they just threw anything they happened to have in their hands down when they were through with it. Occasionally, we saw someone riding his bicycle down the street drinking a bottle of pop, and when he finished, casually throwing the bottle into the gutter, spraying glass all over. Such actions drew not so much as a glance from anyone but us. It was amazing for us, being indoctrinated through media campaigns about the evils of littering, to see such widespread disregard of it among the Chinese.

One thing the mountains weren't, was "turning red all over the place." They were more the "verdant green" the brochure copy had reserved for summer, which surprised us, because we figured the first weekend in October should be pretty firmly autumn. Although we were at about the same latitude as Minnesota, I think the proximity of the ocean must have put us at least a month behind in the change of seasons.

After climbing around the mountain for a couple of hours, we took the bus to our "hotel," which turned out to be more of a country motel. It was privately owned by a farmer, and "rustic" would have been a conservative description. They showed Laurie, the boys, and me to our room: a ten by twelve foot cubicle with two tiny windows, bare concrete floor, and whitewashed concrete walls. We had been in China long enough to realize that privacy was not highly valued, so we weren't surprised that the door to the hallway had a window, but neither curtain nor lock.

Our furnishings comprised four metal-framed cots, a small wooden table, a thermos of hot water, and a bare electric lightbulb hanging from the center of the ceiling. The mattresses were hard straw thatch about two inches thick, covered by cotton sheets. The bedding was soft, sheet-covered, down comforters. The pillows were stuffed with rice hulls that made a grinding noise when we turned our heads, which took a little getting used to. After climbing that mountain, however, we were tired enough to have slept just about anywhere, and it was just fine. The boys loved it—Jesse kept saying we were "camping out."

We were told we would be awakened at 3:30 in the morning, to climb another mountain and see the sunrise. I couldn't hold it any longer—I asked the question: "If the sun won't be up yet, how will we be able to see to climb the mountain?" "No problem," came the cheerful rejoinder, "we brought along two flashlights." "For 23 of us!" I started to scream, then remembered our resolve not to make them uncomfortable by questioning their plans. "That was probably every flashlight they could get their hands on," I told myself, and began preparing myself mentally for death. Laurie, bright person that she is, said, "The boys are

The mountains south of Shenyang "turning red all over the place."

so tired after their climb today, they may not be able to get up that early, so I'll have to stay here with them." Sometimes she's really good—she knew an appeal to children was infallible. I shot her a glance that said, "You'll be sorry when I'm gone and you have to raise two boys all by yourself."

Well, thank goodness somebody slept in, and we didn't get up until 5:00. It was starting to get light, so we didn't make it to the top in time to see the sunrise, but I, for one, had no complaint. I had no hankering whatsoever to climb a mountain by flashlight, and seeing that one did nothing to change my mind—it was even steeper than the one the day before. There were people falling and sliding down and starting little landslides, and other people screaming and leaping out of the way. Nobody sustained any serious injuries, but frankly, I'm not sure how.

I don't know how, as exhausted as he had been the evening before, but Cooper had gotten up and insisted on coming along. I figured I would either have to carry him part way—a thought I did not relish—or we just wouldn't get all the way to the top. I was wrong. Cooper got there—unassisted, and as nearly as I could tell, unwinded—before I did. He had attached himself to a group of young, athletic, Japanese girls, and had chattered nearly non-stop with them all the way up.

It was an hour and a half climb, but once we got there, it was well worth it, because it was absolutely gorgeous. At the top of that really sharp peak, which we were told was the highest point in that mountain range, was a shrine to Buddha carved into the face of the rock. It must have taken months to carve, and I couldn't help but wonder if the artisan had camped up there the whole time, or had climbed up and down every day. Either way, it was an incredible feat, not just of artistry, but of endurance.

On the way up, we had noticed a beautiful, walled compound, which we were told was a Taoist monastery, at the foot of the mountain. It was late morning by the time we descended, and we stopped there. We were to visit many religious sites while in China, but this one was different. There was no commercial feeling about it, but rather a sense of hushed tranquility; no expectation that a host of maintenance people would emerge at night to refurbish the set, but rather a confidence that the well-used surroundings were home to the people who stopped their work when we came in, to smile and wave.

When our guide knocked at a huge, red, wooden door set into the stone wall, the sound reverberated through the stillness inside the compound. We were met by a young monk, who escorted us to meet the master. He was an ancient-looking man, with a thin white beard to his waist—a man of whom National Geographic covers are made. He greeted us calmly—not a display for tourists, but a gracious host to unexpected, but no less welcome, guests. Then he sat with us while we drank the tea and ate the cakes that brown-robed monks had set out for us in their dining room. He grinned broadly when we offered to pay, and said that would not please the masters he served, by whose instructions he and his monks tried to meet the needs of travelers who came to their home.

The old man, who told us he was "in his eighties," and had been a monk "all his life," stood serenely as his tourist/guests snapped photo after photo with him. He then presented us with bags of small, sweet, crab apples and wished us well on our visit to the mountain. He stood in the gate, leaning on his staff, waving each time one of us turned to look back, until we were out of sight. I remember thinking several times on the bus trip back to Shenyang of that old man, and how it is no wonder we Westerners are somewhat in awe of the mysteries of China.

The next weekend, the staff of the Foreign Affairs Office arranged for the foreign scholars to visit a reservoir about a two-hour drive north of Shenyang. In addition to Laurie, the boys, and me, several Japanese teachers chose to make the trip. Only a couple of them spoke any English, but every one of them was friendly and delightful to be with. In return for his teaching them children's songs in English, they taught Cooper how to count in Japanese, which he was still able to do years later.

The reservoir was near a coal mining, steel processing city, and as the bus approached, we could see a huge cloud of smoke for miles. It looked as though the city were covered in dense fog but, in fact, it was acrid coal smoke. We could feel our eyes burning as we drove into the city. Once we got through it and into the hills on the other side where the reservoir was, however, with the exception of a multicolored smear of oily-looking smoke on the horizon behind us, it was a very beautiful area. The water in the reservoir was deep and cold, and of a striking, translucent blue.

We rode around in the bus for a while, looking at the scenery; then parked on the dam and walked down to the water to await the next boat. That was the high point of Jesse's day. He had a full 45 minutes for his favorite activity: throwing rocks into the water. When we boarded a boat for a trip across the reservoir, we were once again shocked at the Chinese' lack of concern for personal safety. They climbed onto that boat, which was much like a small ferry boat, in numbers that seemed to us practically guaranteed to capsize it. Perhaps that's a bit of an exaggeration, but the crew did allow them to keep coming until the gunwales were dangerously close to the water level.

Laurie and I seemed alone in our concern. They clambered all over, sitting on the cabin roof and perching on the railing, looking as if they were going to fall off into the water at any moment. Nobody seemed to care—or even notice—that there were no life boats or flotation devices. Probably twice as many as should have just hopped onto that old, rusty boat that looked as though it would sink at any minute, and set off gaily across that hundreds-of-feet-deep reservoir. Evidence of the childlike nature of their unconcern was the fact that their delight was shared by Cooper and Jesse. Laurie and I assumed we were all doomed.

We need not have worried. Our voyage ended, not amid the waterlogged refuse at the bottom, but on the far shore, at the base of a rather steep hill on which we were told a 16th century emperor and his commanding general had won a major battle. It seems it was such a historical event that either the emperor, the general, or both (our guide told us, but for the life of me, I can't remember) were buried there, and, as was usual in such cases, a temple was erected on the spot.

It was one of the thousands of temples in China that the government had let deteriorate during the Cultural Revolution, but which had since been beautifully restored to their original splendor. We spent a couple of leisurely, sun-soaked hours there, then began the trip home. Part way back, we stopped to eat. The restaurant was in one of the numerous villages we passed through, and it looked like what we Westerners affectionately referred to as a "hepatitis hut."

Our hosts escorted us through the main dining room, which offered little promise of culinary delight, to the ubiquitous private dining room in the back. It was very basic, but much cleaner, and the table was very nicely set. As was to happen so often in China that it ceased to surprise us, from those eminently undistinguished surroundings came a wonderful meal. It included some very nice dishes, including some we hadn't had before. One, for example, was a salad of bean sprouts and tiny little mushrooms, mixed together in soy sauce and vinegar.

We had been led to believe that in China soup was the last course; that when it came, we could count on the dinner being over, and in the unlikely event that we weren't already stuffed, we could fill up on soup. So, it being later than I was accustomed to eating lunch, and my being pretty hungry, when they brought the soup in, I topped everything off nicely, thank you very much. Well, it was at that little country restaurant we learned about "main food."

The Chinese always had a main food. It came at the end of the meal, and was something plentiful and filling—insurance that nobody would leave the table hungry. Many of our Chinese friends treated the meat and vegetable dishes much as we do appetizers, taking very small portions of each—hardly more than tastes—then filling up on the main food. Only in some areas of China was soup used as the main food.

51

Most often, it was rice. Not a rice dish of some kind, just rice—plain, white, sticky, steamed rice. Seldom did we eat with Chinese friends who did not have at least two bowls of rice apiece to finish off the meal. And the stickier it was, the better they liked it. No Uncle Ben's long-grain instant with each grain an entity unto itself for them. It didn't take many meals with chopsticks to understand why, either.

During our year in China, we traveled throughout most of the eastern and northern parts of the country, and in addition to rice or soup, had noodles, jiao zi, or bread in various forms as the main food. Although we liked them all, with the exception of Cooper, we never did get used to the concept. It always seemed to me as though we were having rice for dessert. It never bothered Cooper, because he was going through a stage in which he ate only one dish at a time, anyway. He preferred only one food on his plate at a time, but if forced to have more than one, they simply must not touch each other or the entire meal was ruined.

Well, the main food for that meal was not soup, but jiao zi. Laurie counted. She said they brought in 140. There were 12 of us—a dozen jiao zi apiece. I was able to get two of them down. I don't know how, but the other 11 finished off the rest. Maybe it was the drinks that did it.

Bai jaio (by' joe) was a clear, 160 proof alcohol distilled from sorghum. Almost all the Chinese men drank bai jaio at every formal meal, including luncheon meetings, and I realized early on that I had three choices. One: I could say I hated the stuff, which would have been about like telling a citizen of Paris I hated the wine. Two: I could say I couldn't drink alcohol, which would have been acceptable, but would have put me at a grave social disadvantage. Or three: I could say I loved it, and drink right along with the rest of them. I chose the latter. It tasted rather like kerosene smells, but after about three swallows, it didn't really matter.

The Chinese, delightfully sociable people, considered it impolite to take a drink alone. Even when someone took a sip of water, he usually raised his glass to someone else at the table, who dropped what he was doing to share a drink. It was a warm, friendly custom, but as frequent guest of honor, I was often the subject of such mini-toasts, and sometimes found myself snatching at bites of food between drinks.

We drank bai jaio out of little shot glasses. When someone wanted to drink, he would stand and shout the Chinese equivalent of "bottoms up!" and everyone was expected to stand up, raise his glass, return the shout, drain his glass, and hold it upside down at arm's length, so everyone could see he wasn't cheating. And cheat they did, if they could get away with it.

Chinese men considered it "macho" to be able to hold their liquor, so it was a kind of game to try to get the other guy drunk—especially if the other guy was the guest of honor, and most especially if he was a Westerner. They would always try to fill my glass so that only surface tension kept it from running over, then give themselves three-quarters. If they could slip water into their glass instead of liquor, or sneak a half-shot occasionally, or toss it into the potted plant when nobody was looking, so much the better. I tried to catch each of them just often enough to keep the game fun, but not often enough that they lost face.

The good news was that the glasses really didn't hold very much, so they weren't very big drinks. The bad news was that each person around the table shouted "bottoms up!" in relatively rapid succession, so that before I knew it, I'd had six or seven of those little buggers and it wasn't as easy to stand up the next time someone shouted. I was lucky: at 5 feet 10 inches and 195 pounds, I had a lot more mass than the Chinese to soak up all that booze. Consequently, I never got as drunk as they did, and gained a reputation for having "sea capacity."

The only thing was, like the fastest gun in the West who had to face all comers, all the other gunslingers felt they had to challenge my standing. I noticed that, although the food remained on the table, once they started serious drinking, the Chinese stopped eating. I made sure I ended up with something in front of me that would soak up alcohol, and made sure to keep nibbling at it throughout. In this way, I left China at the end of a year with my dubious reputation intact.

A problem resulted, however. Because I obviously liked bai jaio so much, if there was any left, they always made sure it went home with me. I insisted that it wasn't fair for me to reap such consistent rewards—that I should share the bounty—but to no avail. We always had several half-full bottles of the stuff in the back of our storage closet. It was handy to serve to an occasional guest, and we sometimes poured two or three bottles together to take as a gift when invited to someone's home. We never did that when the invitation was from Chinese friends—I'm sure they would have recognized the blasphemously mixed brands—but we loved to proudly present such concoctions to Western friends and watch them try to keep from cringing.

With a couple of bottles, we mixed in a lot of instant coffee and some sugar, and through a trial-and-error process, came up with Kaluha that, although not as good as regular Kaluha, was better than what we started with. To be fair, I must admit that, as with many kinds of liquor, some of the more expensive, more highly refined bai jaio wasn't bad. Also, I think it was probably an acquired taste, and given a few more years, I probably would have learned to love it. In the context of warm friendships and excellent meals, it really didn't make much difference what we were drinking, anyway.

I had been the guest of honor at several banquets, so I decided it was time to present one in return. Actually, the impetus for my decision resulted from a misunderstanding at a banquet the English teachers from the Foreign Languages Department had given me the week before. We had been doing the inevitable "bottoms up!" routine, and were feeling no pain. We decided it was such fun, and we were all such "old friends" that we should get together for another luncheon the following week. It was my understanding—whether from the fact that their English wasn't great, the fact that my Chinese was nearly nonexistent, or the general well-oiled nature of the conversation—that I was to have a luncheon for them.

So I got together with an interpreter and the head cook at the foreign students' and teachers' dining room, and arranged for my luncheon. I paid them the equivalent of $15, which was to get the six of us eight dishes, including a beautifully presented whole fish. The beer was extra. I paid the equivalent of $1.60 for 20 beers, with the understanding that we would settle the difference depending on what we actually consumed. Now, $17 doesn't sound like much for a banquet for six, but if it's more than 10 percent of your salary for the month, it puts it in a different perspective. I considered it a social obligation, however, and didn't complain.

I met them in their department office at the appointed time, and they said, "Okay, are you ready to go?" I said, "Go where?" They said they thought we'd go to a little restaurant somewhere off campus. "But no," I babbled, "I've arranged the luncheon. It's on me." They said, "No, no, you're a guest in our country, we must treat you." "That's going to be very awkward," I replied (pretty calmly I thought, given the circumstances), "because I've already arranged for it, and paid for it, and they're going to have it set up for us when we get there." "Oh, you can't do that!" they said, to which I replied (bringing out the big guns), "I'm sorry, I already have, so unless you want to waste my money, you've got to come with me."

They came, but they were very uncomfortable with the situation, and kept saying, "You're our guest, we should treat you." And I kept saying, "I'm sorry, I've already paid for it and I don't want to waste my money." We ended up agreeing that we would do it the American way that one time: "This one's on me, but you can treat me next time." So I took them to the dining room and we went "behind the screen," which was the Westerners' phrase for special dinners in the dining room, because the tables for such meals were separated from the rest by ornate cloth screens. The luncheon was everything the head cook had promised it would be, but my guests never stopped talking about how they really wished I hadn't done it. They would not leave until we had arranged for them to give a dinner party, not just for me, but for Laurie and the boys, as well.

———————————

Another celebration in early October was one the Chinese called the "Mid-Autumn Festival," or more commonly, "Moon Festival." Its observance was keyed to the full moon—a sort of harvest moon festival. The major tradition for the Moon Festival was to sit outside, under the full moon, and devour great quantities of "moon cakes." They were large, filled cookies, about four inches in diameter, ranging from about a half inch to two inches thick, with a variety of sweet fillings. Cooper really liked them, so a few days before the festival he ate too many and got sick. When the festival arrived, and everyone was insisting we eat ridiculous numbers of moon cakes to celebrate, he couldn't even look at them.

The day before the mid-autumn festival (I suppose you could say "Moon Festival Eve," although nobody did), we went to my department chairman's home for a dinner to celebrate the holiday, and they sent us home with three boxes of moon cakes. The next evening, the staff of the Foreign Affairs Office arranged for the foreign faculty and foreign students to celebrate by going out onto the flat roof of one of the buildings, where we had a good view of the harvest moon, and eating fruit and moon cakes. Again, the generosity of the Chinese was overwhelming. They sent us home with a couple of bags of moon cakes.

Weeks later, with consistently flagging enthusiasm, we were still eating moon cakes, and trying to figure out what to do with the rest. Laurie came up with what I considered a brilliant solution to the problem. She suggested that if we doused some of the bigger ones with brandy—which was readily available, and surprisingly good—wrapped them in plastic, and put them away somewhere to let the brandy soak in really well (going back every once in a while to give them another dose), that by Christmas we should have some nice little brandied fruitcakes. I still think it would have worked, if only she had thought of it before they started to get all furry.

China's cities were not designed to handle traffic, and as the amount of traffic increased, so did the problems. Some cities—Beijing, in particular, had been rebuilding streets to alleviate those problems. Shenyang had done very little and it showed. In many respects, the problems were less a result of the quantity of traffic than they were the consistency of it. Pedestrians and bicyclists vied for space with horse carts and three-wheeled bicycles with huge loads of things such as telephone poles, scrap metal, truck cabs, steel beams, and things nobody outside China would believe possible to carry on a three-wheeled bicycle.

Cranes jockeyed for position with pickups, dump trucks, flatbed trailers, automobiles, taxis, front-end loaders, and backhoes. Interspersed were farm tractors pulling wagons loaded with corn, watermelons, and all varieties of animals. In short, there was just about any imaginable combination of vehicular traffic, all competing for limited space.

One of hundreds of 3-wheeled bicycles in Shenyang, ready to deliver someone's kitchen.

Our Chinese friends described to us the laws governing traffic in China. They were very similar to those in the States, but it didn't seem as though anyone took them seriously. The only law seemed to be facing the other person down. People in cars or on bicycles darted into the middle of the street and everybody else had to get out of their way. Drivers blew their horns continuously and nobody paid the least bit of attention. They turned left on red lights and right from the center lane. They went against the lights and ran stop signs—all with police officers on every corner.

Usually, the police seemed to be stationed in pairs, and usually the reason seemed to be so they could keep each other company. Most of the time, they were either chatting or reading. Occasionally we saw them engrossed in card games. We saw police stop drivers, usually of large trucks, but we could never figure what those drivers had done that others hadn't. Chinese friends told us that sometimes such procedures were to combat boredom.

It was amazing to us that very few accidents seemed to occur—we saw them occasionally, but none that looked very serious, or as though anybody had gotten badly hurt. The most frequent were between bikes—not surprising, as there were about three million in the city. The riders always seemed to be in pretty good shape, though: standing nose-to-nose screaming at each other.

We had frequently viewed with awe, then, the unfolding drama of traffic in Shenyang, but had never seen what happened at night. One evening in mid-October, we were attending a party on the other side of town. Although we were later to begin riding our bikes everywhere, at that time we were still being ferried on our longer trips by a van from the Foreign Affairs Office. A couple of other Americans got into the mini-van with Laurie, Cooper, Jesse, and me, and the driver started off. One of the first things we noticed was that none of the drivers had their lights on. There was a blackout in that part of the city, so there weren't even any streetlights, and people had, at most, their parking lights on. They were driving at what seemed to us breakneck speed—weaving among bicycles, pedestrians, and other cars and trucks.

The only reason we could possibly imagine that they didn't have their lights on was so they could flash them at people for effect: to scare them into moving out of the way. If that was the case, it failed miserably. People paid no more attention to flashing lights than they did to blaring horns. Occasionally drivers would use horns and lights in combination, for the added startle factor, I suppose, but again, to no avail. About the only result we could see from their driving without lights and occasionally flashing them on, was that they blinded each other because their eyes weren't used to the light.

As with so many things, we scoffed at the unfamiliar, then given more information, realized our folly. After we began riding our bikes throughout the city at night, we realized it was much easier for us to see when the drivers kept their lights off, and as there were far more of us than there were of them, it only made sense that the drivers should accede to our needs. It also became apparent that the flashing lights served as a good indicator to us when there were cars and trucks in the area, and we could exercise added caution. As it was more difficult for the drivers to see us, and as we had more to lose in the event of a car/bike collision, such added caution on our part also made a lot of sense.

It was during the second part of October that the utilities started shutting off. Counting heat, hot water, natural gas, and electricity, we were never without all four at once. Seldom were we without three. Occasionally we were without two. Often we were without one. Electricity was the most frequently delinquent, typically going off about 7:00 a.m. and staying off until about 7:00 p.m. two out of three days. When we realized it was going to be a continuing situation, we purchased a large bundle of candles, which we used at the rate of two or three an evening.

One evening I was making spaghetti sauce in the wok over one of the gas fire-rings. When the gas went out halfway through, I just switched it to the electric oven. Back in the States, I probably would have seen it as a catastrophe, but China had made me more flexible, more patient. We stopped complaining when the electricity went off. We just said, "Oh, there goes the electricity," and went on with whatever we were doing. In China when something didn't go the way it was supposed to, we accepted it, having gained the perspective to recognize that not every little setback was worthy of great expenditures of energy and concern.

We considered ourselves quite fortunate when, about a month later, with no more warning that when the outages had begun, the electricity stopped going off. From then until we left, we had power more consistently than anyone we knew in other parts of the city—with the exception of the American Consulate, of course, which had the same priority as hospitals, police stations, and other emergency facilities. It was unusual then for us to be without power for more than an hour at a time, and no more frequently than once a week.

With the exception of the Westerners, both faculty and students got their boiled water from one of several boilers throughout campus. Some of them had to walk a couple of blocks, at least twice a day, to the nearest boiler. They were housed in buildings about the size of small, two-car garages, and alongside each building was a row of spigots with a shallow cement sink under them. At meal times, there was a steady flow of students and faculty to those spigots. Between meals, and in the evenings, the flow slowed to a trickle.

During the winter, the boilers provided hot water heat for the buildings on campus, as well. In the case of the two buildings that housed foreign teachers and foreign students, from 6:30 to 7:15 in the morning, and from 7:30 to 10:30 in the evening, they also supplied hot water for bathing. Everyone else had cold water only, and had to go to the public bath house—usually once a week—to bathe. It was located near the center of campus, which meant that some people had to go as far as six or seven blocks when they wanted a bath. Our hot water for bathing was pretty dependable. I liked to take my showers in the morning, and there were only a few times when I couldn't. Except, of course when they tore up the supply lines, and we didn't have any hot water for eleven days.

One evening a young man from the Foreign Affairs Office came to our apartment to inform us that for "five or ten days" we wouldn't have any hot water. I asked when that would start. He said it had started earlier that day. I said it would have been nice to know a little earlier, so we could have taken our last baths for five or ten days. He said oh no, we could still take baths, he had brought us some tickets to the public bath on campus.

I asked if he had any idea what kind of reaction we would get if we went as a family with two small American boys to the public bath. He said he thought people would be very interested in watching us bathe. I pointed out that we were not used to having crowds watch us bathe, and we would be very uncomfortable. He said, well of course they are segregated baths, the men go on one day and the women go on another, so I wouldn't have women watching me bathe. I said that would be good, but that having 50 men watch me would bother me, as well. I'm not a prude, but on the other hand, there are limits to my immodesty. He allowed as how that was reasonable, but that there really wasn't anything else he could do. Good point.

We were lucky—there was a boiler adjacent to our building, so I didn't have far to carry water. We cut our baths back to every other day. Cooper and Jesse shared one batch of water, and Laurie and I shared another. The water straight from the boiler was scalding hot, so we could mix two cold to one hot. That meant I could get away with carrying only four 2 1/2 gallon plastic scrub buckets of water upstairs for each pair of baths—assuming we could get by without the kind of bath in which we soaked luxuriantly in a tub full to our chins—and I made sure we could. Cooper offered to let me use his and Jesse's water when they were done. I took one look and decided I'd rather carry water all day than do that. I've never even cared to watch mud wrestling, let alone try it myself.

One Tuesday afternoon in the middle of October, a staff member from the Foreign Affairs Office came to our apartment to ask if we'd like to go to a concert the next evening. Whereas in the States, we would have thought one day very short notice, in China we were impressed with the lead time. We asked him what kind of concert, and he said, "A fiddle concert." After a bit of discussion, we determined there was a traditional Chinese instrument something like a two-stringed fiddle, which performers rested on their thighs, rather than tucking under their chins, but still produced the music by drawing a bow across gut strings.

I said yes, I'd be interested in going, but Laurie and Cooper didn't feel well, so they declined. Jesse decided it was something he couldn't miss, but I said I didn't think a two-year-old would go very well at a classical concert. Our friend from the Foreign Affairs Office insisted it would be no problem. I needn't have worried.

It was an excellent concert. I sat in rapt attention, awed by the performer's skill and how many different sounds he could get from that tiny instrument. Jesse was entranced. He sat, silent, nearly unmoving, throughout the two and a half hour concert. The young man who played the instrument was only 27, but he was every bit as good as any classical violinist I'd seen in the States. There were only two pieces I didn't particularly care for—traditional ones from the Ming Dynasty. In addition to traditional Chinese works, he played a Romanian piece called "The Lark," "The Song of the Gypsy," and several modern compositions that reminded me of Bela Bartok.

We had been in China about two and a half months when Laurie and I realized we no longer thought in terms of dollars, but considered items in the context of their cost in Chinese money. There are three and three fourths yuan, the basic Chinese unit of currency, to one dollar, but for everyday use we had just been figuring four to the dollar. The yuan were divided into ten units, similar to dimes, except that they were small paper notes. They were in turn divided into ten "pennies," which could be either tiny paper notes, or small coins, much like the play money I remembered from my youth. These came in one, two, three, and five "cent" denominations. The notes were various colors, and had trucks, trains, ships, and planes on them, depending on their value. Jesse used to say, "Dad, can I have a ship money?"

When we first went shopping, we were spending money that we had exchanged dollars for, so when something cost five yuan, we automatically converted that to about $1.25, and considered it really cheap. When we started spending money that we had earned at the Chinese rate, however, we thought of something costing five yuan as relatively expensive. The 600 yuan we got each month was anywhere from five to ten times what the Chinese made, but it was much lower than the salary we were used to in the States.

Also, although the cost of living at the level of most of the Chinese we knew was much less than we made, the cost of living at the level we had back home was much more. For example, a pound of peanuts was the equivalent of about 60 cents—cheap by U.S. standards. On the other hand, in terms of Chinese money, it was fairly expensive compared to other foods we could buy for the same amount—five pounds of rice or cabbage, for example. Hamburger was about 90 cents a pound, but we could buy five pounds of fatty pork for that. As might be expected, the food items most common in Chinese diets were the cheapest. Those least common—but often most familiar to us—were most expensive. Consequently, we had to find someplace between that was acceptable, and that we could afford.

The weather during the last half of October was beautiful, and I was homesick for the softball tournaments I was missing back home. Then one afternoon, when I was outside trying to hold my own in a game of badminton with Cooper, a Japanese student approached me, and in very halting English (after all, he was there learning Chinese as his second language), asked me if I would like to play on their baseball team. It seems the Chinese students from a university on the other side of town had challenged the foreign students at Liaoning University to a game of baseball, and they had accepted the challenge readily.

Except the only foreign students that knew how to play baseball, or wanted to learn, were the seven Japanese. With much effort, they prevailed upon the Swedish boy—who had never so much as picked up a ball or bat—but were unable, try as they might, to find a ninth for their team. There's no way they could have passed me off as a student, so I suppose they just figured the other team wouldn't mind, as I clearly did not pose much of a threat.

The Japanese were avid baseball fans, and they had brought to China with them a collection of equipment, including three wooden bats (smaller than most used in the States), some balls (the same size as we use, but with soft rubber coatings about a quarter inch thick), and a couple of extra gloves (small). On the appointed afternoon, our team set out by bus for the trip across town.

In addition to our accompanying fans, we were seven enthusiastic Japanese boys, one Swedish boy who had never played, and one old-timer. I played slow-pitch softball every summer, but hadn't played baseball since I left the Marine Corps in 1967. The Swedish boy spoke good English, so I was able to explain some of the more critical rules to him on the way over. Well, we were going to play a pick-up game with Chinese students, after all. Most people in China had never heard of baseball, let alone played it. How good could they be?

We piled out of the bus, face to face with what must have been the closest thing to a varsity baseball team in northern China. They had uniforms, they had a coach, they had umpires, they had bases, and they had a diamond chalked out on the dirt and stones of their university's central playing field. When we arrived, they were going through very rigorous, coordinated exercises with their coach. I think the Japanese students were very surprised, but they did a great job of being inscrutable. I didn't speak any better Japanese than Chinese, but from the tenor of their conversation, I think my team decided there wasn't much we could do but go ahead with it.

I'm not quite sure how, but we beat them nine to four. I don't know which team was more surprised, but both took it with a great deal of aplomb. It didn't surprise anyone that the Japanese students played well, but the Swedish student who had never played baseball in his life got a hit. The old foreign expert who hadn't played baseball in 20 years hit a single up the middle, got hit by a pitch and walked once, and stole home to score once. All in all, it was a pretty good game

In Shenyang, as in all the major cities we visited, the streets around entrances to public facilities thronged with an amazing assortment of street vendors. There were people giving haircuts—not haphazardly, but whole barbershops set up on the sidewalk. There were shoe repair people. There were people selling exploded corn, and candy, and ice cream, and shish ke-bab. There was a man with an homemade cotton candy machine that looked as though it were made out of spare parts from a rocket ship or something.

There were people selling baked sweet potatoes, and others selling steamed sweet corn. There was a man with a huge, gasoline-powered machine that extruded a kind of corn tube when he stepped on a lever with his foot. Some of them he left about three feet long and straight; others he made into basket shapes by coiling them while they were still hot. We hadn't seen anything remotely resembling it in the States, but the product tasted a lot like corn puffs cereal.

Although outside the zoo was the biggest concentration and greatest variety, such street vendors appeared throughout the city. In fact, we used them as we did convenience stores back in the States. We bought our yogurt from the yogurt vendor outside the gates of the campus, and got our shoes fixed by the shoe repair woman who set up at seven each morning on the entrance steps of one of the dorms. We took the bikes over at least once a week to a little old man with glasses that looked like they had been made from the bottoms of coke bottles. He was brilliant at fixing bikes, using tools many of which I would have throw away at home as being worn out.

Then of course there were the vegetable stands, fruit stands, and bread stands. Instead of driving to the nearest Seven-Eleven, we just walked down the street. After we were there a while, we got to know where the closest stands of various kinds were, when they were open, and which had the highest quality products or services at the best prices. We became discriminating China shoppers. Nothing matched the growing feeling of belonging we got as we began to frequent each person's stand, and began to receive the special treatment reserved for "regulars."

One Sunday, on the way back from an afternoon of playing in the park at the North Tomb, we realized how much we had come to take the street vendors for granted. On the way out of the park we had stopped to buy three tea eggs (hard boiled eggs, with a unique color and taste derived from having been soaked in strong tea), two baked sweet potatoes, and four meat pies (little pancakes with meat and vegetable filling). We had, without a second thought, purchased them at the stands outside the gates and, having leaned our bikes against a tree, all four of us were standing there on the sidewalk, eating. It was like the New York City office worker who, pressed for time at lunch, stops for a hot dog from the stand on the corner.

We took Cooper and Jesse to a Halloween party at the Consulate, where they could go trick-or-treating. There were only eight apartments there, however, and we knew that would never sate their appetite for the traditional Halloween treats, so we decided to dress them in their costumes and take them trick-or-treating in the foreign students dormitory. We were culturally inclusive, knocking on the doors of students from Sweden, Germany, Italy, Japan, Great Britain, the United States, and the Soviet Union.

Of course, the Americans knew right away what was going on, and the British caught on very quickly. The Italians have something resembling Halloween, so it didn't take long for them to get the idea. The

Cooper and Jesse, ready to go out and "rob people" on Halloween.

Germans, the Swedes, the Russians and the Japanese were a bit taken aback, however. Although after a while they all understood they were supposed to put some sort of treats in the boys' sacks, I'm not sure all of them really understood why. I'm sure that to this day, some of them believe that in the United States, once a year, all property laws are suspended, and people are allowed to don masks and steal from others with impunity.

It took us a lot longer to do that little bit of trick-or-treating than it's ever taken before, because we had to explain at almost every door what was going on—often to students that spoke about as much English as we did their language—but the boys loved it. The result was that they have not, before or since, gotten such interesting treats in their Halloween hauls. Most of the students seemed to understand that some kind of edible goodie was called for—some even seemed to have stocked up "just in case"—but one contributed a Kewpie doll piggy bank, another gave a couple of stamps, and yet another, after rummaging through every drawer and shelf in his room, came up with a cloth measuring tape.

One of the Japanese students had been to Beijing a couple of weeks earlier, and for some reason, known only to her, had brought back two panda bear suits. Laurie asked if they were for Halloween, and she said, "What is this 'Halloween'?" That pretty much answered the question.

Well, when she saw Jesse and Cooper in costumes, going from room to room robbing people, she didn't really understand what was going on, but she did recognize an opportunity when she saw it. She got one of her friends, and they each put on a panda suit, so that when the boys knocked on her door, she was ready. Cooper didn't have any problem with it—he knew the Beaver mascot for the football team back home was a person in a beaver suit, so he knew right away (although, with Laurie and me, he had no idea why) that he was looking at two people in panda costumes. Jesse didn't.

Jesse just assumed they were pandas. He thought it was pretty close to the neatest thing he had ever seen that there were two panda bears in the foreign students' dorm. He didn't seem to have much trouble with the fact that they were the first talking pandas he had encountered. But the thing he really had a hard time accepting was that they knew his name. He stood there and looked up at them, mouth agape, and it was at that moment that I understood what the phrase "eyes big as saucers" really means. He answered when they spoke to him—luckily, these Japanese pandas spoke pretty good English—but he never did understand how in the world those two panda bears knew his name.

Jesse's costume was easy—he wanted to be a clown, so we just put him in a pair of his Dr. Denton pajamas, sewed some extra little bows and stuff on them, put some make-up on his face, and tied a bow in his hair. Cooper's was a bit more difficult—he wanted to be a test pilot. We weren't quite sure how we were going to go about making him a test pilot. Well, the Chinese propensity to litter benefited us in this case, because we were able to construct most of his costume from "found" things.

During our walks on campus, we found an old thermos bottle. It was a big one—about two and a half feet tall. The inside was broken, so it was just the shell, which made a dandy "oxygen tank." We found an old corrugated hose that once drained water from a washing machine. That became the hose from his oxygen tank to some old plastic thing we didn't recognize in its former life, but which, with a cord attached to go around his head, made a passable oxygen mask.

The construction workers wore bamboo hard-hats. Actually, "hard-hat" was rather a misnomer—they were really "firm-hats." I can't imagine that they could have kept a falling brick from crushing anybody's skull, and I offer the one we found as "exhibit A." If anyone was wearing it when it suffered the damage it had before we found it, I hope the government took good care of his widow.

We were able to resurrect it with an added layer of paper we had crayoned into a reasonable likeness of camouflage. Thus adorned, it didn't look too unlike a military helmet. A visor, in blue, see-through plastic, attached to an elastic headband (a sun-shade for tennis, perhaps?—surely not headgear for a casino gambler!), with minor reworking, became a set of goggles. In a brown sweat suit; outfitted with all that stuff, "presto" he was a test pilot. He vowed it was his favorite Halloween costume ever. It was a sincere vow—one destined to evoke feelings of warmth in parents—but one that should be viewed in the context that he had made it every Halloween for the five preceding years, as well (he couldn't yet talk for his first one).

The Consulate school was attended by seven students, ranging from first to eleventh grade, and the party was the result of their efforts, with help from their teacher. They had put together suitably Halloweeny refreshments, a haunted house, and an interesting (if not professional) version of the witches' scene from "Macbeth"—rife with "in" jokes. They had made a special effort on publicity for the event, so had drawn the attendance of every American child in Liaoning Provence—all eight of them. With parents and friends, we numbered at least twenty five.

Although they could offer only eight apartments for visitors' to trick-or-treat at, we were awed by the amount and variety of the goodies. We'd been in China for three months, and it didn't take nearly that long to really begin to appreciate the Western candy to which we no longer had access. Chinese candy was mostly of two kinds. There was a sort of sweetened playdough—basically dry globs of sugar and flour. And there was something much like flat chocolate candles—very waxy, semi-sweet chocolate bars.

Neither offered much thrill to our sweet teeth. After several more months, however, we did find a couple of kinds that were really pretty good. "Sport candy" was a kind of firm, but chewy chocolate/caramel with peanuts—like wax-paper-wrapped, bite-sized chunks of Snickers bars. It was not always available. Nor was the hard peanut-brittle-like candy that resembled Planter's peanut bars, which was available in "plain" or chocolate flavor.

Imagine our glee at encountering imported Kit-Kat Bars, Rollos, Milky Ways, Mars Bars, Hershey's Bars (plain, almonds, and crushed peanuts) and—my personal favorite—candy corn. The folks at the Consulate knew what a treat it was for us, and they had so much of it, they just kept pouring it in the boys' bags. We didn't stop them. As Laurie put it: "Far be it from us to interfere with our children's happiness."

There was one apartment where the people weren't home, so they had left a huge bowl of candy corn out for the children to help themselves. I admit it—each of the boys got an extra my-size handful in his bag. It's scientifically proven—sugar deprivation makes grown men do strange things. When we got home, we rewrote a rule. Always before, anything the boys got for Halloween was theirs, to eat (within reason) when they chose. Not that year—the spoils of that Halloween served as dessert for the family for weeks.

Chapter Four
November

Everybody else on campus had heat November first, but for some reason, our heat didn't come on when everybody else's did. I mean, even the other people in our building had heat. We didn't realize that until one day Laurie noticed the radiators were on in the hallway downstairs. I think I've mentioned what a smart person Laurie is. She said, "Wait a minute, if there's heat coming out of these radiators, why isn't there heat coming out of ours?"

I went over to the Foreign Affairs Office and asked when we would get heat in our apartment. The young man said we already had heat—it had been turned on November first. I said ours hadn't been. He said I must be mistaken, we really had no heat? I said nope. He asked for how long? I said forever—we'd never had any heat. He said you mean today? I said no, forever—the heat hadn't come on in our apartment since we'd been there—the last time there was heat in that apartment was probably the previous spring, before they had turned it off. He asked if I was sure. I said yes, I was very sure. I said our radiators were stone cold.

Then he acquired a knowing look and explained that the heat was only on from 6:00 in the evening to 9:00 in the morning. I said ours wasn't. He asked if we had checked between the aforementioned hours. I said we had checked over and over, at all hours of the day and night, and it had never been on. He insisted I feel his radiator to see that it, too, was cold, as it was about 11:30 a.m. I agreed that his radiator was somewhat cold, though not as cold as ours, because his had been warm a mere two and a half hours earlier, and it had been a minimum of months since ours had been. He said he would come over after 6:00 that evening to feel our radiators. I told him he was welcome.

He came over, put his hand on each of our three radiators, and said we had no heat. I said good thinking. He said he would send someone over to look at it. In the meantime, he said he would get us an alternate source of heat—just in case it took a while to fix ours. Laurie gave me a look that clearly said, "Uh-oh." She had been in China long enough to know what that meant. The stop-gap heat source he brought us was a small electric space heater. He said, "Here, this should keep you warm until they get your heat fixed." I said, "Wait a minute—this is it? One space heater for the whole apartment?" He said, "Yes, that's all we have." It was hard to argue with that. It was a game little heater, but badly outgunned. It could either keep one room pretty warm all the time, or, moved from room to room, take the chill off each in turn.

There followed a 3-week process in which 15 times anywhere from one to five men came into our apartment and trooped through all three rooms. Each put at least one hand, and some two hands, on each radiator. Each said, "Maio (May-oh')," which, loosely translated, means, "there isn't any." I always said, "Right." After about the fourteenth time, we didn't bother getting out of our chairs. We just smiled as they went by.

The fifteenth time the repairmen came trooping through—there were five of them that time—each of them put his hands on the radiators. Each of them said, "Maio." Each of them smiled encouragement before leaving. We smiled and said, "Yeah, maio." A half hour later, Laurie said, "Roy, there's heat coming out of the radiators." Sure enough, there was. We never saw anyone actually do anything to fix the radiators, so we decided it must have been a case of "laying on of hands"—it was probably what they had in mind all along: a miraculous repair.

Clothes drying on our radiator after the laying on of hands.

At any rate, we had heat the rest of the winter. Not a lot of heat—generally about 56 degrees in the boys' room (which had a southern exposure), 54 degrees in our bedroom, and 52 degrees in the kitchen/bathroom. I started wearing my longjohns the first of November, not because it was so cold outside—usually in the high fifties during the day. After all, it was a lot colder in northern Minnesota, and I seldom wore them there. They turned the heat off in my office each day at noon, however, and those thick, concrete walls acted like a refrigerator. I never actually took the temperature there, but by late afternoon it got so cold I had to stop working occasionally to slap the numbness out of my fingers.

It wasn't until the nights started getting cold that Laurie and I realized none of our blankets were wide enough. Our hosts had provided all four of us with sets of bedclothes that included a sheet, two wool blankets, a down comforter, a pillowcase, a colorful cotton bedspread, and a terrycloth hand towel with brightly painted scenes of birds or flowers for use as a pillowcase cover.

During the summer and fall, we had piled the blankets and comforters on the mattress and covered them with the sheet, which disguised the fact that the mattress was very lumpy. As the nights got cooler, we sometimes slept under the bedspread. When it got colder, however, we were forced to move under the blankets and comforters. It was then we realized just how hard and lumpy our mattress was, and that, for some reason, it was higher in the middle than the edges. It was also then that we realized our blankets weren't wide enough. The boys had no problem. They had single beds, so all of their comforters and blankets worked fine. Our Chinese hosts had found a double bed somewhere for Laurie and me, however, which we greatly appreciated, except that all of our blankets and quilts were made for single beds.

So we each had our own set of blankets, which overlapped in the middle. When we made our bed in the morning, the combination of graded mattress and overlapping bedclothes made it extremely high and lumpy in the middle, dwindling off to each edge. At night, we tended to move together in the middle, because that's where the most blankets and quilts were. If we clung together, so as not to roll toward the lower edges, we were toasty warm in there, if somewhat compressed from the combined weight of our bedclothes. Sleeping under all that weight probably did wonders for our muscle tone, and it certainly was cozy.

My assistant came to our apartment one day in early November and proudly handed me a slip of paper with Chinese writing on it. He said, "Here, this is for you." Having no idea what it was, of course, but not wanting to seem ungrateful, I said, "Oh, thank you. That's nice." He smiled and waited, knowing what had to come next. He was right.

"Okay, what is it," I was forced to ask. After a few minutes of explanation, it became clear that it was the Chinese equivalent of a gift certificate. In celebration of Teachers' Day—which, as nearly as I could tell, was similar to Mothers' Day or Fathers' Day—the administration of the Chinese department had given one to each faculty member. They had decided that as a foreign expert assigned to the department, I should be included—another example of the kindness and generosity with which I was consistently treated.

The certificate was for 100 yuan—about $25—a sum that would go a long way in a store in China. It was for use at a "sports store," which were rather like sporting goods stores in the States, only with no sporting goods—just sports clothes. They had running suits (or, as they called them, "sports suits"), body suits, t-shirts, shoes, sports socks—that sort of thing. My assistant went along to help me find the place, and to explain to the clerks what I was there for. I didn't see anything I was particularly crazy about, but I didn't want to seem ungrateful. Nothing in the place was made from natural fibers, so I picked out a sports suit—a modest, grey, polyester number—and said, "Yeah, that's nice. I'll take that."

My assistant said, "Okay, what else would you like?" I said I didn't really need anything else, and he said, "But that's only 75 yuan. You've got 25 more yuan." I said, "What if I don't want anything else?" He said, "Oh no, it has to come out to 100 yuan." So I looked around some more. After a while, the clerks—who had been standing around looking nervous—said something to him, and he informed me they were closing in two minutes. Only slightly rattled, I found a shorts and shirt combination that would fit Laurie and said I'd take it. That brought the total to 92 yuan. I was proud of my composure under pressure. I was certain that would be close enough. I was wrong.

"No, no," he said, "it has to come out to exactly 100." I crumbled under the pressure, and admitted there just wasn't anything else I wanted. He said, "Well, here, how about these socks?" I said, "Fine." So they ended up giving me some socks and a couple of handkerchiefs, or something. Anyway, it came out to 100 yuan exactly. The store was closing, they were happy, and it was okay with me. So I got a nice sports suit with Chinese calligraphy on it that I could wear when I jogged back in the States—if only I jogged.

As circumstance would have it, I had the opportunity to wear my new sports suit sooner than I expected. Not long after I got it, my assistant mentioned that many Chinese were starting to play tennis instead of badminton. He said he had played once, had really enjoyed it, and wanted to get a tennis racket and learn how to play. He told me he was trying to save a little from his salary each month to buy a racket.

I asked him how he was doing, and he said he was able to save about two yuan a month from his salary of 56 yuan. I said at that rate it would take him two years. He said, "No, two and a half," and I was struck again by the patience I continually saw exhibited by the Chinese. A young teacher in the States would have been playing for months with a racquet purchased using VISA or MasterCard—and paying 18 percent a year for the privilege.

He and his family had done so much for us that I took the first opportunity to go downtown and buy him a tennis racket. The best tennis racket they had (one of those magnesium alloy things with an oversized head) was the equivalent of fifteen dollars—not much, considering all he and his family had given us. So, I got him that tennis racket. He was beside himself with joy, and immediately asked if we could arrange a weekly tennis date.

The time that seemed best for both of us was after my 2:00 class on Tuesdays. The problem was that because students had very few afternoon classes, there were oodles of them out playing tennis, badminton, volleyball, basketball, and soccer. The space set aside on campuses for such activities was woefully inadequate, so students occupied any spot even remotely large enough for their desired activity. It was next to impossible for us to find space to hit a tennis ball back and forth, but my assistant had an ingenious idea. He said, "Look, the swimming pool has been drained for the season, let's go see if we can play in it."

We checked, and sure enough—there was this big, empty, Olympic-sized swimming pool with an almost-flat bottom. The walls weren't quite as high as the fence around a tennis court, so we had to climb out of the pool once in a while to get the ball, but it was certainly better than the alternatives. Again, as with so many things in China, it sounded strange, but it worked.

By the second week in November, the almost weekly trips the Foreign Affairs Office had been arranging for us had dwindled to a trickle. It was one of these, however, that we found most educational. We went to a town about 60 kilometers southwest of Shenyang to visit a paper factory that produced brown wrapping paper. At the time of our visit, they were adding the equipment to make it the first factory in China to produce newsprint from recycled paper.

The first Chinese factory producing newsprint from recycled paper.

The man who ran the paper factory was famous in China. A reform economist, he was heavily involved in the movement to open China to Western economic patterns, and had instituted many of the processes of a market-driven economy. We had the opportunity to sit and talk with him through an interpreter for a couple of hours, and he pointed out that his factory was a rarity for China, in that it was not government-owned. When pressed on the point, however, he admitted that technically the government owned the buildings and the land, but that they had turned everything over to him, and he ran the factory just as though he owned it.

He explained that any money he made from the operation he could treat as his own, to reinvest in research and development, pay bonuses to his workers, or take more profit for himself. It seemed he was indeed operating as a private entrepreneur. The amount of recent construction and new equipment indicated that he must have chosen to put much of the profit back into the business. He said he could pay his people what he wanted, that the government didn't determine their salaries as they did in most factories. Consequently, he said, they were paid more than most workers of that level in China

The process seemed to be working very well. He had increased production by 100 percent each of the four years he had been manager. The government wasn't about to interfere with that kind of success. If there was anything they were interested in at that time, it was economic

74

development, and he was accomplishing precisely that. They seemed ready to let him move in any direction he wanted.

As usually happened on such "tours," we spent hours in their well-appointed meeting room, then the tour itself took only about ten minutes. The place wasn't very big, and there just wasn't much to see, but they really seemed to be turning out the paper. The factory itself was dismal—it was amazing the quality of paper they were producing, given the antiquated equipment and facilities they were working with. Then they showed us a huge new building that was going up, where they said they would produce newsprint from waste paper. The manager was really excited about that, saying it was going to be a really great new process. We didn't doubt him, judging from how bright he seemed, and how well in hand he seemed to have everything.

We had lunch with the manager, the governor of the county, and the head of the Communist Party in the county. Any doubts we may have had about whether he was being given free reign to run that factory were dispelled at lunch. The local Communist Party director made it very clear that was precisely what was happening, and that it was going to happen more and more in China. That was exactly what they were looking toward, he said: finding people with the talent to operate big businesses at a profit. And, he said, they were going to treat them as entrepreneurs and allow them to make better profits for themselves and their workers.

It was well into November before we realized the wonderful treatment we had been getting from the Foreign Affairs Office was part of a honeymoon, which, as the saying goes, doesn't last forever. It was then they began to withdraw some of the privileges we had been told went with the job. We were told when we came that we would have a car available whenever we needed one—a perk we hadn't taken full advantage of. We rode our bikes almost everywhere. The Consulate, however, was all the way on the other side of town—about a 45-minute bike ride—so, on our infrequent trips there, we had used the university's car.

One of the children at the Consulate had a November birthday party to which Cooper and Jesse had been invited, so we reserved the car to take us. The day of the party, one of the people from the Foreign Affairs Office came to our apartment to inform us that we could no longer have the car for free, and another of "those" conversations ensued. Actually, he said I could have the car for free, because I was a foreign expert and they provided a car for foreign experts. He said Laurie could ride free, because she was the wife of a foreign expert, but Cooper and Jesse would have to pay, because they were neither foreign experts nor wives of foreign experts. I said that didn't make much sense, we couldn't leave our children when we went someplace, so essentially what they were saying was I had to pay for the car.

I asked how much. He said 10 yuan—about $2.50—cheap by U.S. standards, but expensive on our Chinese salary. Laurie was a bit upset, and said, "Wait a minute, we have a letter of invitation from Liaoning University that invites not just Roy, but the boys and me as well. It seems to me that if you invited them to come, you should provide the same services for them that you provide for Roy and me." He said, "You have a letter that says that?" She showed it to him, and he said, "Oh, let me go show this to the administration." We watched him go, satisfied that we had made our point.

He came back about an hour later and said the administration had decided that we must always pay for the car unless it had to do with teaching. I asked what that meant. Did that mean if I went downtown to buy chalk that I could get the car for free, but if we went to the Consulate we had to pay for it? He said well, no, what that meant was we didn't have to pay for the car when the Foreign Affairs Office arranged it, but we did have to pay 30 yuan for it when we arranged it. I said, "Wait a minute, an hour ago it was 10, now it's 30?" He said, "I'm sorry, that's what the administration has decided."

I had to feel kind of sorry for the guy—he wasn't making the rules, but he had serve as the bearer of bad news. So we tried not to take it out on him. He asked what time we'd like the car that evening. I said we wouldn't. He asked if he should tell them to cancel the car. I said yes, to tell them they'd priced themselves out of the market. He said they'd what? I said in the United States, as a capitalist country, people could "price themselves out of the market," meaning they'd asked more than people were willing to pay for their service. I told him that was what his administration had done. He grinned and said he would tell them that. We assumed nothing would come of it, but at least he'd learned a useful English idiom.

The drivers had won again. We didn't for a second buy that stuff about his "administration." Oh, sure, his boss was making the decision, but it was in response to pressure from the drivers. In the day-to-day operations of the country, the drivers were some of the most powerful people in China. Because only they had any knowledge at all of gasoline-powered vehicles, they held a unique power. They knew that without them everything in China would grind to a halt, and they used that knowledge tyrannically. By and large they were imperious, demanding, haughty people. When they said, "Here we go," there we went, and if we weren't ready, we got left behind.

I had drivers pull away when I was talking to somebody with the door open and my leg hanging out. They didn't care. They were ready to go, even if I wasn't. I had to stop talking, get in, and pull my leg in, or have it taken off by the first telephone pole we passed. Given the way the system worked, there wasn't anything that could be done. It wasn't just the drivers, it was all the service people. They knew they weren't going to be fired. They could do their jobs the way they wanted, and only the most powerful government officials—with whom they almost never came into contact—could really do anything about it.

Not having the university car available turned out to be a blessing. Not only did it limit our exposure to the drivers, it also gave us a much better feel for the city and its people. Nothing does the job like getting out among the people on their terms. With the bike the university had provided me, and the one we had bought for Laurie, we averaged two people per bike.

The Chinese had bike seats similar to those we had used back home, that were mounted over the back wheel—except, of course, theirs were made from woven straw or wood, rather than moulded plastic. Nonetheless, they did the job just fine. The Chinese didn't like to use them, however, because they cut down on the carrying capacity of their bikes. Most Chinese bikes had a sturdy rack over the back fender that was where they usually carried their "stuff"—especially heavy or bulky loads. So when they carried children, they usually did so in front of them. We got a little wooden seat at the market for that purpose. It was ingeniously made, so that we could easily remove it when we didn't need it.

These were not the ten-speed bikes we were used to back home. They weren't even the three-speed Schwinn I had used as a boy. Actually, they looked a lot like the old Schwinns—with high handle bars and hard seats—and they were about the same weight. Except Chinese bikes had no gearshifts, we just got on and pedaled. If it was uphill, we pedaled harder, and if it was downhill, we didn't have to pedal as hard—that's just the way it was. They all had locks, most of them a kind we had not seen in the States. They were a lot like one half of a handcuff, bolted to the frame above the back tire, so that when they were closed, they went around the tire between the spokes, and made it impossible to ride the bike.

The Chinese were quite taken by Western, BMX-style dirt bikes—not just the children, but adults as well. It seemed a bit surreal for us to see 50- and 60-year-old women riding their dirt bikes to the market—grandmas perched on high, banana seats, clutching high-rise handle-bars, fat knobby tires humming on the pavement.

Many of the streets were very rough, and the bikes took a real beat-ing. In the States we took our 10-speeds in each spring for preventive maintenance, and that was it. In China we had one of our bikes over to the bike repair guy at least once a week. Chains broke, brakes got out of adjustment, wheels got out of round, or—they didn't seem to know what a lock washer was—nuts and bolts worked loose, leaving some part dragging or rattling. A lot of the Chinese just didn't pay any attention to a wheel out of round, or something wobbling, scraping, or clanking. To ride down the street was to expose ourselves to a symphony of bi-cycles: some of them scratching, some of them clanking, some of them scraping, some of them whistling—each carrying its distinctive part of the score.

A 45-minute bike ride across town really wasn't bad when I was the only one on the bike, pumping the way my body was meant to pump a bike—with my knees straight ahead. But when I had to pump them out to the side to avoid hitting the butt of a little boy (whom I dearly loved, but who was of neither the weight nor the aerodynamic configuration to improve a bike's performance) sitting in front of me, it added a bit to the challenge.

Laurie's bike had a rack over the back fender, and that was where Cooper rode. The racks on Chinese bikes were very much like those on many bikes in the States—flat chrome things with large spring-loaded clips that could be lifted to hold things down. Cooper sat on that rack with both feet off to one side, holding on with one hand on each side of his butt. We had seen Chinese children doing that, and figured if it worked for them, it should work for us. In fact, we saw families of four on one bike, with the man pedaling, the woman sitting on the rack over the back fender, holding one child, a second child perched on the bar in front of the man—what must have amounted to 300 or 400 pounds on one bike.

Actually, the bikes were surprisingly well balanced. With the tires pumped up really hard, they rode quite well. And we did pump the tires up hard—we had no idea how much pressure we put in them because we used hand pumps, and we didn't see a pressure gauge the whole time we were in China. We just pumped until we got tired; then squeezed the tires with our thumbs to make sure they were good and hard. If they weren't, we pumped some more. With Cooper on the back of Laurie's bike, Jesse on the front of mine, and loaded baskets looped over our handlebars and strapped to the rack over my back fender, setting off for a 45-minute trek across town, we never felt more like we belonged.

———————————

When we arrived at the Consulate apartments for the birthday party, we were faced with a food-laden table bearing a big sign that read, "Free Food, Take What You Want." The woman who ran the Consulate school, and her husband, had been sending articles to the States for inclusion in their church newsletter. In one of those articles, thinking it might interest their fellow parishioners, they had listed the food items they were having trouble getting, and had received 25 large boxes of food from church members in response. That was great, except they were scheduled to return home in three months.

The woman said she had calculated that if they each ate four bowls of hot oatmeal every morning for the next three months, they would only have 12 more containers to dispose of when they left. So, knowing several teachers would be coming to the party, they had set their extra food out for us to take. It was as though they had set that table up especially for Laurie and me. We borrowed a couple of large market baskets, and filled them to overflowing with chili powder, ground oregano, black pepper, lemon juice, macaroni & cheese, oatmeal, coffee, and most of the other food items we hadn't been able to find.

Had we been driving a tractor-trailer in the States, we would have had to pay overload fines. Several times during the bike ride home (it took us about half again as long as usual, we were so overloaded) we wished the Foreign Affairs Office had waited a bit longer to withdraw our car privileges. All the effort was worth it, however. With judicious use, we still had some of those precious items left at the end of our year there.

Two things we weren't able to find, and that our friends didn't have on their "free food" table, were mayonnaise and mustard. We bought a bottle of of ketchup in our dining room the first week—why they had ketchup, but neither mustard nor mayonnaise, will always be one of those mysteries of the Orient, but that's how it was. So one Saturday afternoon, Laurie decided we'd been doing without mustard and mayonnaise entirely long enough, and announced that she was going to make some. She had gotten recipes from someone at the Consulate. The mustard turned out extremely well. It was a cross between regular yellow mustard, hot mustard, and that brown mustard with horseradish in it. It was pretty hot, but Laurie and I agreed it was some of the best we'd tasted.

The mayonnaise didn't turn out quite as well as the mustard. It looked like mayonnaise, but it just wasn't the same. After three months without mayonnaise, though, it was good to have something even vaguely resembling it. She made adjustments in each subsequent batch, but never did get it right. It had the texture and the look, and it moistened sandwiches the way mayonnaise is supposed to, but it never had quite the tang it should have.

The staple winter vegetable for the northern Chinese was what, in the States, we called Chinese cabbage, which looked like big, fat stalks of celery. We had eaten it back home, and liked it fine, but nothing had prepared us for the sheer quantity of it in China—it was everywhere. For weeks, we watched a continuous stream of trucks and tractor- or horse-drawn wagons bring loads of Chinese cabbage into the city. It was not unusual to walk down the street and see four or five dump trucks full of Chinese cabbage waiting to be unloaded at a corner market—not a major market, but one of the little ones that occurred every seven or eight blocks.

To prepare the Chinese cabbage for storage, they spread it in the sun for a couple of weeks to dry, and as some friends told us, "to kill the germs." Each morning, they spent hours sorting it, peeling off bad leaves, and spreading it in the sun. Each night, they spent hours piling it up and covering it, until the next morning, when the process began once more. The quantity was astounding. We had to walk in the streets because the sidewalks were covered with Chinese cabbage. It was on every window sill; roofs were covered with it.

As the process went on, the unwanted leaves, which had simply been thrown on the ground, began to rot. The stench was enough to make our eyes water, but that wasn't the worst of it. As they decomposed, the leaves liquified, creating a vile, green runoff. The sewer system—in the parts of the city where there was one—was unequal to that mass of liquid, so it stood in huge, stinking pools that gradually dried up. What remained were large green stains of evil-smelling residue that stayed until covered, mercifully, by the first snow.

After it was sufficiently dry (and sterilized by the sun) they stacked the cabbage in crocks and submerged it in brine—essentially, pickling it. Sort of like uncut sauerkraut. Whereas fresh it had looked like thick stalks of celery, after pickling it looked like limp, thick stalks of celery. I didn't look forward to eating pickled cabbage all winter, but to my surprise I really acquired a taste for it, and actually missed it when spring came and it ran out.

If cabbage is the vegetable of choice for winter in northern China, the fruit is apples. When I returned to my office after lunch one afternoon, I knew somebody had been there. The office doors had big metal bars across them, which slid through heavy flanges fitted with padlocks. The padlock on my door was backward from the way I normally put it on, so I knew somebody had been in my office while I was at lunch. I went in, and found a 60-pound wicker basket of apples packed in straw. I said, "Oh, well, there are some apples," sat down at my desk and started to work. I had been in China long enough to know that it would be much more efficient—and much less frustrating—to let the answer come to me.

Sure enough, after a while my assistant came in and said, "Did you find your apples?" I said, "Well, they'd be pretty hard to miss, but I didn't realize they were mine." He said, "Oh, yes, the department work unit got together, purchased a truckload of apples, and gave each of the faculty in the department 60 pounds of apples. Here is your 60 pounds." I trust I was sufficiently appreciative, but the whole time I couldn't stop wondering what we were going to do with 60 pounds of apples. We probably don't eat that many apples in two years back home.

He told me they were the kind of apples that were supposed to keep through February, and so they did. The last few, however, were getting pretty soft and wrinkly by the time we ate them. We gave some away, but we ate most of them. We ate apples pretty much every morning with our yogurt, and went heavy on the apples when we made fruit salad. We ate apple pie, apple crisp, apple cobbler, and apple turnovers. We ate raw apples, baked apples, stewed apples, and apple sauce. They were good apples, and that helped.

We started eating dried fruit, as well. Most Chinese candy was pretty bad, but the dried fruit—of almost every variety—was excellent. It was pretty expensive, but no more so than the candy (about sixty cents a pound), and we only ate it as a treat.

As it turned out, fruit and vegetables were both in ample supply all winter; especially potatoes and what they called scallions, which were like big, thick, green onions. These they tied in clumps by the green part (which eventually became the brown part) and hung them up to dry—outside when the weather permitted; inside when it didn't. The food transportation system consisted primarily of trucking, and was certainly acceptable (although the highway system was fast becoming inadequate). So most other major fruits and vegetables were also available all year—though not in the same quantity, quality, or variety. And they were a bit more expensive. Any thoughts of gastric martyrdom we had entertained were quickly dispelled.

———————————

With Liaoning Province so close to Korea, one of the large minority populations was Korean. In fact, there was a part of Shenyang called Korean Town. One of our favorite places to eat was a Korean restaurant near the university. The first time friends took us there, we hadn't been in China long enough to see past the way the place looked, and we feared for our health. As with most of the small restaurants, the floors and walls were grungy, the ceilings black from coal smoke, and the windows translucent with grease residue. The waitress wiped our table with a cloth that looked as though it had never been washed. After we'd been in China a while, we appreciated the fact that she had wiped it at all. In many places, they just brushed the leavings of the previous meal onto the floor with their hands.

They brought to our table what looked like a small forge filled with charcoal, and put an inverted cone on top, which created a draft that really got things roaring. Sparks flew up, making little black scorch marks on the pressed cardboard ceiling. The danger of the whole place burning down didn't seem to bother anybody much—except us, of course—we were pretty sure we were about to die in a conflagration of the first order. Nothing so dramatic happened. They took the cone off after a while—the coals underneath were almost white hot—and placed a heavy wire screen on top.

Then they served us a couple of two-pound bowls of marinated meat—probably beef, maybe pork, possibly dog—we didn't know; we didn't ask. It was cut into thin strips, and they showed us how to use chopsticks to pick the strips out and lay them on the screen. It cooked very quickly, because the fire was so hot, and the meat cut so thin, so we had to keep moving it around on the screen to keep it from burning. They had provided each of us a bowl about half full of chopped greens and spices—coriander, chives, hot pepper, mustard, and several other things we couldn't identify—and showed us how to add vinegar and soy sauce, mixing it around so we had a cold, thick, very spicy soup.

They showed us how, when the meat was cooked, to pluck it off with our chopsticks and slosh it around in the soup. The hot meat picked up just enough of the spices, and the soup cooled it just enough to eat right away. It was unlike any taste we had experienced, and it was delicious. To go along with the meat were side dishes of spiced peanuts, and white Chinese radishes and raw potatoes, both cut into strips and spiced. To top it all of, we had hot, spiced noodles in a thin broth. It made an excellent meal, and cost about $8 for six of us.

It didn't take us long to stop noticing what, in the States, would have been considered absolutely untenable hygiene, and to enjoy the excellent food without reservation. We assumed that sooner or later we would pay with bouts of food poisoning, but it never happened, and we left China thankful that we hadn't diminished our enjoyment by being overcautious.

———————————

Meryl and Ruthie, the couple who introduced us to the Korean restaurant, were to become our best Western friends in China. Like about 80 percent of the English teachers in China, they had come there under the auspices of a Christian organization. When I expressed my surprise that China's Communist government would knowingly enter into agreements with Christian organizations, Ruthie said the government officials saw them as a ready supply of dependable, responsible teachers, and that as long as they did not preach the benefits of Christianity to their students, or try to convert them, they were welcomed by the government.

Although part of a Mennonite missionary organization, Meryl and Ruthie had no intention of "converting the masses." They were not ostentatiously "Christian," but were truly good people. Their intention was to impress their students by the way they lived. If someone asked them about Christianity they were happy to discuss their faith, but they were not there to proselytize. They were older than many of the English teachers, and it was clear they weren't there just so they could go back and say they'd taught in China for a year.

In fact, they had made a two-year commitment, and had really enjoyed their experience. Of course there were things about China they didn't like, the same as everybody else. They didn't like having to go without electricity every two or three days. And they didn't like the fact that sometimes the heat went off in their apartment for a day or two and they practically froze. Those weren't anybody's favorite things, but they were there because they wanted to be, and they accepted such inconveniences as tradeoffs for experiencing another culture.

They had learned to cope—had found almost all the necessities—and shared their experience, showing us where to find them, or at least letting us know if they weren't available. It was from Meryl and Ruthie, for example, that we acquired one of our most prized possessions—an oven. Most teachers spent only a year in China, so when they returned to the States, many of them had left things with Meryl and Ruthie. One of those things was an extra oven, which (bless their hearts) they passed on to us. Chinese ovens were electric—similar to small toaster ovens in the States—and cost about $25. That doesn't sound like much for an oven, but it amounted to about one sixth of a month's salary for us.

Some of the ovens had temperature controls and timers—the one we got didn't. We just plugged it in and put things in to bake. If it wasn't hot enough, we left the item in longer. If it got too hot, we opened the door a bit. None of this should be interpreted as complaint—it was very rudimentary, but it was an oven. To people who had not baked for months, it was akin to heaven. The evening our friends brought it over, we baked banana bread. I don't know how good it really was, but to us it was the best banana bread ever. We made three loaves. The first didn't last five minutes, the second we sent home with them, and the third we had for dessert the following evening—except for a few little nibbles I snuck while Laurie and the boys were out for an afternoon walk, and I was supposed to be preparing for my next day's class. To my dismay—though I had (grudgingly) to admit it was only fair—my share after dinner was correspondingly decreased.

The Chinese did almost no baking at home—what baked goods they had they purchased at the market—so we couldn't find baking pans anywhere. What were very common, however, were metal, covered lunch boxes about the size of small bread pans. The Chinese put rice and stir-fried vegetables in them in the morning and took them to work. They could, then, just eat their lunch cold, or if they had some way to do so, could heat it right in the containers, then eat directly from them. We got four of those lunch boxes and lids of various sizes, and they became indispensable to us—not only as baking pans, but as storage containers, as means to transport fragile items on our bikes, as mixing bowls, and even—on occasion—as lunch boxes.

I said we hadn't baked for months, but that wasn't entirely true. We had as utensils in our kitchen two medium-sized sauce pans, a large sauce pan, and a very large wok. We decided one Sunday morning it would be nice to have muffins for breakfast. We mixed up some muffin batter, and gave ovenless baking a try. We put a bit of oil in the rounded bottom of the wok, got it nice and hot over the gas fire ring, and put a dollop of muffin batter in it just long enough to brown it a little.

Then we slid the slightly browned glob up the side of the wok and stuck it there, repeating the process until there was a circle of muffins high up around the edge of the wok. By that time they were getting pretty brown on the bottom, so we turned them over, adjusted the heat to a very low setting, and put a lid on the wok. They were far enough up the side of the wok that most of the heat was dissipated before it reached them, so they were being cooked as much by the heated air trapped by the lid inside the wok. They weren't exactly muffin shaped—in fact, they weren't even close to muffin shaped—more like very small, very thick pancakes, or maybe slightly skinny biscuits—but they tasted like muffins, and that was the important thing.

We had also created a bread-like substance using a steaming process. We put water in the bottom of our wok, placed one of our lunch boxes full of bread dough above the water, put a lid on the wok, and boiled the water. Naturally, the water made steam, which in turn steamed the bread. It wasn't exactly the bread we were used to, but it was pretty good—especially warm, with fresh butter melted into it.

After three months in Shenyang, we had found pretty much everything we needed if it was available. We had even gotten to the point where we had found more than one variety of many items, and had balanced the expense of the better versions with how badly we wanted them. Toilet paper, for example. We paid a premium price (about 25 cents for a roll maybe half the size we were used to back home) for the best toilet paper available in the city, and carried a roll with us everywhere we went. Where there was anything available at all outside our apartment, it ranged from old newspapers to a substance only vaguely reminiscent of toilet paper, of the nickel-a-roll variety.

The closest American equivalent I could think of for our Chinese TP was crepe paper. It was kind of wrinkly like that, but (thank goodness) a bit wider. Often, the perforations were missing, and it tore much like crepe paper—stretching; then snapping when its tensile strength was exceeded, leaving a handful of skinny shreds.

During the late eighties, the Chinese began to export many goods to the States—some people said to the detriment of American producers. Chinese goods imported by American stores basically fell into the "cheap, low quality" category, but those were the best goods produced in China. It was essentially those rejected for export that were kept for domestic sale. Most of the materials and workmanship were fairly shoddy. It was not uncommon, for example, for us to pour a glassful of cold water and have the glass break because it had a flaw in it.

Everyone was aware of the lack of quality control, so part of the process of shopping consisted of culling out the unacceptable items from those that were available. When we went to a government store to buy something, the clerk would automatically pull out ten of the item, and we were expected to sort through them—often with the help of other shoppers—to find the best one. When we bought some plates to replace our first set, each of which had lasted from a week to three months, I looked at 30 plates to find four that were acceptable—without cracks, or gouges in the glazing so deep food would have seeped into the porous centers.

In at least one way, however, lack of quality in Chinese goods made sense—it was a labor intensive society, and one that fixed things, rather than throwing them away. Therefore, the more things needed fixed, the more people could be employed fixing them. It had always bothered me that in the States when I took my shoes to get them fixed, the shoe repairman inevitably said, "They're not worth fixing, it would cost you less to get new ones." I always wondered, if that were the case, how he could make a living repairing shoes. One time I asked him, and he said, "Those are cheap shoes. Some people buy good shoes, and I fix them." Well, I had asked. Still, it seemed reasonable to me that I should be able to buy cheap shoes and still have them repaired cheaply.

In China that was the case. There, I was able to take my cheap tennis shoes to the woman on the corner and have them fixed where they had torn out on the side—five cents (she refused more). She fixed my cheap leather shoes when they started coming apart at the sole—seven cents.

We could count on her. Every morning at seven, she arrived with her shop. It was contained in a wheeled, wooden cube, about two feet on each side. She would pull it from her home to her spot on the corner. There she unpacked her folding stool and one for her customers to use if they chose to wait for the repair. Next came felt booties for shoeless customers on cold days, and the metal shoe tree on which she worked. Then she took out her very small, heavy-duty, hand-powered sewing machine. What she left in the box was an amazing assortment of heels, buttons, taps, thread, leather and rubber pieces, glue, soles, and other potential replacement parts for every variety of (cheap) shoe imaginable. She spent twelve hours on that corner every day we were in Shenyang.

Jesse had a pair of leather boots that wore out at the toe from his crawling around in the dirt. We took them to our shoe repair woman and she said the Chinese equivalent of, "Oh sure, I can fix that." She sewed a rubber patch on the toe—12 cents—and they lasted until he grew out of them. They didn't look as good, of course, but Jesse certainly didn't care. Had it been in the States, we'd have had to buy a new pair of boots for the six months until they no longer fit. We really liked being able to get things fixed instead of discarding them.

———————

We needed to get a winter coat for Jesse. Laurie had brought hers from the States (it was of down, and made good packing around my computer), and Cooper and I were able to find coats in the Shenyang markets. There seemed to be no such thing as practical, warm, winter coats in two-year-old sizes, however. Oh, there were cutesy things with Donald Duck and Mickey Mouse on them. There were light, fluffy, dress coats in fake tiger, zebra, and leopard skin, or in neon orange or lime green. But they were more in the line of costumes than practical winter wear. We had been warned about how cold it got in northern China, so we couldn't understand why there weren't warm coats available for little children.

Then, as it got colder, we saw how the Chinese dressed their children for winter. They bundled those poor little tykes up so they could barely move. They bought coats that were so big they reached the children's ankles. They didn't need mittens, because their hands reached only to the elbow area of the sleeves. More than once, we saw a small child who had fallen down, unable to stand up again without parental assistance. Jesse was a very active little guy. We had found it necessary to pin his mittens on the winter before, to keep him from discarding them so he could grab things. There was no way he would have put up with that kind of restrictive clothing.

We ended up dressing him in longjohns; then a bulky-knit wool sweater, a hooded sweatshirt, and, on top, an old jeans jacket that Cooper had outgrown. He was plenty warm. In fact, he insisted often that he was too warm, and wanted to take something off. There was, however, no way we could convince the Chinese women of that. About the only animosity we encountered during our year in China was from older women who insisted that we were terrible parents for dressing our child so inadequately during the winter. As the weather got colder, these confrontations became so frequent that Jesse picked up the Chinese words for "not cold," and began using them to defend us from such attacks.

As the winds begin to take on a biting chill, we were interested to see whether some of the street vendors would be driven inside by the cold. What we found was that the number of vendors stayed pretty constant. Many of them just wrapped themselves and their goods (if they were of a kind that would freeze) in layers of huge, padded quilts. For others, what they sold changed with the seasons. Whereas, in the summer and early fall there were yogurt and ice cream vendors on almost every corner, during November they gradually gave way to hot sweet potato and corn on the cob vendors. In some cases, it seemed the same people just changed to their winter carts; in others, it seemed to be different people.

The sweet potato vendors had modified 55-gallon drums to create huge ovens. They had cut a circular hole that consisted of about half of one end, set the barrel on end with the hole up, cut small draft holes near the bottom, and welded racks of heavy wire mesh around the inside at several levels from top to bottom. Early each morning, they started a charcoal fire in the bottom, loaded the lowest rack with raw sweet potatoes and the higher ones with those half-baked the day before, and wheeled the whole thing on a cart to their corner.

As the potatoes baked, they were gradually moved from the bottom to the top rack, until, when they were so hot and soft the skins were the only thing holding them together, they were moved out onto the top of the barrel, where they were kept hot from the glowing coals inside. It was an unforgettable experience: pulling over to one of those vendors on a cold day and, for about five cents a pound, buying big, hot, soft, sweet, yellow potatoes. We'd break them open and the steam would roll out, warming our faces. No sweet potatoes, before or since—no, not even those candied ones at Thanksgiving—have tasted as good.

The boys seemed to have the same kind of feeling for the hot corn on the cob. It wasn't exactly like the sweet corn we knew in the States. In fact, it was more like our field corn. It was a lot starchier, and the kernels were a lot bigger and tougher, than our sweet corn. But they steamed it for a long time in burlap-wrapped pressure cookers, until it got fairly tender. It was really pretty tasty, and only cost about five cents an ear. We couldn't get by one of those sweet corn vendors without one of the boys wanting to stop. One of the first Chinese words Jesse learned was the one for "corn."

A street vendor selling delicious baked sweet potatoes.

We were sorry to see the yogurt go. We had gotten rather dependent upon it with our fruit for breakfast. We kept a culture going for several weeks from our last purchased bottle, but when it bit the dust, we just had to do without. By that time, we had started baking bread pudding with fruit in it. That, covered in milk, went a long way toward making up for the lack of yogurt, but it just wasn't the same, and we were glad when the yogurt stands began to reappear the next spring.

We didn't miss the ice cream very much—that from someone who generally ate a helping every day in the States. Chinese ice cream was not the same, however. There were several flavors, all of which tasted faintly of stale tutti-frutti gum. The consistency was more that of mushy popsicles. So, when the ice cream stands gave way to those serving hot noodles with various toppings, it didn't hurt our feelings a bit.

Some of the vendors were seasonal. They made whatever money they could in the summer; then holed up and lived on whatever they had for the winter. Our bike repairman, for example (in the combination of English, Chinese, and sign language at which I had gotten fairly fluent) told me he hibernated for the winter, while one of his grandsons took over his stand. Boy, that had to be a tough job in the winter. It got real cold, and they had to take their gloves off to work on some of the smaller items. What a way to make a living. That's the way the poor people worked in China, though. There was a need for bike repair, even in the winter, so somebody was out there repairing bikes. They were true entrepreneurs: if there was a need, somebody filled it.

We were regular church-goers back home, and by mid-November, really missed the experience. There was both a Catholic and a Protestant church in Shenyang, but services were in Chinese, and we just didn't feel the boys would do very well in a completely Chinese service—it was hard enough to keep them quiet during the liturgy back home. So, when Dave and Linda Benedict, the political officer and nurse at the Consulate, offered a Bible study at their apartment each Sunday afternoon, to which any Westerners in the area were invited, we decided to give them a try. They had two children about Cooper's age, so the prospect of playing with them gave the boys something to look forward to, as well.

When we arrived, workers were unpacking four big, wooden packing crates, about four times the size of those refrigerators come in. They didn't have refrigerators in them, though. They were full of food—case after case of Heineken beer, Coca-Cola, chocolate bars, and everything we couldn't get in China. They were taking the stuff into the Consulate apartments.

We weren't prepared for their apartment. I don't know what we expected—I guess we had just gotten so used to our apartment and the homes of our Chinese friends that they had become the norm for us. The Benedicts' apartment (and as we were to find out, all of those in the Consulate living compound) was like no other we had seen in China—in New York City, or Chicago, or Minneapolis, yes; but not in China. Even by U.S. standards, it was very nice: kitchen, dining room, living room, family room, three bedrooms, three bathrooms. And the conveniences: microwave oven, popcorn popper, ice cream maker, two huge ovens, two huge refrigerators, chest freezer, and a huge color television with a VCR.

Their family was the same size as ours. Their apartment was about four times as large as ours. Their children had at least ten times as many toys as Jesse and Cooper had. They had a McDonald's playland in their back yard. Their rationale for all these things was, "We're going to be here for two years, and we want to be comfortable." We didn't resent the Benedicts' lifestyle. In fact we wouldn't have traded with them. If anything, we felt sorry that they were not experiencing China as we were. They were caring people who were always willing to share, and we came to like them a lot. We questioned how effective U.S. government personnel could be, however, when they were so far removed from the lives of the people in the country where they were stationed.

The driver and the interpreter for one of the teachers came to pick him up after the Bible study. He asked if it was okay to show them the apartment, and the Benedicts said, "Sure, go ahead." Their jaws dropped open. Their eyes widened. They had clearly never imagined a home like that, let alone seen one. I asked the interpreter, after she had been through the apartment, if she could live in a place like that. She said, very seriously, "Yes. Oh yes. I think so. I think I would like a place like this." The effect was simultaneously humorous and touching.

The Benedicts invited us for a Thanksgiving feast that was every bit as good as any at Grandma's house. It had the works: great big, delicious Butterball turkeys, sweet potatoes, mashed potatoes and gravy, cranberry sauce, green beans, stuffing, and corn. For dessert there was pecan pie or pumpkin pie with whipped cream, apple pie with ice cream, and lemon meringue pie. Either it was the best lemon meringue pie I'd ever had, or it had just been so long since I'd had lemon meringue pie that I thought it was. Either way, it amounted to the same thing—great pie. The absence of football on television was more than made up for by warm conversation with friends. It was a Thanksgiving long to be remembered.

We had a white Thanksgiving. In fact, it snowed twice that week. Not very much—the first day was little more than a powdering; the second maybe three quarters of an inch. But it was the kind of snow that was absolutely gorgeous—big, fluffy flakes that drifted down and tickled our faces. We all bundled up and went for a walk in an area of town we hadn't seen before—up and down the little back streets of a poor, residential neighborhood. People looked at us strangely—not un- friendly, just curious. We didn't pay much attention to them. We were in a happy mood. It was a beautiful day: just the right temperature— just cold enough to make our ears and noses tingle. And that beautiful snow made us forget that everything in the city was dirty and polluted, because it was all neatly covered and clean.

For transportation in Shenyang, we could choose between biking, walking, or taking the bus. The buses were usually unbearable. We had just never seen anything as crowded as Chinese buses. People fought to pack inside, and when the bus was fuller than we would have thought possible, they hung from the outside. It created a nearly impossible

Baking one of two huge Butterball turkeys in a real oven in a real kitchen for Thanksgiving at the American Consulate.

situation with children, so we rode our bikes. We weren't really looking forward to bike rides in snowy, sub-zero weather, however.

With the snow came our first exposure to winter bike riding. Again, our assumptions were completely unfounded. We had pictured millions of people laboring to pump through hard-packed, rutted snow, but quickly realized that all the bike paths had been cleared. Later that day, I asked my assistant what had happened to all the snow. He said, "People shoveled it." I said, "When?" He said, "This morning before they left for work." I couldn't believe it— people got out at 5:00 to get everything shoveled in time for the morning rush hour. I'm not talking about shoveling the sidewalk in front of their houses, I'm talking about shoveling entire streets, because bikes took the place of automobiles— there were literally streets full of bicycles.

He explained that work units were assigned sections of streets, and that they were responsible for making sure their section was always clear of snow and ice. If that meant getting up in the middle of the night to get their section of the street shoveled in time for the morning rush hour, that's what they did. He said the only real problem was when they got the kind of wet snow or freezing rain that was very slippery and took a long time to chip off. "That's when burning coal is an advantage," he said, "because when you burn coal you end up with ashes, and you can use ashes on the slippery spots."

Chapter Five
December

One of the things our family really liked was music—mostly classical and jazz—and we didn't expect to get much of that on Chinese radio. So we took with us our tape collection and a good cassette player, as well as a short wave radio with which we could receive Voice of America. Although both tape players and short wave radios were available in China, they were very expensive. Electricity in China was delivered at 220 volts, however, whereas in the States it was 110. That meant to run our tape deck and radio, we needed a transformer that would convert 220 to 110. Such items were available inexpensively in electronics stores in the States, so I bought a couple to take along. They worked fine—for five months. I suppose I should have realized that such small, inexpensive transformers were intended for use on a limited scale—say a month-long trip overseas; not for permanent installation.

One evening Laurie and I were reading and the boys were playing with their toys, when Cooper said he smelled something burning. I looked up to see smoke pouring from the transformer for the tape player. Before I could get there to unplug it, the transformer had burned out completely, and the tape player was fried. We were dismayed. We couldn't afford 550 yuan—about $150—for a new cassette player, but we certainly didn't want to have to do without music for the next seven months.

The solution to our problem came from an unexpected quarter. One of Laurie's English language classes was made up of Chinese faculty from throughout the university, including one from the physics department. When Laurie mentioned in one of her classes what had happened, he told her his students could probably fix our tape player. He said the physics department had an electronics lab in which students did most of the electrical appliance repair for the university. Laurie gave him the tape player at their next class. My assistant insisted we borrow his tape player until ours was repaired. Two weeks later, the physics professor brought our player to class. As it was impossible to get 110-volt parts, he and his students had custom-made them. They had also constructed a heavy-duty, 220-volt transformer for us to replace the one that had burned out.

One day I developed a very itchy rash all over my chest and back, so a young man from the Foreign Affairs Office went with me to the campus clinic. We were ushered into the doctor's office. He looked quite young to have completed medical school, and when I asked later about his training, I got conflicting replies. The young man from the Foreign Affairs Office assured me that their doctors had all completed the same course of studies as doctors in the States. A Chinese friend, however, said the doctors at the university clinic didn't have medical degrees at all, but had taught themselves medicine from books.

Anyway, when we entered his office, the doctor was sitting at his desk, reading what looked more like a medical journal than a comic book. He looked up, rather disinterestedly, and asked what was the problem. My interpreter told him about the rash, and he said for me to pull up my shirt. I did so, and without getting up, he glanced at my chest, said something in Chinese, and returned to his reading. My interpreter informed me that what the doctor had said was, "It doesn't matter."

Well, that didn't make me very happy. If it didn't matter, I wouldn't have been there in the first place. I said—in a tone that pulled the doctor away from his reading—"Well you tell him that's easy for him to say; it's not his chest." The young man from the Foreign Affairs Office looked very uncomfortable, but he conveyed the message. The doctor grinned, and told me to take off my shirt. I did so, and he stood up and walked around me, peering carefully at the rash.

He asked what I thought might have caused it. I said I didn't know, but that I had worn a new t-shirt the day before without washing it first. He said not to wear it again without washing it. I said I'd already figured that out, which the young man from the Foreign Affairs Office didn't translate. I said I had been taking some cold capsules provided by the doctor's clinic. He said to stop taking them. I said I'd already figured that out. The young man from the Foreign Affairs Office looked pleadingly at me and was silent. The doctor sat back down, said, "It doesn't matter," and returned to his reading.

I didn't need a translation—I recognized the phrase from the last time. And the doctor didn't need a translation to pick up on my attitude when I said, "Look, is he a doctor or not? This may not matter to him, but the itch is driving me crazy, and it seems like he ought to be able to do something to help me." The young man from the Foreign Affairs Office, who was beginning to look a bit like he could use a doctor himself, probably softened the presentation, but he relayed the general message.

The interpretation of the doctor's response was rather innocuous—I'm sure he said something more like, "Well why didn't the wimp just say he wanted something to stop the itching in the first place?" At any rate, he scribbled a prescription, which he handed to me, accompanied by a broad grin, and a comment that the young man from the Foreign Affairs Office elected not to interpret for me. On the way out, we showed the prescription to a white-robed person behind a counter, who gave me a packet of small, white pills that got rid of the itch in short order. The rash went away in a few days.

Months later, I learned that the phrase, "It doesn't matter," had many connotations, depending on the context. If we apologized for stepping on someone's toes, they might say, "It doesn't matter." That wasn't to say it didn't hurt, but that we were forgiven. If we invited people for dinner, they might say, "We can't come, but it doesn't matter." That wasn't to say that they didn't want to come, but that there would be another time. In the situation with the rash, the doctor had used the phrase to mean something like, "Don't worry, it's not serious and will go away by itself in a few days."

Although the most common means of transportation in China was bicycles, there were a lot of trucks, buses, and taxis. An increasing number of high-level Party officials and individual work units such as universities and large companies also owned cars. The drivers had to get gasoline somewhere, but I was there almost five months before I saw a gas station. Then, one day a driver came to take me to another university where I was to give a guest lecture. Instead of taking the normal route to his university, he went in the opposite direction.

I tried, through a combination of bad Chinese and (what I considered) good sign language, to find out what was going on. Eventually it became clear—he was going to get gas. As nearly as I could determine, there were only about half a dozen gas stations in Shenyang, a city of almost five million. Because there were so few stations, most drivers carried gas cans with them to get them to the nearest gas station if they ran out. And the nearest one quite likely was all the way across town. The only ones we saw were on the perimeter of the city.

The gas stations didn't look to be much more than that, unlike those in the States that offered everything from groceries to mechanical services. There were repair shops scattered throughout the city, but not many were the kind that drivers took their cars inside to get them fixed.

They just pulled up onto the sidewalk, and the mechanics crawled under the vehicle with their tools. They did major repairs that way—several times we saw them with motors pulled out of cars or trucks, sitting on the sidewalk. The drivers all seemed to have their own tool kits and did most of their minor repair and maintenance themselves. In addition, each of the work units had its own mechanic, or at least someone who, if not a trained mechanic, served in that capacity.

Some of the drivers really knew what they were doing. One especially cold day, when our family was returning from a trip to a neighboring town, the jeep in which we were riding quit. It was very cold and snowy, and we were miles from anywhere, but our driver seemed unconcerned. He climbed out, rummaged around in the back, came up with a minimal tool kit, lay down on his back in the snow, slid under the vehicle, and began working. After a few minutes, he reemerged, piled a couple of old rags in the middle of the road, soaked them with gasoline from the spare can, and lit them with his trusty Zippo.

We thought perhaps he was trying to warm up, but instead of holding his hands over the flames, he reached under the jeep and brought forth the gas line. He had loosened it at the carburetor and the tank, and had removed the whole thing. For the next few minutes, he barbecued its entire length over the flames, which he had to replenish occasionally with additional gasoline. The whole process was going on entirely too close to the vehicle for our taste, and we could envision the flames following a dribble of gas from the fire to the tank, resulting in our immolation. Just as Laurie was suggesting that we move the boys a discreet distance into the neighboring rice paddy (conveniently frozen for the winter), however, he decided medium rare was good for the gas line, and slid back under the jeep to reinstall it.

It didn't work. The jeep wouldn't start. So he did the whole process again—and again. After the second time, we were ready to consider the possibility that the gas line had been falsely accused, but our driver was determined it was the culprit. It was his call, so we kept quiet and waited in the increasing chill. Actually, Chinese jeeps weren't the snuggest means of transport in the winter, so we were dressed quite warmly. The chill had been pretty noticeable even with the heater going full blast; so it didn't really increase that much.

He was right: after the gas line had endured its third barbecuing, it relented and began to work properly again. Our driver remounted, and cloaked in a shimmering robe of triumph (it may have been frost) completed the trip home.

One day in early December, I got a postcard from my friend Sherry Wright. She was a journalist from Kansas who was spending a year in Beijing as an editor for China Daily, the only English language daily newspaper in China. She said she would have a few days off soon, and asked if we'd like to have her come for a visit. She needed to know right away, so she could make plans, so asked that I call her.

No problem—how big a deal could it be to place a call between the two major cities in northern China? I went over to the Foreign Affairs Office and told the young man there that I wanted to make a phone call to Beijing. He said fine, did I want to make it an express call or a regular call. I said well, I didn't know, what was the difference. He said for a regular call I would have to stay around our apartment, possibly all day, because it could take many hours for a regular call to go through. I said how about an express call. He said oh, that could be anywhere from ten minutes to half an hour. I said I'd do that, then. He said it cost more. I asked how much more. He said it cost twice as much: the equivalent of $1.50 a minute for a regular call; $3 a minute for an express call.

If I'd had any ideas about a leisurely chat with my friend, that would have dispelled them, but I figured I could tell her, "Yes, we'd love to have you visit," in less than a minute, so I said I'd make the express call. He took me down the hall to the telephone room, where the woman at the switchboard called the operator and said she wanted to place an express call to Beijing. Then we waited. After a few minutes, I decided I might as well make use of the time, so I ran over to the apartment and got a book.

Two and a half hours later, the call had still not gone through, so I said look, I can't sit around here all day, so maybe I'll try her home number this evening. The young man said fine, that'll be two cents. I asked for what. He said for trying to get the call through. I said wait a minute, you mean I have to pay for not making a telephone call. He said yes, the woman worked very hard trying to get my call through. I said she sat there the whole time, just like the rest of us, and besides, that's her job—this is a socialist country, the government pays her for doing her job.

I know, I know: "Big deal—two cents." Well, it was another of those times when I didn't care about the money. It was the principle of the thing. The longer we were there, the more convinced we became that the people in the Foreign Affairs Office had decided to make as much money as possible off the wealthy Americans, and it got a bit irritating. At first, we accepted each additional charge as legitimate, but after a while, we began to question some of them. We wanted to be sure we were being treated fairly, even if it didn't involve much money.

So, I said I wasn't going to pay an additional cent for her to do her job, for which she was getting paid by the government anyway. Then the young man from the Foreign Affairs Office said actually, it wasn't for her, but for the telephone exchange downtown. He said the university had to pay them for making the connection, even though the call never went through. Well, it sounded a bit suspect to me—why hadn't he just said that in the first place? But what could I say? In China, as in most countries, it is very offensive to accuse someone of lying, so I said fine, and paid up.

I made arrangements to meet him at 7:00 that evening to try again, and went over to the apartment to get my coat and go to my office. Within three minutes, he came dashing into the apartment and said my telephone call had gone through. I said what telephone call, I thought we had cancelled it. He said well, the operator had decided to go ahead and try again anyway (Maybe she was putting her two cents in?). I asked what would have happened if I'd been at my office already. I'd have been paying for a telephone connection that I wasn't talking on—for how long? He said, well, I'd better hurry because I was paying for it as we talked. I got the point.

We ran back over to the other building, and sure enough, Sherry was on the line. When I was done, the young man said I owed $4.85 for the telephone call. I said, you mean $4.83, right, and reminded him that I had already paid two cents. He said I had paid the two cents for not making a telephone call earlier. I said how could I pay two cents for not making a telephone call if I had just finished the call? He thought about that for a while and said he guessed that was right. So he subtracted two cents from my bill.

I thought about it later, and decided that I really had paid two cents to spend 2 1/2 hours not making a telephone call; then a couple of minutes later had paid $4.83 for a call that had lasted less than two minutes. The inescapable conclusion was that, although not making telephone calls in China cost much less than making them, not making them took much more time. Philosophically, I was never able to resolve how much different that was, if any, than using telephones in the States.

Although Sherry's visit was pleasant, it was not without complications. When I told the young man from the Foreign Affairs Office that a friend was coming to visit, he said oh, that's very nice, where will she stay? I said she'd just stay in our apartment—we'd have Jesse sleep with us in our double bed, and she'd sleep in Jesse's single bed. He said well, maybe. I said what do you mean "maybe"—is there a problem? He said well, he'd have to check with the Liaoning Provincial Foreign Affairs

Office. Because she was coming from a different province, the Foreign Affairs Office at the university had to report her presence and how long she was staying. The provincial Foreign Affairs Office would then decide whether it was okay for her to stay in our apartment, or whether she would have to stay somewhere else.

Rather than go through all that hassle, she paid the equivalent of $4 a night to stay in one of the single rooms in the student dormitory. Again, it was one of those things where we said, you have to check with whom—about what? They really did, and they couldn't understand why we were surprised, because they're so used to it. We tried to imagine visiting a friend in a neighboring state, and having to check with a state office there to see if it's okay to stay at the friend's house overnight.

Although her bike was Sherry's primary mode of transportation in Beijing, she was not prepared for riding bike in Shenyang. In Beijing, they had wide bike paths along all the major highways and streets, something often missing in Shenyang. Therefore, we had to compete with cars, trucks, tractors, horses, wagons, and heavy equipment much of the time. She followed me around on Laurie's bike, and did quite well. At one point, however, she said she was afraid that when she got back to Beijing and people asked her what she had seen of Shenyang, she would have to say, "The back fender of Roy's bike," because she had spent so much time concentrating on following me and not getting run over.

In mid-December, I was honored as the first foreign expert to be named advisor to the Liaoning Provincial Translators' Society. I was never sure exactly what that meant, but it must have been an honor, because they had a big meeting to install me in that capacity, with an elaborate banquet afterward. At the meeting, they provided an interpreter for me, who sat beside me and told me what was going on the whole time. I hadn't realized it, but the Liaoning Provincial Translators' Society was an important organization. It had the third largest number of books printed in translation every year in China.

The main order of business at the meeting was discussion of a government funding cut for the translation societies. I got a big laugh when I told them they sounded a lot like numerous cultural organizations under the Reagan administration. Undaunted, they had found a Chinese travel agency to fund them in place of the government. Travel agencies were up-and-coming businesses in China, but public relations was almost unknown, so I couldn't understand what the people at the travel agency figured was in it for them.

As the meeting progressed, however, it began to make more sense. Each year, the translators' societies in China had a national conference. Two years before, it had been in Shanghai (site of the largest society); the year before, it had been in Beijing (site of the second largest society). It looked very much like the next conference was to be in Shenyang. Well, if the Liaoning Provincial Translators' Society were funded by a travel agency, guess who would get all the business from the people coming to the conference in Liaoning Province—a clear case of reciprocal back scratching.

I was introduced to most of the people at the meeting, and it was an impressive group. There were the editors-in-chief of the three major publishing houses in northeast China, several high-level Communist Party officials, various provincial and city government officials, and numerous senior faculty and administrators from area universities. I was flattered that such an august body had invited me to be the first foreign expert to serve as their advisor.

The banquet was the biggest we had attended. There were about 50 people, including Laurie and the boys. As we entered the banquet room, however, the director of the Society, who had arranged everything, took Laurie aside and said, "We are pleased to have you and the boys at our banquet, but Dr. Blackwood will sit at the head table. Could you and the boys please sit at this other table?" They stuck them off with the workers over in the corner. Laurie was a bit chagrined, but there was a tendency for that sort of thing to happen. The foreign expert got all the glory. The wife and children of the foreign expert got to eat well, but they didn't get to do it at the head table—good food, but no glory. That was better than Chinese family members were treated—they were not included at any of the banquets we attended.

One of the things the people in our Foreign Affairs Office did for us that we always appreciated was provide tickets for cultural attractions they thought we might like. Occasionally, an event was a bit of a disaster, but mostly they were wonderful experiences. One such was the evening they took us to see the Shenyang Acrobats—what an experience. We could not believe some of the things those people did with their bodies.

In one act, a woman lay on her back, and an assistant balanced inverted pyramids of six wine glasses filled with water on each of her hands, her feet, and her forehead. She then, very slowly and carefully, rolled from her back onto her stomach without spilling a drop from any of those thirty glasses. Then she slowly rolled from her stomach onto her back again. When she had finished, her assistant, in case there were any doubters present, emptied the water from the goblets into a bucket. It was water, and each glass was full. Now, if anyone had told us that could be done, we would not have believed it. In fact, we sat there and watched her do it, and we're still not sure we believe it.

A guy came out with what looked like a slightly flexible telephone pole, about 20 feet long. He put one end of it on his shoulder, and with his hands, balanced it there, sticking straight up into the air. Another guy came out, leaped up on it, and scrambled to the top like a monkey going up a coconut palm. There he wrapped one leg around it and stretched himself out horizontally from the top of the pole. That was pretty impressive, but they weren't finished. Next, a woman came out, scrambled up the pole, and hung onto the guy that was sticking out horizontally. The effect was of a huge, human, real estate sign. Then, they did all sorts of acrobatic things in the air, supported the whole time by the guy with the pole on his shoulder—amazing stuff.

Every act was equally amazing in its own way. Two "lion tamers" came on with their beasts, and had them jump through hoops, balance on rolling balls, and do numerous complicated acrobatic maneuvers. Each of the "lions" was two men in a lion suit—one as the front legs and head; the other as the rear legs and body. But they were so well coordinated, moving in such complete accord, that it was impossible to see them as anything but huge, highly trained lions.

Two young men came on juggling small pottery jars. They were certainly good jugglers, but we'd seen good juggling before. They juggled bigger and bigger jars, until they were tossing pots the size that small trees are planted in as easily as they had those the size of jelly jars—impressive, but not up to the other acts we'd seen. Then they stopped, faced each other, backed a few steps away, and leaned forward. The one on the left balanced one of the pots—it must have weighed 15 or 20 pounds—on the back of his neck and shoulders.

Then, so quickly we didn't even see how he had done it, except to note that he had not used his hands, he "threw" the pot across to his partner, who "caught" it with the back of his neck and shoulders. His partner took a couple of steps back, and threw the pot back. This time we were watching more closely, for all the good it did—we still don't know how they did it. They just shrugged their shoulders, and the pot launched across the stage. They kept backing up, like children playing that game where they throw a raw egg back and forth until it breaks all over one of them. The difference was, they backed up until they were all the way across the stage from each other and didn't break a thing.

The acts just kept coming. Each, in its own way, was as impressive as the ones before: the 15 women riding one bicycle, the slack-wire artist who stood on his head and juggled, the trapeze act that used people instead of poles to anchor the swing, and many more. We had never seen a circus act in the United States nearly as impressive as any of those. We raved to our hosts from the Foreign Affairs Office about how much we appreciated the opportunity to attend. They were so pleased we were pleased, that the following week they arranged another cultural event for us.

I had been invited to a Chinese opera shortly after arriving, and had accepted out of a sense of duty, thinking that, although I didn't expect to like it, I really shouldn't live in China for a year without seeing it at least once. I loved it, and took every opportunity to listen to it, watch it on television, or attend live performances. Laurie also enjoyed Chinese opera, but the pleasant surprise was that Jesse and Cooper did, as well. It wasn't like American, German or Italian opera—it was fun. The actors wore flashy, interesting costumes and bright, colorful make-up. The sounds they made, their exaggerated actions, and the music that accompanied them were all exciting. It was very theatrical, and many entertaining things happened, even in tragedies.

A few days after we saw the acrobats, a young man from the Foreign Affairs Office came to ask if we'd like to see some Chinese opera. We said we'd love to. What he neglected to mention was that we were not going to see a professional performance, but one by students at the Liaoning Provincial Opera School. They invited us backstage before the show and introduced us to the performers—children from six to 15 years old. The scene was totally unlike the frenzy I'd seen many times backstage in American theatres. Those children were calm and relaxed. The only excitement they showed was when they had their pictures taken with us.

If we hadn't been backstage and seen them, it would have been difficult for us to know that the performance we saw that night was not by professionals. We had to keep reminding ourselves that these were children we were watching. Had we not known, we may have noticed that they were smaller than the professional actors we had seen, or that their voices were not as powerful. But their actions, their facial expressions, the poses they struck, and the way they worked together were, to us anyway, indistinguishable from the professional ensembles we had seen.

Many Chinese operas included a battle scene replete with acrobatic stunts, and the one the students performed was no exception. The acrobatic stunts performed by one of the characters—a sort of ninja or super warrior—as part of the mock operatic battle were the more impressive for the fact that we had seen him backstage, and knew he was about 12 years old. Whether because he knew the performers were children, or because the action was so compelling, Jesse was captivated. As soon as we let go of him, he began to move, trance-like, toward the stage. Laurie went to retrieve him, but the director said it was okay, to let him go.

Cooper getting up close and personal with the Chinese opera cast.

He ended up sitting on the steps to the stage, elbows onstage, chin in hands, for the entire performance.

After the performance, our interpreter introduced us to the woman who had taught the young actors. She informed us that we had just seen their final examinations for that term. We told her we certainly hoped they'd passed with flying colors, and she said yes, she was pleased, they had done quite well.

105

My assistant had invited our family to his home several times, but he came one day with a special invitation: to have Mongolian hot pot with his family. They put a huge pot of water over the fire and after the water was boiling well added noodles, pickled Chinese cabbage, meat, fish, shrimp, vegetables, and a variety of spices. The result was a thick, spicy, soup. Then they sliced raw mutton very thinly and put plates of it on the table.

We used our chopsticks to hold the pieces of sliced mutton in the boiling water until it was cooked—which didn't take long, because it was sliced so thinly. By watching our hosts, we learned to slosh the mutton around until we got some of the goodies from the brew hanging on it; then take it out and eat it. They provided several little dishes containing various kinds of spicy sauces for dipping: one sweet-and-sour, one salty, one soy-tasting, and one peppery. They also provided a ladle, so we could scoop some of the soup into little cup-sized bowls, and every time the mixture in the pot began to recede a bit, they brought more goodies to replenish it.

As if all that weren't enough, they had several other dishes, which they said were fairly traditional with the hot pot. One was chicken, barbecued in a kind of sweet-and-sour sauce, and served cold—delicious. Another was steamed, spiced, green beans. Mongolian Hot Pot was never served in the summer, but was a traditional winter dish. It didn't take long to figure out why—we weren't there ten minutes before the temperature in the apartment went up about five degrees, and people began shedding their outer garments. It got very comfortable. In fact, Mongolian hot pot dinners were the only occasions during the winter when Chinese buildings were what we would call warm by U.S. standards.

———————

Our hopes for a white Christmas were in vain. Actually, by the middle of December, we had begun to think we had been misled about the severity of winters in northern China. We had been led to believe, for example, that they got quite a bit of snow. Well, it had snowed three times by Christmas—none of which would have been able to pass itself off as a self-respecting storm in northern Minnesota.

We'd had a few pretty cold days. It got below zero Fahrenheit for three or four days near the middle of December, and it was hard to find a place to warm up, short of going over to our friends' apartment at the Consulate, where it was really hot inside. None of the Chinese buildings were heated to the degree we were used to in the States. The result was that it seemed colder in China than it did at equivalent temperatures back home.

Jesse checking out the presents under our Christmas bush.

Our preparations for Christmas in China were more extensive than any we'd made in the States—probably a reaction to the fact that we were so far from home and Christmas was so different there. We did a lot to maintain our Christmas traditions. The only time I (knowingly) broke a Chinese law was to that end. On the way home from my office one day, I loitered near an evergreen bush until I didn't think anyone was watching. Then I quickly broke a 2-foot branch from the bottom— in the back, next to a building, where I figured it would go unnoticed. Laurie was skeptical, but decked with homemade decorations, it made a serviceable, if somewhat minuscule, Christmas tree. The boys were delighted.

I came home a couple of days later to find that Laurie and the boys had built a manger scene from playing cards. They had made Mary from the queen of hearts, and the angel from the queen of diamonds. Joseph and (a slightly oversized) Jesus were the jacks of hearts and diamonds. The sheep were cut from numbered cards and covered with cotton-ball wool. They had made four Kings of the Orient instead of three—there are four Kings in a deck, after all. There was no danger of the sheep straying, for they had used the remaining four queens and jacks as shepherds. They had found a small cardboard box for the manger, and had used dead weeds for straw. It wasn't the sort of decoration we could run down to the local store and buy, so it was an especially nice creche, playing cards notwithstanding.

A daily activity that helped get us into the Christmas spirit was watching Jesse and Cooper open their Advent calendar. Merle and Ruthie, about the first of December, had given the boys the greatest Advent calendar we had ever seen. They had wrapped match boxes in colored paper, numbered them from one through 24, and pasted them on a large sheet of colored cardboard. Inside each matchbox they had placed little presents—nothing big: a couple of sticks of gum, or a couple of key chains, or balloons. One of them contained packets of root-beer Kool-Ade, of all things. We had forgotten about Kool-Ade.

They were just little things, but Cooper and Jesse loved them. From the first of the month until Christmas, we had no trouble getting them up and dressed in the morning, because we made a rule that they couldn't open the box for that day until both of them were dressed. It was amazing how much those 24 little boxes did to enhance our spirits during that time.

We put together a list of 17 people—workers in the Foreign Affairs Office, the people who took care of our building, foreign students, other Western teachers, and Chinese friends—to whom we wanted to give presents. After much thought and discussion, we decided to make them holiday gift packages. The packages would include two kinds of Christmas cookies, fruit cake, peanut butter, and two kinds of peanut brittle.

In preparation for making the contents of our gift packages, I went to the market for ingredients. We knew the stuff would be expensive, so we had been saving for a couple of months. It's a good thing we had been, because I spent the equivalent of $20, about what we would normally spend for a week's worth of groceries. I bought eight pounds of peanuts, eight pounds of peanut brittle, four pounds of dried fruit, three pounds of raisins, and three pounds of candied walnuts. In the process, I attracted quite a crowd of Chinese.

I approached the first counter and told the woman behind it that I wanted eight pounds of peanuts. The Chinese words for "eight" and for "one half" are very similar. She scooped me out a half pound of nuts. I said no, I wanted eight pounds. She assured me that was a half pound, and put it back on the scales to prove it. There were hand signals for each of the numbers from one to ten, which Cooper had learned at school and, luckily, had taught me. I had to show her the hand signal for eight to convince her that I did indeed want that much, and wasn't just suffering from terminally poor pronunciation.

I simultaneously accumulated greater quantities of luxury foods, and greater numbers of astonished Chinese onlookers. I didn't begin to have enough Chinese to tell them about Christmas, and how that stuff was going to make Christmas presents for about twenty people. So I just finished shopping, struggled through the crowd to my bike, and pedaled away.

Merle and Ruthie helped us with the baking. They tied their oven onto one of their bikes, loaded their backpacks with ingredients, came over after classes one afternoon, and we set up a cookie production line. We cleared a sort of end table in the living room, and Merle and Ruthie, with indispensable help from Jesse, prepared the ingredients. This was a critical job, and somewhat more complex than it would have been in the States. The raisins, for example, had to be soaked and washed twice to get them clean enough to use. Then about one in three had to have a little, hard, stub of stem removed. To do three pounds was rather time-consuming.

A lot of cookie recipes called for cinnamon, nutmeg, cloves, and other spices. Because we had only cinnamon and cloves, we just used twice as much of them. They were available whole, so the ingredient preparation team had to crunch them up, as well. I had had brought a tool kit from the States that included a hammer. It made a serviceable mortar, with a hard plastic cutting board as a pestle.

Laurie mixed the prepared ingredients in a semblance of the recipe and decided on appropriate substitutes for the (numerous) ingredients we lacked. For brown sugar, we used regular granulated sugar when we could get it. If it wasn't available, we had to crush sugar cubes, which, although more expensive, we could usually get. For powdered sugar, we melted granulated sugar. For baking soda, we used baking powder— at least we think it was baking powder. Laurie brought the resulting dough to Cooper and me in the kitchen.

There we had set up the dining table, leaving just enough room for us to sit on the edge of the bathtub to roll out the dough and create Christmassy shapes with cutters Ruthie had gotten who-knows-where. I put the cookies into the two electric ovens, and tried to make sure—

through a complicated process of plugging and unplugging, and opening doors to various degrees—that they came out somewhere near the fine line between still raw in the middle and burnt crisp. Only about one batch in ten were ruled unacceptable as gifts—but certainly within acceptable range of intrafamily edibility.

Sitting on the edge of the bathtub making Christmas cookies on the dining room table.

We made fruit cakes using gum drops, dried fruits, and candied nuts, and spent hours grinding peanut butter. Laurie and I divided everything, and the boys put it in yellow plastic bags tied with red yarn, both of which we had found at the market. One day at the post office, I had found some postcards of the Disney characters—Mickey and Minnie Mouse; Donald and Daisy Duck; Goofy; Pluto; and Huey, Duey, and Louie—all with Christmas trees on their shoulders and dressed up in Santa Claus suits, saying things in Chinese. My assistant translated them, and, to my delight, they were saying things such as, "Merry Christmas," and what would pass for "Peace On Earth." So we used those as the "to" and "from" tags on the packages.

Christmas shopping was unlike anything we had ever experienced—or ever want to experience again. Laurie and I had often complained in the States of the commercialism surrounding Christmas—how the day after Thanksgiving stores began to bring out their stocks of toys and their Christmas displays. Well, we certainly didn't have that problem in China. The stores were no different before Christmas than any other time, so we had to spend hours going into them one at a time to see what they carried.

It was a half-hour bike ride, one way, to the shopping district and, as we didn't have anyone to leave the boys with, we had to take them along. One of us had to employ diversionary tactics while the other made purchases. It wasn't an ideal situation, but we did what we could. Two days before Christmas, we accepted the fact that what we had accumulated, although it wasn't much, would have to do.

The ranks of presents were swelled, however, by Grandma Susie. My mother sent a "care package" that, like the cavalry of legend, arrived in the nick of time. The slip of paper glued on the outside said the box contained about $38 worth of stuff, and she had to spend about $45 in airmail fees, to get it to us before Christmas. It was money well spent.

Even with a somewhat smaller mound of packages than they were used to under the tree Christmas morning, Jesse and Cooper couldn't complain too much, because it was only one of several celebrations we had. The first came, quite unexpectedly, on December 6, with what in Germany is called St. Nicholas Day. There were several German students on campus, and one of them—a very nice young woman named Dorothy—really liked the boys. She must have let St. Nicholas know there were a couple of American children at Liaoning University who would really feel good if he stopped at their house when he came to visit the German students.

When we returned from breakfast one morning, the boys found outside our door two metal tins about a foot long, six inches wide, and eight inches high; beautifully painted to look like tiny, red, double-decker buses—complete with passengers, and a jolly old driver so lively and quick. One box had a tag that said "To Cooper from St. Nicholas," and the other a tag that said "To Jesse...." They were full of German candy, gum and toys. We got the impression they were the equivalent of stockings left hanging from mantels in the States.

A few days before Christmas, Merle and Ruthie came over with a couple of other English teachers from the Education College where they worked. We had an early Christmas with them, because they were leaving on the 24th to spend the break between terms in Hong Kong and Thailand. We spent a very festive Christmas Eve with my assistant and his family. They had gone to a great deal of trouble to incorporate as many American customs into the celebration as they knew about, or could arrange.

Christmas Day, after opening our presents at home, we went over to the Benedict's, our friends at the Consulate, for a beautiful service, a Christmas dinner rivaling any that Mother used to make, and an exchange of gifts. Then Laurie's parents came on the 28th, and we had a Christmas with them—and anyone who's ever had grandparents knows how special they can make Christmas. So, although it was different from those in the past, our Christmas in China was certainly memorable for the number of friends we got to share it with in very special ways.

For months, we had been working out plans with Laurie's parents, Dick and Lois, to come the end of December and spend the first three weeks of January traveling with us throughout southern China. Someone from the university Foreign Affairs Office had arranged for the provincial government to issue them official letters of invitation. As best we were able to determine, it was possible for them to travel in China without such invitations, but the invitations legitimized their presence, and—in theory, at least—made things go more smoothly.

Grandpa Dick (in his new hat) and Grandma Lois opening Christmas presents with Cooper.

To issue the invitations, the provincial government had requested their "resumes." Both were retired—Dick as principal of a high school, and Lois as an assistant manager of a small department store—and neither had what could be considered an up-to-date resume. They created documents that satisfied the provincial government, however, and the invitations were sent.

The people from our Foreign Affairs Office had reserved for them the room next to our apartment on the second floor of the foreign experts building. It was a very nice room—nicer than those available in all but the most expensive Chinese hotels. It was about two thirds the size of our whole apartment, with a small sun porch and a private bath (no kitchen). It was nicely furnished with overstuffed couch and chairs, coffee table, side board, twin beds, desk and chair, color television, and oriental carpet—all for the equivalent of $15 a night. Although that seemed like a lot to us on our Chinese salary, it was certainly less expensive—and nicer—than a double at Motel Six.

Christmas in China, of course, is not celebrated with nearly the gusto it is in the States, so Laurie and I had to work until the first of January, when our between-terms vacation began. The folks from the Foreign Affairs Office were very accommodating, however, about squiring Dick and Lois around town, and in fact, treated them generally as honored guests.

So during her parents' first day in town, Laurie was teaching. I was taking care of Jesse, and a young man from the Foreign Affairs Office was giving Dick and Lois a tour of downtown Shenyang in a car provided by the university. They stopped at a large traffic circle near the center of the city where, in a park-like setting, resided one of the biggest statues of Mao in northern China. On the South side of the circle was a hotel patronized primarily by Asian businessmen, in front of which was a drive where cars could stop to unload passengers and luggage. The university driver pulled into that drive and stopped, to let Dick get out and take a picture of Mao.

Dick climbed about halfway up the massive front steps of the hotel to get a better angle for his photo, which he was preparing to take when a young Chinese man rushed up behind him and clubbed him on the back of the head with a heavy cane. The force of the blow caused Dick to stumble down the steps, into the side of the van, where he slumped to the ground, unconscious. About 50 Chinese people immediately leaped on the man, pinned him to the ground, and began pummeling him with their fists, canes, or whatever else they had handy.

The police, never far away in Chinese cities, ran over, pulled the people off him, arrested the somewhat battered attacker, and took him away. They rushed Dick, who had regained consciousness by then, to get medical aid—which didn't take long, as the main hospital happened to be less than two blocks away. In the excitement, however, they left Lois sitting in the university car, for about an hour, with no idea of what was going on.

Someone decided that Laurie and I should be notified, so the driver went into the hotel and called the Foreign Affairs Office. Two of the people there set out to find us and let us know what had happened. Laurie was in class, and nobody from the university administration seemed to know where. I wasn't home—I had taken Jesse on my bike to the local post office—so they gave up and started off to join the others downtown.

As luck would have it, just as they turned onto the four-lane highway in front of the university, one of them saw me in the crowd of people riding past on bicycles. They honked their horn and shouted to attract my attention—as well as everyone else's within earshot—stopped in the center of the highway, and both came running over to me, leaving auto, bike, and pedestrian traffic in a snarl. Neither of them spoke any English, and the little Chinese I understood did not include such words as "attacked," "clubbed," or "concussion."

All of the Chinese onlookers, of course, understood perfectly, and were so intrigued that they stopped to see what would happen, further disrupting the situation. Many of them, in a sincere effort to help make me understand the gravity of the situation, began what has to rank as one of the most bizarre games of charades in history. I had gotten as far as somebody hitting his or her head, or somebody hitting someone else's head, when one of my English speaking students happened by, and explained it to me.

Actually, he explained to me what he understood the two people from the Foreign Affairs Office to have understood from the driver who called them, and was inside the car, and didn't actually see what had happened, understood to have happened. I got enough to realize there was some medical problem with one of Laurie's parents, and that I should go with the two people from the Foreign Affairs Office. So I did.

By the time we got there, they had x-rayed Dick's head and neck and found that he didn't have any fractured vertebrae, nor a cracked skull. Several doctors had examined him and determined that he didn't have a concussion. In fact, as nearly as they could tell, he was none the worse for wear. In fact, Lois was probably in worse shape from the trauma of spending an hour not knowing what was going on. At any rate, we all agreed they had probably had enough excitement, and postponed the remainder of their Shenyang tour until the next day.

The incident was considered important enough that the police chief for Shenyang had come to the scene, and after everything settled down, he asked Dick if he had gotten his picture of Mao before he'd been hit. Dick said he wasn't really sure, so the police chief insisted he take another, just to erase all doubt. After getting Dick situated and stationing a police officer behind him to ward of any potential attackers, the police chief hurried across to get in the picture. As a consequence, Dick is probably one of a handful of Americans who have a photo of the police chief of Shenyang waving to them from in front of a statue of Mao.

We never understood why Dick had been attacked. We didn't see or hear about anything else like that happening in the year we were in China. There was much speculation. Someone said that perhaps his assailant was one of the rare Chinese who did not like foreigners. Dick had been wearing a Russian-style hat, and someone said perhaps the man hated Russians for some reason. Someone else said perhaps the man had been offended by the fact that Dick was taking a photo of Mao's statue. The most likely reason, however, was probably the official one put to us by the police: "He was a crazy man."

The police wouldn't give us any more information about the man, and we were never able to find out what happened to him, but everyone we asked said it would certainly be a long time before he would have the opportunity to hit anyone else—if ever.

Happily, that was the low point of their visit. In fact, it guaranteed them royal treatment. Word of the incident spread throughout officialdom, and city and provincial dignitaries contacted Dick the whole time he was in Shenyang to make sure he was okay. He was. The only residual effect was that his right leg felt a little numb for a few hours, and then a little tingly for the rest of the day. And who can blame him if, throughout our trip that followed, he sometimes looked furtively over his shoulder before bringing his camera to his eye, or if some of the resulting photos weren't quite in focus—as though he'd taken them a bit quickly; then hurried on.

Chapter Six
January

Travel in China was not easy. Oh, it would have been no problem if we had wanted a pre-packaged tour through an established travel agency. Had that been the case, they would have made all the arrangements in advance, and all we would have had to do was follow our guide around with the rest of the tourists. There were two problems with that scenario: 1) it offered no flexibility—we would have gone where the guide said, and when, and 2) it would have cost a lot more money than we had. A very nice travel agent told us he could arrange a trip for us in which all expenses would be covered for the equivalent of $500 a day—about five times what we had. That left the other possibility: arranging travel ourselves. Which brings me back to the fact that travel in China was not easy.

We couldn't book hotel rooms ahead of time, nor could we reserve plane or train tickets in advance. So we just had to cope with each situation as it came up. What we did to increase the odds that things would work out in various situations, and to decrease the odds that we would go insane trying to communicate, was take my Chinese assistant along. We had to pay his expenses, but Westerners who had traveled in China—especially those with families—said we'd save money just by having a Chinese speaker with us. They were right. It was probably the single best decision we made all year. I couldn't count the times (nor would I care to) that having him along saved us from camping out in train stations—or worse.

Our Foreign Affairs Office contacted people in the Foreign Affairs Offices of universities in the cities we would visit. They gave us letters of introduction to the ones they were unable to contact. We realized early in the trip that introductory letters were usually very helpful. The higher the status of the person signing such letters, and the more specifically addressed, the more they helped. An I.D. card that indicated my foreign expert status, and one that showed I was a professor at a Chinese university were occasionally helpful, as well.

Although our trip with Laurie's folks was to hit mostly the tourist spots in the South, we began by heading north. January 1 we took the train to Harbin (Har bean'), a city of about a million and a half in the northernmost province in China. Each January, Harbin had a celebration called the Ice Lantern Festival. Now, most people have seen or heard of cities in the States that have ice sculptures to celebrate some sort of a winter festival, but the Ice Lantern Festival was in a completely different league.

Each fall, as soon as the river froze to a sufficient depth, all the carpenters in Harbin were assigned to work on the ice sculptures. That meant that for about two months, several hundred highly-skilled men worked full-time cutting huge blocks of ice from the river and moving them up onto the bank. There they had set up large circular saws, much like those in Minnesota lumber mills. After cutting each block to roughly the size called for in the overall plan, they moved it to the location where it was to be used.

Once on location, the blocks were used to construct ice sculptures—some small and intricate; others two or three stories tall and hundreds of feet across. Whether small or gigantic, each was beautifully carved, and shaved crystal clear—not a ripple of imperfection showed. These pieces were scattered throughout the city, but most—hundreds of them—were concentrated in a city park about four blocks square.

After constructing them, the craftsmen had drilled into most of them at regular intervals, inserted what looked like strings of colored Christmas lights, and poured water into the holes. After the water froze, the imbedded lights were almost invisible in daylight. We went to the park late in the afternoon, and were there when the lights came

A 3-story ice edifice at Zhaolin Park, in Harbin.

on at dusk, creating a dazzling array of multi-colored structures. Some of the pieces were made only to be looked at, but others were buildings such as castles that we could walk around inside. Some had clear ice roofs through which shown the stars and the lights of the structures around them. We felt like flies must, crawling around inside a brightly-lit crystal chandelier.

Some of the structures were made to be climbed on. Several were huge slides, as though the proprietor of a carnival water slide had forgotten to turn off the water when the park closed on Labor Day, and the children could slide on its icy slope all winter. There was one ornate structure where we could climb a 50-foot set of stairs, and once at the top, could descend by any one of four slides. Cooper and Jesse wore me out climbing to the top; then sliding in various configurations (me sitting with Jesse on my lap and Cooper standing behind, Cooper and Jesse sitting and me standing behind...) down first one slide, then another, then another, then another. When I could do no more, they cajoled Dick and Laurie into repeated descents.

Among the pieces were very life-like animals, frozen in mid-leap. Tastefully confined to one corner of the park were the commercial offerings, much like colorful floats in some huge parade—marketing efforts, carved in the shape of company symbols. One was a huge truck, "Shenyang Motor Company" carved in Chinese characters on its side; another a huge pack of cigarettes with the name of the company emblazoned on it. There were beer cans and liquor bottles, 25 feet tall, ablaze with light—very ornate, very festive, very tacky.

We stayed in a small, two-bedroom apartment in the guest house at the Harbin Institute of Technology. At the equivalent of about $25 a night for seven of us, it was the least expensive place we stayed. As we traveled, we found a great variety of available accommodations—from the very swank, very expensive joint venture hotels such as the Great Wall Sheraton, which had been built primarily with foreign capital, to the very un-swank, very inexpensive Chinese guest houses.

Many Western tourists and business people who went to China wanted to stay first class; they provided much of the business for the joint venture hotels. Chinese tourists and business people, generally, did not have that much money, so they stayed mostly in the guest houses. Those of us who had been paid in Chinese money for several months found the guest houses more in our league, as well. The joint ven-

119

ture hotels operated just like expensive hotels everywhere, but the guest houses took some getting used to.

Each time we checked in, there were three standard questions we learned to ask. The first was, "How much is this going to cost us?"—because there was a real range of prices, and they didn't necessarily seem keyed to quality. The second was, "When is the hot water on?"—because we generally had hot water for only three or four hours at night, and an hour or two in the morning. That became such an expectation that when we were told at one place that it was on all the time, we asked again, on the assumption that either they had misunderstood the question, or we had misunderstood the answer.

The climate in China was quite a bit like the United States. In Shenyang and Harbin it was similar to northern Minnesota, so we needed warm clothes for the time we were there. In the southern part, however, where we were to spend most of January, it was quite warm. There, we needed pretty much the same clothes we'd have worn on a vacation in the southern states. Nowhere we stayed were the rooms heated 24 hours a day. South of Beijing they weren't heated at all, despite the fact that winter temperatures sometimes dipped below freezing. We didn't bother asking about room heat—it didn't really matter. When the heat was on, great. When it wasn't, we put on more clothes.

The third question we learned to ask was: "When is the dining room open?" We found early in the trip that, unlike in hotel restaurants in the States, we couldn't just walk in whenever we felt like eating and order. The dining rooms might be open for lunch from 11:30 to 12:15, and if we weren't there, we didn't get lunch. In some places, we had to let them know a day in advance which meals we would be eating in the hotel. As we traveled, we learned that, generally, the further north we went (the further we got away from tourist centers) the less expensive everything was, and the nicer we were treated.

It was often difficult to get train tickets in China, and we expected that to be a problem. We were pleasantly surprised to find, however, that the people in the Foreign Affairs Office at each university where we stayed had special access to tickets. They had to pay fees—possibly in the form of bribes to the right person—to have tickets set aside, and those fees were passed along to us. They usually only amounted to about $1 a ticket, however—well worth it to make sure we got to our next destination on schedule. We never had any real trouble getting train, boat or plane tickets.

Most of our travel was by train, on which there were four classes of tickets: hard sleeper, soft sleeper, hard seat, and soft seat. We traveled hard sleeper on the overnight train trip from Harbin to Dalian (Dahl yen'), the last time we did so when we had a choice. It wasn't that we needed more luxury, it was just that we had no privacy.

In hard sleeper, one side of the car was all windows, with an aisle along that side. The other side had partitions at right angles to the wall about every eight feet. The resulting cubicles were about eight feet square and 12 feet high, open on the end facing the aisle. On the wall opposite the aisle, were a window and a small wooden table, attached to the wall, with one leg on the outside edge. Each cubicle contained six bunks about seven feet long by three feet wide. The top two had only about three feet of headroom, leaving enough space for the bottom one to be about two feet off the floor, and still allow enough room to sit up without hitting the one above.

Instead of mattresses, the bunks had about two inches of padding, covered with vinyl—hence the name, "hard sleeper." Each bunk had a sheet, a pillow, and a quilt. During the day, luggage, personal belongings, pillows, and quilts were stored on the top two bunks. Three passengers used each sheet-covered bottom bunk like a bench: sitting up straight, without a back rest, or half reclining against the partition behind them. At night, luggage and shoes were stored on the floor between the bottom bunks, and pillows and quilts were distributed. Passengers lay down in their clothes, used their coats as either extra pillows or extra covers, pulled their quilts over them, and went to sleep. Each cubicle had one overhead light, which was extinguished by the conductor, leaving sleepers—especially those in the top bunks—to cope with the aisle lights, which were left on all night.

Westerners seldom traveled anything other than soft seat or soft sleeper, so we were a bit of an oddity, and news of our presence didn't take long to spread throughout the train. Soon people began to stop and watch us, especially Cooper and Jesse. The first one, it was kind of fun to have somebody stop and talk to the boys. The second one, well, okay. The third one, it started to get pretty old. After the 20th person in two hours, the boys just didn't want anything more to do with it. They were cowering under the bunk and screeching at people—which the Chinese thought was hilarious. It didn't make for a terribly pleasant ride to Dalian, so we decided that from then on we would go soft sleeper when we could.

Soft sleeper cars were similar to hard sleepers, except that the cubicles were enclosed, each had four bunks instead of six, and everything was generally much more plush. The enclosed rooms were much like those in old train movies: wood paneled, with sliding doors. The bunks had soft mattresses, and the top ones folded up during the day, allowing the bottom ones to be used as sofas. There was padding on the walls of the bottom bunks, so passengers could lean back in comfort, and there were luggage racks built out over the aisles, so suitcases didn't have to be moved around each morning and evening. The table was larger, and covered with a linen cloth. Each bunk had a reading light; each room a table lamp, separate switches for the overhead lights, and large thermoses of hot water, which were kept filled by conductors.

As there were four bunks in each soft sleeper compartment, we just bought a compartment. Laurie, Dick, Lois, and I each got a bunk. Jesse slept with Laurie, and Cooper slept in the luggage rack. It was just his size, and he liked the idea of having his own bed. My assistant got either a hard sleeper or a soft sleeper ticket, whichever was available. He spent all day in our compartment anyway, playing cards, talking, and reading; going to his bunk only to sleep at night. We still had plenty of contact with Chinese travelers when we went for walks with the boys, but we had much more control over how much contact, and when.

Hard seat cars were traditional passenger cars, with an aisle down the middle and a series of hard, double, vinyl-covered seats facing small

A very un-luggage-like Cooper, retiring for the night in his "bunk."

wooden tables down each side. Although hard seat tickets were very inexpensive—perhaps $2 for a 12-hour trip—they did not guarantee a seat; only the right to get on a train car where people almost certainly outnumbered seats. Friends told us they had stood for up to 30 hours at a time. This was the way most Chinese traveled, and when the gates opened to allow access to trains, the resulting stampede—with everyone trying to get in before all the seats were taken—was a sight to behold. More than once, we saw parents throwing their children through open windows, so they could stake out a space for the family. Aside from the fact that soft seat cost quite a bit more, the differences were that a soft seat ticket actually bought the right to a seat, and that seat was padded.

———————

We didn't go to Dalian because we particularly wanted to visit there, but rather to catch the boat to Shanghai. As we were going to be there anyway, however, we decided to stay a a couple of days to have a look around. It would give us a chance to see the coast. It was a good choice. We stayed in the guest house at the Dalian Foreign Languages Institute. It was only a couple of miles from the train station, so Dick, my assistant, and I walked there to hire a car.

We had learned in Harbin that the best way to acquire transportation was to hire a car and driver for the day. Actually, the seven of us couldn't fit into a car, so we had to get either two cars—which was expensive—or a van. In fact, what we did was compromise between comfort and expense, and hired what the Chinese called mini-buses. They were built like the vans in the States, only about three-quarter size. They were pretty cramped for seven plus a driver, but we could hire them for $20-$30 a day, depending on the city. The driver would take us anywhere within the greater metropolitan area and wait for us while we were there. We were expected to buy his meals during the time he was driving for us. There was sometimes an additional charge to go to a site very far outside the city, and we were expected to buy him a pack of cigarettes in that case—preferably American.

In Dalian, our driver took us on a quick tour of the city, drove us down to see the docks, and dropped us off at the museum for an hour. Then he did something that convinced us he was a kindred spirit. Despite the fact that it was a cool, gray, drizzly day, he took us to the seashore. There was a road along the shore just south of town, and it was a beautiful drive. It reminded us of the road along the coast of northern California: all curves, and cliffs, and waves scattering seagulls when they dashed against huge boulders on rocky beaches.

Because of the ameliorating affect of the ocean, Dalian has a winter climate similar to Portland, Oregon: occasional wet snow, but mostly cool drizzle. We stopped several times and walked down to the deserted beach. In traveling during the winter, we had traded a bright, warm summer day overrun with tourists, for a damp, dingy winter day rich in its own kind of private beauty. It was a great trade. The whole coast of northern China was ours, to do with as we chose. We drove along part of it. We walked along part of it. We stood on parts of it, collecting mist until it dripped from our hair. It was an afternoon unlike any other we spent in China, and ranked right up there in the competition for most memorable.

We caught the boat to Shanghai at 8:00 the next morning. It was about the size and shape of those sometimes pictured in advertisements for cruises on the Caribbean. That was where the similarity ended. It had once been white, but had long since surrendered to rust and other stains any such pretensions. The accommodations might graciously have been termed "basic." The toilets (Asian-style) were not clean. The rooms were not clean. The food was not good.

In a typical Chinese anomaly, there was no first class. Second class cabins contained two built-in double bunks, a tiny built-in closet, a built-in bench seat, a small, shelf-like wooden table attached to one wall, a wooden chair, and a wash-one-hand-at-a-time-size sink. These accouterments were contained in a metal room about eight by ten feet, and seven feet tall, with one small porthole on the outside wall. The classes went down to sixth, in which ticket holders had the right to enough floor space on which to lie down. We took second class.

The metal walls, floor, and ceiling may once have been green. It was hard to tell. If there had ever been heat, it had stopped working— probably about the same time the paint had ceased to serve its function. When Lois lifted one of her bags onto the table to get something out of it, and it trailed a stream of water, we realized the room leaked. The leak wasn't very bad—until we left the harbor. Once we got out into the waves, some of which splashed over the side onto the deck, we began to take on water in earnest. We were never in danger of sinking, but there was always enough water gurgling from one side of the cabin to the other to make keeping our feet dry a practical impossibility.

We checked the menu from the dining room, and were surprised at how inexpensive the dishes were. Then we ate some of them and understood why. Luckily, we had long since learned not to count on the availability, quality, or affordability of food while traveling in China, and always carried a small duffel bag stocked with food. Its contents didn't offer great variety—usually bread, fruit, peanuts, smoked sausage, instant coffee and tea, hard boiled eggs, soup noodles, and hard candy—but there were many times we were glad we had it—on the boat from Dalian to Shanghai, for example. It was far from the best part of our trip, but it was bearable. For 38 hours we bore it.

As we chugged slowly into Shanghai harbor at 10:00 p.m., Laurie described the view as "glorious." The lights of the city glistened in the water and gleamed dully off the hulls of ships from several countries as men worked at their loading and unloading. She said that experience alone made up for the past two days of discomfort. The rest of us weren't entirely convinced.

We were told that for the equivalent of about $5 we could keep our cabin until 6:00 a.m. Compared to about $30 a night at the cheapest place we'd be able to find in Shanghai, we decided that was certainly a good deal. So we stayed on the boat overnight. What they failed to mention when making the offer, was that they would be unloading and loading the ship the whole time we were trying to sleep.

Had we been on the harbor side, it might not have been so bad, but we weren't. Our cabin was immediately adjacent to both a loading ramp and a crane. Our tiny porthole, which had done a woefully inadequate job of admitting light throughout the trip, did a magnificent job of admitting noise. It had never occurred to me how much noise people unloading and loading a ship must make. We had what could only be described as a fitful night's sleep for our $5—except Dick, of course, who's a world-class sleeper. He could just as easily have slept through their loading and unloading him.

We got through the night, and the next morning at 6:00 we got off the boat. We had arranged for a driver to meet us, but he wasn't there. About 7:00, we decided he wasn't going to show, so we started looking for a taxi. Now, the docks, as in most cities, were not in the most fashionable section of town, so the taxis in that part of town were, as a consequence, not the most fashionable taxis.

Throughout China, there were ubiquitous little work vehicles: small, 3-wheeled scooters, built on motorcycle frames, powered by motorcycle engines. Some had enclosed one- or two-seat cabs. Over the back wheels, they had little truck beds—some open; others with metal or canvas tops. They hired out for all kinds of hauling jobs, and we sometimes saw them carrying prodigious loads. The one we ended up with had a canvas cover over the bed, and wooden benches along each side. I don't know if I'd call the load the seven of us and our luggage made "prodigious," but there certainly wasn't any room to spare. It felt like we were being transported throughout town in a large wheelbarrow.

After forty minutes of watching Shanghai out the back flap of that tiny covered truck, we arrived at the guest house of Shanghai International Studies University, where they supposedly expected us. We didn't consider the absence of a car to meet us an auspicious omen, however. When we told the woman at the desk who we were, she said what are you doing here, you're not supposed to be here until the ninth. We said this is the ninth. She looked at the calendar and said oh, you're right, it is. They were a day off on their whole operation, but they found rooms for us.

It was one of the most expensive places we stayed—the equivalent of about $35 for the seven of us—but the rooms were very nice: three good-sized bedrooms, a small kitchen, and a private, Western-style bath. The food was excellent. We really went overboard on our first breakfast there, because it was the only place we had stayed that had truly Western-style breakfasts: mushroom and cheese omelets, fried eggs, soft-boiled eggs, ham, bacon, and toast. We spent the equivalent of about $10 for the 7 of us—about twice what we spent on most other meals.

Shanghai was not one of the most scenic places in the world—just a big international city—but at twelve and a half million people, it was the biggest city in China, and no tour of the country would have been complete without at least stopping there for a look. Tourists usually took the boat tour up and down the Hwang Po River, but we had just spent 38 hours on a boat, so we didn't feel we needed that. Instead, we went to a jade and ivory carving factory. It was the highlight of our stay in Shanghai. We had seen jade and ivory carvings in stores, and although they were very nice, they seemed a bit expensive. After watching them being produced, we understood why.

The first step in the process was to create an ornate drawing on paper. Although some of the carvers created their own designs, they were more often created by an artist—someone who, as a carver, had exhibited outstanding design talent—then given to a carver to make three-dimensional. To do that, the design was transferred with pencil onto a rough block of jade or quartz, or part of an elephant tusk. Each carver sat at a station with a small lathe-like machine. Some had little burr wheels attached directly to the lathe. On others, the grinding disk was powered by a flexible shaft attached to the lathe chuck, rather like a large Dremel set, or a dentist's drill.

Using only those little grinding wheels, sandpaper, and pumice for the final polishing, the carvers created incredibly ornate pieces. Some consisted of three or four hollow, filigreed balls, each inside a larger filigreed ball. They accomplished this by grinding the design into the

126

surface of the outside ball; then, inserting tiny grinding tools into the various holes, working slowly until a slightly smaller sphere separated from the inside of the first. They then smoothed the inside surface of the larger, and the outside surface of the smaller sphere, and working through the holes of the outside sphere, ground the design into the surface of the next. They repeated the process until the fourth ball, in the center, had been hollowed out. The finished pieces were very fine and airy—when held up we could see completely through them.

Other pieces were much larger—some two or three feet tall. They often represented mountains—complete with winding trails and houses, and hundreds of tiny trees and flowers—populated by hundreds of animals and people. Each tree had hundreds of individually carved leaves. Each person, although no more than an inch tall, had a face that exhibited individual features. In the reception area, a carving of that sort was on display, only it was made from a single piece of jade about seven feet tall, and about four feet across at the base. It was enclosed in a glass case, and sat on an ornately carved ebony base. We were told that it took six carvers working full time more than a year and a half to complete.

Watching the painstaking process for a couple of hours engendered an appreciation for the unique nature of each piece. We would watch a carver work on a half-finished piece for a while, then say, "That's nice. How long have you been working on it?" She would say, "Four months," and "nice" suddenly seemed an inappropriate modifier. We began to appreciate why some of their pieces sold for the equivalent of $100 or $150; in fact, we went away marveling at how inexpensive they were.

Just as everywhere else in China, Cooper and Jesse were a real hit with the carvers. Each time we entered a new room at the stone cutting factory, work slowed to a crawl, while the carvers gathered around the boys, talking to them, delighted when Cooper replied in Chinese. Each time we left a room the boys had more little pieces of jade, amethyst, or ivory that workers had stuffed into their hands or their pockets when the bosses weren't looking. Everybody wanted to give them presents. Cooper ended up with a small collection of semi-precious stones and ivory given to him by carvers. Some of the pieces had been hastily shaped into hearts, animals, or flowers by workers who would have been punished had they been caught by their managers.

We had not planned to stop between Shanghai and Guilin (Gwee leen'), but we kept hearing great things about Hangzou (Hawn joe'), so decided we had enough time for a side trip there. The problem was that because we hadn't planned the visit in advance, we hadn't arranged for a place to stay there. We mentioned our problem to the people in the

Foreign Affairs Office at Shanghai Foreign Languages Institute. They said no problem, they had friends at a university there, and we could stay in their guest house.

They wrote their names, and the names of the people we should see at the university in Hangzou. They said, find these people and give them our names. They'll take good care of you. We thanked them and asked for the phone number of their friends, so we could call ahead. They said oh no, you don't need to call ahead. Just show them our names when you get there. We said okay, fine.

We hired a car at the train station in Hangzou to take us to the university our friends in Shanghai had told us about. We had no trouble finding the people they had said to find, and gave them the piece of paper on which our friends had written their names. They said oh, so-and-so sent you. That's great. That's fantastic. But we don't have any rooms—there's a convention going on here. We'd love to help you—we'd do anything we could to help you, any friends of so-and-so are friends of ours—we just don't have any rooms. In fairness to our friends and their friends, however, they were very helpful. After much effort, they found us rooms at a Chinese hotel.

The decision to visit Hangzou was a good one. The city was built around a couple of mountains and a big lake, and was one of the most beautiful we saw in China. It was also there that we had a unique experience. During our first night there, as we slept, a cold front from Mongolia pushed the snow belt south almost to Guilin. These southern cities almost never experienced snow, but when we got up the next morning, about four inches of fluffy, moist snow covered everything. Hangzou was far enough south that it had palm trees and others that never lost their leaves, but stayed green all year. They were an amazing sight with their mantles of pristine snow. The effect on the residents was as though someone had declared a holiday. Everyone was outside—walking, building snow people, and having joyous snowball fights.

We hired a delightful young couple with a van to show us their city—a task they accomplished with charm and vigor. They seemed to know just the kind of places we would enjoy, and just the kind of restaurants we liked. The best of many good experiences in Hangzou was our visit the silk weaving factory, where some of the finest silk goods in China were produced. They started with the cocoons of the silkworms. About 20 cocoons were placed in each foot-square bin of water. Hundreds of these bins, two deep, were situated waist-high along several aisles in a huge warehouse-like building. Above the bins, about eye-high, a series of spools were spinning.

Cooper instructing some new-found friends in Hangzhou on the fine art of snowman construction.

The workers, most of them young women, were responsible for finding the end of the thin filament that made up each cocoon, joining about ten of them together, running them through a guide that twisted them into a single strand, and starting the strand around a spool. Each woman was responsible for a station about ten feet long, that included about twenty spools. She had to keep track of the 200 cocoons feeding those spools, noting when one was nearly depleted, and before the filament spun off, replace it with the end of a new one. If she missed, she had to stop the operation and back it up to the place where the thread became one strand short, wind the new strand in, and start the spool spinning again. The dexterity and speed with which those women worked was awe-inspiring.

Once the silk thread was finished and dyed, it was transported to what they called automatic looms, where it was woven into fabric of various patterns. The process began with an artist drawing a design on a piece of paper, which they enlarged onto huge grids so each stitch was clearly visible. Then they punched holes in stiff cards and attached the cards together to make strips hundreds of feet long. Those strips were fed through card readers that operated the looms, causing them to create stitches in such a way as to replicate the original design. The process looked like a mechanical precursor of computerization.

Although the resulting material wasn't exactly hand woven, there

129

was an operator at each loom making sure it worked properly. And they were kept busy—it looked as though the looms were pretty crude, and as many were idle, being repaired or adjusted, as were working. Yet, as so often was the case in China, from this seemingly inefficient, ineffective process came some of the most beautiful silk we had ever seen.

To make decent connections to Guilin, it was necessary for us to backtrack to Shanghai, where we had two hours for dinner before re boarding the train. During those two hours in Shanghai, we had one of the most frightening experiences of our year in China.

Across from the Shanghai train station was a large, multi-story market. We were in for a 2-day train ride and needed to replenish the contents of our food bag. So we left Jesse and the luggage in the station with Dick and Lois, and Cooper, my assistant, Laurie, and I went out for a quick bowl of soup and some groceries. The market and its restaurants were packed. As we wandered around, we were approached by two young men and a young woman who invited us to eat at their restaurant. They said it was nearby, so we agreed to follow them.

We followed as they led us away from the busy, lighted market, and down a street in a residential area. We began to get apprehensive as they negotiated a series of dark alleyways through a neighborhood of shabby, single-story houses with outdoor water supplies. Just as we decided we had been Shanghaied, they stopped at one of the little houses and ushered us inside. It was the home of one of their brothers, and consisted of two rooms. They lived in one. The other, furnished with two small tables and several stools, was the restaurant.

We joined two old Chinese men for egg-drop soup, a couple of vegetable dishes, and beer. When we finished, the young people led us back to the market, wished us well, and began recruiting their next customers. We plunged into the throng inside the market to do our grocery shopping. As we wandered from counter to counter, checking out our options, Laurie stopped occasionally to remind Cooper to stay close so he wouldn't get lost. The third time she turned to check on him, he was gone.

We had read in the newspaper about children (especially boys) being kidnapped. Laurie was sure that Cooper—with his dark hair, light skin, blue eyes, and ability to speak Chinese—had been too much for someone to resist. I thought it more likely that he had just gotten interested in the contents of one of the vendor's stalls and hadn't noticed when we moved on.

We retraced our path, my assistant repeatedly asking if anyone had seen Cooper. The longer we looked, the more panic-stricken we became. My assistant ran out to the street to look. Someone brought a couple of security guards. As the Chinese in the market learned of our plight, they joined the search. Laurie decided to look on the floor above, but as she started up the stairs, one of the security guards met her on his way down and told her Cooper was not up there. After 15 minutes, there were so many people searching that we couldn't imagine he could still be in the building.

We were at a loss for what to do next. Then Laurie realized it was almost time for our train, and her parents must be worried about what had happened to us. My assistant ran across the busy, six-lane street to the station to tell them what had happened, and to contact the police. He returned, and with tears in his eyes, told us that Cooper was with Dick and Lois. When he couldn't find us, he had threaded his way through dense traffic to the station, where he knew his grandparents were. As word spread throughout the market, the tense atmosphere eased. As we left, many shoppers smiled, waved, patted our arms, or otherwise let us know of their relief for us. With shaking voices, we reminded Cooper what to do if he got lost. He didn't need to be told again the rest of the trip.

We were just in time to catch the train to Guilin. Although little more than a poor farm town, Guilin was situated in one of the most beautiful geographic areas of the world. Few photo spreads of China are without at least one scene of Guilin. It is the area of China where mountains emerge directly from flat land, like huge, calloused fingers bursting without warning through the earth's crust to reach hundreds of feet into the sky. These spiny peaks are riddled with all sorts of caves and strange looking rock formations. A beautiful river winds through it all. The people from the Foreign Affairs Office had bought us tickets for the river boat, to best experience the unique geography of the area. What a trip—six hours of beauty, interrupted only for a delicious meal of Mongolian hot pot.

It was in Guilin that we saw many of the sights National Geographic teaches Americans to expect in China. "Coolies," for example, wearing pointed straw hats—bamboo yokes over their shoulders with heavily-loaded baskets on each end—moving in those funny little, quick, gliding steps. We saw guys with incredibly well-muscled legs, pedaling around with two or three people in their rickshaw-type bicycles. And we saw the fishing cormorants.

Each fisherman had a narrow bamboo raft, and one or two of the water birds, which looked like small, black-and-white herons. The men would pole their rafts out into the river; then push a cormorant into the water with their pole, and make it swim around and catch fish for them. The birds, which seemed to be semi-domesticated, were attached to the rafts by long cords, and they had bands around their necks so they couldn't swallow the fish they caught. The only thing they could do was take the fish back to the man on the raft.

Those bamboo rafts were some of the least-sturdy water craft we had ever seen. They were constructed from three or four bamboo poles, maybe eight or ten feet long, lashed together, with both ends curved up slightly. So, they were only about two feet wide, and floated very high in the water, giving them a high center of gravity. The people poled them while standing, surfer-style, about two-thirds of the way back. We'd go by them in the river boat, and our wake would bounce them around, but we never saw anybody go in. We figured they'd had a lot of practice.

I did see one guy almost lose his raft, though. He must have gotten his pole stuck in the mud, or between two rocks, and he almost ended up—Tom Sawyer fashion—hanging on his pole with his raft floating downriver. He freed his pole at the last instant, however, regained his balance, and poled nonchalantly on—a bit too nonchalantly—I'm sure he knew I was watching. I swear he almost started whistling; looking like, "Who, me? Oh, I meant that."

A couple of days in Guilin were enough, though. Once we'd seen the natural wonders, we felt everything else in the area paled by comparison. When we got ready to leave for Xian (See on'), we were pleased to find that the folks from the Foreign Affairs Office had already bought our plane tickets for us.

With the best of intentions, the director of the Foreign Affairs Office at the university where we were to stay in Xian had sent two luxury cars to meet us at the airport and drive us less than a mile to the university. We were tired from our trip and hours spent in airports, so we were glad to have transportation waiting. Then we found that we had to pay the equivalent of about $25—ten times what we would have paid a private driver. We asked why so much, and were told we had to pay for the five hours the drivers had sat at the airport, plus the meals they had eaten while they waited. It had never occurred to them to drive the short distance back to the university and return when our plane came in. They were government drivers. They had been told to go to the airport and pick us up, so that is exactly what they had done.

An argument ensued, which I lost. The only satisfaction I got was that I paid them with Chinese money instead of Foreign Exchange Certificates. FEC was supposed to be used exclusively by foreigners in China, and was supposed to be worth the same as Chinese money. In fact, however, it was worth about twice as much on the black market. The reason was that FEC was convertible to other currencies, and Chinese money was not.

Many young Chinese men made a good living by taking advantage of the disparity in real value between the two currencies. They loitered in areas frequented by foreigners, and when the opportunity arose, approached them, intoning, "Change money?" "Change money?" It happened to us occasionally in Shenyang, but much more frequently in the South, where they were often very insistent, sometimes following tourists for blocks. We were approached so often on our trip to the South, that Jesse picked it up. He asked me for some money, so I gave him a small Chinese bill. He would walk around with it, and in a good imitation of the young men, chant, "Change money? Change money?"

As a foreign expert, teaching at a Chinese university for the year, I was paid mostly in Chinese money, so the government had issued us what were called "white cards," which allowed us, despite the fact that we were foreigners, to spend Chinese money, and to pay domestic, rather than tourist, rates. We had learned early how to say, "I have only Chinese money," and that, coupled with pulling out a few Chinese bills quickly discouraged money changers.

When I lost the argument about having to pay extra for their waiting at the airport, then, it was with full knowledge of the probable effect that I very conspicuously ignored my FEC and handed the drivers Chinese money. They were upset, and insisted that, as I was clearly a foreigner, I had to pay them in FEC. When I showed them my white card, however, they realized that I was fully within my rights.

In Xian, we discovered an alternative to hiring a van for the day to see the sights. In each of the tourist cities there were many Chinese, as well as Western, tourists, and they didn't have as much money as the

Westerners. A day-long Western tour in one of those cities cost $25 to $50. The same tour for Chinese was a tenth as much. The difference was in quality: the buses weren't as nice and they weren't heated, parking lots for Chinese buses were further from the sites, the lunches weren't as posh—that sort of thing.

We decided all those niceties weren't worth the difference in price, and as we had white cards, we could go the cheap route. In Xian, for example, we paid the equivalent of $2 apiece for a tour of the terra cotta warriors, two temples, a hot springs, and a museum. Of course, we had to leave when the bus did, but that would have been true on the comfy, heated buses as well, only for $30 apiece.

At first the people looked at us a little oddly, wondering why in the world Westerners would choose to go on a less-than-luxurious tour. Once they realized that we knew what we were doing, however, and hadn't just wandered onto the wrong bus, they were very friendly, accepting us as just part of the group. In addition to seeing the same things for a lot less money, it was nicer than a Western tour because we didn't feel as estranged from everybody else. We felt a little closer to our surroundings—sometimes a little too close.

The real disadvantage to the Chinese tours, we found, was that the Chinese were very pushy. They didn't line up for anything, but pushed en mass. When they got on a bus, even when they knew there were enough seats for everyone, they got into shoving matches to try and get on before anyone else. Rather than try to compete with that, we stood back until all of the Chinese had fought their way on; then took the seats that were left. Sometimes the conductor or the driver would move people around so we could have seats together. When they didn't we just interacted with the people around us.

The terra cotta warriors were an underground, life-sized army of horses, wagons, chariots, and men. Each was individually crafted from clay, with unique features. An emperor had ordered the army sculpted to guard his tomb. The story has it that the hundreds of artisans who created the figures were sealed in with them to die, so the location would remain forever secret. It probably would have, if a peasant hadn't come across it hundreds of years later, while digging a well.

About half of the figures had been excavated, and the rank upon rank of warriors in full battle dress made a unique and amazing sight. They were covered by a huge metal building, about the size of a football field. We could walk around the part of the site that had been excavated, and on catwalks built over the warriors, some as close as a few feet. There were signs at particularly interesting spots, with explanations of

Laurie, Cooper, and Jesse at one of the statues (wire-clad to deter climbers) flanking the Sacred Way to the Ming Tombs.

what we were looking at. There was also a museum nearby, with exhibits covering the entire history of the site in great detail.

Another unforgettable experience in Xian was our visit to a cloisonne factory. We had seen cloisonne pieces in stores, souvenir shops, and tourist bazaars. When the proprietors had assured us they were handmade, we had looked at them and smiled knowingly, thinking, "Sure, they are. A hand pulled a lever on a machine to stamp them out in a factory somewhere." Well, they had been created in a factory, but one in which things were made by hand.

We spent one whole afternoon watching young women make cloisonne. The process began, as with most artwork in China, with an artist creating a design on paper. The design was then transferred to a copper piece—anything from tiny thimbles or earrings to huge, human-sized urns. Two popular items were plates and vases. The design was replicated using epoxy glue to attach tiny copper twists, maybe an eighth of an inch wide, to the surface of the piece. They then filled the recesses created by the copper twists with various colors of ground glass mixed in water. This glass and water paste was applied with a spatula in the larger areas. Many of the designs were so intricate, however, that the colored paste had to be squeezed into the tiny openings with eyedroppers, or inserted with the tips of pins.

Next they blotted the water out of the mixture with soft clothes or paper towels—leaving the ground glass stuck in the recesses—and glazed the piece in very hot ovens. They repeated the whole process several times. Each time, through three or four glazings, depending on the design, the surface got smoother and the colors brighter. Finally, the piece had the look of brilliantly multicolored, polished crystal.

I asked one woman how long had she been working on that dish. She said two months—very matter of factly, not like it was any big deal. I was impressed. As we were leaving, we stopped at the outlet store, and I kept thinking about how every one of those pieces had been created with painstaking labor and artistry by someone using her hands and skills that had taken many years to develop. I wanted to buy Laurie something. The prices ranged from about $5 for a set of small earrings, to $2500 for a huge, exquisite urn. She wears them often, and they look great on her.

The train ride from Xian to Beijing was another long one—we got into Beijing early evening of the second day. Despite prearrangements, the woman on duty at the university where we were supposed to stay had never heard of us. She was very accommodating, however, and after half an hour on the phone, found us rooms in a Chinese hotel nearby. As Chinese hotels went, it was quite nice, but it was being renovated.

The Chinese went about the renovation process a bit differently than we were used to from the States. They didn't close down or block things off, they just renovated in the midst of everything. They tore up that hotel and put in new wallpaper, floors, ceilings, water pipes, light fixtures, and everything else while we were staying there. They didn't actually tear up our rooms, but they did tear up the hallway right outside our rooms. There were times when we had to climb over bundles of old wallpaper that had been stripped off the walls and were blocking the hallway.

By the time we got to Beijing, we'd learned how to get around on city buses and how to catch Chinese tours, so we hired cars only when we really needed them. Of course, the buses were not nearly as comfortable—in fact there were times they got so crowded we gave up and flagged down a taxi. On the other hand, Dick and Lois said several times they were glad they had chosen to come and see China with us instead of doing it on a Western tour, because they saw the country and the people in a whole different way than Western tourists usually do. They seemed to mean that positively most of the time.

For about ten cents apiece, we took city buses downtown to Tiananmen (Tee en' uh man) Square and the Imperial Palace. Tiananmen Square was a huge, open area, paved with stone slabs, where a million and a half people could gather for official celebrations. It was flanked on the north by the the Imperial Palace, the Forbidden City and a huge park. We spent a whole day exploring them, and felt we had seen little of what was there. To the east of the square was the People's Museum, a huge building that housed their equivalent of the Smithsonian Institute. To the south was Mao's tomb and a monument to the Communist revolution; and to the west was the Great Hall of the People, their equivalent of our Capitol Building.

In the center of it all stood the Monument to the People, which looked like a miniature Washington Monument, and held a message to the Chinese people from Mao in his own calligraphy. The Chinese said the Monument to the People was the center of Tiananmen Square, which was the center of Beijing, which was the center of China, which was the center of the world, which was the center of the universe. We were impressed.

Our hotel was only a few stops on the bus line from the Summer Palace, so we took the city bus there. It consisted of hundreds of acres, including a large lake and a small mountain. Almost all of it was swept, raked, pruned, groomed, and trimmed, as though it were one huge back yard. There were so many buildings that they were under constant renovation. In the years it took the carpenters, masons, and painters to work their way to one end of the grounds, the structures on the other end deteriorated to the point where they needed work again. It was at the summer palace that the empress dowager once spent the country's entire naval budget constructing a huge, ornate, concrete boat. Word has it that her admirals were not pleased, but none of them had the nerve to tell her so.

One day we took a Chinese bus tour to the Ming Tombs, the Great Wall, and a couple of temples for the equivalent of $2.50 a person, including lunch. Granted, it was far and away the worst meal we had in China, but one of them had to be, so why not a cheap one? Besides it was good that our worst meal came during a Chinese bus tour, because then we didn't have time to eat it anyway. The Chinese could eat a meal faster than any human beings we had ever encountered, and they were especially fast when they were anxious to get on with something—like a tour.

We got our soup and bread (buffet style), found a place to sit, said grace, and looked around to find ourselves alone. Knowing Chinese drivers weren't noted for their patience, and not wanting to be stranded miles from the city, we gulped a few mouthfuls of (awful) soup, pocketed our bread (also bad) for later, and headed for the bus. Actually that driver was pretty patient—he let us get to our seats before lurching off toward the Ming Tombs.

The Ming Tombs, the underground palace for the bodies of the Ming emperors, was the most over-rated tourist attraction in China. Oh, they were situated in a nice park, and the half-mile approach to the park was flanked by wonderful stone statues on each side, every 20 feet or so, but the tombs themselves were a bust. They were deep underground, however, so we didn't know that until we had bought our tickets, and climbed down there. We walked through them quickly; then spent the rest of our time sauntering along flagstone paths and relaxing on carved stone benches in the park. It was the only site we visited on a Chinese bus tour where we didn't feel rushed to catch the bus.

In contrast, the most awesome experience I had in China was walking on the Great Wall. It was the only thing created by humans that the astronauts said they could see on the earth from outer space. It was maybe 50 feet high and 20 feet wide, built from blocks of stone about two by two by three feet. Just hewing those blocks from solid rock, with nothing but the hand tools they had available, was a prodigious accomplishment. The surface was wide enough, and smooth enough, that columns of horsemen could ride four abreast.

I walked that surface, on undulations created by millions of feet for hundreds of years. I struggled with steps worn concave by men coaxing horses up their 45 degree slope. I stood at one end of the mile or two of restored wall north of Beijing, and stared at the unrestored grandeur of the rest, snaking through the mountainous landscape to the horizon. I tried to imagine the 3,000 miles of stone that stretched beyond that horizon—and I couldn't.

After five days in Beijing, Dick and Lois caught their flight back to the States, and Laurie, the boys, my assistant, and I took the overnight train to Shenyang. When we arrived at 8:30 the next morning, we were exhausted. The next-to-last thing in the world I wanted to do right then was haggle with one more driver for a car to take us to the university, but the last thing I wanted to do was camp out in the train station. So (once more into the breach), I took a deep breath and went out into the parking lot—where the first driver I saw was the one for the university van. The folks from the Foreign Affairs Office (bless their hearts) had sent him to wait for us.

He took our bags from us and threw them into the back of the van, we climbed in, and within half an hour we were in our apartment.

Cooper and Jesse had been great travelers: adjusting well to new situations, coping with problems, and maintaining cheerful dispositions. We got home, and they fell apart. Within half an hour every toy, every book, everything in the place small enough to carry, was spread throughout the three rooms of our apartment. The boys were screaming, crying, shouting, and fighting with each other. All in all, it was a pretty miserable first day back. We went to bed very early that evening and slept late the next morning. Things weren't so bad the second day. By the third day, we had pretty much recovered. It was a good thing, because the next day we left for our trip to the North.

Chapter Seven
February

Whereas our trip to the South had been to all the places people visited when they went to China, our trip to the North included places no Westerners had been. What a different experience it was. In our southern trip we were tourists. In our northern trip we were guests. Many people we met told us they had only seen Westerners on television. Granted, we were oddities, but the relationships we established were personal; not based on our buying something.

The trip was a result of a fortuitous meeting with the father of one of Laurie's graduate students, Zhao Xian, or David, as he preferred we call him. Most Chinese students, as part of their study of the language, chose English names for themselves. Some of them liked using those names with their Western friends. A couple of months after our arrival in China, David's father visited him at the university, and David introduced him to us. During the conversation, Mr. Zhao (Djow) had asked what we were going to do during the break between terms. We told him Laurie's folks were coming and we were going to travel in southern China. We said something about being a bit disappointed that we would be visiting only tourist sites, and not getting to see "the real China," as it were.

He welcomed us to his home in the North, and we said we would love to come. After being in China longer, and learning that, "Welcome to my home," meant something more like, "I hope you are enjoying China," we worried that what we had thought was an invitation hadn't been at all. At the time it happened, however, we were too naive to realize. After we got to know David better, we asked him, and he assured us that his father really had meant it as an invitation. At any rate, we assumed the invitation (if it had been one) was for a couple of days. As time progressed, however, we found he had planned a major tour, and wanted us to come for three weeks.

As a chief engineer for the Ministry of Forestry, Mr. Zhao was one of the primary people responsible for fire protection in northern China. Nobody could hold a much higher position without being a member of the Communist Party. He explained that the Ministry of Forestry had several large units throughout the northern provinces of China and Inner Mongolia. Attached to each unit was a contingent of army officers and enlisted men assigned to the forestry ministry as fire fighters. His job required him to travel among those units, so he had more mobility than most Chinese.

February was a very slow fire season, so Mr. Zhao had made arrangements for us to travel to several of the cities where the ministry had forestry units. The directors of those units, who were his friends, had made arrangements for us to stay either in guest housing if their unit had it, or if not, in local hotels.

Our first stop was Qiqihar (Chi' chi har) because David, who was traveling with us, had gone to college there, and he wanted to stop and see a couple of his former teachers. The city had a small ice festival, of which the residents were very proud. After having seen the one in Harbin, it was hard for Laurie and me to get too excited about it, but Cooper and Jesse loved it. There were a couple of ice slides on which they spent hours playing with the neighborhood children.

On our last evening there, one of David's former teachers (his favorite, I bet) invited us all to her house for jiao zi. We sat around eating and talking while her husband, who said almost nothing all evening, cooked and served—very unusual for China. On the bus back to the hotel, David told us that her husband was the brother of Li Peng, the man who had headed the army under Mao Zedung. Li had allegedly engineered an unsuccessful assassination attempt on Mao, and died in a mysterious plane crash shortly thereafter. David said few people even realized Li Peng had a brother, and that he lived as a relative recluse, content to keep it that way.

From there, we took the train to Nenjiang (Nin jung'), where Mr. Zhao lived. As with many Chinese families, not all of David's lived in the same place. His mother, who was a school teacher, had taken a job in a city near Beijing, and their young daughter had gone to live with her. They felt attending a more urban school would increase the daughter's chance of getting into a good college. To us it seemed a drastic step. The status of the college from which people in China graduated, however, probably was the greatest factor affecting their futures.

Many Chinese families, therefore, lived apart for years to benefit one or more of their children. David, for example, had been raised by his grandparents in Beijing, to better prepare him for college. One of his brothers lived with Mr. Zhao and worked for the public relations office of the forestry ministry. A third son was at the aviation college in Beijing, and would probably return to live with their father and work as a pilot with the forestry ministry after graduation. As with Christmas or Thanksgiving in the States, however, families tried to get together during Spring Festival, and David's brothers, sister, and mother were all at his father's house when we arrived.

142

Spring Festival was what we knew as Chinese New Year, and was like a combination of Christmas and New Years in the States. Most schools back home took vacation from just before Christmas until just after New Years. Spring Festival was much like that, except it was more than just a vacation. It was a continuous celebration. Officially, it lasted five days. In fact, it lasted 15. The Lantern Festival, another important holiday, was only two weeks after Spring Festival, so it must have seemed like a good idea just to connect the two. For 15 days, people stayed home and prepared special food. The only thing they did outside their homes was walk around town and visit their friends and have cookies and tea and shoot off firecrackers. Nobody did any work.

We got to Nenjiang about 5:00 p.m. The compound where Mr. Zhao lived was about 15 kilometers out of town. The plan was that we would call from the downtown office of the forestry ministry in Nenjiang, and he would bring a car to pick us up. We hired a little 3-wheeled taxi, piled into the back with our luggage, and with exhaust fumes pouring in on us, chugged a few blocks up the street to forestry ministry's office.

We called over and over, but nobody at Mr. Zhao's compound—a village of 650 people—was answering the phone. The director of the forestry ministry office in Nenjiang decided that the woman who was supposed to be operating the switchboard at the forestry compound must have started her Spring Festival a bit early. To us, that meant we couldn't get in touch with Mr. Zhao, which meant we had no way to traverse the 15 kilometers to his home. We were saved by guan xi (gwan' she).

Everything in China was based on relationships. It was a way of life. People were constantly working to enhance their relationships with other people. Guan xi, loosely translated, meant "pull"—the result of those relationships. It ranged all the way from close friendships developed during the course of many years, to the crass selfishness involved in the establishment of what the Chinese referred to as "back doors." If they couldn't get something done through regular channels, the Chinese would buy gifts—often Western cigarettes or liquor—and bribe officials with them.

They were subtle bribes, and because China was a gift-giving culture, it was sometimes difficult to tell where the gift giving left off and the bribery began. It was never as direct as saying, "I'll give you these cigarettes if you'll do this for me." It was more like, "I've been thinking about you. I know you smoke, and I know you like good cigarettes, so I thought you'd like this carton of Winstons (worth about $25). They're

143

a gift from me to you." Then, a couple of days later, "You know, I have this problem, and you just happen to be in a position that you might be able to help me."

Often, people developed back doors for future use. Someday when they had a problem, they might be able to solve it through a back door they had established with someone. Most guan xi, however, resulted from legitimate relationships established through years of association. People became close, and naturally wanted to help each other when they could.

The forestry ministry offices were on the second floor of the building, with a small general store downstairs. The Ministry of Forestry probably owned the building and the store, so the store manager was likely a ministry employee. At any rate, he came upstairs to meet us. When he saw we were having trouble, he asked what the problem was. We explained, and he said he might be able to help. He called a friend at the Nenjiang phone exchange, who contacted the operator at the forestry compound in such a way that she thought it was a long distance call from the national office of the Ministry of Forestry. They were able to get in touch with Mr. Zhao, who immediately came to pick us up.

By the time the store manager's guan xi got us through to Mr. Zhao, it was about 7:30, and we were getting pretty hungry; especially the boys. We hadn't eaten because David said his father would certainly have dinner prepared for us when we got there, and would be disappointed if we'd already eaten. As we waited for Mr. Zhao and the car to arrive, the director of the forestry ministry office pulled a bag of peanut brittle from his desk drawer and asked if we would like some.

Cooper and Jesse both said yeah, great, and simultaneously plunged their hands up to their elbows into the bag. I said, sure I'd like a piece, and wasn't far behind them digging in. Laurie was a bit more genteel, but still said yes thanks, and took a piece. He looked horrified. He sat back, and his mouth dropped open. He was clearly stunned at our display of barbarity. We had forgotten that tradition dictated three refusals when offered something. It was basic etiquette to say, "Oh no, no thank you. Oh no, I couldn't. No please," until the offer was withdrawn—in which case, they didn't really want you to have it in the first place, or repeated for the fourth time—in which case, it was okay to accept.

We were done in by three facts. First, it was a custom that, although we knew about it, wasn't second nature to us. Second, the custom was adhered to much less in the South, where we had just spent the past three weeks. Third, we were very hungry. David explained to him that, in the West, if you offered people something and they said, "No thank

144

you," it meant they really didn't want it, but if they did want it, they said, "Thanks," and took it. He still looked a bit skeptical, but there followed a good discussion about things Western—in which he was very interested—and I think that by the time Mr. Zhao arrived, we had salvaged our guan xi with him.

The forestry compound where Mr. Zhao lived was a small village in which everyone worked in some capacity for the Ministry of Forestry. On one edge of town was a large airfield. It was deserted while we were there in February. Mr. Zhao said, however, that during the two "fire seasons"—mid summer and late fall—it was a fully-functioning field. He said they served several spotter planes, and at least one large transport plane, used to carry firefighters to the places they were most needed.

To our surprise, the compound was situated on a huge, treeless plain. We naturally expected it to be in a forest—after all, it was the major forest fire prevention unit for the entire province. Mr. Zhao said the nearest forest was about 100 kilometers away. We asked why in the world they built the unit there, instead of near the forest, where it would have been most useful. He said that was a good question, which nobody seemed to be able to answer. He said that 30 years earlier, when they had built the unit, he had argued long and loud to put it in the forest. However, somebody with guan xi must have stood to gain by its being near Nenjiang, so that's where it was built.

Mr. Zhao lived in the first private house we had been in. It was in the middle of one of eight almost identical brick row houses, with about 12 units in each row. Each unit had a tiny backyard/garden defined by the house at one end, a brick storage shed at the other, and a short, wooden fence or brick wall on each side. They had no real front yards, but were set back about four feet from very narrow dirt streets. Half of the area between the house and street was taken up by tiny, enclosed porches. The other half, in most cases, was fenced and used either for storage or to raise animals. These row houses made up most of the compound.

Surrounding them were various other brick structures: several individual houses, a community outhouse on each edge of town, a school, a store, a recreation building, a telecommunication building, a bath house, a dining hall, a garage, a power station, and—largest and most impressive—the administration building. Scattered around their perimeter were a motley collection of gardens, root cellars, small barns, storage sheds, and livestock pens. These pens held chickens, pigs, sheep, goats, a few cows, and—occasionally—a mule or a horse. About a quarter of a mile away were the barracks where the firefighters lived during the fire seasons.

Mr. Zhao's house consisted of an entryway and five rooms, each about 10 by 12 feet. The back of the house, which consisted of a living room in the center, and two bedrooms—one heated and the other not—had wood floors painted in glossy red enamel. The entryway, with a kitchen to the left and an unheated storage room to the right, had raw concrete floors, shiny with a patina from years of tracked-in dirt. Mr. Zhao was very proud of his wood floors, so to keep them in good shape, we all left our shoes in the hall.

Every time we wanted to go into the front part of the house, then, we had to put our shoes back on, leaving them at the living room door when we returned. When everyone was in the house, there might be 20 shoes of various sizes piled outside the living room. It would have been unreasonable to expect people, each time they left the room, to sort through all those shoes and find their own. We'd just slip our feet into whichever shoes were closest. Given such freedom, of course Jesse chose to clomp around in my hiking boots, laces flapping. Cooper would shuffle around in Mr. Zhao's or David's shoes. That left us, if we wanted to go anywhere, to try and squeeze into whatever smaller ones were left.

They had one cold water tap in the kitchen, but no drainage system, so they used an enamel wash basin as a sink. They had a couple of galvanized, 2-gallon buckets on the floor nearby. After washing dishes, hands, or vegetables, they poured the dirty water into the buckets. Several times a day, they emptied the buckets in the street. During the summer, that served to keep dust down, and any vegetable peels made good pickings for the many chickens, ducks, and geese that wandered the streets in search of just such delicacies. In freezing weather, however, the resulting ice would have made the streets quite treacherous, so they added an important modification.

During the winter, they used coal for cooking and for heating their homes. They carried the coal cinders to the intersections of the village streets, and dumped them in such a way as to create reservoirs, rather like shallow swimming pools. Then they poured the waste water into those pools. The process made the intersections quite narrow, but there was so little traffic it hardly mattered. We asked Mr. Zhao what happened in the spring, and he said it got pretty muddy for a few weeks when the pools thawed. He said that after it dried up a bit, they brought in big trucks and front-end loaders to haul away the mess. Laurie and I agreed that we were glad to be there while it was still frozen.

Mr. Zhao was not happy with the situation. He took me to the edge of town and showed me a large sewer line the Japanese had put in when they had operated an airfield there during the war. He said that every year he conducted a campaign to get the men of the village to repair it, dig a sewer system in the village, and connect the system to the line the Japanese had built. He made no effort to hide his irritation when he told me that the men of the village did not think the problem warranted the effort it would take to solve it. He was sure he could get the necessary materials, but they would have to do the digging by hand, something they weren't willing to do.

One thing we were not looking forward to during our stay was using the community outhouses. They were brick sheds, about eight by twenty feet, divided into men's and women's sides by a brick wall in the center. The concrete floors in the large, open rooms had about four slots along one wall. They opened into a large pit that was dug under half the building, and which extended beyond the wall, allowing access from behind by the men with the "honey wagons." They came around periodically to empty the pits of what was euphemistically called "night soil," and transported it to gardens, where it was used as fertilizer.

Because he knew we were not very comfortable using communal toilets, Mr. Zhao had designed a sort of port-a-potty for us. He had cut a hole in the seat of a backless chair, installed a toilet seat, and painted the whole thing with red enamel—left over from the wooden floors, judging by its shade. Under the chair he had installed a reservoir ingeniously fashioned from a large plastic "jerry can." Once or twice a day, he or one of his sons emptied it at the community toilet. The system, although it caused a lot of work for Mr. Zhao and his sons, functioned very well, and illustrated not only his talent as an engineer, but his his generosity as a host.

They heated their house, as did everyone in that part of China, with the same stove they cooked on. Actually, "stove" is a bit of a misnomer. It was a knee-high concrete box with holes and removable iron covers, much like those in old, cast iron wood stoves. They could burn wood or crop residue, but most people used coal, pouring it on top of the fire through the holes on the cooking surface. Iron doors in the front gave access to a cinder pit.

The flue went into a double masonry wall between rooms, wound back and forth through the wall, and exited through the roof. They had a water pipe embedded in the concrete around the fire chamber, so on especially cold days, hot water could be routed to radiators for supplemental heat in the rooms. There was also a tap from which they could draw hot water for cooking or cleaning. So, through a very efficient system, one stove heated their home (three rooms, anyway), their food, and their water.

Their stove had two burners, on one of which a huge pot of water always simmered, because as with most places in China, the water was not potable until it had been boiled. It was convenient for brewing tea or instant coffee, and it kept the humidity in the house at a nice level all winter. What was not convenient, was cooking on a knee-high stove.

Laurie and I cooked a Western meal for David's family while we were there, and we agreed that it was a real pain (literally) to bend over that stove and cook a meal. but they did it, and Chinese cooking was generally much more time consuming than Western. We usually ate two meals—at about 10:00 a.m. and 4:00 p.m., and there were days when Mr. Zhao and/or his wife started cooking our second meal right after breakfast. Granted, because it was a holiday, many of the meals were probably more elaborate than usual, but still, we were amazed at the amount of time they spent preparing food.

In addition to the stove and the wash basin, the kitchen contained a two by four foot counter, a small cupboard that served as both pantry and utensil storage, a wooden table, and two wooden chairs. In the summer, their refrigerator was the root cellar they had dug at the edge of town. When it got colder, they used the unheated storage room across the hall from the kitchen. In the winter, they also used the sloped roof of their front porch as a freezer. In preparation for the holiday, it was stocked with a small deer and several pheasants. Mr. Zhao was very embarrassed that he had not found time before we arrived to dress the deer, so it had to lie around inside thawing for a couple of days before he could do so.

To do laundry, Mr. Zhao had a tiny agitator-type washer. We filled it with hot water from the tap near the stove; then added soap and clothes. Because the dirty water had to be carried out by hand, we did several loads in each batch of water. He had a large washtub that we used to rinse the clothes, twisting excess water out of them by hand. A couple of clotheslines strung along each side of the heated wall did a great job for drying.

The old woman who lived in the house next door was out of town for Spring Festival and let David's family use her house. Essentially, everybody spent the day in Mr. Zhao's house, but the whole family went next door to sleep, leaving Laurie, Cooper, Jesse, and me with their house to ourselves. It was very nice. The last thing they did each evening before they went next door was bring us a couple of enamel dishpans full of warm water to wash with before we went to bed. And that was the extent of our bathing for the five days we were there. There was a public bath house in the village, which was open each Saturday for men, and each Sunday for women, except during Spring Festival, of course, when nobody worked—including the people in the bath house. The boys loved it.

On the evening before the official festival, everybody went to bed at 6:00 p.m. and slept until midnight, at which time we got up and went outside to set off firecrackers. It was not unusual for each family to spend the equivalent of a month's wages on fireworks. Every family in town had simultaneous fireworks displays—about 100 of them. It's a wonder Jesse and Cooper didn't suffer major damage to their necks, the rate they were swiveling their heads, trying to see all the explosions at once.

The Chinese would never have passed a Fourth of July safety quiz. Otherwise intelligent, decorous people lost all sense of caution when exposed to fireworks. David, a bright graduate student, showed the boys how, by holding them just so, he could let firecrackers explode in his hand without blowing his fingers off. It was no wonder that every few weeks China Daily carried a story about someone being killed by fireworks. One was an account of how a bride and groom, and most of their retinue had perished when the van full of fireworks they were transporting to the wedding exploded from a carelessly discarded cigarette.

After the fireworks were expended—with only minor loss of hearing and scorched fingers on the most intrepid young men—we went back inside to welcome the new year by eating indecent quantities of jiao zi. We were told that if they were the first thing consumed by every member of the family (and guests) in the new year, it assured good luck for the family.

One day Mr. Zhao asked if we would like to go with him to visit his brother, a retired farmer in a village about five kilometers away. We said sure, that would be great. So he, Laurie, Cooper, Jesse, and I piled onto bicycles and set off across a rutted, snow-packed, dirt road through the middle of barren, wind-swept fields. On the way there, Laurie reminded me how many times, from the comfort of a bus or train, we'd looked out the window and seen people riding their bicycles over snow-packed dirt roads in the middle of nowhere, and said to each other, "I wonder where in the world they're going?"

The name of the village was "Red Star," one of thousands in China that proudly bore the name. Mr. Zhao's brother lived in a three-room, mud house, with a thatched roof and dirt floors. The first of the ten by ten foot rooms was the kitchen, with a fire of corn stalks burning in the concrete stove. In addition to the stove, it was furnished with a set of open, wooden shelves with a few utensils on them, and a small wooden table. The second room was almost filled by a large, concrete sleeping platform, called a "kang" (cong). The only other furniture was a small, unpainted, wooden table and two wooden chairs. We didn't go into the third room, but got the impression it was a living room.

Mr. Zhao's brother wasn't home. He was working in a mine that the village operated about 100 kilometers away. Mr. Zhao said that because there was a limited amount of suitable farm land around the village, the older farmers had to retire and let the younger men take over their land. For many of them, who still had children living at home, their retirement pay wasn't adequate, so they had to work. He said his brother had to work during Spring Festival because he had been fined by the government for having too many children. The family had a hard time surviving on his regular salary, so he was earning extra money during the holiday.

Mr. Zhao's sister-in-law invited us in and ushered us into her bedroom, where she moved bedclothes aside to make room for us on their kang. After a few days in that part of the country, we no longer thought it strange to be entertained in our hostess' bedroom, seated on her bed. It was proper etiquette—we were guests, and that was the warmest place in the house. What we had found was that Mr. Zhao's heated wall was the exception—in most homes the flue, instead of going through the wall, went through the sleeping platform.

Constructed of mud or concrete, some kangs had wooden tops, others did not. In either case, the family spread their quilts on it, and they all slept there. Mr. Zhao said he used to have one in his house, but he tore it out and replaced it with beds. He said he hated kangs, because they were always too hot when he first went to bed. They got too cold in the middle of the night, and then when somebody got up and stoked the fire to start cooking breakfast, they got too hot again.

His preferences aside, it was proper to entertain in bed, so there we sat, talking with his brother's wife, eating sunflower seeds (throwing the shells, as was traditional, on the floor), and drinking tea. It was considered impolite not to insist that guests have a snack, even if all they had was sunflower seeds and tea. As we talked, Mr. Zhao's niece gathered the neighborhood children, none of whom had ever seen Westerners. They filed respectfully through the room, staring quietly but intently. One beautiful girl Mr. Zhao said was a teenager, but she didn't look to be more than nine or ten. She really liked Cooper and Jesse, and wanted to know if they could go next door to her house for a while. We said okay, so they went with her.

A few minutes later, Cooper and Jesse came running back and said, "Dad, Mom, come on, you've got to see this, come look, come look." We went to the house next door, and there in the kitchen was a huge sow with about ten or twelve nursing piglets. The girl's mother was cooking dinner on the stove a few feet away. The boys, of course, thought it was great, and wanted to know if we could get one when we got home.

After the five days of Spring Festival, Mr. Zhao announced that we were going to Heihe (Hay' huh), a city on the Amur River, which forms the border with the Soviet Union in the far northeast of China. We said great, when do we leave. He said the jeep's out front. So, the driver, Laurie, Cooper, Jesse, David, Mr. Zhao, a friend of Mr. Zhao, and I all squeezed into a jeep for the 5-hour ride to Heihe. Incidentally, stories about Chinese people being small are over generalizations based on the people from southern China. It is seldom true of people from the North. The generalization, however, aptly applies to their jeeps.

There was one way to get from Nenjiang to Heihe, and that was a dirt road, which in the winter became one of the roughest I had ever had the misfortune to travel on. To say that traffic was thin would be an understatement—essentially, we were the traffic. We asked Mr. Zhao if it was always so sparse, and he said that it was especially so because of the holiday. He said we were lucky to have gotten a car—that he had used his guan xi, and we would still have to give our driver the equivalent of about $20 and a couple of packs of cigarettes.

Heihe, not surprisingly, exhibited a lot of Russian influence. People kept trying to speak Russian to us, and were surprised to find that we

The seven passengers and driver blocking out the jeep in which they had just spent the past five hours.

were Americans. In fact, they weren't only surprised, they were pleased. Their attitude toward Americans was much more positive than toward the Soviets.

Mr. Zhao's friend had come along to visit relatives, so he stayed with them. The rest of us got rooms at the Heihe Guest House. The manager showed Laurie and me two rooms and asked which we preferred. We were standing in the second of the two, when suddenly, before we had a chance to consider the question, he began talking urgently to the hostess, who quickly escorted us back to the first. He told us they had realized the second was not suitable because it had a black and white television. This despite the fact that the one they put us in had a hole we could have dropped a bowling ball through in one corner of the bathroom floor.

We generally didn't pay much attention to television, but in Heihe they had one Soviet station, and we were fascinated by the difference between Soviet and Chinese television. Chinese television consisted primarily of historical dramas, soap operas, variety shows, children's programs, educational shows such as English classes, and a few cartoons. On the Soviet channel the night we were there, they had a body building show, an international beauty contest, and a couple of very interesting movies. The next morning they had movies, and a very upbeat aerobics show, with attractive, shapely, young men and women dressed in fashionable exercise outfits. We weren't surprised when they told us people in Heihe seldom watched the Chinese channels.

Our second day in Heihe, we took a 30-kilometer side trip, southeast along the river, to a town that was 70 percent Man nationality—one of the 52 recognized minority groups in China. We drove into the little village, and the driver pulled the jeep to the side of the road. The men got out, looked around, and said, "That looks like a good house over there." They walked up to the house, and without knocking, pushed the door open, stuck their heads in, and said, "We're thirsty and tired and we'd like to rest for a while." The head of the household said, "Please come in."

Laurie and I pushed our mouths closed with our hands, held them until we were sure they'd stay, and at the urging of everyone, entered the house. I kept thinking to myself what would have happened if, in a town in the States, we had walked up to somebody's house, opened the door, and said, "We're thirsty and tired and we'd like to rest for a while"? Traditionally, however, the Man were obligated to serve visitors, no matter how unexpected.

We all went in and sat down, and they served us candy and cookies and tea. We stayed and talked for about three hours. The head of the household had finished high school; then gone away for two years of "normal school," to learn how to be a teacher. With that background, he taught all of the classes in the village school. We had no doubt he could do it—he was a very knowledgeable, eloquent man. He gave us a fascinating history of the Man nationality, including an explanation of how the primary colors in their costumes indicated how directly they were descended from the emperor's line.

We returned to Mr. Zhao's home the next day, where we stayed another day. We then took the train to Jagdaqi (Jog ah dotch' ey), one of three cities we visited in Inner Mongolia where there were major units of the Ministry of Forestry.

We arrived about 8:00 p.m. One of the foresters met us at the station with a jeep, and drove us to the compound, which was about five kilometers out of town. They had a delicious late dinner ready for us, and had rooms for us in their guest house. Again, the facilities were very basic: we slept in a 10 by 15 foot room furnished only with four iron cots, used the community toilet, and ate in the dining hall with the foresters. They were very embarrassed, insisting that their facilities were terrible, and apologizing profusely. We assured them they were wonderful.

Part of the tradition in China, and especially in the North, was to be very apologetic for serving so poorly—no matter how good the service was. Guests, in turn, were expected to insist that they had never been better served—no matter how poor the service was. Given the effort put forth to take care of us, we seldom had to do anything but be honest. The Chinese in inner Mongolia served us gorgeous banquets and apologized for having nothing to feed us. It seemed almost laughable to us, but it was just part of a pleasing tradition of modesty.

The next morning, one of the foresters took us on a tour of the city. As we were driving around, we noticed a building that looked very Western, and very out of place, so we asked what it was. Mr. Zhao explained that the unit at Jagdaqi had an ongoing program with Canadian fire fighters, in which the Canadians came over and taught them how to fight fires. When they saw the facilities for the first time, the Canadians refused to live there, so the Canadian and Chinese governments together paid to send a pre-fabricated house from Canada. The Canadians didn't trust the Chinese to construct it properly, so they sent their own carpenters, as well, to build a it in the parking lot of the Jagdaqi Guest House.

We didn't go in, but Mr. Zhao said it was a completely Western house, including thick, wall-to-wall carpeting and imported Canadian furnishings. Laurie asked what the Canadians did with the house when their firefighters weren't there. He said it sat empty; they had a caretaker for it. I felt secure in the knowledge that the ugly American syndrome included all Americans; not just those from the United States.

They were very good to us in Jagdaqi—we had a wonderful time, and met some interesting people. I spent a couple of hours, for example, talking with a man who had the rather misleading title of "Political Instructor." In fact, he was the most powerful person in the compound.

There was a general misconception in the States that the Communist Party governed China. In fact there were various levels of government offices (supposedly independent of the Party) just as there were in the States. At each level of government, however, there was a Party member who held the real power. For example, Party Secretaries were equivalent to mayors. Although the mayors supposedly governed their municipalities, in reality, they only carried out the Party Secretaries' wishes. In the military, although there were base commanders, it was the Political Instructors who held the real power on each base.

The Political Instructor I talked with was a general, and he was surprisingly forthcoming about his job. He told me he was responsible for "thought control." I asked how he did that. He said he had classes two afternoons a week and passed out tracts that the men were required to read—that sort of thing. I said, "You spend two afternoons a week in political indoctrination?" He said not always, sometimes he was busy and didn't have time, so he had the men clean up the compound instead.

———

Our next stop was Yakeshi (Yock' uh shuh). It was still on the Chinese government's closed list, so officially we weren't allowed to go there, but official lists didn't mean much in the face of guan xi. One of Mr. Zhao's friends, a high-level member of the local Communist Party, had used his guan xi to set up the visit for us. We arrived at Yakeshi about 4:30 p.m., and checked into the local guest house. That evening Mr. Zhao's friend gave us the most lavish banquet we had in China.

Mr. Zhao told us later that it cost the equivalent of about $55 a person. That was pretty pricey even by Western standards—in China, it was extravagant. Many of the dishes were fresh seafood. There weren't many seas around Inner Mongolia, so fresh seafood didn't come cheap. The wine we had seen for sale for $90 a bottle. During the dinner, David leaned over and whispered, "In China, this is what we call 'eating Communist.'"

The next morning after breakfast, we were trying to decide where we ought to go first, when Mr. Zhao got a phone call. He said he and David had to leave for a few minutes, but would be right back. About half an hour later, he came back and sheepishly informed us that we had to be out of town by noon. It seemed his friend had made a critical omission from the guest list for the banquet the night before. He had forgotten to invite the head of the the district Foreign Affairs Office—the person responsible for all foreigners in the area.

The man had been proud to have Westerners stop in his district, and had come to the guest house the night before to meet us. When they told him we were at a banquet, it was a great loss of face for him (a terrible fate for a Chinese official), and he was furious. In revenge, he used his authority to kick us out of town. He said if we weren't gone by noon, that Mr. Zhao and David would go to jail, and that we would have to pay a large fine. There was a train to Hailar (Hi' lar) at 11:30 a.m. The only tickets we could get for the 6-hour trip were for standing room in the hard seat section.

Mr. Zhao's friend came to the station to see us off—an act that

155

David told us required much courage, as he had been shamed by his inability to counteract the director's demands. He tried to get us soft seat tickets to Hailar, and when he couldn't, he felt even worse. At least he was able to get permission for us to wait in the soft-seat waiting area. It was a very nice room, with carpet, upholstered furniture, and a color television, instead of the wooden benches in the noisy, dirty, concrete barn that served as the main station. We all told him how great that was, but it didn't seem to do much good. We figured we'd seen the beginning of a long-running animosity.

Riding hard seat on a Chinese train is something everyone should get to experience at least once in life—it made us appreciate all the little things we tended to take for granted. Actually, the trip to Hailar wasn't as bad as we expected. Laurie was holding Jesse, so a man got up immediately and gave her his seat, under the unwritten mother-holding-baby law. A woman scrunched her husband and daughter over to make room for Cooper, under the unwritten special-consideration-for-children law. A young man even tried to give me his seat under the unwritten (and only adhered to rurally) be-nice-to-foreigners law, but I wouldn't take it. After all, there wasn't that much difference between liberalism and socialism. Mr. Zhao, David, and I stood about half of the way; then we were able to get seats.

While we were in China, even government officials had begun to admit publicly that crime had been increasing during the past few years. I carried our passports and most of our cash in a money belt—it was a cash economy, so travelers checks and checking accounts were not common. The little money I needed for daily expenses, I folded and kept in a front pants pocket, with my handkerchief tucked in on top of it—not an easy target for pickpockets. I usually kept my white, green, and red cards in my hip pocket. In crowded situations, however, I'd put them in my front pocket as well, making them harder for someone else to get at.

In the excitement of being run out of town that morning, however, I had forgotten to switch pockets with them. As I stood in that crowded car, in a crush of humanity, reveling at experiencing "the real China" I felt a hand in the pocket with my ID cards. I reached back and slapped it as hard as the limited space would allow, and turned to face a young man. He was nursing his hand, talking to me in Chinese, and trying to make it look as though he had been jolted against me by the movement of the train. But I knew, and he knew that I knew, he had been trying to pick my pocket. I immediately moved my cards to a front pocket, and

man really had liked us, and had appreciated the gifts. Normally, during the tourist season, he would have charged us the equivalent of about $135. That information put a whole new light on things. It hadn't been so expensive, as sheep bones and kidneys go, and it really had been a memorable afternoon.

We had to change trains in Qiqihar on our way back to Shenyang, so Mr. Zhao contacted a friend who managed a guesthouse there. She agreed to arrange for our train tickets from Qiqihar to Shenyang, and said we could stay there on our way through. Mr. Zhao went directly back to his home from Hailar, and David, who needed to pick up some books in Qiqihar, went there with us, before returning to his father's home for the rest of his term break.

When we got to Qiqihar, we took a taxi to the guest house. As soon as we had checked in, we asked about our tickets. The woman said that because she hadn't had our cards, they wouldn't sell her the tickets. She introduced us to the driver for the guest house, who said to give him my passport, green card, red card, and white card, and he would take care of it for us. I didn't want to seem ungrateful, but that would have left me nameless in China, a situation with which I really wasn't very comfortable.

David, who knew my opinion of drivers, assured me it would be okay, so I gritted my teeth and handed them over. The driver returned later that day with my cards and two hard sleeper tickets—both for top bunks. He said that was all he could get. The train didn't run the next day, so our choice was to sleep two in a bunk or wait around in Qiqihar two more days before we went home. Laurie decided we should take them. She said that it wouldn't be a comfortable trip, but at least when we got off at the other end, we'd be home. The driver said we should meet him in the lobby at 10:30 p.m., and he would take us to the station.

When he arrived that night, he had four Chinese men with him. He said we should give them our tickets; he had a letter for us that would get us on and get us bottom bunks. I thought that sounded a bit fishy, so I said why didn't we make sure we had those nice bottom bunks first; then we'd give those nice gentlemen our tickets? David must have done a good job of translating—the innuendo wasn't lost on the driver. He laughed and said okay, he'd come with us into the station and take care of it there.

I don't know where a driver for the forestry ministry guest house got so much guan xi, but we saw it at work that night. When we got to the station, he didn't even slow down at the main entrance, but pulled right up to the door of the soft sleeper lounge. He took us in and said something to the woman in charge of the lounge. She unlocked the door, and without even asking to see our tickets (the only time that happened in our year in China), ushered us out onto the platform.

The driver went with us onto the platform, which he shouldn't have been allowed to do. He talked with the head conductor—a difficult thing to do right before a train took off, as he was a busy man just then. The head conductor took our tickets and the letter. The driver told us we were all set; to follow the head conductor, he'd take care of us. We thanked him and offered him some money, which he refused. He said it had been a pleasure to help us, smiled, waved, and trotted off. My attitude toward drivers was more generous after that night.

The head conductor put us on a special car, which was reserved for train employees. It was only about half full. We had a compartment to ourselves, with six bunks for Laurie, Cooper, Jesse and me. The four Chinese men that got on with us had another compartment with six bunks to themselves. On top of all our other good fortune, none of the four men smoked. The chances of finding a group of four Chinese men none of whom smoked were minuscule—an estimated 80 percent of the men in the country did. We enjoyed a pleasant trip back to Shenyang.

We had sent a telegram from Qiqihar to let the people in our Foreign Affairs Office know when we would get back. There was no way we thought it would actually get to them on time, given the usual performance of telegrams in China. They were cheap, though, so we figured, "Why not?" When we arrived in Shenyang, we carried our bags out to the parking lot, and I started looking for a taxi—and there was the university van. The driver helped us load our bags into the van (something he didn't usually do—he must have missed us) and drove us to our apartment. It had been a wonderful 25 days, but it had consisted of even less luxurious living than we had been used to in China. We were exhausted, and it was good to be home.

We encountered many problems while traveling in China: hassles with petty bureaucrats, difficulty getting train tickets, rudimentary lodging conditions, and arguments with drivers and ticket sellers who wanted to charge us more than they should have. Despite those inconveniences, the six weeks we spent traveling (especially the three weeks in the North, where we were less tourists and more people) were the best of our year. For every situation that made us question why we had bothered to leave home, there were at least two of consummate value. For every person who caused us problems, we met two or three who gave us delight.

Chapter Eight
March and April

I came back to the university to step into the middle of a battle between the Chinese Department and the Foreign Languages Department about who was going to have me as foreign expert spring term. The woman who had been teaching English and American literature in the Foreign Languages Department had notified them that she was not coming back second term. Naturally, that left them with a real void in their literature classes.

I was scheduled to teach Western literature in the Chinese Department, so the people in foreign languages decided the solution to their problem was to transfer me to their department. The chairman of the Chinese Department wanted to help, but he didn't want to lose the status of having a foreign scholar in his department.

After several meetings, they decided that I would officially remain a foreign expert in the Chinese Department, and keep my office there. I would teach one 2-credit course on theories of Western literature in the Chinese Department. In addition, I would teach one 2-credit graduate seminar on the American novel, and one 4-credit course on readings in Western literature in the Foreign Languages Department. In return for this doubling of my teaching load, they increased my salary from the equivalent of about $160 to about $215 a month.

Laurie had some new and some returning students in her English conversation classes spring term. Cooper started back to kindergarten. The way they treated the children in kindergarten seemed to us a strange combination of regimentation and lack of restraint. Cooper was supposed to be there at 8:00 a.m., but we got him there anywhere from 10 minutes before, to a quarter after, and it didn't seem to make any difference. The lessons had never started. The children would always be running around, the teacher either laughing and playing with them, or talking with another teacher while keeping an eye on them. Laurie's background was in child development, so she requested, and was granted, permission to observe Cooper's class. She said the lessons were very short, and were surrounded by a lot of what seemed to be free play.

On the other hand, the children were required to do things a specific way. For example, Cooper came home crying one day. Laurie asked him what was the matter, and he said he had gotten a bad grade on a picture he had drawn. She asked to see the picture. It seemed pretty good: the standard pond-with-fish-jumping-flowers-and-grass-around-it-sun-shining-airplane-strafing-everything landscape one might expect from a six-year-old boy. Laurie asked what the teacher hadn't liked about it, and he said there had been no airplane in her's.

We didn't really understand what that meant until we learned how much different the educational process was in the United States and China. The over-riding difference was that creativity was encouraged in the States, whereas mastery of form was valued in China. The teacher would draw a picture on the board, and the children were expected to copy that picture as closely as possible. The highest grades were awarded those most like the original. What we saw as Cooper's creativity, they saw as lack of discipline in mastering the assignment.

That striving for consistency was so prevalent that Cooper was not allowed to use a pencil tablet we had brought from the States because it was different than those the other children were using. His teacher showed us examples of the "proper" materials we should get him, and even told us which store we should buy them in. One of the requirements was an art book, which had the pictures already lightly drawn in them. The children then traced over the lines to complete their art work.

The children were assigned seats and cubby holes in which they kept their belongings. They washed their hands before they ate, and each child had to have a hand towel of a specific size. We sent a canteen full of water with Cooper each morning, but that wasn't acceptable. We had to buy him a metal cup with a lid that was the same as everybody else's. If he wanted a canteen of water as well, he had to keep it out of sight in his book bag.

The result of that kind of education was that the students in Cooper's class all knew their addition tables better than he did, but they didn't understand math as well—they had just memorized the tables well. They could all draw better than Cooper in a particular, stylized way, but they didn't exhibit as much creativity. They could all sing a few songs better than Cooper, but they only knew those few songs.

One of Laurie's students asked if Cooper had taken music lessons when he was younger. That seemed a strange question to us—he was only six years old. We had just started considering that he might want to take music lessons when we returned to the States. The idea that we hadn't considered lessons for him by the time he was six seemed odd to Laurie's student. By that age, Chinese children had been practicing something for years. As soon as they could pick up a violin, or sit up straight enough to reach a piano, they started music lessons.

All but the poorest parents had their sons and daughters take some sort of lessons—whether dance, music, or art—and they were very proud of what their children accomplished. Laurie and I were amazed at how well even the very young children of our Chinese friends could sing and dance (and they had them perform for us if we gave them even a smidgen of an excuse), until we realized they were all performing the same pieces. They had learned them well, but so had all the other children that age in town.

They tried their children out on several things. If they seemed to exhibit a talent for something, they developed it; if they didn't have a talent for it, they dropped it. What the child enjoyed had little to do with it. One of Laurie's students, for example, said her brother was an artist. She said she'd always wanted to be an artist, but she couldn't be, because her father had told her she would never be any good at it, and had made her stop taking lessons. She borrowed several of Jesse's books, and said she hoped someday to write children's books that her brother would illustrate.

When children seemed exceptionally talented at something, they were taken out of regular schools, and sent by the government to a special school to develop that talent. So, if a child had a particularly good voice, she might be sent to a school to learn Chinese opera. Once there, she might study only Chinese, math, English, and music. From the time she was six years old, then, she knew what her life would be. The choice had been made for her.

Laurie and I saw the results of regimented early schooling in our college students. They had been conditioned to learn in a particular way, and they found it almost impossible to do it any other way. For example, I had a modern American novel class of 18 graduate students. I was really pleased when I went the first day and found they had scheduled the class in a small conference room where we could sit around a table, rather than in one of the lecture halls. Such an arrangement was conducive to the discussion appropriate in a graduate class. Discussion did not come easily, however, and the third class meeting the class leaders came to me and said they would like to move to a different classroom.

I said okay, where did they want to move to. They said there was a small classroom in the graduate student dorm that would be very good. The next time we met, I entered that room to find rows of desks and chairs facing a raised podium in front of a large blackboard. The lectern was four feet wide, two feet deep, and chest high. I think they were just uncomfortable sitting around a table with their professor. They needed to be lined up, facing front, their professor on a platform, separated from them by an imposing lectern.

I had met some of the graduate students who would be in this American novel class. Their dorm was right next to our apartment building, so we had spent hours, while Cooper and Jesse played with their Chinese friends, talking about China, the United States, and the world at large. They were very bright, energetic young people, and I looked forward to lively discussions about the novels we were to read—questions of style, discourse about greater meaning, and disagreement on fundamental principles. It just did not happen.

Even when they asked questions—which wasn't often—they expected direct, no-nonsense answers. I tried saying well, that was a good question, what did everybody think? Nobody would respond. They just couldn't transpose their lively conversation to a classroom setting with a focused topic. There I (the professor) wasn't supposed to ask them what they (the students) thought. I was supposed to tell them what to think.

The fact was that they were taught much differently than we were in the States, and that fact had ramifications that permeated every aspect of their lives. Their art, literature, and theatre—in fact their entire culture—reflected the emphasis on likeness and discipline imbued in them throughout their educational experience. Even their personal mannerisms were affected.

When we saw old people walking, it was invariably with their hands clasped behind their backs, staring at a spot ten feet in front of them. We wondered why, until we saw Cooper's kindergarten class, under the watchful eye of their teacher, learning to walk just that way.

Although we were about as far north in Shenyang as we would have been in northern Minnesota, our proximity to mild ocean currents brought spring earlier there than we were used to back home. With spring came the change of street vendors. One morning in March, the hot sweet potato vendors were gone, and the yogurt vendors were back. The old man who had done such a fine job of keeping our bicycles repaired was working again, as well.

It was a good thing he was back, because one day, on my way to get Cooper at kindergarten, the front wheel of my bike locked. Jesse was on his bike seat in front of me, and both of us went over the handle bars. To keep him from landing on his head, I grabbed him with my right arm. Although that fatherly gesture kept him from getting hurt, it cost me dearly.

166

I landed squarely on my left elbow, and a searing pain shot all the way to my eyeballs. Jesse was unhurt, but started token-crying from surprise. The Chinese passersby ignored me, but immediately surrounded Jesse, showering him with sympathy. My elbow was badly scraped, but I was in good shape compared to my bike.

The force of the sudden stop had not only twisted the front wheel, but had also bent both the front fork and the frame so much that the back edge of the front wheel overlapped the frame by four inches. I figured that bike was a goner—there was no way anybody could fix it, short of replacing the wheel, fork, and frame, and that was most of the bike. I decided I'd better get a professional opinion, however, so I carried it four blocks to where the old man had his repair cart set up.

He was an engineering genius. He took the fork off, put it in his vice, and worked on it for about an hour. He kept looking at it, sighting down it every which way, laying it on the level surface on top of his cart, looking at it again, turning it over, and pounding on it some more. Finally, he was satisfied that it was straight. I thought okay, that was the fork, but what could he do about the frame?

What he did was take a 3-foot tempered-steel rod and a 4-foot length of quarter-inch steel cable to a nearby tree. He laid the rod vertically against the side of the tree and secured the top of it by wrapping the cable tightly around it and the tree. Then he pulled the bottom end of the rod away from the tree enough that his assistant could slip it through the sleeve at the front of the bike frame through which the top of the front fork normally runs. They slid the bike, upside down, to the top of the rod, just under where the cable held it firmly against the tree. The bike, then (minus handlebars, front fork, and front wheel), stuck out—back wheel up, seat down—horizontally from the tree, held there by the rod running through the sleeve on the front of the frame.

The old man steadied the bottom of the rod against the tree, while his assistant pulled down on the back of the bike. As I watched, I tried to remember what I had learned in high school physics. They had made the bike into a lever, with the fulcrum at the point where it intersected the tree. The bike, minus front wheel, must have been about five feet long. According to my calculations, the force exerted on the bent part of the frame where it was secured to the tree must have been—a lot.

The assistant pulled down until the old guy shouted the Chinese word for "that's good, that's enough." Then they unwrapped the cable, pulled the bike off the rod, and turned it over. The only way I could tell it wasn't brand new was that the paint had flaked a little where it had been bent and then pushed back. He reinserted the fork, put the handlebars back on, hooked the brakes up again, and reinstalled the (still bent) front wheel. He turned the bike over and rested it on the handlebars and seat. Then began the painstaking process of straightening the front wheel.

With a tiny, homemade spoke wrench, he went around and around the wheel, loosening some spokes and tightening others. Ever so slowly, I began to notice a change. Some time after the wheel began to look straight again to me, he began to check it periodically by holding onto the fork and sticking his thumb out until it just brushed the rim. Then he would spin the tire and feel where it rubbed harder on his thumb. There followed more loosening of some, and tightening of other, spokes; then a repeat of the thumb test. When he was finally satisfied that the wheel was running true, he turned the bike over and cleaned the whole thing with a damp rag.

When he got to the spot where the paint had flaked slightly from the strain of straightening the frame, he paused, clucked his tongue, looked up, and said something that sounded apologetic, as though any imperfection must be his fault. I assured him that I was more than pleased with his work, minor imperfections notwithstanding. He charged me the equivalent of $3 for two and a half hours of mechanical virtuosity. The bike rode better than it ever had.

———————————

Spring was the most beautiful time of year in northern China. Its progression was accompanied by an increase in one of the Chinese' favorite leisure activities—strolling. Evenings at the university were once again filled with the murmur of couples, families, and small groups of people meandering around campus, chatting. As our family strolled with the others around campus, we were struck by how green everything was, where only a couple of weeks before it had been gray with a film of coal dust. Apple and peach blossoms were so thick they looked like the snow loads we had expected, but never saw on trees during the winter. They made the air tangible with moist aromas. The only thing that detracted from an otherwise idyllic setting was the wind.

To some degree in the fall, but much more so in the spring—accompanying the seasonal climactic change—strong winds blew from the northwest. With the winds came a gritty haze of fine loess soil, carried from the plains of Mongolia. A film of dirt replaced the layer of coal dust on everything. Some days, warm spring rains washed our world, and if the wind didn't blow, it glistened in amiable spring sunlight.

On bad days, though, when the wind was especially strong, we felt as though we were being sandblasted. We could almost feel the skin on our faces tighten, as our pores clogged with silt. Most of the women and children, and a few of the young men, fought back by tying brightly colored chiffon scarves over their heads. There were times, riding my bike, when I caught a glimpse of one of those apparitions overtaking me, and the story of Ichabod Crane pursued by a pumpkin-headed rider imposed itself momentarily on me.

My major, ongoing area of research for years had been how the United States was portrayed in the media of other countries. A year in Shenyang seemed like a perfect opportunity to look at the U.S. in Chinese newspapers. I analyzed China Daily, which was the only major daily in English. Two Chinese friends agreed to examine three of the major Chinese papers.

Many librarians in China had been promoted to their positions directly from peasanthood during the Cultural Revolution. They had been told by those who placed them in their positions that their primary objective was to protect the holdings of the library. I didn't really blame the Chinese for that attitude. They had very little foreign exchange with which to purchase new materials, and they'd had little more than a decade to restock hundreds of thousands of books that were destroyed during the Cultural Revolution. Motivation aside, however, the result made it very difficult to conduct research.

Of course, the best way for a librarian to protect books to keep them in the library—which Chinese librarians did very well. That was a complete surprise to me when I began my research. The first time I went to the library to check out some back issues of China Daily, I approached the woman responsible for them and relayed my request. She said she was sorry, they weren't available. I could see them on the shelves behind her, and I told her so. She turned to look at them; then turned back to me and said no, she was sorry, that wasn't them. I said but, I could see them. She said (without turning to look that time) no, I must be mistaken, that wasn't them.

Such inaccessibility of library materials had become an expectation for Chinese scholars, so many academic departments had established their own reading rooms. The Foreign Languages Department had back copies of China Daily in theirs, and readily gave me permission to use them. Any time I had a couple of hours free, I went there and collected data from a few issues. Shortly after spring term began, I went to the reading room, spoke to the woman responsible for the material, and walked straight to the place the back issues of China Daily were kept. They were gone.

I told the woman (with a note of urgency in my voice) the China Dailies for 1988 were missing. She said (calmly) yes. I asked (with greater urgency) where were they? She said (still calmly) she had sold them. I asked sold them? She said yes, the secretary to the president of the university had needed them for insulation in the ceiling of his home. I said but, she had known that I needed them for my research. She said yes. Clearly the materials in departmental reading rooms were not conserved with the same vigor as those in the library. I accepted defeat in the face of overwhelming cultural odds, mumbled as sincere a "thank you" as I could muster under the circumstances, and left. My restraint was rewarded, and catastrophe averted, when I found the issues I needed in another department.

My Chinese friends were allowed access to the papers they needed at the library as long as they didn't leave the room. One day one of them came to my office with some good news and some bad news. The good news was that he had finished gathering data from his two papers for the first half of 1988. The bad news was that the librarian would not allow him access to the papers for the second half of the year. I asked if there was anything we could do about it. He said if I went with him and presented my official card to the librarian, she might relent.

It was during the next hour that I learned "no" in China (given the right conditions) didn't exactly mean "no." We found the proper librarian—not an easy task, given the fact that there were hundreds, each with immutable power over his or her own minute area of responsibility. I presented her with my "official" card: my business card, in English on one side, and Chinese on the other. She scrutinized it, and my friend informed her that 1) I was a very important "vice president of journalism" from the United States, 2) I was working with the "high-level administration" of her university on a joint research project, and 3) the papers in question were vital to the success of the project. She said "no."

My friend spent the next ten minutes making small talk with the librarian about her children, and the "no" became "maybe." The next ten minutes they spent talking about my children. I knew that despite my lack of fluency, because at one point I was called on to exhibit their pictures—she was appropriately impressed. The "maybe" became "probably." There followed ten more minutes of talk about my friend's children. The "probably" became "yes." The librarian brought the papers out, and the "top-level, joint research project" continued. I came to understand—even to appreciate—that strange, time-consuming process, but my type A personality precluded my ever being any good at it.

All went well for two days. Then my other research assistant came to my office to tell me that he had some good news and some bad news—same story; same librarian; different paper. Astonishingly, ransoming those papers required the same process. She looked at my "official" card as though it were the first time she had seen such a thing. The only difference was that the "no"/"yes" mutation that time didn't take quite as long.

A process that I had taken for granted in doing research in the States was photocopying. I quickly learned to do without it in China. There were very few copiers on campus, and time on those had to be reserved far in advance. What the Chinese often did instead was silk screen. I saw a worker one day who was in the process of making 150 copies of a 25-page document—screening it one page at a time. He put in a blank sheet of paper, closed the frame, ran the roller back and forth to coat it with ink, rolled it on the screen to squeeze ink through onto the paper, opened the frame, and took out the paper—over, and over, and over.

I ran statistical analyses of my data and composed a list of questions based on the findings. Then I made appointments for the first week in June, 1989, with the editors of the papers studied, for the purpose of asking them those questions. It was not to be.

Chapter Nine
April and May

On April 15, Hu Yaobang (Who Yow bon') died. He was the government official who had been kicked out of office for supporting student demonstrators in December 1986 and January 1987. Although we didn't know it at the time, his death was to have a profound effect on our stay in China.

By mid-April, the weather was beautiful—dry and sunny, with just enough rain to keep everything clean and green. The winds had abated, and it was as though the sand had scoured the air. It was cleaner than it had been all year. The campus looked the best it had, as well. Mid-April must have been spring cleaning time—staff, students, and workers were all cleaning. The students threw the accumulated trash from the winter out the newly-washed windows of their dorms; then came out and raked it into piles and burned it. The front-end loader came and picked up tons of ashes that had accumulated outside the heating plant next door to our living quarters. When that was done, they hauled away the trash, bricks, and dirt left over from construction the previous fall and winter. Then workers came around to shovel, rake, and sweep.

I was out riding around on my bike with Jesse one day, when we saw a guy in a front-end loader working on campus. Jesse loved front-end loaders, backhoes, and cranes, so we stopped to watch. When the driver saw Jesse sitting there watching him, he stopped and asked if he wanted to go for a ride in the front-end loader. Does a bear like honey? Of course Jesse wanted to go for a ride in the front-end loader. I figured as long as I was right there watching, it wouldn't hurt to have him sit on the driver's lap, and it would certainly be a thrill for him. Little did I know.

First Jesse found the horn button. The driver thought that was pretty funny. Then Jesse pulled the lights on, and the driver got a chuckle out of that, too. Then he showed Jesse how to start the thing, and moved his seat way back so Jesse could stand up in front of the steering wheel. Then the guy just leaned back in his seat and let a two-year-old drive his front-end loader. As soon as Jesse realized he was really controlling it, he started turning the steering wheel back and forth like crazy. He had that huge piece of construction equipment weaving back and forth down the street, with people, cars, and bicycles scattering to get out of his way.

The driver was laughing—that was the best time he'd had for ages. Of course Jesse was having the time of his life. It was just me who was having a conniption about the whole thing. But all I could do was ride alongside them on my bicycle, hoping he wouldn't run into anything. After about a block (which seemed like five miles to me) the guy put it in reverse and Jesse backed down the street the way they had come, both of them laughing and carrying on. It took a few years off my life, but they came back unscathed, and we didn't have to scrape anybody off those huge tires.

On April 17, students in Beijing started demonstrating, calling for an end to government corruption.

Spring in China, as in many other countries, is a time for cleaning, and the university went at it with a vengeance. The general clean-up was enhanced by the fact that China was experiencing a shortage of scrap metal, so some abandoned structures that had stood around for years as eyesores were dismantled. One of them was across the street behind our apartment, so we had ample opportunity to watch the process. When they tore the building down and carried the bricks away, we were a bit curious about why then, when they had obviously been available for years. That got them down to the basement, however, and it was then we realized it wasn't the bricks they were after at all.

We watched (off and on) for three days, while six men with sledge hammers worked ten hours a day smashing the concrete support posts and foundation into small enough pieces that they could extract the reinforcing rods. We couldn't believe they were spending all that time just for that little bit of steel. Cooper's Chinese had gotten really good, so we took him over and had him ask them what they were doing. Once they got over their glee that Cooper could talk to them in Chinese, they told him they were smashing the concrete so they could get the reinforcing steel inside it.

Because of a shortage of wood, most of the telephone poles in China were cast from concrete. We saw them replace several on campus, and when they did, they just left the old ones where they fell. One day I was walking home for lunch, and saw a couple of workmen smashing some of those concrete posts. Often, instead of hauling trash away, they just dug a hole and buried it, so I thought maybe that was what they were doing. On the way back from lunch, however, I saw them loading the reinforcing rod from the poles onto a cart, and hauling it away. Nobody had told them what to do with the concrete chunks, so they left them where they lay.

April 22, was Hu Yaobang's funeral. Students throughout China erected memorial wreaths, many with banners attached bearing political slogans. Many of the trees on campus had white crepe flowers—a sign of mourning— tied to their branches. In an attempt to avoid trouble, the administration began locking students into their dorms after 10:00 p.m. Some of them threw bottles and burning papers from their windows.

Cooper showing off his Chinese to a group of young postal workers. They were thrilled.

Before coming to China, we had heard a lot about the "military presence" there. People who had visited China said that everywhere they went, they saw multitudes of soldiers. They were right—we saw people in military uniforms all over. Closer inspection, however, revealed that many of them were police, forest rangers, and postal workers. Many more government workers than we were used to wore military uniforms, so it looked like a lot more "army" people than there really were.

When their uniforms wore out, the government supplied new ones, so people tended to wear them all the time. At tourist sites, we often saw people in uniform who were clearly visiting from some other part of the country. Also, for at least part of their freshman year, college students wore uniforms as part of a compulsory service program. It would have been hard, however, to imagine a less-threatening army than those 18-year-old boys and girls, running around in their uniforms, holding hands, laughing, and playing volleyball.

When we first arrived at Liaoning University, we were surprised to find that, as with all colleges in China, there was an army barracks right on campus. The soldiers were not part of an ROTC program, but a regular army unit of about 50 men. We were even more surprised when we found that they were there as a custodial force. They dug ditches, pruned hedges, weeded flowers, planted trees, raked leaves, swept streets, and cut weeds. They certainly didn't look very ominous, straggling down the street, their rakes and shovels at "port arms."

The motto of the People's Liberation Army was, "We serve the people," and we were given every reason to believe they took it seriously. Every encounter we had with the PLA was positive. They were some of the most helpful, generous, friendly people we met in China. We once saw a group of Western college students who had a short time to get on a train, and were having difficulty with their luggage. Several young soldiers hopped off the train, cheerfully picked up the students' luggage and carried it on for them, just to be helpful.

Every time we walked by their barracks on campus, the soldiers called for us to come over and spend some time with them—singing, playing games, or just talking. They never let Jesse and Cooper pass a place where they were working without taking a break to talk with them, carry them on their shoulders, and share some treat with them. Such things made what was to happen in Tiananmen Square even more difficult for us to comprehend.

On April 27, students at Beijing University, with the help of people from outside the campus, broke through a government blockade, and organized an orderly march through the city. They were joined by workers, and media reports estimated participation as high as half a million people. The government began moving more soldiers into Beijing.

One night we were awakened in the middle of the night by a tremendous din, most of which consisted of what sounded like fire sirens. We sprang from our beds to see what was the matter. There were a couple of little private restaurants on the corner about half a block away, and by opening a window and leaning out, we could see that one of them was on fire. Within a few minutes, two fire trucks moaned by in the street below. Of course Jesse and Cooper wanted to get dressed immediately and go down there (actually, they would have skipped the getting dressed part) but Laurie and I wouldn't hear of it. We promised to take them over right after breakfast for a look.

We joined the crowd the following morning, and found that the whole kitchen and part of the dining room had burned. About half the roof was gone. As we stood there, a group of men began to work on it. In four days, they had it rebuilt and back in operation. Had it been a government enterprise, it would have taken four months, but as a private concern, they didn't want to be out of business any longer than necessary.

A professor from Denver came to Liaoning University for a couple of weeks in April, and the first time he went to the market, he saw a stand where they were selling turtles. He said one of them wanted to get away so badly, that he decided he had to help . So, he bought it and brought it back to his apartment with him. After two days, he realized the folly of his ways, and was desperate for some way to get rid of it. Then he hit upon the perfect solution. He brought it (and a couple of bottles of beer to soften me up) over to our apartment to "show it to the boys."

They liked it so much (of course) that he felt he had to offer it to them (of course). They wanted it (of course), and said, "Oh Daddy, please, please, please." So I said, "Okay" (of course—that's a Daddy's job). So we got a turtle. He was only about four inches long (luckily), and lived in the bathtub—except when Laurie or I took baths; then we put him in a bowl and set him on the washing machine. The boys shared their baths with him, but only after Laurie determined conclusively that it was not a snapping turtle.

He seemed happy enough. Who knew how to tell if a turtle was happy? He ate a little lettuce every once in a while, and every morning after I finished my bath, I rinsed the tub and left some clean water in it for him. The tub didn't sit quite level, so there was always a puddle at one end for him to drink from or swim in. The faucet didn't shut off completely, so he'd waddle over and let it dribble on him when he felt like it. All in all, he had it better than ever before. He'd had a pretty tough life—he was missing his left rear leg, and had a hole part way through his shell where some shell borer had worked on him. He lucked out, because something stopped it. He had a deep indentation, but it hadn't quite gotten to him.

After we'd had him about a month, for no apparent reason he stopped eating and began to look sickly. We had no idea what to do, so we convinced Jesse and Cooper that he needed his freedom. One sunny morning, we put him in a paper bag and rode our bikes way out into the country, where we found what seemed an ideal habitat for a small turtle and released him. He turned and shot us a grateful look just before waddling out of sight into some tall weeds.

On April 29, China Television began carrying live broadcasts from Beijing of discussions between student and government leaders. From then until martial law was declared, the media grew more and more open, carrying more news, and more uncensored coverage of events than ever before in the country's history.

May first was National Labor Day, and we all had a long week-end. The folks in our Foreign Affairs Office arranged a trip for the foreign students and teachers to Dandong (Don doong'), a city on the Yalu River, which formed the border between North Korea and China. They got us soft seat tickets on an express train, and we happened to get a new car, so the trip down was quite luxurious. The countryside we traveled through was very pretty, including some beautiful, mountainous terrain.

We stayed at the Dandong Guest House, a villa-style hotel that had been created by converting a 4-block area of the city that was once stately, private houses into guest residences. The facility looked just like a residential neighborhood, but the houses were all divided into rooms and apartments for the hotel.

The first day, we visited North Korea. Actually, we didn't set foot in the country, but we did take a cruise up and down the river. The boat, through a long-standing agreement with the Koreans, crossed the river to the North Korean side. Things looked pretty dismal over there— much less developed than the Chinese side. We came within fifteen or twenty feet of a Korean gunboat, however, and that was kind of exciting, although all they did was wave.

The other thing we did that day was visit the Azalea Festival. The whole town was decked out—potted azaleas all over. As with the ice sculptures in Harbin, however, there was an official place where most of

What our guide on the Yalu River assured us was a Korean gunboat coming out to check on us.

the display was concentrated. It was a huge field house, and in it, in addition to a general display of untold varieties of azaleas, were numerous special "theme" displays. Laurie said they reminded her of the garden club displays back at the Beltrami County Fair in Minnesota.

The boys' favorite memory of Dandong was the ice cream. In Shenyang, and throughout the rest of our travels, the ice cream we had encountered left us cold. It was generally a mixture of milk and ice, frozen, popcicle style, onto bamboo sticks, and tasted a lot like Tutti-Frutties. Dandong ice cream was more like the soft twist cones at Dairy Queen—a bit more like ice milk, and pretty tasty. It was a hot day, too, so that helped.

The next day, they rousted the group out early, and drove us in a bus, 45 kilometers, to climb a ridiculously unnavigable path carved into the side of Phoenix Mountain. Laurie and I decided that our parental responsibility had to kick into overdrive somewhere, and that was it. We didn't take Cooper and Jesse up. Everyone that went said we had chosen wisely—they were petrified, because they could have fallen to their death at any time. One woman got so terrified that she froze, and could go neither forward nor back. A man got in front of her, another behind, and one pushing the other pulling, forced her to safer ground.

Right next to Phoenix Mountain was Xian Mountain, which had a narrow dirt road to a television tower on top. Laurie, the boys, and I hiked about four kilometers up its twisted, hairpin curves, back and forth through dense woods. It was calm and beautiful. We even glimpsed occasional animals and birds. The path up Phoenix Mountain

Cooper and Jesse hard at work backstage at the Azalea Festival.

was jammed. In contrast, we saw only a handful of people all morning. Near the top of Xian Mountain was an open gate, with a big sign in huge, red Chinese characters. It probably said something like, "Danger; No Trespassing; Keep Out; You'll Be Shot On Sight," but I couldn't read Chinese, and the gate was open, so Cooper and I went on through.

Jesse was pretty tired, so Laurie stopped to let him rest. Cooper and I, however, were determined to go all the way to the TV tower. About half a kilometer further, we rounded the last corner, and there near the base of the tower was a People's Liberation Army barracks. The soldier who was leaning against a retaining wall, gazing at the magnificent view, looked a bit surprised to see us.

A set of steps led around their barracks to the top of the mountain, and I asked him in pantomime if it was okay for us to go up there. He motioned for us to follow him, and started up the steps. He took us all the way to the base of the antenna, and the view was breathtaking. We were looking down on the people on top of Phoenix Mountain. The soldier told us Xian Mountain was the highest spot in Liaoning Province, but people weren't allowed up there because of the military radar station he and his men were responsible for guarding.

We shouted to Laurie and Jesse, who were waiting on the road far below, then started back down. When we reached his barracks, the corporal invited us in for some tea, and as he'd been so nice to us, I didn't see how I could refuse—besides, I wanted to see the inside of a PLA barracks.

"Barren" was the adjective that sprung immediately to mind—"filthy" followed immediately. It was an essentially deserted brick building. Its two large, and two small, rooms all had bare concrete floors. The two large rooms were squad bays, their walls devoid of any decoration. One was empty; the other contained about ten metal cots. The only other furniture was three wooden chairs. On one sat a color television, which all the soldiers were gathered around. At the foot of each bunk was a duffel bag, in which I assumed were all the soldiers' belongings.

One of the small rooms was the most filthy indoor bathroom I saw in China; the other was a kitchen of sorts, with a cold water tap, a gas fire ring, and a small, scarred, wooden table. I assumed their meals were brought up to them, because the kitchen looked unused for anything but boiling tea water. Cooper and I sat on the cot hurriedly vacated for us, and accepted the tea they brought us. We watched television with them, and Cooper answered their myriad questions for about ten minutes. Then we explained that Laurie and Jesse were waiting for us below and we had to leave. Most of them walked with us to the bend, where they all stood and shouted goodbyes, waving until we were out of sight.

By the time we climbed back down the mountain, it was almost 2:00 p.m., and we were exhausted, thirsty, and hungry. The foreign affairs people had brought box lunches and canned sodas for us, so we got ours, found a fairly isolated picnic table out of the sun, and sat down to eat.

We no sooner sat down than we were surrounded by half a dozen young men. They were so pushy that when I opened the bag containing my lunch, I had to wait until three of them checked to see what I was going to eat before I could get close enough to see it myself. Another, while I was coping with my lunch observers, opened a bag, took out some bread and meat, made a sandwich, and started feeding Jesse. There was no malice intended, they were just being friendly. They were so excited about interacting with us that they didn't even notice for a few minutes that they had taken all the seats, and Laurie was standing.

All of them were talking to us in Chinese. Cooper was trying to interpret for all of them at the same time, and was getting frustrated. Finally, one of them realized we were trying very hard to be nice, and that it was becoming quite a chore for us. He spoke to the others, and they went away until we'd had our lunch and a chance to rest a bit. Then they came back and talked with us some more, and each of them got pictures with Jesse and Cooper.

One of the young men, in particular, kept coming back to get one or the other of the boys to stand in front of a scenic spot for a picture with yet another friend. Then we noticed that he had started an impromptu business in which he would approach people, and for a small fee, would arrange for them to have their photo taken with a young American boy. The next time he came back, we told him that was the last time, that Jesse and Cooper were getting too tired. He beamed and said okay, no problem.

By then, the others had returned (all alive) from Phoenix Mountain, exhausted from the rigorous climb in 85-degree heat. They had been much more exposed to the sun than we had, because there had been far fewer trees on their path. The Chinese man who had gone as their guide flopped down in the shade near me, gasping. He looked as though he were going to have a heat stroke. I peeked, and sure enough, there were his longjohns hanging out from beneath his pants.

After everyone had finished lunch, we piled onto the bus and began the hour and a half drive back to Dandong. After about half an hour, the driver turned off the highway, and drove about ten kilometers to a little country town, where he stopped the bus in front of a big building bearing a sign that said "Dandong Hot Springs Hotel." They had arranged a room with a private bath for each of us. The tubs had been filled with water from the hot springs, and we had an hour to soak and relax before continuing, much refreshed, to Dandong. We returned on the express train to Shenyang the following day.

On May 4, in response to student threats to demonstrate if a list of 12 demands weren't met, police cordoned of Tiananmen square, but student demonstrators broke through and occupied the square.

Competition was something Chinese college students were not as enamored of as were their counterparts in the States. The first thing college students in the States did when they got hold of a volleyball, baseball, basketball, or football, was choose up sides and have a competition. That seldom happened in China. We watched young people hitting volleyballs, soccer balls, and tennis balls for hours, but they just hit them back and forth for the pleasure of it. When people played tennis, they didn't try to keep the ball away from each other, or see if they could get the ball in bounds where the other person couldn't get to it. They hit it back and forth so that it was easy for the other person to return it—to, rather than away from, each other.

In the paved courtyard in front of our building, it was common to

182

see anywhere from three to eight students standing in a circle, hitting a volleyball back and forth to each other. If one person hit the ball a little hard, so that another couldn't get it, she would apologize; then both would laugh. They played for exercise, and as something fun to do together. The competitive element was practically nonexistent.

One game the younger boys played that did get somewhat competitive was called "piagis" (pee ah' gees), after the playing pieces. They were little, cardboard disks, anywhere from one to four inches in diameter, with colored pictures on them. The decorations were often of ancient warriors, but Cooper had some with Mickey Mouse and Donald Duck, some with cars, and some with animals.

We asked Cooper how to play the game, and he explained that the idea was for the first player to lay one of his piagis on a level surface (they usually hunkered down and used the ground). The second player then flapped one of his piagis down so as to try to make the first player's piagi flip over. Laurie and I each tried it many times, and found that it took, shall we say, a unique talent. If the first player's piagi flipped over, the second player got to keep it, and try again on another of the first player's. If it didn't flip over, then it became the first player's turn to try and flip one of the second player's over.

When he first started playing, we had to buy Cooper new piagis every couple of days, because he was supplying all the other boys on campus. After a few weeks, however, he began to get the hang of it, and we had to resupply less often. Then he began to catch onto the finer points of the game.

I came home from work one evening to find him busily coloring the backs of some of his piagis with thick layers of wax crayon. To others, he was glueing a second layer of cardboard on the back. He was applying gummed stickers to the backs of others. I asked him what he was doing, and he said he was making them so they would be more effective. I asked if that wasn't cheating, and he assured me that it wasn't. "All the guys do it," he said. "It's part of the strategy." It must have worked, because we noticed his stock of piagis growing. In fact, we didn't have to buy him any more before we left.

On May 13, some students occupying Tiananmen square began a hunger strike.

Students gathering for a protest demonstration in front of the government building in Shenyang.

On May 14, Students in Shenyang organized a march to the government offices, where they held an orderly demonstration. Northern China was very conservative, and this was the first time in history such a large demonstration had taken place. When it was finished at about 9:00 p.m., a fleet of government buses took the students back to their universities.

On May 15, Gorbachev arrived in Beijing. China Daily reported that the number of students occupying the square had risen to 100,000 and the number of hunger strikers to 3,000. Although not officially cancelled, classes were no longer held at Liaoning University.

On May 18, Gorbachev left Beijing. Government representatives visited hunger strikers, both in the square, and those who had been taken to hospitals. The largest protest march in Shenyang's history took place. Although it was organized by college students, they were joined by school students from kindergarten (including Cooper, with his entire class) on up, teachers, administrators, and workers from the city. Many students stayed in the courtyard in front of the government offices, and began a hunger strike in support of the protesters in Beijing.

On May 20, martial law was declared. Orders to clear the courtyard in front of the government offices in Shenyang were obeyed. Orders to clear Tiananmen Square were not. China Television no longer carried direct news, only speeches by government officials, interspersed with the regulations of martial law.

On May 23, an estimated one million people in Beijing marched in support of those occupying Tiananmen Square. For the first time since

1978, China began jamming Voice of America broadcasts, but were only successful on some frequencies.

On May 28, an unofficial work slowdown that had been building for weeks came to a climax. It was estimated that as many as a million of Shenyang's four and a half million people were milling about in the streets.

On May 30, many declared what had by then become known as "The Democracy Movement" dead. Many students had already gone home, and more followed.

Chapter Ten
Week of June 4

Early on the morning of June 4, soldiers of the People's Liberation Army attacked the people in Tiananmen Square with small arms, automatic weapons, jeeps, and tanks. The Chinese called it "a war against their own people."

Throughout 1987 and 1988, and for the first five months of 1989, the Chinese media had become increasingly open in their news coverage. My research on how the U.S. was portrayed in Chinese newspapers during 1988 certainly showed more about the U.S. in Chinese papers than our papers carried about China during the same period. In fact, Chinese papers carried quite a bit about what was happening throughout the world. It seemed to be fairly straightforward, unbiased coverage—a bit propagandistic perhaps, but not much more so than what U.S. newspapers carried about other countries.

Some of their "news" was certainly blatant propaganda, but those were mostly domestic stories about the "glorious" workers, and how they were exceeding their quotas—that sort of thing. People didn't pay much attention to that stuff, but there was also a lot of quite useful economic and political news. They carried very little spot news: murders, rapes, and automobile accidents. But they did report on natural disasters such as floods, earthquakes, and forest fires.

Their television news had begun to look a lot like Western news programs. They had a half hour of local news, and a half hour of national news on two channels at about 6:00 p.m. and 10:00 p.m. One of the channels carried ten minutes of news in English at 6:30, and the other 15 minutes at 10:30. Most of it was political, economic, and public interest information—things such as Reagan and Gorbachev meeting, a flood or an airplane crash somewhere, or a legless person who had become a great skier.

In 1989 they had only been carrying that kind of news on Chinese television for a few years. Before that it had all been blatant propaganda. The change was drastic during the year we were there, culminating in live coverage of the demonstrations in Beijing and the meetings between students and government representatives. Every day they had news conferences, with both Chinese and Western reporters attending, and every night they had footage of the student demonstrations.

When they declared martial law, however, all that changed. Suddenly, domestic news was replaced by a wearying repetition of speeches by government leaders, and specifications about the rules of martial law. Reporters could no longer get near Tiananmen Square. A couple of Laurie's students went to Beijing for a few days, and when they returned, they told us the square was ringed by tanks and soldiers. Differences between the previous coverage of incidents in Beijing, and the pre-written, pre-taped, propagandistic speeches were obvious. It was a clear indication that something was wrong—something had changed.

Then, immediately following the massacre in Tiananmen Square, China Television reverted to the format they had been using before martial law was declared. People had begun to equate that format—quite similar to the one used for network news programs in the States—with honest, open coverage. Although the format was the same, however, the content wasn't. It consisted almost entirely of government propaganda, with no consideration of truth.

For example, on the evening news two days after the massacre, a reporter announced that fewer than 200 people had been killed in Tiananmen Square, and that only 23 of them had been students. In contrast, reporters for Voice of America and British Broadcasting Corporation were reporting Red Cross estimates of 3,000 to 4,000 killed, most of them students. A couple of weeks after we returned to the States, we saw a rebroadcast of a Chinese news program in which a government official announced that not one person had been killed in Tiananmen Square.

Numerous times during the week following the massacre, we saw on television a long "documentary" piece that had been put together by the government propaganda office to explain the events leading up to what they called the "incident in Beijing." It began with scenes of attractive young soldiers standing around chatting, then cut to "hooligans" throwing rocks and bottles. The next scenes were of the attractive young soldiers wounded and bleeding, ostensibly from wounds incurred from those bottles and rocks. Next, they showed some civilians—whom they said were students—throwing Molotov cocktails at an army truck, stopping it, smashing the windows, and pulling the driver and passenger out and—according to the announcer—beating them to death.

The announcer reiterated other such atrocities by "students and hooligans." Then we were shown scenes of how the students had desecrated Tiananmen Square: the squalor and filth in which they had "chosen" to live, and the problems the government was having, trying to maintain hygienic conditions despite overwhelming odds. There followed more scenes of students perpetrating violence against passive soldiers; then, finally scenes of troops pouring out of the North Gate into the square, weapons blazing. Any scenes of people being harmed by the effects of their gunfire, however, were carefully exorcized. I don't think anybody really believed that story, but it was the only one being offered.

A day or two after the massacre, one of the women news anchors for China Television began to wear a charcoal-colored suit when she read the news. Speculation abounded that she was doing it as a protest against the killings. The rumor became so widespread that government authorities had her read a statement on the news to the effect that she had been presented her new suit by the government so that she would appear more respectable, and could perform her job more effectively. She ended by thanking the government for caring so well for her and the rest of the citizens of China.

Clearly, the impact of the massacre was not as great for us in Shenyang as it was for people in Beijing, but the most common topic of conversation among foreign students and faculty all week was whether we should leave China.

Wednesday, the U.S. State Department began issuing a Class One Advisory, recommending that all Americans in China leave the country as soon as possible. They made arrangements for several shuttle flights a day from Beijing to Tokyo for the evacuation of U.S. citizens. We got word from a friend at the Consulate in Shenyang that the Consul General had been instructed by the Embassy in Beijing to send all dependents of the Counsel officers to Beijing for evacuation on a special plane that Friday.

The vice president of Liaoning University called the foreign students and faculty together Wednesday afternoon to express what was obviously a sincere concern for our safety, but he said he felt there was no real danger. He told us his only concern was that we might be injured accidentally if we got involved in a large crowd outside the university. He said, and we had been given no reason to think otherwise, that there was no animosity on the part of Chinese people toward Westerners. On the contrary, Westerners who had been near some of the demonstrations said they were greeted enthusiastically by both students and workers.

Some of the foreign students and teachers took part in the demonstrations. All of us were asked what we thought about the situation. People wanted to know if we favored the demonstrations. Laurie and

I decided that, although we wanted to let our students know they had our moral support, we should not become directly involved in what was really none of our business, so we were very circumspect in our discussions.

A young man from our Foreign Affairs Office rushed breathlessly into our apartment Thursday morning, to inform me that I had a call over in his office from some people at my university. The director of our International Studies Program was calling at the behest of our president and vice president to convey their strong recommendation that we return as soon as possible. They had told her to inform me that any extra expenses we incurred would be reimbursed by the university—a sure sign that they were truly worried.

I told her that the official stance of the Chinese government, and therefore the administration of Liaoning University, was that there was no problem, that we were in absolutely no danger, and that we should stay and continue to teach our classes. This despite the fact that there were only about 500 of the 7,000 students still on campus, and it had been weeks since any of them had showed up for classes. In fact, they no longer even bothered to unlock the classrooms. I told her I was concerned that if we left then—a month before our contract was up—our hosts might consider that we had broken our contract without just cause.

They had the Chinese exchange scholar at my university in the States speak to the director of Liaoning University's Foreign Affairs Office. She explained what a bleak picture the U.S. media were painting of the situation, and how everyone was concerned that we were in great danger. After about ten minutes of her impressing on the director the concern for our lives on the part of people back home, the conversation concluded. The director hung up the phone, turned to me, and said she had arranged for my family to visit the city zoo the following morning. I was stunned. I didn't know how to respond. I said that was very kind of her, and I was sure we would enjoy it. We did, although it was our third visit, so the novelty was somewhat diminished.

Thursday, the foreign students and faculty at Liaoning University received word from an American reporter in Shenyang, that the troops of the People's Liberation Army had surrounded the city and were preparing to move in the next Saturday at dawn. She said Liaoning University was targeted for an attack because some of the student leaders of the protest movement lived in the graduate dorms there. The German, Swedish, Italian, and Belgian students were instructed by their government officials to leave as soon as possible, as were most of the foreign students in the city.

Cooper, Jesse, and friends at the zoo, where there, at least, all is calm and peaceful.

Most of the foreign faculty and students at Laioning University who hadn't already done so, made arrangements to leave on a Friday flight to Dalian, where they would connect with a flight to Tokyo. A friend from another university in Shenyang came over to tell us that almost all the American faculty at the other universities in town had bought tickets for a Friday morning flight to Guangzhou (Gwon Joe'). From there, they would connect with the train to Hong Kong.

The Gillette Company, which had more American employees than any other business in town, chartered a plane to take their employees out. The few seats that were available, they gave to some visiting professors from Colorado. There was a rumor that the American Consulate was bringing in a plane to fly all of the Americans in the city out. We checked with the Counsel General, and he said that had been considered, but they'd decided not to do it. He said that if any Westerners in town felt they were not safe, they could come to the Consulate and stay there. That wasn't a particularly alluring invitation, because all he was offering was floor space and a public bathroom in their office building, but several of the German and Belgian students accepted it.

Laurie and I talked it over at length, and decided, for several reasons, that the best thing for us to do was stay at Liaoning University. First, the government of China (most likely) did not want us to get hurt. Certainly the administration of Liaoning University didn't, and were doing everything in their power to make sure that didn't happen.

191

Second, so many people were trying to get out of China that all the planes, trains, airports, and stations were overflowing, and the transportation system—which wasn't great under the best of conditions—was in an even greater state of turmoil. VOA and BBC were carrying reports of people sleeping in airports and train stations for days before getting tickets, something we didn't want to subject the boys to if we could help it

Third, we had prepaid tickets for July 17 from Beijing to San Francisco on CAAC, and then from San Francisco to Bemidji on Northwest. If we changed the date, it would have cost nearly $5000. Although my university had said they would cover the cost, we just didn't think it necessary.

In fact, we thought the most likely scenario for Shenyang was that things would go on much as they were for a while; then gradually cool off. On the other hand, we'd heard of fighting between various factions of the army, and that a civil war wasn't out of the question. If that happened, we figured danger to us would still be minimal, but that international travel might come to a screeching halt, leaving us stranded in China for the duration—not a pleasant prospect.

The situation in Shenyang during the week following the massacre was surprisingly peaceful, although there were orderly demonstrations. Every morning at 5:00, we were awakened by a broadcast, which was amplified so that it reached every part of campus. It originated in a student dorm room, and alternated between news bulletins—some of them from VOA and BBC; patriotic music—including the "Internationale" from the French Revolution, the 1988 Olympic theme, and the Chinese national anthem; then announcements by the students about strikes and demonstrations.

Following the broadcast, organizers got all the students up who would go with them, and gathering students and workers as they went, marched through the city. The bus drivers and trolley drivers supported the students, and they would stop their vehicles, completely blocking major intersections. One morning, we saw this happen at the intersection of two of the biggest four-lane streets in the city.

Traffic came to a standstill, and backed up for many blocks in every direction. The policemen responsible for traffic flow at the intersection saw there was absolutely no way they could maintain control, so they went to the police booth on the corner and pulled out a bench and a sign, which they dragged into the middle of the intersection. They erected the sign—which said "road closed" in large Chinese characters—sat down on the bench, lit cigarettes, and watched the chaos from the best seat in the house.

People couldn't get to work on sidewalks, bike paths, or streets, so they gathered by the thousands at clogged intersections, where students seized the opportunity to tell people their version of what was going on. Chinese students were greatly respected by the working people, because they were considered the most intelligent, knowledgeable people in the country. The workers were much more likely to believe what students told them than what they heard from government leaders. For many of the workers, those student announcements were their only news about what had been happening.

The official word in China was that almost everybody in the cities had television and radio, but in fact, many of the poorer workers didn't have access to the media. Those who did, recognized the fact that they were only getting the Party line. Before the massacre, people listened to what they were told by the Chinese media, and what they were told by any foreign media to which they had access. They then drew conclusions that fell somewhere between. Because their media had become so blatantly propagandistic, however, nobody believed anything they heard there any longer.

It was primarily students and professional people who had access to short wave radios, and could listen to the Voice of America and the British Broadcasting Corporation. When they broadcast tapes of that information, hundreds—in some places thousands—of people stopped to listen, blocking sidewalks, bike paths, and streets. They were hungry for credible information about what was happening in their own country.

Another way they distributed information was a resurgence of "large character posters," as were used during the cultural revolution. The posters appeared in various central locations, which came to be known as "freedom walls," or "democracy walls." They were replaced each night, and were used to exhort people to continue the struggle, or to give synopses of the latest news. Each morning, hundreds gathered in front of them. Only those in the first few rows were close enough to read the posters. Some read out loud for the benefit of those standing 40 or 50 deep behind them.

Hearing them read was enough for some people; others waited patiently until they could work their way in close enough to read the posters themselves. Sometimes, after reading about new government atrocities, people would denounce their Communist Party membership, some even burning their membership cards for the cheering crowd.

One of Laurie's students, who had been in Beijing on the fourth, came back with a 6-minute audio tape of the attack on Tiananmen Square. It was obviously very confusing, with the sound of many weapons firing in the background, and people running and screaming. Chinese friends interpreted what they could for us, breaking into sobs in the process. It was pretty dreadful—many of the sounds were clearly of people dying. The students set up a dubbing facility in one of the dorm rooms, from which came a continuous flow of copies of that tape. They were distributed throughout the city, so people could hear what had really happened.

Some eyewitnesses to the massacre had taken photographs, which they smuggled to friends in the States. Their friends, in turn, faxed thousands of copies of the damning photos back to machines in Chinese cities. Each morning, much to the consternation of the government, more of those copies were prominently displayed on lampposts and walls throughout the country. Faced with photos of the bodies of young men and women torn by automatic weapon fire, it was difficult for people to believe their government's version of events.

The day after the massacre, one of the Japanese students who was at Liaoning University to learn Chinese, but who really wanted to be a photojournalist, went to Beijing. While there, he risked his life to take dozens of photographs—including bodies still lying on the sidewalk from the day before—that showed devastation wrought by government troops in what had clearly been a needlessly brutal crushing of dissent.

Faced with such evidence of their government's actions, many of the workers in Shenyang went on strike, and joined the demonstrations. Although the city was not crippled by the strike, it certainly slowed things down. Critical functions such as communication and utilities were no worse than usual. Transportation was affected more than anything else. In addition to the problems caused by drivers going on strike, the need to detour around demonstrations and roadblocks also made travel in the city quite difficult.

Within the walls of the campus, it was extremely peaceful, the weather was beautiful, and people were out strolling around. There was little indication that anything was wrong. Then, occasionally, something would happen to remind us that beneath the calm were serious problems. I was walking home from my office for lunch one day that week, and as I passed the tennis courts, I heard a bottle smash on their blacktop surface. I looked up and saw a second come sailing out of the graduate student dorm across the street, arc over my head, and shatter on the courts, narrowly missing two young men who had put up a net and were playing badminton.

They stopped playing, and as I watched, a group of 15 or 20 male graduate students came out of the dorm. Without saying a word, they walked across the street, took the rackets away from the young men, took their net down, and returned to their dorm. I thought their actions a bit extreme, but my assistant explained that the student leaders had put signs up a couple of days earlier, forbidding anyone from taking part in fun activities, because of the gravity of the situation.

Thursday afternoon, Laurie's sister called from Montana to inform us that my mother and all of Laurie's family were very concerned for our safety, and asked that we come home as soon as possible. To help us do so, she worked with a travel agent almost full time for two days. Using her charge cards, she had for us at various times: four prepaid tickets for Canadian, Northwest, Pan Am, or United to Tokyo, Hong Kong, Vancouver, or San Francisco waiting at Dalian, Beijing, Shanghai, or Guangzhou. She called us several times to explain, but we weren't sure we ever understood exactly which tickets for where were waiting for us at which airport.

Given the concern for our safety being expressed by families, friends, colleagues, and government bureaucrats, Laurie and I decided to rethink our position. I couldn't do any more on my research, as it necessitated interviewing the editors of four major Chinese newspapers, and they were either dead, deposed, or otherwise not talking. Almost all our students had left campus, and the ones who hadn't were hardly interested in attending classes. It looked as if we would have little to do but sit around for another month. There was at least a possibility that we were in some danger. We decided to go.

No classes had been held for three weeks. Had we stayed we would have been the only foreign teachers or students to do so. Representatives from our university had told the administration of Liaoning University how much they wanted us to return. Despite overwhelming evidence to the contrary, however, they refused to acknowledge that there was a problem, and considered our decision to leave a month early a breach of our contract.

Of course, in China, the decision to leave and the act of leaving are separated by a huge gulf of uncertainty. Thursday afternoon, I took our tickets to the CAAC office to see if we could book a flight out. It was a 45-minute bike ride across town in the rain. Despite the fact that I arrived at 3:00 p.m., and the sign on the door clearly said they were open from 1:00 until 4:30, they just as clearly weren't. I hung around for an hour and saw no sign of life, so I went home and returned the next morning.

The good news was that it wasn't raining. The bad news was that it was still a 45-minute bike ride. The good news was that the office was open. The bad news was that it was the wrong office. The right office was an additional hour and fifteen minutes on the other side of town, at the airport. When I got there, I felt very healthy, but I was in no mood to be toyed with. They didn't toy with me, but told me very directly (and very firmly) that getting from Shenyang to Beijing would be no problem—for some reason, it wasn't a very popular destination just then—but the first seats available from Beijing to the States were in mid-August.

We spent much of the rest of Friday trying to call CAAC in Beijing to see if we could get on a flight out the next week. The result of our efforts (each time we finally got through) alternated between getting no answer, and getting a recording saying the number had been disconnected. We had better luck arranging for a place to stay. The Holiday Inn Lido was a very nice joint venture hotel and apartment complex about halfway between the airport and downtown Beijing. Many of the foreigners who worked in Beijing lived there, so we figured it was probably the safest place in central China. The young woman who answered the phone said, yes they did have double rooms available, and yes she would reserve us one for Sunday—just like back home.

Laurie and I discussed it and decided that surely some of the Americans who would have used those reserved seats to the States had already left on evacuation flights. And some of the Chinese who would have used them must have found their travel plans in disarray following the "incidents" in Beijing. We decided to go to Beijing and take our chances on getting one of the three flights to the States the next week.

On Saturday, university officials announced the dissolving of the Students' Autonomous Union, which had been responsible for leading the protest movement in Shenyang. Police had been cracking down increasingly on dissent all week, and by Saturday almost all the students had gone home, people had gone back to work, life was back to "normal," and the arrests had begun. Before we left Shenyang, we learned that a couple of our students had been taken from their dorm rooms the night before.

Unlike previously in China's history, however, the people weren't helping police find the "criminals" and "hooligans" they sought. When police came to a neighborhood looking for someone, the answer they were likely to get was, "No, we haven't seen him since June 4. Is it possible he was one of the very few people killed in Tiananmen Square?"

Cooper bidding a fond farewell to his teacher.

The university driver took us to the Shenyang airport 5:30 Sunday morning, where we purchased tickets to Beijing and boarded the plane. Twenty seven of the 180 seats were occupied. We arrived at 11:00, and I headed immediately for the international ticketing counter of CAAC.

I was intercepted by a young man intent on offering his services as a taxi driver. I asked how much to the Lido, and he gave me a figure at least twice what it should have been. I pointed that fact out to him, and he said he was afraid of getting shot—a concept he conveyed by pointing his fingers and making "pkew, pkew" sounds with his mouth. I laughed and asked how many taxi drivers so far had given their lives in efforts to transport Americans from the airport to the Lido. He grinned and said something beyond the scope of my Chinese or his English, but which I guessed to be: none, but with his luck, he'd be the first. But he cut his price in half. I told him he had a deal if he would wait until I concluded my business with CAAC.

The young woman behind the counter asked how she could help me. I showed her our tickets, and asked when the first seats were available to San Francisco. She consulted a computer and said Wednesday. I asked if there wasn't anything before that, because I had two small children (accompanied by a display of their passport pictures), and we needed to leave as soon as possible. She "Ooh"-ed and "Aah"-ed at how beautiful Cooper and Jesse were, and after numerous questions and answers about them said there weren't any flights before Wednesday. I said I had seen a brand-new CAAC schedule that showed flights Monday and Tuesday, as well. She said yes, but they went through Tokyo, and our tickets were for a direct flight. I asked if it wasn't possible to change. She said I would have to talk to her supervisor, who wasn't there just then, I should come back in half an hour.

I did so, and her supervisor asked how she could help me. We went through an identical process: Wednesday, small children, "Ooh," "Aah," Tokyo, "...possible to change?" She looked at our tickets and said they couldn't be changed; that I'd have to buy new ones at a cost of about $3000. I said we couldn't afford that, so we'd take four seats on the Wednesday flight. She said there were only first class seats left on that flight, and that it would cost us about $2400 to upgrade our tickets. I said we couldn't afford that, wasn't there anything else she could do to help us. She said that if we didn't mind leaving Monday, she could get us seats, but they would be on a direct flight from Beijing to San Francisco. I bit the inside of my cheeks to keep from screaming, and croaked, "Oh, that would be very nice, how much extra would it cost?" She said it wouldn't cost any extra. I asked if there were four seats available. She said yes, would I like them. I said yes, please. Nobody shot at us on the drive to the Lido; in fact we saw very few people in uniform.

The room was $120 U.S.—more than I had ever paid for one night's lodging—but we figured it was as safe as we could get. Besides, we had saved the administration of my university several thousand dollars by using our original plane tickets, so we didn't think they had any grounds for complaint. It was a great transition period for our return—it could have been a Holiday Inn anywhere in the States, except a bit more luxurious. We swam in a pool for the first time in a year. I nursed a tall, cold scotch and soda at the bar. The boys had chicken nuggets for dinner, and Laurie a mushroom and cheese omelette and hash browns for breakfast. Laurie and I watched hour after hour of English language news on CNN. And we all sat, transfixed, before a couple of offerings on the movie channel in our room.

The next morning at 11:00, we boarded a CAAC plane at the Beijing airport. We learned later that we were among the last hundred or so Americans to leave. Our "direct" flight to San Francisco was interrupted only twice—by a 2-hour layover in Shanghai, and a 4-hour layover in Tokyo. Because of the combination of date and time changes, we collapsed into our own beds in Bemidji at midnight.

Epilogue

One evening about a week after we got home, Laurie and I were reminiscing about the previous year. We remembered a day in early April when the "what will we do?" syndrome had hit. Everyone we had talked to said it would happen sooner or later: "What will we do when we get back to the States? Where's the first place we're going to eat? Should we go to McDonald's right away, or should we go someplace fancy?" We were like children anticipating a birthday. It had nothing to do with whether it was better in the States—it was just so different. We began to remember ordinary things we had done back home—things we hadn't done for so long we didn't even miss them any more: going swimming at the university pool, window shopping on a hot afternoon in the air-conditioned mall, renting a couple of videos with no redeeming social value.

Then Laurie had said, "Of course you realize that we won't be back in the States two weeks before we'll be saying, 'Boy I wish we could stop at that little Korean restaurant on the corner by the market. Their noodles were so good. And that one Szechun place over by the Medical University—remember their whole fish in oyster sauce?'" It had made us sad to realize that, although we would be going back to many things we greatly missed, there would be many things—and people—from China that we would miss just as much, maybe for the rest of our lives.

Our students often asked us which we liked better, the United States or China. The temptation was always to take the easy way out and answer that we liked both countries equally, but in different ways. That wasn't true, though. From nearly all the criteria by which we had been taught to judge, China was not as "good" as the United States. China was a developing country; the United States was one of the richest countries in the world. China was a Communist autocracy; the United States was a Democracy. It would have been silly for us to try and pretend we thought China as good. We couldn't even consider the question objectively. We were products of American culture. We'd spent most of our lives there. We liked it. We were unquestionably ethnocentric.

On the other hand, we realized that not everything in the United States was good, and that not everything good was in the United States. One of the first things most Chinese did was apologize to us because they couldn't offer us the things we were used to. Of course they couldn't, but we didn't expect them to. Nor did we want them to. Had we wanted two cars, a 7-room house, a video recorder, and unlimited access to indecently over packaged consumer goods, we'd have stayed home. We were looking for things they did have, many of which we'd never have back home. In fact, our experience has changed all three of us in ways that will affect our view of how we fit into our own culture. It will also change how we interact with people who are different from us—culturally, socially, ethnically, economically, and just personally. In short, I believe our year in China has made us more accepting of others, and that can only be a good thing.

II
THAILAND

Introduction

Our year in China was so fulfilling that we were committed to spending a year in another country five years later, so in 1992, I began putting out feelers for possibilities. As a member of the International Communication Association, I had made numerous personal connections, and received their newsletter, which included international openings. By Fall of 1992, I was considering several possibilities, but wasn't really excited about any of them. I wasn't due for another paid sabbatical for five years, so this leave would be unpaid. Some of the positions I would have liked did not offer realistic stipends, so were not under consideration. I presented a paper at the annual convention of the International Communication Association in St. Louis that Fall. At dinner the first evening, I noticed that many tables were occupied with members I knew, but one table had only one woman sitting at it. She looked Asian, and uncomfortable with the prospect of interrupting the interaction at other tables where the people were obviously familiar with each other. I approached and asked if I could join her. Her warm "Please do" clearly expressed relief at not having to dine alone in unfamiliar surroundings. I found her interesting, among other reasons, because she was from Thailand, and I was fascinated by her discussion of the Thai culture. She seemed pleased when I suggested that we share a table the next day. In fact, we sat together at every meal during the conference. At some point in our conversation, I mentioned that I had taught in China for a year, and that my wife and I wanted to spend one of every five years in another country. She asked when the next time would be, and I told her I was looking for a position for the next year. She responded immediately with, "Why don't you come to my school?" I said that would certainly be a possibility, and she told me she would speak to her department chair as soon as she got home. When I got home, I looked up her "school," Chulalongkorn University, and found that it was named after a former king of the country, and was universally considered "The Harvard of Southeast Asia." I received a letter from her within two weeks with a list of information her dean would like me to send her. After about a month of communication, I received an official invitation to spend the next year as an "honored international scholar" at their university. The bad news was that my school year ended—as did the boys'—in May, and theirs began in June. The boys were less than thrilled to have their summer vacation cut down to a couple of weeks, and it didn't leave us a lot of time to make all the arrangements necessary to move for a year to a country halfway around the world. But we did it.

Chapter One
June

Students in Thailand had the right idea about how to treat faculty. Every time students passed their professors, they weied (pronounced like the letter Y)—put their palms together as in prayer, fingertips touching their noses, and bowed slightly. Before classes started, all 150 new students in the Faculty of Communication Arts held a ceremony for the professors. We sat on stage in a small auditorium. Twenty pairs of students came forward with flower arrangements, took off their shoes, came up on stage, knelt before Buddah to present the flowers, and then walked across the stage on their knees to where the dean sat. They weied her, touched their foreheads to the floor in front of her, and presented the flowers to her. She accepted them; then passed them to another student, who arranged them on a table on the floor in front of the stage. Meanwhile, the students who had presented her the flowers walked the rest of the way across the stage on their knees and exited. After all the flowers were presented in this way, to the accompaniment of live music and poetry, all the students lined up and knelt before Buddah; then walked on their knees before us, weied us, touched the floor in front of us with their foreheads, and presented a wrist to have us tie a piece of

Students presenting flowers to the dean and their
professors at the beginning of the school year.

white yarn around it for good luck in their studies. Then they each walked the rest of the way across the stage on their knees and exited.

As respectful as Thai students were, however, they just weren't very good students. From kindergarten on up, they formed two expectations: 1) they would work very hard, get into the best college they could, and coast; and 2) their job as a student was to come to class, memorize pertinent facts from the teachers' lectures, and reiterate them on the exams. As with many other Asian systems, they had a great command of the facts, but if they could generalize from them, it was purely by accident. Classes generally met once a week for three hours, or twice a week for two hours. Many students dropped my class because they weren't prepared to meet my expectations that they think, and not just memorize. Even those who dropped my class, however, responded well to me. They were quick to say that they would like to learn to think, but just as quick to admit that they weren't well prepared to. Those who hung in there were probably interested in going to graduate school in the States, and knew they would have to learn our methods.

We enrolled Cooper and Jesse at Satit Chula, the demonstration school for the Faculty of Education. The language of instruction was Thai, but most of the teachers (or if not, then the student teachers) knew enough English to translate at least partially for the boys. They were learning English, math, and Thai, but not much else. It was indispensable for the contact they got with Thai children and customs, however. The boys were chagrined when they learned they would have to

Cooper and Jesse in their school uniforms. As a Cub Scout, Cooper got to wear the bandana and cap.

206

wear uniforms to school: white short-sleeved shirts with the school insignia sewn in blue on the left breast and their names in Thai on the right breast, black shorts, black tennis shoes, white socks, and a black belt with the school insignia on a silver buckle. Then they found out every student up to graduate school wore uniforms—in both public and private schools—and they didn't mind so much.

It took Jesse all of a week and a half to get lost. Laurie taught at Bangkok University until 5pm on Tuesdays, so I picked Jesse and Cooper up alone at the Chulalongkorn demonstration school on campus at 3 p.m. I took my eyes off Jesse for less than 15 seconds, and he was gone. We were still on the fenced school ground, however, complete with two uniformed guards at the gate (who wouldn't let us out unless the boys and Laurie or I all showed our photo IDs), so I wasn't really worried. After a half-hour search turned up nothing, two students told us they had seen Jesse outside the school heading in the direction of our apartment—a half-hour walk through downtown Bangkok. The teachers said that was impossible, he couldn't have gotten out the gate. I said they didn't know Jesse. Cooper and I walked to our apartment but didn't find him, either on the way, or there. I left Cooper there, and walked back to the school. They hadn't found Jesse, but a university guard said he had seen him walking by himself across campus toward the gate. They called both university security and the Bangkok police. By this time, it had begun pouring rain (we were just starting the rainy season). I started back toward the apartment again, asking everyone on the way if they had seen a little foreign kid by himself. I traced him to within about three blocks of our apartment; then lost him. I went the rest of the way to the apartment to see if he had turned up there. He hadn't, but Cooper said they had called from the school to say the police had found him and had taken him there. He had missed a turn, and ended up about five blocks off course—after having crossed two six-lane streets during rush hour in Bangkok, where the traffic is (defensibly) claimed to be the worst in the world. The police officer said Jesse didn't seem upset about being lost, but said he was very thirsty, and asked for something to drink and some candy. I walked—through the rain—back to the school to find that he wasn't there, but at the police station. After another half-hour wait, the police delivered him, and we walked once more to our apartment. At least it had quit raining by then. Laurie had just gotten home when we arrived at 6:30, so she hardly had any time to be worried, but I felt like I aged several years in those three and a half hours and ten miles of walking. When Jesse's teacher asked him the next day if he had learned anything from the experience, he told her he had learned that it was interesting at the police station, and wondered if he might work there part time while he was in Thailand.

Laurie taught English pretty much full time: Monday, Wednesday and Friday at the Chula Demonstration School; and Tuesday and Thursday at Bangkok University. I taught one course in Journalistic Writing in English at Chula, and guest lectured in numerous other classes. Professors were so poorly paid there, that all of them "moonlighted" at other schools, so they arranged for me to teach a course in Public Relations or Advertising for the graduate school at Bangkok University, and a course in International Media for Dhurakij Banbhit, another private university in the city.

The weather in Thailand was great—if you like 90 degrees and 90 percent humidity, with intermittent rain. We had just started into the rainy season. We had an apartment within a half-hour walk of my office and the boy's school. We were told it was the best school in the country, but that didn't mean much to Cooper and Jesse, as the instruction was all in Thai, and they couldn't understand much of that. We were learning, though—I concentrated on food terms, for obvious reasons.

I thought it was about 90 degrees, but in fact it was much hotter and we had just gotten used to it. After we had been there a couple of weeks, we were in the process of unpacking some small stuff, and putting it on some shelves when we came across a thermometer we had brought from the States. In our air conditioned apartment, which we had come to think of as cool and comfortable, it was eighty-five degrees. About the shelves—we had assumed (first lesson: don't ever assume anything about another culture) the apartment they got for us would be furnished. Not. It had three beds, two end tables, three hassocks, and a (small) refrigerator. Just a refrigerator; not a kitchen. We learned that few people in Bangkok—even those who lived in much more upscale apartments than ours—had kitchens. There were inexpensive restaurants and food stands on every block, and people generally either dined out, or stopped at food stands for take-home. We eventually found that wasn't a bad idea, as it cost about the same as buying groceries and cooking at home. At the time, however, we were dismayed that our apartment had no sink, no oven, no counters, no cabinets—no kitchen. We bought a table, some shelves, a hotplate, and an electric wok. We used the bathroom sink to wash dishes, but it was a step up from our China bathroom/kitchen.

The "make-do" kitchen in our apartment.

Luckily, furniture in Thailand was very cheap. We got five sets of rattan shelves (about 3 feet long, a foot deep, and 4 feet high) for about $20 each. We also got a couch, two chairs, and a coffee table for about $150—new. They weren't great quality, but they were fine for a year. They said they'd deliver them that Monday at 5 p.m. They didn't. We called and they apologized and said they'd be there Tuesday at 5 p.m. On Wednesday, still no furniture. Thailand is an incredible country. 1) I had some business cards printed with English on one side, and Thai on the other. I had to sign six separate sheets of paper to get it done. 2) We had to get a dozen little 1-inch by 1-inch photos taken for various ID cards—we needed a separate one for everything. Turned out they wouldn't do for my work permit—I needed a 5-cm by 6-cm one for that. 3) On a single day shortly after our arrival, I saw an elephant strolling down one of the main streets of Bangkok, holding up a two-block line of Mercedes, BMWs, and Volvos. Amazing.

When our furniture still hadn't arrived by Friday, a Thai woman Laurie worked with in the language lab at Cooper's and Jesse's school was determined she would speed up the process. She called the company and spoke sternly to them—well, as sternly as Thai people ever spoke. It came about 4:30 Sunday evening, of all times. As a result, though, the apartment did feel a bit more like a home. At least we had someplace to sit besides the kitchen table.

The next Saturday, we were treated to a bus trip of about three hours to an adjoining province where we toured a huge petrochemical plant.

It was them (National Petrochemical Company) who footed the bill for a group of teachers from the demonstration school and a group of army officers (some combination). We rode out in an air conditioned bus, with sandwiches and pop; saw one of the smoothest multimedia presentations I had seen in a while (that almost convinced me the petrochemical industry did not then, nor had it ever polluted the environment); climbed to the top of an observation tower for a beautiful view of the presumably unpolluted ocean in those parts; visited a demonstration school we assumed the company was pumping money into; stopped for half an hour at a "fruit fair" (which we had been told was the purpose for the trip); and came home. It was a full day—we left at 7 a.m. and got back about 8 p.m. It was fun, except that I got food poisoning (probably from the ham salad sandwich I had for lunch on the bus) and thought I would die from about 2 p.m. onward. From about 5 p.m. onward, I sort of wished I would. Sunday I was much better, however, and Monday I felt fine. The boys adjusted well to their new surroundings. They spent all Sunday afternoon at their friends' house. Laurie was teaching a lot of English and not getting paid much for it, but she felt good about being included in the activities of the group of Thai women who taught English at the demonstration school. The boys weren't learning as much Thai as we had hoped, because most of the teachers knew enough English to help them, rather than forcing them to learn Thai.

By the end of June the morning walk to work was getting cooler (about 85 degrees) and pleasant. I got up at 6:00 and showered, then made breakfast while Laurie showered. We got the boys up about 6:45, and tried to get started for work/school about 7:10—pretty difficult with Jesse dinking around. On mornings, though, when we got off on schedule, we had time to stroll leisurely through the grounds of the national sports complex (people out jogging, exercising, riding bike, and just walking; as well as playing soccer, tennis, and basketball) and across campus. People in our neighborhood had started to recognize that we were long-term, and not just tourists, and I got the feeling they reacted more positively to that. They were especially warm to the fact that Jesse and Cooper were going to a Thai school (as evidenced by their uniforms). We were starting to feel comfortable going to neighborhood restaurants—some of which were really just street vendors with facilities set up on the sidewalk for cooking noodles and a couple of tables set up in a nook with a tarp over them. We had learned enough Thai to order what we wanted (sort of; sometimes), and were beginning to develop preferences for the cooking or the people at some of the places over others—starting to feel part of the neighborhood—it felt good.

Chapter Two
July

When we switched from temporary to extended visas, we had to register at the U.S. Embassy. They were much less cordial than at the Consulate in Shenyang when we were there. It was pretty clear that there were a lot more 'Mur'cans in Thailand. While at the embassy, we learned that there would be a big blowout in the expatriate community for the Fourth of July—we decided to skip it. We missed the Water Carnival and fireworks over the lake back in our home town. It was a pretty lazy Fourth of July weekend in Bangkok: no fireworks; no parties—almost like they weren't interested in celebrating U.S. independence—go figure. We had a Thai couple (Chub and Oy) with whom we had become friends over. They had a boy (Gokkoi) about six months older than Cooper, and another (Gokkow) about six months younger than Jesse. I made them a good-old Fourth of July picnic meal: hamburgers, corn-on-the-cob, potato salad, and watermelon. They brought Carlsburg beer (a big deal, as it had been available in Thailand for only about a week at that time), Pepsi, and home-made ice cream (coconut with little pieces of vegetables such as corn and green beans in it, but, hey, it was home-made). We had a great time.

July 8 was graduation day at Chulalongkorn University. The students who had finished their senior year back in March all returned with their families for the weekend, and took part in various traditional activities all week. On graduation day, they all put on white suits with a sort of gauze, full-length coat (white, with wide gold stripes on collar and cuffs—sort of like an airline pilot's) and gathered in the main auditorium (just the students and faculty, the parents and friends sat outside and watched on closed circuit TV) for a four-hour ceremony that culminated with the king of Thailand giving them their diplomas. In case there was any question about whether that was the most prestigious university in the country, that answered it. I spent about an hour and a half standing on the second floor balcony of the cafeteria, watching festivities preceding graduation for the students in the Faculty of Communication Arts. The first year students had been practicing cheers and songs for weeks, and they roamed around until they came upon a graduating senior who wasn't otherwise occupied; then they surrounded him/her and cheered or sang. The "otherwise occupied" that students might have been was either receiving huge bunches of flowers and balloons, or having their photos taken in front of backdrops especially constructed by each of the grades for that purpose. The flowers and balloons were bestowed on the graduates by family and friends, as well as the lower-level students, all of whom came with several bunches to give away to any graduate they came across who looked as though he/she could hold more flowers. By the end of an hour, most of them couldn't. They had such huge armloads, they either had a friend or family member help carry them, or just stored them temporarily somewhere. The whole atmosphere was one of joy—much more so than in the States. Later, when the King conferred their degrees, it was very serious and traditional, but the morning was really fun.

Some kind of virus—one that resulted in a sore throat and hacking cough—made the rounds in early July. I fought it off, but Cooper succumbed to it. He woke up one morning sounding like he had a barking dog living in his throat, and with a bit of a fever. He allowed as how he could go to school though. I thought the decision probably had to do with the fact that he had become one of the champion ping-pong players at the school, and he didn't want to miss the chance to play with his friends. I gave him my number, and told him if he got any worse, to give me a call, and I'd take him home (Laurie was teaching at Bangkok University, across town). One nice thing about being in Thailand was that the pace of life was much more civilized. Whereas at my university in the States, it would have been almost impossible for me to cancel everything to go and be with a sick child, in Thailand they would have thought it very strange if I didn't. There are many things about the cultures of "developing" countries that put ours to shame.

A professor from New Zealand came in the second week in July. He shared my office for about six weeks. He was doing research on the media in Asia, and setting up a "virtual university," in which students would be connected electronically. I met him at his hotel on a Saturday afternoon and showed him around for a couple of hours. We went out to dinner with Chub and Oy and their boys that night, and they took Cooper and Jesse home to stay overnight. Laurie and I took advantage of the situation to sleep in Sunday morning. We walked to Maboonkrong, a huge shopping center (eight stories tall; a block wide) with dozens of food booths on the seventh floor. We had Sunday brunch there—Vietnamese egg rolls, Vietnamese pancakes, and iced coffee—$3.20 for both of us. It was really nice spending some quiet time together. We then walked over to Chub and Oy's house where the boys were playing. We went with them to another huge, Western-style department store, where they did some shopping and we followed the boys around the game room. After that we went home and I cooked supper. We had the new guy over for a Western meal--barbecued pork, sweet potatoes, salad, string beans, and fruit.

The following week Laurie added another three hours a week to her teaching load. Three managers at Krung Thai Bank wanted English lessons. Their bank was on the way to work/school for us, so she began stopping there from 7:30 to 8:30 Monday, Tuesday, and Wednesday mornings. They payed her $12 an hour, which we added to our travel kitty. We planned to travel for three weeks to the north of Thailand in October, and three weeks to the south in March, and were a bit worried about money, as we really didn't have a very good feel for how much the travel would cost.

The third weekend in July was a great one for us. Sunday we took a bus all the way to the south end of town, then caught a water taxi up the river all the way to the north end of town. We then caught another bus back to within a few blocks of our apartment. We did all that without help from any Thai friends—just Laurie, Cooper, Jesse, and me—and we didn't get lost. We left about 11:00 a.m., and got back about 3:00 p.m. We ate lunch at a Thai restaurant (hole-in-the-wall type) down by the river. They had no English menu. We ordered all in Thai, and had four different dishes, plus ice and pop. Including stops once for ice cream and once for pop during the afternoon, the whole outing cost us less than 200 baht ($8.00). Sunday evening we had David, who lived upstairs, and his girlfriend, Sara, who was visiting from New York City for a week, for dinner—fried chicken, hamburgers, salad, fruit salad, and mashed potatoes. Not bad for one hot plate and one electric wok. Monday Laurie and I played hooky most of the day. We went to a photo exhibit on campus—it was on the environment, and had begun at the Earth Summit in Rio and toured major cities of the world for a year. It was very impressive. We then walked to the American University Alumni Association, which was a library, bookstore, auditorium, and English language school. We joined the library, and got on their mailing list for activities (concerts, plays, and the like).

The next week things started getting pretty busy for me. The man who taught photo editing came to my office, informed me he was going out of the country for the rest of the term, and asked if I would take over his class. It wasn't too bad, as I had taught both photo editing and newspaper design in the States, but it took time preparing lectures and assignments, and then grading the students' work.

It seemed as though they were always having some sort of celebration at either the university or the boys' school. One morning Laurie and the boys took part in some sort of teacher appreciation day. The boys had to bring flowers to present to their teachers during the ceremony. Actually, we were never quite sure what was going on until after the fact; although many people spoke good English, the ceremonies didn't really translate because they were unlike anything in our experience. The students asked me about every other week to cancel class to allow for some sort of event. I did it the first couple of times, but then drew the line. I told them they would have to figure out some mutually acceptable time to reschedule. As a result, I often had class at noon instead of lunch.

Students preparing to present flowers and gifts to Laurie, their honored English teacher.

On July 22 I received a fax from the vice president of my university in the States informing me that following consultation with my dean, she had decided to approve my request for an unpaid leave to spend a year teaching in Thailand. Oh, good. She asked that I send them something in writing letting them know whether I accepted. After due consideration, I decided I would.

That Friday was Jesse's birthday, so we took some goodies for him to share with his friends at school. One of his teachers gave him a Chula baseball cap. He invited four of his friends from school and two from our neighborhood to a party Saturday afternoon at 2:00. We took him to McDonalds for lunch—first time we'd been there since coming to Thailand, so it was a big treat.

The McDonalds we could only afford on special occasions such as sons' birthdays.

By 2:00 we had all the games and party decorations up in the cafeteria of the apartment building, but nobody showed. Luckily, we remembered the Thai tendency to be late, and promised him people would come; and they did—just before 3:00. One of our friends had given him a huge birthday cake, so we all had cake and pop, and played silly games 'till our eyes bugged out. All in all, it was fun. When Chub and Oy came to pick up their boys, they invited us out to dinner for Jesse's birthday. Needless to say, we accepted, and saved the spaghetti fixings for Sunday evening. They took us to a good seafood restaurant near the university, and we had a great dinner. Chub had invited one of his friends from college with whom he still kept in touch. He also had two boys (5 and 7) so it became a pretty rowdy group. I suggested the three of us take our younger sons and open a demolition business. No building in the world could survive their combined onslaught. Actually, it was refreshing to find others with sons like Jesse; it gave us a common bond; sort of like soldiers in a war. We got home late, so slept in Sunday; then took it easy all day.

It was near the end of July, and we were supposed to be in the rainy season, but it hadn't rained for more than a week. When it did rain, it was only once or twice a week for less than an hour. We'd only had two rains in which I could see the makings of a monsoon. They kept saying, "Any day now...."

We were witnessing some of the less positive aspects of "development" in Bangkok. Over the weekend two students at a local college were killed in what could only have been described as a "rumble" between the students of two tech schools. Really remarkable, considering the Thais aversion to conflict of any sort. Ah, Westernization: Levis, Coke, and ego-based riots.

It took eight separate forms (about 19 pages of paperwork) but I finally got registered for a work permit two weeks after I had started working. Being registered for a permit in Thailand, however, is a far cry from actually getting one. The third time I went to pick up my permit, they wanted to see my passport (a photocopy they had made during an earlier visit was in front of them), so I had to go back a fourth time. Just to be safe, I took all of our passports—none of which they looked at, all of which they kept. Nor did I need to be there, which they had insisted on. A secretary from our office who had accompanied me on that trip chatted with a bureaucrat, the bureaucrat stamped some papers in about four or five places, and we left. If I hadn't spent a year in China, which was far worse (at least the bureaucrats were pleasant in Thailand), I would probably have been upset. As it was, I was just bemused. It took another 15 days get the actual permit (at a cost of $40) but at least they returned our passports, as well. Two weeks in a foreign country without passports was a bit disconcerting. For one thing, we needed them to extend our visas for the year. Laurie and I weren't supposed to work or get paid until our extensions came. In fact, it wasn't clear whether we were even in the country legally without them.

The professor from New Zealand who was sharing my office for a month was treated to a trip to the Bridge on the River Kwai one weekend. He said it was very like an Oriental Disneyland in a cemetery. He was a bit upset—said they made us act very appropriately when we visited their temples, and here they were dancing, playing, and climbing all over the tombstones of British, Australian, and New Zealand soldiers who had died there during the war. I assured him they meant no harm—just a matter of intercultural misunderstanding. When in Thailand....

In Thailand, the last weekend in July ran from Saturday to Tuesday. As nearly as I could figure, it was the beginning of what seemed to translate as Buddhist Lent. It was a time when all the monks retired to their temples and didn't come out for three months. It was supposed to be a holy-of-holies type observance. A lot of young men also tried out the monkhood during that time—some just to experience it; others to see if they might want to be monks. Some of the faculty arranged a trip to Ayutthaya, commonly called "The Old City." It was about a 2-hour train ride from Bangkok. They scheduled it for Sunday and Monday. They said not to try traveling on Saturday or Tuesday, because everybody in Thailand would be, and everything would be even more of a snarl than usual—hard to imagine.

Well, we had quite the fun-filled long weekend holiday. Cooper spent the whole four days with Chub, Oy, and their boys at their rubber plantation in the south of Thailand, swimming, riding bikes, playing, and all that stuff that 10- (almost 11-) year-old boys have fun doing. Laurie, Jessie, and I spent Saturday sort of hanging around until dinner time, when we had Vera—a German woman, married to an American, who lived in Washington, DC, and worked for the EC in Thailand—over for dinner. She was very interesting, and we had fun. Sunday we took the bus to the zoo, where we spent about four hours. In addition to looking at the animals (Jesse's favorites were the huge snakes and the ancient chimpanzee who moved only one arm, but never missed a peanut), we had lunch and rode the paddle boats. There was a big fountain in the middle of the lake, and of course Jesse insisted we go under it again and again. Although the boats had awnings over the passenger compartment, we were well soaked by the time our half hour was up. After we left the zoo, we were walking to the bus stop, when a tuk-tuk (a little, open-sided, 3-wheeled taxi) stopped, and the driver offered to take us to the shopping center near our apartment for ten baht—about one-sixth what it should have cost. We informed him that I was a professor at Chula, that we had been here a couple of months, that we knew some Thai, and that we knew he was up to something fishy. He confessed, saying that on the way, we would stop at a swanky jewelry store that catered to farangs (foreigners), where we would act like we spoke no Thai. He said we didn't have to buy anything, just "Look all the same you want to buy." We weren't really interested, and told him so, but he entreated us so winningly, finally admitting that if we would look around for twenty minutes, they would give him a $12 commission for bringing us in. He was so funny, and pleaded so insistently that we said we would do it if he would take us on to the shopping center for free. He agreed, and we went to the jewelry store, which turned out to be a lot more interesting than we expected. We didn't buy anything, but we did have fun looking.

Our entrepreneurial tuk-tuk driver, happy to take us to a pricey jewelry store.

Monday we got up early and walked over to the railroad station, where we met a couple of the faculty in my department at 8:00 for a trip to the ancient capital of Ahyutaya—about a 2-hour train ride. When we got there, we hired a pick-up with padded bench seats in the rear for about $25 for the day. We were able to squeeze in the Summer palace; a great historical museum; the old, walled part of the city; and three wats (Buddhist temples). The first contained the largest Buddha in Thailand, the second was one of the oldest in the country, and the third—which was on an island that we got to on an old cable car—was the only Gothic wat in the country—maybe the world. It looked for all the world like the protestant church you would find on the center square of any little New-England town.

The only Gothic wat in Thailand.

We took the train back to Bangkok, arriving about 8:00—quite a full day. Tuesday we got up late, had a leisurely breakfast, and took the bus over to Lumpini Park—the biggest park in Bangkok. We spent about three hours there, just playing, walking, and sitting. We walked home by way of Sam Yan market, where we stopped for lunch and to buy some peanuts and fruit. Cooper got home shortly after we did. We traded stories, had supper, and the boys went to bed early. Laurie and I spent the evening reading; then went to bed a bit early ourselves. It was amazing how much reading and talking we got done when we didn't have a television.

Chapter 3
August

Everybody in Bangkok was all atwitter about Michael Jackson coming to town August 25 for a stop on his "World Tour." There was some question about whether the National Stadium was sound enough to hold the 45,000 people they had sold tickets to. They decided it was, and the show would go on. I had seen the place, and I fully expected at least one section to collapse, killing and injuring hundreds, if not thousands.

With two months "in country" we had begun to realize the benefits of eating out, so at least two or three times a week we ate dinner at a little place near our apartment. A brother and sister had appropriated part of the alley behind their video store for a "restaurant." They had stretched tarps over part of the alley and each evening, set up four or five collapsible tables and stools under the tarp. They rolled a large cart out to the end of the alley. The cart was ingeniously constructed so that when it was unfolded, it becomes a sort of portable kitchen with a huge pot set on one gas burner, and an equally large wok set on another. Each day, they went to the market down the street and bought ingredients for that evening. The brother waited on tables and washed dishes, while the sister cooked some of the best food we'd had on those two burners. One night, as we waited for our food, a torrential downpour began, accompanied by strong, gusting wind. They had a large umbrella set up over the cooking area, but it didn't cover the cook, so the brother stood with an umbrella over his sister while she cooked. Neither it nor the tarps under which we ate kept anybody really dry. As we sat there in that alley, eating dinner, with the gusts of wind blowing rain on us, a sense of great joy overcame me. Laurie asked what I was grinning about, and I said, "This is why we're here." Cooper said, "Why, Dad, to eat under a leaky tarp in an alley in a rainstorm?" I said, "In a way, yes." It was the epitome of the experience we had come to Thailand for. Never, if we lived to be a hundred years old, would we have experienced that, or many other situations in the United States. It was not specifically to eat in an alley under a leaky tarp that we had come there, but it was to expand possibilities for our lives. I'm not sure that can make sense to someone who hasn't had some similar experience, but trust me, it's real.

The next Saturday morning at 7:30, a couple of faculty from Comm Arts picked us up at our apartment in a department van and we spent the day touring part of Thailand. First we went to a beach about an hour's

The cook at our favorite eatery, working in her alley kitchen.

drive southwest of Bangkok. It was supposed to be so thick with oysters that if we poked a stick into the sand, oysters would pop up around it. "Supposed to," because our driver miscalculated the time; when we got there the tide was in—no beach at all. A very pretty scene, looking out over the ocean, though. We planned to come back later, when the tide was out, but there just weren't enough hours in the day. We never did get back there. Next we drove about 40 km west to a big lake with a network of canals around it on which operated a huge floating market. We paid 300 baht ($12) for a woman to paddle us around the canals for an hour in a narrow, flat-bottomed punt. Actually we didn't pay for anything but souvenirs all day. The whole thing was paid for from a departmental budget for that purpose. There were many tourists milling about, but the faculty with us were Thai, so we got special treatment. The woman took us up a series of little side canals that we had almost to ourselves. We stopped at a boat on which another woman had set up a little noodle restaurant and got our lunch, which we ate while cruising around the canals. We returned our dishes on the way back. The only time we got out of our boat was to visit a place where they boiled coconut flowers down very much like maple sugar. We bought a bag of yummy candy made that way—so sweet it made our mouths ache.

After the floating market, we stopped at King Rama II Park, a very pretty provincial park, the main attraction of which was a replica of King Rama II's home, of wood, in the traditional Thai style. We had it almost completely to ourselves, and it was wonderful to stroll around

The floating market at Rajchaburi.

imagining ourselves as members of the King's family. Our final stop was in a small town that was the site of a wat that was both the oldest (although rebuilt several times, so it didn't look old) and the largest in the country. It was truly awe-inspiring. My favorite part was a wonderful, secluded garden with huge trees, flowers, fountains, grottos, and even a couple of small caves. There, as everywhere we went, the Thais were enamored of Jesse's boundless energy. They said, "He's a naughty boy," but they loved it. He must have been the most-photographed farang in the country. I felt kind of sorry for Cooper—he was always very well-behaved, and what did it get him—ignored, basically. We got home about 6:00, had some noodles at a stand across the street, and relaxed for the evening. Sunday afternoon, we went to a play presented by the students of the Faculty of Communication Arts—my department. It was in Thai (naturally), but we certainly picked up most of what was going on. Basically it was a comedy about a young guy trying to become a singing star. It was really quite good, although Thai drama was acted in a much less subtle style than we were used to in American theatre— more like Chinese opera without the music, or even the old vaudeville slapstick. As part of the plot, several rock songs were performed—the boys' favorite parts. It did get a touch long: about three hours overall. They were sponsored by several companies, including Xerox, Levis, and Close-up Toothpaste, so the quality of the tickets, programs, and sets were very professional. The acting and directing seemed quite good, but again, it was hard for us to tell, given the unfamiliar style.

Well, it finally happened. It was bound to with traffic as crazy as it was. Jesse and I were hit by a car on the way to school. Neither of us was badly hurt: Jesse a bit of a scuff on one knee, and me a bit of a kink in my lower back. We were crossing the second of two busy streets to get to school. It was clear both left and right, but as we started across, a guy pulled out of the gate of the campus directly across the street from us. I was holding Jesse's hand; he was sort of dragging along, as usual. I was looking to my left to make sure we would get across before any cars got to us. The guy in the car was looking over his shoulder to make sure he would be able to get out into the stream of traffic. We both turned back at the same instant he reached us. I was almost clear of him, but my reflex action, when I saw he was going to hit Jesse was to turn back and put both my hands on his hood to try and stop him—fat chance. Luckily, he was going very slowly, and slammed his brakes on quickly. The force of the car, as I was off balance, anyway, lifted me off my feet and pushed me back a few feet. He hit Jesse on the right knee with his bumper (resulting in the scuff), and knocked him back about four feet and to the ground. Cooper was further back, so he wasn't involved. My immediate reaction was fear and anger, and I glared at the guy through his windshield for a second before going to pick Jesse up and carry him into the campus. I sat him down and checked his knee; then had him stand and make sure it worked OK. By the time the guy got to us, it was clear Jesse wasn't hurt. The poor guy was terrified. He left his car in the middle of the street with the door open—it's a wonder it wasn't smashed by the time he got back. He was just a young guy—maybe 26 or 27. His face was all white and he was shaking. He kept offering to take us to the hospital, and telling everyone how sorry he was. I was sure the fact that we were farangs had a lot to do with how upset he was. I felt really sorry for him, though. Given time to think about it, I realized it wasn't really his fault—just a case of bad timing; a true accident. I assured him over and over that it was OK, that we would be all right, that we weren't angry. He gave me his card and said if anything was wrong to call him. I did call him a couple of hours later, just to reassure him that there was no problem. He offered to come to our home to apologize again, but I assured him that wasn't necessary. He was clearly more affected by the whole thing than either of us. At least both Jesse and Cooper were much more careful when crossing the streets after that. Maybe it was a blessing in disguise.

That Friday, we were taken out to dinner by a woman who taught at the boys' school and her husband, who was on the faculty of Open University in Bangkok. They had a boy Cooper's age and a girl Jesse's.

They were all really nice, and we got along very well. The food was great. The next day after lunch, we were walking around the neighborhood, and just happened to run into them again. They were on their way to lunch and then to Central Department Store—a huge Japanese store. They invited us along, and when we told them we had just eaten, insisted we come with them and at least have dessert. So we rode with them (in their Mercedes) to the restaurant (which turned out to be in the department store). After we ate (them lunch; us dessert), we spent a couple of hours window shopping (mostly in the bookstore); then said goodbye and walked the mile or so back to our apartment, arriving just in time for the party.

August 12 was the Queen's birthday, so it was a holiday for everybody. The bad news was that as it was her 61st birthday (not an even ten, or "cycle" as the Thais called it) so there were no fireworks. The good news: it was also Sammy's birthday—the man who owned our apartment building. So he had a whopping big party—complete with food, drink, games; the works. Both Jesse and Cooper won prizes—Jesse a little stuffed dog that squeaked when squeezed, and Cooper a flashy t-shirt. Needless to say, both were quite happy. It was hard to tear them away to bed at 9:00, as the Thais let their children stay up 'till all hours ("But, Dad, they get to, why can't we?). A good time was had by all, and we got to meet some people who lived in our building whom we never saw otherwise (with everyone's busy schedules) except coming and going.

Saturday one of my students invited Cooper and Jesse to go see "Jurassic Park" with her. She didn't have to ask twice. As it was only about $1.60 for a ticket, we said OK. Laurie and I took advantage of the lull to have a nice lunch together at a local noodle stand, then relaxed for a couple of hours and read. We spent the evening together, and slept in Sunday morning. We had been looking for a satisfactory place for church, but everything was either in Thai, very fundamentalist, or three-hour services, which we just couldn't see trying with Jesse. We had a couple of children's inspirational tapes that we played for the boys, but we had to start holding family church—not really what we preferred, but better than nothing.

Sunday afternoon, we met Chub, Oy, and their boys for a picnic in the city park. We brought potato salad, fruit, and ham sandwiches. They brought fried chicken, Pepsi, and dessert (fried bananas and some sort of sweet balls rolled in roasted coconut, which we ate with lettuce and chili peppers (strange, but tasty). While we ate, we watched a sporting event nearby. Eight guys stood in a circle about 15 feet in diameter, and hit a ball woven from bamboo, and about half the size of a volleyball, into the air. About 20 feet up, over the center of the circle, was a net that looked sort of like three basketball hoops turned up on edge and hooked together so that standing under them, they formed a triangle. A net bag hung under the whole affair. The idea was for the members of the team to keep the ball in the air, hitting it with anything but their hands, and to try to put it through one of the three hoops into the net. They wore pads on their foreheads, and getting it in with their heads must have been easiest, because they were only allowed to do that one time apiece. When each guy got it in using his head, he had to remove his head pad, and had to use only elbows, knees, shoulders, and feet after that. They got points each time the ball went into the net, and the number of points (from 10 to 15) depended on how fancy the hit was that put it there. They had 40 minutes to accumulate score, then after a short break, another team started. Three teams played while we were there, the highest score being 462; the lowest 214.

After our picnic (which ended just in time, as we no sooner got in their car than it began to pour) we went to what the Thais called a fair—a kind of exposition of Thai-made products, all of which were for sale at reduced prices. Evidence of the increasing disposable income there were the hoards of people that rushed to spend money at such fairs—or anywhere goods were for sale, for that matter. Laurie said that every Monday, women asked her where she shopped that weekend. They thought it strange when she told them we didn't spend our weekends shopping. After the fair, we took the scenic route home—scenic because workers had strung hundreds of thousands of lights, in myriads of colors and displays, along the main streets surrounding the castle, in honor of the queen's birthday. It made any Christmas display I'd seen in the States pale by comparison. We got home about 9:15, so put the boys immediately to bed, and struggled to get them up for school at 6:30 the next morning.

The middle of August, I started teaching at Bangkok University: Interpersonal Communication, from 6:00 to 9:00pm. Traffic was terrible; especially during rush hour, so I left at 4:00pm—plenty of time to ride a bus the 10 km to BU, have dinner there, pick up the material I had left to be photocopied for my class, and get to class early. I caught a bus about two blocks from my office—and sat for 15 minutes waiting to get through the first intersection. The bus quickly became packed, and it began to pour, so we had to close all the windows. It became stifling, and everyone was soon dripping sweat. I finally decided the only way I was going to make it on time was to walk the final two km. The rain had eased up to a steady drizzle and I arrived (only moderately damp) at 5:45—fifteen minutes to eat, pick up my copies, and find the room I would teach in. I grabbed a couple of chicken legs and an iced coffee in the first floor cafeteria, climbed the stairs (no elevator) to the third floor to get my copies, then on up to the fourth floor to the room they told me I would teach in—it didn't exist. Back down to the office to find out why. They had given me the wrong room number. I got the right number and climbed back upstairs. By that time, I was pretty soggy from a combination of rain and sweat, but I did get there just in time (thank goodness the room was air conditioned, or I wouldn't have made it through the evening). Two students were there. While the other 10 straggled in during the next 15 minutes, I ate my dinner and waited. I knew it was common for Thais to be casual about getting anywhere on time, but it was still frustrating to bust butt like that; then have students come when they felt like it. I told them I'd really like to try and start on time; that if we did, I'd try to make sure we ended by 9:00; but if we didn't, I wouldn't feel bad about keeping them as long after 9:00 as we started late. I think they got the message, but traditionally Thai classes sort of started whenever—often the professors straggled in 15 or 20 minutes late, as well. As it was the first class (traditionally reserved for administrative details, rather than a "real" class) we finished by 8:15. I expected, that late, to have no trouble with crowded busses or traffic, but I was wrong. I stood about half of the way back, and didn't get home until 9:45. I slept soundly, anyway, and I just kept reminding myself how much they were paying me—I was getting almost as much for one 3-hour class a week as I did full-time at Chula. Besides, it was nice to have such a small class of grad students for a change.

Our visas were going to run out on the 29th, but nobody seemed worried about it except us. To get them renewed, we needed 1) our passports, 2) 3,000 baht ($120), 3) two photos of each of us, 4) a letter from the manager of our apartments saying we really lived there, and 5) a letter from the administration at Chula saying I really worked there. I had collected all but the last, which they kept saying I'd get "tomorrow." When I finally did get it, and took everything to the the proper office, they told me we needed birth certificates for the boys and our marriage certificate, as though we carried them with us when we travelled. I told them we had to provide them to get our passports in the first place. They relented, and insisted on only the passports, the money, the photos, and the letters.

We had a relaxing weekend for a change. Saturday mid-day, we took a bus to the east side of town to check out a new park the queen had built there. The park was very nice, with a pretty lake and a couple of very nice playgrounds for the boys. It wasn't nearly as crowded as most Bangkok parks on weekends. Because it was fairly new, however, the trees were all small, and so shade was at a premium. Luckily, Saturday was cloudy and not too hot. The park was in a real swanky area where most of the expatriate Westerners and many wealthy Thais lived, so we strolled and looked at how the other half (or in that case, about one-hundredth) lived. There were some very ritzy places: swimming pools, tennis courts, three-Mercedes garages, etc. Made us feel a real part of the majority lower class.

Jesse and I stopped by the National Stadium on our way to school Monday morning. They had the stage, lights, screen, and speakers up for the Michael Jackson concerts Tuesday and Wednesday. Judging from the size of the speakers, we weren't going to have any trouble hearing him from our apartment five blocks away—in fact they would probably hear him at the airport 20 km away. In addition to the hundreds of posters of The Michael adorning the city, his photo was on the front pages of all the newspapers Monday morning, running around seeing Bangkok and being seen by Bangkokians over the weekend.

When I arrived at the universityTuesday morning, I (as well as everyone else in the Mass Comm department) was faced with a strange sight. The man who started the Faculty of Communication Arts way back when, had died recently, so the alumni decided to erect a monument in his memory. They had finished it over the weekend, and had the official ceremony Monday morning. It was awful: a three-story tall, blue-and-white, metal pencil perched on a concrete eraser in front of the Mass Communication building, complete with a clock and speakers for piped-in music and announcements. It was hard to tell who hated it most—the faculty or the students. To make matters worse, they had ripped some beautiful flowering ivy off the wall behind it to make it stand out more, and cut down three nice trees in front of it so we could see it better (as if anybody wanted to). The students put up protest signs, saying they preferred the ivy and the trees, and because they said the pencil was befitting of a kindergarten, they brought in a set of teeter-totters to place in front of it.

The teachers asked parents to take their children home early, to avoid the crush of people waiting to get into The Michael's show. Both were sold out—about 40,000 people at each, with tickets ranging from $50 to $100. As expected, Monday's concert was an incredible hassle for us residents—traffic snarles, security, and all. We had to detour around the area when we walked home from school. Also as ex-

*The monument (of questionable taste) in memory of the
founder of the Mass Comm Department.*

pected, we had no choice but to hear the concert at full volume in our apartment. To our relief though, for only one night. The Michael just couldn't handle concerts two nights in a row—he called in sick. He was getting a million bucks a show; 40,000 people (some of whom had flown from Japan and other surrounding countries and had reservations to fly back on Wednesday) had paid $50 to $100 each, and had been waiting at least four hours in a torrential downpour to see him; 2,000 cops and army personnel had to be kept on standby a couple of extra days; people had driven hours through unbearable traffic; other events had to be cancelled; and he was screwing up every imaginable schedule in a huge city; but he didn't feel good. But at least the stadium didn't collapse, and there weren't any riots in which people were injured.

The end of August we went with the second grade teachers from

Two of hundreds of posters advertising The Michael's stop in Bangkok on his "World Tour."

Cooper and Jesse's school to Hua Hin, an ocean resort town, for the weekend. The teachers were having a curriculum development retreat, and they invited us along to reward Laurie for the time she was spending teaching English to their students. The school paid for all our expenses. Hua Hin was a busy resort town, mostly for wealthy Thai people from Bangkok, many of whom had weekend condos there. Our hotel was small (probably 40 rooms), but very nice (Hilton quality). The rooms were normally about $60 a night, but the school had a "special relation-ship," so they paid only about $35. They told us if we ever wanted to go back, to let them know, and they would make the reservations at that price. It was really very nice: right on the ocean (private beach, so not at all crowded), nice swimming pool, snooker room, nice dining room, etc. We left Bangkok in air-conditioned vans about 7:30 a.m. on Saturday, and arrived there about 10:30. We went down to the beach and swam and collected shells until lunch at noon. After lunch, the teachers had to work, but the principal took us on a tour of the local sights for a couple of hours. When we returned, we spent the rest of the afternoon in the pool. After dinner, we went back down to the beach and picked up more shells. By that time, Jesse, Laurie, and Cooper had about 50 shells each. I said I thought we could take about five apiece back. I didn't count, but it looked more like 15 apiece when we got home (but small ones, as Jesse quickly pointed out). Breakfast was at 7:00 the next morning. We spent most of the morning in the pool. After lunch, we checked out and headed home, with detours to stop at a Thai cotton fabric outlet famous for its Southern Thai patterns (we bought nothing), and a bakery famous for various Thai baked desserts (we bought samples of several). All of the teachers bought virtually tons, and passed everything out all the way back to Bangkok. We sampled dozens of baked goods. Some we didn't particularly care for, but most were quite good. One was little balls, about an inch in diameter, made of flour, crushed nuts, sugar, etc; covered in shaved, toasted coconut. I popped one into my mouth, and was rewarded by a rush of sweetness—followed by a distinct (though not unpleasant) burning from the crushed chili peppers mixed in with the crushed nuts. It took some getting used to, as we just didn't usually think of candy as being hot. It was quite a bit like those hot cinnamon candies, although coconut, rather than cinnamon. We got back home about 5:00 Sunday afternoon—tired and sunburned, but happy. We noticed the next morning that almost all the second grade teachers were late for school.

Chapter 4
September

Although August 31 was Cooper's 11th birthday, we celebrated it Saturday with a party, presents, and his choice of where to go for lunch. He chose Pizza Hut. It was our first time there since coming to Thailand. Jesse had chosen McDonalds for his birthday in July. I had to admit, it was kind of fun to go Western once a month or so. That's not nearly as often as most of our Thai friends. When they took us out to dinner, we had to tell them that we really would rather eat at Thai restaurants. Cooper was so well-behaved that all his teachers really liked him. Consequently, he got several presents from them. Of course Jesse was envious, and was a terror all day. Number one on Cooper's wish list was Michael Jackson's "Dangerous" tape, so we felt compelled to have it among his presents, despite the fact that it was almost certainly the start of (between the two of them) about a decade of having to listen to whatever was new in rock music. Oh well, I guess they'd spent about that much time listening to my music.

Cooper celebrating his birthday with friends from school.

One evening, just after dinner, I got a terrible toothache. It was one of those where you'd rather die than have it go on overnight. Just across the street from our apartment was a "dental clinic." It was open until 8:30, so I went over there. Nobody spoke English, so I mimed "toothache" to the old Chinese dentist. He sat me in his chair and prodded in the area I indicated. When he tapped on a tooth and I muffled a scream, he said, "Aaaahhhhh!" He rubbed some clove oil on the gum around that tooth, called his daughter (who looked about 12) to assist him, set out some instruments, and started drilling. Ever had a root canal done without novocaine? I'll tell you, I knew there was somebody there. After he had the old nerve completely cleaned out and the hole filled, he dug under the gum around the tooth with all manner of instruments. Through sign language, he let me know that it was infected, and he had to get it cleaned out. I think he got all the infection and part of the jawbone. He gave me three different kind of pills and told me to take one of each at mealtimes. Then he charged me the equivalent of $20 dollars, told me to come back in two days for a checkup, and sent me home. Where he dug around in the gums was a little sore the next morning, but other than that, it was fine. It certainly beat the ache that was there the night before.

We started home schooling the boys in September. Although attending a Thai school was fine for math, Thai, learning the customs, and making friends, it wouldn't have done much to help the boys pass their competency tests in American history, science, and English when we returned to the States. So, before we left, Laurie had gotten all the books they would be using in their school back home, and we started working with them to make sure they wouldn't miss anything while we were gone for the year. I had them for social studies and reading on Tuesday and Thursday evenings, and Laurie had them for English and science on Monday and Wednesday evenings. They got Friday evenings off, and we both worked with them on Saturday morning. If they got everything done for the week, they got Sunday mornings off. Sort of filled up our already pretty-busy schedule. I was a bit surprised at how well they took it—especially Jesse. I assumed they just weren't challenged enough at school, and welcomed a chance for some real schoolwork.

Friday I spent most of the day in a seminar on Native American literature. A guy named Lance Henson, a Cherokee from Oklahoma who seemed to travel around a lot giving lectures on Native American issues, was the primary presenter. He was very good. Just political enough to keep the representative from the U. S. Information Service antsy, but not enough to really upset anyone. The Thais were quite sensitive to such tensions, so it didn't take much.

Faculty attending a seminar on Native American Literature.

Saturday we took a boat to Ayhuttaya, the old capital of Thailand (or Siam as it was known then). Actually, we took the boat to the summer palace, which was just outside Ayhuttaya. It was about a 2 1/2 hour boat ride up the Chau Phrya, the main river in Thailand. A fascinating ride, with great scenery, shifting from city high-rises, to suburban sprawl, to country life. The castle was nice, but not really worth the $2 they charged farangs to get in. That was one of my pet peeves, by the way: having to pay farang gate charges. I was working for the year as a professor in a Thai university, making Thai wages; I should have payed the same as Thais to get into things. Oh well, "mai phen lai," as the Thais said: "never mind." If I had spent enough time in Southeast Asia, I probably would have become a patient person (say another decade). It was the boat trip, however, that was really fine; especially the last half hour, when it poured rain of monsoon quality. Almost everyone went inside, but Cooper, Jesse, and I, as well as a young man from Holland, stayed on the top deck, protected by a canvas awning without sides. With the wind whipping around, we got pretty wet, but it was easy to see the attraction the sea used to have for young men. I felt like Cap'n Ahab or somebody, and it was all I could do to keep myself from bellowing, "Thar she blows!" Everyone thought we were pretty strange already, though, and I was afraid such an outburst would have made me certifiable.

We didn't have much of an insect problem. Mosquitos were surprisingly scarce. The ones we had were nasty, though—actually one type was. One type was big, very slow, and easy to snatch out of the air. The other was very small, silent (no whine to give them away), and could chew on us in about four places before we realized they were even there. What we did have were hoards of teeny little ants that got into everything that wasn't securely closed, and gigantic cockroaches—as in 2-3 inches long. The best thing I could say about them is they were the clumsiest cockroaches I'd ever seen. They'd get to running and trip over their own feet, ending up on their backs. They couldn't turn over by themselves, and expired within about eight hours. Sometimes we'd come home after being at school all day and find ten or twelve corpses throughout the apartment. They seemed to come in cycles. Most days there were only two or three.

Cooper got sick and went home from school early Monday. Laurie said he upchucked four times during the 30-minute walk home. Of course the next morning on the walk to school, Jesse had to point out all four places to me. When I got home from Bangkok U at 10:15, Cooper was half asleep, hanging off the edge of the bed, with his head draped over the barf bucket. Some kind of stomach flu, I guess. With the re-

A couple of "cowboys" at "The Western Hollywood Stunt Show."

silience of youth, he was OK the next day, except for a tender stomach. He went to school Tuesday and Wednesday, and then played hookey Thursday and Friday to go with our Thai friends to Pataya, a beach town near Bangkok. Chub had a conference there all week; Oy and the boys took Cooper when they went down to join him on Thursday. Jesse and Laurie spent Friday with the Satit Chula kindergarteners at Safari World and The Western Hollywood Stunt Show.

We'd have had to give our first-born child for a jar of pickles in Bangkok, so we bought some small cucumbers at the market and made three jars of dill pickles Saturday morning—just like "Little House on the Prairie." Then Laurie, Jesse, and I (Cooper was still at the beach with our friends) walked to Sam Yan market to buy peanuts so we could make peanut butter (same recipe as in China five years before), and a pot so we could make chili. While we were on our way home, it began a torrential downpour. Luckily, we were only a few steps from the Comm Arts cafeteria, so we stopped for lunch. After lunch, it was still pouring, so we spent about a half hour in my office, reading and playing computer games. Laurie and Jesse really enjoyed Safari World yesterday. I asked Jesse if any dinosaurs attacked them, and he said they didn't have any, but a giraffe put its face right up to the window next to him.

We were into finals the end of September, with a three-week break between terms beginning October 9. I walked to the train station and bought round-trip tickets to Chiang Mai, the end of the rail line in the north, near the border with Mianmar. The Thais, incidentally, refused to call it that—it was still Burma, as far as they were concerned, and there was no love lost between the citizens of the two countries. There was a long history of aggression by the Burmese against Thailand. I got second class, air conditioned, sleeper tickets for all four of us for about $135 round trip.

That Monday, I got knocked down by a bus on my way to teach at Bangkok U. When the bus stopped, a bunch of people rushed to get on, and I brought up the rear. As I started to get on, a woman who had been trapped inside by the rush tried to get off. I was hanging on to the railing in the doorway, and stepped back down to let her off. As I did so, the driver took off (they sometimes didn't even come to a full stop if there weren't a lot of people getting on or off). Well, I was half in and half out, so the edge of the doorway caught me on the shoulder and knocked me flat on the sidewalk (Luckily he hadn't stopped out in traffic as they often did). The people in the bus and those at the bus stop all started shouting at the driver, and he stopped. I got up, dusted myself off, and climbed on. He wouldn't look at me in his mirror, so after a while, I stopped trying to glare at him and just sat down. Other than a little scrape on my shin, and another on one of my knuckles, I didn't seem any the worse for wear the next day.

Neither Cooper nor I felt real great the next weekend. I wasn't sure whether it was a reaction to the malaria medicine we were taking in preparation for our travels, or some flu bug that was going around, but we both had general aches and lack of energy. At any rate, we took it pretty easy over the weekend. Saturday we went grocery shopping. That meant going to the nearby street market for veggies, meat, eggs, fruit, and staples; then walking about a half-mile to Mahboonkrong Department Store. The prices there were about the same as back home (except for imported stuff, which was very expensive—cheese, for example was about $4 for eight ounces), but much higher than the street market. We got stuff there we couldn't get at the market, such as jelly, yoghurt, butter (cheaper than margarine), bread, and honey syrup (maple syrup was too expensive). We bought good, lean beef and pork, and ground it ourselves for hamburger and sausage. The water in Bangkok was not potable, so everyone had to either boil their water or buy bottled water. Although water was cheaper at the department store than other places, we usually chose to buy it at a little convenience store just around the corner from our apartment, rather than carry it the half-mile home. We paid about a dollar for six 1-liter bottles (which we used at the rate of about two bottles a day). That was only about a dime more than we would pay at the supermarket, and it was worth that not to have to lug it home (or listen to Cooper bitch about lugging it, which was even worse). The pickles that we had made the weekend before (and agreed to let age for three weeks) made it three days before we "just tested" the first jar. We decided they were great—plenty aged—so we were on jar number two the next day.

After doing home schooling most of the morning, and reading and playing games most of the afternoon the next Saturday, we all needed to get out of the apartment, so we caught a number 15 bus to Lumpini Park, which was a very nice, but heavily-used city park about five miles from home. There, we watched while the boys played in the playground, walked around and enjoyed the (relatively) cool evening, and spent a half-hour killing our legs on the paddle boats. There was a small lake in the middle of the park where, for 80 cents each, we could rent paddle boats for a half-hour. We got home about 6:30, had ham sandwiches (at $3 a pound, our treat for the week), read for a while, and went to bed early. Sunday we hung around home, doing cleaning, laundry, and the like most of the day. One of Jesse's teachers came over for dinner to celebrate her 45th (Laurie guessed 27th; I guessed 34th; she loved us both) birthday. At her request, I made meatloaf, mashed potatoes, and salad—no small feat with one electric wok and one hotplate and skillet. The boys had gotten her a handkerchief (in a bright whale, tiger, giraffe, elephant, etc. pattern; Jesse's choice, as he said he knew she loved animals), and a small picture frame with photos of Cooper and Jesse. She was single, lived by herself, was very quiet, and was going into the hospital for an eye operation the next week, so I think it really meant a lot to her. She wasn't able to watch TV for at least two months, so she insisted we borrow hers in the meantime. So, we could watch our choice of five channels, none of which we could understand a word—with the exception of the news in English from 6 to 6:30 a.m.

Chapter 5
October

Midterms were over on October 8, and our 3-week travel break began. We caught the overnight sleeper to Chiang Mai at about 7:00. In the Chiang Mai station the next morning, we were besieged by taxi and tuk-tuk drivers—as farangs always were. They saw us (generally rightly so) as easy money. Drivers always asked about twice what a trip was worth, and farangs who didn't know better paid up. Those who had been in the country a while (especially if they knew some Thai) rode for about the same price as Thais. Tuk-tuks, the small, three-wheeled taxis, were named for the distinctive sound they made when running: "tuk-tuk-tuk-tuk." They generally cost much less than regular car taxis. Regular motorcycles were even less, but only people with a death wish paid to ride them. Anyway, we were besieged by taxi and tuk-tuk drivers. We were very lucky, and chose an older man who turned out to be wonderful. He was kind and gentle; a good driver (many weren't—some had bought their licenses), with a great sense of humor. He liked the boys as much as they liked him. He offered his services to show us the sights in and around Chiang Mai for 300 baht (about $12) a day—8 a.m. to 6 p.m. It was a great deal, so we used him three of the four days we were there. A friend had arranged for us to stay at the Mineral Resources Ministry guest house for free. It was very basic: two bedrooms and a bath. One of the bedrooms had an ancient air conditioner that worked, but sounded like it would shudder to a stop at any second. There was no water one day, and the beds were super hard, but it was sure worth the price.

The first day, we took a bus into town and spent the afternoon just walking around looking at the sights, and visiting the local Tourist Authority of Thailand office for maps and descriptions of what we should see in the area. The morning of the second day, our driver took us to see elephants working, to a national park with a series of ten beautiful waterfalls, to an orchid farm, and to a butterfly farm—where they also raised scorpions (Jesse's favorite), which they dipped in gold and sold as jewelry. That afternoon, he took us to factories where we watched them carve teak and rosewood furniture, produce leather goods, make ceramic pieces, and build and paint silk and paper umbrellas. The second day, we went to the most impressive wat in the area, which we got to by riding in the back of a pickup up a mountain, taking a cable car up a cliff, and walking the last 350 steps—but it was worth it. Then we spent most of the afternoon at the zoo, and visited the university's museum on the hill tribe cultures. There were about 15 or 20 distinct tribes in the hills of northern Thailand. They ranged in size from a couple of hundred to tens of thousands of people. We took a small cooler, and a backpack of food for breakfasts and meals on trains and buses, but for lunches and dinners, we sampled the various regional specialities. Basically, I loved Thai food (including the very hot dishes), Laurie liked most of it, but not the really hot stuff. Cooper liked some dishes, and Jesse had a few dishes he would eat—none spicy. The Thais ate the same thing for breakfast as they did for other meals, and the boys just couldn't handle that, so we had Western breakfasts—which translated to yoghurt, fruit, and peanut butter and jelly sandwiches when we were traveling.

We took a regular bus to Chiang Rai on Tuesday, Oct 12, arriving there late morning. We found a mid-range hotel for 500 baht (about $20 for air-con, private bath, and hot water), and walked around town for a while, just to get our bearings. Then we hired a tuk-tuk to take us around to see the sights (mostly wats) the rest of the afternoon. We asked what else there was, and he said "nothing." We had planned to stay until the next afternoon, so weren't sure what to do the next morning. Laurie had picked up a brochure for a tour service at the bus station, and one of their morning tours looked interesting: a boat trip on the river, visit to a Karen (hill tribe) village, and elephant ride—back by noon. We had always avoided tours because they were too polished and inflexible (pick you up in their fancy white van and herd you around, hollering at you through a bullhorn), but we decided to at least check on the price. The "agency" turned out to be a little one-woman, store-front operation—anything but polished. She had a sister who was a student at Chula (she said), so she gave us a special (she said) price: 1500 baht for the whole family (about $60). Fifteen bucks apiece seemed pretty reasonable, so we went with it. She said she'd pick us up in front of our hotel at 8:30 the next morning. She arrived in a tuk-tuk, took us to her office, where she got off and and a little old emaciated guy (who turned out to be our English-speaking guide) got on. He took us to the river where our boat awaited. It was just the four of us, our guide, the boat driver, and his little boy in the boat. It was an old "long-tailed" boat, badly in need of a coat of paint. Long-tailed boats were so named because they had a four- or six-cylinder auto engine mounted at about a thirty-degree angle on the stern, with the drive shaft entering the water about fifteen feet behind the boat, and the propeller on the end of it. They were quite powerful, and could really scat—the boys loved it (me too). The guide began a standard recitation about the nature of the Thai language until Cooper and Jesse began to talk Thai to him. Then he said something the the effect that we were clearly not unschooled tourists, loosened up, and we all had a great time. It turned out he was the guide for the author of our guidebook when he went to the north, and he showed us his name in the acknowledgements.

Jesse helping bring our long-tailed boat into the dock.

The engine on our boat conked out three times on the way upriver, and once on the way back—not too polished for us. We traveled about a half-hour (not counting engine repair time) up the Mei Kok River (a main tributary of the Mei Kong) to a Karen village. By the time we got there, all the other tourists had come and gone, so we had the place pretty much to ourselves. It wasn't exactly pristine. Many of the houses had been converted into shops, selling local crafts. They were of high quality and quite reasonably priced, though, so we bought several souvenirs. Also, our guide took us on a little hike off the main street, so we got to see the part of the community "less traveled," as it were. We had lunch at a little place with a porch that overhung (and looked as though it would fall into at any minute) the river. After lunch we took a short elephant ride around the area (short in distance; not time—those suckers were slow), and returned by boat to town.

Children playing, still in traditional dress, after the tourists have taken their posed photos and left.

Because of the breakdowns, we were a couple of hours late getting back, and had missed the bus back to Chiang Mai. No problem. Unlike in the States, most such things were very flexible. They just gave us tickets on the next available bus and called it even. It was a very nice air-con bus, but about halfway back, in the mountains, I noticed it began making noises uncharacteristic of a healthy bus (or a healthy anything, for that matter). They weren't loud, and nobody else seemed to notice, but I told Cooper I'd be surprised if it made it all the way back. I wish I had been wrong, but about a half hour out of Chiang Mai, it quit. The good thing about an air-con bus is that it is cool when the air-con is on; the bad thing is that if the air-con goes off, you can't open the windows, and it gets real stuffy, real fast. We all climbed off and waited beside the road while they tried to fix the bus. When it became clear that wasn't going to happen any time soon, people began getting their own rides the rest of the way—some flagged down cars, some paid taxis, some caught local buses. We waited. There were Chiang Rai to Chiang Mai buses every half hour—air-con on the hour; regular on the half hour. So after about a half hour, the regular bus stopped and picked up those of us who were still waiting. It was old, hot, rickety, and noisy, but it offered one advantage our new air-con bus didn't: it ran. By the time we got back to our guest house quarters in Chiang Mai, the water was back on, and even fairly warm, as the tank had been in the sun all afternoon, so we took warm showers before supper and bed.

Thursday was only a partial day in Chiang Mai, as I had booked us on the overnight sleeper to Bangkok, which left Chiang Mai at 4:30pm. When our driver picked us up at 8 a.m., he had a mystery package, about the size of a clock radio encased in styrofoam. He took us about 25 km out into the country, where we drove thousands of feet up a precipitous mountain road, and walked up 385 steps to the mouth of a cave. We then walked another 185 steps down into the cave. It was a natural limestone cave that had been made into a wat, complete with a huge reclining Buddha that had to have been built there, because there's no way they could have gotten it in—the tunnel in was small enough that we had to bend double a couple of times to get through. After the cave, he took us to a beautiful park where we learned the contents of the mystery package. The park was a hot springs site, and the driver had brought half-a-dozen eggs for us to cook in the springs. They were supposed to cook in seven minutes, but the springs must have been off their feed, because it took more like a half hour. We didn't mind, because that gave us time to wander around the lush grounds and see the geysers.

When we got back to town, we stopped at a cotton weaving factory, then dropped Laurie and the boys at a native crafts shop for souvenir shopping, while I picked up our luggage at the guest house and replenished our food supplies at the local market. We got to the train station in plenty of time, and were on our way home to Bangkok. We got in at 6 a.m., and spent the day washing clothes and resting up for the next leg of our journey.

Back in the middle of September, several Thai friends had talked about taking us various places during break. The Thais seldom followed through on such offers, however, even when we made it very clear that we'd like nothing better (sort of like "Let's do lunch sometime."). We had to stay open to the possibility, however, as it would have been a grave insult if someone followed through and we then said we couldn't do it—even if they waited until the last minute to get back to us with definite plans. In fact one of our friends did approach us on the day we left for Chiang Mai, wondering when we would like to travel to Trat Province, on the Eastern border.

We had left some time after our return from the North for just such an eventuality, so on the 16th she drove us to Klong Yai, a small town near the eastern end of Trat Province, where her older brother lived. He was the Agricultural Extension agent for the province, and as such, quite an important man. We stayed the afternoon and night in his house; only a year old, and quite nice—with much beautiful carved wood. The next morning, he took us to a tiny fishing village all the way at the eastern end of Thailand, where a power boat waited to take us out to one of the many islands in the area. The island we visited was Ko Kong, where his brother-in-law had a resort. Not a fancy, posh resort, but more of the cabin-on-the-beach type. It was very nice, though. Laurie, Cooper, Jesse, and I had a cabin built on stilts over the river— sitting room, two bedrooms, and bath; fan-cooled. The main dining area for the resort was built out over the river as well, and had open sides—great atmosphere, with the fishing boats putting by as we were served a lunch of the best seafood we had ever eaten.

Twenty minutes after we arrived, we were all sitting in that dining area having drinks, when someone asked how we liked Cambodia. I replied that we hadn't been to Cambodia. They laughed and said, "No, you are in Cambodia now." And I had left my visa in my Sunday pants. Turned out Thais didn't need a visa for Cambodia, and didn't realize we did; we knew we needed a visa for Cambodia, but didn't know that's where we were going. It didn't seem to bother anybody else, so Laurie and I tried not to let it bother us either. That afternoon, our host suggested we all pile into the boat and visit the (Cambodian) mainland. "Sure," we said ("Might as well be hung for a horse as a colt," I always say). The Cambodians were too busy just getting by to care anything about us. It was as close to anarchy as I'd ever seen. There didn't seem to be any government: no police; the few soldiers we saw were in partial uniform and didn't seem to have any leadership; all the official buildings, including schools and army quarters, seemed to be padlocked; many of the cars had no license plates; nobody seemed to be taking care of public roads, grounds, buildings, or facilities. Not a very nice place to visit, but I certainly wouldn't want to have lived there.

Monday morning, we drove back to Bangkok, with a detour to visit "Oasis Sea World." It was fun in a quaint, campy sort of way, but Shamu it wasn't. The show consisted of about 15 bottle-nose and half a dozen of what Jesse termed "no-nose" dolphins. I don't know what they were; they looked like miniature whales: about four feet long and black. They sure could squirt water from their mouths, though. One of the acts consisted of them squirting their trainer on cue, and then turning on the audience, scattering them, screeching. Guess what Jesse and Cooper's favorite part of the show was. It was fun, but when we finally pulled into Bangkok at 10:30 that night, I think everyone (all of the adults, anyway) sort of wished we had skipped it and opted for an earlier ETA. We spent two days in Bangkok, so I could grade midterms from my graduate class at Bangkok University, which had been proctored in my absence; then delivered to my office at Chula. A note of explanation about schedules: Most universities (including the undergrad classes at BU) were on a schedule that put first semester from June through September, and second semester from November through February, with finals and semester break in October. BU's grad classes, however (to coincide with those in the States), ran from August through November and January through April. So, my semester break at Chula coincided with my midterm break at BU, and vice-versa. Anyway, I graded exams for two days, and we set out for the Northeast on the morning of the twenty-first.

Cooper watching as our shuttle boat approaches the floating restaurant.

The next Saturday at 6:00, Chub, Oy, and their boys picked us up in their car and took us down to the river, where he had made reservations on a restaurant boat. We had a great meal, while chugging up and down the Chao Pryha River, which runs through Bangkok. We could even forget how dirty the city was, and how polluted the river. When seen at night, the lights made both quite beautiful. Still, I wouldn't have wanted to fall overboard. There were a couple of wats along the river that were especially beautiful when lit up at night.

We didn't get back until about 11:00. The boys stayed overnight at their house, so Laurie and I had the luxury of sleeping in Sunday morning. At 10 a.m., we walked about a half mile to a modern shopping mall, in which the fifth floor was all food establishments. We had a great brunch of Vietnamese pancakes, spring rolls, and iced coffee—all for about $2.00 each. Then we really splurged and went to Dunkin' Donuts (they had one on each floor—as well as Pizza Huts) for donuts and coffee—about the only place we had found to get anything resembling American coffee. Thai coffee was very strong and bitter. They (and we) generally drank it with a lot of milk and sugar. I didn't drink much coffee, but when I did, I liked it black, so Thai coffee just didn't do for me most of the time. We walked back home and prepared the makings for hamburgers, baked beans, and salad for dinner.

At 1:30 we were supposed to meet another couple with a boy Cooper's age and a girl Jesse's, to go see the wat that housed the emerald Buddha. As we were walking down the street, on the way to pick Jesse and Cooper up, I thought I very faintly heard someone calling, "Dad." I stopped and looked around. On the other side of the eight-lane street, half a block behind us, were the boys, hanging out of Chub's car, yelling at me. They had forgotten about our plans, and were on their way downtown to a huge park, where they planned to fly kites and ride bikes. If Cooper hadn't seen us walking, it could have been a real mess. As it was, we took the boys, and as the parkwas right across the street from the wat with the emerald Buddha, promised to look for Chub and Oy after we had seen the Buddha. We walked on to our other friends' apartment. It turned out that the dad had work, and the son had homework. As the mother didn't drive, we took a cab. When we got there, we found that although Thais got in free, farangs had to pay 125 baht ($5) apiece for adults—including Cooper, who, although he was only 11 (hardly an adult) was more than 150 cm tall. I was upset. I could maybe see it for tourists, who are in and out in a few days, spending their American or Eurodollars, but I was teaching at a Thai university for a year, earning Thai wages. We were living in a Thai apartment in a Thai

248

neighborhood, and eating Thai food. Our boys were going to a Thai school, and we were with Thai friends. We spoke a reasonable amount of the Thai language. We showed them our ID cards to confirm all of the above, and even argued the point in Thai, but they were firm—polite, but firm. They said for an exception, we would have to get a letter from the Minister of Culture. We didn't see how we could do that in the two hours before closing, so gave in—partially. I had seen the darned thing when I was there in 1969, and didn't figure it had changed much in 25 years, so I paid for Laurie and Cooper and went to the park across the street to wait for them. I found Chub and Oy and their boys over there, and we talked and ate, and watched a magician and people flying kites. Altogether, I was sure I had a better time (for free) than the rest of the family. When they came out, we all went to a nearby food stall for pop. Then we said goodbye to Chub, Oy, and their boys, and went with our other friend and her daughter to our apartment, where we met her husband and son for burgers and beans. The burgers were a big hit with them, although nobody but the dad was crazy about the beans. After dinner we played a little Chinese poker (talk about a cross-cultural experience) and they went home. We got the boys to bed, cleaned up and went to bed ourselves—exhausted, but content with our life there.

We left Bangkok for Khon Kaen early on Thursday, Oct 21, by express train, air conditioned, second class. On the trip, which took most of the day, we met a Dutch couple and their two adopted Korean children, who were about Cooper and Jesse's age. Jesse wanted to play with them, so he approached them first with English. When they didn't understand, he switched to Thai. When they still didn't understand, he got very confused. Their parents, who spoke fluent English, explained that the children had lived in The Netherlands since they were babies, and spoke only Dutch. Well that was OK, then, as long as the boys understood the situation—they just proceeded in sign language, and that other secret language all children share and adults will never know. They hadn't brought any food with them, so we shared lunch from our cooler and pack: ham or peanut butter and jelly sandwiches, supplemented by corn-on-the-cob from a vendor that got on at one one of the stops. At each station, vendors clambered on, selling everything from liquor and cigarettes to fried chicken and candy. Some got off as the train started up again; others rode to the next stop, where they caught the next train back. We were warned by the state health doctor before we left the States not to eat food from such vendors, but that's like saying we should spend three days at the beach, but not go wading. We might as well have stayed in the States as gone to Thailand and not eat food from vendors—it was a big part of the culture. People didn't eat at home much, and much of what they did was snack all day.

We arrived in Khon Kaen about 4:00 that afternoon, found a hotel, and walked around the city. I liked it as much as any of the places we had visited. It had a very rural, small-town feel, but was scattered with very interesting restaurants, hotels, and clubs. There were also a couple of nice large parks, one complete with a quite big lake. The next morning, we took a songtoew (a pickup with the bed covered and bench seats installed, used in many smaller cities in place of, or in addition to, city buses) about 5 km out of town to Khon Kaen University, where the Satit games were being held. About 125 children from the sixth through the twelfth grade at Satit Chula (the boys' school, and the one where Laurie teaches English) were participating. When the teachers who had accompanied the students saw us, they practically swooned in delight. They considered it a great honor that we had taken time from our vacation to come and see the children compete.

Three cheerleaders from Cooper and Jesse's school at the Satit Games.

Actually, we didn't get to see much of the competition (although I did get to see the women's basketball team win 72-10; they were very good, and went on to win the tournament), because the teachers took us to the booths of traditional Thai crafts spread throughout the campus in conjunction with the games. They spent hundreds of baht buying us traditional Thai clothing. We were a bit embarrassed by what we felt was excessive generosity, but it defied custom to refuse gifts. A couple of things were at work: in addition to their feeling honored by our presence at the games, the gifts were traditional Thai crafts, of which Thai people were very proud. Also, they were very grateful for the English teaching Laurie did for free, and wanted to repay her a bit. That evening, they picked us up and took us about 15 km out of town, where they were all staying at the Agricultural Ministry's conference center, for a fine dinner and party.

The net morning, we visited a very nice natural history museum, and explored the city. What we did (as in most places we visited) was just get on the first bus or songtoew that came along, and rode it to the end of the line; then caught another; and so on; until we recognized that we were within walking distance of our hotel, at which point we disembarked. It was an inexpensive and effective way to see a new town. The drivers sometimes treated us as though we were crazy (or lost) but we didn't see that as a problem. After lunch, and restocking our food supply, we left for Udon Thani on a regular, non-air conditioned bus. The kind that served so well to check our fillings—if they were still in when we arrived, we could be sure none were loose.

We got to Udon Thani in the middle of the afternoon of Oct. 23. As the bus station was all the way across town from the hotel we wanted (a fairly posh one this time, as we—read Cooper and Jesse—wanted a swimming pool) we got off the bus at a traffic light. A tuk-tuk driver pulled over and asked where we wanted to go. I told him, and he asked 50 baht. That was ridiculously high, and I told him so—our hotel was only about ten blocks away (we would have walked if not for our luggage). He wouldn't go below 40. I was bargaining with him and getting nowhere, when a pedicab driver stopped and asked where we wanted to go. We told him, but added that there was no way he could get us in his little bicycle-powered rickshaw. He said he and his friend would take us for 20 baht. I said that was still 40 baht—too much. He said no, 10 apiece; 20 total. So we rode two to a pedicab, with our luggage piled on our laps. Cooper and I and our luggage had to weigh more than 300 pounds, but it didn't seem to bother the guy—I wished I had his leg muscles. The whole way to the hotel he kept berating that tuk-tuk driver for asking such a ridiculous price. After a relaxing (but squashed) ride to the hotel, we checked in. A double was 850 baht ($34); cheap in the US, but a luxury hotel by Thai standards, and expensive on my Thai salary. We had budgeted 1000 baht a day (including train and bus tickets but not souvenirs and gifts), so we went considerably over for the two days we stayed there. We made it up other days, though, and came in on budget. I didn't have my bag set down before Jesse had his suit on and was saying, "Come on, Dad, let's go swim." We spent the next two or three hours in and around the pool. The only thing that kept me from wrinkling up like a prune was the fact that the pool closed at 6:00. That, and the fact that there were several young Americans in it. Jesse and Cooper introduced themselves, and learned that the young folks were Peace Corps volunteers, spending some time there in intensive language classes before being dispersed to rural sites throughout the country. The boys spent most of the afternoon and evening with them (including going on "a date" as Jesse put it, with one of the young wom-en for ice cream after dinner), giving Laurie and I a much needed break.

One way we were able to keep travel costs down was that we could eat dirt cheap. We usually spent between $3 and $4 for all four of us; never more than $6.50, and that for a really good dinner. We could have gone to fancy hotels and spent $50, but the food wouldn't have been any better; we'd have just been paying for the atmosphere. Sunday morning, we caught a regular bus and went about 35 km east; then a songtoew 6 km north, to Ban Chiang, a tiny village that was the site of a former ar-chaeological dig that was world famous. It was where an American ar-chaeologist had found remains of a civilization that was making bronze tools, and was believed to be as much as 5,000 to 7,000 years old. That pushed the date for the bronze age back considerably, and gave rise to speculation that civilization may have begun in northeastern Thailand and moved to Mesopotamia, rather than the other way around, as had been thought before. They had constructed a very nice museum. The exhibit was especially good, because it had been put together by the Smithsonian as a traveling show, and had appeared in major museums all over the world. In addition to displays that clearly showed the his-tory and culture of the people, there were many beautiful examples of the pottery for which they were noted, and which the people in the area still made—large pots and bowls of natural clay color, with either red or white swirled designs; some embossed with patterns made by pressing rope or roughly-woven cloth into the wet clay. They had also construct-ed an impressive "open-air museum" by roofing over the original site of the dig, with many of the skeletal remains, pottery pieces, and tools intact, just as they were uncovered. The boys were more impressed with the souvenir stands in the village. We took a songtoew and a bus back to our hotel and swam for the rest of the afternoon; then made plans to travel on north to Nong Khai, a small city on the Laotian border just across the Mekong River from Vientiane.

We arrived in Nong Khai in late morning. Our guidebook showed an interesting place to stay that was within easy walking distance of the bus stop, even with luggage (two carry-on type bags of clothes, a two six-pack size cooler and a day pack of food, and a small bag of the boys' personal "stuff," which we let them pack on the condition that they had to carry it). We got off the bus, and repeatedly saying "mai crap" ("no thanks"), made our way through the swarms of tuk-tuk and taxi drivers. The guest house was really nice—sort of like the old-style motels in the States, with separate cabins. We had a screened sitting room, a private bath with hot water, and an air conditioned room that served as bedroom, kitchen, and dining room—all for 450 baht ($18). As was our custom, we spent the first afternoon just walking around town to get our bearings, and to get a feel for the place. Our first stop was a little restaurant that sort of perched on a crumbling bank overlooking the Mekong River. As we ate, we watched the Laotians going about their business. We then walked along the edge of town next to the river, which was a huge market selling everything, but mostly souvenirs and crafts. Ever since he could talk, Cooper had been asking for a Swiss Army knife. Well, at this market, he found a Swiss Army knife rip-off—the kind that weighed about 17 pounds and included a small bulldozer (certainly not what I considered a pocket knife)—for such a ridiculously low price (85 baht; the real ones were 2500 baht in Bangkok) that we felt we had to get it for him. He immediately began thinking of every possible way to get us lost in the jungle, so he could use it to save us (presumably by constructing a road out to civilization). Of course, it wasn't five minutes before he started saying, "Boy, I sure wish I had a belt sheath for this." (as I said, it wasn't really a pocket knife). After walking around for about an hour more than my legs could take, we returned to our rooms and rested for a while. Actually, Laurie and I rested while the boys did everything they could to keep us from resting.

That evening we splurged on dinner, having it on a floating restaurant that spent a couple of hours cruising up and down the Mekong. As the border is down the middle of the river, and as we cruised very near the Laos side, I suppose we were technically in Laos, although certainly not as illegally as we had been in Cambodia. When we docked, it was beside a wat on the grounds of which a carnival was in full swing.

Buddhists have a completely different attitude about both their religion and its physical manifestations than do Christians. Buddhism is much more firmly entrenched in their everyday lives, with numerous appearances daily, but seldom the somber ritual of our weekly church services. Such rituals are reserved for special events, every couple of months or so. Also, with the exception of the interior of the main temple, the grounds of their wats are treated much as parks, or common areas, and serve more practical functions than do our churches. Anyway, the boys were excited about the carnival. I gave them each 50 baht ($2), and they spent the next hour on bumper cars and in shooting galleries. They were both pretty impressed when I tore the whole center out of a paper target with fifteen shots from a pellet pistol—Marine Corps training's practical application in civilian life.

We slept in the next morning; then set out to find the national historic park near Ban Pu. Our guidebook warned us that it would not be easy, as it was situated way out in the boonies, but it also said it was well worth the effort. Also, the people at the Tourist Authority of Thailand office in Khon Kaen had encouraged us not to miss it. A songtoew driver offered to take us there, show us around, and bring us back for 600 baht—a very good price—but we decided to try it by local bus. By the end of the day, we weren't sure it was worth it. We ended up spending about 300 baht, and it took us about eight hours of travel for an hour and a half at the park, but we surely did experience an aspect of Thailand seldom seen by tourists. There was no bus directly to Ban Pu, so we took one to a tiny village in the middle of nowhere, and changed buses. During the half-hour wait between buses, we were assailed by several tuk-tuk drivers at the bus stop who said they would take us there and back for 300 baht. As it was 10:30, and they were all sitting around drinking Mekong whiskey, drunk as the proverbial skunks, we decided to wait for the bus. Seeing that they couldn't sell me on a tuk-tuk ride, they then proceeded to try and sell me the young woman who was with them. She was young and pretty, so when one of the drivers asked me, "soi mach?" (very pretty?), I said, "soi mach." When he asked me if I wanted her, I said no, and he asked why not, if I thought she was pretty. I paused a moment, thinking—not about whether I wanted her, but about how to answer; I'd dealt with enough drunks to know that I needed to be a bit careful. I pointed to Laurie and said, "Soi mach." They all thought that was a hoot—that I would prefer my wife over that young, pretty girl, but they relaxed a bit, anyway. Then they started in again on why we wouldn't hire one of them to take us to Ban Pu. A scrawny little ancient woman with an incredibly wrinkled face and two teeth, both stained black from chewing betel leaves (of which she had a huge mouthful), stepped in and gave the drivers a verbal dressing down. She told them (we assumed—even if we were fluent in Thai, I don't think we could have understood her around all those gummed-up leaves) to let us alone; that they were no-account drunks, and that they should all go home and sober up; then get some honest work. That was certainly the tone, anyway. They laughed, and teased her, but Thais did respect old people, so they also let us alone from then on. She then turned to us, saying something like, "Don't pay any attention to those drunken bums; you stick with me, I'll take care of you and your two cute boys." I bought her an iced coffee, we got on the bus, and in a few minutes we were on our way. She told us when to get off—which turned out to be about three stops too soon, but it was a pleasant walk. By then, it was lunch time, so we had something to eat in a little hepatitis hut.

Then we set about trying to find a bus to the national park. Well, the long and short of it was that there wasn't a bus to the park. We had two choices: take a bus for 20 baht that went within three km of the park and walk from there, or hire a tuk-tuk for 150 baht that would take us there, wait for us, and bring us back. We chose the latter. Actually, he took Cooper and Jesse there. The park was on top of a mountain, and the tuk-tuk just didn't have the power to get up there with all of us aboard; in fact, even after Laurie and I got out, it was still having problems, so we had to push for about 100 yards, until he got up enough steam to make it without us. We waved to the boys as they disappeared around a bend, and walked the last half mile. When we arrived, the poor driver was taking a terrible ribbing from the employees of the park, and was suffering terminal embarrassment because his tuk-tuk lacked the power to get the job done. We assured him it was no problem, and went inside to drip sweat around while we looked at the displays explaining the background of the park. It really was worth all the effort. We saw cave paintings thousands of years old, incredible rock formations, and the remains of a thriving civilization that had carved dwellings and wells out of solid rock.

After only an hour and a half there, however, the park people told us that the last bus to Nong Khai left Ban Pu at 4:00, and as Ban Pu was 14 km back down the mountain, we'd better get going if we hoped to catch it. We did hope to catch it, so we got going. We almost made it. As we drove into town, the driver started waving and shouting so much that I thought he must be friends with everyone in town; then I realized he was trying to get the attention of the conductor in the bus about a block in front of us. Through signs, he let us know that it was the one

One of the many amazing rock formations at the national historic park near Ban Pu.

we sought—the last to Nong Khai. He couldn't get their attention, and we were losing them, but not to worry. They would stop at the last bus stop on the edge of town to drum up more business. We assumed that both drivers and conductors got a per-head commission, because they sometimes stopped for half an hour and tried to talk people into going with them. They'ed slow down and try to get people walking the opposite direction to get on and ride back the way they had come. So we would have plenty of time to catch them when they stopped. They didn't stop. As we watched them fade into the distance, our driver said, "Mai phen lai" ("no problem"—sure, no problem for him, he lived there). He took us to another stop, where a bus was getting ready to leave. We asked where it was going, and were told Udon Thani. We informed him that Udon Thani was south; we wanted to go north; that we had stayed in Udon Thani two days before, but all of our luggage was now in Nong Khai, 65 km north of Udon Thani. He said, "Mai phen lai (they said that a lot), that we could take the Udon Thani bus east to Route 2, where it turned south to Udon Thani. There, we could get off and catch the next bus traveling north from Udon Thani to Nong Khai. We looked at our map, and he was right, a bit out of the way, but it could work. He took us to the (deserted) bus stop at the "T," dropped us off, and left. It wasn't until then that we realized we were well and truly alone, as in we could hear the sound of our breathing, and nothing else. We were on a deserted plain that stretched to the horizon in every direction. Then four things happened that brightened our day: 1) we heard the distant sound of a vehicle approaching, 2) when the vehicle appeared we could make it out well enough to see that it was a bus, 3) it was headed in the right direction, and 4) it stopped and let us on. Actually, although it was longer by that route, it took about the same time as it had getting out there in the morning. Back at our hotel, we asked the people at the desk where and when we could catch the air-con bus to Nakhon Ratchasima the next day. They said we were in luck, the station was only two blocks away, and the bus left at 8:30 a.m. We asked if they were sure about the departure time—as it would be an all-day trip, we wanted to be sure and catch an air-con bus, and not have to spend all day in a local that stopped every fourteen feet and considered pigs and chickens valid riders. They said absolutely—8:30 on the dot. Just to be sure, we got there half an hour early. "The bus to Nakhon Ratchasima?" the people at the station said, "Oh it left at 7:30." Mai phen lai.

We caught a regular bus to Udon Thani at 8:30, and planned to transfer there to an air-con the rest of the way to Nakhon Ratchasima, so we told the conductor we wanted to get off at the air-con bus terminal in Udon Thani. He told us that would be the second terminal. When we got to the second terminal, we asked again to be sure, and both he and the driver assured us that was right, so we got off. We asked at the information booth where to get the air-con to Nakhon Ratchasima, and were told we would have to go to the air-con terminal across town. Just then a driver approached us and asked where we were going. When we told him, he said we should go with him. He said that although his bus was not air-con, it was new and comfortable, and it would only take five hours to Nakhon Ratchasima. We asked when he was leaving, and he said, "Now." We decided to take the sure thing, and loaded up at 10:00. Fifteen minutes later, we pulled out—and went to every other bus station in town (including the air-con), picking up people before leaving town at 11:00. We stopped what seemed like every 10 feet, and were still hundreds of km from Nakon Ratchasima after the promised five hours. In fact, we pulled into town at 5:30, after nine hours in buses and bus stations. We decided it would be a good time to splurge on a hotel with a pool.

We were only staying overnight there, on our way to Ubon Ratcha-thani, on the Laotian border to the east, where an annual Thai/Laos celebration was to begin the next day. Our guidebook showed two hotels with pools—one a bit cheaper than the other, so we tried it first. It seemed very nice, and the woman at the desk was very accommodating. We could get a double for 700 baht ($28). As I was filling out the registration form, Jesse asked about the pool. "Oh, I'm sorry," she said, "our pool is closed for renovation." Oops. We explained the situation, and she very nicely suggested that we stay at the other hotel in town with a pool. She said it would be 50 baht more, but the boys would really like their pool. She even called and told them to expect us. When we got there, they too were very gracious. "We'll take you right up to your rooms," the manager said. "Oh one double will be fine," I said. "Oh no," she said. "There are four of you, so you have to have two rooms." It turned out they had a rule: no more than three people to a room. It didn't matter that the rule was to keep young travelers from trashing their rooms like dorms. It didn't matter that we were a family of two adults and two children. That was the rule, and they were bound by it. We would have splurged 750 baht, but there was no way we could go 1500—even Jesse and Cooper understood that. So we went to a third hotel. This one was only 350 baht—air con, private bath, hot water, but no pool. We had passed the low point of our trip, and the day was even at least partly salvaged when we went out walking at dinnertime, and stumbled quite by chance onto what we were told later was the best restaurant in town. For the equivalent of $6.50, we had an excellent meal outside in a relatively cool, beautiful evening. The next morning, we had time to walk around town a bit before catching the train to Ubon Ratchathani at 11:30. We also stopped in the VFW Cafeteria, next door to our hotel (complete with retired U.S. Army types sitting around drinking coffee and telling war stories), and ordered eight sausage patties from which to make sandwiches later on the train. I went to the ticket window at the train station and asked for two adult and two children, air-con, second class, to Ubon Ratchathani. I was told there was no air-con on that train—bummer. Oh well, then two adult and two children, second class. I was told they couldn't sell me second class. We had to buy third class, standing-room tickets, get on the one second class car, and hope there would be seats, at which time we could pay extra to the conductor and upgrade to second class—double bummer. Well, we had no choice, so that's what we did. Of course there were no seats in either second or third class when we boarded the train at Nakhon Ratchasima about noon on Oct 28. People were even sitting between the cars. We stowed our bags behind the last sets of seats in second class, made room for Jesse and Cooper to sit on them, and Laurie and I stood in the aisle. The sausage from the VFW Cafeteria made delicious sandwiches, but we'd have enjoyed them more in more comfortable surroundings. The conductor came by and told us we could have the first four seats when people got off. It was a five-hour trip to Ubon Ratchatani. Laurie and Jesse got seats after about an hour, and Cooper and I after about two hours. The boys complained the whole time about not having seats—until I had paid extra for seats for them, of course; then they spent the whole time running around and playing; anything but sitting in their seats.

We got into Ubon Ratchatani about 5:00 p.m., and started trying to find a hotel. The first two we tried were full, and the people there said we would have a hard time finding anything because of the festival. We had noticed a listing in the guidebook for a hotel called "The Ubon," which was described as "going continuously downhill." We figured any available rooms in town would be there. They had rooms, and must have reached their low point, because they had started remodeling. The good news was that the plumbing was brand new; the bad news was that half the walls were still torn out to put in the new plumbing. Overall, it wasn't really that bad—we'd stayed in a lot worse in China. In fact, it was comparable to some of the best places we had stayed in China. A big surprise bonus: it was only one block from the grounds where all the festivities were being held. We lucked out for dinner again, and chose a place that served us the best dum yam (a sort of spicy seafood soup) we'd had. We were told later that restaurant had the best dum yam in the whole province. After dinner we walked over to the festival grounds. It didn't take long to realize that things wouldn't really get going until the next day. None of the pavilions were ready for visitors. It was just as well, because about the time we got there, it began to rain—the only rain we had during our whole vacation, with the exception of while we were driving back from Trat Province, and a short shower one evening while we were at dinner. It wasn't very heavy, and actually felt pretty good, so we just walked in it. That was not something the Thais generally did, so we got a lot of puzzled looks. We returned to our hotel, dried off, and relaxed for the rest of the evening.

The next morning we walked around town; then went back to the festival, which by then was in full swing. We ate, watched a parade, ate, visited the pavilions to look at various Thai and Lao crafts, ate, shopped for souvenirs and gifts, and ate. That afternoon we took a local bus a few miles out of town to a very impressive temple in the Khmer style. As we were walking around the grounds there, we found stored a huge float that the monks had entered in a parade some years before. It was the size of Rose Bowl type floats, only instead of being made from something as mundane as flowers, or crepe paper, or paper mache, it was carved entirely from wax; and it was unbelievably ornate. It comprised (among much else) a warrior astride a horse, dragons, and flowers. Every square inch of it was carved in intricate patterns. We returned to town by bus, and Laurie graciously volunteered to take the boys back to the festival so they could ride the rides and spend their money at the shooting galleries (the same ones we had been to in Nong Khai, by the way—the girls that operated them shouted and waved at the boys). I graciously volunteered to go back to the room and take a nap before moving our stuff down to the lobby for storage until our bus left for Bangkok at 8:00 p.m. As it was about a nine-hour trip, and as the only thing available on the train was second class, without air-con, leaving at 6:00 the next morning, we decided to try what they billed as "The V.I.P."—an overnight, air-con bus. Good choice. Although Laurie and I only got about three hours sleep apiece, the boys slept like the proverbial logs. Outside the bus station on the north side of town, we flagged a taxi and told him where we wanted to go. He said 300 baht ($12). I laughed, and said we'd go by the meter. When we pulled up in front of our apartment, it registered 89 baht ($3.50). Although Laurie and I were pretty beat, we were glad we'd chosen the bus. By spending the night on the road, we had an extra day to recuperate from our odyssey before we had to start back to school on Monday. We spent Saturday and Sunday resting, replenishing the food supplies we had depleted in preparation for being gone, washing clothes, and generally putting all the things back in order that inevitably get messed up in three weeks on the road. Monday morning at 6:00, the alarm rang, and we were back into our ordinary life in Bangkok.

Chapter 6
November

The weekend of the 13th and 14th we took part in a road rally to Pattaya, about 150 km east of Bangkok. The rally was put on by the PTA of Satit Chula, where the boys went to school, as a fund raiser. The entry fee was 5,000 baht ($200), and there were more than 50 cars. In addition, several big companies helped sponsor the event, contributing lots of money, as well as products. Each car had big stickers on it advertising the sponsors: Marvel Comics, Thai Petroleum, Singha Beer, Janzen Sportswear, Bridgestone Tires, etc. They looked very professional. Cooper rode with three young men in a new Toyota Corolla (car #4). Laurie, Jesse, and I rode in the school van with the principal, two vice principals, and three teachers. They had actually entered the competition, and we were #13. They said that as it was the thirteenth of November, the two unlucky numbers canceled themselves, and became lucky. Maybe there was something to that—we took third place. There were six checkpoints, and each held new challenges. Each car started with 100 points, and every time they failed a challenge, they lost points. At the first checkpoint, drivers had to toss a ping-pong ball into the holes of a Coke carton. Each hole was labeled (0-25), and they lost the number of points on the label. If they missed three times, they lost 30 points. We were timed between some checkpoints. Between some, we had to answer a list of questions from signs along the way. Between some, we had to find letters of the alphabet that had been painted on telephone poles, bridges, and the like, and write down what color the letters were; or find a letter of a given color, and record what letter it was; or find a particular letter of a given color, and tell where the letter appeared. Between two of the checkpoints, we were given an hour to eat, but we also had to find a list of items, as in a scavenger hunt. I think we were the only car that found one of the items—a fruit that was out of season. Most of the people in our van were just having fun, and didn't really care about winning, but our co-pilot was serious (having fun, mind you, but wanted to win). He spent his lunch hour walking around town until he found some of the fruit on a tree in a private yard. He knocked on the door, and asked the owners if he could buy one of the fruit. When they heard what it was for, they just laughed and gave him one. They asked if he wanted more to give to other participants, and he said absolutely not. We ended up with 75 of our 100 points—having lost 10 in the ping-pong toss, so only 15 the whole rest of the race.

Well, it was a huge success—everyone arrived happy and excited. We checked into one of the many luxury hotels in Pattaya (the PTA paid all our family's expenses in gratitude for Laurie's teaching their children English). We swam all afternoon, then went to dinner and the party following. It was an excellent dinner. The party had its moments. They awarded very nice trophies for first through third place, the group of entrants who "tried the hardest but had bad luck," the family that had the "best rally costumes," the person who had the "best party costume" (a little girl in a tu-tu), and "most beautiful car." Then they had several

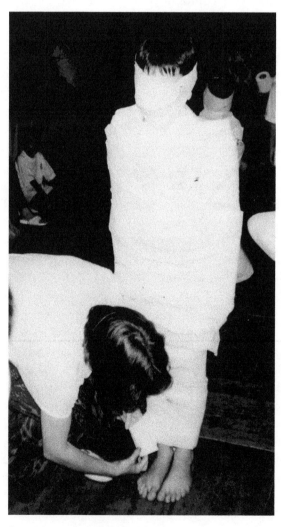

Laurie preparing Cooper to be crowned
"most beautifully wrapped."

children's games. Both Cooper and Jesse won prizes for being among the last six children left in a game in which each child tied a balloon to his/her right ankle; then all tried to break the others' balloons. Jesse won mostly because just before the game began, he reached down and pulled his balloon up to his knee—pretty hard to step on it up there, the sneaky little cuss. Cooper and Laurie won prizes in a weird contest in which the parents wrapped the children in toilet paper until the music stopped; then the crowd cheered for the child they considered "most beautifully wrapped." Go figure.

The children (and most of the adults—certainly I) were then entertained by a quite good magician. Cooper decided that's what he waned to be when he grew up. Jesse scoffed, "Aw, it's just tricks." At about 10:00, the emcee announced that the children had been entertained enough, and it was time to entertain the adults. What followed was a sort of cabaret show, with (relatively) scantily—clad women dancing and lip-synching singing, young men doing rap dancing, and young men dressed as (relatively) scantily-clad women dancing and lip-synching singing. Most of the children sat right down front and enjoyed it every bit as much as they had the magician. Laurie took (dragged, to be more precise) the boys up to bed. I followed soon after, on the pretense of helping her get them to bed. The party went on until 1:00 am.

The next morning we had breakfast and swam some more. We were to go back with the van at 10:00, but some friends offered to take the boys back with them, so they could stay a couple of extra hours and swim with their boys. We didn't mind—it made our ride back all the more relaxed. We asked one of the assistant principals what time we would get back, and she said about 3:00. We thought that odd, as it was only about a two-hour drive, and we were leaving at 10:00. On the way, however, we made three scenic detours, on one of which we stopped for an excellent seafood lunch overlooking the ocean. We also stopped twice to "shop for items famous in the area." We had forgotten the Thai custom: whenever they travelled, they stopped at local markets to buy locally-produced presents for their friends back home—nice, huh? We got home at 3:00 on the button. Our friends delivered our boys and theirs at 4:30 and left. The boys all played together until 7:00, when I fed everybody. Their parents picked them up about 8:00, and we went to bed, exhausted, shortly after. Another restful weekend. Luckily for Laurie and the boys, they didn't have school Monday. Unluckily for me, I did—plus night class at Bangkok U. I got home about 10:00 p.m., wired, and in no way ready for bed. Laurie, ever sympathetic, said that's what I got the big bucks for.

We had no school at Chula from Friday, Nov. 19, until Sunday, Nov. 28, because of the University Games (an Olympic-style sporting event entered by universities throughout the country), which were held at Chula that year. The boys were out of school even longer—their vacation began on the 13th. Actually, Cooper had to go in two days that week to practice. The third, fourth, and fifth graders presented a couple of original Thai dances at the opening ceremonies—attended by His Royal Higness the Crown Prince, so they were a big deal. They actually kept 800 kids at school for two full days, practicing. After the first practice, he brought his costume home: traditional baggy pants in glittery electric blue, neon pink silk blouse, glittery gold sash, white socks, and white gloves with bells. Imagine 800 of those little suckers lined up in one place, jingling. He had to be at the school at 2:00 on Friday, despite the fact that the celebration wasn't scheduled to begin until 3:00, the Prince wasn't supposed to arrive until 5:00, and they weren't on the program until 5:30. Of course the program started late—Laurie, Jesse, and I got there at 4:00 and they were just getting going; His Royal Highness got there fashionably late—6-ish. The kids didn't get on until about 7:30—800 children between nine and eleven years old, forced to wait in their fancy costumes for five hours. It was quite a spiffy show, if a bit slow—much in the style of opening extravaganzas for the Olympics: singers, dancers, musicians, parade of athletes, acrobats, the works. Most impressive was the section of bleachers about 150 by 75 feet, packed with Chula students holding flash cards. At various times during the festivities, they spelled out "Chula," in both English and Thai, and the names of the five corporate sponsors—complete with the Coke logo in Thai "bubbling" up across the section; created several truly beautiful scenes in vivid color of the Prince and Princesses, and the King and Queen; and pictured a couple of colorful scenes of athletics. When the runners ascended to light the flame, they responded with a scene that depicted a runner lighting a flame—complete with flickering flame. I couldn't imagine getting that many U.S. college students together with enough discipline to learn all those routines, let alone sit for five hours, packed together in a hot stadium, and run through them with remarkable precision. When their time finally came, the 800 costumed cherubs filed onto the field in a huge "X," and ran through their routine. It drew much applause from the audience, much of which consisted of 1600 parents (rather like the "Sound of Music" syndrome—get enough kids on stage, and you've got a guaranteed audience).

Cooper in his traditional Thai dance costume, practicing with 799 other students.

Chub and Oy had invited us to go with them to visit her folks for a few days in Songkhla. Given a choice between that or spending the next ten days watching college sports, we chose the trip to the South. I had a makeup class at Bangkok University on Saturday morning, so we decided to take a sleeper leaving Bangkok at 3:15 p.m. At 10 a.m. the morning before, we found that the water in our apartment had mysteriously disappeared. All of the other apartments had water; it was only ours that didn't. They tried all day Friday to restore it, to no avail, but at 10:00 p.m., assured us it would be on by morning. It wasn't, and we had to prepare for our trip by carrying buckets of water from the hose outside. Just before we left, I told them we would be gone a week, and asked if they thought that would be long enough to take care of the problem. My sarcasm was wasted. They smiled and assured me it would be. I smiled and assured them it had better be (very un-Thai).

Chub made the arrangements, and got six berths for the eight of us. As their 6-year-old still slept with his mother, he assumed Jesse did too. So he did Saturday night on the train. When we got to the station, another surprise awaited us: he had gotten non-air conditioned. The boys were really upset, but I made them promise not to say anything. It was OK until we went to bed; then it was stifling. When they turned the seats into bunks, they put the windows 3/4 of the way up, and pulled louvered, screened vents all the way down, effectively shutting off most air to the bottom bunk, and all to the top. There were signs in Thai, Chinese, and English under each window that said, "Do

265

not open windows while asleep." Cooper ventured that he had heard of people walking in their sleep, but never opening windows. We made it through the night; if not refreshed, at least not completely exhausted. We got into Hat Yai Sunday morning about 8:00, and hired a taxi for 90 baht (about $3.50) to take us the 25 km to Songkhla. The drivers wanted us to take two cars, as there were eight of us with all our luggage (not an unreasonable request, to my way of thinking), but Chub would have none of it. He had made it clear from the beginning that, with the exception of the train tickets, they were not going to let us pay for anything; we were their guests—a very common tradition in Thailand. I didn't feel, therefore, that I should venture an opinion, so I kept my mouth shut and scrunched in with everybody else. When we got to Grandma and Grandpa's, we were all ushered (one at a time) into the bathroom to "freshen up"—which to Thais meant a full shower; usually before every meal and at bedtime. It was well past my breakfast time by then, and Chub and Oy took Laurie and me out to eat, leaving everyone else for Grandma to take care of. Everyone else, incidentally, consisted of Cooper and Jesse; Chub and Oy's two boys; Grandpa; Oy's younger sister, who lived at home; and her younger brother, who was also visiting from Bangkok for the week. That was 12 of us staying in their (small) 3-bedroom house. Laurie and I got one bedroom, Cooper and Jesse got one, sister slept on the living room couch by the TV (which she seldom looked away from), and everybody else slept on the floor in Grandma and Grandpa's room. Guests in Thailand were treated like royalty.

Grandma and Grandpa had a small motorbike instead of a car, so Chub hired a couple of motorcycle taxis to take Laurie and me to the restaurant, and he and Oy took Grandpa's. I hadn't ridden on a motorcycle since I was a teenager, and I remembered why I never learned to drive one. After a brunch of noodles and rice, Oy took the motorcycle back home, and Chub walked with us via the scenic route through the old part of the city. It was a very nice old fishing port; very little industry, so consequently almost no pollution. We returned to the house and relaxed for a while before setting out for a market on one of the islands in the bay. We hired a songtoew to the island, walked around for a while, and hitched a ride in a private pickup going back. After a lunch of noodles in a local shop, we spent the afternoon swimming in the ocean. To be more precise, the boys and I spent the afternoon trying to stand up under the onslaught of waves created somewhere offshore by tropical storm Kyle; while Chub, Oy, and Laurie (along with numerous other passers by) questioned our sanity. Dinner was an all-evening affair of excellent seafood at a restaurant on the beach. The next morn-

I, with Cooper, Jesse, and friends, wait to be pummeled by the next big wave.

ing, Chub took Laurie, Cooper, Jesse, and me on an extended walking tour of the city. We were treated to lunch at another excellent seafood restaurant by one of Oy's high school classmates who owned her own business. After lunch, the boys would have nothing but a repeat of the previous day's "swim." The only difference was that this time Laurie temporarily lost her grip on sanity and joined us (fully clothed, as she had not brought her suit that afternoon), and it began to rain and blow quite hard. Two things Thais don't do is swim in the ocean when it is rough, and spend time outside when it is raining. So we had the whole beach pretty much to ourselves, except for an occasional driver who stopped on the nearby road to stare.

By special request, I cooked hamburgers for dinner Tuesday evening. Chub and Oy and their boys had been to our apartment for burgers a couple of times, and thought the rest of her family might enjoy them. With the exception of Grandma, who was a vegetarian, they were right. I assumed the fact that Grandpa had four was more than just politeness on his part. Chub and Oy and their boys were going on to another city to spend some time with his brother, so Laurie and I and our boys decided to stop at Ko Samui—a popular, resort-filled island—for a couple of days on the way back to Bangkok. The next morning at 8:00, we hired a taxi to Hat Yai, where we had reserved seats on an air conditioned van to Surat Thani and the ferry to Ko Samui. We were to arrive on the island by 4:00; 4:30 at the latest.

In Hat Yai, we caught the van on which we had reserved seats, and they assured us that it would take us directly to the ferry dock at Surat Thani, where we would catch the 2:30 ferry for Ko Samui, arriving there at 4:00. The van ride was comfortable, except that the driver, as did most Thai drivers, kept pushing on the gas and letting up; pushing on the gas and letting up; pushing.... At noon, he pulled into a restaurant in a tiny village and said we had 10 minutes for lunch. We noticed there were five other tour vans there as well, and when we asked about prices, we understood. Everything was half again as much as it should have been, but most of the foreign tourists didn't realize how overpriced it was, and were chowing down. There was no place else to eat anyway, so they didn't have much choice. I was sure the drivers got a kickback from the restaurant. I told our driver that we would not pay such prices, and we broke out our cooler. We set up at a table and made some ham, and some peanut butter and jelly sandwiches. Thais from the restaurant gathered to watch, and were curious about what the peanut butter was, but nobody said, "Hey, you can't do that!" (or the Thai version of it). After more like 15 or 20 minutes, the driver climbed in and leaned obnoxiously on the horn until everyone reboarded, and we continued. We arrived in Surat Thani at 2:15, but instead of going to the ferry dock, he took us to a little hole-in-the-wall tour office and told us to get out. There was an Italian couple and their 5-year-old daughter along, and they got very abusive, saying they paid to go to the ferry, etc. In the end, all their complaints amounted to nothing, and they got out too. We waited 20 minutes; then another van picked us up and took us across town to a somewhat larger tour office, where we waited another 20 minutes. While we were waiting, a 30-ish man dressed as a quite handsome woman (not at all uncommon in Thailand) asked if we had a place to stay on Ko Samui. I said that as we had expected to get in at 4:00, we thought we would wait until we arrived. It was very off-season, so there would be no problem. He said that, in fact, we wouldn't get in until 7:30, and suggested we make reservations with him. I suspected some sort of scam, but he seemed on the level, explaining that the resorts gave him a percentage of any bookings he made, so he had to keep people happy. He asked what we were interested in. I told him air-con, private bath, hot water, nice beach, and swimming pool; between 500 and 800 baht if possible. He showed us a brochure for a place that met all those criteria, and we took a chance and booked one night at 800 baht ($32). He promised us someone would meet us at the pier with free transportation, as the resort was halfway around the island from where the ferry would dock. I told Laurie I'd believe it when I saw it. After the 20-minute wait, they ushered us onto the regular Surat Thani to Ko Samui local bus, which took us to the vehicle ferry, 30 km back toward Hat Yai, where we'd started at 9:30 a.m. By the time we got on the ferry, it was 6:00, and we were again glad we had our own food along.

Just as the guy had said, we didn't get to Ko Samui until 7:30, and just as he had promised, there was an air-con van with "World Resort" painted on the side waiting for us at the pier. After a half-hour ride, we arrived at the resort, checked in, and were shown our bungalow. It was everything he had promised, and we upped our estimate of human nature a notch. The resort was fairly isolated—about 1 1/2 miles from the nearest village—so rather than try to find someplace else, we had a late dinner in their open-air restaurant on the beach. The food was pretty good—expensive, but we expected that. By breakfasting from our cooler in our room, and having cheap lunches ($3.50 for the four of us) in town, we were able to have expensive dinners ($12.00 for the four of us) at the seaside restaurant. We had the people at the desk make ferry and train reservations for a sleeper leaving Surat Thani at 5:50 Friday afternoon and arriving at Bangkok about 5:00 a.m. Saturday. Then we spent all day Thursday, and Friday morning, swimming in the ocean and the pool, playing the Thai version of bocci ball, walking on the beach, exploring the neighboring villages, eating, and just generally relaxing. It was like a second honeymoon—with children. Only two incidents marred the calm. Cooper stepped on a piece of glass that drinkers had broken on the pool apron the night before, cutting his foot badly enough that he limped for a couple of days. Then while exploring the area near the back of our bungalow, the boys stirred up a nest of some kind of tiny bees. They swarmed all over them in the hundreds, scaring them nearly to death, and sending them screaming for the water. Before they got too far, Laurie, I, and a couple of resort employees caught them. When they realized they weren't being stung (If he had been, Cooper would have gotten hives, swelled up, and had a hard time breathing), the emergency abated. The bees were still terribly annoying, as they stuck firmly anywhere they landed, which was mostly all over the boys' clothes and hair. It was a real chore getting them all off and getting the boys cleaned up. Friday about noon, we checked out, caught a songtoew into town, had lunch, and boarded the ferry. We got to the mainland about 4:15, so assumed we had plenty of time to make the train, as they were supposed to have a bus waiting to make the connection to the station. Even when there was no bus waiting, and we had to wait 20 minutes for it, we assumed we still had plenty of time. It wasn't until we had been riding on the bus for an hour, and still no station in sight that we began to wonder. We made it—pulled into the station at 5:40, got on the train, sat down, and left. No sweat. The trip home was uneventful, and we arrived at our apartment about 6:00 a.m., to find that we had no water. They told me they were waiting for "a part" that should get there "any day." Fortunately, it did arrive that morning, and we had water for late showers.

As we were gone on Thanksgiving, we postponed our celebration until Sunday, the 28th. That was also the date of a huge Thai celebration, Loi Kratong, which served to thank the major rivers for providing water for our use, and to apologize for treating them so unkindly in return. So, we had an intercultural day. Our friends, Chub and Oy, and their sons came over to our apartment for Thanksgiving dinner, which I prepared on one hot plate and one electric wok. The lack of an oven precluded turkey and pumpkin pie, but we had chicken, mashed potatoes and gravy, squash, sweet potatoes with sugar and honey glaze, stuffing, green beans with chopped onions and ham, and fruit salad. I shopped Saturday, and cooked pretty much all Sunday morning. Just before they came, I went out and bought two roasted chickens, then when they got there, began the process of reheating everything. We had a steamer that fit on top of the electric wok, and we borrowed another that fit on top of our big stew pot. Thus, I could reheat four dishes at a time—one in the pot and one in the steamer over it; one in the wok, and one in the steamer over it. Amazingly, everything turned out well—and was hot. Even without the turkey and pumpkin pie, it was unmistakably a Thanksgiving dinner—everyone left the table stuffed, and we had leftovers for dinner Monday night. After dinner, we did dishes; then sat around and chatted while the boys played in the other room.

At about 7:00 we left to attend a Loi Kratong celebration. The primary components of the celebration were fireworks (which began the first of the month, and built to a climax Sunday evening that made the Fourth of July in the States pale by comparison—I mean, we're talking big-time incendiary here; many fingers and other body parts blown off each year), and the floating of hand-made boats on the various canals, ponds, and rivers of the country. "Boats" didn't really do them justice; the most mundane were beautiful, and some were incredibly ornate. Many people worked for days on theirs. They were supposed to be constructed completely of natural materials—mostly flowers and banana leaves—usually with a chunk from a banana tree as the base. Chub and Oy took us to a huge park (what they referred to as an "open temple") about 15 miles northwest of Bangkok, where there was a major Loi Kra-

*First prize winner at the Loi Kratong celebration:
a 10-foot Thai temple constructed of thousands of flowers.*

tong celebration scheduled. We were not disappointed. It was the site of what was referred to as "the Big Buddha," for obvious reasons—it was about three stories tall. Although Loi Kratong was supposedly not a religious ceremony, as with so much else in Thailand, Buddhism and the rest of their lives were intertwined. So people were crowded around the foot of the Big Buddha, offering flowers, candles, and incense. Others were setting their boats afloat in the numerous ponds that were always part of the landscaping of parks and temple grounds there. Others were setting off enormous quantities of fireworks. Others had brought picnics, and were spread out on woven straw mats. And others, such as us, were just walking around, trying to take it all in. Over it all was the amplified voice of a monk, speaking continuously in Thai. I asked Chub what he was saying, and he replied, "Oh, I don't know; we don't listen." After a few minutes, in which he stopped to listen, he said the monk was essentially preaching a sermon about good living. Part of the festival was a display of the boats that had won prizes in various age categories—much like at a county fair in the States. First prize in the open category was in the shape of a traditional Thai temple, about ten feet tall, and constructed entirely from orchids and other vivid flowers. It was truly awe-inspiring.

By the time we left at 9:00, traffic into the temple was lined up two and three abreast much of the way back to Bangkok. We were glad we had come early. As it was, it took us 20 minutes to get out of the temple, and another hour to travel the 15 miles back home. There were 2.5 million cars and 2.6 million motorcycles in Bangkok, and all of them seemed to try to drive on the streets and sidewalks at the same time. As there was almost no off-street parking, when people needed to make a delivery, or run into a store for a minute, they pulled up onto the sidewalk, leaving the street for those of us who were walking. If traffic was too badly tied up to make any headway, motorcyclists thought nothing of driving on the sidewalk instead, until they got past the jam. Many people had installed overhead doors on the first floor of their houses or store fronts, and parked in their living rooms or their stores at night. Any time we left Chub and Oy's house in the evening, if we turned and looked back, we would see him open the overhead door on the front of their house, drive their car into the living room, and close the door behind it. When cars, trucks, and buses stopped at an intersection (and I had been stopped at intersections in buses for as long as 45 minutes), the spaces between them immediately filled with motorcycles—it looked like pouring water between rocks. On the first day of school the year we were there, a pickup, which had been modified with benches in the back, was hit from behind by a ten-wheel truck. Four of the 24 school children (between the ages of 8 and 11) in the back of the pickup were killed. One had both legs amputated later, and three others were still in the hospital a week later. The driver of the big truck left it and escaped on foot—which was almost always the case with the person at fault in a serious accident. Often they didn't want the police to find out that they had bought their drivers licenses. There was no way to describe the traffic situation in Bangkok except as a form of anarchy.

Chapter 7
December

The boys did their home schooling Saturday morning, while I went to the market, and made peanut butter and pickles. Then Cooper and I walked to a shop about a mile and a half from our apartment to buy a birthday present for one of his friends with whom he was to spend the rest of the weekend. At 1:00 his friends parents picked him up, and we were left with only Jesse (which was plenty). At 3:00 we walked to the university pool, where we met Chub and Oy, and their boys. Laurie swam with the boys until about 5:30, while I went for coffee with our friends. We then went together to the cafeteria at the women's dorm for dinner. After dinner, we went in search of lights. Sunday was the king's birthday, so many big businesses and government offices were decked out in lights that made our Christmas displays in the States look meager by comparison. First we drove down Wireless Road (Chub had taken a new job, and had a larger car, so we weren't as crowded), where many of the posh hotels and embassies were lit up in glorious displays. Some of the stores were also decked out in Christmas lights, so the combinations were quite spectacular. Next we tried to drive past the palace, but traffic was so bad we gave up after spending half an hour and getting no closer than three blocks. We went instead to the main office of Thai Farmers Bank (As I am neither Thai nor a farmer, that's the bank I chose as appropriate for my account). It was amazing. The building sat in a small, park-like setting, which was ablaze in strings of literally millions of tiny white lights—the kind some people used on their Christmas trees. The neighborhood for blocks was brighter than day, and hundreds of people—mostly couples with children and groups of teenagers—were milling about in a truly carnival atmosphere. We (double) parked and mixed in with the crowd. I don't think I had ever seen so many lights in one place at one time. It was dazzling. I wasn't sure whether I was proud to claim it as my bank because of the wonderful display, or ashamed at how blatantly they were squandering energy (I had the same dilemma in the States about Christmas lights). Next we tried the palace again, but still in vain. We did get close enough that time to see that it was lit for blocks around much as it had been for the queen's birthday. By that time, it was 9:30, so we started for home. On the way, however, Chub and Oy insisted we stop for dessert. They went to a stand that served Thai desserts (which were truly awful—the only Thai food we really didn't like—stuff like kidney beans in sweet coconut milk, or globs of sweetened, sticky rice flour in some kind of slimy black liquid (it tasted even worse than it sounded). Luckily, there was an ice cream stand nearby, as well, which Laurie, Jesse, and I went to instead.

Sunday morning I went to the supermarket for yoghurt, milk, butter, and bread. The rest of the morning was relax time. Jesse went to his girlfriends' apartment—some high school girls whom he thought were just the berries. Much of a Thai person's future was linked to which college he or she attended. To get their children into the best colleges, which were in Bangkok, parents sometimes sent their children to the best high schools, which were in Bangkok. Often, that meant the children lived with relatives or friends there, but if that wasn't possible, several families from outlying towns might go together to rent an apartment for three or four of their children to share. As Suwanna Apartments, where we lived, was near several high schools, many of the apartments were occupied by groups of teenagers. Jesse's four "girlfriends," for example, shared a one-room studio apartment that he said was about the size of our living room. Anyway, while he was up there playing video games with the girls, Laurie and I read.

Cooper and Jesse clowning with three of Jesse's "girlfriends."

276

After lunch, we walked a couple of blocks to the National Stadium, a huge Olympic-style sports complex that was built for the 1965 Asian Games, and renovated for the 1978 games. It was in almost constant use for national, university, or city competitions (or Michael Jackson concerts). That weekend was the national sports competition between the physical education departments of the various universities in the country. As with all such events, they took advantage of the fact that so many people were gathered in one place, to sell stuff. So there were dozens of booths set up, offering everything from food to sporting gear, to Thai crafts. We "window" shopped; watched soccer, target shooting, field hockey, and several Thai games; and snacked. Jesse bought a hand-carved wooden rooster (It looked like a hen to me, but he insisted it was a rooster). I cooked supper, and we spent a relaxing evening reading and playing games.

The Thais loved their cars. Even more than in the States, they served as symbols of status and mobility. Most were Hondas, Toyotas, and Mitsubishis; but about every tenth one was a BMW, Mercedes, or Volvo. This with sky-high prices. A Honda Civic that would have sold in the States for $10,000 (very basic) would have been $20,000 in Thailand—if you could find one, which would be difficult. Nobody was interested in a basic car. They were all loaded: air conditioning, power everything, cloth or leather seats, carpeting, rear spoilers, pin striping; the works. There were more motorcycles than cars in the country, and most of them cost nearly as much as we would have paid for a car in the States. Pickups were also very popular; especially with the young men. Nissans, and Toyotas dominated. The more lettering there was on a vehicle (with the exception of the really classy ones), the better they liked it. For example, a truck or car might have painted on it (from the factory), "New Generation Power," "2.5 liter GLSi Fuel Injection," and "Positraction Active All-Wheel Drive." Then the driver may have added stickers advertising anything from sporting gear to alcohol, as well as Garfield, Spiderman, or Mickey Mouse stickers. The first thing they did in the morning (or their maid did, if they had one) was go out and wash their car or motorcycle. And "washing" meant inside and out—including the trunk, engine, and undercarriage—as well as polishing the chrome, and applying Armorall to the dash and tires. If the car had been washed in the past couple of days, and so wasn't dirty, they just wiped it with a damp cloth; or if it really wasn't dirty at all, they just dusted it with a feather duster. Every car had a cleaning kit in the trunk; or in the case of trucks, tucked behind the seat, or for motorcycles, somewhere on board. Truck drivers or taxi drivers, who may not have had running water at home, drove around until they found puddles large enough in which to wash their vehicle. After a heavy rain, we saw them lined up for access to the biggest puddles, just as you would at a car wash on a nice Saturday in the States.

Most people left the plastic covering on the interior of a new car until it wore out; then they either bought seat covers, or some stretched t-shirts over the back of their bucket seats and put towels on the seat part. People made a living sewing dash covers out of either fake fur or a plush, crushed velvet material. Some people didn't drive their new car any more than they had to until they'd taken it in to be fitted for a dash cover. Many people, when they parked, covered their vehicle with a nylon cover; some lifted the wipers off the windshields, so they won't deteriorate from the heat. Almost all cars and trucks had very heavily tinted glass (some so much that we couldn't see in from outside), either factory installed, or applied as a stick-on film. Many people had installed window-shade like devices (that stuck by suction cups to one edge of the glass) on both their windshields and their back windows, which they pulled as sunscreens when they parked. Others used the more conventional sun shades that just propped between the dash and the rear-view mirror. Few cars—including the BMWs and the Mercedes—had their original wheels and tires. They had been replaced with custom chrome wheels and low-profile racing radials. There were nearly as many beautifully restored old cars as there were new ones, but we almost never saw the kind of junkers on the streets that were common everywhere in the States. Volkswagen beetles were the car of choice for restoration. There were literally hundreds of them in Bangkok. Some were in showroom condition; others had been painted a really vivid color, and had leather interiors with hardwood trim, racing radials on custom wheels, altered suspension so they rode very low, air conditioning, cellular phones, and full power accessories.

Because traffic was so terrible in Bangkok, and because lots of the more well-to-do folks had moved out to the suburbs to escape some of the pollution, many of them had to leave home very early in the morning, and return home very late in the evening to avoid rush hour. It was not uncommon for a family to get up at 4:30 a.m., leave home at 5:00, arrive at the children's school at 7:00—where they all ate breakfast (The school cafeterias were open 6:00 a.m. to 6:00 p.m. for that purpose), mother and father left the school at 8:00 (after the worst of the traffic had cleared), dropped mother off at work, and father took the car on to work. In the evening the process was reversed, with mother and father arriving at the children's school about 5:00 (the kids had been through with school since 3:00, and had been playing or watching videos since then), where they all ate dinner and left for home about 6:30, arriving there at 8:30. Clearly, they spent more time during the week in their car than they did at home, so they had their cars equipped much like a detachable room of their house—especially those who had vans. The passenger area probably had a stereo—either cassette deck or CD player—with custom speaker system, including jacks for headphones; a small color TV, VCR, and video game setup; additional interior lights; and some sort of food storage—either a cabinet, a refrigerator, or both. The children and mother probably spent the two-hour (often more—I knew some families who drove four hours one-way every day) commute in the morning sleeping. The children did their homework on the way home, with mother's help. If they had no homework, or if they finished before they got home, they either watched videos or played video games the rest of the way, while mother read or listened to music. Father probably got the paper read, and possibly some work done that he had taken home from the office, while they were stopped (for as much as a half hour at a time) in traffic. That's if it didn't rain. If it rained during rush hour, they could add probably two hours to the commute time. So, it was clear why Thais—if they could afford it—were willing to pay $50,000 or $60,000 for a car. After all, it was the one room in which they spent the most time.

We had Friday, Dec. 10th, off for Constitution Day, so did home schooling with the boys Friday, instead of Saturday, morning. The older son of our friends, Chub and Oy, came over to play with Cooper about 11:00. Their younger, who makes Jesse look almost angelic by comparison, couldn't come over, because he hadn't finished his homework (a perpetual condition). Chub and Oy picked us up at 1:30, and all eight of us piled into their Toyota Corolla and drove across town to a new department store, which as a promotion, has brought a dinosaur show in from Japan. Ever since "Jurassic Park" showed in Bangkok, anything having to do with dinosaurs was a sure sell. That show was no exception. Traffic into the place was even worse than the usual horrible Bangkok jams, and parking was almost non-existent. I had to get out and push some cars around to make space. The Thais consistently double- and triple-parked, leaving their steering wheels centered and their transmissions in neutral when they got out and locked their doors, so that if they were blocking someone, their car could be rolled out of the way. We were lucky, and although the line of people was very long when we got there, we were the last ones in to the next walk-through. They were showing "The Land Before Time" while we waited, so it wasn't bad at all (except that I had to hold Jesse on my shoulders so he could see the TV over the crowd). The show featured 40 mechanical, moving, roaring, tail swishing (on some), eye blinking (on others), clawing, approximately life sized, rubber skinned, pretty fakey-looking denizens of the past. Jesse's verdict: "OK (yawn)"; Cooper's: " Booorrring." Laurie and I were somewhere between. We had to act thrilled, however, as we were Oy's guests (to the tune of about $3.50 per adult and $1.50 per child). Actually, as she was a frequent purchaser of stocks at the Thai Stock Exchange, the tickets were complimentary (which made me feel much better about the whole thing). It was just fun being with our friends, though—our boys and theirs had become bosom buddies. It was a good thing we liked being with them, as we spent 1 1/2 hours driving there, and 1 1/4 driving back (all for a half-hour show).

We got back just in time for Laurie and Jesse to walk over to the University, meet one of Jesse's teachers (who just got out of the hospital last week following an eye operation), and walk her back to our apartment for dinner. As we hadn't had time to shop, Cooper and I did that in the meanwhile. We all got back at the same time, and I prepared spaghetti, salad, and garlic bread. Saturday morning we shopped for groceries for the rest of the week. Then I prepared the fixings for hamburgers and potato salad, as we expected Chub, Oy, their boys, and her parents and sister for dinner (hamburgers were the one Western food that almost all Thais, including the old ones, seemed to like). They picked us up at 3:00, and we drove (in two cars—I was a bit surprised that they didn't try to get all 11 of us into one) about 15 km out of town to a huge arboretum, where they were conducting a plant sale that covered several acres. Oy's father had taken up gardening in a big way after he retired from the customs office, so he was in hog heaven. There was plenty of room for the boys to run around and play soccer, and everyone else just strolled through the lovely grounds, enjoying the (relatively) cool afternoon, and the stunning array of bushes, trees, and flowers. There were thousands of people there, but the place was so huge, that it didn't really feel crowded. Many of the people were concentrated at the steps of a museum honoring the King, where the Army band, accompanied by a variety of singers, was playing a mixture of traditional and modern Thai music. Laurie and I spent about a half hour in the museum. We were impressed—the King really was a pretty all-round talented guy. It was no wonder the people loved and respected him so much.

We didn't get back to town until about 7:00, so our friends decided to have us over to help them consume some of the enormous quantities of food Oy's family had brought with them. As is traditional, they had brought boxes and bags of stuff for which their part of the country was noted. About 9:00 we started the 20-minute walk home with an extra boy—quite a notable step. Although both Cooper and Jesse had spent the night at their house several times, their boys had been very leery of spending the night at our house. Their older boy had been invited to take part in an exchange with the middle school in our home town, and he would be living with us for the next year, so I guess he decided he might as well try it out. It went well (he's was easygoing as their younger boy was wired). About 1:00 the next afternoon, the rest of the gang trooped in and we lunched on 'burgers and 'tater salad; then took off to visit one of the many mansions of former kings. In the Thai custom, it would be very disrespectful to expect a new king to live in the house of a former king, and it would be almost as disrespectful to let the house of a former king fall into disrepair, so they had made them into museums and tourist attractions. The one we visited was especially nice, as it was all of teak, and for some reason, didn't seem to draw the crowds of farangs some of the others did. We got there just in time for the 3:00 tour in Thai, which all but Laurie and I went on, and the 3:15 tour in English, which we opted for. The place supposedly closed at 4:00, but really, they just stopped letting people in at that time, and let those of us who were already in wander around until about 5:00. Our friends dropped us off near our apartment at about 5:30. We dined well on leftovers from the long weekend, and went to bed early.

The next morning, in the hour before we left for school, in addition to breakfast, we managed to get in the Tooth Fairy, noticing the new boxes under the Christmas "tree," have Advent devotions, and open that morning's Advent box. A few words of explanation: the Tooth Fairy did come to Thailand, and in place of his tooth, left in a glass of water on the refrigerator the night before, Jesse found a gold-centered ten-baht piece (worth 40 cents) the next morning. Instead of a Christmas tree (real ones were few and far between there, and we refused to have a fake one), Laurie had made a Christmas-tree-shaped Advent calendar, about 3-feet tall, and bedecked with wrapping-paper-covered match boxes for ornaments—one for each day from the 1st through the 25th of December. Inside each match box, which they open following Advent devotions, was a treat for the boys. In an effort to add to the Christmas-y feel in that snowless environment, we had also been adding a package or two every few days to the small-but-growing-pile under the "tree." It certainly wasn't like home, but then that's not why we were there.

Our Advent tree, with its growing pile of (small) presents.

Our Christmas break in Thailand was the shortest we'd ever had. I left work at 5:00 Friday afternoon, and was back at 7:40 Monday morning. But our Christmas (what there was of it) was nice. Actually, it was quite a bit like many other of our weekends, only with presents. Most of the parties were the next week—the Thais did New Years with much more elan than they did Christmas. We did attend a party the Tuesday before Christmas, at Bangkok Christian College (one of our friends was on their board of directors). It began with a 4:30 service (which started at 5:20), followed by dinner; then a sort of amateur variety show that was the mainstay of so many Thai parties. Our friend had class until 7:00, so he was to meet us there at about 8:00. Our friend's wife was to go with their two children and Laurie, Cooper and Jesse by cab at 4:30. I had class until 5:00, so I was going to walk the two miles after class. Our friend wouldn't hear of that. His wife drew me a detailed map, and told me to take a #2 air-con bus. So I did. The problem was the #2 air-con bus didn't go where she said it did, and by the time I realized that, I was all the way downtown, and had to walk about three miles back. I got there, tired and footsore, just in time for dinner. It's difficult to convey the spirit of a Thai "party." They set up a stage, and performed a highly structured sort of show that included karoke singing (very popular there) by most of the honored guests (often including Laurie and me), distributed gifts for everything from having a star on the underside of one's chair to wearing the most beautiful traditional Thai costume. They presented awards to women who were "old, but still beautiful"; men who had been married the shortest time; couples who were dressed the most like twins; people who were wearing the most of a certain color; people who had a certain color on, but out of sight; basically, any silly excuse they could think of to award prizes. They often had arranged for several children to sing and dance as part of the program. The whole thing was presided over by a master or mistress of ceremonies (sometimes both) whose job it was to keep everyone having a good time. Some in the audience took great pleasure in participating enthusiastically; others didn't pay any attention, but drank and talked among themselves at their table, or made the rounds with their drinks to chat with friends at other tables. My Thai friend told me that much business was conducted after everyone got "loosened up" a bit. That took, a while, as they drank the weakest drinks I'd ever seen—one capful of Black Label or Passport Scotch to a full glass of soda. Laurie and I dragged the boys away at 8:40, as they had to go to school the next day. Thai children were allowed to stay up until all hours, even on school nights (say midnight, when they would be getting up at 4:30). Then they slept any time they had a spare moment: on busses, in cars, after lunch, between classes, during classes.

We were invited to another Christmas party on Christmas Eve at 5:00—that one for the teachers and their families at Satit Chula, where the boys went to school and Laurie taught. It was very much the same, but without the church service preceding it. As this one was on the grounds of a public school, we drank only soft drinks. I danced to traditional Thai music (they insisted—it certainly wasn't my idea of a good time); then we led the assembled multitude in a rousing rendition of "Jingle Bells" (again, they insisted); all without benefit of proper "loosening up." It was a real flashback for me—of Christmas 1968, when a friend and I who were traveling throughout Southeast Asia, divided a huge watermelon among dozens of Thai waifs and taught them to sing "Jingle Bells" as our Christmas celebration (no presents that year).

Showing off my Thai dance skills as backup for the karaoke singer.

We got the boys to bed about 9:30, after they had each put one of my socks out (mumbling a bit because all my really big wool ones were back in Minnesota). Then we wrapped a few last minute presents and "Ma in her kerchief and I in my cap...settled down for a long winter's nap," to allow Santa to come. The pile under the tree had swelled to impressive proportions with the addition of many presents to Laurie from her students, to all of us from folks at the party, and to the boys from their teachers and friends (not to mention the boxes from friends in the States). At (a quite reasonable) 7:00 the next morning, the boys began trashing the place in an action they called "opening presents." We had prepared them with many comments about how we couldn't take much back to the States with us, so they weren't (visibly) disappointed that

Our Christmas day visit to jolly old St. Nick near our local Pizza Hut.

they got nothing "big." They did get books, small toys, plastic models, small Lego sets, candy, collection books for their coins and stamps, and jig-saw puzzles. Laurie got a belt of Thai silver, a "Chulalongkorn University" t-shirt, and an appointment book for 1994 (plus an incredible assortment of "stuff" from her students. I got an elephant hide wallet and a variety of cheese, candy, crackers, and olives—food that we couldn't afford to buy there that I had been pining for. Saturday afternoon we went to Pizza Hut for our "traditional Christmas dinner." On the way there, we stopped to visit a very large Santa.

On the way back, we stopped at Chub and Oy's, and dropped the boys off to play. At 10:45 they brought our boys back and left their older to stay overnight. We'd gotten word of a church that had English services of reasonable length at 10:00 Sunday mornings, and had planned to go there on the 26th, but because the boys had been up so late, and because we had one extra (who was Buddhist), we decided to wait until the next week. Chub and Oy picked us up at 1:00 Sunday afternoon, and we all went to a small restaurant that specialized in Southern Thai food. Oy was from the South, so she knew where the best ones were. We then spent the afternoon at a temple famous for its huge "reclining Buddha." It was a very large temple, and quite beautiful. As with many of the temples, the tourists rushed in, looked at the major attraction, and rushed off to the next one. In fact, many of the most beautiful parts of those temples were missed by most farangs. We spent a couple of hours wandering with our friends through the less-traveled parts, enjoying the relative quiet and slow pace within noisy, hustling Bangkok. We spent the evening at home with the boys repairing broken Christmas toys, putting together jig-saw puzzles and models, and reading new books. It was certainly not the "biggest" Christmas we'd had, but it was just as blessed.

Chapter 8
February

One Friday evening, some of my students took Cooper, Jesse, Laurie, and me out for an end-of-the-semester dinner. We went to a very nice Chinese restaurant, and had a wonderful meal. I didn't know how much it cost; they treated us, but I assumed they got a good deal, as the restaurant belonged to the uncle of one of my students. In keeping with the social whirl, Saturday evening, one of the professors in the Faculty of Communication Arts and his wife took us to a nearby coastal province, where we went to a seafood market; then met some friends of theirs and their friends' daughter for dinner. Their friends' daughter had graduated from college the year before, and they wanted to pick my brains about getting her into a grad school in the States. I got the better of the deal—it was a great seafood dinner for only talking about grad schools for a while. Sunday afternoon and evening, the boys went over to Chub and Oy's house to play with their boys, so Laurie and I took advantage of the lull to do some clothes shopping for her, relax over coffee and donuts at Mr. Donut, and attend the last of three "Concerts in the Park" by the Bangkok Symphony Orchestra. That one comprised a sort of "Best of Concerts in the Park" program, as it included a mix of pieces from the other two. Monday was uneventful. As Laurie's dad was coming in Tuesday night, and we were going to travel for a couple of weeks, Tuesday morning we walked a mile and a half to the AUA library to exchange books (the ones we had would have expired by the time we got back). On the way there, we stopped to admire several spirit houses—they were sort of Buddhist versions of Catholic shrines in the States, only much more ornate.

Laurie, Jesse, Cooper, and I planned to travel to the South in April, so I had to go to the train station and get tickets. If I had waited until less than a month before the date we wanted them, they'd have been sold out of second class and air-con, so we'd have ended up riding sixteen hours on third-class wooden benches (or standing, as third class tickets would have gotten us on the train, but would not have reserved us seats. We'd done that, and preferred to avoid a repeat if possible.

Just as I was getting ready to leave for the station, one of the professors from my department came in and informed me that the payroll office wanted me to open an account at Siam Commercial Bank so they could deposit my pay directly. I told her that I already had an account

A typical Thai spirit house on a side street in Bangkok.

at Thai Farmers Bank, and was happy with the current arrangement, in which I picked up my check from the payroll office and deposited it in my account myself; besides, I added, I would only get three more checks, and it seemed silly to change the process at that time. If they had wanted me to have my account at a particular bank, why hadn't they told me that nine months before? Or if they wanted to deposit my check directly, why couldn't they do it in my already existing account? She was sympathetic, but said there was nothing she could do—if I wanted to get paid, I would have to open an account at Siam Commercial. I decided discretion was the better part of valor (in other words, "retreat"), and agreed to do so. Turns out that the closest branch was about halfway to AUA, so I had walked past it twice already that morning. I walked to it once again—about 3/4 mile. When I got there (hot, sweaty, and unhappy with being coerced into having to be there at all) the clerk asked me for my passport. I told him that I had been living in Thailand for nine months, and was not in the habit of carrying my passport around. I offered an official letter from Chula that verified that I was a professor there, instead. He took it to his boss and returned a few minutes later to inform me that it wasn't enough. If I wanted to open an account, I would have to have my passport. I didn't want to open an account, so I left. I said nothing, as I was afraid of what might come out if I stopped gritting my teeth and opened my mouth. I walked to the nearest bus stop from which I could get a bus to the train station—about 1/2 mile. At the station, I stood in line for a half hour before being told that although we could get second class air-con sleepers for the trip back, we would have to settle for second class fan sleepers on the way down. It would be Thai traditional New Year, and everybody would be traveling, so I was lucky to get that. Then another half-mile walk and a bus trip back to my office. Counting the mile and a half each way to school and back to the apartment, I figured I got in a refreshing seven or eight miles in 95 to 100 degrees. The university money handlers did relent, and let me pick up my last three checks in person. But my day was just getting nicely started.

Laurie's dad was coming to visit from the States, and had written, saying he would arrive at 11:45 p.m. on the 9th. I had called United Airlines, just to be safe (better safe than sorry, after all). Oh, no, they had said, he's arriving on the 8th. So, at 10:00pm, I caught a taxi to the airport (120 baht), and hung around watching people until 11:45. Then I moved up to the area where incoming passengers passed on their way out of customs. I knew it would take him probably an hour to clear customs, but I didn't want to miss him. I stood there on my 8-mile-weary feet until 1:15, when it became pretty clear that everybody was ashore who was going ashore. Then I hunted down the United office in the bowels of the terminal building to find out the terrible news: he had fallen from the plane over the Pacific; he had suffered a heart attack and been rushed directly to the hospital (or, worse yet, morgue) on arrival; the drug-sniffing dogs had caught him trying to smuggle 10 kilos of uncut into the country. None of the above. He would arrive on the 9th—just as he (unlike the United Airlines representative) had said he would, proving that sometimes, contrary to popular opinion, it is possible to be both safe and sorry. Not a good day for the home team. Back down to the taxi stand. By then, it was 1:30, and they all wanted 400 baht to take me back to town—including the metered taxis, who weren't allowed to do that. I refused, saying it had cost me only 120 baht coming out, and I wasn't going to be cheated going back. I was spoiling for a fight by then, anyway, so it gave me the opportunity to vent some spleen; and on deserving recipients, at that. My venting was cut short, however, when one of them agreed to take me "on the meter." We pulled out of the airport, and came to a screeching standstill. All of the truck traffic that was not allowed into the city during the daytime was backed up for miles. I had visions of the meter reading 1000 baht by the time we got back, but the blockage eventually dissipated, and by the time we arrived at 2:15, I only owed 130 baht. I gave him 150 to reward his honesty, and staggered in to bed. But first, I had to explain to Laurie what I had done with her father. Of course, my adrenaline level was still so high that I didn't get to sleep until about 3:00. I picked Laurie's dad up that night (uneventfully), and we spent the next ten days taking him to many of the places we had visited previously.

Chapter 9
March

My driver's license would have expired on my birthday (March 17), and if I had waited until we returned to renew, I would have had to take the driving test. So, my accountant back in the States (who was handling our business while we were gone) talked to the folks at the Motor Vehicle Bureau, and they agreed, under the circumstances, to issue me a new license (without a photo; I'd have to get the photo added when I returned), if I would get an eye exam from a qualified doctor in Thailand. My CPA sent me the form, and I set out to get an eye exam. First I tried the clinic on campus, but they said they didn't have the "equipment" to do the job. I said all they needed was one of those charts that hang on the wall that I could look at with one eye; then the other. They said they didn't have one. Next I went to a shop where they sold glasses. They said they had all the equipment, but nobody licensed to examine eyes in the States (how many people in Thailand would have been?). I explained that it was just a formality; that all I needed was somebody to check my eyes and sign the paper saying that I wouldn't mow down pedestrians if I got behind the wheel of a car (a foreign concept there). He allowed as how he wouldn't really feel comfortable signing such an official document as I needed. So, on to the hospital. This was the largest hospital in Thailand—similar to the Mayo Clinic in the States—for an eye exam. I entered and approached the reception desk. The receptionist took me to another desk. The nurse there took me to another desk, where I paid 20 baht (80 cents), and the woman there took me to another desk. At each of these stations, I explained that all I wanted was to have somebody check my eyes and assure the Minnesota DMV that I could see well enough to drive. At each of the stations, they filled out more paperwork. Finally, they sent me to the second floor—Preventive Medicine. I handed them the wad of paper, and explained that all I wanted was.... They said they didn't have anyone there qualified to look at my eyes, and sent me to the eleventh floor—Specialized Medicine and Optometry. I approached the nurses (five of them) behind the desk, handed them my wad of papers, and explained that all I wanted was.... After several minutes of telephone calls and urgent consultation, they told me the doctor who handled eye diseases wasn't in (I realized that it was Wednesday afternoon—their doctors must have trained in the States, with Wednesday afternoon golf as part of the curriculum). They said they would make an appointment for me to see him on Friday. I tried one more time. "There is nothing wrong with my eyes. I can see just fine. I just need someone official to tell the people in the Minnesota Department of Motor Vehicles that, so I can get my driver's license renewed." "If there is nothing wrong with your eyes, why are you here?" It occurred to me that Thais must not need to be able to see to get a driver's license—that would have explained a lot about the traffic problem. I took out my license; I showed them the expiration date; I explained that if I waited until we returned to renew, I would have to take the driving test; I explained that if one of them would let me cover one eye at a time and read that chart on the wall over there (I paused and did so, just to prove that I could, but they stopped me part way through); and sign the sheet of paper I had brought with me (which by then was buried amidst many other sheets of paper, so I dug it out to show them); I would go away and leave them alone, and could get my license without taking the driving test when I returned. "You mean there's nothing wrong with your eyes?" "Right." "You mean you just want us to verify that there is nothing wrong with your eyes?" "Right." "Oh, we can do that; no problem." "Now?" "Of course." "Wonderful." "Please have a seat over there and wait." After about 15 minutes, a nurse took me into a darkened room, and I repeated my performance with the wall chart. That time, she let me do the whole thing. I thanked her, thinking I was done, but she led me to another room, where another nurse spent 15 minutes having me find colored "X"s, "O"s, and triangles in a comprehensive color-blindness test. She took me to another room, where a doctor, conducted a complete eye examination—peering into each eye with piercing lights, having me look through complicated equipment, moving her finger about and having me track it with first one eye; then the other. Finally, she filled out three forms, which she inserted into my, by then, fat file, and signed (at last) the form from the DMV that said that if I ran down pedestrians it wouldn't be because I hadn't seen them. By the time I got back to my office, three hours had elapsed, but I could rest easy in the assurance that my eyes were perfect. Actually, they weren't—I cheated. I had an astigmatism in my left eye that made it impossible for me to read more than half the numbers on the 20/20 line of the chart, but I read them with my right eye first, and, following the logical assumption that they would say the same thing for my left eye, simply repeated from memory what I had just said. I feel safe in confessing this now, as I'm sure the statute of limitations has expired.

Our friends bidding us and their older son goodbye at the Bangkok airport.

The first week in May, Chub and Oy, their sons, his mother, a nephew, Laurie and I, and our sons piled into two cabs for our last trip together. The five of us (Gokkai included) bid them a tearful goodbye, and boarded a plane for the States. After one transfer in Minneapolis, we landed in Bemidji at 8 p.m. We fixed Gokkai a temporary bed on the sofa and retired to our own beds for the first time in almost a year.

III
BULGARIA

Introduction

Unlike our years in China and Thailand, we had time to spare before we needed to report to the American University in Bulgaria. We took advantage of that extra time by purchasing Eurail passes and spending several weeks taking the "scenic route." The passes allowed us to pay a greatly reduced fare for 21 days of unlimited train travel. We flew to Frankfurt, Germany, with a 2-day stop in Iceland; then travelled by train and ferry to France, Switzerland, Spain, Italy, and Greece before ending up in Bulgaria.

Chapter 1
August

Our Hotel in Paris (the Vieille) was only a couple of blocks from both the North and the East train stations (I never did figure out how the "north" and the "east" stations could be so close together). We had a small, garret-like room with sloping walls on the sixth floor. Access to it was via a tiny elevator that only held two people at a time as far as the fifth floor; then up a narrow, winding stairway to the sixth floor. The room was cozy with all four of us in it, but it did have a private bath and a wonderful view of the ventilation shaft.

Our first day in Paris was a Tuesday, and all the museums were closed, so we bought a 2-day bus pass and spent the day visiting the traditional tourist sights of the city. My favorite part was just traveling by bus throughout the city and seeing the various neighborhoods. Many of the buildings were of monumental proportions, and although taken for granted in Paris, if plunked down in a city in the States, would have been tourist attractions in their own right. We went first to the Eiffel Tower, and as it was still very much the tourist season, lines of people waiting to ascend to the top were almost a block long. Cooper was determined to climb it, however, so the rest of us wandered around watching people for the hour and a half it took him to stand in line for a (ridiculously expensive right to climb four billion steps) ticket, ascend to the top, look at the views, and descend to ground level. While we waited for him, we noticed a figure wrapped in gold lame', wearing a gold King Tut mask, standing on a gold-painted box. The only time the figure moved was to bow deeply from the waist each time someone put money in the basket at its feet. I saw some guys standing around who seemed to know what was going on, and (as I am wont to do—which drives Cooper crazy) approached them and struck up a conversation. They said they and the young man in the gold suit were from Bangladesh, that he was one of two who took 1-hour turns in the suit for about ten hours a day, earning them each an average of 10 francs (about $1.60) a day—tough way to make a (meager) living.

The morning had been quite warm and sunny, but the afternoon turned very chilly and rainy. As we had limited time in Paris, however, we couldn't waste any sitting in our room waiting for the rain to let up, so we went to the Arc d'Triumph anyway. To do so, we took a bus

299

A golden King Tut near the Eiffel Tower, unmoved by passersby.

within about ten blocks of it and did something I'd wanted to do for as long as I could remember: strolled down the Champs Elyse'es. Granted, it was raining fairly steadily, which didn't help, but even in the best of situations, I would have been disappointed. I expected something a bit more intimate; It's just a huge, congested boulevard. The central walking street in Blagoevgrad (the city in Bulgaria in which we lived for the next year) was more like what I had envisioned: intimate outdoor cafes, street musicians, and food carts. Even with the rain, crowds at the Arc d'Triumph were dense. That time Jesse made the climb, and again we spent about an hour and a half people watching while we waited for him. He said the masses inside made it slow going, and the humidity made it a bit uncomfortable and claustrophobic, but that the view from the top was marvelous. The view from underneath was no slouch, either. Much of our waiting time was spent admiring the intricate reliefs carved into every surface of the huge stone monument. Also, while we waited the ceremonial guard came and lit the memorial flame at its base.

Our last stop of the day was Notre Dame. As with many of the sights throughout Europe, it was being readied for "Europe 2000," so much of its facade was obscured by scaffolding. We didn't spend much time inside, as the crowds milling about discouraged any contemplative efforts. Also, it was quite dim inside, and the crowds made it difficult to get close enough to the religious art to really appreciate it. There was a long line of people waiting to ascend the tower, and the boys allowed as how they'd pretty much had enough climbing for the day, so we passed on that.

The next morning we bought passes and set off museum hopping. Our first stop was the Museum of the Middle Ages (at Jesse's request, as he expected every sort of armor, and knightly weapons fit for King Arthur's Round Table). The museum was housed in the Cluny Monastery, and offered, in fact, a marvelous collection of religious art from the 11th through the 13th century. It also housed many huge, ornate pieces of furniture from the wealthy households of the period. There, as with many of the places we visited, we were struck by the sheer wonder of such ageless beauty, and reminded of just how young, and in many senses immature, our own culture was. The most famous exhibit was a series of five tapestries depicting "The Lady and the Unicorn." In marvelously muted colors and fine workmanship, they told the story of the lady's immersion in the senses, and her eventual renunciation of the sensual. The museum also offered an archaeological bonus, as part of it was constructed over some ancient Roman baths.

We went next to the Louvre'—my biggest disappointment in Paris. With at least a week, and one hundredth the number of people, I'm sure it would be wonderful. As it was, every time we paused to try and appreciate a work, we were nearly trampled by mobs of "art lovers," usually being herded around by professional guides whose monotonous spiel about what their charges should be seeing, and what they should think about it, was less than uplifting. Appreciation of the "Mona Lisa," for example, was enhanced by a thick sheet of bulletproof glass, as well as restraining ropes that kept potential viewers back at least 15 feet. The throngs gathered to get a glimpse of the masterpiece, however, made anything as close as 15 feet out of the question. That same mob made contemplation of any other pieces in the room impossible as well. I

The plaza outside the Louvre, with people gathering to watch a solar eclipse.

stopped to take in the grandeur of a piece on one wall that must have been 15 by 25 feet and depicted the coronation of an emperor. Within seconds, I had been jostled by several patrons, most of whom looked at me as though I were crazy for actually stopping in the middle of the room. We did find a few exhibits that, as they didn't contain any world-famous pieces, weren't quite as crowded, and so were much more pleasant to spend time with.

The real highlight of the Louvre', however, was that our visit happened to coincide with a solar eclipse. We gathered with hundreds of others in the courtyard to watch as all but a tiny sliver of the sun disappeared. They had been selling special glasses in the pharmacies, but all the ones we found were either closed, or had sold out. Jesse was sorely disappointed that we had to be content with looking only when the cloud cover allowed it.

After lunch, we walked to the Orsay Museum, which was as enjoyable as the Louvre had been disappointing. It's scale was not intimidating; it wasn't as well-known, so less crowded; they limited the number of patrons allowed in at the same time; and, in my humble opinion, the pieces were as good as in any museum in the world. They were showing a special exhibition of the impressionists, and we were able to linger over works (both well-known and not) of masters such as Degas, Monet, Van Gogh, and Renoir. I entered one room, and there was "Whistler's Mother," just hanging there unannounced, unadorned, uncrowded—delightful. Jesse's quota of appreciation for classic art was a bit shy of the rest of ours, so while Cooper and Laurie spent more time in the Orsay, I took him across the street to the Legion of Honor Museum—talk about uncrowded; only four other people came in during the hour or so we were there. It was right up Jesse's alley: weapons, medals, coins, uniforms, and models and paintings of famous battles. It really was very nice, on a modest, unassuming scale.

The whole time we were in Paris, Laurie and I kept lobbying to sit down for a nice dinner at an outdoor cafe, but by the end of each day we were exhausted, and were just glad that the hotel restaurant was convenient, inexpensive, and offered good, simple food. Laurie and I did manage a couple of coffees one morning before the boys got up. At $1.50 a demi—I suppose it was just as well we never got to do wine and French cuisine; we probably couldn't have afforded it anyway. We had reservations on an overnight sleeper to Spain that left at 11:30 , so we took a taxi at 9:00 to Austerlitz Station to await its departure.

As it was the height of the tourist season in Spain, Barcelona and the other coastal towns were overflowing. Madrid was too far to get to and ever hope to have any time at all for Italy and Greece. We were about ready for a smaller, more out-of-the-way place, anyway, so we opted for Zaragoza, which the guidebook described as "the most Spanish of all the cities in Spain" (whatever that meant). Accommodations on the German trains were the best anywhere we traveled, and they went gradually downhill as we progressed from Germany to Switzerland, France, Spain, Italy, Greece, and Bulgaria. The Spanish trains were not great, but I could finally communicate without having to depend on people speaking English. In fact, I was pleasantly surprised at how well my less-than-fluent Spanish served us. I fell into the category of "terrible vocabulary and grammar, but doesn't let that get in the way of being understood." I mean, verb tenses are nice, but who was going to misunderstand if I said "I go now," "I go tomorrow, " or "I go yesterday"? I may have sounded silly; they may have laughed; but they did understand, and that's what I was after. In fact, I was surprised to discover that my Spanish not only served well in Spain, but better than English in Italy as well.

We called La Penzione Magnificat from the train station, and reserved rooms. We took a taxi there, and found it was on the third floor of an old 5-story apartment building on a narrow street only two blocks from the central square in the old part of the town. We could walk everywhere but the train station. We got two clean, airy double rooms for 60 pesetas (about $45) a night—about half what we had been paying in Germany, France, and Switzerland. The bad news was that we were also in the center of the night-life district, and the young people of Spain tended to party from midnight until 5:00 a.m. every morning. It was too hot to close the windows in our non-airconditioned rooms, so we just had to try to ignore the noise and sleep as best we could. We had decided to stay in Zaragoza a couple of days; then move on to the north of Italy—maybe Florence or Genoa. We had learned that it was best to return to the train station on the morning of our first full day in a city to make reservations to our next destination, for although our rail passes meant we didn't have to pay for tickets if we could get them, they didn't necessarily mean we could get them.

Thursday morning I caught a city bus to the station to see what I could arrange to northern Italy Friday night or Saturday morning. I had practiced on the bus and was sure I had gotten the Spanish pretty close, so knew I was in trouble when the ticket agent laughed at my request. As it happened, we had not taken the Feast of the Assumption (tied with Easter as the biggest religious holiday of the year in Spain and Italy) into consideration in our travel plans. The agent informed me that weekend travel was out of the question: nothing available Friday; nothing available Saturday; nothing available Sunday. Wait, if we weren't too particular about where we ended up, he could get us to Barcelona Sunday afternoon, where we could change to an Italian train that would get us to Genoa sometime Monday morning. My inquiry about sleeping arrangements on the overnight train drew more mirth. The best he could do was four of the six seats still available in a no smoking compartment. I took them and considered myself lucky. As so often happened, what seemed at first unfortunate, we soon realized was a stroke of luck. We couldn't have picked a better place to be stranded for the Feast of the Assumption. One side of the main square was dominated by one of the oldest, most venerated cathedrals in central Spain, and people had traveled for days to be there for the celebration. Many had held off baptizing babies just to have the ritual performed in that church. The side of the square opposite the church was lined with hotels, shops, and restaurants. At one end of the square was a huge, modern, marble fountain constructed to serve more as a series of waterfalls than as a fountain, per se. At the other end was a cathedral that had served during the Moorish occupation as a mosque. Consequently, it displayed a fascinating layering of architectural styles and ornamentation. It had been built as a relatively modest Roman Catholic church; then had added a moorish-style minaret and had been faced with glass tile and other Moorish decoration. After the Moors were driven out, the facade was chiseled smooth, and Roman Catholic architectural detail reintroduced. The rest of the exterior, however, was left in the quasi-Moorish style to

*The glass pyramid in Zaragoza's central square;
covering the remains of a Roman city.*

which it had been adapted during their occupation. The interior was a strange amalgamation of cultural and historic styles, as well.

The center of the square held a strange, modernistic glass pyramid, surrounded by fountains and pools; impressive by day, and more so by night, as it was beautifully lit. It took us most of the first day to figure out that this structure housed the entrance to the remains of an impressive city that was built when the Romans occupied that part of Spain. As the Spanish city had been constructed over it, the excavated remains were deep below the square. We were impressed both with the forum and marketplace that had been preserved as an underground museum, and with the quality of the displays. We could walk around among what was left of the original shops, warehouses, and baths; and could view parts of the old streets and water and sewer systems. The educational displays explained quite a bit about the daily life of the Romans who had lived and worked there.

We visited the main cathedral Saturday, and were struck by its opulence. We could certainly understand Luther's objection to how much wealth the Roman Catholic church expended just on maintaining such buildings. The mammoth main alter, which looked as though it was seldom used for worship, was constructed of marble, gold, and silver. A smaller, more accessible alter was slightly less ornately appointed in silver and carved hardwoods. The pipe organ and choir loft were also huge and ornate. Most of the main iconography was dedicated to Mary, with the small side chapels each dedicated to a separate saint. Only one of the alters was dedicated to the crucified Christ.

Much of our time in Zaragoza was spent just walking around the old part of the city—looking at the architecture and watching people—and enjoying the numerous excellent cafes and restaurants, almost all of which had tables outdoor under awnings, trees, or grape arbors. We were also pleasantly surprised at the number and quality of the museums. One of the nicest museums we visited in Europe was in a beautifully preserved mansion, and housed much of the sculpture of Pablo Gargallo. The building was delightful and empty of other tourists, the sculptures were beautifully displayed—incorporating working drawings and rough miniatures of the finished pieces, and admission was free. Gargallo' s work was truly impressive. Many of his works were in the Louvre, and many of his other pieces (in my humble opinion) were good enough to be. We also visited the Paulo Serrano Museum—lots of modern paintings—and a gallery that housed the work of a wealthy man who had been an art critic and had amassed a huge and varied collection. It was interesting to see some beautiful pieces by unknown artists, some definately-less-than-beautiful works by artists who didn't deserve recognition, and several early pieces by artists whose later work was world-famous and incredibly expensive. The temporary exhibit at this museum was a collection of 77 of Goya's drawings. His unremittingly black view of the world was divided into three sections that depicted the death and mayhem of war, the death and mayhem of natural disasters, and the death and mayhem of bullfighting. After slowly, carefully studying about half the sketches, we'd had about all the death and mayhem we needed for one day, and walked quickly past the rest.

We caught the train to Barcelona Sunday afternoon, and switched to the Italian train to Genoa, where my awareness of the diminished comfort of train by country held true. We shared our (cozy) 6-seat couchette compartment with a delightful young Italian couple who were on their way back from vacation to their home in Genoa. Before we left the station, a mass of college students on their way back to school after traveling for the summer—with tickets, but not seat reservations—crowded into every inch of the passageways, space between cars, and any other area the conductor didn't keep shooing them out of. A trip to the bathroom at the end of the car meant walking over dozens of reclining bodies. To make matters worse, most weren't the least bit interested in whether they were in a no-smoking car. Jesse, especially, hated smoking, and I had to restrain him from trying to throw college students twice his age (and size) off the train. We were thankful that the couple who shared our compartment didn't smoke. It drizzled much of the trip, so it was impossible to open the windows for fresh air, and the atmosphere deteriorated steadily to hot, clammy, and generally unpleasant. Our compartment mates and the boys (as seems to be universal with young people) were able to sleep much of the time, but Laurie and I had a lot of time for solitary reflection.

By the time we reached Genoa, it was obvious that we would not have time to stop anywhere but Rome and Athens if we were to make it to Bulgaria in time, so we decided to just catch the next express train to Rome, and hunkered down among the throngs of students to wait. When the proper (I thought) train arrived, we boarded and within a couple of minutes, were on our way. I admit I thought it a bit strange that very few of the waiting students rushed aboard with us, but was so relieved that we weren't going to be crowded that I didn't give it much thought. Well, in my defense, although it may not have actually been a train to Rome, it was, in fact, a train toward Rome. It was, not to put too fine a point on it, a (very) local train, and what we had gained in elbow room, we lost in time. We were on the right track though, and (after sitting on a siding to watch the—very crowded—express whoosh past) we just kept switching to the next local that would take us (unremittingly) to our destination. One of them, incidentally, must have passed close to Pisa, because we got a pretty good look at what was unmistakably the Leaning Tower. We arrived at the main station in Rome about two hours later than we had planned—after 32 hours on trains and in train stations, and about nine without eating. I had called ahead (in Spanish) from Genoa to reserve rooms at the Penzione Albert, but the owner expected us by 8:00. I called from the station, and she said it was alright; she had saved our rooms (bless her). We took a taxi, and with great difficulty, as it was at the end of a tiny cut-de-sac in a residential part of town, found Penzione Albert by 10:30. We put our packs in our room, and assailed by doubts magnified by our landlady that we would find anyplace to eat open that late, set out in search of food. After wandering for a half hour, we came across a wonderful Chinese restaurant that seemed in no danger of closing in the immediate future, and feasted on delicious (and inexpensive) Chinese food and (for Laurie and me) well-deserved beers.

The next morning we were excited to see the wonders of Rome—but first we had to take care of business: arranging the next leg of our trip, by train and ferry, to Athens. As we had bought both Europasses and Balkan passes for the trains before we left the States, and as we had been told that the ferry tickets were covered if we were going on to Greece, that should have been no trouble. Rome had a great subway system (called "Metro") that lay under the majority of the city in a huge "X" shape, and had stops within easy walking distance of almost everything worth stopping for (including one within two blocks of the pension at which we were staying). The center of the X was directly under the central train and bus stations, which made it even more convenient. We took the metro to the train station to reserve tickets to Brindisi, where we would catch the ferry to Patmos, Greece, and connect there with the train to Athens. I got an uneasy feeling when they told me at the train station that they couldn't make the reservations there because they didn't know when the ferry left Brindisi. They sent us out into the sweltering heat (it was one of the hottest Augusts in recent history in both Italy and Greece) to a travel agency about four blocks away. When we got there, the office had just closed for their 2-hour lunch, so we spent the time visiting a couple of cathedrals in the area.

When the agency reopened, they told us of course they could book us train tickets to Brindisi, but they needed to know which ferry we'd be taking. When I asked our choices, they said that although they had a schedule, they didn't know which of them were already full; we'd have to go to the ferry office about six blocks away and book our ferry tickets first. After several wrong turns, we found the ferry office tucked away in a back alley. The woman there was very nice; she said they would be happy to book us tickets, and that there was no problem getting on any one we wanted, as it was off-season, and there was plenty of room (they didn't know this at the travel agency?). I said fine, our tickets would be included (with an additional service charge, which for the four of us was about $120) in our Europasses. She said no, they were only included in our Europasses if we had added Greece. I said we had Balkan Passes for Greece and the other Balkan countries. She said she'd have to see the paperwork (which, of course, was back at the pension). At least the Metro was cool. After the 40-minute round trip, we took up where we had left off. I showed her the paperwork, which said that if we were going on to Greece, the ferry was covered. She said only if we were using the train system when we got to Greece. I said we were. She said she'd have to see the paperwork for the Balkan Passes. After the 40-minute round trip to get our Balkan passes, we took up where we had left off.

I presented her the paperwork for the Balkan Passes that showed we were going to use the trains in Greece. She said no, that didn't count, because they were separate Balkan Passes, and not add-ons to the Europasses. I said so what, it's the same company. She said it didn't matter. I said (of course, I had maintained a calm, quiet, and respectful manner throughout) wait a minute, you mean to tell me that if we go from Italy to Greece and stop, the ferry's covered, but if we go on from Greece it's not? She said yes. I gave up. We had been in Rome almost a full day by then, and had seen their Metro system, several travel offices, and a couple of small churches. I couldn't take it. OK, I said, how much? After some calculations, she said $143. I said wait a minute, are you telling me we've gone through all this hassle for $23? She said yes, it's off-season prices. I said why didn't you tell me. She said (I swear she did) you didn't ask. So, then we had ferry tickets and could go back to the travel office and get train reservations—but only as far as Brindisi; we'd have to get reservations for the Greek train when we got to Greece (of course; why would I have thought otherwise?).

We took the Metro, and spent the rest of the afternoon in the area of the Coliseum. It was staggering for us northern Minnesotans, for whom a "century" house was impressive, to stand amid structures thousands of years old and try to understand that they really were used by people. We were especially impressed by the Forum, with its evidence of layers of civilization: Christian churches built on Roman temples built on other structures. We walked about six or eight miles, and in the process, stumbled on several impressive monuments, buildings, and ruins. Among them was a large field encircled by an earthen embankment, on which children were playing soccer, and around which adults were jogging. In using it to try and get our bearings on our map, we realized that it was the site of the Circus Maximus. Although the sight itself was not at all impressive, the concept amazed us that here, as well as throughout the city, such antiquities were simply taken for granted—part of their everyday lives. We also saw a huge monument nicknamed "the typewriter" because of its general shape. We thought it must have been in honor of Italians who had died in war, as it housed both their equivalent of the tomb of the unknown soldier, and a small military museum. The museum was cool inside, so we spent more time than necessary to see the exhibits. One of the most interesting was Italy's first 2-man submarine, which they used (if my Spanish interpretation of the Italian text served me well) mostly to sneak into harbors and plant mines on Allied ships.

We had dinner that evening in a small family-style restaurant near our pension. The boys had pizza, and allowed as how Pizza Hut's was better. We explained that, just as the Chinese food in the States had been Americanized to suit Western tastes, it is unreasonable to expect real Italian food to taste anything other than Italian.

The next day we set out to try and follow a couple of the walking

One of Dali's melting clocks, outside an exhibition in Rome.

tours in a brochure we had found. We failed miserably to follow any one of those laid out in the brochure, but in our stumbling around, did manage to somehow come across most of the important sites described in it. As with most of the European cities, Rome was "sprucing up" for the Year 2000 tourist season, and many sites were partially obscured by scaffolding and people working on restoration. We saw what we could of Michelangelo's Moses, Rachel, and Leah in the Church of St Paul. Moses was the only one not partially obscured, and they had him set in an alcove behind thick plate glass, with lights on a timer that only came on when we inserted a 10 lira piece. We found the Trevi Fountain, which we joined the other tourists in helping finance the city government by throwing coins into. Nearby was a Dali exhibition, with three of his pieces outside to advertise it, including one of the melting clocks, and the woman's torso cut and offset at the waist with bugs crawling on it. They also had a huge portrait of him with his famous quote about not being crazy. We would like to have gone in, but at $15 apiece, decided to skip it (much to Cooper's dismay).

One of the other sites we found quite impressive was "The Rotunda," a huge round building, built like an igloo—completely open inside, with a hole in the roof. It was another religious edifice the Christians had rebuilt from an ancient Roman structure. As we lingered in the cool dimness, we realized that the shaft of sunlight through the roof moved across the interior, lighting various beautiful works of art in turn. It would have been great to be able to spend a day there, noting each of the pieces as it became illuminated. The last site we intended to spend time at was St. Peter's Basilica and the Vatican museum. By the time we arrived at 4:00, however, the museum was closing, and the boys couldn't go into St. Peter's because they were in shorts. We just wandered around in the plaza and looked at the Vatican from outside—which was pretty impressive in itself. Laurie was very disappointed at missing the Michelangelos, and even considered trying to get back the next morning before our train left. I talked her out of it by pointing out what a mess it would be if we missed the train and subsequently the ferry, and asking if she wanted to go through that booking process again.

We packed the next morning, and picked up some food at a local market. We'd learned not to count on the availability, quality, or price of food on trains or ferries, so always tried to carry emergency rations. We got some bread at a bakery, and at a nearby meat counter, saw what looked to be lunchmeat. I talked with the young man behind the counter in a mixture of Spanish and English, trying to determine what it was, and if it was precooked. He said it was precooked, but he couldn't come up with the word in either English or Spanish for what it was, and I didn't understand it in Italian. Finally, in desperation, he put his hands in his armpits, flapped the resulting "wings," pulled his chin back, puffed out his cheeks, and in a very deep voice, said, "big chicken." We were delighted with his efforts, and I knew that from then on, no Thanksgiving dinner would pass without our remembering the "big chicken" sandwiches we had in Italy.

We caught the train to Brindisi at 1:00. It was to arrive at 6:30, and the ferry wasn't to leave until 8:00. We had been told by the people where we reserved our ferry tickets in Rome that their Brindisi office was "just across the street from the train station." We envisioned a train station near the harbor, and a dock-side office, so expected no problem. Sure enough, we found their office just across the street, where they checked our tickets and told us to proceed "about 300 meters" down the street, to their "other office," where they would assign our cabins. OK, so the train station wasn't quite on the harbor, and their "other office" was dockside, right? We eventually realized that "about 300 meters" in Italy and Greece was a phrase that might translate loosely as "not too far." In fact, it was a half-mile walk with all our baggage.

The woman at the "other office" assigned us cabins and told us to proceed "about 300 meters" to the harbor where the ferry was preparing to leave in about a half hour. The harbor was about 3/4 mile away, but it was huge, and although we passed many ferries on the way, ours was the last in line—another 1/4 mile away. I felt really sorry for Laurie, because I could see she was really struggling; especially the last 1/4 mile. I couldn't slow down, though, because I still had to get our pass-ports cleared at the police station before we could board (besides, I was pretty much running on fumes by that time myself). I told Cooper and Jesse to hurry ahead and leave their bags with me while they went back to help their mother. I didn't realize it, but the food bag, which she was carrying, had ripped and scattered food all over. She probably would have had to abandon it, except a nice couple who were strolling along the dock took pity on her and helped her until Jesse and Cooper got back to her. When we got on the boat we were told our cabin was up three narrow, steep, flights of stairs. We probably would not have made it if a couple of porters hadn't helped us up the last one and down the hallway to our room. One of them saw how exhausted I was, and told me I needed to quit smoking. When I told him I didn't smoke, he scoffed at me and said he was as old as me and wasn't having any trouble with my carry-on bag. I couldn't decide whether to invite him to go back to the train station and carry both it and my pack the mile and a half in 45 minutes, or to just throw him over the side. I decided I didn't have enough steam left for either, and let it pass. We were all drenched in sweat, so we dropped our bags in the cabin and went topside. We were among the last to board, so were soon underway, and it wasn't long before the cool evening breeze had us feeling much better. I was sure, though, that years later, when I recalled the most pleasant times of my life, that trip from the train to the ferry in Brindisi, Italy, wouldn't make the top ten.

Chapter 2
September

We arrived at the Blagoevgrad train station early on the morning of September 3. Shortly after disembarking, I realized that I needed to use the "facilities." No problem, train stations always have them. The bad news: the station was locked. The good news: they were in a small (very basic but unlocked) concrete building next door. Sitting outside the building was a little old lady with a small pile of toilet paper in front of her. It seemed use of the toilets was free, but the toilet paper wasn't. In the two and a half hours since we had crossed the border, I hadn't learned enough Bulgarian to understand how much it cost, but that didn't matter, as I had no Bulgarian money anyway. Cooper ran to the bank across the street to change some money, but it was closed. I made an unsuccessful attempt to pay with some of the Greek coins I had left. I offered her an American dollar—probably worth more than she made in a week. By that time, it was becoming pretty clear that my negotiating had taken on an air of urgency. She refused the dollar, but handed me a wad of paper and motioned for me to go on in. She didn't understand the words, "Bless you," but I'm sure she got the idea. The next morning, after we had been able to change some money, I went back and offered her a handful of Bulgarian coins. She took one of the smallest ones, smiled, and said what I assume was "Thank you" in Bulgarian.

After I exited the "facilities," we approached a taxi that was sitting in front of the train station. I told the driver that we wanted to go to the American University in Bulgaria. He motioned for us to get in. I asked how much—a silly question, as I had no idea 1) how far away the university was, 2) what the going rates were for taxis in Bulgaria, and 3) whether he would accept Greek or American money. He said he would take one dollar. That seemed like a pretty good deal to me. I paid him, we loaded some of our belongings for a year in Bulgaria into his tiny trunk, some onto his tiny roof, and the rest on Laurie, Cooper, and Jesse's laps. I climbed in front, and we took off. Four blocks later he stopped and motioned for us to get out. I looked around and saw nothing resembling a university. I pantomimed that information to him, and he pantomimed back that the large building he had parked behind was said university, that he couldn't drive in front of it, and that we would have to lug all of our belongings around front by hand. He could see that I was skeptical, so he offered to help with the lugging.

The American University in Bulgaria, housed (ironically) in what was originally Communist Party headquarters in Blagoevgrad.

Sure enough: the other side of what appeared to be a rather nondescript structure was an impressive front facade with "American University in Bulgaria" engraved on it. I thanked him, but offered no tip, as I figured he made out pretty well at twenty five cents a block. Well we were there. I climbed the impressive steps to the equally impressive front door—which was locked. We sat patiently with our baggage on the impressive steps for two hours, when someone showed up for work and unlocked the door.

The American University in Bulgaria was housed in a six-story building situated on the west side of a football-field-sized plaza, in a space that had once housed hundreds of private homes. When the Communists took over, they had razed all those homes to erect a building to house the offices of the Communist Party in Blagoevgrad. After the Communists left Bulgaria, the university took over the top five floors. A movie theatre, a restaurant, and the city library occupied the first floor. Movie theaters in Bulgaria played mostly American movies (subtitled) with the original soundtracks played at maximum volume. I had a 3:00 class scheduled for a room directly over the theatre. I was a half hour into my first class when the 3:30 movie started. It was so loud that I had to cancel class. I got the Dean, took him to the classroom, and asked him if he would be guest lecturer for my next class in that room. We went back to his office and he assigned me a new room.

The plaza was paved with marble, granite, and other stone in various sizes and textures (from rough cobblestones to polished marble slabs a yard square) in a complicated, multicolored, geometric pattern. On the north side of the plaza were the city theatre (where all the major stage performances were held), and what we assumed was a government office building. Most of the east side (opposite the university) was taken up by the entrance to the walking mall, with a bank and a night club to its south. The plaza was actually two stories, as a section about 50 feet square was sunken in the middle, with wide granite staircases at each corner. In the center of the sunken area was a large, beautiful fountain, and on the east and west sides were waterfalls cascading into large reflecting pools. Around this sunken pavilion, under the plaza above, and behind the waterfalls, were numerous shops, including a bingo palace, a cybercafe with interactive video games (Jesse's favorite hangout), a couple of restaurants, a shoe store, a photo shop, a home decorating center, and a couple of clothing stores. At one point, Jesse had to seek a new place to play video games, as his favorite was closed by the government. I asked a Bulgarian student about it, and he said they closed it because it was owned by "fatnecks." I assumed he had mistranslated something, and asked him what he meant by "fatnecks." He told me that was slang for the mafia types, and that left me just as puzzled. He explained that while the Communists were in charge, they spent huge amounts of money financing the Bulgarian olympic weightlifting team. He said it was the only sport in which Bulgaria won medals—often gold. The men on the team were treated like movie stars; and were given houses, cars, and huge allowances by the Communists. When the USSR folded and the Communists withdrew, the money dried up. The weightlifters, all of whom were extremely muscular (and had fat necks) were left with nothing but their size and strength. They used those assets to develop a powerful mob that eventually ran many illegal businesses.

The walking mall was shaped like an "L," with the university at the west end of the long leg, which extended about eight blocks east. There, at the "heel" of the L, was the main square of the city. It was about a block square, and with all of the other squares and walking malls, was paved in a manner similar to the plaza in front of the university. When Bulgarians said "I'll meet you at 8:00," if they didn't specify where, we took it for granted they mean that square. At virtually any time from 6:00 a.m. until 3:00 a.m. it was busy with people, either waiting for

315

A view of the less-than-attractive exterior of our quite nice apartment.

someone, or standing around smoking, eating, and talking. From there, the short leg of the L extended south for about six blocks, with what they called "the river" (but which, back in Pennsylvania where I grew up, would barely have qualified as a self-respecting "crick") running along its east side. Three bridges crossed the river; one at each edge of the city, and one near the center; and there were pedestrian bridges every couple of blocks.

The open air market ran for about six blocks along the east side of the river, and it was to the east of the market that our little neighborhood nestled into the side of the mountains that ringed the city to the east, north, and west. In addition to the primary "L"-shaped walking mall, all of the streets that adjoined the long leg of the L from the west were closed to traffic and paved for pedestrians. Each of these branches ended in either a small park or a paved square. An asphalt walking/biking path ran along the river from the south edge of the city to a small lake in a large park about five kms to the north. We walked it up and back in the fall, and it was lovely.

On the south end of the plaza was a nice park about three blocks in size, and the biggest, most expensive (but definitely not nicest) hotel in the city. It was government run—a holdover from the old Communist system, and was as inefficient as that sounds. We could attest to that, as we stayed there for the first week we were in town, while we found an apartment. Our apartment was the second floor of a house. The first floor was a storage area and workroom. The third floor was where the grandma of the owner lived. The house was somewhat less than impressive from the outside, but it was solid, and our apartment was much nicer than either of the ones we had in China or Thailand. It had a roomy living/dining room, a real kitchen, a bathroom, and two nice-sized bedrooms. We had to go through the boy's to get to ours, but that was a minor inconvenience (at least for us).

Blagoevgrad, with a population of 71 thousand, was tucked into the end of a valley on the south edge of a mountainous region, so all of the neighborhoods on the north, west, and east sides climbed quickly uphill. That meant the 3/4-mile walk from the university to our apartment on the far east edge of town started with a pleasant stroll along the eight blocks of walking mall. The middle was a relatively steep section of narrow streets, some with; some without narrow sidewalks, and the last few blocks comprised hundreds of very steep, very uneven stone steps. To say that our apartment was on the far east edge of the city was a bit misleading. The first morning we were there, we were awakened (well, Laurie and I, anyway) by a very loud noise that sounded almost like a lion's roar. We got up, dressed, and set out on a walk around the neighborhood to see if we could find out what it was. Three blocks up our street (which was the last on the east edge of town, and our apartment was on the east side of it) We came to a large set of gates with a sign (in Bulgarian, naturally) over them. We could not read the sign (naturally), but given the scene inside the gate, we were pretty sure it said "City Zoo." The space behind the gates covered a large area on the edge of the city, including the area directly behind our apartment. We visited it several times in the following months. It wasn't very well maintained, and most of the limited assortment of animals were pretty mangey, but they did have two very loud lions. As with most things, we eventually got used to their presence, and were no longer awakened by their morning "yawns." In fact, the zoo housed a minority of the animals in our neighborhood. Virtually every family (including granny upstairs) had a back yard full of at least chickens, and some with goats and pigs, as well.

All of the fountains, pavilions, squares, and walking malls were very nice, except that—as with all the infrastructure in Bulgaria—too little money was budgeted for their upkeep, and they were, generally, quite the worse for wear. Also, as we had found in all the countries in which we had lived, people had not yet taken on themselves personal responsibility for keeping public areas clean. Consequently, they thoughtlessly dropped trash wherever they happened to be. Women were paid to sweep the public areas, but they couldn't possibly keep up with the amount of litter generated. People who worked in the businesses swept in front each morning when they opened, and many of the babas (grannies) came out at least once a day and swept the sidewalk and street in front of their homes (Laurie said Bulgaria would have fallen apart if it weren't for the babas). The problem was that most of those people didn't actually pick up the trash, they just swept it away from in front of their building.

Bulgarians had no concept of making the risers of steps consistent heights. Until we got used to it, we kept stumbling going up and down stairs. The sidewalks were mostly made from hexagonal concrete pavers about 10 inches across, and were anything but smooth. The pavers were cocked at every angle, with many missing. Daydreaming while strolling along wasn't safe—we could have found ourselves on our butts, with twisted ankles (or worse). When we first got there, Laurie and I were walking on the pedestrian mall, chatting. She was looking at me, rather than where she was going. I shouted at her just in time to keep her from stepping into a hole about two feet square and a foot and half deep, right in the middle of the sidewalk. Add the fact that many homes and business had no parking spaces, so people parked on the sidewalks, blocking them to pedestrians in many places. Mostly, people walked in the streets, which were generally either cobblestones or asphalt, and usually marginally better than the sidewalks. Except for a few main streets (along which they seemed to concentrate on keeping the sidewalks in better shape) there was very little traffic, anyway.

One very civilized aspect that we found we could afford in Blagoevgrad that we we never could in the States was a combined haircut, head massage, manicure, and hand massage. Like so many things we experienced in every country in which we lived, we stumbled on it by accident. Laurie and I were on one of our extended weekend rambles. We were in a neighborhood on the far side of town from ours, when we noticed a little "salon," a designation we had not seen anywhere else in town. They had lots of barbershops, but no other salons. We were intrigued, and both ready for haircuts—we had been wary of the barbers, based on some of their work we had seen. On the other hand, we didn't feel we could afford a salon. We decided to at least ask. We entered, and were surprised at how modern and well-kept the shop was. We were approached by a young man who asked us in impeccable English if he could help us. We asked him how much for a haircut and he told us the equivalent of $1.50 in leva. We were greatly surprised and told him that would be fine. I went first. He sat me in a very comfortable barber's chair, put an attractive cape over my front, and begin cutting. At the same time, a young woman pulled up a stool, sat down, and began giving me a manicure. I had never had a manicure, figuring I could cut my own fingernails, thank you. I didn't know what I had been missing. She finished the manicure before he finished the haircut, and began rubbing a very soothing in and massaging my hand. Before I could say anything, he assured me it was part of the package. Before he started a very relaxing head massage he said, "This too." While they did the same with Laurie, I asked him where had learned such good English, and where he had come up with the salon idea. He told us he had wanted to be a barber in Blagoevgrad, but wanted to be better than their typical barbers, so he had studied English; gone to Boston, where he went to barber's school; and taken a job on a cruise ship. After four years, he had decided he was ready to return to Blagoevgrad, and open the best shop in town. We told him we admired his initiative and thought he had certainly succeeded in his effort. We returned at least every two weeks, whether we really needed a haircut or nor.

A young man named Ivo, 31, was the consummate entrepreneur; the new Bulgaria personified; the founder and president of Mariana Club, named for the woman he lived with. Mariana Club was, basically, Ivo, and he was, basically, a fixer. He was retained by the university to look after new faculty for their first three months: find them apartments, shop for them, deliver pizza to them, negotiate in Bulgarian for them—fix things. After three months, the faculty could retain him for 50 leva (about $30) a month to do the same sorts of things, or they could pay him per job. We preferred to learn our own way around a new culture—after all, that was a big part of why we were there. If we had wanted convenience, we could have stayed home. He did help us find an apartment, and he found us a (very hard to come by) used VCR that played both Western- and Asian-style video tapes—for 150 leva (about $90). There were three reasons for purchasing a VCR: 1) the only TV channels we got were in Bulgarian, and 2) we wouldn't have wanted to watch them even if they had been in English. Actually, both those reasons were for not watching TV. The third reason was for buying the VCR. When I was meeting with AUBG's provost about details of my employment, he mentioned that he had a huge collection of video tapes, and we were welcome to borrow them. He was British, so they were in English. He was crazy about several American actors (Clint Eastwood, for one), so many of the movies were from Hollywood. Ivo got us the

VCR that week, so starting the next Monday, the provost would bring in several movies and TV episodes each week. I would pick them up. We would watch them during the week. I would exchange them the next Monday. It was like having our own video rental store, only free.

In mid September we spent three days in Nesebar, a small town on the Black Sea coast. Actually, we were in the old section of the city, which was on an island connected by a causeway to the mainland. We hired Ivo to arrange for accommodations, and to drive us there. Some trips we took on our own. For example, when we wanted to spend a weekend in Sofia, or another nearby city, we just caught a bus, and arranged for a room when we got there. As Nesebar was all the way across the country, however, we felt we would have spent the three days just trying to get there and back, so we hired Ivo. He took us in his ten-year-old Audi (which he kept in great shape, and charged us about $200. The room was about $24 a night, and food for all of us was about $40 a day. It was worth every penny. The weather was hot and sunny, and the Black Sea was cool and refreshing.

We left Blagoevgrad at 7:00 Friday morning, stopping on our way out of town for a Bulgarian-style breakfast of pastries, yoghurt, and soft drinks. The pastries were of three general types: sweet sugar-coated, chocolate- or vanilla-filled; flaky cheese-filled (either a salty goat cheese much like feta, or a milder cow cheese more like parmesan); or meat-filled (one of several kinds of sausage ranging from one much like a hot dog, through more brat-like, to the hardest, saltiest salami we'd ever have wanted to put our mouths to). Ivo, Cooper, and I had the salty goat cheese ones; Laurie and Jesse opted for the sweeter ones. Laurie had yoghurt, Cooper and I had grapefruit Fanta, Jesse had Coke, and Ivo had a disgusting drink, called boza, that Bulgarians loved only because they started drinking it as small children. It looked like light brown chocolate milk; was made of some sort of flour, sugar, and water; and tasted like something they might have scooped out of the retaining ponds at a fish farm that hadn't been kept up like it should have been. A baba who ran the cafe (as they called them) told me it was the booze that helped the young girls grow "here"—pointing to her chest (which offered evidence for her argument)—and the boys "here"—pointing lower. her cafe was near a school, and while we were there the men who supplied her with boza delivered four cases of it in 1/2 liter bottles. She said they might last her the day if the students weren't too thirsty.

We took the mountain road through south central Bulgaria, stopping at a ski resort where the king used to maintain a weekend retreat. After the Communists took over, they confiscated it and made it into a Communist Party weekend retreat. When the Communist Party was thrown out, the Bulgarian government took it over and made it a government weekend retreat. When the government decided to restore property to its rightful owners, they gave it back to the former prince, who was then living in Spain. They were waiting to find out whether he planned to make it into a princely weekend retreat, or allow the government to keep it for—well, whatever they wanted to do with it. When it wasn't serving retreat duties, the folk could get in to see it, and it was a hoot. It had been kept pretty much as it was when old King Ferdinand had it, complete with several 1912 Siemens electric heaters that still worked. The bulk of the heating duties, however, fell to 50 tile-covered radiant heaters—each unique. The first room inside the front door looked like the captain's cabin of a sailing vessel—for good reason, as that's what it was. It seems the King wasn't too shoddy at cards, and had won it in a game. He had it transplanted to his retreat lock, stock, and bunk beds. The walls of most of the rooms were covered with trophy heads, and dozens of mounted birds that were about the size of large hawks and looked like a cross between wild turkeys and eagles. The caretaker said they were very popular game birds, but he believed they had become extinct—no doubt. One of the rooms, the one that had a fireplace of the stand-up-in-it variety, contained a table about three feet in diameter. It's top was inlaid with tiny pieces of various colored woods in a delicate and extremely complex pattern. The caretaker said that a prisoner had spent more than a year crafting it; then presented it to the king with a request for his freedom. The king said the crime was to have such an artist locked up, and had him released.

After an hour or two driving through the beautiful Balkan Mountains, we stopped for lunch in Plovdiv, the second largest city in Bulgaria; then drove on to Nesebar, arriving there about 5:30. We had three rooms with a bath down the hall on the second floor of an old house. We explored the old city and the Greek and Roman ruins, swam, rested, drank, ate, and generally had a good time. None of our meals were inside; all were within sight of the sea. One particularly fun one was breakfast Saturday. We had pastries, coffee, and soft drinks at an outdoor cafe that was in the Y of the two main streets of the old town. While we were there, they were holding a race for the young people. As nearly as we could tell, the younger age groups ran 400 meters, with the older groups progressing in distance to about 1/2 mile on a circuit that took them past our cafe each 400-meter circuit.

The house in which we stayed in Nesebar.

We (reluctantly) left Nesebar at 8:00 Sunday morning for the long
drive back. This time we took a more northerly route, stopping at a
town in central Bulgaria they call "Guns and Roses," (an intentional
pun on the seventies rock band) because they produced Kalashnikov
rifles and rose oil there. We took a side trip up into the pass that led to
Romania, to see the battleground where the Russian army, supplemented with Bulgarian volunteers, held of the advancing Turkish hoards in
1894 to win independence for Bulgaria. Well, at least the northern
half—the southern half stayed, at least nominally, under Turkish rule
for several more years. Anyway, this battle was a real rip-snorter. The
Russian army had tens of thousands of Turks bottled up in a city south
of there, and if that part of the Turkish army had broken through, they
would almost certainly have united with their countrymen further north
and won the war. The ragtag group of Russians and Bulgarians were
greatly outnumbered and outgunned, so they kept retreating northward
until making a final stand on that mountain top. They picked a good
spot. I wouldn't have wanted to try and take it, even when we were
there, with steps built to the top. The Turks were obviously more determined. They just kept coming, until the defenders began to run out of
ammunition. Instead of surrendering, as the Turks expected, however,
they began throwing stones, and even the bodies of their dead com-
rades down on the advancing Turks. A famous Bulgarian poem said the
Turks were demoralized because they had never had to fight both live

The Freedom Monument, built in 1890,
near the town of "Guns and Roses".

and dead soldiers before. They were nothing if not determined, how-ever, and kept coming. In what must have been a truly dramatic finish, the calvary—in the form of a fresh unit of the Russian army—came thundering to the rescue at the last moment, and drove the Turks back. That was in August, and the Russian generals, who were in command, stationed an ill-equipped unit of the Bulgarian army there to hold the pass that winter. It was a terrible winter, and about as many of those men died of starvation and exposure as had in the battle the preceding summer. So the monument (being Bulgarian) concentrated on those men, as well as the Bulgarian volunteers killed by the Turks. They didn't say much about the Russians, except that they were stupid to put such a poorly supplied group of Bulgarians up there to perish during the winter.

In general, the Bulgarians clearly distinguished between "Bulgarian" monuments and "Communist" ones. They characterized the latter as a big waste of money that would have been better spent improving the lot of the people. We drove by numerous impressive Communist monuments. When asked about them, Ivo either dismissed them outright, or said they were to commemorate some Communist or other, and were of no importance. He could go on at length, however, about the events and people commemorated by the Bulgarian structures. In fact, a couple of weeks before our trip, they used a lot of dynamite (they were sturdy) to completely demolish a Communist mausoleum in Sofia. That weekend, it was the site of the first annual city-wide beer fest. My students said it was a fitting symbol of the new Bulgaria that was replacing the old.

After a great lunch in a restaurant that used to be a museum dedicated to the rose oil industry, we were on the road again. That more northern route took us to what Ivo called "the only highway in Bulgaria." He had a point. It was their only four-lane freeway, and if what we experienced was any indication, the only road on which they spent any money for maintenance. At speeds of 80-90 mph, the trip back to Blagoevgrad from there was much quicker than it would have been going back through the mountains. On the outskirts of Sofia, we were stopped for speeding. Ivo said the police officers made him their usual offer: give them a 5,000 leva (about $3) donation to help with their living expenses, and he could go. I asked if he had, and he said no, he had told them to go ahead and give him a ticket. He was counting on the fact that as he was from out of town; they wouldn't want to mess with the paperwork. He was right. They just gave him back his license and passport (which the Bulgarians had to carry with them at all times) and told him to get out of there.

As it was Sunday evening, we met a steady stream of traffic for miles outside Sofia. Ivo said it was all the people who claimed to be Sofians coming back from where they were really from. As one might expect in a country where a driver could get out of any traffic violation with a $3 bribe, most drivers didn't pay the least bit of attention to the laws. Many times we had to leave the road or slow almost to a stop to avoid being hit head-on by someone passing illegally. It was also common to see people passing on the shoulder, driving the wrong way on a one way street, and ignoring red lights or stop signs. We made it home by 7:30 without being killed, however, and ended the weekend with a dinner of reheated sloppy Joes. The water was off (a not uncommon occurrence), so that was about all we could do, short of going out to eat, which none of us had the energy left to do. Luckily, the water was back on by morning, so we didn't have to go to work and school completely slimed.

Incidentally, it was at about that time that I realized I had become "acclimated" enough that I began to refer to the old and new leva interchangeably. The government had decided that it was ridiculous (I had to agree) to have 1,800 leva equal to a dollar, so they began printing new money in which 1.8 (new) leva was equal to a dollar. Actually, one new leva was equal to one deutchmark, but as 1.8 deutchmarks were equal to a dollar.... We were caught in the middle, as both types of bills were being used until the first of January, when we had to use only new leva. Add to that the fact that the old coins had 10, 20, and 50 stamped on them, and they were worth one-hundredth the value of the new coins— which were about a fourth the size, and had 1, 2, and 5 on them. It's confusing reading about them; we had to use them. Anyway, 1,000 old leva were the same as one new leva. I had gotten it screwed up a few days earlier, when I went to the bank to withdraw $800 worth of leva for us to live on for the next month (it was a completely cash economy). I asked for 15,000 leva. I couldn't believe it when she said they didn't have that much cash in the bank. After a little math, I realized that I had asked for the equivalent of $8,000 instead of $800, subtracted a zero, and was given my 1,500 leva. I still couldn't believe, incidentally, that they didn't have $8,000 in cash on hand at the bank.

Chapter 3
October

The second week of October was semester break for us, and we took advantage of the opportunity to see some of Bulgaria. Sunday afternoon we took the bus to Sofia, about 150 km north. We found a room in the Tsar Assen Hotel, a tiny place with only four rooms. It was situated within walking distance of the whole downtown area, where almost all the galleries, theatres, museums, and parks were. It was also on the inside of the block, away from street noise; was very clean and well kept; and a room for the four of us (with private bath) was only $55 a night. Sunday afternoon we went to the National Historical Museum. We had gotten very official looking letters—in Bulgarian, replete with stamps and signatures—saying that I was a professor at AUBG, Cooper was a student there, Laurie was a teacher at a Bulgarian high school, and Jesse was a student there. We presented them at all the ticket booths (where foreigners generally paid from twice to ten times the Bulgarian price), and it was fun watching the reaction of the people who sold tickets. They had no idea what to do. Some just gave us back our letters and waved us through; others charged us the Bulgarian prices, and still others just charged us a token fee. The result was that for the week we paid a total of about 10 leva ($6) for tickets that would otherwise have cost us about $50.

The Historical Museum was quite impressive. During the Communist regime, they had spent millions of dollars collecting the best exhibits from all over the country, to create a wonderful national museum representative of the rich and varied cultural history of the region. They confiscated the building, which was gorgeous, from the national attorney's organization. When we were there, the mayor, who just happened to be an attorney, was pushing to spend millions to decentralize the collection and return the building to its "rightful owners." The people were irate about it, but it was a very real possibility that it would happen.

We then visited the Sheraton Hotel, which was built around the remains of some ancient Roman baths, and a new fountain nearby that was computerized to change spray patterns in time to blaring rock music. Now that was a dichotomy that we saw as representative of Bulgaria at that point in its history. We walked on the "yellow brick road," so called because it was made from yellow bricks given to one of the former kings of Bulgaria by one of the former rulers of Turkey (evidently in

The exterior of the Archeology Museum in Sophia, inside which was displayed pieces from Absolut Vodka's international advertising campaign.

one of the sparse moments when they weren't at war). The archaeological museum was proudly marketing a temporary exhibit that we simply could not miss. We got to experience a display of eight-foot posters collected from Absolut Vodka's international advertising campaign, the chief attraction of which was the new one for Sofia itself. Now that was something we didn't get to see every day (especially not in an archaeological museum) yet another representation of the "new" Bulgaria. They had moved all the antiquities against the walls to make room for the posters, and the juxtaposition lent a surreal quality to the experience. My favorite piece was the 12-foot replica of an Absolut bottle (of clear glass) they had placed over the 10-foot marble statue of what looked like a Thracian goddess. The upstairs gallery featured an impressive display on a series of digs going on in south central Bulgaria. They had found a unique set of pits that seemed to be part of some religious rituals, but not used for burial, as had been the case for similar sites.

From there, we visited the most famous non-sight in all of Bulgaria. A few weeks before Sofians (mostly younger ones) had destroyed the most famous Communist mausoleum in the country. The event had made a big splash in the international news, and since then, most visitors to Sofia had gone to see the spot where the mausoleum wasn't. They were in the process of constructing what looked like it would be a very nicely landscaped park.

Monday—in response to a special (and oft repeated) request from Jesse—we went to the National Military Museum. It had to be the least well-funded entity in the country. The gate was open, so we went in, but all the buildings were locked. We spent about fifteen minutes touring the several dozen implements of war outside. They ranged from a horse-drawn cannon of Crimean War vintage to a MIG-19 jet fighter from WW II. The extent of their upkeep seemed to be occasionally dabbing some olive drab paint on the worst rust spots. The good news (for Jesse) was that he was allowed to clamber over them all. His favorite was a small anti-aircraft gun—sometimes referred to as an "ack-ack gun," from the distinctive sound they made when fired (I knew this from military service, not because Jesse actually fired it). He did sit on it, however, and using the appropriate wheels, spun it 180 degrees while raising and lowering the barrels through a 60 degree arc. After about 15 minutes, I found someone official who unlocked one of the buildings and watched us closely while we looked at a very nice collection of uniforms, flags, weapons, and other memorabilia from several armies and several wars—all tucked very efficiently into a single large room. It was a bit spooky seeing a British helmet with a jagged bullet hole through it: knowing it was almost surely a Bulgarian bullet that had put it there.

After the attendant had locked the building securely behind us and disappeared again, we spent another hour inspecting the outside exhibits before having some lunch and moving on to the National Polytechnic Museum. We were a bit surprised that much of the food in Sofia was quite different from that available in Blagoevgrad, only 150 km south. Oddly, Greek food was more in evidence further north, so we had gyros, which we had not seen in Blagoevgrad. Their pastries were generally of the much sweeter varieties as well, so it wasn't easy for us to find those with meat and cheese that we had become accustomed to for breakfast. The Polytechnic Museum was a bit far to walk, so we decided to take a tram. We had been told that we should just get on and buy tickets from the conductor or driver. We got on a number seven, which went within a few blocks of the museum, tried to buy tickets until we reached our stop, and disembarked without being able to. There were some college-student-looking young women there—most of whom we had found could speak some English—so we asked them how we were supposed to get tickets. "Oh, you just get on and buy them from the driver or the conductor," they replied. OK.

The Polytechnic Museum was featuring three exhibits. The first was photos of "One Hundred Years of Progress in Sophia." It was interesting, but (for us) not very informative, as the explanations were all in Bulgarian. Only in the tourist attractions most frequented by foreigners was any English used. We had learned the Cyrillic alphabet fairly well (I say "fairly well" as an average of Laurie's "quite well," Cooper's "passable," my "getting by," and Jesse's "hardly at all."), so could generally make out how the words were spelled. That helped, however, only for words that were derived from English. "PECTOPAHT," for example, translated as "RESTORANT, "—helpful; but it didn't do much good to know that "CEPEHE" translated as "SERENE" unless we also knew that was a kind of cheese. The other two exhibits were more accessible, as they were on the development of holograms, and early versions of common electronics and technology. They had displayed, for example, prototype versions of the computer, which Bulgarians insisted was invented by a Bulgarian. For some reason, which for us remained a mystery, they also had on display an absolutely flawlessly restored 1928 Ford—apropos of nothing, and with no connection to any of the other exhibits (As far as I knew, they didn't claim Henry Ford was Bulgarian). Despite the distance (about three miles), we decided to walk back to our hotel, winding our way through some of the back streets to get a feel for the city (Some of the winding may have been because I got lost, but everyone agreed that it was a nice walk).

Tuesday our luck with the weather ran out, and it rained pretty continually. We were determined not to be confined to our room, however, and spent the day instead getting pretty thoroughly wet. We visited the street bazaars (where the merchants didn't let a little rain deter them from the prospect of making a few leva). Laurie and I bought some hand-made lace and some small icons and pieces of art—keeping in

The Alexander Nevsky Memorial Church, built in 1912 as a memorial to Russian soldiers who died in the Russo-Tuirkish War.

mind that we'd either have to pay to have any purchases shipped back, or carry them for a month through Eastern Europe on our way back to Frankfurt to catch our return flight. Jesse got some coins for his collection, and he and Cooper both got some hand-carved, painted wooden bottles of rose oil.

We also visited several churches and the National Art Gallery. The most memorable church was the Alexander Nevsky Memorial Church, built in 1912 as a memorial to Russian soldiers who died in the Russo-Tuirkish War. The building, with seating for 5,000, took craftsmen from six countries 30 years to complete. We saw it as a classic example of the permanence of Russian influence in a country that was no longer part of the USSR.

We didn't expect a lot from the art gallery, because our guidebook said it was "pretty pedestrian." Well, either we were more easily pleased than the writer, or s/he didn't know whereof s/he spoke. Not all of the pieces were impressive, but some were magnificent. One, called "In the Field," pictured a young peasant woman who had stopped plowing long enough to nurse her baby. Her face left no doubt whatsoever about how tired she was—and expected to be for as long as she lived.

Tuesday evening we went to a party at the home of an artist named Natalia Himmirska, whom we knew because she commuted to AUBG twice a week to teach art, and we had invited her to dinner a couple of times. As it was the first time we had been invited into a Bulgarian home, it was a special experience for us. She and her husband were both fascinating people. She was born in Russia and had paintings in galleries in three countries. He was the Bulgarian Minister of Defense, had a doctorate in classical poetry, and had just published a bilingual collection, which, in my humble opinion, was quite good.

When we returned to Blagoevgrad, the water was off for a couple of days. I think I liked the water outages in China better. At least there we could count on it being off several hours every other day or so. In Bulgaria, it would stay on for two weeks, or until we let your emergency supply dwindle, whichever came first. Then, just as we were lulled into complacency, it was gone. So, when it came on, we filled everything in our apartment that would hold liquid with water. Well, not everything; it was time for the bottling of the new wine, so we had brought back a couple of bottles from Sofia, and our landlady had presented us with a 3-liter jug of hers. We were not about to empty them just on the off chance that we might need some water.

We called Ivo to take us to the Rila Monastery, which was considered the most impressive in the country, and was only about 35 km away. He had just returned from a few days in war-torn Kosovo, where he had taken a couple of photographers. We were worried because the killing of a Bulgarian in Kosovo had been in the news only days before. They made it back safely, however. We had debated whether to take a bus up, walk around, and take a bus back, but we had been told that the connections were sporadic, and that we might spend more time on buses and waiting for them than we would at Rila. So we shelled out the 50 leva ($30) for the day—good decision. Ivo started by taking us to a restaurant way back in the woods, where we ate lunch outside in the sunshine, overlooking a beautiful valley, complete with noisy stream and "trees turning red all over the place," as we remembered from a Chinese brochure we saw once (not about Bulgaria, about China, but it seemed apropos to the situation, nonetheless).

From there, he took us to a trail that wound steeply up a rocky mountainside about half a mile to the tomb of St. John of Rila. He was a holy man who had lived as a hermit in a cave up there. Ivo said that some detractors had thrown him off the edge, and people swore that at the place where he landed leaves on the ground still occasionally seeped blood. We went into the mouth of the cave; then exited through a hole in the roof, which (legend had it) if we could get through meant we were without sin. Both Cooper and Jesse seemed quite surprised when I

A small portion of the ornate murals in the Rila Monastery.

.made it without a hitch. I said it was because my heart was pure; Jesse said it was because I'd lost about 15 pounds since we left the States. Next, we climbed further up the mountain to a grotto, complete with icons, spring, and gurgling brook. There, following Ivo's instructions, we 1) wrote wishes on slips of paper, 2) rolled them up and wound them with loose threads from our clothes, 3) stuck them among the thousands of others in the cracks between rocks surrounding the spring, 4) took drinks from the spring, and 5) tossed coins into the water. A complicated process, but a small price to pay for world peace, or, in Jesse's case, the new computer game that some stranger would bring to our door soon. By that time, we had been there a couple of hours doing neat stuff that we never would have known about if we hadn't gone with Ivo, and hadn't even gotten to the main attraction.

Rila Monastery lived up to its reputation as the most notable example in Bulgaria. It was a walled compound about a city block in size, with two stories of monks' cells, bakeries, kitchens, and common rooms constructed against the inside of all four walls. In the center of the compound was the church, completely covered, inside and out, with murals of Biblical scenes, likenesses of the saints, ornate circles of life, scenes of the "deserving" climbing ladders to heaven and the "undeserving" being thrown into the depths, and just general decorative paintings.

We bought a loaf of special Rila bread to take back to our landlady's mother, who lived upstairs from us, and were preparing to leave when Ivo said, rather offhandedly, "Well, that's all, unless you'd like to see the tomb of a Western journalist." "Do you mean James Bouche, the British journalist who lived in Bulgaria for 20 years, wrote for "Time," spied variously for both the CIA and the KGB, and is the only Western journalist buried in this country?" I guessed, astutely. Did I, a journalism professor, want to visit his tomb? Well, "duh," as the boys would say. It was about 100 yards up a path into the woods outside the walls of the monastery, and was a rectangular marble sarcophagus about 8 x 12 feet, surrounded by a low, black, wrought-iron fence. It was kept up neither better nor worse than any of the other tombs we'd seen. Someone had placed a flower and a plastic cup of coffee at one end, the significance of which I was sure we'd never know. We spent Wednesday night in our own beds. Grandma practically had to be beaten into submission before she'd accept our gift—and after the untold bags of tomatoes and peppers we'd graciously accepted (and heroically tried to consume) from her.

Thursday we caught the 1:30 bus to Sandanski (about 45 km south), intending to connect with a local bus from there to Melnik (about 15 km southeast, and only 20 km north of the Greek border. Our plans were thwarted by the fact that we had, it seems, missed the last one, so we hired a taxi instead. Two offered to take us; one for 20 leva ($12), and the other for 15 ($9). It was a decision made easier by the fact that we were living on a decreased income, while at the same time trying to save enough for future travel. We had been told by the people who had made arrangements for our room that, "Melnik is a tiny town where everyone knows everyone else, so all you'll have to do is ask to find the home in which you'll be staying." We, therefore, just had the driver drop us in the center of the (admittedly small) town. After walking the length of the main street twice, and asking four people, we were finally directed to the home where we would be staying. Our "room" was, in fact, two large, sunny sleeping rooms with three

beds in each; an even larger, sunnier sitting room; and a bathroom, for which we paid a total of 80 leva ($48) for two nights. An additional

18 leva ($11) bought us breakfast Friday morning. Our hostess served it on a large coffee table in the sitting room at 9:00. It consisted of: a huge bowl of fresh yogurt each (we stopped her before she brought Jesse one, as the only yogurt he'd eat was processed and mixed with sugar and fruit); one pot of coffee, another of hot milk, and a third of tea; a banana each; a pot of fresh honey; and two dozen fresh-baked pastries that were about four inches long and the consistency of fry-bread. Everything was delicious.

Chapter 4
November

November 1 was a national holiday in Bulgaria, so all the schools were closed, and we spent the day wandering around town in our shirtsleeves. Actually, we didn't spend all day outside. We started after breakfast at the regional museum in Blagoevgrad. It's pretty nice for a small town; a mixture of natural history, antiquities, and cultural artifacts. It gave us a pretty good feel for where we could go in the region to see good archaeological sites.

The next morning Laurie and I were having our usual leisurely weekend breakfast of pastries and coffee at an outside cafe, when we heard loud rock music from a few blocks away. Such music usually signaled a special event, so after we finished eating, we strolled over to see what was going on. It was coming from one of the main squares downtown, which the police had roped off, and on which they had set up two lines of orange cones such I had seen on car shows in the States, when they tested vehicles for maneuverability. People were registering at a nearby table, and were showing officials that the lights and brakes on their cars were in working order. Parked in the center of the square, under the statue of one of Bulgaria's famous freedom fighters (of which there is no shortage, as they have spent the vast majority of their history fighting for freedom from one ruling group or another) was a Lada, the multiple decals on which identified it as the Bulgarian international road rally car.

About the Lada: It was the Russian equivalent of the Volkswagen, keeping in mind that, whereas the Germans were noted for their engineering and auto making, the Russians...well, the Russians just weren't. The poor little Lada was the brunt in Bulgaria of many jokes. Probably the most pointed was the one about the two guys who were racing their Ladas, and the loser accused the other of cheating by carrying his part way. Be that as it may, the Lada was omnipresent in Bulgaria. As we walked around, observing the activity, it gradually dawned on us that they were actually going to hold an automobile race in the main square of downtown Blagoevgrad. We determined that it was to begin at 10:30. As it was 9:45 at the time, we hurried home to get the boys and returned for the action. By the time we got back, the race was about to start. Twenty people—most young; all but two male—had entered their private cars (or in one case a small pickup, one case a company

One of twenty cars in a race taking place in the main square of downtown Blagoevgrad.

car, and two cases taxies) in a race that consisted of starting at one end of the row of cones, weaving through them to the other end (about 10 cones away), turning around, and weaving back through them to the original starting line. If they lost control, they had two rubber tires on each corner of the base of the statue to minimize damage should they hit it, and absolutely nothing but a rope to do the same for the crowd gathered around the square to watch. We set up next to a lamp post, figuring we could jump behind it if one of them headed for us. Besides, what with all the weaving, they couldn't

muster too much speed, and, after all, most of them were Ladas. It would have about like getting hit by someone on a bicycle, anyway. The whole thing lasted about 20 minutes, nobody got hurt, and those who won seemed equally pleased with the glory and the prizes, which comprised new parts for their cars.

On the way home we stopped at the little store down the street from our apartment to buy a loaf of bread for dinner. It had gotten so we didn't think it was strange any more to walk in, break a loaf off the

Laurie with her friend Kalinka and a "baba", outside the shop where we bought our fresh-baked bread.

bunch that were still stuck together just as they came from the oven, pay 450 leva (25 cents) for it, tuck it unwrapped under an arm, and carry it home. It didn't even bother us when we saw shoppers before us squeeze several of the loaves to make sure they were fresh. Almost everything in Bulgaria came in minimal (or no) packaging, and consequently when we emptied the trash each week, it consisted of two small plastic bags full. Eventually, Laurie became good friends with the woman, named Kalinka, who worked in the little store, and whom it turned out lived a couple of houses down, and across the street from us. She was a wonderful source of information about customs we didn't understand (although because she spoke no English, and our Bulgarian was limited, we often needed to get her nephew, whose English was passable, involved). As Laurie's Bulgarian improved, the nephew's involvement decreased.

By the middle of November we had become good friends with Natalia and her husband, Krassin. He had been invited by the president of the university to present a reading of his new book at AUBG. As the audience would be made up of both English and Russian speakers

(Bulgarian was an offshoot of Russian, so Bulgarians were fluent in both), Krassin asked me to follow his Russian readings with the English version. The event was attended by most of the movers and shakers in the city, and was covered in a lengthy article in the newspaper. What follows is the first three of paragraphs:

"Krassin Himmirsky opened the November 11 Blagoevgrad presentation of his first English/Bulgarian collection of poetry, Time Bomb, in three foreign languages. He greeted the audience gathered in the Red Room at the American University in Bulgaria in English, Russian and Indonesian. Born in Varbitsa, Bulgaria, Himmirsky graduated from Moscow University and has served as Cultural Attaché and Charge d'Affaires in Washington, D.C., and Jakarta. Being a diplomat, however, has not prevented him from writing.

Time Bomb is Himmirsky's seventh book. Composed of both old and new poems, it is divided into three sections: "Time Bomb," "Urban Mystics" and "Martian Girls." Himmirsky read the poems in Bulgarian, and AUBG's Balkan Scholar in Journalism, Roy Blackwood, presented the English translations. The poem that opened the reading was also titled "Time Bomb." This poem was about the death of the poet's father, a WW II veteran, to whom the book is dedicated.

Himmirshy wrote the rest of the new poems constituting the first section of the book in response to what he calls "the recent Balkan wars." He visited Bosnia and Herzegovina many times during past two years as an international observer. The poems depict the horror and violence of war contrasted with undying trust in humanity.

On November 16, we e-mailed our Christmas letter:

Dear Family and Friends,

Welcome to beautiful Blagoevgrad, Bulgaria. It is mid-November and we're thinking of friends and family in the U.S. as we begin to look ahead to the holiday season. We are in our third overseas adventure—this time enjoying the people and culture of Eastern Europe. We had time to see a little of the beauty of Germany, France, Switzerland, Italy, Spain, and Greece before settling in for our year in Bulgaria. Unfortunately, it was the "what day is this and where are we" type of whirlwind tour. We saw a tiny bit of many places we know we could easily have spent a month in and every place made us want to go back. We are now settled into teaching (Roy at the American University in Bulgaria) and studying (Cooper at AUBG, too, and Jesse at the foreign language high school). Laurie is trying her hand at teaching English there. We're trying to get all the subjects needed for Bemidji Middle School during home schooling time. It can be a real struggle to have the time and energy to do both. Second semester we may drop the commitment here and spend our time on the stuff for home. Our time could be a little more flexible that way.

A brief recap on the year—Roy enjoyed his turn as Department Chair at Bemidji State, and will return to it when we go back in July. They said they would refer any difficult items to him here and so he has kept in touch with some unfinished business. He didn't get a chance to work on the '51 Chevy this year because our summer was cut short with what we needed to do to get ready for this leave. He did manage to get some fishing in, and I don't think he lost a single rod. We had several great fish-fries with walleye and northern. The boat motor conked out again, so it put an early end to the water ski season for the guys. The guy who fixes the motor was swamped and promised Roy he'd have the work done by July 4, 2000. Works for us. Here, he's ended up with a busier schedule than he had signed on for. A faculty member quit unexpectedly and left many classes that needed covering, so Roy will be teaching four courses instead of two.

Cooper had a busy year with his show choir competition and choir tour. He has really missed the show choir, and hopes to be in it again when we get back. He is in choir here, and is taking voice lessons. He will have concerts at the end of November, and a recital in the spring.

He was selected to sing with the Minnesota All State Lutheran Choir last June. It was a wonderful experience working with excellent directors and spending three weeks with great kids. He is hoping to send a tape for the auditions this year and be in the group again next June. He is taking college level courses here and is finding that in college, the teachers don't tell you everything you need to know. There is a lot of additional reading and synthesizing that needs to be done. As usual, he has found something else to be busy with—the college newspaper, "The Aspector." He's learning how to do computer layout and is thinking he'd like a good camera to try his hand at photography. We've tried to keep him focused on what he needs to do to be covered for his senior year. We will look for instrument lessons during the second semester to get him limbered back up for band.

Jesse enjoyed band and choir in middle school, and was disappointed that the school here doesn't have them. He's technically in eighth grade here because the seventh grade has four hours of English each day and then math, physics, chemistry, and literature in Bulgarian. We didn't think he needed that much English and he still wouldn't be able to do the Bulgarian work, but the upper courses don't really overlap with what he'd be doing at home. So we've traded some social interaction for the academics, at least for the first semester. His biggest complaint is that he can't understand his teachers' English. He is thrilled that computer game technology is available here, and game rooms are popular and fairly cheap. (His favorite was raided and shut down by the economics police for either having computers without serial numbers or pirated software.) He has found that the kids here are just as enthusiastic about computer games as his friends at home are.

Laurie is teaching English at the language school, working with the 7th, 8th, and 9th grades. The school has been in an uproar this year because many policies were to have been changed by order of the Ministry of Education, but the necessary machinery was not in place for the school start up. Textbooks were to have been revised and with both English and Bulgarian editions, but it took weeks for the new Bulgarian texts to come out, and the English versions aren't out yet. The students are much like American students, not wanting to work any more than they have to and willing to take advantage of any ambiguity. Students must test into this school, and seem to think that once they are in they needn't do anything else. Her plan to work there to meet people and get to know the culture better has not yet panned out.

We've had time to travel some here in Bulgaria. We didn't really appreciate Bulgaria's long history before coming here. But in traveling, we've seen Greek and Roman ruins, Byzantine churches, Thracian tombs, Copper Age artifacts, and examples of the bustling trade routes that included the wine trade in the middle ages. It has been fascinating, and again we realize how little of the world we know. We've gotten a very small sense of the extent of the Roman Empire—from the ruins of Caesar Augustus in Spain to the city walls on the Black Sea of Bulgaria. As always, there isn't enough time; money; or convenient, efficient transportation to see all there is to see in the country we're visiting.

Love, Roy, Laurie, Cooper, and Jesse

The AUBG choir, of which Cooper was a member, took part in a concert one night. It was part of "Czech Days in Blagoevgrad," and was primarily organ pieces by Czech composers. The choir sang one piece a cappella, and two with organ accompaniment. The concert hall, upstairs in the huge Communist-era opera hall, held about 200 in a balcony and main floor. Over the proscenium was a brightly-colored painting of epic proportions; in the best Communist tradition. It portrayed a variety of people engaged in performing and appreciating the various high arts. It was a bit overpowering, but as the concert proceeded, I grew rather fond of some of the folks in it. The organ was of Czech manufacture, and was one of only six pipe organs in the country. The pieces were played by the only person in the country who taught organ classes, and his students. They varied from powerful and flawless (him) to meek and not-so-flawless (one of his lesser accomplished pupils). The AUBG choir was no match for the the university choir back home, and maybe not even the high school choir, but it was still quite good. The balcony was horseshoe-shaped, and the organ, strangely, was situated in the left leg as we faced the stage. This positioning resulted in a situation in which, if we wanted to hear the music balanced in each ear, we were forced to sit sideways in our seats. Of course most concert goers were too proper to contort themselves such, but I was not. The only time the position of the organ worked even close to well was when, for the pieces with both organ and choir, the singers adjourned to the right leg of the balcony and were led by their director from across the room with the organist. The stereo effect—singers in one ear, organ in the other—was interesting, if a bit nontraditional.

The concert would have been a lot more enjoyable had the room been heated, even a bit. As it was, it really was colder inside than out. The organists said the only way they could play was that they had taken an electric heater into the loft, and they gathered around it, warming their hands between pieces. Even worse than the cold was the uncouth behavior of many of the audience. People talked, ate, drank, smoked, and entered and exited throughout the entire performance. The doors to the left rear were locked. I knew that because several people rattled them back and forth trying to leave through them in the middle of the organ pieces. When it became clear they couldn't get out there, after discussing what they should do in stage whispers for some time, they proceeded across between the seats, whispering and giggling the whole time, to exit through the doors at the other side of the room. Of course, any people sitting in the rows they traversed had to stand to let them through—the first time I'd witnessed a "wave" at a music concert. I finally asked (between pieces) a group of the worst offenders to either adjourn to a cafe to laugh and talk or keep quiet so the rest of us could enjoy the concert. They seemed surprised that anyone would actually speak to them such, but were apologetic, and quieted down a couple of decibels.

I taught an extra class for the last half of fall semester, and all of spring semester as well. One of my esteemed colleagues beat up a student. The student said he had hit him ten times; the professor said it was only "about twice." His classes were temporarily cancelled because "he would have the flu all week." By the end of the week, it became clear that he had returned to the States. The president got a request to "extend his medical leave" so that he could get further tests for his acute sinusitis. It seemed those tests revealed that he wasn't fit to return to Bulgaria, so he submitted his resignation, which the president accepted immediately. Needless to say, the student government was screaming in protest that the professor got away without being appropriately censured. The administration said that because the professor had left, it would probably be impossible to conduct an investigation that would ensure due process for everyone involved. In the meantime, the rest of the faculty were stuck with his courses. I was asked to take over the newspaper lab, the class in which participants were responsible for producing the student newspaper. They had already published four of the five issues for that semester, and a search of the professor's office and computer files uncovered complete grades for his other two classes, but nothing for newspaper lab. The secretary e-mailed him, and he sent students' grades for the first four issues. I graded them for the fifth issue, and derived their final grades from a combination of his and mine. The whole situation arose from what the professor perceived as a battle between the official student newspaper and an alternative paper started by some of the older students the year before, when the official paper quit publishing. The professor was convinced that the alternative paper's staff was out to get both him and the student paper, a claim I never saw as valid. A student that he had kicked out of one of his classes for plagiarism posted a harsh satirical web page about him, and he assumed that some of the staff of the alternative paper were involved. The first one he came across bore the brunt of his rage. After he returned to the

States, he sent a long, very harsh e-mail message to all the servers on campus satirizing the administration, the students, the faculty, the staff of the alternative newspaper, and me, because I had released the content of an earlier e-mail in which he had threatened to find the "slimy little bastards" responsible for the web page "and break their faces." He overlooked one of the primary tenets of satire, however, which is that if you blast everybody, there's nobody left to laugh. Consequently, what support he may have had evaporated.

The Balkan Scholar Award at AUBG existed to attract senior scholars from the States to the university. The expectation was that they would be on sabbatical, so AUBG could pay them a minimal salary for teaching only two courses a semester. I was to cover two sections of a beginning reporting class with a limit of 15 students in each. After I got there, and we decided that Cooper would take courses at AUBG, we agreed that I would teach a third class in return for his tuition. That class was cultural reporting, with a cap of 35. When I added newspaper lab, I was teaching a full load. I was certainly a bit busier than I expected to be, but enjoyed myself greatly.

Most of the classes were an hour and a half, either Monday and Wednesday or Tuesday and Thursday, with very few classes on Friday. Most of the faculty elected to pack all their classes into two days, with five days a week outside the classroom. I preferred to have two on Monday and Wednesday, one on Tuesday and Thursday, and when I added newspaper lab, it met Wednesday evening and Friday midday. In China and Thailand students worked very hard in elementary through high school, to be admitted to the best colleges, then coasted. The students at AUBG were some of the best in Eastern Europe, and were working to be admitted to Western graduate schools. Consequently, their work was generally of a higher quality than I was used to. They had all scored very high on their ACTS and their work generally reflected their intelligence. They also had very high TOEFL scores (most of them had graduated from English language high schools). Still, they were writing college-level work in a second language, and much of my time was spent working with them on the subtleties of the language. Many of them planned to work in positions in English-speaking countries, or in positions that would require extensive use of English, so they were generally eager learners and willing to work hard. Still, I got the distinct impression that many of them had been riding on their reputations, and that grade inflation was a bit of an expectation. When I announced their midterm grades, and they found that only two or three in each class were getting "A"s, several were getting "C"s, and a couple even had

"D"s, I had many visitors during office hours. The conversations often began with them informing me that they were "A" students. After I explained that for me "A" meant a student was doing excellent work in all aspects of the class, we settled into my explaining what they could do to improve. In almost every case, it was just a matter of them applying themselves more. Once they realized the fact that I would only be there for a year didn't mean my classes wouldn't be rigorous, or that I wouldn't have high expectations, the biggest hurdle was crossed. When I told them they could expect such rigor in the graduate programs they were preparing for in England or the States, the matter was settled.

"Blue Streak" (a police/chase/shoot-'em-up/action/comedy) opened the next weekend at the Cinemax. Jesse looked it up on the Internet and found it had a PG-13 rating, so he was all hot for me to take him to the 3:30 showing that Saturday. On weekends the Bulgarians (hence we) moved all their meals later—breakfast about 10:00, lunch about 3:00 and dinner about 8:00. I wasn't about to watch a movie on an empty stomach, so I had to find somewhere I could get an "early" lunch.

In November, President Clinton visited Bulgaria—the first president to do so. Jesse's class at the Foreign Language High School wrote (or someone wrote it in their name) the following letter to him:

> Dear President Clinton,
> Welcome to Beautiful Bulgaria! We hope your stay in our country will show you the beauty of our natural setting and our people.
> As you know, Bulgaria has a long history, longer than that of the United States, and has had periods of world greatness. We hope that in the coming century Bulgaria will be able to continue the stability it has had through the last four wars in the Balkans, and soon will be allowed to resume a position of strength in Europe.
> As young people of Bulgaria, we are concerned that selfishness and corruption will compromise our future. We do not want our natural resources and brain power exploited only for the benefit of a few within Bulgaria, or only for trans- or multinational companies. Our nation's needs are great: more and better transportation, more jobs, better schools, easier access to Western Europe, to name only a few. We want to be assured that in meeting these needs we will have a sustainable future for all Bulgarians; one that preserves the beauty of our natural environment and the dignity of our people. Bulgaria is more than

its world class athletes and its natural resources. It is a nation of resourceful people that has endured changing fortunes but is ready to take steps into the twenty-first century. We hope that the rest of Europe and the United States will walk with us into our future.

Respectfully,
Grade 9 Students
Foreign Language High School
Blagoevgrad, Bulgaria

On November 27 it finally got below freezing. It was about 20 degrees the next morning, and all the puddles had skins of ice on them. Some of the cars had the frost scraped from their windshields. It snowed for the first time the next day—quite heavily; in big, wet flakes—but as it was by then above freezing, it didn't stick; we were back to bare ground the next day. Laurie and I had our usual Saturday (and Sunday) breakfast the next morning. The boys always slept in on the weekend, so we went out for pastries and coffee. At about 2,700 leva (less than $1.50) for both of us, how could we afford not to? That morning Laurie had a banitza chocolat with her cappuccino and I had a piece of "pizza" and a makitza. Banitzas were about four inches wide, ten inches long, and two inches thick; made from many layers of paper-thin dough; and could be either plain or filled with goat cheese—either serene (like feta) or cascaval (sort of like mozzerella)—or chocolate cream. She had a banitza because they were out of the kifla chocolats she preferred. Kiflas were large croissants, that came plain or chocolate-filled, sprinkled with seeds such as sesame or sunflower, or coated on top with serene or cascaval cheese. Makitza (my favorite) was fry bread, just like we got back in northern Minnesota, with or without a sprinkling of powdered sugar. Makitza chocolat was just folded over a healthy slathering of chocolate cream.

Pizza places were abundant, and they served something much like Pizza Hut's thin crust—except that no self-respecting Bulgarian would consider eating one (including Hawaiian, with ham, pineapple, and cherries) without a thick coating of ketchup, mayonnaise, or a mix of both.

The "pizza" chunks from the bakery, however, were pizza in name only. They were about 8-10 inch squares of bread dough, 1 or 2 inches thick, coated with just a touch of tomato sauce; a sprinkling of goat cheese; and one or two toppings such as chopped ham, mushrooms, black olives, tomatoes, salami, or cucumbers; and a sprinkling of seasonings. We didn't order what we wanted. We just asked for pizza, and took whatever rendition happened to be up at the time. As with all of the pastries, it was either warm or cold, depending on how long it had been since it came out of the oven—unless they weren't busy, in which case they might pop it in the microwave for us. They had many other pastries, so it took us quite a while to learn the names of them all. The women at the bakery window thought it was a hoot when I would step up and order, "Edna makitza, y edna makitza chocolat, y edna pizza, y edna... that thing, right there; no, more to the right; yeah, that one."

Oddly (to us, anyway) no place served both pastries and cappuccino. The bakeries had a few outside tables, so weather permitting, we could stay and eat our pastries (although hardly anybody did; they almost always ate them while they walked). The only thing most of them had to drink, however, was boza, a truly revolting (to us; the Bulgarians

The 8-block walking mall downtown where many of the bakeries and cappuccino shops were located.

drank it like we did milk) drink made from millet, that resembled nothing more than buttermilk mixed with muddy water. We found a cafe near the bakery that, while the weather was warm enough, we took our pastries to and sat outside, where we ordered our cappuccino. The first day it got a bit nippy for outside dining, we went inside, and were politely informed (we figured out after a while) that, although we could do that outside, it wasn't permitted inside. It was just as well, as the place was small and had terrible ventilation, so the cigarette smoke was unbearable. After several weekends of searching, we found a place (Pizza Italiano) where we could take our pastries inside and order cappuccino. The good news was they had better, cheaper (35 cents a cup) cappuccino; good ventilation; more room; and a better view of passing humanity through huge picture windows.

The day before Thanksgiving, we had a couple of faculty over for "Thanksgiving dinner" (a Russian who lived in Sofia and came to AUBG Thursday afternoons for Friday classes, and an American who taught business that semester). We served them a traditional dinner, except that we had chicken and saved the turkey for the real Thanksgiving. The university administration had taken orders and shipped in a bunch of frozen turkeys for us from France. They were a bit expensive—25 leva ($15.00) for an 8-pounder—but we figured we could make the sacrifice for tradition. We had invited four American students, four Peace Corps volunteers, and the French teacher from the English Language High School. We got a chicken too, as we were not sure that, even with all the other food, eight pounds of turkey would stretch enough for 13 people. I told Laurie to just mix the chicken in with the turkey and nobody would know. I'm not sure how she did it, but somehow she found (or managed to replace) most of the critical ingredients for the traditional items. We were without sweet potatoes and replaced cranberry sauce with a sort of pineapple chutney, but what they called "tikva" was close enough to pumpkin that I certainly couldn't tell the difference. In fact, either because of the substitution, or (more likely) because of the fact that it was there, I liked that "pumpkin" pie better than those back home.

After our traditional Thanksgiving dinner for most of the Americans in town.

Chapter 5
December

Every day when I left the university, they had added a bit more to the Christmas/New Year decorations on the square and the walking mall. They had strung little colored lights and pennants on the buildings and between the light poles; some in the shape of Christmas trees and wreathes; some spelling out the Bulgarian equivalent of "Merry Christmas" and "Welcome 2000." Colorful banners were hung down many of the light poles, or strung between them, across the street. I also noticed they were building about two dozen little wooden booths. When I asked a student about them, he said, "Oh, those are Christmas booths." Sure enough, they finished them off with colored lights and tinsel; a little Christmas tree on top of each. Laurie, the boys, and I were interested to see what "Christmas booths" would be. When they began occupying them, we were disappointed to find, as Laurie put it, "the usual." They were offering nothing we couldn't get at the market or any of the little storefront shops. A couple of them had a few kitsch ornaments (just too cute for words), but they were "Christmas booths" in name (and decoration) only. They built some pretty impressive stone gateposts at each end, however, and at the end of one row of booths, a little stone house with a red tile roof. Jesse was convinced that it would house a Santa, prepared to hear the Christmas wishes of all good little boys and girls. He was right about the housing part, but wrong about the wishes. Mostly, Santa just smiled, waved, shouted "Merry Christmas" (in Bulgarian), and generally spread good cheer.

Well, we got our white Christmas. It snowed about two inches during the night Monday, and was cold enough—between five and 20 degrees—to stick. The problem was that before it got cold enough to turn to snow, we got a lot of rain, which covered everything with a layer of ice under the snow. We took the bus to Sofia Tuesday morning, and transferred there to a Plovdiv bus. The 100-km trip to Sofia usually took less than two hours, but because of the ice and snow (which increased to about five inches in Sofia), it took almost three. Although it was the main corridor to Greece, and one of the main highways in the country, the road to Sofia was not as good as any of the two-lane asphalt back roads in northern Minnesota—narrow, and with no shoulders a good part of the way.

The highway to Plovdiv was much better—four lanes most of the

Santa spreading Christmas cheer on the walking mall in Blagoevgrad.

way—and had been plowed, so the trip from Sofia to Plovdiv was little more than the usual two hours. The average temperature of the two busses was quite comfortable: freezing to Sofia, and sweltering to Plovdiv. We took a taxi from the main terminal in Plovdiv to Puldin Tours, a small travel agency. I had contacted them the week before, and they had agreed to reserve us "a couple of rooms in a private home near the center of town." We introduced ourselves, and the young woman telephoned the man we would be staying with to come and escort us to his home. I paid her 109 leva (about $65) for our rooms. Mr. Kotev arrived, and walked with us about two blocks to an apartment building, where we took the elevator to the ninth floor. He spoke no English, and with our limited Bulgarian, it took us some time to realize that, in fact, we had rented an entire two-bedroom apartment for two days—complete with satellite TV (much to our dismay and the boys' delight) and a bottle of his homemade plum brandy in the refrigerator, which he insisted that we help ourselves to. We did, and it was delicious.

We never could agree about whose apartment it was. Clearly, their son—who was a junior at Plovdiv University—lived there, and was staying with friends for the duration, but Laurie and Jesse thought that the man and his wife lived there and were staying with friends or relatives as well. At any rate, we couldn't decide whether to feel guilty for getting such great accommodations so cheaply, or good because we probably paid their rent for the month. Mr. Kotev recommended a small restaurant nearby, so we went there for dinner, and were pleased. We let the boys watch television until quite late, based on their promise that they wouldn't complain if we left early and didn't return until late the next day.

The apartment was about a 15-minute walk across the river to the old part of town. We set out the next morning, stopping at a kiosk along the way for breakfast of pastries, coffee, and juice. One of our guidebooks recommended a walking tour of the city, and so we tried to follow it, but the map they provided was not very good, and was out of scale, so we kept getting lost. We finally just got our bearings from the three hills around which the city is built, and made up our own walking tour. It wasn't nearly as efficient as the one in the book (we probably walked seven or eight miles), but we did see all the major sights eventually. Plovdiv was the second largest city in Bulgaria at about 165,000, but more importantly, it was the site of some of the oldest remains of Roman and Thracian civilizations, as well as some wonderful 18th and 19th century houses and churches. Those were collected in a section built on one of the hills, intertwined with narrow cobblestone streets overhung with balconies and bays extending from the houses. They were clearly not designed for motorized traffic, and in numerous places chunks of the overhangs had been knocked off and replaced (or often not) many times. The ornate architecture and colorfully painted structures lining steep streets was a bit like sections of San Francisco—only older and more scrunched together.

One of the main streets in the center of town had been closed to traffic, creating a very nice walking mall. At one end of that mall was a section of an open-air Roman theatre that had been excavated and incorporated into the surrounding structures. Stairs at each end of the excavation allowed access to the ancient theatre, and a beautiful basement restaurant had picture windows along one side that overlooked it. At the other end of the pedestrian mall was a huge paved square

A winter view of one of the restored Roman coliseums incorporated into the more modern elements of Plovdiv.

bordered by many of the municipal buildings and statues, as well as a large, beautiful park and a fountain. One of the buildings on the square housed a new McDonalds. Of course that's where we had lunch—no way we could have kept Jesse out of there, considering it had been more than six months since his last Big Mac.

We also found the most complete restoration of a 3,500-seat Roman coliseum in Eastern Europe (very impressive), and several centuries-old orthodox churches. To warm our feet up, we spent about half an hour in the archeological museum—the natural history museum was closed, despite a sign to the contrary. We had learned not to bet the farm on the accuracy of signs in Bulgaria. We would have missed seeing many worthwhile sites if we had taken the "Closed" signs for granted, and not tried the door and found it unlocked. We climbed to the top of two of the three hills around which the city was constructed, and which afforded spectacular views of the city and surrounding countryside. At the top of one was a beautiful old clock tower (maybe 19th century), and at the top of the other was an even older tower that our guidebooks and maps oddly didn't identify, but which looked like some kind of watch-tower. Many of the houses in the old section, although clearly once quite grand, were deserted and in grave disrepair; but many others had been, or were in the process of being, restored to their former grandeur.

They didn't do much in the way of snow removal in Bulgaria, and the temperature was right for the four inches of snow from the night before to create about two inches of cold slush through which we walked for hours. Even the most intrepid northern Minnesotans need to restore feeling to their toes occasionally, so at one time we began to search for the natural history museum as a toe-warming refuge. We eventually found it (hence discovering the spurious "open" sign), but not before unintentionally discovering many other parts of the city (I had always maintained that it was impossible to get lost if we didn't care). In this process (evidence to support my thesis), we came upon a rather unassuming church. When we crossed the street to see if we could make out the Bulgarian sign on it, an old couple came out and insisted that we come inside and look around. It was just as unassuming inside. In fact, I'd have to say it was the most unassuming church building we had seen in the eight or nine countries through which we had traveled since August (and we had seen a bunch). On the other hand, we were amazed to find that in this bastion of orthodoxy, interspersed with the occasional mosque, it was a Lutheran church. So amazed, in fact, that we at first assumed that our faulty Bulgarian had failed us. Nope—when asked to repeat himself, the old man clearly said "Lutheran." He and his wife (we assumed) were excited to learn that we were Lutheran, as well, and took us out back, where they swept the snow from two modestly Lutheran-looking tombstones. They were for the missionary ("killed by bandits" in the late 1800s) who had built the church, and his wife who, as her death was a few years later, and it didn't specify, must not have been "killed by bandits" (at least not the same ones at the same time).

We returned to our apartment that evening, cold, wet, and exhausted, but chuck full of history and culture. After another nice dinner at our neighborhood restaurant and a couple of hours of satellite TV, we flopped into bed. Actually "flopped" better described only Laurie's and my actions, as we had lucked into one of the old-style beds, with something like heavy chicken wire strung on the frame, covered by a 3-inch thick mattress pad. The resultant situation dictated that we spent as much time crawling up out of the middle and getting resituated as we did sleeping. It certainly made us appreciate the new-style box springs and mattress layout we had back in Blagoevgrad. The next morning about nine, Mr. Kotev and his wife either came by to pick up the keys or to move back into their home. We said goodbye and caught a taxi to the bus station. The driver cheated us by driving the long way around, resulting in twice the fare we had paid the other direction. I didn't say anything because my Bulgarian wasn't good enough to encompass effective bitching; because I was in a good mood and didn't want to spoil it; but mostly because he'd cheated me out of a grand total of about $1.20, and it just wasn't that big a deal. It used to bother me when people thought they were getting away with cheating the stupid foreigner, but I had come to feel that it just wasn't that big a deal—and we probably deserved it anyway, for being so rich to begin with.

We arrived at the bus station in Sofia just in time to miss the 1:00 bus to Blagoevgrad, so had some lunch and waited for the 2:00 bus. As so often happens, what at first seemed like a misfortune (missing the bus) was in fact a wonderful opportunity. As we waited, I had a chance to observe the incredible process around us. What I referred to the Sofia "bus station," was, in fact, an open area about the size of a football field; no building functioned as what we would normally think of as a bus station. The field was surrounded by kiosks from which people sold reserved tickets for the various private lines served by the "station," food, drinks, groceries, clothes, cigarettes, and every other manner of stuff that people might need while traveling. The field itself was full of rows of busses—about 40 or 50 of the big Greyhound type, in six rows of about seven or eight across. Between the busses was just enough room for people to get their luggage into the bins underneath or get between the busses, but not both at the same time. Between the rows was barely enough room for a bus to pull out of or into a space without hitting one of the other busses. In fact, several times busses were not quite able to get in or out until another driver interrupted his loading to move a few feet.

Add to the mix hundreds of people getting on and off busses, all of their luggage, delivery trucks, and taxis and private cars dropping off and picking up passengers. Over and over I saw bus drivers maneuver their huge charges within not feet, but inches, of other busses, cars, people, piles of luggage, and kiosks. The most amazing thing was that, with very few exceptions, no voices were raised in anger; nobody threatened anybody else; nothing that sounded like strings of invectives was uttered. In fact, more often, I saw people leave a pile of luggage to go off and get something to eat, trusting that everything would be there when they got back. Often their luggage would not be exactly where they left it, because to keep it from being run over, some stranger had moved it out of the way. As we waited for the next Blageovgrad bus to arrive, it became obvious that we were not alone; in fact, it became obvious that there were more people gathering than would fit on the next bus. Bulgarians did not stand in line. Instead, they crowded in a mass toward the door through which they all wanted to go. Even at the theatre, where everyone had a reserved seat (and they were meticulous about making sure they sat in the seat with the number that matched the one on their ticket), as soon as the doors opened, they swarmed in an unruly mass toward them, and pushed their way in as soon as they could get there. We always just hung back until everyone else was in; then strolled in and found our seats—made all the easier, as they were often the only empty ones left in the section.

The situation at the bus station was different, however, as we were trying to get on a bus for which there were no reserved seats—tickets had to be purchased from the driver as we got on the bus. The fact that we had been there first would make absolutely no difference to the mob trying to get on before us. We decided that the only way we could avoid missing the next bus (and who knew how many to follow) was to play by the Bulgarian rules. When the bus pulled in, Cooper and I surged with the rest of the mass toward the door. In fairness to us, we did not really push ourselves, but let those behind us push us forward. Nor did we trample any little old folks or mothers with babies; but rather, did our best to let them in front of us and keep the crush of others off them. We got on somewhere near the middle of the pack, bought four tickets, put our packs in three of the seats and me in the fourth, and Cooper made his way back to the front where he passed two of the tickets to Laurie and Jesse outside. When he had sold all the tickets, the driver informed the remaining people outside that they would have to wait for the next bus. As they drifted away, Laurie and Jesse got on, presented their tickets, and took the two seats we had saved for them. Throughout that process (which in the States would surely have been accompanied by much shouting and swearing, if not worse), nobody gave any outward signs of ill will toward the others involved, and those who did not get on accepted their fate with resolve, if not good will. Traffic was terrible in Sofia, so it took us about an hour just to get out of town, but once outside the city, things loosened up and we were in Blagoevgrad by 4:30. After dinner at the Chinese restaurant near the university, we made our way, slipping and sliding, up the hill to our home, where we settled in for the evening, and prepared for Christmas Eve the next day.

Unlike in China and Thailand, I was employed in Bulgaria by an American-run university. That fact resulted in some negative aspects (it diminished day-to-day contact with the culture of the country), and some positive (smoother administrative process, Thanksgiving turkeys, Christmas trees). The university had taken orders in the middle of November for Christmas trees. They were a bit pricey, but saved me sneaking a branch from one of the bushes in town, so we ordered a small (read less-expensive) one. They were delivered to the university a week before Christmas. My progress was followed with much interest as I carried it home over my shoulder. Although somewhat sparsely decorated (mostly paper snowflakes) it added a festive air to the apartment. As with our gift exchanges in China and Thailand (with the knowledge that we would have to carry everything that wasn't either consumable or otherwise use-up-able back to the States) we used discretion in our choice of gifts. It was a calm, mellow Christmas day, but given the pace of our travels before, and the ones we knew were coming up, it was just what we needed. We left the next morning for two weeks in Turkey and Greece, returning January 8, in time for the startup of spring semester classes.

The first leg of our trip to Turkey was to catch the 10:00 a.m. bus in Blagoevgrad for the 2-hour ride to Sophia. There was a nightly bus to Istanbul, which cost slightly less than the train, and took a couple of hours less, but we preferred trains for long rides, as we could get up and move around. Therefore, on arrival in Sophia, we negotiated the tunnel that connected the bus and train stations, which were separated by the 6-lane bypass around Sophia. The tunnel was more like an underground market; lined on both sides with stalls selling everything from food to all kinds of consumer goods. At the train station, the sixth window we tried was the one to buy sleeper tickets to Istanbul. Unlike information booths in Western Europe, those in Eastern Europe didn't necessarily contain people who spoke English, so the only responses we got to "Istanbul?" were fingers pointed or hands waved in a general direction. When we finally found the right window, buying the tickets was pretty straightforward. I gave the woman 192 leva (about $28 each) and she gave me four tickets for two adjoining compartments with two beds each and a sliding door between.

What should have been a 9-hour trip from Sophia to Istanbul took about 16 hours, for two simple reasons. First, the "train" to Istanbul from Sophia was, in fact, one sleeper car attached to the end of a train to one of the eastern Bulgarian cities. At some time in the middle of the night (timed to happen just after we got used to the movement of the train and fell asleep), we stopped and our car was uncoupled and left to sit on a siding somewhere in east central Bulgaria. After a couple of hours, the Orient Express, on its way from Romania to Southeast Asia, stopped and picked us up. That didn't sound like a big deal, and it probably wasn't to those who knew what was going on, but to those of us who didn't, it was somewhat disconcerting. Anyway, as we sat there, heat seeping from every crevice in the car, with no umbilical cord to an engine to replace it, we realized why they had kept the heat turned all the way up in our car during the first part of the trip.

Just long enough after we got going again to get back to sleep, we stopped at the Bulgarian border. There, four times, border patrol officers took turns pounding on our doors, shouting "policia" or "passaporta," shining lights in our faces, peering into our compartments, and looking at our passports. Why four times? We never knew. It took them about an hour to thus sufficiently torture everyone on the train. Just long enough after we got going again to get back to sleep, we stopped at the Turkish checkpoint (about 3:00 a.m. by this time). There we all had to get dressed, get out of the train, and go into a building, where we stood in line for about a half hour to have our passports checked. We were told that we needed to go stand in another line, where we bought visas, for a whopping $45 apiece—the single greatest expense of the trip. At least they stuck colorful stamps (like large postage stamps) in our passports, rather than just whacking them with a rubber stamp.

Then we got to go back and stand in the first line again. The good news was that by that time almost everyone had gone through that line, so we didn't have to wait nearly as long. We got back on the train, undressed, got back in bed, and were wondering why the Bulgarian border patrol got on the train and the Turkish border patrol made us get off, when the Turkish border patrol got on. A repeat of the torture at the Bulgarian checkpoint followed, only in Turkish this time. All told, the delays amounted to about seven hours—plus the 9-hour train ride—so we arrived in Istanbul at almost 10:00 am. We then became millionaires by going to the nearest ATM and getting $400 in cash—about 200 million Turkish lira. Now that took a while to get used to. Next we took a tram (a million lira for the four of us—the cash flowed like water) to the Sultanahmet district (the old town) where we had reserved a room (bathroom down the hall) in a pension at $5 a bed per night.

After a short rest and sprucing up a bit, we ate and walked around the area. We couldn't have picked a better spot to stay—in addition to being able to see the Aegean Sea from the window of the third floor common room in the pension, we were within walking distance of almost all the major sights of Istanbul. That afternoon we saw what was left of the hippodrome, where the Romans once held chariot races, and a couple of impressive obelisks. One of them was of smooth marble with ornate inscriptions, that was thousands of years old, and looked like it had been made a year ago. The other, about 50 feet away and about the same age, was of the same style, but constructed of blocks of rough stone that looked like they had been cut from hardened lava and had been there since God was young. A block away, we came upon the remains of a Roman amphitheater that had been made into a city park, complete with multi-level patios, fountains, and benches. Just as in many of the other ancient cities we had visited, the antiquities there were taken very much for granted by the people—children climbed on Roman walls like jungle gyms.

And what delightful people they were. Often those who approached to ask where we were from were trying to get us to visit their carpet shops or restaurants, but occasionally they just wanted to be friendly or to practice their English. Even the salesmen approached their job with lively good humor and, when told firmly that we weren't interested, either just chatted for a while, or thanked us politely and bid us a pleasant day. One young man who stopped to talk with me told me that he had been watching NBC news on satellite TV (lots of people in Istanbul had lots of money), and had seen that the U.S. State Department was issuing warnings to citizens overseas to beware of terrorist attacks around the new year. He said he just wanted to assure me that we had no worries in Istanbul, as they really liked Americans; especially since Clinton's visit. Not once while we were in Turkey did we feel in any way threatened. It wasn't unusual for the people in small villages to be friendly, open, and honest to visitors, but we were impressed by the fact that we got that feeling from the people in a city the size of Istanbul. We couldn't pause to refer to our map for more than a couple of minutes without someone stopping to ask if he or she could help. At one time, when we were trying to decide whether we could take a shortcut through the courtyard of a small mosque, a man came out and offered to show us around inside. As we were looking around, he told us that although most people knew that the famous Ayasophia was built by Constantine as a Christian church, few realize that only a couple of blocks from it was a small mosque, built originally as a church, and known locally as "Little Ayasophia." He had the keys to it, and proudly showed it to us as well.

We spent most of the next day at Topkapi Palace, and most of a day wasn't too much to spend there. It was a magnificent complex of buildings and park-like grounds that covered much of the area of the old city between the Aegean Sea and the Bosphorous. Most of the buildings were set up as museums; each concentrating on some aspect of the culture of the time. Among the most impressive pieces were huge jewel-encrusted thrones (which, although beautiful, certainly looked uncomfortable). We also saw the huge topaz—as big as a person's hand—the theft of which comprised the plot of the movie "Topkapi." We had wanted to spend time in the famous archeological museum on the grounds of the palace, but the entrance fee was exorbitant, and so many of the buildings were closed for restoration that we decided it just wasn't worth it. By the time we left the palace, it was mid-afternoon, and we were

Our (unlike China and Thailand) real Christmas tree.

famished, so we set out to find a place to eat. On a side street nearby, we came across a tiny restaurant that served "donar kabobs," the Turkish equivalent of Greek gyros. We looked in, but the few seats were taken. Before we could leave, however, the owner grabbed us and ushered us up a winding wrought iron stairway to a small, low-ceilinged room that looked like something out of "Arabian Nights." We sat on low benches with pillows and Turkish carpets and marveled at the amount and variety of clutter that contributed to the unique atmosphere. We signed a Bulgarian bill and left it under the glass on the tabletop with others from throughout the world.

The cozy upstairs dining area of a tiny restaurant in Istanbul.

After a yummy lunch, we set off in search of what used to be known as the "Egyptian" market, but was then called the spice market. Much of it was in a huge covered bazaar, with shops spilling out onto the streets and squares for blocks in every direction. The stalls offered every manner of goods, but it didn't take long for us to see where the market got its name: many of them were packed with barrels, bins, boxes, bags, cans, and jars of every size and shape, all overflowing with every type of spice imaginable. The mixture of aromas was enough to make us lightheaded. Of all the sights, sounds, and smells, I think the one that impressed us most, however, was in a cheese shop: a complete goatskin, slit down the belly to reveal that it was stuffed completely with snowy white cheese.

As it was Ramadan while we were there, the devout Muslims were fasting from sunrise to sunset—about 5:00 a.m. to 5:00 p.m. As the time to break their fast approached each day, the shopkeepers began to pay increasingly less attention to customers, and increasingly more to preparations for their dinner. Beginning about a quarter to five, we had to be careful not to be run over by delivery people laden with huge trays of food, rushing from shop to shop, delivering dinner to the shopkeepers who couldn't leave. Simultaneous with the sound of the cannon announcing the end of fasting for the day, virtually everyone began to eat. Shops either locked their doors for a half hour, or proprietors just refused to acknowledge anyone silly enough to come in. If tradesmen were working at someone's home, they stopped while the homeowner

A view of the classiest portion of the Grand Bazar in Istanbul.

served them tea and something to eat. After dark we got round-trip tickets for one of the ferries to the Asian side of the city, and spent about an hour on the water, sitting on deck looking at the lights of the city and sipping tea. They actually had someone who came around selling little glasses of (very inexpensive) apple tea on the ferries.

On the 30th we went to both the Blue Mosque, one of the most famous in the world, and the Ayasophia, built by Constantine as the largest Christian church in the world after he moved the government of the Roman Empire to Constantinople (now Istanbul). The Blue Mosque was where all the Muslims in Turkey tried to get to at least once to worship during Ramadan. Consequently, we couldn't get near it five times each day for a half hour. It was open to the public at other times, however. As with all the famous religious sites we had visited, whether in China, Thailand, or Europe, the courtyard was more a souvenir bazaar than a holy place. The clamor of people hawking their wares faded, however, as we entered the mosque itself, and a calm stillness prevailed that attended sacred spots everywhere. The few people who spoke did so in whispers, including the guides; everyone's movements slowed; people seemed to relax. The atmosphere enhanced our appreciation of the huge domed interior, resplendent in multicolored tile; dark, intricately-carved wood; and wall-to-wall Turkish carpet. We saw the spot high on one wall where, several years before, thieves had stolen about

15 of the estimated three million unique aquamarine tile. We were told that they sold them to a museum in London for $15,000 apiece.

Chapter 6
January

The end of Ramadan that year was the weekend of January 7-9, and as that coincided so closely with the start of the new year, they did it up good in Turkey. Several people told us officially they were holding back because of mourning for those killed in recent earthquakes, and because they didn't want to spend a lot of money on fireworks and the like, when it should be sent for earthquake relief. It was hard to imagine, however, that the air of festivity that prevailed could have been greater. During the week we were in Istanbul, booths were erected on both sides of the street for two blocks on the West side of the Blue Mosque. Each night, more and more people crowded into the area to see the clowns, eat, drink, buy stuff, play games, and just generally celebrate.

There was virtually no parking except on the sidewalks, so traffic jammed up for blocks around. It didn't help that when the sidewalks became parking lots, people were left with only the streets in which to walk. The police were out in force, but as nearly as I could tell, they were mostly just celebrating with everyone else. On the rare occasion when they tried to give orders, I didn't notice anybody paying much attention. One officer must have been told to keep cars off the sidewalk in front of the mosque, but by the time he got there, half a dozen were already parked; their owners long gone. The idea of getting a tow truck in was laughable, so he set about keeping the remaining sidewalk clear. As it was the only area that was clear, however, every driver was trying to park there at once. While the officer was urging one to move along, another was parking, locking his car, and skedaddling before the officer could turn his attention to him. Like any good Turkish policeman, he soon decided to accept the combined will of the people and turned his attention to celebrating as well. After all, this was the city where the mayor publicly described red lights as "a suggestion."

The Ayasophia was a truly impressive edifice, built completely from stone; much of it imported from other countries. Most of the upper walls and the entire dome were covered with what were once magnificent religious murals and mosaics. Many were painted over when it was transformed into a mosque, and the crosses carved into the stone were all chipped away. Many of the faces of the saints, Christ, Mary, and the disciples had been destroyed as well. The greatest destruction, howev-

365

er, had been from nature; mostly leaks in the thousands of lead sheets covering the roof. The building, no longer used as a mosque, had been declared a national treasure, and in 1992 a massive restoration project was begun. Oddly, one of the most striking elements of the interior was the massive scaffolding, which covered one fourth of the floor space, and rose to the dome, about 200 feet above. All they had been able to accomplish was to stabilize most of the deterioration of that quarter of the dome, and through chemical and physical analysis of the materials, to determine some steps that might be taken to best restore the work. Another big problem was that movement from earthquakes and natural settling of the massive structure was threatening its physical integrity. In several places bowtie-shaped chinks had been chiseled out of the walls, and electronic devices inserted to monitor their movement.

On the premise that we couldn't visit Turkey without looking at Turkish carpets (and the double rationale that their showroom was in a restored Turkish bathhouse and that they were supposed to teach visitors about the carpets without subjecting them to a hard sell), we visited the government showroom. We weren't disappointed in either case. The bathhouse was beautiful. It was built much like a mosque, but without the minarets (the tall, slender towers from which the calls to prayer were sounded) or interior embellishments. Architecturally, the interior was beautiful: the smooth, curving lines of arched doorways echoing the line of the domed rooms. The walls, however, were all pure white plaster, which set the vivid colors of the carpets off beautifully. The manager was very friendly and helpful, filling us in on the basics of how to tell quality handmade carpets with natural dyes from those made on mechanical looms and colored with chemical dyes. We noticed, however, that her presentation and tour of the showrooms seemed a bit rushed, and, although we hadn't expected a hard sell, had expected her to show some interest in our buying something. Then we noticed the time—five minutes to 5:00. The cannon sounded just as we were leaving, and when I stuck my head back in to inquire about whether they would be open the next day, I interrupted her meal.

The next day, equipped with our newly acquired knowledge, we went to the carpet store of a young man we had met and liked, to take him up on his offer of "tea and conversation," and to convince him that we could not afford a carpet. Of course he convinced us that we could not afford not to buy one. In truth, it didn't take much; I think we had both already bought one in our minds and just needed someone we liked and trusted to tell us so. It was a small one (about 5X7), and comparatively inexpensive: if we thought of it as 380 million lira, then $650 (including shipping) didn't seem like so much. It took us about three hours to actually decide which one we wanted from the dozens on display (any one of about 20 would have been great), and it was dazzling.

We spent that entire afternoon at the Turkish Military Museum, partly to appease Jesse, who was tired of looking at all the "boring stuff" and wanted to spend some time viewing weapons of destruction, and partly because a couple of people had recommended the concert of traditional military music that took place there every afternoon at 3:00. The place was about the size of the Pentagon, and was clearly funded with part of the defense budget of the country. As the museum had been converted from the grounds and classroom building of the military academy where Ataturk ("Father of Turkey") went to school, they took great pride in it. Rightly so—it was impressive in both the quality and quantity of its displays. After a couple of hours even Jesse began to pass glass cases full of weapons with only a cursory glance. He said that he had seen enough for one day. The rooms were arranged in roughly chronological order, and showed (exhaustively) Turkey's involvement in military campaigns throughout history. One of the most extensive displays (not surprisingly) featured their defeat of the ANZAK forces at Gallipoli, which I was pretty familiar with. I didn't realize, however, that Turkish troops fought with the UN forces in Korea. The concert was every bit as good as we had been led to expect. Turkey claimed theirs was the historical advent of military bands, created to instill awe in their enemies. It instilled awe in us, at any rate, performing music unlike any we had heard before.

As it was New Year's Eve, we went out for a nice dinner and then celebrated in our usual way: I went to bed and was asleep by 11:00 (what millennium?) and Laurie took the boys out to see the celebration. They said the fireworks weren't anything special—not as good as some we'd seen back home. Besides, I got to see it all on Euronews the next day—fully rested.

We had planned to spend five days in Istanbul; then travel to Greece and spend five days in Thessaloniki, but we liked Turkey so much that we decided to spend our whole time there. We had made reservations for an overnight bus to Cappadocia, leaving at 10:00 from the main bus station, so we had to catch a minibus from Sultanahmet at 7:30. That gave us one more day to see the sights of Istanbul. We spent part of it in the underground cistern a couple of blocks from our pension. We had hesitated to go there, as the entrance fee seemed high just to see a hole in the ground where the Romans had stored water—besides most of the water was long since gone. Compared to what we had slapped

The head of Medusa supporting one of the columns in the underground cistern in Istanbul.

our VISA card down for the day before, though, it seemed silly to quibble, so we splurged—good choice. In fact, it was much more than just a hole. The dozens of massive stone columns supporting the vaulted roof were worth the price of admission alone. They were all different: some very plain and elegant, others ornately carved. We were awed by the artistry expended on something they knew would be out of view, submerged in water. The bases of two of the columns were heads taken from a set of five statues of Medusa and transported hundreds of miles for their new purpose. The subdued lighting, the cool, moist atmosphere, and the sound of water dripping into the remaining three feet of water under the catwalks we were traversing all made for a sort of unique, eerie beauty.

That afternoon we went to the National Mosaic Museum, mostly because it was cheap and close by. Our guidebook didn't have much to say about it, and we had been unimpressed by its exterior several times when we had walked by it. We approached and peeked in the door. It looked very modern and quite small. The man in the ticket booth just inside the door saw us and said, "Much more inside; very nice." Well, why not? We had to do something until time for our bus, and we couldn't make dinner last that long. Another good choice—it must have been one of the best-kept secrets in the city. We stepped inside the lobby and found that the "museum" was an excavation of part of a Roman castle, comprising the most complete (and beautiful) set of mosaic floors from that period in the world. Our only quibble was that after we had gone through the whole display, we found the final room contained a detailed explanation of how complicated and extensive the restoration had been. After spending twenty minutes there, we felt compelled to retrace our steps and go through the whole thing again—with greatly increased appreciation of what we were seeing. That worked fine for us, as we were the only people in sight, but it probably caused problems during the

A section of mosaic floors from a Roman castle.

369

height of the tourist season. Or maybe they didn't get enough business even then to be a problem. If that was the case, it was a shame, as we decided it was a site we were very glad to have stumbled upon.

At 7:30 we caught our minibus to the main bus station, and were staggered by its size and complexity. Nothing in our experience had prepared us for such a station. It was like a major airport in the States, only with three times as many busses as planes at the arrival and departure points all at one time. We saw gates numbered as high as 150, and each had a bus parked in it. In addition, hundreds more busses were parked in every available space of the three-tiered facility—some loading or unloading; some being serviced; some sitting idle. Luckily our shuttle dropped us right at the gate we needed, or we never would have gotten out of town. We had no idea whether we would stop on the 12-hour trip, so we bought some emergency rations and settled into our reserved seats—a bit narrow, but otherwise fairly comfortable. The fact that we didn't see a toilet on board seemed to indicate that we would surely be stopping, but we had learned to take nothing for granted. We all got off and paid our 20 cents each for a last visit to the facilities in the station. Shortly after we re-boarded, we were off for the interior of Turkey.

We needn't have worried about bathroom facilities on the long bus ride—we stopped for 15-30 minutes every two or three hours, whether everyone was asleep or not. The stops were surprisingly modern, with restaurants, snack bars, convenience stores, and restroom facilities. In fact, they were essentially like any truck stop on major highways in the States, only instead of several semis, there were several buses in the lots. In fact, I neglected to note what color our bus was at the first stop, and had to look into several before finding the right one to reboard. At first, we were very antsy about getting off, as we had no idea how long we would be stopped, so we took turns keeping an eye on the drivers, on the theory that we weren't going anywhere without at least one of them. There were two on all the long trips; one driving, and the other sleeping in a cleverly designed compartment for that purpose, which took up part of the space under the bus that would have otherwise held luggage. These little bunk compartments were accessible either from outside, or from a small door on the wall of the exit stairs halfway back the bus. One time we could count on stopping was between 4:00 and 5:00 a.m., so the driver (and anyone else who wanted) could have a big meal in preparation for fasting until sundown. Unlike in Thailand, the drivers in Turkey were not only sane, but seemed quite competent. Not once in all the hours we spent on Turkish buses did we feel in danger (whereas in Thailand we seldom felt we weren't).

Dawn revealed a dry, rugged landscape reminiscent of the Dakota badlands. As we got closer to our destination, Urgup, the formations became increasingly extreme, and we began to notice caves cut into the sides of some of the rock faces. Cappadocia was an area about 200 kms across in central Turkey that was famous for its rock formations, a result of volcanic eruptions, followed by millions of years of erosion by wind and water. It was a stronghold of early Christianity. When the persecution of those people began, they dug underground rooms connected by tunnels, in which to hide. Over decades those refuges became whole underground cities. We arrived at Urgup about 7:30 a.m., and had about two hours at our hotel to get cleaned up and eat before our tour bus picked us up. That is we'd have been able to clean up if we could have gotten into our rooms. Usually that would have been the case, but the hotel was packed with folks from Istanbul who had come out on a special excursion to celebrate the New Year, and who wouldn't be leaving until later that day. So, we had an hour to sit in the lobby waiting for the dining room to open, and an hour to eat a continental breakfast of a hard-boiled egg, tomato slices, goat cheese, olives, bread, butter, jam, and coffee or tea. We managed to get it all down in the allotted time. To their credit, however, when someone checked out of one room early, they got it cleaned and ready for us to at lest stow our belongings before we left on the tour. When we returned that evening, they had a second ready for the boys.

We usually shunned tours, as they just didn't offer the flexibility we wanted. We had made an exception in this case, however, for several reasons. First, the area, as I mentioned, was quite large, creating transportation problems for individual travelers unfamiliar with the local system. We would have spent much of our two days just arranging to get from one place to the other. Second, the cost of the tour covered round-trip transportation to the area, local transportation to the main sites, two hotel rooms, breakfasts, lunches, and entrance fees to the sites (which were as much as $5 or $6 apiece in some cases). When we added up all those costs, it came to almost as much as the 170 million lira (about $340) we paid for the two-day tour. Third, the tour group consisted of the four of us, a South African doctor named Colin, and a young Turkish couple the first day, and just us and Colin the second. It was a small enough group that we got plenty of personal attention. In fact, the guide changed the set itinerary a couple of times, at our request.

A white, 10-passenger mini-van picked us up at the hotel about 9:30. Our first stop was a scenic overlook, to give us a feel for the geographic anomalies of the area. With a gorgeous, rugged backdrop, and the second highest peak in Turkey in the distance, our guide gave us an interesting talk that provided historical and geological context for what we would see during the next two days. In fact, all of his exposition was good: long enough to be helpful, but not so long as to make us impatient to move on. The two most impressive stops of the day were the underground city built by the Christians, and a long hike along a river at the bottom of a canyon.

The underground city was the largest of a couple dozen in central Turkey. It stretched over several kms, and was seven layers deep. Only three of the layers had been excavated, and the area we covered was probably no more than half a km, but it was still exceedingly impressive. We toured dozens of rooms, connected by hundreds of yards of corridors, all hewn from hardened volcanic ash. The corridors were anywhere from 10 feet high to so low we had to duck-walk for several yards. The rooms ranged from 25 feet across to maybe 5 feet. The largest were meeting rooms; the smallest used for storage. Between were kitchens, larders, sleeping rooms, churches, dining rooms, and wine preparation rooms. The latter were marked by large depressions around the edge of the floors, fashioned to hold the bases of huge jugs called "amphoras," containers for the wine. They also had coffin-sized niches cut into the walls in pairs, one slightly higher than the other and connected by short, pipe-like tunnels. The higher of the two was where the grapes were smashed, and the juice ran down into the other, where it was ladled into the amphoras. Many of the tunnels had occasional slots cut into the side, and huge stone wheels set in compartments to one side. If they were attacked, the residents could run down these tunnels, and roll the stones into place, sealing themselves in and blocking the tunnel.

After a couple of hours as tunnel rats, we were quite ready to return to the surface. We stopped next at a site that looked like the Grand Canyon, only smaller, and with much more greenery. We descended to the level of the river on a flight of steep steps, where we visited a couple of the half dozen chapels carved into the base of the cliff along a stretch of several kms. As with all the formerly Christian sites we visited, the once magnificent iconography, although still impressive, was greatly diminished by the efforts of vandals. What followed was an invigorating hike of about an hour and a half along the river bottom, with beautiful vistas rising on both sides, made more interesting by the occasional caves hewn into the walls of the canyon. One of them, our guide said, was the remains of an ancient theatre. We couldn't imagine what a theatre would be doing carved into the rock 50 feet from the bottom of a gorge in such an isolated setting. There it was, however, testament to

Laurie traversing one of the tunnels in the largest underground city in central Turkey.

how little we really knew or understood the past. The path itself wound through trees and bushes along a small, clean, fast-moving river. As we got further from the entrance, evidence of other hikers grew less, and the path narrowed. It was splendid; Laurie and I tarried, and would have made an afternoon of it, but the others wanted to move along. As it was, the guide came back a couple of times to ask if we were alright. We assured him that we were better than that. The weather had been comparatively mild for our whole time in Turkey, but that afternoon was so pleasant that we stripped off our jackets and tied them around our waists. At the end of the trail was a wonderful little town with a small restaurant down by the water. There we sat, at picnic tables under huge trees that looked like cottonwoods, to eat a late lunch. After all the exercise, we were famished, and were struck by the discipline of the young Turkish man, who sat apart from us, observing his fast. Laurie and I would have liked to spend more time exploring the little village, but we were getting short on time, and miles to go before we slept.

On our way back to Urgup, we noticed several ruins at intervals along the highway. When we asked about them, our guide said that the road we were on had once been part of the spice route from the East, and that what we had noticed were the ruins of "caravansaries," the truck stops of the day. They were built every twenty kms, the distance a caravan could reasonably travel in a day. The next one had been reconstructed, and we stopped to see it. These caravansaries were stone forts, about 50 yards square, with massive walls, intended to offer safety from the bands of thieves who were after the wealth of spices carried by the caravans. One huge, thick gate offered entry; a stone watchtower rose from the center of the courtyard. It was in this courtyard where the people slept on hot summer nights. In winter, they took advantage of the warmth of their animals, sleeping with them in the large, covered rooms surrounding the courtyard. The owners of these caravansaries kept their huge storerooms filled with the provisions necessary to wait out possible sieges by

The entrance to a restored caravansary near Urgup.

bands of thieves. In fact, every contingency was prepared for within the walls, including a small mosque for daily prayers.

Our guide had warned us about our last stop of the day. We had told him as we set out that morning that we weren't interested in shopping, so he had skipped all those stops. He told us, however, that we would have to make one: at a topaz factory. He said he used to work there, they were his friends, and they would be upset with him if he bypassed them. We weren't thrilled, but said OK. In fact, it was quite nice. The manager took us into their workshop, showed us the raw stone, and gave us a short lesson on what topaz was, the various types, and how it was prepared. We watched a worker turn a raw block into a rough egg on a lathe; then move to another station where, in several steps, he sanded and polished it to the finished product. When he was done, he turned and, much to Jesse's delight, presented the glossy egg to him. That priming us to buy something completed, we were ushered into the showroom, served apple tea, and encouraged to "look around." The manager assured us that we were under no obligation, but of course if we saw anything we liked.... In fact, I did give Cooper 2 million lira ($4) to buy two fist-sized topaz apples for his favorite teachers back in the States, but they certainly didn't get rich from us. Our guide (who was a real hoot—he'd announced to us early on that he was both an alcoholic and a "nicotineaholic") jokingly berated us, saying his commission wouldn't be enough to buy one drink, let alone get him drunk when we got back.

He found enough somewhere, though. He had told us at one time during the day that his boss, the owner of the travel agency, owned a traditional Turkish restaurant, and had asked if we were interested in having dinner there. He said a five-course traditional dinner would be less than 10 million lira ($20) for all four of us. As our hotel was on the edge of town, and we'd have quite a hike to eat anywhere but the hotel dining room (a fate we generally chose to avoid) we asked him if there was a bus that would take us near his boss' restaurant. When he said he would pick us up and take us back to the hotel in his boss' BMW, we leaped at the offer. Had we know the condition he would be in, we might not have been so willing. He weaved all over the road, and I thought I would have to grab the wheel a couple of times to keep him from sideswiping some parked cars. He neglected to slow down for some speed bumps that almost put our heads against the roof, but in fact, the worst he did was fail to make one curve, running up on the sidewalk with the right front tire on the way around. We were fine, but I wouldn't have taken odds on whether the boss noticed a distinct shimmy in the front end the next time he got his Beamer up to speed.

Jesse throwing a pot at a ceramic factory near Capadocia.

The dinner was all our guide had promised. The restaurant was closed for Ramadan, but the boss' wife had come in and cooked the meal especially for us. She'd done herself proud. Each course: cheese, soup, salad, traditional Turkish stew, and dessert, was delicious. We might have preferred that the boss not sit with us the whole time, but his conversation was interesting, and at least he didn't chain smoke as he had while we were in his office that morning. After dinner, we were not disappointed when he told us that our guide was in no condition to drive us back, so he would take us himself. On the way, he told us that, although our guide was quite good, he always drank up his pay for the day, and never worked two days in a row. Sure enough, the next morning when the minivan arrived, it was with a different guide.

Our second day in Cappadocia began with a stop at another scenic overlook (this time with the third highest mountain in Turkey in the distance), and another short history/geology lesson. Short was good, as our luck with the weather had run out—it was cold, snowy, and quite windy. We were glad we had done the two-hour hike the day before, while it was still nice. We visited several sites where whole villages had been carved into the sides of steep hills formed from solidified volcanic ash. Then we went to a site that was created by the early Christians in the area as a sort of commune. The area, which was maybe a km across, had been declared a national treasure by the government, and was being made into an outdoor museum.

It contained several chapels, workshops, living quarters, wineries, storage spaces, kitchens, and a large communal eating area. In the dining room were a table and benches, about 20 feet long, carved from the rock. As with the other sites, many of the once magnificent iconographic paintings had been damaged by vandals. In some cases, extensive damage had been inflicted by subsequent residents, who had adapted the spaces to their needs—such as livestock stables—by carving additional space from the rock, obliterating what had been there. Consequently, some of the chapels had beautifully painted ceilings, with rough-hewn walls below.

This guide's obligatory shopping stop was a pottery factory—it was in his hometown. Again, it wasn't nearly as bad as we feared. We were met by the manager and taken to the factory, where a woman demonstrated how they made plates on an electric pottery wheel. We then were shown the steps pieces went through—drying, glazing, painting, and firing—before they were complete. As in both China and Thailand, we were awed by the fine work being produced hour after hour, day after day, by the people in those small factories. Next, we went to a separate room where a young man demonstrated their manual wheel. Naturally, he made it look effortless, but those of us who had taken college pottery classes knew better. Jesse hadn't, and so didn't. The manager overheard his comment to Laurie that he thought he could do that. When the young man finished his sugar bowl (the lid, which he had turned separately, naturally fit perfectly on the first try), the manager handed Jesse an apron and invited him to try.

I suppose when I was that age I was cocky enough to step just as confidently forward as he did. I was torn between wanting to see him get his comeuppance and not wanting him to be hurtfully embarrassed. I shouldn't have worried; they knew exactly what they were doing. They had years of experience prepping fathers like me to buy the goods on display in the next room. The young potter gave Jesse just enough leeway to let him realize that it was anything but easy as it looked, but just enough help that he wasn't embarrassed. In fact, the resulting bowl was quite passable—until he let Jesse cut the bottom out of it with the wire used to separate pieces from the wheel. Jesse, without hesitation (as was his wont) announced that it was a flowerpot, complete with drainage hole, and just needed the tray for underneath. Of course Jesse wanted to keep his creation. He was earnestly trying to convince us that the transportation of a raw clay vessel throughout Europe would be no problem, when the potter, who understood not one word of the discussion, ended it by recycling the piece into the large glob of clay beside the wheel.

The number, variety, and beauty of the pieces in the showroom were awe-inspiring. Again, I satisfied neither the manager nor my sons by putting up about $4 for two beautiful mugs they could take home and use for hot chocolate and apple tea. I was glad I didn't spend more when neither of them made it two full days unbroken. After lunch in a local restaurant, we made a couple more stops at sites similar to those we had already seen, but enough different to make them worth stopping for. Then we headed back to Urgup, where we caught the 4:30 bus to Ankara. There, the travel agency owner said, he had made reservations for us with Kamel, the largest bus line in the country, for their 10:00 overnight to Canakkale.

About halfway to Ankara, we faced a tragedy of the first order when Jesse realized he had left his fanny-pack (or "bum-bag" as two Australians we met called it) in the restroom at the bus station. He demanded that we turn around immediately, a command the driver fortunately could not understand, as I doubt he would have taken kindly to being highjacked by a 13-year-old. We had noticed that the driver had a cell-phone (after all, Turkey was a good prospect for inclusion in the European Union), and found someone who could translate a respectful request that he call back to the station and have someone check the restroom for Jesse's bag. Of course it wasn't there, and Jesse spent the rest of the trip to Ankara accepting the fact that his onyx egg, Turkish additions to his coin collection, and other valuables were forever lost to him. When we got to the station in Ankara (an only slightly smaller version of the one in Istanbul) we were immediately accosted by a man who wanted to take us to the counter where we could purchase tickets for Istanbul. We told him we were going to Canakkale, not Istanbul, and he wanted to take us to the counter where we could purchase tickets for Canakkale. We told him we had reservations on Kamel lines, and he insisted yes, yes, that was where he wanted to take us.

Naturally we were suspicious, as we couldn't imagine anyone spending their nights at the bus station, generously volunteering help to weary travelers. We figured we were OK, though, as long as we carried our own bags; stayed in the crowded, brightly-lit station; and kept our wallets securely on our persons. He took us to one in a row of nearly identical ticket counters, and presented us to the man behind the counter, who immediately began making out a receipt for tickets to Canakkale. Observant one that I am, I noticed that the huge red letters over his head said "Truva," not "Kamel." He, the man who had escorted us there, three other men behind the counter (one who said he was the driver), and several onlookers then began insisting either that "Truva" (it didn't help any that in English it means something like "Trojan Horse") was either the same as, or a subsidiary of, Kamel; or that it was just as good only cheaper; or that the Kamel bus had already left; or something; all in rapid Turkish, which we wouldn't have understood even if it had been slow.

Cooper and Laurie, meanwhile, had been casting about in vain to find the Kamel counter. I resorted to insisting that they were charging us twice what they should have (generally a safe bet in Turkey). The ticket agent insisted that the 36 million lira he was asking was right—9 million apiece (about $18). He grabbed a man who was waiting to buy a ticket to Canakkale and asked how much he expected to pay. The man grinned and said 5 million lira. I thought the ticket agent would belt him, but everyone just started laughing, and the customer assured me, in halting English, that 9 million each was fair. Just to show us he was a nice guy, the ticket agent knocked 2 million off the price. I gave him the 34 million and one of the men came out from behind the counter and showed us the right bus. Sure enough, it said "Canakkale, 22:30 p.m." on a sign in the window. We stowed our packs onboard, grabbed a bite to eat, went to the bathroom, and took off, the man inside who had assured us that he was the driver (sure enough) driving.

We arrived at the bus station in Canakkale about 7:30 a.m. and called the Yellow Rose Pension, where we had reservations. The owner picked us up, took us to his place, checked us in, and we never saw him again. From then on we dealt with his 18-year-old son and his wife. Our guidebook said the facilities at the Yellow Rose were "adequate," but the people "could be a bit more friendly." That about said it all. Of all the places we stayed, it was the one to which we would be least likely to return. The weather had turned quite cold, and there was no heat in our rooms. When I mentioned that fact, the son said, "No heat until 5:00 " He neglected to mention the fact that they turned it off from about midnight until 5:00 every day. We did have two doubles with baths, however, and plenty of hot water. When we got there, only two space heaters were on: one in the office, and another near the TV in the common room. That one wasn't very efficient, so we spent a lot of time huddled around it, reading or watching CNN—until the second day, when it reached maximum inefficiency and quit altogether. After that the boys spent a lot of time in the office watching the son play computer games. Laurie and I read, huddled under blankets in our room. Occasionally Jesse and I went outside and played ping-pong to warm up. Actually, we didn't spend that much time at the pension, as we were out and about most of the time.

The first day we spent some time just exploring the town; then went to the archeological museum, where many pieces from Troy were displayed. It was a surprisingly modern, well-kept museum for such a small town, and we were impressed with many of the displays. We hadn't gotten nearly enough sleep during the two overnight bus rides in the past three days, so we had dinner and went to bed relatively early. The next morning we went to Troy. As it was only about 15 kms from Canakkale, and we were told a minibus ran there regularly, we decided to make our own way, rather than taking a tour. Sure enough, the bus was easy enough to find, and quite inexpensive: only a couple of million lira ($4) for all of us. There was no admission fee, and we were the only ones there for about the first half-hour. Four other people came and went in the next hour, leaving the place all to us again. Our guidebook had told us not to expect much. Since it had been written, however, a German university, funded by a huge grant from Mercedes Benz, had spent three years excavating, documenting, and identifying. The result was a fascinating and educational site that took us hours to walk through. First was a climb up into the Trojan Horse—not the original of course, but an artist's rendition of what it must have been like, given existing information. For one thing, I'm sure the original had no rows of windows along the sides from which to appreciate the view.

Next we stopped at a small museum that had been created (with Mercedes Benz money) to tell the story of how Mercedes Benz money had made it possible to enjoy the wonders of Troy. In fairness to them,

An artist's rendition of the Trojan Horse (with windows.)

the money had been well spent. The displays were quite interesting and educational, and they only mentioned the funding source a few times. The city of Troy was actually a site that exhibited about seven distinct periods of the rise and decline of an urban center. The German archeologists had done a good job of exposing areas that illustrated the similarities and differences in those periods, and of reconstructing parts of the major structures that gave a feeling for some of the former grandeur. A series of educational stops with signs explaining what we were looking at helped a lot, as did the fact that Cooper had just finished an anthropology course in which they studied Troy extensively. It was sort of like having a guide in the family. After a few hours, when we decided we had seen all there was to see, we started looking for transportation back to Canakkale. There was none. We asked a caretaker, and he told us we had to walk to the nearest village (only about a half-mile away) to catch a bus. The sun had come out, and the walk was quite pleasant.

The proprietor of a (noticeably under patronized) souvenir store in the village told us the next minibus would be by in 20 minutes. About a half-hour later one came. When we asked the driver if he was going to Canakkale, he said sure. As I always did (just to be safe), I asked how much. He said 10 million lira (about $20). I said that was ridiculous, we had paid only 2 million to get there. He explained that we had come in a public bus, one of two that shuttled between the villages and Canakkale, and that one of them had broken down, so the other wouldn't be there for about 45 more minutes. He said his was a private bus, and they charged more. I told him not to me they didn't; we'd wait for the next public bus. He said we could catch a public bus in about five minutes at the intersection with the road to Canakkale, which was about five kms away. He said he had to go out to the main road anyway, so would take us there for four million lira. I said if he had to go there anyway, he may as well take us for two million, rather than not take us for nothing. He thought about it, seemed to see the logic, and told us to hop in. He was right: we waited only about five minutes before a bus came by on its way to Canakkale, and we waved it down.

Back in town, we had lunch and spent most of the afternoon at the military museum, which occupied the grounds of an ancient fort built to guard the mouth of the strait. We spent some time in a building that was dedicated almost exclusively to glorifying the Turkish victory at Galipoli, which was directly across the strait. Next, we explored a reproduction of the minelayer that snuck out the night before a famous naval battle and laid the mines that destroyed several of the British fleet not long before the ANZAK invasion. It was a reproduction because, when Turkey gained independence just after WW I, they needed all the money they could get to jump-start their new government, so they sold the original (as they did with most of their war-time fleet) to a shipping company. After decades of duty as a small private freighter, it sank near shore in the Aegean. It had since been salvaged, and there was some talk about fixing it up and putting it on display in place of the reproduction. It was in pretty rough shape, however, and restoring it would have been an expensive proposition. Finally, we explored the fort, which in a couple of places had huge chunks missing, thanks to bombardment from the aforementioned British fleet. To Jesse's delight, it was chock full of old weapons and other military gear. It was unheated, and cold as the belly of a seal, however, so even the draw of massive firepower soon waned, and we moved on.

Back at the pension, we made arrangements for seats on the 10:30 a.m. ferry across the strait, where we would connect with the bus to Istanbul. When we left the next morning, our hosts made one last gesture of "could-be-a-bit-more-friendly"-ness by absenting themselves completely from the scene. We left our keys on the desk in the office (along with the business cards they had given us earlier, as we could think of no use for them), and didn't let the front door hit us on the butt as we left. The ferry trip and bus connection were uneventful. We shared the bus with about a company of Turkish soldiers, whom we decided were stationed at Canakkale, and were on their way home on leave to celebrate the end of Ramadan. As we got within 50 kms or so of Istanbul, we noticed that every square foot of the Aegean shore (and for hundreds of yards inland) was taken up with summer homes—some just unassuming cottages, but plenty of the gotta-be-rich-to-own-it variety. We couldn't imagine who could afford all those second homes—until we took a boat ride on the Bosphorous the next day and saw the hundreds of first homes that could only belong to the wealthy. We arrived at the gargantuan Istanbul bus terminal on the edge of the city by mid-afternoon, and caught one of the free minibuses operated by the overland bus lines to take passengers into the city. We went to the train station to get sleeper tickets on the overnight train to Sofia. They were sold out.

No way were we going through the process that would be required to go back out to the bus station, find the right counter, determine what time the next bus left for Sofia, buy tickets, find the right gate, and get on the bus. We took the easy way out, and reserved sleeper tickets for the next night. Then we caught the tram back to the Sultanahmet district (our old stomping grounds) and honored the owner of the Nayla Palace Pension with our presence for another night. We took advantage of our extra day in Istanbul (which started as drizzly, and worked itself into a steady rain by early afternoon) by riding the tram to the west end of town and back to the east end. There we intended to buy tickets on the government-run ferry for a two-hour sightseeing trip up the Bosphorous and back. Before we could get to the ticket window, however, we saw that the pier where said ferry should dock was conspicuously empty.

As Laurie and I were wondering if the absence of a ferry might put a dent in our plans for a ferry ride, we were caught up in a whirlwind in the person of a man who asked us with machine-gun rapidity whether we wanted to take a boat ride up the Bosphorous, told us that his boat was docked close by, said they were getting ready to leave immediately but that if we hurried we could still make it, and asked us for 40 million lira for the privilege. He paused only momentarily when I told him to go ahead and leave, unless he was planning to take us all the way back to Sofia, because that's what he'd have to do for the $80 he was asking. How much were we willing to pay then, he wanted to know, but quickly, or we'd miss the boat. Half that, I said. He couldn't afford to take us for that. Goodbye, then. How about 30 million for a full two hours in a small boat that would stay in close to the shore for maximum sightseeing potential? That was probably too much, but it was raining quite steadily by then, and lacking the government ferry, we were pretty much at a loss for another way to spend the afternoon. I got the "O" part of "OK" out before he had grabbed us and started rushing us through a break in the fence to a small boat tied up at what seemed suspiciously like part of the dock where the government ferry should be. There was nobody else on the boat, so we couldn't understand the rush to leave. Rush there was, though. We no sooner got on board than he asked for our money so he could get off and we could cast off. I had my wallet out before I realized that we had planned on leaving Turkey the night before, so had not gotten more Turkish lira. I only had 25 million lira. I informed him of that sad fact, and we started to get back off. He wouldn't hear of it. He took the 25 million, probably gaining respect for me as a master bargainer to come up with such a ploy. He got off, and we were in the process of casting off when he returned with a distinguished-looking middle-aged French couple to add to our group. I must admit, I was glad to see them, as it meant the involvement of another nation's embassy if ransom negotiations were necessary.

We were only about a hundred yards out when we realized why they were in a hurry to get going: the huge government ferry was pulling into the space we had vacated only minutes before. The French man introduced himself and asked how much we had paid. I told him, and he said they had paid about half again as much as we had. I'm not sure if that means we got a good deal, or if he got cheated even more than I had. Probably a bit of both, but in the end, it was worth it. In the government ferry, we would have been four of many tourists on a huge boat in which we would have sat inside and peered through foggy windows at the distant shore. As it was, we were a group of six on a small boat with only the captain (I use the term loosely). We could feel the vibration of the engines pulling against the current as we moved slowly upstream, so close to the shore that we could see architectural details of the buildings. We stood on the open stern under a canvas cover, with unobstructed views on three sides.

And what great views they were. The Bosphorous upriver flows through some of the nicest parts of Istanbul: lush green parks set on hillsides rising up from the river; large, beautiful, very expensive homes on the river, some with boathouses nearly as big as our house in the States; and gorgeous wooden houses in the old style—some beautifully restored, and others not. Many were in the disrepair brought on by decades of sitting empty. The Turkish government, however, had declared them national treasures (the equivalent of the National Historic Register in the States), and wouldn't allow them to be torn down or altered externally. They had put new red tile roofs on them, and they awaited owners wealthy enough to take on the costly task of renovating them to their former beauty. After a great two-hour river tour, we returned to the area from which we had embarked. There seemed to be no open dock space, however. Our "captain" putted around until, as what seemed a last resort, he put in near the end of a concrete pier that looked like it had once been a commercial dock, but had long since outlived its useful life. It was raining, and we were blocks from the tram that would take us back to our neighborhood, but it seemed our only alternative was to go home with the driver, so we got off.

We arrived cold and wet at our pension, took a bit of time to warm up and dry out, then went out to a very nice but inexpensive Indian restaurant we had discovered, for our last dinner in Istanbul. After dinner we picked up our bags, said goodbye to our host, and took the tram to the train station, where we boarded the sleeper car and set off for home. It was a Turkish sleeper, and none of the compartments had sliding doors between, so Laurie and I took one compartment and the boys took another. Inside our compartment, above the door, was a sign that said, "Dear passengers, please make the payments to the conductor of sleeping cars requesting receipts for the service prices mentioned below to be collected per night in our express train." We read it several times, and understood it no better (in other words, not at all). Nobody, including the conductor, either offered or requested payments or receipts at any time during the trip (which we decided was probably a good thing). During the night, we went through the same stops and checks we suffered on our way into Turkey—only in reverse order, and without having to buy visas. We slept better, partly because we knew what to expect, and partly because we were exhausted from our trip. The only excitement resulted when we stopped in Plovdiv the next morning. After we sat for a while, Laurie decided to see if she could find someone who could tell us whether we had time to get off and buy a cup of coffee. She came back in a few minutes and said she didn't think it would be a problem, as our car was sitting in the middle of the station by itself, in elegant simplicity, disconnected from both other cars and engines.

Eastern European conductors seemed to operate on a need-to-know basis, and had a hard time understanding why, as long as they had things under control and knew what's going on, it should be any business of the passengers. What did they think they were going to do about it anyway? Say, for example, the train broke, what did the passengers think they were going to do, get out and fix it? Laurie eventually found someone who had asked, and said we would be there at least an hour. As that seemed plenty of time, she got off and got us some coffee. In the meantime, a young man introduced himself and his traveling companions as members of the Turkish national ski team. He said they had brought no food with them and had nothing but Turkish lira, which were no good, as we were in Bulgaria. In fact, I later found, they were no good almost anywhere but Turkey. He asked if I had any Bulgarian money that I would be willing to change for Turkish. I changed about $10 worth for them, and Cooper got off with them to help them find some food. No sooner had Laurie gotten back on and Cooper gotten off, than we felt the jolt of an engine coupling to us, and we began to move. We had visions of Cooper and the Turkish ski team, stranded in Plovdiv, three hours by bus from Sofia, five from Blagoevgrad. They looked less happy about it than we did. I told Laurie that, as the ski team had to get to Sofia, I was sure that, however they did it, they'd take Cooper with them. I said we could wait in Sofia, one of us at the bus station, and the other at the train station, with Jesse serving as messenger between. We would just wait there until Cooper arrived, either by bus or train; then go on to Blagoevgrad.

In the time it took to decide that, we had been moved out of the station to a switch yard, shuttled to another track, moved back to the station, and uncoupled one track over from where we had been. Cooper and the ski team, much relieved, got back on and seemed content to stay on until we left for real about an hour later. The rest of the trip to Sofia was uneventful. We switched to the Blagoevgrad bus there, and were home in time for dinner. My only problem was what to do with the $80 worth of Turkish lira we had left when we got back. I assumed one of the many money changing services would do what they do best—change it. Nope. Well then, surely I could deposit it in my account at the bank in Blagoevgrad. Nope. As it happened, one of the faculty at AUBG was Turkish. In fact, in addition to her apartment in Blagoevgrad, she had a house in Istanbul and visited there at least once a month. She said she'd be happy to buy my Turkish lira, and would even give me the going exchange rate.

During January, coinciding with the middle of winter, the Bulgarians spent a week dedicated to driving out the evil spirits of winter, so that spring could come. I was in my office one day, when I heard a commotion out on the street: shouting, singing, and drums beating. I went to my window to see an old rattletrap bus disgorging people in every manner of costume. They got organized, and began to march around to the plaza on the other side of the building, I donned my coat and hustled downstairs to see what in the world was going on. It was a group of about 50 from a nearby village, come to drive away the winter spirits. I asked someone why they were doing it in Blagoevgrad, and not in their village. I was told that after all the work they'd put into their costumes, they wanted an audience, and as this was probably everyone from the village, there was nobody left there to watch. In addition to about half the folks who were in traditional Bulgarian garb; and a horn, string, and drum band of about half a dozen; there were four or five who were dressed all in goatskins, with huge, elongated heads, who looked something like abominable snowmen. There were also men dressed both as old women and pulchritudinous young nurses, attending old men on stretchers. Several teen-aged boys were dressed in rough, woodsman-like outfits, and carried huge, wooden, plier-like instruments, which they chased young women with, trying to grab them by the ankle. The remaining folks, mostly young boys (all the young girls were dressed in traditional garb), were dressed as warriors, with swords and shields. They marched around to the plaza, where they danced to the increasingly rapid tempo of the music. The goatskin costumes must have become unbearably hot—they certainly began exuding a strong smell of goat—and the young men in them eventually were forced to shed their heads, probably just to get enough oxygen. After about a half hour of frenzied cavorting, they finally stopped abruptly, and were invited into a couple of nearby cafes for refreshments. It would take an intrepid winter spirit to have withstood that onslaught. It must have worked, because spring arrived with not an evil spirit in evidence anywhere.

Chapter 7
February

We set out for spring break in northeast Greece on Sunday, February 27, by catching the Sofia to Thessoloniki bus when it stopped in Blagoevgrad at 2:30. It was a 3½ hour drive, but Bulgarian and Greek customs checks added an hour and a half. We tried to look at it as a chance to get out and stretch our legs—a lot. Our travel agent, Mario, had phoned ahead for reservations at the cheapest hotel he could find—two rooms at 15,000 drachma ($45) each per night. He was appalled when we insisted that he change them to a hotel mentioned in our guidebook that was 6,000 drachma ($18) a room per night. He called, but wouldn't make the reservations until the person from the hotel assured him that it was not a place frequented by "ladies of the evening." We arrived in Thessoloniki at 7:30, and walked 15 minutes to the hotel. It was ancient, and in much need of repairs, but spotlessly clean and reasonably quiet; and the people who ran it were wonderful. Not a lady of the evening showed her face (or anything else). We certainly didn't regret the change.

As we'd had nothing but snacks since lunch, we set out immediately to find a place to eat. After a less-than-satisfying (but filling) supper at a cafeteria, we walked around a bit and came across a chunk of the city wall from Roman times—unrestored; just sitting there minding its own business; everybody but us taking it very much for granted. It staggered my mind to see people who were walking their dogs stop to let them pee on this thousands-of-years-old piece of history. A couple of blocks from our hotel, we found a sandwich and pastry shop, where we had great cappuccino and hot chocolate; then went to our rooms, read for a while, and went to bed.

Monday morning I went to the station and got tickets for the train to Alexandropolis on 2:00 Tuesday. When I got back to the hotel, we returned to the sandwich shop for breakfast. The Greeks, as with most Eastern Europeans, usually did not eat what we thought of as breakfast food, but had pastries or sandwiches instead. After breakfast, we went to the main branch of Mario's travel agency and introduced ourselves to Tom, the American who ran it. He was nice enough, but we got the distinct impression that he would have been of greater help if our travel plans had been somewhat more upscale. He did call ahead and make reservations for us at a hotel in Alexandropolis—for which we had given him the name and phone number. Our next travel step secure, we began exploring Thessoloniki, the second-largest city in Greece, and an important port on the Aegean Sea.

We went first to the White Tower, so named because at one time it had been painted white, long since reverting to it's natural gray stone color. It was built as a lookout tower, and had served variously as a barracks and a prison, but when we were there, was a museum—one that was closed on Mondays. Undaunted, we moved on the archeological museum, which was not closed. At the ticket desk, I flashed our Bulgarian letters that identified me as a professor, Laurie as a teacher, and Cooper and Jesse as students. We figured they wouldn't cut much ice outside Bulgaria, but to our surprise, got us all in at no charge. We paid no entrance fees for any of the museums or antiquities we visited the whole trip. In fact, at some of them, we had a hard time finding anyone to open them. Some said we were their first visitors for weeks. It was very much off-season.

After the archeological museum, we walked throughout the city, using our map to locate antiquities and churches. We found the old Roman forum and amphitheater, tucked away in a walking mall between two of the main streets in the city center. After lunch of gyros, sitting at a table in the sun in front of a little shop, we visited the spectacular Church of St. Dominic. Much, but only part, of the spectacle arose from the iconography and architecture of the building. The rest was a result of the knowledge that it was rebuilt in the late forties, after a fire destroyed virtually the entire structure. They cleaned out the charred remains, thoroughly cleaned the parts of stone pillars and walls they could save, and rebuilt the church on what remained. The difference between the two parts was clearly visible. After sitting for a while and taking in the ambience, we were ready to leave, when Laurie discovered the stairs down to the catacombs. They, alone, were worth the price of admission (had we paid any). Again, the restoration work was impeccable, leaving clear evidence that the "modern" church had been built directly on top of an ancient Roman structure.

After a visit to the covered market, we returned to our hotel to rest a bit before dinner (well-earned, as we had walked 5-6 miles). Cooper commented that we had really gotten out of shape; we were walking twice that far each day in Rome and Athens last fall. We found a small seafood and pasta restaurant for dinner; then gave the boys some money to go find ice cream, while Laurie and I returned to "our" sandwich shop for cappuccino. We went to bed fairly early, as we wanted to get in some more exploring the next morning before leaving for Alexandropolis.

The next morning after breakfast, we returned to the White Tower, which was open—at least part of it was. The wide spiral stairs around the outside wall gave access to six floors, the first three of which advertised an exhibit of historical photos, but which were locked and dark. The fourth and fifth contained quite nice exhibits of iconography, but we had seen so many truly splendid pieces by then, that we were not easily impressed. The sixth floor was a café, which was closed, but from which we could get onto the wide walkway created by the fact that the room on the top floor was significantly smaller than those below it. We spent a long time just lounging in the sun, looking out over the city on one side and the Aegean Sea on the other. On the way to the train station, we stopped at three more churches that weren't too far out of our way. We had just enough time for a late lunch before catching the 2:00 train to Alexandropolis.

A direct line between the two cities would probably have resulted in a 3-hour trip, but the track went north almost to the Bulgarian border before turning east, and later curving back south to the seacoast. Even the inner-city train, which made few stops, took 5½ hours. The locals would have taken more like 7½. Our guide book said the hotel in Alexandropolis was only a block north of the bus station, which would have been fine had we arrived by bus. As we came by train, however, we first had to find the bus station. We spent about a half-hour, and (as we realized the next day, after we had found a map) walked about four times further than we'd have needed to, but eventually found the bus station, and subsequently, the hotel. Once there, we had a pleasant surprise. The hotel was described in the guidebook as somewhat shabby, but they were in the middle of a complete renovation. They had completed the third and fourth floors, and our rooms were on the fourth. They were waiting for the summer tourist season to raise their rates, so we paid only 7,000 drachma (about $20) per room, with private baths. By the time we got checked in, we were nigh unto starving, so we set out to find a restaurant—preferably seafood, as Alexandropolis was a fishing port.

We eventually came to conclusion that the Greeks didn't really eat. Instead, they spent their time sitting in bars and cafes, nursing tiny cups of mud-like coffee, and glasses of ouzo (a sweet, liquorice-flavored liqueur) or retsina (a dry white wine that tasted a lot like pine pitch)—both of which I relished, incidentally. We found dozens of little cafes, before we finally gave up and ate burgers and fries at an American-style fast food joint. Wednesday morning I went to the ferry office and bought tickets on the noon boat to Samothraki, with return at 8:00 a.m. Friday. We spent the morning finding someplace for a breakfast of gyros (difficult); then another for cappuccino and hot chocolate (easy), which we drank sitting on benches along the shore. We wandered around town until time to catch the ferry; then made our way to the docks and boarded. At noon, as they were casting off, one of the crew shouted that someone else was coming. About two blocks away, an old man, obviously drunk, was carrying a heavy suitcase toward the dock. Preparations for departure ceased, and the crew members all began to shout for him to hurry; they had to leave. Well, he was too old, too loaded down, and too drunk to move at more than a snail's pace. Finally, a couple of the crew members ran to him, took his suitcase, grabbed him under each arm, and virtually carried him to the boat. It made us five minutes late getting started, but funny thing, nobody seemed to mind. We in the States could learn much from those in other cultures, if only we weren't too sure we're right about everything to pay attention.

As soon as we got out of the harbor (before that for some of them) all the Greeks had ensconced themselves firmly in the plush lounge areas inside, smoking, drinking, eating, chatting, reading, and playing cards. It was a beautiful day, but Laurie and I and the boys were the only people on deck. We spent the entire 2½ hours there, enjoying the fresh salt air, looking for porpoises (of which we saw none), and watching the city recede as the island drew closer. Samothraki was a volcanic island, with the remains of the volcano that created it still very much in evidence as a huge snow-capped peak that took up about half its land mass. We docked at the port city, which was made up of about 15 blocks of houses and shops, three streets deep along the shore. To say that they weren't geared up for tourists would have been a huge understatement. We walked the length of the main street (along which most of the shops and offices were closed) twice, looking, in vain, for a place to eat. About the only thing open were the coffee shops and bars, of which there were about two per block. Finally we found the ferry office open, and decided to check with the clerk on whether there was a more direct way back to Thessoloniki than to return to Alexandropolis by ferry and connect by train. He said that during the summer there were ferries direct to Thessoloniki, but as it was off-season, there were only two ferries a day to Alexandropolis.

We asked if he knew of any place we could stay. He made a phone call, and told us we could get two very nice rooms in a pension for 8,000 drachma ($24) apiece. We said that would be fine so, leaving his office open, he took us out front, loaded us into his car, and drove us to the pension. It was a beautiful, white, 3-story house on a hill just outside of town, with a magnificent view of the Aegean. It looked as though it had just been renovated, and I think we were the first occupants of the rooms. They were nice-sized, with private baths, satellite television, and the most comfortable beds we had slept in since leaving the States. The only problem was that they were sweltering. We had to leave the windows open to cool it off enough to sleep. There was also a small kitchen and dining area that the landlady said we were welcome to use. As we had nothing to use in it, however, we asked if there were any restaurants open downtown. She said only the "Scorpion" was open off-season, and gave us directions. We made the 15-minute walk downtown, and found the restaurant (which we had walked by twice, but hadn't realized was open).

As we sat looking at the menus (with listings in both Greek and English), the waitress approached, and in a New England accent, asked if we were speaking English. I said yes, and so are you. She said yes, she was born and lived her first 20 years in Connecticut. As theirs was the only game in town, we ate all our meals (except breakfast, for which they weren't open) there for the next two days, and got to know the family pretty well. The mother (who ran the restaurant and cooked) and father (who ran a sheep farm), and their daughter (who was the other waitress) had moved to the States 25 years before. The second daughter was born there. After 20 years, they moved back to the island because both the woman's brother and mother had become very ill. They rented the restaurant, and had been operating it for the past four years. We assumed their sheep farm, being on an island, was small, and were amazed to hear they had thousands of sheep. We were further amazed when they told us that Samothraki contained the greatest concentration of sheep and goats in all Greece. That explained the odd smell we had noticed, and the fact that for the two days we were there (even when we hiked for an hour up into the mountains), we were never out of range of the melodious tinkling of the bells many of the critters wore around their necks. The family's 20 years in the States was reflected in their menu by such items as New England style pizza. That's all Jesse needed to hear to make his culinary choice. Cooper and I opted for seafood: fresh calamari; tender and sweet; the best I'd had for years.

We asked the mother if there was someplace we could get a bus schedule, and she asked if that was how we planned on getting around the island. When we told her it was, she said she wouldn't recommend it, as the busses ran infrequently during the off season. She said she would loan us her car, but her husband needed it for the next couple of days. She recommended that we rent a car, but we said we didn't think we could afford it. She said she had a friend who might rent us one cheap, and gave him a call. A few minutes later, he came in and, after they talked for a couple of minutes, she said he would rent us a new compact for 10,000 drachma ($30) a day. I said I didn't have an international license: "No problem." I said I didn't have insurance: "No problem." As there didn't seem to be any reason not to, we rented the car from 5:00 Wednesday for 24 hours. I gave him 10,000 drachma and my passport to hold, and he gave me the car keys. I had not driven a car for seven months, and it wasn't quite the same as riding a bike. For one thing, there's no emergency brake to remember to release on a bike, nor is there a clutch you have to let out at the right speed while depressing a gas pedal the appropriate amount. I made it out of his sight before he could change his mind, however, and it wasn't long before the old skills began to creep back.

We got gas—a shock compared to what we payed in the States. I got a half tank, and was astounded to find that it cost me as much for gas as it had for the rental. As it happened, we could have gotten by with about a fourth the amount of gas I bought. There just weren't very many kilometers of paved road on the island—and after a look at the unpaved ones, we decided not to go there. Wednesday evening we drove on very narrow, winding roads across one end of the island to the only sand beach. Jesse saw how much sand he could pack into his shoes by running up and down the dunes. The rest of us just appreciated the sunset, accompanied by crashing surf and tinkling bells. We then drove to the end of the road inland where the "hora," or old town, was situated. By the time we got there, it was getting too dark to really appreciate it, but we could see enough to know that we wanted to come back the next day. We returned to our room, where we rested a couple of hours before going for supper. Laurie and Jesse had Greek pasta, Cooper paid tribute to the quality of the calamari by having it again, and I had grilled lamb—delicious.

The folks at the Scorpion had told us they weren't open for breakfast, so the next morning we set out to find something else to eat. Had we wanted Greek coffee, or retsina, or ozuo, or pop, we'd have had our choice of several establishments, but we were had hard pressed to find food. Finally, an old woman, who had seen us try several cafes, asked if we were looking for food. When we said yes, she told us to follow her. She took us down a side street to a little hole-in-the-wall bakery, where we purchased delicious meat pies and cheese pies. We supplemented these with some fruit from a nearby market, and went back to one of the cafes that had outside seating. There we ordered cappuccino and hot chocolate and had our breakfast in the sun. The drinks, as was often the case, cost as much as the food. We decided the reason the Greeks seldom seemed to eat out was that they couldn't afford to both drink and eat, and clearly saw drinking as the higher priority activity. After breakfast we drove to the "Sanctuary of the Great Gods," the original site of "Winged Victory," before she was moved to the Louvre. We had been told it was open only mornings off-season, so went there first to be sure not to miss it. The sign brazenly stated the hours were 8:30 a.m. to 3:00, and everything was just as brazenly locked, despite the fact that it was squarely within those times. We looked around, and could find nobody to let us in; then I noticed that, although the gate was chained, complete with padlock, it was not locked.

We (mostly I, with Cooper strongly dissenting) decided to "break in." After all, I reasoned, the sign said they were open, and as the lock wasn't "closed," didn't that constitute "open"? Cooper wasn't convinced, but went reluctantly along. Boy, were we glad we did. It was a truly magnificent site—better than Troy, and rivaling those in Athens. We learned afterward, when someone showed up to open the museum, that the site was the location of an ancient religious cult, and that nobody was thought to have lived there. All that was left of the adjacent city were extensive chunks of the walls. Evidence, I suppose that, just as in many periods of history, those folks put more money and quality work into their religious sites than they did their dwellings. The museum was small, but interesting. It illustrated that the site had, in fact, been used by at least three civilizations for religious purposes. In fact, Phillip of Macedon met Olympia, his future queen, when they were both there as initiates.

The entrance to a nearby 10th century fort was securely locked, so we had to be content to view it from the highway. Truth be known, I wasn't too disappointed; it looked pretty well decayed, and it would have been quite a climb. From there, we visited "The Murderer's Tower," the origin and purpose of which were shrouded in mystery. It was on the beach, and looked much like a sort of defensive embattlement: about 15 feet in diameter, and perhaps 30 feet tall, but with no door. There were a couple of windows about halfway up, though, and as the mortar between the stones was quite eroded, Jesse and Cooper climbed up and in. They said we weren't missing anything by not seeing inside; that it was pretty empty, so they took pictures from up there, we took pictures of them up there, and we left. We drove along the narrow highway, which threaded its way between the cliffs and the shore, to a turnaround about a fourth of the way around the island. In the States we sometimes saw signs that showed huge boulders falling on cars, presumably to warn of

Cooper amidst the ruins at Sanctuary of the Great Gods on the island of Samothraki.

the danger of falling rock, but we never really saw any falling (or even fallen) rock. That was not the case on Samothraki. The narrowness of the road was consistently exacerbated by the presence of a great deal of (some very newly looking) fallen rock. And I'm not talking little stones here; a couple were of a size that would have taken a tank to move them. Speaking of tanks, the views were terrific, but none as unexpected as when we rounded the corner of a cliff to be faced with a fully-camou-flaged tank dug into the dirt on the beach side of the road, overlooking the sea. It looked for all the world as though they believed invasion by the gunboats of a hostile navy was imminent.

On the way back we stopped at a trailhead with a sign that announced that the path led to a lake and waterfall. As it was the nicest afternoon we had experienced for weeks, we decided there could be no better way to spend it than hiking up the valley along a beautiful creek. The hike was wonderful, and it felt great to be outdoors in nature after a winter spent mostly in the city. An hour's gradual climb along paths clearly used more by sheep and goats than by humans brought us to a dead end. The path very definitely ended abruptly against a sheer cliff. Cooper volunteered to cross the creek on a fallen log and climb the not-so-sheer cliff on the other side, to see if there was any reason to go on. His gesticulations when he got there left no doubt that there was. The rest of us crossed on the fallen log and climbed the cliff. There we discovered, literally beneath our feet, a small lake confined on all sides by cliffs, with a beautiful stream of water cascading into if from about fifty feet above. After a suitable time spent communing with nature, we safely re-crossed the creek and made our way back down the valley to the car.

We went back to town for a late lunch, and had just enough time to return to the old town for a look around. In daylight, we realized that it was protected by its own ruins of an ancient fortress. We parked the car and climbed through a warren of narrow cobblestone streets. After many wrong turns and much trial-and-error (plus a couple of encouraging signals from old women who leaned out their windows to watch our progress) we made our way to the top. The wind was so strong that, had we gotten too near the edge, we would literally have been blown off. After spending another half hour wandering through the streets and walkways (usually it was hard to tell the difference), we found we were fast running out of time, and had better get going if wanted to get the car back in time. On the way out of town, I took a wrong turn. In my defense, our map was out-of-date, and the road, according to it, wasn't even there. By the time we found our way back (which, in truth wasn't much of an orienteering feat, as there really were a limited number of options), I had to hustle to get the car turned in on time. I handed him the keys precisely on the minute, however, and he casually walked to his unlocked car, which was parked on the street, and got my passport, which had been lying on the dash for the past 24 hours. I tried not to cringe noticeably.

We walked along the beach, sat on the seawall and drank cappuccino and hot chocolate, and returned to our rooms to rest for a while before dinner. We went to bed early, as we had to get up in time get ready and to catch the 8:00 ferry. It was a stormy night, and we were awakened several times by tremendous flashes of lightning, followed by deafening claps of thunder. Those pyrotechnics were followed by a torrential downpour that caused me to lie awake trying to decide how we were going to get to the ferry in a few hours without getting thoroughly soaked in the process. We had learned how to call a taxi in similar situations in Blagoevgrad; knowledge that, unfortunately, did not transcend borders. As with so many worries in our lives, however, I need not have bothered. Morning dawned thoroughly laundered but clear. We walked to the dock, stopping on the way at the little bakery for meat pies and sesame rings. As we approached the ferry, we were told by one of the dockhands that it would not sail until 10:00. That fact did a couple of things. First, it settled the question of whether we would take the (faster) bus or the (slower, but allowing Jesse to move around and not go completely bonkers) train to Thessoloniki, as, by the time we got to Alexandropolis, said bus would be long gone. Second, it gave us plenty of time for a leisurely breakfast. So leisurely, in fact, that Cooper, Jesse, and I got in several hands of hearts before we boarded.

The weather had been great, but seeing that we were safely aboard the ferry, the wind began to blow, and it began to rain; a situation that prevailed pretty much the rest of the day. As we were on boats and trains almost all that time, however, we minded but little. Well, maybe Jesse and Cooper minded some, as they found it necessary to go on deck several times during the crossing to "get some air," and presumably look at the beautiful whitecaps resulting from the prevailing wind. Neither of them actually got sick, but I did see what is meant by the phrase "green around the gills." We docked at Alexandropolis, where we made a damp, hurried trip about four blocks to the train station and booked seats on the 2:00 train to Thessoloniki. We had just enough time to cross the street to a little restaurant for a nice lunch before the train arrived. We got to Thessoloniki at 9:30, and Laurie and Cooper ran across the street to buy gyros while Jesse and I bought tickets for the 10:00 sleeper to Sofia, which stopped in Blagoevgrad at 5:30 in the morning. We had our dinner on the train and went to bed. The trip was uneventful, other than the hour and a half stop for Greek customs and the hour stop for Bulgarian customs to interrupt our sleep. When we arrived at Blagoevgrad, we got a taxi to our apartment, where we went back to bed until 10:30 a.m., before deeming ourselves fit to arise and begin resting up in preparation for starting school again on Monday.

Chapter 8
March

The first week of March was when people began to expect to tie their martinitzas to bushes. Martinitzas were made from red and white yarn. Most were simple braided cords people tied around their wrists, but some were little tasseled bows people could pin to their jackets (mine was the latter). People gave them to all their friends on Baba Marta (Grandma Marta's Day—March 1). Mine was given to me by Natalia on the day she came down from Sofia to teach her art class at AUBG. Laurie had one given to her by her friend Kalinka, and the boys each had several given to them by their school friends. If people got several, they pinned them to various jackets or sweaters, to be sure to have one with them the first time they saw a stork returning for the season to nest. That event signaled the true advent of spring, so to celebrate, they took off their martinitza and tied it to the nearest bush for good luck and to ensure a nice summer. If they were one of the fortunate few whom a pair of storks chose to honor by building a nest on their property, they were assured of maximum luck for as long as they stayed—which was usually for some time, for unless they were disturbed, they returned to the same nest every year. Having storks nest on their property was considered so auspicious that people would build a new chimney before they would disturb a pair that had built their nest in the original.

The Bulgarians' was a pretty superstitious culture—but in a generally charming way. The second Sunday in March, for example, was the day for cutting all the brush back—not before; not after. What they cut, they allowed the children to drag into huge piles, and as soon as it got dark, light it on fire. In my experience children, given the choice, would drag brush (or anything else, for that matter) as little as possible before piling it. The result was that those huge piles of dry brush, rather than being built in the center of huge open areas, were disconcertingly (at least Laurie and I were disconcerted, although no Bulgarian adult was noticeably so) close to the surrounding buildings. At about 7:00 they were all relatively simultaneously set ablaze. As far as we knew, nobody was left homeless, but we were still glad one of the buildings they were disconcertingly close to was not ours. After the fires had burned down to less-disconcerting proportions, the children (oldest first) began jumping over them—to bring them health for the rest of the year. As the fires became less and less disconcerting, younger and younger children traversed them, right down to the toddlers. That was also the weekend when people were supposed to visit everyone they knew—especially family members—to ask their forgiveness for any harm (intentional or un-) they had done them during the past year: a sort of annual jubilee of the spirit. Laurie and I allowed as how this fell firmly into the category of something we in the States would do well to emulate from a "less developed" culture. I'm sure not everyone took advantage of the opportunity. In fact, as is usually the case, it was probably those who least needed forgiveness who were most prone to ask it. Be that as it may, it was a wonderful idea.

Laurie and I often took long weekend strolls (sometimes as much as three hours). I mentioned that fact while having coffee with a couple of faculty in the university lounge, and they asked where we walked. I said throughout and around the entire city, and one of them said, "Not in the Gipsy section, I hope?" I said yes, we lived near the Roma neighborhood and so walked there often. Both of them began to tell me how that was not a good idea, as it was dangerous for anyone not Gipsy to go into their neighborhood. We could expect to be overrun by beggars at best, and beaten and robbed at worst. Granted, most of the people asking for money on the streets of the city were Roma, but Laurie and I saw that as no different from members of minority groups in every country we had visited (or in the States, for that matter). In fact, we made sure to carry a some change just for that purpose. I thanked them for the advise, and promptly dismissed it. Laurie and I intentionally walked throughout the Roma neighborhood, and although we had been approached with requests for change in other areas of the city, we had never been approached in their neighborhood—it was clearly a matter of pride for them. In fact, we had been invited to stop and join them in their festivities, and had shared food and drink with them on several occasions.

One Saturday, while walking in the Roma neighborhood, we rounded a corner and came upon a couple of men cutting down a tree. It was in a relatively built-up area, and the tree was too tall to fell from the bottom without hitting something, so the middle-aged man had climbed about halfway up, tied himself to the tree, and was attempting to saw through the two-foot-thick trunk with a handsaw. We heated with wood for about ten years, so I had cut many a tree in my time, some of the early ones of which did not fall quite where I intended; a few with moderately disastrous consequences. One memorable one for example, requiring men from the electric company to come out on a Sunday and repair downed power lines. I could see, then, that these guys intended to fell the top half of this (30-foot) tree in a direction opposite to that which the tree was wont to go. In fact, the direction it was about to fall would likely take the cutter, some electric lines, and a nearby chicken coop all out in one fell swoop. I tried to tell them that, and they showed me that they had planned for that eventuality. They had tied a rope to the trunk about four feet over the cutter's head, and the old man on the ground was going to pull on it to force the tree to fall in the direction that it would not want to go. It did not take a physicist to see that all that was going to do was add the old guy to the causality list.

I tried to warn them, but they would have none of it. Then a neighbor, whose chicken coop was in mortal danger, added his voice (stridently) to my side of the equation. Then the tree added its two cents, in the form of cracking sounds. When the cutter found that his saw was inextricably bound into the cut from the pressure of the top half of the tree, he realized it did not bode well for him, the wires, or the chickens. He began to yell for the old man to pull. Against my better judgement, I threw myself into the breach, grabbing the end of the rope with the old guy. Laurie (whose judgement was virtually always better than mine) joined us. To my great surprise (and need I say relief) we were able to coax the falling tree, if not in the direction they wanted, at least enough away from the direction it wanted to save all in peril (barely). It was certainly much too close for the neighbor whose chicken coop had been grazed by the falling limbs, and he let everyone know so, in no uncertain terms. Laurie and I left them to their neighborly discussions, and continued our walk.

A guy who lived down the street from us got a job for which he needed a truck. On the way to school the one morning, I saw him sitting out on the street with a cutting torch, removing all of his van from just behind the front seat back. On the way home that night, I noticed that the unwanted body parts had been removed, and part of what had been a side wall cut to fit and welded behind the front seat to enclose the cab. The remains had been dumped unceremoniously on the sidewalk nearby—as were the remains of ever so many things, forcing pedestrians to spend more time walking in the street than on the sidewalk. Luckily the paucity of auto traffic seldom made that displacement a problem. The next day he had replaced the rear of the vehicle with a truck bed that he had acquired somewhere. Vans in Bulgaria were not the take-the-kids-to-soccer mini-vans like people drove in the States, but large, commercial-type delivery vans. The result, then, was similar to what we used to call "stake trucks" where I grew up in Pennsylvania—a regular farm truck. The left-over sheet metal from the van comprised its first load. I assumed it was sold for scrap. Before, I seldom saw this guy outside his house, and his truck, in its former incarnation seldom moved from its parking place on the street (actually partly on the street; mostly on the sidewalk). After, most mornings on my way to work, I saw him starting his truck and driving away—to his new job, I assumed.

One evening after dinner, I was setting up the VCR so we could watch a Clint Eastwood western, while Laurie washed dishes. With a lot of stress in her voice, she called me into the kitchen. I hurried in to find her holding a dishtowel tightly around her right hand. A glass had broken and cut her. I had her unwrap the towel enough to realize it was way above my pay grade. She sat down, dishcloth held tightly, hand over her head, while I called an emergency number the folks at the university had given us. I told the person who answered what the situation was, and she told me to come to the university where they would have a doctor waiting. I asked if someone couldn't pick us up, and she said she was afraid not. I called Ivo to see if he could, and got no answer, so we set off in the heaviest rain we'd had for weeks. When we got closer to downtown, we were able to get a taxi. When he saw the situation, the driver didn't even try to hit us up for the foreigner price. When we got to the university, a doctor they kept on call for just such emergencies looked at Laurie's hand and told us to go to the hospital. I tried Ivo again, and got him. He rushed over and took us to the "hospital," which was more deserving of "clinic" designation. They had called ahead from the university, so a (very young) man who was dressed like a doctor was waiting for us. When we arrived, he took a couple more quick drags; then dropped his cigarette on the floor and stepped on it. He took us to the "emergency room"—a cot, counter, pan of water, and several medical tools. With Laurie lying on the cot, me sitting on it beside her, and a young nurse to assist him, the doctor had just enough room to move between the counter and the cot. He unwrapped the towel and gave Laurie a shot to deaden the area. While he prepared a needle and thread, the nurse swabbed the area with a lot of iodine. Just as she finished and turned away, a very large bumble bee flew in the open window and landed on Laurie's chest. She and I froze, so as not to antagonize it. The nurse turned back, noted it, rolled up a piece of newspaper that was lying nearby, swatted it, threw the corpse out the window, and held Laurie's arm while the doctor put four stitches in her hand. Ivo had waited for us and took us home. Laurie saw the university's doctor to have the dressing changed and the stitches removed. He said the young doctor hadn't done a very good job on the stitches, and she would probably have some wrinkles there. He was right.

March 17 was my birthday, and Laurie took it as a challenge, for my present, to create comestibles we had not experienced since leaving the States in August. She invited five of Cooper's friends: two exchange students from the States and three from Romania; a couple who were professors at Potsdam State in New York, teaching at AUBG spring semester; and Kalinka, her Bulgarian friend who worked at the neighborhood grocery store. One of the disadvantages of teaching (and studying) at an English language school, was that we learned much less of the language than we had in China and Thailand. For that reason, none of us or our other guests spoke more than a smidgen of Bulgarian, and Kalinka spoke almost no English. Laurie hesitated to invite her, because she was afraid Kalinka would be uncomfortable. She was such a neat person, however, and so expressive, that she was generally able to communicate pretty well despite language barriers. It was the right decision—she had a great time, and everyone seemed perfectly at ease with her. I brought the professor couple home with me after work, and when we came in, Laurie had an amazing spread of appetizers laid out on the coffee table: peanuts, both black and green olives, fresh vegetables and yogurt dip, crackers and two kinds of bread, pretzel sticks, spinach dip, seafood spread, and liver pate'.

In the kitchen, she had prepared bowls of shredded Romaine, onions, red peppers, and Caesar dressing, and was grilling blackened chicken breasts for blackened chicken Caesar salad—one of my favorites. She had even found anchovies, as I am one of the rare breed who relish the disgusting, hairy little creatures. She couldn't decide whether to make chocolate cake, banana bread, or cheesecake for dessert, so she just made one of each. For drinks, she had wine, beer, pop, and juice, as well as (especially for me) vodka and tomato juice, and all the necessary ingredients for bloody Marys—including Worcestershire sauce, which I didn't think existed east of France. Everyone raved about everything, wondered at how she had been able to put it all together; and ate far more than we should have. People gave me enough chocolate to last several weeks (even sharing it with the boys), and the evening was generally an unqualified success. Kalinka raved so much about the cheesecake (which they didn't make there, although the ingredients were inexpensive and readily available) so much that we sent a quarter of it home with her. Laurie and I stopped at the store to say "Hi" to her on our way out to breakfast the next morning, and she started raving about the cheesecake all over again. Laurie promised to translate the recipe into Bulgarian for her, no mean feat, as it required looking up each ingredient in the Bulgarian-English dictionary she carried.

Chapter 9
April

April, at AUBG was encompassed by an incredible collection of arts events that covered almost every evening, titled "Arts 2000." One of the events was a visit by William Meredith, a famous American poet, and one of my favorites when I was studying poetry in college. He was there with his partner, Richard Harteis, a not-so-famous poet who had spent his life basking in Meredith's reflected glory. Meredith was 80, and had suffered a stroke, so Harteis was more nurse at the time. One of the reasons for their visit was to launch Harteis' new novel, "Sapphire Dawn." The folks in the university's activities office asked me if I would do a dramatic reading from it as part of the festivities. I said I would, and then read it. I should have done it the other way around—it was terrible. The best thing I could say about it was that it was only 144 pages. I worried what I would say if he asked my opinion of it, as dissembling isn't one of my strong points. Of course one of the first things he asked was what I thought of it. In a flash of sheer brilliance, I said, "It sure is a fast read." I meant, "Thank goodness it's only 144 pages." What he heard was, "It's very exciting; a real page-turner." I read a (very short) section. He was pleased. He presented me with an inscribed copy. I told Laurie that I would treasure it forever—from its place on the shelves of the AUBG library, to which I donated it the next day.

The next Wednesday evening we went to the performance of a guitar quintet from Sophia, Thursday evening we went first to the performance of a string quartet from France; then to dinner for an artist from Sophia. Friday evening we attended the opening of his exhibition; then a reception after. Monday evening we went to the opening of an exhibition by an art student at AUBG who had been working a couple of hours a week with Jesse. She was pleased when we complimented her on her work. She had done some very nice religious icons (oil on wood) in the traditional style. She was the youngest artist I had met who still did them. Tuesday in Varosha (the Old Town) from 3:00 to 6:00 , they presented what they billed as an "Art Happening" (a word I hadn't heard since the early '70s). They had all the art studios and schools (about four of the first and two of the second) in that area open for visitors, and continuous performances of traditional Bulgarian music and dance groups. I recognized most of the people there as being from the university. I didn't know if it hadn't been publicized in town, or if people other than academic types just weren't interested. The next Wednesday and Friday were Cooper's final recitals, with others who had been taking voice lessons from the choir director.

We went to a play the next Tuesday evening that was part of the "Arts 2000" festival at the university. It was called "Going to Pot," a comedy translated from French, and it was hilarious. Even the fact that it was only the "final exam" for an acting class, and thus not very professionally done, did little to detract from the wonderful writing. The main character was a businessman who manufactured pottery. He learned that the army planned to provide each of its men with their own chamber pot, and invited the man to lunch who was responsible for selecting the firm that would manufacture those items. If his firm were chosen, he would become rich. The problem was that he was having a hard time convincing the man that pottery chamber pots would be better than porcelain. He seemed to think that pottery would be too prone to breaking. Meanwhile, the businessman's wife was still in bathrobe and curlers, cleaning the bathroom, and more concerned with the fact that "baby" (who was seven) hadn't "gone" yet, than in making a good impression on their very important visitor. As the plot progressed, she brought baby (played by a college student), and the laxative that he refused to drink, into her husband's office. There, through a series of misadventures, both the husband and his important visitor (but not baby) eventually drank some of the laxative, with the expected consequences. The funniest scene was one in which the businessman tried to convince his visitor that his pottery was unbreakable by throwing it up in the air and letting it land on the wooden floor. Of course it shattered all over. The humor was greatly heightened by the fact that the visitor was a very nice man who wanted very much to believe that the pots were, in fact, unbreakable. His astonishment when the first one shattered was hilarious. The businessman explained that it must have been a flaw in production; that it happened to "about one in a thousand." The best line in the play came when they threw the second pot, it shattered, and the visitor very quietly asked, "Two in a thousand?"

Wednesday evening we attended the most fun musical event I'd been to in years. It was a percussion ensemble from Plevin, a town in northern Bulgaria. The performers were students of a special music school there, and ranged from 11 to 17 years old. They played xylophone-type instruments in five sizes, from bass to soprano in sound, as well as a whole range of drums, bells, triangles, cymbals, and every other sort of noisemaker imaginable, including plastic bags. Their music ranged from Scott Joplin's to J. S. Bach's, and included two jazz pieces written

Cooper and his vocal classmates practicing for their performance at Arts 2000.

by the performers. One boy, whom we found out later was 12, played a couple of solos so complex that the sticks he was using became a blur. Part of the group's appeal was that they were obviously having so much fun; the whole time they played, they kept grinning broadly at each other and at the audience. I looked around, and the entire audience was grinning as well. We wouldn't let them go until they had played two encores, one of which was the '60s hit "Tequila." They said they were cutting a CD in May, but weren't sure it would be out before we left, so we gave them my cards for both AUBG and in the States, and offered to give them enough money to send us one when they were available. The director refused our money, saying that, as we would be their best fans in the States, they would send us one for free. I wish they had, it would have been the best cure I can imagine for getting rid of a bad mood.

Cooper was taking voice lessons and an ear training course, and was a member of the AUBG choir. Thursday he and the other voice students gave a recital as part of their final exams. Cooper must have been the most versatile of the two men in the class, as he sang the male parts in all the duets, trios, and quartets with the women. They sang everything from Verdi operas to Russian love ballads. He also sang a couple of Frank Sinatra-type numbers (against his will, but on the insistence of his voice teacher), and a couple of Russian ballads (one had something to do with a lover pining away under a weeping willow tree, I think). Laurie and I thought he did a great job—based, of course, on our extensive knowledge of classical Russian music, and having nothing whatsoever to do with our being his parents. Jesse deemed his performance, "OK, I guess." His professor must have come down more in his parent's camp, as he got an "A" for the course, and was told that his Russian accent was "quite good." Friday evening he sang again—just he and a woman who was doing her senior recital. They performed a series of solos and duets.

Laurie, Jesse, and I went to Sofia that weekend—Cooper had to stay home and study, as he had finals the next week. We caught the 8:10 a.m. bus, arriving in Sophia at 9:45, and got off at the closest stop to our hotel: about a 15-minute walk. After checking in and dropping our packs, we took a cab across town to the American College in Sophia, which was, by Bulgarian logic, an English language high school. It had about 500 students, equally divided between the sons and daughters of well-to-do Bulgarians and those of internationals working in Bulgaria. It had an excellent reputation, and we would have sent Cooper and Jesse there except for two considerations: 1) we couldn't afford it, and 2) we didn't come to Bulgaria as a family only to live in separate cities. Our friend, Natalia, who taught the art courses at AUBG on Fridays, spent the rest of the week teaching at the American College in Sophia, and had invited us to their annual arts fair. When she had first talked about ACS, I imagined a college campus; then she explained that it was a high school, so I changed my mental image to one building, and thought nothing of it when she said it would be easy to find her there when we arrived. When the cab driver dropped us at the gates and we walked a quarter mile in to the eight or so buildings clustered around a couple of large quadrangles, and when I saw these quadrangles held hundreds of people, I reassessed how easy finding her would be. We spent half an hour looking through the buildings and grounds and asking people who said they knew her and assumed she was there, but didn't know where. Then we decided to just have fun, and trust that we would run into her. We had chicken sandwiches for lunch and our first Dunkin' Donuts in several months for dessert. We admired the various displays of student art. As we were having another dessert (this one ice cream sundaes) we saw Natalia across the quad, and sent Jesse to grab her. She showed us around her office and classrooms; then we went to the auditorium for the students' annual variety show. After three scenes from "Fiddler on the Roof," which had been their spring theatre production, we left to help Natalia set up the "Kids' Art Contest," which was her primary responsibility for the day.

Laurie and I helped her run the contest, doling out paper and art supplies, while Jesse created an entry for the contest. After two delight-ful hours of sitting in the sun, chatting, and watching young minds cre-ate, Natalia declared the contest closed, and we gathered the 15 entries for her to judge. Jesse won first prize in his category, over my protests. Natalia said his was clearly the best entry in that category, and she wasn't going to deny him first place just because we were her friends. He was delighted, as were all the young artists, when we stood on the steps of the building, displayed their works to the assembled multitude of appreciative parents, announced the names of the winners (which, through judicious use of fourth places and multiple ties, amounted to everyone who entered), and awarded them their prizes of candy bars, jigsaw puzzles, and ballpoint pens. After cleaning up and stowing the supplies, Natalia took us to visit her friends who teach at ACS, and live in one of the houses on campus for visiting faculty. She then drove us downtown to her apartment, stopping on the way for dinner supplies. Within two blocks of each other, we stopped at a supermarket every bit as modern as any in the States, and an open-air market just like any we had seen in developing countries throughout the world. We spent a wonderful evening in her kitchen, preparing, cooking, drinking, eating, and talking. At 11:00 we made the 15-minute walk to our hotel, with the understanding that I would call the next morning and arrange to meet for the day.

I called the next morning at 9:30, and got her answering machine, so we went to a neighborhood bakery for breakfast. I called again at 10:00, and got her answering machine, so we had coffee and tried to find the English language Lutheran church to attend Easter services. We didn't find it, although we did find the Bulgarian Congregational church. We weren't sure whether they were celebrating Palm Sunday or Easter, but we knew whichever it was it would be in Bulgarian, so we skipped it. We got two chances at Easter that year. Our "regular" Easter was that Sunday, which was the Orthodox Palm Sunday (or in their case, more like Weeping Willow Sunday, as that's what they use instead of palm fronds). Orthodox Easter was the next Sunday. I called again at 11:30 and Natalia answered, sounding none too sprightly. She said she'd need an hour to get ready, but when I told her we had to get our packs out of our hotel room so the owner could go to Weeping Willow Sunday services, she said to come on over and relax while we waited for her there.

We got started about 12:30, with the intention of visiting a couple of art galleries before catching the 4:00 bus back to Blagoevgrad. We only got a couple of blocks, however, before being stopped short by (of all things) a combined celebration for Mickey Mouse's birthday and the reading of books. It was taking place in a park that, until the September before, surrounded the mausoleum of a famous Bulgarian communist leader. When we were there, it surrounded more park, as that was what they put there after razing the mausoleum. Now that's progress: from communism to Mickey Mouse in one decade. Anyway, they had erected a large stage, complete with a monster sound system—the Bulgarians were big on monster sound systems; for cars, movie theaters, nightclubs, and (evidently) Mickey Mouse birthdays. Hundreds of people had gathered to watch and listen (or in the case of many, sell all manner of goods to those watching listeners). The Mickey Mouse part of the festival clearly dominated, as the books part was confined to one corner of the park, where several booksellers had set up tables piled with their wares. The crowd was pretty sparse in that corner, drawn Mickey Mouse-ward by the hype of free "stuff" from numerous sponsors—including Volvo, Ford, McDonalds, and KFC. We stopped long enough to watch an 8-year-old girl in a lion costume recite a poem in honor of Mickey (the logic escaped me), and a couple of traditional folk dance groups (again, the Mickey connection was a bit murky). When the techno-music band started, we were drawn inexorably away. As we left, we were treated to half a dozen horseback riders in what appeared to be Medieval costume (not a mouse among them) parading around the perimeter of the park. Pursued by the techno-beat, we made our way toward Sofia University, and the first of the galleries we intended to visit.

As the techno-sounds faded in the distance, they were replaced by a cacophony of bells. Straight ahead, in the tower of the most famous cathedral in Bulgaria, back-lit by the sun, three men were beating exuberantly (and with little apparent design) on the bells with what appeared to be wooden mallets. Their Weeping Willow Sunday service was letting out, and they were marking the event for all to hear. I wondered what it would sound like the next Sunday, on Orthodox Easter. I made the mistake of stopping, enthralled, to listen, which gave Laurie, Natalia, and Jesse time to wander into the nearby market. By the time I found them, Laurie was negotiating for a set of nested Russian dolls, and Jesse was wondering whether he could have his allowance for the rest of our time in Bulgaria to buy an antique knife. We finally got to the gallery, and stopped in the vestibule to figure out how much time we had to spend there. If, afterward, we were to walk to a restaurant, have lunch, walk to Natalia's apartment to get our packs, catch a taxi, and get to the station in time to catch the 4:00 bus, we had exactly a half hour to take in three floors of art. I spent the time in two exhibits: one of Gillray's colored woodblock prints of political satire from the late 18th and early 19th centuries, and one of Japanese prints, mostly from the "Thirty-six Views of Mount Fuji" and the "Fifty-six Stations on the

Tokigawa Road." Both exhibits were wonderful, and deserved a couple of hours each.

We had lunch at a Chinese restaurant that had replaced a Russian restaurant after the fall of communism in Bulgaria made all things Russian very much passe—except, of course, Natalia, whom nothing could have made passe. We were well on schedule, on our way to her apartment to get our packs, when we passed (well, not-quite-passed) the Sofia City Gallery, which had a sign out front announcing a temporary exhibit of one of Natalia's late friends. Nothing would do but that we stopped for "at least a moment" to see "at least his best pieces." It was time well spent—his "best pieces" really were fine, and the rest were pretty darned good, as well. We spent 15 minutes looking at what should have taken two hours, and were once again on our way. We got our packs, got a cab, and got the 4:00 bus (because, as it happened, it was actually the 4:15 bus) to Blagoevgrad. We arrived just before 6:00, bought a roasted chicken ($2.50) and a loaf of bread (40 cents) at the market, went home, ate, watched some TV, and went to bed.

Although the regular Easter bunny couldn't find us in Sofia, one did visit us the next weekend. We had no Easter baskets, as they weren't much in evidence, so we ended up with Easter treats in Christmas stockings—we had those, as I wore a couple every day (we washed them thoroughly). Laurie's friend Kalinka understood that our Easter was a week later than her Easter. She wanted our Easter to be just as special as hers, so she and her family took us out to dinner that evening.

April was always the time in our year's stay in another culture when we began to realize that we just didn't have much time left—we had only two more weeks of classes at AUBG; then finals week. We stayed in our apartment another month after the semester ended, however, and made short trips throughout Bulgaria, Macedonia, and Albania. The week after Easter we went to Bansko. The boys had heard that Bulgaria had good skiing, so they were excited when the university organized a ski trip to Bansko over the break in January. The trip, however, was cancelled because of a lack of equipment and funds. We did want to visit the mountains, so the week after Easter, we hired Ivo to take us to the Pirin Mountains and Bansko. The snow had melted on some of the main trails, making them difficult for hiking, but Ivo wanted us to see the 1200-year-old fir tree on the way to Mt. Vihren. It was massive, and could have held our whole crew of five, but Cooper was the only one to take it on.

Cooper perched on a limb of the 1200-year-old fir tree near Bansko.

We stayed that night in the one room upper level of a chalet-type guest house. It was definitely off-season, and we seemed to be the only non-residents around. We did our usual walkabout, and came across a fascinating sight of some women using the community "washer." An icy stream had been diverted into a huge wooden bowl. The women had thrown in a load of heavy woolen rugs and some detergent, and the force of the moving water spun everything around in the tub, much like a huge automatic washing machine. When they decided their rugs were clean, they let the soapy water run off into the stream; then plugged the outlet and let the tub fill with fresh water for the rinse cycle. Their dryer wasn't quite as impressive: they hung the rugs over nearby rocks and let nature take its course. The town also offered some beautiful churches, an interesting "old town," and an impressive monument to Paissii Hilendarski, the author of the first Bulgarian history in 1762.

Women in Bansko washing their rugs in the community "washer."

The train station at Valiko Turnovo.

Chapter 10
May

We returned to Blagoevgrad for a few days of rest and laundry; then took a train to Valiko Turnovo, an old city with a medieval fortress on one side of the river. It was the site of a rebellion against the Byzantine Empire in the 1100s. They touted a light and sound show dramatizing the defeat of the Turks. We expected tacky, but (just in case) had dinner across the river at an outside cafe with a good view. As it got dark, the show started, and was, in fact, very impressive.

Tryavna, a nearby village, was listed as a "museum town," so the next day, we took a local bus there and found an inexpensive place to stay. We wandered around town that afternoon. There were several small villages near Tryavna that our hostess said were good examples of life in the 1800s, so the next morning, we took a minibus to one of them. We spent several hours looking at the houses and local crafts. When we were ready to return to Tryavna, one of the locals told us the next bus wouldn't come by for two more hours. He said, however, that there was an excellent hiking trail that would take us the ten miles back to Tryavna. He said it was well-marked with blue blaze marks, and showed us the first one at the edge of the woods. It was a beautiful day, and we all agreed that a hike was a good idea. All went well for about seven miles, when we stepped out of the woods into a very large open field with not a blue blaze to be seen. We were discussing what to do when we were approached by a group of youngsters coming toward us, led by a college-age woman. We asked her if she spoke English, and she said yes, she was from the United States. We said we were too, and asked what part of the States she was from. She said Bloomington, Minnesota— about 250 miles from our home town. After we had all agreed that it was a small world, she pointed us in the right direction, and we finished our walk back to our overnight quarters.

The next morning we took the train back to Blagoevgrad, where we relaxed for a few days. Cooper performed with the AUBG choir for the Southwestern Bulgaria choir festival in Blagoevgrad on May 18 and 19; then went on tour with them throughout Macedonia May 21-23. Laurie, Jesse, and I headed to Melnik, billed as "the smallest town in Bulgaria." We were actually more interested in the surrounding countryside: sandstone hills that had eroded into columns and finger-like bluffs. Melnik had once been a busy city with a majority Greek popula-

The first blue blaze on the 10-mile trail back to Tryavana.

tion on a major trade route. As trade routes shifted, it dwindled, until, by the time we were in Bulgaria, it was a small village. It's major source of income was a large wine cavern just outside of the town, where very good wine that was exported throughout Europe was made and stored. We sat in the coolness of the cave and drank a couple of glasses of very good (but quite reasonably priced) red wine; then bought a couple of bottles to take back to Blagoevgrad. We spent the afternoon in a house museum above the cavern. It had belonged to a wealthy wine merchant, and was replete with beautiful stained glass panels and ornately carved wooden walls and ceilings. The next morning we had breakfast in a little bakery on the main (only) street, and were delighted to be curbside (actually, it was dirt, with no curbs) when a couple of shepherds drove their flock through town on their way to pasture. After breakfast we set out to find the path up the steep bluff on the edge of town that led to the ruins of a 13th century house that had been built during Melnik's heyday. We looked for some time without success, and finally decided to go back to the house where we were staying and ask our hostess. As we approached the house, we noticed a tiny sign that pointed to the path directly behind the house. We managed to scramble up the rocky switchbacks that led to the top.

The ruins of the house were interesting, but we could only walk around the outside, which didn't take long. Then we noticed a path that (according to the sign) led to a monastery four miles away. Our map showed a bus stop just past the monastery, so we decided to hike to the monastery, then take the bus back to Melnik. The path was rugged, but the weather was beautiful when we started. The path stayed rough, but the weather changed for the worse. By the time we reached the monastery, it was raining pretty hard, so we looked at it as we walked by on our way to the bus stop. There was also a small store and trinket shop, and as it was raining quite hard by that time, we went shopping. It took us quite a long time to decide what we wanted—in fact the rain had stopped by the time Laurie settled on a bag of tea herbs. Our timing was great. We had just enough time to sit in the newly-emerged sun long enough to dry out (sort of) before the bus arrived, and it got us back to Melnik just in time for dinner.

The next morning we returned to Blagoevgrad, where we made a quick turnaround, and set off with Ivo for Macedonia, where we met up with Cooper, separated him from the choir and spent a few days traveling throughout Macedonia, before having Ivo drop us at the border crossing into Albania, where we spent a few more days; then returned for the last time to Blagoevgrad. From there, we took the bus to Sofia, where Cooper flew out on June 5, connecting in Frankfurt with his return flight to Minneapolis. There he hooked up with folks from the Minnesota All-State Lutheran Choir for their music camp and tour of Minnesota. Laurie, Jesse, and I caught the train to Romania June 6, and spent the next 24 days wending our way through Romania, Hungary, The Czech Republic, Slovakia, Austria, Poland, and Germany. We caught our flight from Frankfurt to Minneapolis on the 30th, where we met Cooper, having missed his final concert by two days—because those of us in the family who had earned money had stay out of the States at least 330 days to get tax breaks.

IV
KYRGYZSTAN

I retired in the spring of 2005, but had an offer to teach at the American University in Central Asia in Kyrgyzstan, starting that September. Cooper had just graduated from college and gotten married, Jesse had just graduated from high school and was looking to start college, and we had just sold our house. Laurie and I were discussing whether it was realistic to even consider a year abroad, when I said, "Any time we start a sentence with 'Do you remember when...', it inevitably concludes with 'China', 'Thailand', or 'Bulgaria' in there somewhere." We decided to take the offer in Kyrgyzstan. We assumed the boys would pass on it, but that we should offer to have them go with us. They all three said yes (including Annie, our new daughter-in-law), so we left in August. But a lot happened before then. In 2001 we had bought 6 1/2 acres of woods on a little lake 10 miles out of town, and planned to sell our house in town and build there when I retired. When we decided to go to Kyrgyzstan, we figured we'd rent our house (as we had the other three years), build on our new property when we came back, then sell our house in town. When a couple who went to our church heard we were going away for a year, they offered to buy our house. We were hesitant, but they made us an offer we couldn't refuse. So we decided to change the order: we'd build on the lake property, completing the outside so we could store our belongings in it; sell our house, with the closing date on August 1; and go to Kyrgyzstan immediately, leaving us a month to get settled in before school started.

Then I got a grant from the Soros Foundation, which meant that instead of $200 a month and free Russian lessons, I would get an additional $6,700, an apartment, round-trip air fare for three of us, medical and dental for three of us, and thousands of dollars to cover additional costs. The Soros people said we should get there on the 16th. That meant we had to move out of our house on the first. The house we were building would make a fine storage unit by the end of July, but would lack a few amenities (like water and electricity) so we couldn't live there. We were homeless for two weeks. While we were in Bulgaria, Natalia, our artist friend, had asked me about the possibility of coming to my university in the States to teach. As it happened we did have a one-year position open in our art department, so I put her in touch with a friend, who happened to be the department chairman. She was hired for the position. They really liked her, and she ended up being hired in a permanent position. She was spending the summer in Bulgaria, and wouldn't be back until September, so was happy to lend us her apartment for the first two weeks of August. One problem solved. I rented a semi trailer; we moved our stuff into it; after the closing, we moved it out to the new house, where it sat until we got the garage part finished; at which time we moved everything into the garage, locked it up, and left. Second problem solved.

Chapter 1
September

We got to the Bemidji airport at 4:00 a.m. on Monday the 15th for our 35-hour trip to Bishkek, by way of Minneapolis, Toronto, and Moscow. The last two legs were on Aeroflot, the official Russian airlines. Despite the fact that we had been warned by many to expect problems with Aeroflot, they were great, including the food, which was the best on the whole trip. I'm not counting the 9½ hour layover in Moscow as their fault. And what a layover it was. The Moscow airport was like nothing more than a large shopping mall (although not as large as one might expect for a city that size) with exits to runways—except they didn't offer as much seating as most shopping malls. Nine of ten people had to sit or (in many cases) lie on the unfinished concrete floors. The only good thing about a 9½ hour layover was that after about three hours we had seniority, so had inherited seats (which, in fact, weren't much more comfortable than the concrete floors). They were in the form of metal seats, attached six abreast, bench style—except seldom were more than three of the six useable. At one point, a maintenance man came by and shooed people off one of the more damaged units. He took it off to one side and began dismantling it. We said, "Great, at least we'll have a few more seats when he gets it fixed." Who said anything about fixing it? After he got it apart, he loaded the parts on a baggage cart and took them away, never to be seen again. People spread out newspapers and lay down in the space where the seats had been.

When we had checked in at Bemidji, they told us our bags were checked through to Moscow for sure, but we should check there to be sure they would go through to Bishkek. Some would call me a doubter; I prefer to think of myself as thorough. At any rate, I checked (just to be sure) at each stop (it wasn't like we didn't have plenty of time, with at least three hours at each). At Toronto, guess whose bags (all ten of them) were riding merrily around on the carousel in the baggage claim area. We used about an hour of that layover rechecking our bags—after schlepping them all the way across the airport to a different terminal. So, basically, the trip was uneventful until we got to the airport in Bishkek (at 4:00 a.m., after 35 hours in transit). I had been sure to let them know on what flight we would be arriving on the morning of the 16th, so they could meet us with the promised van, and take us directly to our apartment. The problem was, we had crossed the international dateline.

So we arrived on our 16th, to find no van, which had waited two hours for us the morning before—on their 16th. OK, pop quiz: you are in an airport in a country where you have never been; they speak a language you don't understand; it's four in the morning; besides yourself, you have four others for which you are responsible; you have 16 pieces of luggage (counting carry-ons) one of which contains all of your money, passports, visas, and all other critical documents; twenty porters and taxi drivers have homed in on you and are shouting, trying to wrench your bags from you, pushing you in various directions, and generally attempting to extract as much money from you as possible. What do you do?

An angel in the guise of the head porter shouted them all down; pushed them back to give us breathing room (and control of our bags); and in a bit of broken English on his part, a bit of five-year-old Bulgarian on ours (which we had found was as understandable as Russian in most cases), but mostly great pantomime, got a handle on the problem. I had the cell number of one of the Soros officials, so the porter used his office phone to roust her out of bed. He arranged for two cabs to take us to a hotel, where we met her. I expected her to be grumpy, but she was very gracious—just glad we had gotten there safely. They had no idea where we were. When we hadn't shown up the morning before, she had tried to call me at my home and office numbers, and had e-mailed. We had no home phone, as we had no home; I had no office phone, as I had no office; and although I did have e-mail, I had been in transit, with no way of checking it. We finally collapsed into our rooms at about 8:00 a.m. At 9:00 a.m. I got a call from another Soros official saying that we should check out of our rooms after lunch, and she would meet us to take us to our apartment. We did, and she did.

Other than the fact that we had to carry hundreds of pounds of bags up 63 steps to it, our apartment was great—well, relatively speaking, of course—much better than China; better than Thailand; on a par with Bulgaria. It had three bedrooms (a rarity in Bishkek), living/dining room, kitchen, and bath, as well as small balconies off the kitchen and one of the bedrooms. Laurie and I got the smallest bedroom (as in room for twin beds, a nightstand, and a large dresser). Cooper and Annie got the largest one, and Jesse got the one with the balcony. We were on the fourth floor in a building that was in the center of a block, so despite the fact that we were in the center of the city, it was relatively quiet. We had cable TV, with several news channels, ESPN, and the National Geographic channel in English. The phone line was digital, so we got high-speed Internet. But one of the best things was that every morning during breakfast, from our kitchen window, and even more from the

The hotel where we stayed for a few hours on arrival in Bishkek.

balcony, we had a glorious view of the mountains. They looked like they were about half a mile away, but were more like 20 miles. We were in the process of unpacking and putting our stuff in the proper places, when Jessie swaggered into the room wearing a suit he had found in his closet. It fit him perfectly, but was of the most garish orange and black striped crinkly velveteen any of us had ever seen. Jesse loved it. We all told him that wherever he wore it he'd have to go solo.

Laurie and I never locked our home—neither our houses in the States, nor our apartments in any of the other countries in which we'd lived. One night, less than a week after we had moved into our apartment in Bishkek, I was awakened by something bumping the foot of my bed. It was about 2:00 in the morning, and very dark, so all I could make out was a shadowy figure standing there. I assumed Jesse had gotten up to go to the bathroom, and, half asleep, had gotten confused in his new surroundings and wandered into our bedroom by mistake. I said something like, "What's the matter guy, are you lost?" The drunken grunt I got in return was distinctly not from Jesse. Laurie had woken up by this time, and we both realized that, somehow, a drunken man had stumbled up four flights of stairs, opened our apartment door, wandered into our bedroom, and was standing very unsteadily at the foot of my (which he probably thought was his) bed, trying to figure out why there was someone besides him in it (Thank goodness that realization came before, and not after, he climbed in with me). I jumped out of bed and (talking calmly to him, as he was probably more frightened, and certainly more confused, than I was) guided him out the front door into the hallway, where I left him while I reentered the apartment, and closed (and locked) the door. I'm not sure if he ever found the right apartment, but at least he was gone the next morning when we left for the university.

The Soros Foundation required everyone in the region who was receiving funding from them (about 50 of us) to attend a week-long conference. That meant, in addition to those of us from the U.S. and Canada, scholars (mostly people who had gotten masters degrees from schools in the States) from Kyrgyzstan, Uzbekistan, Kazakhstan, Tajikistan, Turkmenistan, and Mongolia. The sessions, as usual with that type of gathering, were pretty much a snooze. The good news: the conference site was the Royal Beach resort on Lake Issyk-Kul, a beautiful spot that was a fine place to be before and after sessions. Also, the food was great. But the real benefit was getting to meet all those folks from all over Central Asia. The lake was about a four-hour drive east of Bishkek, in a high mountain plain. It was huge, and the second deepest in the world. The scenery for the first two hours was about like driving across North Dakota; then we traversed a mountain pass, snaking along a river that would offer some great white water rafting. In fact, one "guest house" on the way advertised just that. The other side of the pass returned to North Dakota-like terrain; then the lake. The problem was, except for the eastern end, which snuggled into the mountains, it was just dirt; then water. There wasn't really any impressive scenery; it was mostly stuck in the middle of a large, arid, over-grazed plain. The resort was one of the posh new ones, built after the fall of Communism, and by U.S. standards, quite inexpensive—$60 a day per person for a room, three meals, and all the swimming and lying on the synthetic beach we could take. Of course the price didn't really matter to us, as Soros was picking up the tab. The food was great, although hamburgers and lasagna for breakfast took a bit of getting used to.

In the States when we think of universities, we usually picture several buildings spread over a campus, even if they are set in a city. Many universities in other countries match that description, as well—the universities where I taught in China and Thailand, for example. The university in Bulgaria, however, was a single building. AUCA was in the center of Bishkek, and was two 4-story buildings, side by side, on one side of a large public square, with a main street running in front of it. On the other side of the square, running along the sidewalk, were dozens of colorful banners on tall white poles. As far as we knew, they had no particular meaning, but were just to brighten the square (which they certainly did). As in the other three countries we had lived, native English speakers (especially Americans) were in great demand, and Laurie had no trouble finding teaching positions to supplement our income. On the morning of our first day in Bishkek, I got a call from the president's secretary, asking me to come over and meet members of the administration. She asked that Laurie, Cooper, and Annie come along as well. By noon, all three of them had jobs teaching English at the university.

Laurie, Cooper, Annie, and I were all considered "part-time," as we each taught three classes, and four was considered a full load. I taught one required intro to mass comm class to 25 first year students, one elective public relations class to 15 sophomores and juniors, and one required theory class to seniors. As with students everywhere, they were a mixed bag, but by and large, they really were the best and the brightest from Central Asia (Mongolia, Kazakhstan, Kyrgyzstan, Uzbekistan, Tajikistan, Turkmenistan, and Afghanistan). I expected them (as were students in China, Thailand, and Bulgaria) to be very good at memorizing; not so good at thinking, but was pleasantly surprised. They were more ready to question, discuss, and analyze than were my students in the States. On the other hand, they had clearly not been held to task in terms of getting to class on time, meeting deadlines, or in some cases, avoiding plagiarism. In my class of 25, there were mornings when I started the class with nine or ten. I recognized that it was, to a great extent, a cultural difference, but, as I pointed out to them, they had chosen to attend an "American university," because they wanted to study in an American atmosphere, most of them with the intention of going to graduate school in the States. I made it clear, therefore that they had to play by my rules. I was told that the plagiarism problem resulted from the fact that, in high school, they were taught that a good paper was derived from copying experts on a topic. Be that as it may, they were given specific training when they came to AUCA on how to avoid plagiarism, and (as I required so much writing in all my classes) I covered it extensively the first day of class. I warned them that the only thing easier than recognizing when a student switched from his or her writing to someone else's, was recognizing when a student who was not writing in his or her first language switched to someone's writing who was. Still, I had to fail one or two students every week or two for plagiarism. The first time, I failed students on the assignment; the second case resulted in failure for the class. In 25 years, I had never had to resort to the latter—until the second week of October. The good news is I think that extreme action finally got their attention, as I only got one plagiarized paper after that. I don't want to sound negative about the students, though, because overall, they really were delightful: eager to learn and ready to work hard. Actually, my hardest job was explaining to students unused to getting anything but "A"s that getting an occasional "B" from me did not mean they were in danger of failing.

Bishkek was a beautiful city, taken as a whole—set at the base of a range of snow-capped mountains, and chock full of an enormous number of trees (mostly oaks and cottonwood).

Most of the housing center-city was ugly, Russian-style concrete apartment buildings, with little to recommend them architecturally. On the other hand, they were interspersed with more green space than I had ever seen in a city. These parks and boulevards were much more lush than we expected in such an arid climate, as they had developed a maze of irrigation ditches throughout the city. Because it was so close to the base of the mountains, the entire city listed to starboard, as it were, allowing a brisk flow of water dependent only on gravity. Somebody upstream was responsible for redirecting the flow daily, as we noticed that the various ditches seemed to be flowing in a somewhat weekly cycle. Further downstream, in the various neighborhoods, the flow control seemed much more competitive, with people out diverting it to their (or, more accurately, their greenery's) advantage by blocking ditches, digging side trenches, and constructing what I was willing to bet were unauthorized dikes. They had people responsible for maintaining the green spaces, and the beautiful flower beds. Some of the rose gardens were hundreds of feet long. The scent in the early morning (before the pollution index climbed) was wonderful. Also adding to the overall charm of the city was the plethora of what Cooper referred to as "uplifting Communist sculptures." Some people found them overbearing and intrusive, but I had to go with Cooper on that one. They may not have been "uplifting" per se, but I did think they added a lot to the ambience of the city; especially the smaller, less dominating pieces scattered unobtrusively throughout the parks.

One of the true delights of walking in Bishkek, or most cities outside the States, for that matter, were the street vendors. They were scattered along every major street, and especially along the sidewalks in the parks, selling everything from a vile alcoholic concoction made from fermented mare's milk, to photos they took of people sitting on, or standing beside everything from stuffed animals to a shiny (but totally gutted and inoperable) BMW convertible, and everything in between. We wanted to get Cooper a card for his birthday, so walked to a nearby street bazaar. There we found a vendor with cards for all occasions—in Russian, of course; we were in a Russian-speaking country, after all. Laurie could remember enough Bulgarian, which was enough like Russian, to find a card that she was reasonably sure said "Happy Birthday," and had a cartoon frog on the front that we agreed looked strikingly like Cooper. What else it said, we had no idea, but figured the students in his conversation class could interpret it for him. I got to thinking maybe we should be sure it wasn't inappropriate for young college students, so asked a bilingual professor in my department to translate for me. She said it was difficult, as it depended on uniquely Russian humor, but it went something like this: (outside—under the Cooper-looking frog) "For your birthday, I have composed a poem especially in your honor. It didn't scan very well"... (then inside) ..."but that's OK, it's all bullshit anyway. Have a happy birthday." I allowed as how maybe he'd better not take it to his conversation class after all, but she said, "Oh, no, they'll love it." She was right: he did and they did.

The concentration of housing also created a very compact city, easy to walk around in. Well, easy in the sense that everything was pretty close together. That brings me to the phrase I used before: "a beautiful city—taken as a whole." The infrastructure, as in most developing countries, was terrible. We simply could not walk without keeping our eyes on the ground in front of us much of the time. The only place the sidewalks (if they existed at all) were decent was in front of restaurants, bars, and some of the more up-scale shops, where the owners had laid them new, as part of the décor of their establishment. Otherwise, they were a hazard to navigate. It was not unusual to be walking along, and suddenly be faced with a two-foot deep hole, where the sidewalk had simply fallen into the sewer below. Stairs were a special challenge. Each step was a different height and depth, and often sloped toward the back, making us feel as though we were about to fall on our face going up, or on our back coming down. The streets were a bit better, but not much. Being a pedestrian was further complicated by the fact that drivers would as soon hit us as not. Their attitude was that if they had a car and we didn't, they were clearly higher on the social ladder, and would get in very little trouble if they mashed us like bugs. I was not just imagining this. On the way in from the airport, at 5 a.m. on a nearly deserted four-lane street, our taxi driver was in the center lane. He saw a bicyclist ahead on the right edge of the outside lane. He swerved into the outside lane and blasted his horn until we passed the poor old guy on the bike, then he swerved back into the center lane and continued on his way.

It's good that Bishkek was a nice city to walk in, as walk we did. Other than the four-hour bus ride to the conference and back, I wasn't in a motorized vehicle for weeks. Laurie and I walked a couple of miles a day during the week, and more like 5-10 miles a day exploring and shopping on Saturdays and Sundays. Jesse had "a friend who just happened to be a girl," and she came over for dinner one night. After dinner, we left at 8:00 to walk her home. We got back at 10:00. Her (Americanized) name was Selby. She was Turkmen, and had spent a year in Pennsylvania as an exchange student. She was pretty sure we wouldn't be able to handle her Turkmen name. I said we'd like to try, so she told me what it was. I repeated it exactly several times (I was sure), and she almost hurt herself trying not to laugh. To spare her internal injury we agreed to use the Americanized version. She was studying at AUCA with her brother and two cousins, and the rest of her family was in Turkmenistan. Her mother sent us all camel's hair bracelets to ward off evil spirits. I wore mine one day and had to take it off, it itched so much. It gave me a whole new appreciation for St. John's wardrobe. I might have been able to take the locusts and honey, but a camel's hair bathrobe—no way. Lucie, a Swiss professor in my department, said I should be careful; she thought that if the father of a young man wore one of those bracelets that was a gift from the mother of a young woman, it meant the young man and the young woman were engaged. I'm pretty sure she was kidding, but it gave me a good excuse to take it off. We were happy to see that Jesse was making friends, and starting to fit into college life there. He went to Issyk-Kul the next weekend on a trip for students arranged by the university. He was officially a student, as he not only passed the TOEFEL (the English language exam required of all applicants), but got the highest score ever recorded by an applicant to AUCA. So, I guess all those years speaking English finally paid off.

We got a notice from the post office that we had something there; to come and pick it up. When I had cleaned out my office at Bemidji State, I had ended up with a half-ton (literally) of journalism books, so we had boxed them up and sent them to AUCA as a donation to their journalism department. We had sent the 18 boxes from the Bemidji post office about a week before we left. They told us it would take four to six weeks, and as it had been about five weeks, we assumed that's what was waiting for us at the post office. Said post office was about a mile from the university, so we arranged for a van to take us at 11:00 a.m. to pick them up. In fact, the chair of the department was so excited to be quadrupling their library, that she arranged to send a man to help us carry the boxes. We went downstairs at 11:00, and sure enough, there was the AUCA van waiting for us. Everybody but the driver piled in and waited. The driver stayed outside and waited. It seems the university president had preempted us. We were waiting for him to take us to the post office; he was waiting to take the president to lunch. I went back upstairs, and was told, "Oh yes, we forgot to tell you, you will go to the post office later." I asked when later, and they said that it depended how long the president took to eat. I told them that wouldn't work, as I had a class that afternoon until four. They said they would reserve the van for Monday morning. I said that would be fine. When I got back to my office about ten after four, I was informed that I was late; the van was waiting downstairs. Now, Sarah, a friend who often brought her church youth group from Indiana to Bemidji during the summer to work on Habitat houses, had e-mailed to tell us she'd sent a care package containing a coffee maker, some good coffee, and some spices (we considered nominating her for sainthood). As she had sent it only about two weeks before, however, we knew there was no chance it would be there yet. The department office manager, the driver, the guy to help carry the boxes, Laurie, and I all trooped into the post office and I produced my passport and signed their documents. When the woman brought out the first of the 18 boxes, and handed it over, we waited expectantly for her to go back and get the rest. She asked something in Russian, which I assume loosely translated as, "Well, what are you guys all standing around looking silly for; take your box and go." We looked at the shipping label. Sure enough: "one coffee maker, coffee, etc." The good news was that the guy they sent to carry boxes had no trouble handling it in one trip. Needless to say, we (mostly I, as Laurie had suggested we check first to make sure it was the books, and I had scoffed at her) felt pretty silly. They assured us it was no problem (which, in Russian is "nyet problema," by the way, so we were pretty sure we understood correctly). I did agree, incidentally, to walk over and check the next time we get a notice, before arranging for the van and the carrying guy, and getting everybody's hopes up—although, Laurie (under pressure) did admit privately that she was just as pleased as I that it was Sarah's package, rather than the books.

Just as in China, Thailand, and Bulgaria, they swept the sidewalks every morning in Kyrgyzstan. I was bemused one morning, on my walk to the university, to see a water truck equipped with high-pressure nozzles, cleaning the streets. The nozzles were directed such that all the debris from the street was blown up onto the sidewalks. Whereupon, the little men (they are generally women in China, Thailand, and Bulgaria) responsible for the sidewalks promptly came around and swept said debris back into the streets.

Many of the huge, beautiful trees that lined the streets of Bishkek were oaks, and September was the time of year when oaks, in an effort to procreate, dropped abundant acorns. Some of those acorns, naturally, hit cars that were parked in the shade under the oaks. The result was a relatively continuous blaring of car alarms throughout the city. Obviously, it had gotten to the point where everybody ignored them. I'm certain that every car thief with good sense realized that, and it was the prime season for chop shops to ply their trade.

Speaking of cars, several years ago, when the EU countries tightened their emission control standards, hundreds of used Mercedes (that no longer met the standards, and that would cost thousands of dollars to bring up to snuff) became available at cut-rate prices to people in countries that cared more about development than the environment—a match made in heaven with the former Soviet bloc countries. The luxury car of choice in Kyrgyzstan, then, was the Mercedes. Well, actually, those favored by the truly "upwardly mobile" were the four-wheel drive sport utility vehicles, fully equipped for African safaris. At the other end of the spectrum were the Ladas, the much-maligned Russian-built burros of the auto world. I was delighted to hear the same story I had been told in Bulgaria, about the two men who had a race with their Ladas. The loser was irate, shouting at the winner, "You cheated; you carried yours!" Every morning the market teemed with them, pouring in from the countryside, crammed (inside, trunk, and roof) with every manner of produce. We saw one with an entire living room suite—couch, two chairs, coffee table, and end tables—tied to its roof. Between the two extremes were Toyotas, Hondas, BMWs, and Audis. Most people didn't have any car, however, so either walked, occasionally took a taxi (we could get almost anywhere in the city for a dollar or two), or (most likely) rode one of the hundreds of mini vans that followed set routes and would stop anywhere along that route to pick up or discharge passengers.

One day I took a 2-hour break from work to attend a local beer fest. As with most events we attended, it was serendipitous. I was sitting in my office, when I realized that rock music and all manner of amplified shouting was wafting through my the window on the breeze. I couldn't tell from whence it came, but it certainly sounded intriguing, so I called Laurie and asked if she et al wanted to come down and check it out. Et al didn't (the boys are a bit stick-in-the-mud-ish at times), but she did, so we set off in search of the source. Turned out it was a beer fest on the main square, in front of the national museum, with tents representative of all the local brews, plus Eckes, from Turkey. They had a covered stage set up, with an emcee, live music, and every manner of scantily-clad young woman scampering about. Included in the scampering was a dancing act to recorded Spanish music, that comprised a male and two female dancers in traditional-looking, although scanty (for the women, anyway) Spanish garb, and two cheerleaders, complete with pom-poms. Another dancing act featured three young men in hip-hop garb, danc-ing (quite well, actually, if you like that sort of thing) to hip-hop music. They were joined on stage by three young women (platinum blonde, red, and black hair) dressed in sort of mini-skirted nurses uniforms. It was a bit hard to tell, actually, as they kept them on for but a moment, before shedding them, leaving themselves in lime green bikinis. Lau-rie and I had somsis (triangular meat pies that looked a lot like apple turnovers) and beers; then I suggested that we'd seen more than enough scantily clad females and dragged Laurie away (wait, maybe it was the other way around).

We celebrated our one-month anniversary in Kyrgyzstan by going to a dance "spectacular" (that's how it was billed) and out to dinner. The spectacular wasn't quite. It was sponsored by the French and Ger-man embassies. As nearly as we could tell from the introductions (in Russian, German translated into Russian, and French translated into Russian), the choreographer was German, and the cellist was French. Both improvised; either his playing to her dancing, her dancing to his playing, or (my bet) a bit of both. Then a bunch of her students, and (we assumed) a bunch of his students came on stage and (we assumed) im-provised to each other. Laurie thought it was "interesting." Jesse opted for "weird." Annie said she'd seen worse (citing a 4½ hour post-mod-ern, discordant quasi-opera she'd once taken in at the Lincoln Center). Cooper said he liked that it was short (1-hour-ish). I'd always been a bit leery of the do-whatever-you-feel-like-and-call-it-art school of culture, but there was one section in which the dancer and the cellist interacted in a playful manner (she pretending to help him play; he pretending to hit her with his bow) that I sort of liked. Dinner was at a local cafe (pretty much like any small restaurant), of which there were about one every other block. The menu was in Russian, but we (especially Laurie and Cooper) had transliterated our Bulgarian and learned enough "real" Russian to make out pretty well. Cooper and Jesse had lagman (home made noodles covered with a thick sauce of meat, onion, tomato, garlic, and pepper chunks). I had aslan foo (cold, spicy Chinese soup made with the same kind of noodles). Annie had guy fan (pretty much the same as lagman, only on rice, instead of noodles). Laurie had goulash (nothing like what we called goulash the States: meat and vegetables grilled and served in a little brown gravy with a side of rice). With the bread, beer, bottled water, coke, and tip (10 percent automatically added on), the bill came to 473 soms (at 40 soms to a dollar, that was about $12 for the five of us). That wasn't much, but of course our perspective changed when we were pulling down a whopping $200 a month.

Jesse showing off his treasured (by him only) new suit.

Chapter 2
October

Laurie and I went on a weekly trek to buy cereal—about three miles round trip. Jesse was a real cereal hound. He generally had at least one large bowl for breakfast; then at least one more as a snack sometime during the day—usually just before he went to bed. The rest of us had an occasional bowl, so that amounted to a lot of cereal in a week, and it wasn't easy to get in Bishkek—they used it more as a dry snack, sort of like we would potato chips or peanuts. We could get it in small, snack-sized boxes at several nearby stores, but it was very expensive that way. We found a store about three blocks away that had two kinds (one sort of like chocolate flavored corn flakes that Jesse really liked, and one sort of like regular corn flakes that I liked) in bulk, so we bought it a kilo (about two pounds) at a time. The woman obviously thought there was something very wrong with us. The first time, she refused to sell us a whole kilo of each, assuming that our Russian wasn't good enough to understand just how much that was. She would allow us only a half-ki-lo of each. When we came back three days later and wanted another half-kilo of the chocolate kind, however, she relented and began selling us a kilo at a time. The problem was, we bought her out in three weeks, and she didn't seem to be able to get any more. So, the closest we could find it then, was a store about a mile and a half from our apartment. They had about five kinds, but Jesse only really liked two of them: the chocolate flakes and a sort of sweetened oat or wheat stars. The first time we went there, the young woman didn't believe we could really want a kilo of each, and wouldn't sell it to us until she found an English speaking manager who confirmed that, yes ("for some strange reason only Americans could understand," I'm sure she added in Russian) we really did want two kilos of cereal. I made Laurie carry it, and walked a bit away from her so when everyone looked at her like she was crazy for even being in possession of that much cereal, I could look around and whistle like, "Her, oh, I'm not with her; I've never seen that crazy woman before." She's took to carrying a black cloth bag big enough to hold two kilos of cereal with nobody the wiser. Our new supplier was a big store, and when we bought them out of both kinds a month later, we weren't worried, as we were sure they would get more in soon. When we showed up a week later, the English-speaking manager (who was very nice to us in a "be kind to the feeble minded" sort of way) assured us they would have more of both the next week and sold us a half-kilo of some little chocolate-filled-pillow-shaped stuff that Jesse accepted in the meantime.

One thing I liked as much as Jesse liked cereal, was ice cream, and—unlike China, Thailand, and Bulgaria—they had good ice cream in Kyrgyzstan. Just about every block in the downtown area, some little old lady (bless their entrepreneurial little souls) would come out each morning and set up a stand where she would sell something—usually homegrown produce or homemade crafts. Some of them, though, could get ice cream at a cut rate (probably from a relative who worked some-where in the manufacturing or delivering process). They would drag a small freezer out, and (depending how close they lived to a good sales spot) anywhere from ten to hundreds of feet of extension cord, and some had as many as 25 various kinds of popsicles and ice cream bars, cones, and sandwiches for sale at 5 to 15 soms (12 to 37 cents). One of my favorites was Smack, a delicious vanilla ice cream bar dipped in chocolate and rolled in sesame seeds. We usually patronized the lit-tle old ladies, rather than the (less frequent) trailers with the walk-up windows from which we could order scoops of ice cream in cones. We actually liked those better, but we generally couldn't see into the tubs to point at the kind we wanted, and the only flavor I knew how to say in Russian was chokolat' (an indication of just how meager my command of the language was), and that wasn't my favorite. I wished I knew the Russian for stuff like "cappuccino chocolate chunk," or "cherry Garcia." On the other hand, their flavors at the stands generally ran to the less exotic. Conversely, the bulk ice cream at the market came in numerous varieties of here-to-fore (by us) un-sampled complexity. We bought them based exclusively on the picture printed on the lid. They came in 1/2 liter, one-liter, 1 1/2 liter, and two-liter aluminum containers that looked like small, flimsy versions of the pans the church ladies back in the States brought their hot dishes in, except the top edges crimped over flat cardboard lids. Well, more accurately, we bought them based on the picture and our recollection of how the last purchase of that picture tasted. It wasn't as easy as it might sound. As I said, they came in very complex varieties, which made the pictures 1) very complicated, and 2) remarkably similar. It helped if we bought the two-liter size, as the pictures were larger (a handy rationale, anyway), but even then, about the best we could be relatively sure of was that it had either a vanilla or a chocolate base. We knew the Cyrillic for "chocolate," so the process of elimination principle came into play. I hated banana ice cream, so I learned to recognize (and avoid) that. We considered saving the lids (with pictures) of our favorites, so we could take them with us to compare, but the ladies who ran the shops thought were a pretty questionable bunch anyway, and we were afraid that we might just put us around the bend with them. We couldn't have them refusing us service; after all, we did buy our food there.

On the way back to the apartment one day, I was starving and wanted to stop for lunch at one of the plethora of wonderful outdoor cafes. Laurie said she was probably hungry, but couldn't tell because she had to pee so badly. In the States, we'd have just stopped somewhere to use the "facilities," and then gone on to lunch. It wasn't quite that simple in Kyrgyzstan. They had public restrooms (few and far between) but we had to hold our breath when we walked by them (and they were underground), let alone actually trying to go into one. And most of the cafes did not have restrooms. Luckily, we were near Silk Way, one of

The American University in Central Asia.

The row of banners across from the university that added color to the square.

439

Some of our favorite bread being loaded into a Lada in front of a neighborhood bakery, for distribution to neighborhood cafes.

the very modern, very upscale new department stores. It had four floors: half cell phone stores, and half everything else (as with all the up-scale department stores). At one end of the first floor they had (semi) public restrooms. "Semi" because first, not just anybody could get by the guards to enter the store. They had a discerning eye for anyone who didn't look upscale. Second, only the upscale (and we counted ourselves firmly in their midst) were willing to pay two soms (it was only about five cents, but that was a lot of money for most people in Bishkek) to use the bathroom. We were. After that distraction was taken care of, Laurie realized she was, indeed, ready for lunch. We split a draft beer and each had a serving of lagman boso. The lagman part was soft, thick noodles (like spaghetti on steroids) tossed in a bit of oil with small pieces beef (or chicken, or mutton) and chopped vegetables, and a lot of garlic. The boso part meant it was served "dry" on a plate, rather than with a soup base in a bowl. On the side we had a basket of a special kind of bread that all of us really liked. We hadn't learned the name for it, because we hadn't really needed to. Generally, when we ordered bread with our meal, it was what we got, and anyway, all the bread there was so good that it didn't really matter. In the market, they had numerous stands that sold only that kind of bread, so all we had to do was tell them how many loaves we wanted. Actually, they had about three varieties, so we had to either point or take the one they gave us by default if we didn't specify. It was baked in little one-room neighborhood bakeries, in brick ovens heated by open fires. We didn't have any trouble telling where those bakeries were, as we could smell them for a block in every direction—two blocks downwind. The loaves looked sort of like great big bagels (from eight to 16 inches in diameter, depending on the variety), except the hole in the middle (about 1/4 the width of the loaf) didn't go all the way through. It was blocked on the bottom by dough about the thickness of a medium-crust pizza. It cost about 12 soms (30 cents) in restaurants; about eight soms (20 cents) in the market.

We found several local dishes that we liked. First, a steamed dumpling (of a size that we could hold—if they weren't so hot—about three in one hand), stuffed with ground meat (usually mutton). Second, a version of lagman served on rice instead of noodles (a favorite of Annie's). Third, a cold Chinese noodle soup (a lot like lagman, only fewer noodles, more chopped veggies, and soupier; very spicy, with quite a bit of vinegar in it—actually, nobody liked that one but me. Jesse's and Cooper's favorite was what they sometimes referred to as a hamburger, other times just as a sandwich. They started with a hamburger bun and added shaved meat (beef, chicken, or mutton) off a loaf just like the Greeks used for gyros, mayonnaise, shredded cabbage and carrots, tomato slices (except Jesse said "nyet" to the tomatoes), cucumber slices, French fries, and ketchup. The rest of us decided they weren't bad when we got used to them. At some stands we could get them with shredded lettuce instead of cabbage and carrots; minus the cucumber slices, the French fries, and the ketchup.

One class of food they had a lot of were pieces of fried or baked bread stuffed either with cheese, meat, or something sweet. In the case of the something sweet and the cheese, they sometimes overlapped. One dessert that both Laurie and I liked a lot was sort of like a (hand-sized) turnover, filled with a sweetened cheese about the consistency of a cottage cheese/cream cheese mixture. For lunch, we often had just a couple of the meat or cheese pies. They were quite filling and delicious, and at 10 or 12 soms (25 to 30 cents) apiece, we couldn't beat the price. They also had a staggering variety of baked goods. I think Annie was addicted to a delicious tort-like thing, filled with what seemed to be a kind of custard, and topped with berries and powdered sugar.

One morning as Laurie and I were having breakfast in our kitchen, with the door to the balcony open for the fresh air and the view of the mountains, we heard amplified music coming from the direction of the park to our south. True to our philosophy that anytime you hear loud music in a developing country you should follow it, we set out right after breakfast. On the courtyard of the Kyrgyz National Theatre, two blocks from our apartment, was a huge bank of loudspeakers, from which issued a seemingly random mix of country, jazz, semi-classical, and rock music. The streets in front of the theatre had been roped off and volleyball, basketball, and football (which people in the States know as soccer) courts/fields were marked off. On a nearby table were numerous trophies, t-shirts, and certificates. We ensconced ourselves at an outside table of a nearby café and ordered coffee to wait and see what transpired. Between 8:30 and 9:00 men swept the leaves and acorns from the delineated areas, much to the consternation of a growing number of rag-tag looking groups (teams?) that were trying to practice on them. At 9:00 a man whom we were led to believe was the director of the Kyrgyz Olympic program stepped to the microphone and began to speak. The by then significant number of (mostly middle aged) folks dressed in varying renditions of sporting gear stopped practicing and gathered to listen. His short welcoming speech was followed by a couple of others; then a stirring (and very loud) recorded rendition of the national anthem. Then (accompanied by the blaring mix of music described earlier) everyone broke up into teams and began competing. We watched for a while; then made our weekly trek for cereal. On our return trip we stopped to see if anything new had been added. It's good we did, or we would have missed the entertainment spectacular. It seemed every amateur dance team and vocal ensemble in the city (if not for miles around) had been enlisted to perform simultaneously with the sporting events. For example, some large person in a muppets-style costume, complete with oversized head and three-fingered hands danced to "Itsy-Bitsy, Teeny-Weeny, Yellow, Polka-Dot Bikini," backed by four very young, very amateur girls. It was a sight to behold, represented the flavor of the entire proceedings. As nearly as we could deduce; given that 1) the coming Monday was Professors Day, so it wouldn't be too off-base to assume that weekend was some sort of educators weekend, 2) the contestants looked like they could have been school teachers (granted, they could have been a lot of other things as well), and 3) Laurie was able to make out a few of the words (in Cyrillic) emblazoned on their t-shirts and the huge banner stretched between two trees; and

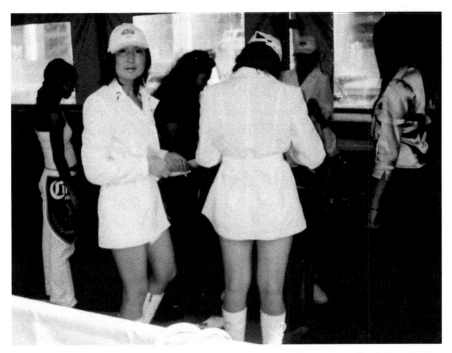

*A couple of the less-scantily-clad waitresses
in a food booth at an exhibition in the Sports Palace.*

although none were conclusive evidence for, neither were they evidence against our theory: it was some sort of celebration of sports (that part was pretty easy) in education (a bit more of a stretch, but quite possible). Whatever it was, it fell firmly into the category of "a real hoot."

A week later, we went to our usual cereal supplier. Had we been naive enough to expect them to have been resupplied with Jesse's favorites, we would have been disappointed. We settled for—more to the point, Jesse had to settle for—the un-chocolate-covered-corn-flake-like version. We then headed off to the sport palace, where we had noticed a new banner earlier in the week announcing some sort of exhibition (we couldn't make out just what kind of exhibition, but figured, as the last one—agricultural products—had been free, it wouldn't hurt to give it a look). Well it wasn't (quite) free, but cost us each 5 soms (about 12 cents) admission. Turned out it was a sort of mish-mash of mostly home goods, but with a liberal dash of food, a few stalls with automotive goods, and a pretty impressive fashion show of career apparel. If nothing else, our question of where the waitresses in one of the tents at the beer fest two weeks ago had gotten their very garish and equally revealing costumes was answered. Given the crush of humanity at the event; coupled with the Kyrgyz propensity to ignore personal space (to the

443

extent of thinking nothing of planting their hand firmly in our backs and pushing us if they didn't feel we were moving along fast enough); and the fact that many of the women had obviously come to save some money on show specials (rendering us virtually defenseless, faced with the bludgeoning power of their heavy packages); and others had seen fit to bring one or more of their small children (which we had to be on constant guard to avoid crushing, or at lest poking their eye out with an errant finger), it wasn't right at the tip-top of my favorite activities of the week. Still, it was an experience that I quite possibly would not have had if I'd spent the year in the States.

I had been playing the ugly American, complaining that the university staff had made no effort to let us know about any cultural events going on in the area, let alone helping us experience any. In response to my complaints, they announced that they had arranged a trip for the new international faculty to Ala-Archa, a national park situated in a nearby mountain gorge. We met (extra jackets, water, and lunches in hand), as instructed, at the university at 10:00 on Saturday morning, where we piled into a mini-van and set off. After about an hour of driving through ever more impressive mountain scenery, on ever less impressive roads, we arrived at a beautiful spot where the road ended at the confluence of two glacial gorges. The woman who was serving as our guide said that there was a very nice restaurant nearby, and that if we would let her know what we wanted for lunch she would put our orders in so that our lunches would be ready after we finished hiking. She seemed a bit taken aback when we informed her that we had brought our own lunches (as we, but obviously not she, had been instructed). She then told us that the gorge to the left was more rugged and more beautiful, and reached the glacial face in five kilometers; and the one on the right was less rugged but less beautiful, and reached that glacial face in seven and a half kilometers; and that we had two hours to go as far as we liked on either one, eat our lunches, and get back to the van. Well, obviously, if we stood a chance of making it to the face of either glacier in that time, it would have to be the nearer one, so the hardier of us set off up the left gorge. Well, yes, it was beautiful, but in a rugged vs beautiful contest, rugged would have won hands down. If I remembered what I learned in my undergraduate geology minor, the left gorge was significantly younger than the right one, as it comprised two things: water and rock—more specifically, very cold, very fast-moving water, and stretches of loose (break-your-ankle-unstable) fist-to-head-sized stones, alternating with stretches of very stable car-to-house-sized (virtually un-navigable) boulders. Of course this ruggedness quotient did not make itself clear until around the first bend, by which time we were pretty well committed. Suffice it to say that we did not make it to the glacier face. We did, however, make it out of sight of the others before stopping for a leisurely lunch; then scrambling, goat-like back to the beginning of the other trail. As we still had some time, we walked up it a ways before returning to the van. We felt a bit betrayed by the descriptions we had been given. The second gorge was way less rugged (as in possible to hike up), but every bit as beautiful, and I was convinced that we'd have made it, if not actually to the glacial face, at least close enough that we could have lied about it with a semi-clear conscious. The trip home was uneventful, and after two extra-strength aspirin and an equal number of equal strength drinks, I was able to get to sleep. The next morning it took only the aspirin to get me up and moving.

We were pleased (as was Jesse) to find, on our next weekly cereal hunt, that they had chocolate flakes. We knew without even looking, as the young woman who always waited on us began beaming the moment she saw us. She was very pleased to show us that the chocolate flakes had, indeed, arrived. If the Kyrgyz weren't so reserved in public (a holdover from the Communist era), I'm sure she would have broken out with the Russian version of, "Tah-Dah!"

In mid-October, Jesse was thrilled when he was asked to be "co-singer" in a rock band—the only one (they claimed) in Kyrgyzstan with a native-English-speaking (singing) vocalist. As nearly as we could tell, he owed his newly-found fame not to whom, but to what, he knew—specifically, a kitten. He was on his way to an 8:00 class one morning, when he heard a plaintive mewing issuing from behind one of the classroom doors. It was locked, so he talked his teacher into getting the key and opening it. The mewing, not surprisingly, was coming from a kitten. What was surprising was the presence of that kitten in a locked classroom, in a university building guarded 24 hours a day, seven days a week, by at least two seemingly able-bodied men at each door. But, there it was, and there Jesse was, and Jesse being who he was, just leaving it there and re-locking the door was not even a consideration. The only two options, as he saw them, were 1) feed it, give it water, and hold it until he could find someone to adopt it; or 2) feed it, give it water, and hold it until, failing to find someone to adopt it, he could convince his pushover parents to let him bring it home, "just until he could find someone to adopt it." Surprisingly, we were spared the latter, as he found the cute little beast a home with the two "Gothic Girls" as they were commonly known, for the obvious reason that they were probably the only two young women in the country who looked as though they could sprout fangs and go for the jugular. Actually, it turned out (as it so often does) that looks were deceiving. They were both very sweet. They had just spent a year in the States, and it was "the look" they brought back with them. It took all day to find a home for the kitten, but in the process, Jesse met virtually every woman at the university (and even a few of the men), who stopped to talk to and pet the cute little thing. Long story short, one of them invited Jesse to audition for her band.

The guards mentioned earlier were also the keepers of the keys. We faculty, not being deemed responsible enough, were not permitted to have keys to the classrooms, or even to our offices. Instead, each morning at 7:15-ish, when I got to the university, I had to sign out the key to my office with the guards at the door. They were also supposed to check my ID each time, but (thank goodness) stopped that farce after about two weeks. We were supposed to keep our offices locked when we went out, so, as I shared an office, I was expected to either hand off the key when I left, or if my office mate wan't there, turn the key in at the guard station. Then when she came back, if the door was locked, she was supposed to run downstairs and get the key, or alternatively, go to get the key first, and if it wasn't there, assume that I was in the office so she could get in. It was, obviously, a needlessly complicated system (even worse for those who were four or five to an office), so we just made copies of the keys for everybody. The first person to arrive checked out "the" key and left it lying on a table near the door, and the last person out checked it back in.

As it was October (very cold by Kyrgyz standards; nicely cool by ours) it got ever more difficult for Laurie and me to find cafes where we could have our Saturday and Sunday morning coffee outside. Virtually all that offered only outside seating had closed for the year. Most of the ones that had seating both inside and out had moved all their tables and chairs inside. The ones that still had outside seating clearly intended for it to be used in the afternoon, after it warmed up some. They seemed to have a hard time believing we wanted to sit out there in the morning, when it was, after all, cold.

Jesse's "friend-who-just-happens-to-be-a-girl" invited us to go with her to a free display of contemporary art titled "In the Shadow of Heroes." We understood that it was in the national museum, so weren't surprised when she suggested we meet there at 11:00. We were surprised when she started to lead us directly away from the entrance to the museum. In fact, the display was in a series of tunnels and rooms excavated under Ala-Too, the main square, where Lenin's statue once proudly stood, arm extended (presumably) over the populace gathered in the square before him (before he was ignominiously moved to a smaller square about two blocks away—where, ironically, his arm now points directly at AUCA, across the street). The tunnels and rooms housing the exhibition looked suspiciously like they had once served as a dungeon, which (if that were, indeed, the case) was apt, given the content of most of the "pieces." Although some were large photographs, and a couple were sculptures, most were videos—either shown on large-screen TVs, or projected onto walls. Actually, my favorite, titled "Black Square," was shown on a small screen set into the wall and matted to look (at first glance) like the only painting in the show. Closer inspection revealed that it was a mass of insects that started out as a black square on a white background. The swarm slowly lost its shape, becoming, eventually, an amorphous mass. I certainly liked it better than the video titled "I Love Naomi, Naomi Loves Fruit," in which a college-age woman, sitting on a toilet explained in Russian (with English subtitles) the reasons she loved the black American model Naomi Campbell. After each reason, a computerized image of Naomi was shown, illustrating the truth of the young woman's statement. For instance, she told us that Naomi loved fruit, followed by Naomi lying in a bed of fruit. A cartoon balloon appeared containing the words "I love fruit," then the pieces of fruit begin to drift up and disappear into Naomi's mouth. I liked that one better than the scratchy black and white video of a young man getting dressed up in a tuxedo, apparently preparing for a big date, who then went into his back yard and hung himself from a tree. I didn't like that one better than anything else. Actually, it was a much better show than I'm able to make it sound. Granted, it was very strange, and overall, a bit depressing, but it really was interesting, and I did like much of the work.

Afterward, we went to a café for lagman. That in itself was not unusual, as virtually every café (and there was one about every other block) served lagman, but this one had a window wall, behind which we could watch them make the noodles. We got seats right on the other side of the glass. It was fascinating, and the lagman was some of the best we'd had. The next day, Laurie and I had lagman for lunch. It may seem strange that we would eat the same thing several days in a row, but when you consider there were numerous versions (vegetarian, chicken, lamb, pork or beef; either in a soup base, without the soup, fried, or served with the noodles and sauce separate; with short noodles, long noodles, one really long noodle, or rice instead of noodles; and each café or restaurant made its own version—sort of like chili in the States), and all of them are basically pretty delicious, it gets more clear how we could have eaten it every day and not gotten tired of it.

That Saturday morning I went in to my office to catch up on some work. After about two hours, the security guys started pushing me to get out of there, as there were several hundred protesters in front of the parliament building next door. The guard at our front door claimed they had been drinking (almost certainly true), many of them had guns (probably not true), and it could get nasty (highly unlikely). They were really pushing me to leave, but I wanted to get my work done, so I told them that if anything flared up, they could hustle me out the back door. They agreed, and left me alone until I left two hours later. I walked by the parliament building on my way home, and except for the (rather lethargic) police presence, it looked more like a very large picnic. When it started to rain, the throng got eminently peaceful. In fact, pretty much everybody not intimately involved pretty much ignored it. The next day, when the sun started shining, things perked up a bit. I had pretty much a grandstand seat from the window of my second floor office, and it was basically just a crowd of people listening to someone talk into a microphone and then chanting for a while. As nearly as we were able to gather, they represented two factions: one was against the prime minister, calling for his ouster; the other was for him, encouraging him to hang in there. At any rate, there was no indication that it was anything other than an internal dispute, and nobody outside the two factions was in danger of any sort. The university administrators weren't taking any chances, however, and cancelled classes for four days.

We took advantage of the break to take a four-day trek around Lake Issyk-Kul, the second biggest (after Lake Titicaca) alpine lake in the world. We generally didn't like tours, so had considered using public transportation, stopping at three towns and finding places to stay for the night, and finding the local attractions on our own. We decided, however, that we would probably spend more time handling logistical problems than actually taking in the local attractions. We had met, Eleanora, a graduate student at a university in Bishkek, who payed for her schooling by operating a one-person travel "agency," and who had offered to arrange the four-day tour for the five of us for $900, everything included. We thought that seemed pretty expensive at first; then we got to figuring how much it would cost if we did it on our own, and decided it would probably be worth the extra few hundred dollars to be able to relax and enjoy the trip. We decided to give her a try. She and our driver, Sergey, picked us up Wednesday morning at 10:30 in a very comfortable Toyota mini-van (a bit short on leg room, but nothing we couldn't live with), and we set off. We stopped after a couple of hours for lunch: tea and bread, served by an old woman in a roadside yurt. It was a bit lame and touristy, and we were afraid we had made a mistake.

*Jesse showing off his resemblance to one of the balbals
in a field near Cholpon-Ata.*

Our worry was misguided, however.

We spent the first night at Royal Beach Resort, a relatively posh, modern complex on the north side of the lake, where I had attended a conference the first weekend in September. We got there about 3:30, so had time to walk into the nearby village and back; then relax a while before a delicious dinner of chicken and rice (preceded by soup and salad; followed by dessert and coffee). Breakfast at 8:00 was hot cereal and a lukewarm hamburger. Near the village of Cholpon-Ata, we drove up into the foothills of one of the three mountain ranges in view at all times, to a several-acre site replete with petroglyphs, carved stone heads, and the remains of some stone walls and alters. The heads were about two to four feet tall, and were carved totem-like stone markers called balbals. We were guided through the site by a very knowledgeable, Russian-speaking woman, whose explanations lost something in translation by our guide, whose English left something to be desired: "Is a deep (with impressive antlers) on a big bone (as in boulder)." She was a sweetie, though, and her English was mostly endearing. When she was concerned about whether Laurie's jacket was adequate, she asked, "Do you cold?" There were times we would have liked a bit more eloquent explanations of what we were seeing, but we kept reminding each other

Jesse riding into a rugged gorge in the Chong AkSuu Valley.

that her English was far better than our Russian.

At Grigorievka, we drove several miles up into the Chong Ak-Suu Valley. The main highway was significantly worse than any of the blacktop roads in the States, so any time we "drove" somewhere off the main highway, the dirt tracks over which we crept were of the five-mile-per-hour-creaky-wooden-bridges-over-which-you-hold-your-breath-and-squeeze-your-partner's-hand-tightly variety. Ella (for short) had arranged for us to ride horses further into the gorge from the point that Sergey decided he would risk his van no more, but said mounts had not yet arrived. She and Sergey stayed to set up a picnic lunch, while the rest of us set off on foot with the understanding that the man with the horses would catch up with us. The good news is that he did. The bad news is that he had only three horses for the five of us. Jesse, Cooper, and Annie all agree that the horseback ride into the gorge was one of the high points of the trip. Laurie and I agreed that the hike was pretty darned nice, too.

After our picnic, which comprised enough delicious food for any dozen of Attila's horde (true for every meal of the trip), we set off for Karakol (on the far eastern end of the 100-mile-long, 40-mile-wide lake. Just before we entered the town, however, we took a side trip to the Przewalski museum. Przewalski was the man who, between 1870 and 1885, made four major exploratory expeditions throughout Eastern Asia, settled in Karakul at the end of his fourth trip, and died of typhus at 49 after drinking water from the Chuy River. The Karakolians were so impressed with him (despite that one significant lapse of good judgment) that they renamed the city after him. Ten years later (presumably tiring of being Przewalskians), they reverted to the more easily pronounced Karakul. The little museum was truly fascinating, and we would have liked to spend more time, but for the fact that several of us were in danger of succumbing to hypothermia in the unheated space. Also dusk was fast approaching, and as the building seemed without the benefit of electricity, we felt we had best find our way outside in the remaining light.

From the Przewalski museum, we went to a guesthouse in Karakul for the night. It wasn't of the quality of our rooms at the Royal Beach, but still quite nice. For dinner Ella took us to a restaurant where she said we could get excellent Russian food. She recommended their specialty: pelmeni (sort of like tortellini in a light broth). We had bought uncooked pelmeni in the market and prepared it at home, and it had been pretty ghastly, so we were a bit leery, but when in Kyrgyzstan...." We (actually, Laurie and I—the young ones were less adventuresome) gave it a try. It was delicious.

Friday morning we awoke to a breakfast at the guesthouse of hot (well, lukewarm) tuna and macaroni, and cold (well, lukecold) coleslaw. After breakfast, we toured (outside—we couldn't go in, as we weren't Muslims) a mosque built by a Chinese architect and 20 Chinese craftsmen. They started it in 1906, taking one year just to carve the pieces and another three to assemble them—entirely without nails. It looked like nothing more than one of the many Buddhist temples in China, but, except for a 10-year hiatus when the Bolsheviks made it into a storehouse, served as a mosque—men only. The women's mosque was several blocks away, and several steps down on the impressive architecture scale—in fact so far down it was indistinguishable from any of the thoroughly unimpressive houses and shops that surrounded it. From there we moved on to the Holy Trinity Cathedral—inside too (after the women covered their heads) despite the fact that we were only Lutheran. It was an Orthodox church that started as a yurt with the founding of the town, and was in its fourth iteration, following destruction by both earthquake and fire. As equal opportunity repressionists, the Bolsheviks tore off its five beautiful gold onion-shaped domes in the 30s, and made it into a nightclub. It had been restored (including the domes) except

Cooper demonstrating his artistic talent laying out a small ala-kiyiz in the artists home/ studio near Karakul.

for exterior paint, and (especially the murals of the saints) cut quite the impressive figure.

Next, Ella announced, we would visit a handicrafts showroom. Here we go, we thought, junk city, where she earned a commission by leading the rich foreigners to the alter of commerce. She may have gotten a commission, but we were dead wrong about junk city. It was a small workshop and showroom, run by a woman and her daughter. The quality of their goods (most produced by the two women, some on commission, but none mass produced) was exceptionally high, and the prices exceptionally low. The moment we walked in the door, I was drawn to a beautiful shyrdak, a hand-sewn rug made from three layers of heavy felt. The one that kept whispering my name was about 5½ feet by nine feet; and was charcoal, green, and red. We had seen some similar in Bishkek, but of lesser quality, for $400-$600. We bought that one for $140. As an added bonus, it turned out it was made by a woman who was the news anchor on the local television station. Ella tried to move us on to the city museum, but we rebelled. Instead, we spent another hour, fascinated, as the woman showed us how she made shyrdaks and chiys, decorated panels made from reeds woven together with wool cords (sort of like some roll-up window shades in the States, only much classier). She then took us across town to her home, in which her husband had his studio. He was an artist who, instead of oil paints or watercolors, created his art with wool, resulting in a piece (to be used as either a rug or wall hanging) called an ala-kiyiz. Some of the wool he used in the natural color of varieties of sheep; some he dyed. He sketched his designs with colored pencil on poster board; then transferred them to a fluffy mat of wool three layers thick. When we got there, he had laid out a beautiful, freeform, pattern (mostly natural colors, but with bright splashes of dyed wool) in the driveway. It was about six by nine feet, arranged on a chiy that extended a foot or two all around it. To illustrate the process, his wife helped Cooper lay out a small ala-kiyiz, about a foot and a half square. When I asked how he got from the fluffy mat before us to a solid felt rug, he said something that Ella translated as, "I kick it." Taking into consideration Ella's endearing (although—when we really did want to know the details of an artistic or historic process—maddening) way with English, I assumed she meant that he placed it in some sort of press. Well, they then poured boiling water on it (and Cooper's), rolled them tightly into the chiy, rolled the chiy tightly into a sheet of canvas, and begin kicking the whole thing up and down the driveway. While he did that for 20 minutes—the first of two times they did the wetting/rolling/kicking process—his wife took us on a tour of their house, which doubled as a gallery for his work. By then Ella said we wouldn't have enough time to visit the city museum. That announcement had the effect of telling someone who had just finished a bottle of expensive Champaign there wouldn't be time for a quick beer. The experience was head and shoulders above everything else on the trip (well, for Laurie and me, anyway; the young folks stuck with the horseback ride).

We liked the man's work so much that we commissioned him to do a wall hanging for us. He asked us what we would like as the subject of the piece, and we were at a loss on what to tell him. He showed us a sketch of a piece he was considering. It was to be about two feet by four feet, all in natural shades of wool from black to a grey so light it was almost white. The content was a semi-realistic portrayal of the field we had visited the day before, with to bulbuls in the foreground, and three wild horses running across the barren field in the background. We

*The little old guy in his traditional eagle hunter's robe
and hat holding his falcon.*

were so taken by it that we agreed immediately, and asked how much it
would cost. When he told us the equivalent of $60, we didn't hesitate.
He said he would have it done in a couple of weeks, and would deliver
it to us in Bishkek.

Our next stop was a dusty little village about halfway down the
south side of the lake, where we were to experience eagle hunting. It
sounded a lot better than it panned out. Ella knocked on a gate and a
little old guy in a cheap suit appeared. When he saw us, he scuttled back
inside, reemerging decked out in traditional eagle hunter's robe and hat.
He took us into his eagle-falcon-dog-sheep-and-goat-ravaged back-

yard, where he displayed an eagle and a falcon that were as impressive as their surroundings were un-. He said something that we didn't catch, grabbed the falcon and a burlap bag that Ella said he said contained two pigeons, and set off for his Lada. The best part of the whole experience (Cooper and Jesse wholeheartedly agreed; Laurie and Annie remained non-committal), was what followed. He opened the driver's door and unceremoniously tossed the pigeons into the back seat. He then just as unceremoniously tossed the falcon into the front. It flapped its way over to the headrest of the passenger seat, where it found purchase for its talons, and subsequently, at least a fraction of its dignity. We followed in the van, stopping on the way out of town to pick up the old guy's grandson, who plopped unconcernedly into the passenger seat, eye-to-beady-eye with the bird. Therein, the high point of the experience. We drove on to a field (barely) outside town. We climbed a (small) hill. We watched as the grandson released an obviously nearly comatose pigeon that sat on the ground looking dazedly around. We watched as the little old guy released the (admittedly impressive looking) falcon. And we watched as he missed the seemingly drugged, certainly stationary pigeon, and had to go back for it—not even flying, but hopping. He was pissed when the old guy hurried down and took the corpse from him (like he deserved it), so he would still be hungry enough to attack the second (just as groggy) bird. This one didn't fly either, but at least he glommed it on the first pass. Then we all stood around like gawkers at a train wreck and watched him rip his ill-gotten gains to shreds.

That bit of psudeo-Kyrgyz culture out of the way, we headed for our next guesthouse, which turned out to be decidedly less posh than the last, let alone Royal Beach Resort. The showers were downstairs, in another building; and the toilet another half block further on. The mattress pads were so thin that Cooper and Annie chose to put both of theirs on one twin bed and snuggle in. Laurie and I, firmly into the sleep-better-on-a-hard-bed-than-a-tightly-packed-one stage of our lives, and Jesse, in the "neah" stage of his, chose to make do with our beds as they were. After dinner of a decidedly American-ish stew, we all (exhausted) tumbled (gingerly, so as to avoid bruising) into our beds. Following a breakfast of hot cereal, lunchmeat, cheese, bread, cookies, and hard candy (most of which found its way into Jesse's pockets "for later") we headed home. The last leg of the trip could only be described as "long." It traversed the decidedly least scenic part of the lake and the lake-less home stretch into Bishkek. The best thing that could be said about it was that we did not stop in some lame tourist-yurt for tea. We arrived home tired but happy, ate out (as nobody seemed to have the slightest inclination to cook) at a local Chinese restaurant, watched a no-redeeming-social-value movie, and retired to our very own beds.

Two weeks later, we got a call from the artist in Karakol, informing us that he had finished our hanging and had brought it to Bishkek; would we meet him in front of the State Museum of Fine Arts that evening. We said we would, and despite our experience with the lateness of Kyrgyz folks, were there a few minutes early. We waited a half hour; then decided we must have misunderstood, and he had said "in," rather than "in front of" the museum. We entered, paid the small fee, and were pleased that it was the opening of an international exhibit called "The Horse in America and Kyrgyzstan." It was an extensive show filling three of the rooms of the museum with some very fine pieces of art. When we walked into the second room, I was a bit ahead of Laurie. When I said, "Laurie, come here," there must have been something in my tone of voice, for she hurried over—to find me standing, stunned, before our wall hanging. We were standing there, trying to get our heads around the fact that a piece of art that we owned was on display in the national art museum of Kyrgyzstan, when the artist approached us, smiled, and said, "I hope you don't mind waiting a couple of months before you take it home." We didn't.

Our weekly cereal treks took Laurie and me about a mile and a half south of our apartment. About three fourths of the way there last weekend, a well-dressed man, probably in his late thirties, approached us and began speaking in Russian. He asked us (we thought) whether we spoke Russian, so we said no. Then he asked us (we thought) where we were from, so we said the United States. Then he asked us (we thought) if we were tourists, so we said no, we were professors at AUCA. Then he asked us (we thought) whether we wanted to rent an apartment, so we said no, we already had one over on Orezbekova Street. Then he told us (we were pretty sure) that we were headed in the wrong direction; that Orezbekova Street was about a mile northwest, so we told him we knew that, and were walking to a store another half mile further south to buy cereal. He looked at us as though we were from another planet, shrugged, said something (which we thought was have a nice day), got into a nearby Mercedes, and drove away. As we continued walking, Laurie and I realized that just before he approached us we had been looking at a street sign (one of the few) trying to 1) interpret the Cyrillic, and 2) memorize the name of one of the cross streets. In light of this realization, we reconstructed the exchange, and came up with this likelihood:

Him: Can I help you find something?
Us: No, we don't speak Russian.

Him: So, you aren't lost?

Us: No, we're Americans.

Him: I have my car right here, would you like a ride somewhere?

Us: No, we're professors at the American University.

Him: Do you live in an apartment nearby?

Us: No thanks, we already have one on Orezbekova Street.

Him: Orezbekova? That's all the way on the other side of town, and you are headed directly away from it. Are you sure I can't give you a ride?

Us: We know; we're going to the store to buy cereal.

Him: OK, I give up, you guys are even crazier than the other Americans I've met.

Us: Thanks, you too.

One day near the end of October, our office manager informed me that the 18 boxes of books (that I had sent the last week in July) awaited us at the post office, and that a van would meet us downstairs at 11:00. It was 10:55—not bad lead-time for Kyrgyzstan. I reminded her that we were talking about a lot of heavy books and, as my experience had taught me, that Kyrgyz drivers were not lifters, and wondered if anyone (other than me) was going along who was. She said that oh, yes, two men would come along to carry the boxes. I went up to the English office and got Laurie (just in case), and we got downstairs just as the clock struck 11:00. At 11:15, I went back upstairs and asked the office manager how long we should wait for these supposed men and their phantom van. She said, "Oh, are they down there already?" I said, "No, that's the point—we are; they aren't." She said, "Oh, let me call." She did, spoke at some length in Russian, hung up, turned to me, and said, "They are somewhere." She suggested that we wait in my office and they would call her from downstairs when they arrived. I allowed as how that sounded good, so we did. At noon, I went back to the journalism office to tell her we would be in the cafeteria eating lunch. Nobody was there. We went downstairs to find the van (empty) sitting out front. As we pondered the situation, the driver approached (I recognized him by the fact that he unlocked the van and got in without so much as acknowledging our existence). I asked him if he was going to the post office and he said (I thought) that he was. I asked him where the two carrying-types were and he had no idea what I was talking about. Now, I had gotten Laurie just in case, but I had learned long before that the key to successfully taking advantage of a person's good nature is not to take too much advantage, and I intuited immediately that we were way over the line there. I had noticed the department chair having lunch in the cafeteria, so threw the situation into her lap. She went to the nearby office of the guy who was the boss of the guys who carried stuff. When she returned, she said they were sending only one carrying guy. We returned to the van, the carrying guy (who, in fairness was almost big enough to count as two) arrived, and we set off (only an hour and a half late). The driver parked about a block from the post office, and both he and the big guy poo-pooed my efforts to convince them that we really were picking up a lot of books.

We went in with the big guy and watched him spend about ten minutes getting anyone to admit that 1) we were there to pick up mail, 2) they were there to give people mail, and 3) there was any logical connection between those two concepts. That step accomplished, he and the young woman from the post office who had been first to relent set about figuring out how to get the books from where they were in the bowels of the post office building to where they needed to be in the relatively distant van. But first the paperwork. Fifteen minutes later (given that her schlupping a half ton of books up to her window wasn't even a consideration), she led us into the aforementioned bowels. The post office had a little-known rate called "M-Bag." To get that rate, each box had to be sealed inside a canvas bag, and 18 of those bags awaited us. When the big guy saw the 18 very large canvas bags, I could tell by his expression that he finally got it.

The young woman undid the drawstring on the first bag and dumped the box out onto the floor. To be more accurate, she dumped a couple dozen books and the remains of what once was a box onto the floor. Realization began to dawn on the big guy's face. When he saw that the contents of the second bag had fared no better than those of the first, he began pleading with her not to open any more, but to let us take them bags and all. There followed a surprisingly short, and surprisingly unheated discussion, the result of which was that she agreed. I didn't understand the language well enough, but I was beginning to understand the culture well enough, to be pretty sure that he promised her something to sweeten the deal. He went to inform the driver that they were, indeed, picking up a lot of books, and that he would have to get a darned sight closer than he was. The good news was that he got right up beside the post office. The bad news was that he was on the other side of the post office from where the bags were piled. The good news was that the big guy carried two bags for every one Laurie and I each carried. The bad news was that 18 divided by four was still four and a half trips. It was almost worth it to see the driver trying to figure out how he was going to get all those bags, plus the four of us into that little van, and realizing that, despite the fact that I was both an American and a professor, perhaps I hadn't been so far off in the warnings at which he had so recently scoffed. He did get all the bags in, however, and we did have (barely) enough space to get in ourselves. As soon as we started back, the big guy got on his cell phone, and I could tell with certainty that he was demanding that every able-bodied man in the physical plant be waiting at the university to help unload and carry those bags to the journalism office on the second floor. Four of them were, and they made fairly short work of it (although I noticed that the big guy opted for the old one-bag-at-a-time routine this time—I thought I had noticed him fading a bit on the last trip at the post office). The "I told you so" center of my brain got a further warm fuzzy as I watched realization dawn on the faces of the department chair and the office manager (the same department chair and office manager who had scoffed at my questioning whether so many books would fit comfortably in such a small office). The only person seemingly completely undismayed by the finally fully comprehended mass of books seemed to be the vice-president for development. She came to my office to assure me that I was no more than one small step below the gods in the estimation of those charged with administering the institution. So, if it is better to give than to receive, I was approximately a half ton to the good.

Chapter 3
November

We had two holidays the first week in November, and both of them involved gatherings of people. That, however, was absolutely all they had in common. November 3 was Orozo Ait, the end of Ramadan. November 7 was the eighty-somethingth anniversary of the Bolshevik revolution, officially known in Kyrgyzstan as Day of October Socialist Revolution. I was unable to find anyone who could tell me why the Day of October Socialist Revolution was celebrated in November. In fact, I had no idea why they celebrated it at all, as they were very proud of the fact they had thrown off the chains of communism (read socialism), and were embracing democracy (read capitalism). In fact, several people I talked to said that the holiday had been banned in Russia, as well as many of the former Soviet Bloc countries. Be that as it may, November 7 in Kyrgyzstan was Day of October Socialist Revolution. I got the feeling they still celebrated it just so they'd have one more holiday.

On the morning of the third, Laurie and I had set out for a walk when we heard amplified chanting from the main square, so (following our any-time-you-hear-amplified-voices-or-music-or-both-follow-the-sound-because-it's-sure-to-be-something-interesting theory) we headed in that direction. We noticed that the streets and sidewalks on all sides were clogged with parked cars, and people were hurrying toward the square (far more cars and people than were in evidence at any time during their independence day celebration). Then we noticed that it wasn't people, per se, but men and boys who were doing the hurrying; not a woman in sight. As we approached the square (about two blocks away) police shooed us off, so we were forced to observe from a distance. We got close enough, however, to see that thousands of men and boys were crammed into rows in the square, with more filling in the streets and sidewalks leading to it, all responding to the call to prayer—the chanting we had heard. They all had spread their prayer rugs facing the booth to the west that presumably held the mullah who was leading the prayer. Actually, he must have done a lot more than just lead prayer, as his voice went on for about an hour before the assembled multitude actually knelt and prayed (which only lasted about five minutes). Given how little use the mosques seemed to get, we assumed it was sort of equivalent to Easter and Christmas back home, as far as peak attendance went. As Orozo Ait was supposed to be accompanied by maximum good deeds and unfettered giving, the streets and sidewalks surrounding the square were full of all manner of beggars, in every stage of decrepitude, all of whom were being studiously ignored by most of those hurrying to prayer. In fact, well into the prayers, a well-dressed man in a late-model Mercedes came speeding through the beggars, blasting his horn, narrowly missing several who had leapt, shuffled, or hobbled out of the way (depending on their degree of decrepitude). He screeched to a halt in the middle of the street, as close to the praying throng as he could get, and ignoring the police officer who was clearly telling him he couldn't leave his car there, rushed to join in the last minute or so of the prayers. As soon as they finished, he rushed through the beggars back to his car and (scattering beggars in all directions) careened away, in good graces with Allah for yet another year.

Laurie and I spent the next weekend in Talas, a town in the northwest of Kyrgyzstan. We went with three other women on the AUCA faculty (Lucie, my office-mate; Elmira, our department chair; and Marie, a visiting professor teaching research methods) and a woman (Gulnara) from an NGO responsible for preserving holy sites in Kyrgyzstan. Lucie, Elmira, and Gulnara were going to hold a focus group in conjunction with a research project they were conducting. Marie was going as an unofficial consultant in the research process. Laurie and I were going because we wanted to see Talas, and it was the perfect opportunity, as Gulnara was familiar with the area, had made all the arrangements, and had offered to show us around during the time they weren't conducting their focus group (which would take only Saturday morning). It didn't make us feel bad that we would miss attending the new AUCA president's official inauguration.

Those of us from AUCA were to meet Friday at noon in front of the university, and take a taxi to the West Bus Station, arriving at 12:15. There we would meet Gulnara and hire a mini-van for the 200-mile ride to Talas. We actually got to the bus station at 12:15, as four of us were Westerners and Elmira went to graduate school in the States, so we all had some understanding of the concept of being on time. Gulnara was Kyrgyz, so we weren't surprised when she wasn't there. Elmira, as the native Russian speaker (Lucie was semi-fluent; it was her fourth-best language of the seven she knew), negotiated with the drivers. After five minutes of verbal sparring that seemed to us to border at times on fisticuffs, she told us we had engaged the services of a nearby van, and that we should put our bags in it, which we did. We asked how much it would cost us, and she said she was offering them 400 soms apiece from the six of us (a total of about $60), and they wanted 500 apiece. I asked if maybe we shouldn't wait until that issue was settled before we loaded our bags, and she said, "Nah, they'll come down." We settled in to wait for Gulnara. After a few minutes, a man got into the van and asked us to move so he could back it out. I asked Elmira where he was going, and she asked him. He said to check the air in the tires. All four of the Westerners said some version of, "Not with my bags, your not." He looked appropriately hurt that we didn't consider him a paragon of trustworthiness, but stopped, and we unloaded our bags. He shut off the van and climbed out. I asked Elmira, she asked him, he told her, and she told us that he had decided to wait until we left for Talas—yeah, right. He never did check the tires, as far as I saw.

By 1:00 Gulnara still hadn't shown up (bordering on late, even in Kyrgyzstan) so Elmira decided to walk to the other end of the "station" (really just an unofficial spot along the street near the edge of the city) to see if just, perchance, she was waiting for us there. Sure enough; in a few minutes she returned with the missing Gulnara in tow (without her bag, however). It seemed she had hired a van at the other end of the station, had loaded her bag, and was waiting for us. Her driver suggested that he get gas while they waited, and she bought it. Elmira re-entered negotiations with our (prospective) driver. They settled on 430 soms apiece. We piled into the van. We drove to the other end of the station in the vain hope that the driver of the other van had not absconded with Gulnara's bag. Lo and behold, he hadn't. He returned it to her. She said he wasn't even angry about the mix-up that had lost him the job; we all felt appropriately ashamed that we had ever doubted him for a moment. She loaded it into our van. As we settled in to take off, a man came over and began to talk with Elmira and Gulnara. It seemed he wanted to ride with us to Talas. They told him the van held six and the driver—exactly how many were already in it. He said he knew that, as it was his van, and that he would provide his own seat. A long, seemingly very complicated discussion ensued. Of course virtually every discussion seemed pretty complicated, as we could understand only about every 20th word. The short version we got in translation was that the young man behind the wheel was not a "qualified" driver—a fact that did not instill much confidence in us, as we had been told the route to Talas was a dangerous one that wound through the second highest pass in the country. He had a valid license, however, and the owner (whose name was Dulat) was a "qualified" driver, but the Kazakh police had confiscated his license (for some undisclosed, but—he insisted—unjust reason) and had not yet returned it. He proposed to ride along, the "unqualified" young man driving during the less-demanding, more-likely-to-be-stopped-by-police-checking-for-licenses part of the trip; he driving during the vice-versa part. Given, with his proposed scenario, what seemed a precipitously less-likely chance of driving over a precipitously steep cliff, we relented. We all felt significantly better, as well, when further discussion with the Russian speakers revealed that a more accurate translation would probably characterize them as "more-" and "less-experienced," rather than "qualified" and "un-." That settled, the owner hurried away, returning quickly, carrying his "seat": a tiny wooden bench, about a foot tall and 18 inches wide. It fit neatly in the aisle beside the second seat, but I couldn't imagine (as he was a pretty good-sized guy) that he fit nearly so neatly on it.

Finally at 1:15, only an hour late (pretty good, by local standards) we set off, Kyrgyz pop-rock blaring from the speakers about a half-meter from my face. I wasn't crazy about pop-rock music in the States, but I'd have taken it hands down over Kyrgyz pop-rock (that is, I would if I'd had a choice). The good news was that we soon left Bishkek, and consequently, all radio signals, behind. The bad news was that I had no sooner expelled a sigh of relief as the last dim vestiges of static faded away, than the driver popped in one of his two tapes of Kyrgyz pop-rock. Turned out each tape was a half hour per side. Turned out the trip (which, being about 200 miles, we naturally assumed would take about four hours) took six hours. Suffice it to say that a week later, some of those songs were just beginning to fade from my memory.

Not far outside Bishkek, the road (a pretty decent—by Kyrgyz standards—narrow, two-lane blacktop) began its increasingly steep ascent into the mountain pass. It reminded us a lot of the road from Red Lodge, Montana, over the Beartooth pass to Yellowstone Park. After uncountable hairpin turns, we arrived at the 1.5 km (very dark, very narrow) tunnel that signaled the 12,000-foot apex of the pass. Drivers in the tunnel all kept to the center, headlights on full bright until the last possible nano-second, when they (sometimes) dimmed their lights swerved enough to (barely) miss each other. It might sound as though such actions were unique to tunnel driving, but in fact, they were accepted practice at night on every highway and byway of the republic. Partway down the other side of the mountain, the driver stopped at a roadside vendor to offer us the opportunity to partake of a refreshing draught of kymyz, the Kyrgyz national drink. Kymyz was fermented mare's milk, and it tasted every bit as good as that sounds. It brought to mind a mixture of 1/4 cup of vinegar mixed into a quart of buttermilk, with a pinch of mold spores added, and strained through an old leather shoe. They said it was an acquired taste. Laurie and I took their word for it.

Laurie trying fermented mare's milk for the first (and last) time.

Two hours of the trip was over the worst dirt road I had experienced since…well, since the last time we took a road trip outside Bishkek, and that was on our trip into the Chong Ak-Suu Valley, on a dirt track not intended for regular travel. The road to Talas, on the other hand, was smack in the middle of the primary international route between the capital cities of two Central Asian nations: Bishkek, in Kyrgyzstan, and Tashkent, in Uzbekistan. They had planted large signs of the "pardon-the-inconvenience-of-our-construction-dust-while-we-make-improvements-to-better-serve-you" kind at each end of the worst section of road. The problem was that 1) the "inconvenience" had been going on for years; 2) judging from the dearth of construction equipment and personnel in evidence, it would go on for many years more; and 3) the "inconvenience" comprised crawling along at 10 to 30 miles an hour, swerving incessantly back and forth, and bouncing disconcertingly up and down, so that we got a clear feeling of how those bobble-head dolls on people's dashes must feel, and scraping bottom far too frequently to be at all comfortable—all with a glaringly noticeable absence of guardrails between us and the yawning void below. If, however, the kilometer of glossy blacktop near the halfway mark of the two-hours of end-to-end jolts was any indication, the great grandchildren of the Kyrgyz citizens "inconvenienced" by construction dust had a lot to look forward to. When we were there, however, all it did was torture travelers with a glaringly clear portrait of unfulfilled potential.

At 7:15 we pulled into beautiful downtown Talas. We couldn't really see it, as darkness had spread its silky wings, but we knew it had to be beautiful, from the three neon fireworks bursting repetitively at the top of tall poles over the central square, reflecting eerily from the bronze face of the huge statue of the city's favorite son and its claim to fame: Manas himself. It would be impossible to overstate the importance of Manas in Kyrgyz culture, history, and literature. He was sort of like Columbus, George Washington, Abraham Lincoln, Paul Bunyan, Pecos Bill, and Johnny Appleseed, all rolled into one. The Manas cycle of legends is 20 times longer than the "Odyssey," and just as epic in proportion. It tells of the exploits of Manas, a larger-than-life warrior, in claiming and defending from all comers the homeland of the Kyrgyz people—important stuff. Somehow, a 14th Century tomb just east of Talas had become accepted as Manas' tomb. Everybody seemed to realize that it wan't (in fact, it was the 1334 burial site of the daughter of a regional governor). That did not, however, stop the government from constructing (and people from flocking to) an extensive complex comprising a museum; a sculpture court; an arena for horse games; a path up a nearby hill topped with a large monument; buildings for killing, cooking, and eating sacrifices; a restaurant; and (of course) numerous gift shops. The main draw, however was the mausoleum wherein the body of Manas himself would have lain, if 1) he ever had a body, 2) anyone knew where it was if he did, and 3) nobody else beat the citizens of Talas to it.

We had dinner at a very nice cafe. The Kyrgyz differentiated between levels of service, variety of offerings on the menu, ambience, and cost by calling high-end establishments restaurants, and everything else cafes. In fact, the real defining factor seemed to be cost, and therefore the social standing of the patrons. For us, social standing fell far below cost on our list of priorities, so we almost always ate at cafes, and many of them were as nice as most of the restaurants. After dinner we walked a block to the fourth-floor apartment Gulnara had arranged for two nights at 250 soms (about $6) a person. It wasn't elegant, but certainly serviceable. I coped with sharing one bathroom with five women by using the Blitzkrieg method: getting up early, getting in fast, and getting out quickly. Laurie got up and used the bathroom as soon as I was done, so she and I were out walking around town by the time the others got up. It didn't take all that long to walk around town—twice. By 10:00 Saturday morning we had done just that, and were seriously wondering whether the battering we had taken on the trip up had been worth it. We had arranged to meet the others after their focus group meeting, for lunch at the café where we had eaten the night before.

Both the driver and Dulat had proven to be very personable, as well as being prepared to offer us reasonable rates both to drive us around Talas and for the return trip to Bishkek, so we had engaged them for the weekend. The others had used them to get to their focus group and back. When they arrived at the café, we couldn't help noticing that they had added another person. We couldn't help noticing because the additional person was quite noticeable: a scrawny old guy with no front teeth, and a wispy white goatee, dressed in traditional cloak, hat, and high black boots. He was clearly joining us for lunch, and, as it turned out, was the primary reason Laurie and I eventually decided the battering on the way up had indeed been worth it. During lunch Gulnara explained that he was both an Islamic mullah and a guardian of an important traditional Kyrgyz sacred site. We had known that most Kyrgyz people were Muslims, but what we didn't know was that many of them also accepted a traditional spirituality, much of which was based on hundreds of sacred sites throughout the country. Exactly what made those sites sacred wasn't clear, as the reasons are generally lost in the clouds of time. With most, however, it seemed based in good part on the presence of fresh water—not surprising, given the fact that the Kyrgyz people were historically nomads in an extremely dry country. Anyway, it seemed there were three kinds of Muslims in Kyrgyzstan: 1) those who believed in both Islam and the Kyrgyz traditional spirituality ("believed in," rather than "practiced," as very few seemed to work very hard at the practice of either); 2) those who believed only in Islam, but were tolerant of those who believed in the Kyrgyz traditional spirituality; and 3) those who believed only in Islam, and thought those who believed in the Kyrgyz traditional spirituality were sinners. As the run-of-the-mill believers didn't generally vest a whole lot in the process, the divisions didn't cause much dissension there, but the same could not be said of the mullahs. Those who were both mullahs and guardians caught a lot of grief from those who didn't accept the possibility of being both. Gulnara explained that the scrawny old guy (actually, he only looked old; I found out later he was four years younger than me) as a guardian, was greatly bothered by the fact that some mullahs could not accept his dual practice. As a cultural anthropologist, Gulnara began studying the sacred sites as an academic interest, but gradually came to see herself as a "dual" believer. She said she considered the guardian a sort of friend and mentor; lucky for us, as he agreed to take us to his site, which was not generally visited by Westerners or non-believers.

He lived in a village a four-hour hike from the site, and walked to it and back at least two, but usually three times a week. For our visit, he (never having actually done so himself) allowed us to drive almost all the way to the site, and walk the rest of the way. That would have been all well and good if we had been driving an Abrams tank. As it was, our driver was able, through an impressive display of either courage or lack of good sense—after traversing a log bridge that threatened to collapse at any moment (three of the group insisted on getting out and walking across on the way back), driving several yards up a fairly virulent creek, and skittering semi-sideways on a slope we probably had no business being anywhere near—to get his poor old Chrysler Town and Country within a good, strenuous hour's hike up the gorge. But only after working out an arrangement with the clairvoyants. It seemed a group of about a dozen clairvoyants had arrived from Bishkek with a sheep they were intent on sacrificing at the site; then camping overnight, following whatever rituals attend such sacrifices. Gulnara felt we had first dibs, and was loath to share the experience with the clairvoyants (nothing against clairvoyants, per se, she just thought it would wreak havoc with our karma). It would have been a simple decision for the guardian—we were there first, he had an agreement with Gulnara, he was her mentor—except that one of the clairvoyants happened to be some kind of mucky-muck in the regional government. We hadn't actually seen these folks—they were out of sight (whether intentionally or un- was never made clear to us) in a brick building about 100 yards away. The negotiations (which took about 15 minutes) transpiring through the guardian (who scuttled back and forth between our respective redoubts) resulted in a compromise. They agreed to give us an hour's start; Gulnara agreed to let them send a couple of young guys on horseback up with their provisions and the sheep. An hour would have been more than enough time to get in, see the site, and get out, but we didn't just look, we took part in many of the sacred rituals, as well.

The first 10 minutes of our hour we spent standing beside the van listening to the guardian tell us the history of traditional Kyrgyz spirituality in general, and his sacred site in particular. It was fascinating, and he was a great storyteller. He would probably have gone on for the full head-start hour, if Gulnara (in the interest of maintaining karmatic separation from the clairvoyants), hadn't bustled us up the path. The driver stayed with the van, presumably to protect it from any passing marauders. Dulat, it seemed, had become a full-fledged member of our little band of pilgrims. After about five minutes, we stopped at a wooden bench and a circle of stones to pray (the guardian prayed; we listened). It seemed it was the ancient burial site of a child, which for some reason, should not be passed by believers without offering a prayer. Said offering complete, we hiked on.

The guardian telling us the history of traditional Kyrgyz spirituality in general, and his sacred site in particular.

Next we stopped in a dry stream bed, and on the guardian's instruction, gathered seven small stones apiece. We carried them a bit further; then stopped in front of a steep rock face about 30 feet high, with ten holes no bigger than bread boxes ascending in a vertical row up its face. He explained that we were to take turns tossing our gathered stones at the rock face. The rules: 1) the higher a tossed rock lodged on the rock face, the more respect we commanded; 2) each rock that came to rest in one of the holes meant that we would be granted a wish; 3) if a rock rolled back to the ground, all bets were off for it; and 4) if a rock ended up bouncing off to the left of the rock face, we were either unworthy, or bad things would happen to us. He explained that we shouldn't really try too hard, as the results were not in our hands, but were determined by the gods, or spirits, or some other forces at work in the universe. I took this instruction seriously, and just sort of casually lobbed my stones in the general direction of the rock face. Consequently, I commanded virtually no respect whatsoever, should not hold my breath in expectation of wish fulfillment, and was generally unworthy in all aspects of my character. It wasn't these revelations, so much, that bothered me, as the fact that not one of those present (including Laurie) seemed the least surprised by them. Everyone else then took a turn, with variously better results. Then a young woman (who had been flitting around near the edges of our karma—with, seemingly, no ill effects) stepped forward and blew the rest of us out of the water. The guardian explained that she was Afghan, and had been there five days, following his spiritual advice and taking part in various rituals, in an effort to shake off some unspecified, but presumably serious, illness that had been causing her to waste away for some unspecified, but presumably extended, length of time. He said we shouldn't feel bad that she had so handily shown us up, as she had been practicing a lot during her stay. Now, that little piece of information certainly left me feeling, at best puzzled, and at worst betrayed. Here I had been, naively counting on the spiritual forces to guide my tosses, assigning their errancy to a general shortcoming in my character, and he was telling me (too late to do anything about it, after some girl had—on false pretenses--shown me up) that practice, skill, and concentration were the determining factors.

We proceeded, grumbling (all of us proceeded; only one of us grumbled). A bit further on, the young woman stopped to pick up a log—not a stick, or even a branch—a full-fledged, Y-shaped log that must have weighed 50 or 60 pounds She was small—maybe 105 pounds, and it became clear that her intent was to carry that heavy, unwieldy piece of lumber the rest of the way up the trail (the steepest, roughest part of which was yet to come), as evidence that her faith had made her well. The steeper and rougher the trail got, the less I grumbled about her stone tossing finesse, until, finally it became clear to me that she deserved all the respect, fulfilled wishes, and general good karma the spirits could spare. She switched shoulders a few times, and even set her load down for a few seconds to catch her breath, but she wrestled it all the way to the top, smiling all the way (albeit a bit strained at times). When we reached the cave at (what we then thought was) the top of the trail, and she finally dropped it, we all gave her a standing ovation. Rather than collapsing in a quivering heap in the corner, she set about building a fire to brew tea for us. While she set about her task, the rest of us proceeded around the corner, where a small waterfall spurted over a ledge about 20 feet above. After pausing to pray (again), we all walked under the falls (a quick, light shower). A short way up the path we came to a crude handmade ladder propped against the face of the cliff. After climbing it and traversing one last section of path, we arrived at a truly beautiful pool of crystal water eroded into the center of a huge boulder. It was clearly the major sacred site. The guardian prayed, and we all drank from the pool. Then we took turns kneeling beside him with his prayer beads draped over the backs of our necks, while he placed his hand on our backs and "read" us. The three Kyrgyz (including Dulat, who by then had become one of the group) said he was startlingly accurate with them. He seemed to have trouble with us foreigners, though. He told me my that my grandparents were nobility (they were, as my fraternal grandmother used to say, "poor white trash," and as my maternal grandfather said, "dirt farmers"); that I was an only child (my brother would undoubtedly disagree); that Laurie and I had only one child (ditto for Jesse and Cooper); well then only one child was living with us (two, unless you count daughters-in-law; then three). Given that track record, I din't think (based on his firm instructions to stop taking "all those pills that I depend on") that I would give up the one-a-day vitamin.

We returned to the cave for tea and bread and one last prayer. While we were there, two young men on horseback arrived with the provisions (including a very large black sheep draped over the back of one of the horses) for the clairvoyants (who, given the elapsed time, could not be far behind). Their imminent arrival, however, no longer seemed a concern, presumably as we had completed any rituals for which conflicting karma might have been a problem. The condition of the sheep, however, was. I assumed it had been drugged to diminish the trauma of its ride up the gorge, but Gulnara said that was not the case. She said it was near death, as the clairvoyants had transported it from Bishkek, kept it overnight, and sent it with the young men up the gorge, all without food or water. We all allowed as how that was at least spiritually amiss, if not downright cruel. On top of everything else, it was black, which Gulnara told us the guardian said was tacky (that wasn't exactly what he said, but that was the idea: not forbidden, but certainly not the best choice). We set off back down the trail, passing the clairvoyants on their way up. Dulat seemed unduly anxious to get going. We assumed that was so we could get back out on the highway before it got dark. That may have been part of it, but it wasn't the biggest part. Once we got into the van and on our way, Gulnara informed us that he had been so incensed at the clairvoyants' treatment of the sheep that he had put it out of its misery—effectively co-opting their sacrifice; making it ours. I could imagine how happy that fact had made them when they discovered it. Back in Talas, we had dinner at the café. Gulnara announced that she would be going to another sacred site the next morning, and asked if any

Two young men delivering the sacrificial sheep the clairvoyants had transported from Bishkek.

of us would be interested in going along. Several of us said we would, and she said she and Dulat would pick us up at 6:00 a.m. The several quickly dwindled to Laurie and me.

We were ready at 6:00, fully expecting time for a leisurely cup of coffee, but Gulnara (very un-Kyrgyz-like) was there right at the appointed hour. We set off in the dark, winding around through the southeast quadrant of town, finally stopping at a seemingly deserted place where the fields began. I was wondering 1) why we had needed to start so early for such a short trip, and 2) how we were going to see the site anyway, as it was still completely dark, when Gulnara informed us that we were trying to find the home of her assistant in Talas, as she was going with us. Technology came to our aid in the form of cell phones (or, as they called them, mobiles), which virtually everyone above the indigent class in Kyrgyzstan had (except Laurie and me). Gulnara called her assistant. They decided it would be too difficult for us to actually find her house in the dark, so they just stayed on their phones, exchanging information about where we were in respect to where she was until we saw her shadowy form (backlit by the feeble sunrise) emerge from beside the road. She clambered aboard and we set off, I (incorrectly) assumed, for the sacred site. In fact, following Gulnara's assistant's directions, we retraced our path (only much more directly) to the apartment building we had left half an hour before. We turned into an alley across the street, stopped, and opened the door. I was thinking, "Now this is really ridiculous, if the sacred site is in the center of town, directly across the street from our lodgings." Gulnara's assistant got out, approached a nearby cottage, and began pounding on the door. Gulnara explained that we were picking up a "builder" who was going along to see what sort of improvements were needed on the sacred site. The builder (after several minutes of intermittent pounding and waiting) appeared and came out to the van. He and Gulnara's assistant got in and I settled in for the trip to the sacred site. We sat and they talked. He got out and went back into his cottage. Gulnara explained that he had agreed, two days before, to go along to the sacred site, but as he had no phone (probably the only builder in Kyrgyzstan without a cell phone), they hadn't been able to get ahold of him to tell him what time we were leaving (I would have thought Gulnara could have walked across the street and told him, but maybe she didn't realize where he lived). He had assumed that we would be leaving later in the day, so wasn't ready, and would take some time to get so. Luckily the driver had his Kyrgyz pop-rock tapes to entertain us while we waited.

The good news was that by the time we finally got there we had plenty of light by which to view the sacred site. "There" was a tiny village comprising a single rutted dirt track between a couple dozen ramshackle cottages. We stopped near the far edge of town. Laurie asked if we'd have to walk far to the sacred site, and Gulnara replied, "Not far." We got out, tightened our shoelaces, made sure we had a bottle of water along, and crossed the street and entered the front yard of one of the cottages, where we gathered around a hole about two feet in diameter, filled with water. it was about as far conceptually from the sacred site we had visited the day before as it could get and still be part of the same civilization. I looked at Laurie, and she looked at me, and it took a concerted effort on my part to keep a straight face. On further reflection, however, and with more information, the concept became easier to accept. We stood there, listening to the gathering villagers (exhibiting,

Kneeling on the floor of the "guardian's" tiny home with what her village had to offer spread out before us.

clearly, a great deal of concern) talk with Gulnara, her assistant, and the builder about how the site could be improved. As we did so, several old women came and knelt over the hole to fill plastic jugs with water, and a dog came to drink from the pool (relieving himself right next to it when he had drunk his fill). As the villagers engaged in animated discussion, Gulnara broke away to explain to Laurie and me that this, in addition to being a sacred site, was the only source of clean water for the village. It was getting easier to see how it might have come to be considered sacred. It seemed that one of the primary concerns was how to make it easier to use as a source of water for the village, without profaning it by putting in a pump or some other mechanical device. After everyone had said what needed to be said, the guardian (the woman who owned the property, and in that case "guardian" only in the sense that she took care of the site, rather than being a holy person as well) invited us in for "tea." As always in Kyrgyzstan, an invitation for tea included (even in the poorest households) as lavish a spread as they were capable of. In that case, we sat on the floor around the perimeter of the main room, leaving enough space in the center for a 4-foot square of oilcloth laid out to serve as our table. On it our hostess placed homemade bread, honey, sugar candy, salads, cookies, and tea. Gulnara, as was proper for the guests, added cookies and candy from a bag she had brought for that purpose. As we ate and drank, a little old barrel-shaped woman came in and began the impassioned relating of what was clearly a complicated story of some sort. Gulnara explained later that one of her sons had been dying. The doctors had no idea how to save him. A holy man told him to spend one day a week for three weeks at this sacred site, praying and performing a series of rituals. By the end of the three weeks, she said, he had fully recovered. It took a half hour for the old woman to tell her son's story, and I took advantage of the opportunity to observe our surroundings.

The room was heated (after a fashion) by a wood or coal fire in a concrete box built into one corner. There were no electrical outlets, but two sets of bare wires stuck out of the concrete walls. The few electrical appliances (a television, a table lamp, and a hot plate on which she had heated the water for tea) had no plugs; just bare wires that were twisted to the outlet wires when they wanted to "plug them in." As the water was heating, we could see that the connection must not have been as tight as it might have been, for sparks were arching between two of the wires. The furniture comprised one small table (about 3 feet by a foot and a half); and a chair that looked as though it had seen many years of hard use, and been repaired numerous times. There were a couple of shelves on one wall that had been fashioned from pieces of a cardboard box, attached with nails along the inside edge; with pieces of string from the outside corners at an angle to the wall to hold the outside edge up. Clearly nothing on them was very heavy. I kept feeling a draft on my feet, and when I looked closely at the nearby window, realized that two of the panes were smaller than the space they were intended to fill, leaving voids about an inch by six inches along their edge. With the exception of one piece, the art on the walls consisted of small pictures cut from magazines. The exception was that one whole wall was taken up by a giant poster of an elegant, modern, Swedish-style living room done in various shades of tan and gold, an immaculate lawn, visible through a huge picture window, falling away to a beautiful seashore. If everyone in the village had sold everything they owned, they would not have had enough to decorate that one room, let alone the house in which it must have been included.

Following tea and prayers, we set off (only an hour behind schedule) to meet the others at our apartment. Gulnara said we simply could not do so, however, without stopping at another sacred site, as we would pass right by it. It was right beside the road, and it would be at least a slight, if not a sin, to zoom by without so much as a quick stop and a prayer. That site comprised nine springs welling out of a cut bank beside the road. The stop and prayer were both quick. Dulat had become so much a part of the group that he led the prayers. After commandeering the clairvoyants' sacrifice the day before, he must have figured he'd earned at least some of the trappings of sanctity. The extra sacred site stop only set us back another 15 minutes. We met the others, gathered our bags, and left the apartment.

Before doing so, however (we had all been in Kyrgyzstan long enough to have learned a few basics) we took advantage of the clean bathroom. Laurie was the last to do so, and I was waiting for her near the door. Instead of the characteristic flush before she reappeared, however, I heard a loud crash (of the uh-oh-something-is-definitely-not-right-here variety). I rushed over, asking what had happened. She opened the door and showed me. The toilet was of the type with a large cast iron water tank hung high on the wall, and when she had pulled the string to flush, the tank had fallen, hitting her on the right hand; then smashing the porcelain toilet to smithereens. Her hand was in far better shape than the toilet, but she still sported some pretty flashy shades of green and purple for a week or so. Everyone else had already gone down to the van, so I got the water shut off; then went down to deliver the bad news while Laurie mopped up as much of the mini-flood as possible. I explained to Gulnara what had happened. Gulnara got the caretaker from next door and explained to her what had happened. The caretaker was scared to death that she would lose her job, but Gulnara assured her that she would point out to the landlord that it had resulted from negligence on the landlord's part, and that she should be thankful 1) that the tank (which weighed about 25 pounds) hadn't fallen while someone was sitting on the toilet, and 2) that Laurie and I were not vindictive, and would not be suing for damages.

By the time we were ready to leave, it was noon, and we hadn't eaten lunch yet. Gulnara informed us there would be no place to eat between there and Bishkek, and wondered if we wanted to wait (six hours) until we got back to eat. There followed a stunned silence, during which we all wondered whether we'd heard her right. Then Lucie (always decisive where food was concerned) responded unequivocally that such a possibility was outside the bounds of rational consideration. Those who understood that she meant "absolutely not" agreed. Other than 1) starting late; 2) being just as torturous as it had been on the way up; 3) presenting several instances when we weren't sure we would avoid ending in a fiery heap at the bottom of a canyon; 4) offering one more opportunity to experience very loud, very repetitive Kyrgyz pop-rock music, the trip back was pretty uneventful. Good news: we weren't very hungry when we got back to Bishkek. Bad news: we were very late (which wasn't really a very big deal, as Monday was a holiday).

On Monday morning (the seventh), Laurie and I were setting out for a walk (actually for our weekly cereal hike, as we had been in Talas all weekend, so hadn't had time then), when we heard amplified uplifting music. The music was emanating from two huge speakers on top of a cute little green antique car that looked for all the world like those conveying pre-war socialist leaders in the old news reels. Said little green car was parked on the small square between the university and the statue of Lenin that used to adorn the main square, but had been relocated following Kyrgyzstan's turning from the communist path. The top of the little green car was quite crowded as, in addition to the speakers, it sported two huge communist flags and an equally huge red and yellow banner proclaiming (I assume) that communism was, in fact, not dead, but merely awaiting appropriate conditions for its resurgence. The crowd was significantly smaller than that of Orozo Ait (by several thousand), and comprised primarily of geriatric but very determined communists and their grandchildren, who were excited to be able to march around to loud, uplifting music, carrying large photos on sticks of a funny-looking old bald-headed guy with a pointy beard, and large bouquets of flowers. It didn't hurt that several of them got to talk into the nice television lady's microphone, either. What the crowd lacked in size, it made up for in lackadaisical-ness. What it lacked in organization, it made up for in joviality. No police shooed us away. In fact, the few police there seemed more intent on their private conversations, than on anything going on around them. After an hour or so, most of the people who had drifted over to the gathering began to drift away. All in all, Laurie and I were ready to make a rather confident prediction that the government of Kyrgyzstan had little to fear when it came to imminent overthrow by the Communists in their midst. In fact, the general attitude of camaraderie evidenced by those in attendance gave support

A meager crowd of Communists in front of the Kyrgyz government building, celebrating the anniversary of the Bolshevik revolution.

to the theory put forth earlier, that the major purpose of the day was to provide another opportunity to do something besides go to work.

Fat Boys, a local café and major hangout for expats, had a bookcase full of mostly mysteries they had collected over the years. We could either check them out (library-like), or exchange some of ours for some of theirs (the only reason Laurie and I ever went there). We went there for that reason Friday, and on the way in noticed a flyer on their bulletin board urging us to buy 2006 Habitat for Humanity calendars. As well as supporting Habitat backing the States, we had helped build Habit houses, so I approached the young woman at the bar and asked how much they were. She said 50 som (about a dollar), so I told her we'd take ten. She paused, and I could tell she was checking her mental Russian/English dictionary to make sure she had understood correctly. "You want ten calendars?" she asked hesitantly, taking no chances. "Yes, please," I replied, in my most reassuring tone. She looked inquiringly at a (fat) man who, it turned out, was the owner (which, to my mind, didn't adequately explain the name of the place, as he had clearly been a man for years, and probably never plural). He came over and calmly (being 'Murican himself, and therefore, not taken aback by our vagaries) informed me that they had only eight, but could get more within a few days. I assured him that eight would do nicely. He sent the (still incredulous) young women somewhere in back to get them. She brought them back and (hopefully) offered to make it nine by adding the one hanging on their wall. I assured her that, no, eight would be just fine, and gave her the 400 som. Laurie and I exited with our books and our calendars, leaving the owner to attempt to explain to her our strange ways (or not, as he saw fit).

The Sunday before Thanksgiving was beautiful. I walked to AUCA from the apartment wearing only a light fleece jacket, and sat in my office with the window wide open. It felt more like late April than less than a week before Thanksgiving. We had a family tradition of inviting anyone we knew whom we thought didn't have another invitation. That year, though, it seemed all of us had been inviting people separately, and when we got to talking about it, realized that it had sort of added up. It was Kyrgyzstan, so some of them wouldn't let us know for sure until sometime Thursday morning. We just figured on 16, and would have lots of leftovers if people bailed out. Given the fact that we had a complete service for six, one skillet with a handle, one skillet without a handle, one large pot, two small pots, one pizza pan, one cookie sheet, six feet of counter space, three burners, and a 15" by 15" oven, preparation would be fun. Also, when our family of five sat down to dinner, the dining/living room was pretty full, so it would definitely be snug. But our attitude was that's what Thanksgiving's all about. If it's not crowded, you must be doing it wrong. We ended up with 12 for Thanksgiving dinner: the five of us, four of Jesse's friends from Turkmenistan, and three faculty from the States. We boiled potatoes in the large pot, waiting until the last minute to mash them (an empty wine bottle worked well for that). We made gravy in the small pot. We used both the handled and the handle-less skillets to steam fresh cauliflower. Laurie had made a pumpkin (actually tikva, which is a type of orange squash, but tastes very much like pumpkin when baked) dessert the night before, so we could use the cake pan for stuffing (which we did, covering it with tin foil and baking it in the oven). We had heard that we could get a turkey at one of the markets near the edge of town, but it wasn't clear whether they would kill it for us. It was clear that they wouldn't gut or pluck it, however, and we didn't relish the idea of 1) bringing a turkey (dead or alive) home on the bus, or 2) cleaning it in the courtyard of our apartment building when we got it there. So, we went out to the market and got three roasted chickens. I carved them, stacked the meat on the pizza pan, covered it with tin foil, and put it in the warm oven with the stuffing after it was done baking. For appetizers, we put together a relish tray of green and ripe olives, radishes, and pickled baby pattypan squash. Also, Laurie had found pretzels in the market, and made a sort of hummus dip out of chickpeas. We washed dishes as we went along, so had both serving dishes and spoons (some borrowed from a friend in a neighboring apartment), as well as counter space in the kitchen to set up a buffet when all was ready. We had put both leaves in the dining room table, and set the kitchen table at one end. Covered with a large cloth, and set with all our dishes and some borrowed from the friend, it looked downright Thanksgiving-ish. We broke out the chairs stored in one of the bedroom closets, and had enough, with three left over (why we had 15 chairs to begin with was anybody's guess). So, once again, we managed to share food and warmth with friends on a day that our family set aside to reflect with joy the abundance that God had given us, and with sorrow how many weren't so fortunate.

Chapter 4
December

I made shorpa (similar to New England boiled dinner) for supper one evening. After we ate, I was sitting in the living room reading, and Laurie was doing the dishes. When I heard her say, "Uh-oh," I figured something wasn't quite right. I was relieved when she stuck her head in and told me the hot water wouldn't shut off. I told her it was no big deal. We could call the landlord the next day and tell him the faucet was dripping. He would get someone to put in a new rubber washer within the next week or so. "No," she said, "I mean the hot water won't shut off at all." I went into the kitchen to have a look, and sure enough, the hot water was poring full-tilt from the faucet, and (of course) it didn't turn off any better for me than it had for her. I crawled under the sink and discovered there were no shut-off valves there. The good news was that all the water pipes (our walls being solid concrete) ran inside the room, so I was able to trace them back toward the source far enough to find shut-off valves behind the refrigerator. While I dragged the fridge out enough to gain access, Laurie called the landlord and told him the problem. He said he would be over in a few minutes. I found that the handles on the shut-off valves were loose on the stems, and did absolutely nothing resembling shutting off (or, for that matter, even slowing) the flow of water. Having no tools with which to work on the shut-off valve, I retraced my steps to the faucet. By fiddling with it, I determined that if I pushed down on the handle very hard without twisting, I could stop the flow. The problem was there was no way I could maintain the force necessary to stem the flow for any reasonable time. I ask Laurie if there was a stick around that I could break off to length and jam between the handle and the shelf about three feet above, to maintain the necessary pressure. She rooted around in the hall closet and came up with just what I needed, and darned if it didn't work.

When the landlord and his 20-something son got there (his "few" minutes translating to about 30), he was very relieved, and told us he had expected to find the kitchen flooded. He removed the stick and tried to shut off the faucet. It didn't work any better for him than it had for us. They did have the tools necessary, however, to make the shut-off valve do its thing. They took the faucet apart and found the stem stripped and turning freely inside the casing, rather than tightening down to plug the hole. They had several old parts, none of which fit, so they put everything back and told us they would send a "master" over the next day to replace the faucet. They asked that somebody stay home until he did so. Laurie said somebody came about 11:00, looked at the situation, and told her in Russian what she took to be that he would get the replacement parts and come back. He didn't. The landlord came about noon, and she told him about the guy who had come (and gone). The landlord tried unsuccessfully to call him, and left. He returned about 1:00 with another guy who looked at the situation; then he and the landlord set off to find replacement parts. Laurie asked what she should do if the first guy came back, and the landlord, on his way out the door, just smiled and shrugged. She took that to mean, "A new faucet on the sink is worth two people hunting for one at the market." I would not have been surprised had I gotten home and found the sink exactly as we'd left it that morning. If so, I would not have been at all upset—increased patience is one of the byproducts of living in a non-Western culture. Besides, we'd still have had hot running water in the bathroom, a few short steps away. As it happened, the first "master" came back about 3:00, installed the new faucet, gave us a bill for the landlord, and left. When the landlord and the second "master" came back later, we gave him the bill, and let him, the first "master," and the second "master" work it out in their own inimitable Kyrgyz way.

One Saturday morning in early December Laurie and I stepped out on our balcony for a breath of fresh air, and noticed a flurry of activity in the yard below. From where we were, it looked like a couple of men were building a yurt. But we couldn't think why anyone would want to build a yurt in the front yard of an apartment, unless they were homeless. More to the point, we couldn't figure why the owners of the apartment building would let homeless people build a yurt in their front yard. On my way to the university, I stopped to ask the men why. They spoke only Russian, and my command of the language was somewhere in the one percent range. Even if the answer were a simple one—which I couldn't believe one with a yurt in it would be, I wouldn't have understood. I thanked the men (one of my few Russian words) for their valiant efforts, and went on to the university. There I was able to find someone who both understood what they were doing, and could explain it to me in English. Someone (she said) in our building had died, and the men were building a yurt in which to keep the body for three days. During that time members of the family would take turns sitting with it 24 hours a day. Friends could visit to view the body, pray, and keep the family member on duty company. So basically, it was the equivalent of a 3-day wake and visitation.

Men building a visitation yurt in the front yard of our apartment building.

Virtually all the buildings in Bishkek were surrounded by fences, and virtually all that weren't unadorned concrete, were either white, brown, blue or green. Not counting the newest, fanciest ones, which tended to be bright yellow with bright green or bright red roofs. The oldest "Russian style" houses were log, covered with wood lattice, covered with concrete stucco. The newer ones, as well as the apartment buildings, comprised heavy concrete frames filled in with brick and covered by the same concrete stucco. The older apartment buildings fell generally into a category graciously referred to as "utilitarian" (read "incredibly ugly"). The newer ones (which were almost exclusively "upscale," leaving the old ones for the less upwardly-mobile) were more varied, both architecturally and structurally, with brick, metal, tile, and stone facing interspersed with the stucco. Most of the old concrete monstrosities had balconies; a nice touch, except the apartments were generally so cramped that as soon as they could afford to, residents enclosed their balconies to provide more living space. The newest houses were also quite varied in style, but still generally used the same concrete, brick, and stucco materials. Roofs were generally either standing seam metal or concrete tile. Some of the newer ones used heavy 3' by 3' plastic sheets formed to look like the concrete tile. The older Russian style houses were often decorated with formed concrete ornamentation on both horizontal and vertical structural columns. Owners of some of the newer ones, in an effort to maintain that traditional look, but avoid the expense (as building costs had gotten much higher) either scratched or painted geometric, curvilinear, or floral patterns on them.

One cultural difference we found very hard to get used to (coming from the Midwest, where everybody looked us in the eye and greeted us) was that the Kyrgyz people (probably a holdover from communist times, when they found it safest to keep their heads down and their mouths shut) seldom made eye contact and virtually never spoke to us. Even people we knew lived in the same apartment building, whom we saw often, coming and going, avoided looking at us or speaking. I decided early on I wasn't willing to accept that particular custom, so I learned the Russian for "hello" and "good morning/afternoon/evening," and started speaking to pretty much everyone I met around home or school. The result was interesting. Many continued to act a bit like I had a communicable disease, but with others, I made great inroads. For example, the old guy who swept the sidewalk and street outside the fancy restaurant near our apartment. I saw him every morning on my walk to work. When I first started speaking, he ignored me. After about a week, he started grunting in reply. About two weeks later, he started responding, but if I said "good morning," he responded with "hello," and vice versa. After about a month, he started responding in kind, but with no real warmth. Eventually, he actually started saying it like he meant it, and sometimes even added other stuff (to which I, of course couldn't reply, as I had no idea what he's saying, so I just smiled and nodded. He probably figured out that I had exhausted my meager supply of Russian. The man who swept in front of the Parliament building next door conscientiously responded with whichever greeting I didn't use. I switched every morning, and so did he. It became one of my favorite bits of humor of the day, brightening the dullest mornings. The guards at the front door of the university generally acted pretty gruff, and treated people as though they were doing them a favor letting them in. I read somewhere that Kyrgyz men often showed friendship with their equals by shaking hands, and if they wanted to convey greater warmth, shook hands with both of theirs. I decided to see what would happen if I started shaking hands with them. At first, they were obviously astonished; I was probably the first professor who had approached them as equals. Very quickly, however, it became clear that they were pleased with the process. They all became very friendly and helpful toward me, and several of them started using the two-hand grip with me.

Another difference in the Kyrgyz culture that drove me crazy (I had grown to accept it in China, but that was more than 15 years before) was how they had no concept of personal space. They decided they were going to walk from one place to another along a predetermined course, and woe to anyone who got in their way. Actually, it wasn't quite that bad; they usually moved just enough at the last second to avoid full head-on collisions, just brushing us enough to let us know they really should have had uncontested right to that space, but had deigned to let ushave a sliver of it. The university buildings (judging from the narrow hallways) were not designed to have hundreds of people moving from one class to another all at the same time, so it was a real crush every hour and a half when they did. Still, it never occurred to students that stopping to chat in the middle of said crowded corridors might prove inconvenient for said hundreds, and they did so consistently. People seemed to have no idea that moving around without paying the least bit of attention to where others were in respect to you would inevitably result in unnecessary collisions, nor did they exhibit any sense of responsibility when they caused such collisions. They would walk out of a side corridor or a doorway without looking, smack into someone; then look at the other person like s/he should have known they were going to do that and somehow avoided them.

The traffic lights in Kyrgyzstan had an extra stage compared to those in the States. From green, they flashed twice, turned yellow, then turned red. Whereas in the States, we generally took a yellow light to mean, "hurry up or you'll have to stop for red," there they often stopped when the green flashed, and virtually always on yellow. Conversely, we virtually always waited for green to go, but there, they watched the green in the other direction and went on red when the green started to flash. Consequently three cars would have run the red light by the time it turned green. It seemed to work OK, as everybody was playing by the same rules (except us—we almost got run over several times until we learned them). Crosswalks had no meaning whatsoever there, to either drivers or pedestrians. The drivers didn't stop, and the pedestrians didn't use them. Given the fact that in a collision between pedestrian and automobile, the pedestrian was clearly the loser, it was just accepted that it behooved people to stay out of the way of cars.

The next Monday, as I sat working at my computer, I heard a loud "crack," not unlike a nearby gunshot. It sounded as though it had come from outside, so I jumped up and hustled to the window to see what was going on out there. Just before I threw open the sash I noticed that it had been, in fact, that very sash that had emitted the "crack." We had double windows (metal frames, with thermal glass) that were hinged on the sides and swung inward (or in the case of the one in question, used to swing inward). The hinges on that one had decided the weight of the window was too much to hold up, and so had quit. The result was that all three of them broke, allowing the bottom corner away from them to drop against the marble sill, giving off the resounding "crack" that had so effectively gotten my attention. The windows were wired with the kind of alarms that had sensors glued to the glass, and the only thing holding the hinge side of the window in place (sort of) was the wire connected to that sensor. As Lucie's desk was immediately under said window, when she arrived later, she was (understandably) a bit nervous about the tentative nature of the situation. She called the "techniques" (as they referred to the repair people), and spoke expressively and at length with them in Russian. Whatever she said must have gotten their attention, as they came over right away (an event that, although not unheard of, was unusual). They inspected the situation, and (Lucie gave me a somewhat emotional translation after they left) declared the hinges broken. She said of course they were broken, that's why she had called them. She didn't need them to tell her they were broken, she needed them to do something about it. They wanted to know what we had done to break them. She told them that I had been using my computer on the other side of the room; did they think that might have done it? Although I appreciated it later in translation, the irony was wasted on them; they were not amused. They said they would have to get repair parts, gathered up the handful of broken pieces from the windowsill, and left. We (silly us) waited for them to return and install the replacement parts of which they had spoken. Two weeks later, when they came back to fix it, the wire still held, and Lucie looked with less frequency (a bit resignedly, although just as nervously) over her shoulder at it. The only thing that had changed was that she had stuffed some paper in the worst of the gaps to help stem the tide of cold air flowing about her person.

Unlike the American university where I taught in Bulgaria, AUCA did not order Christmas trees for us, so I resorted to the same tactic I had used in China. We had a 2-foot Christmas branch that I surreptitiously liberated from one of the evergreen trees in the courtyard of our apartment building. I put it in a water bottle, and set it on the dining room table. Jesse and Laurie made decorations out of green and red construction paper and silver candy wrappers. Jesse's favorite was the Yeti he cut out of green paper (which, at about four inches high, also happened to be the biggest thing on the tree). Every evening he added several more links (alternating red and green) to the paper chain he made. He was delighted when Laurie found him a glue stick, saying that was much easier than Scotch tape for joining the links. We also had an Advent wreath (of sorts). Laurie and I bought five tall, skinny candles at the Orthodox church a few blocks from our house. We were probably supposed to take them into the church to light them, but nobody chased us down when we walked away with them. We filled a large sardine tin with coarse salt and set the candles four around the outside edge and one in the middle. It made for a pretty compact Advent wreath, but it did the job The candles must have had a pretty high wick to wax ratio; they burnt down pretty fast. By the time we did a nightly reading and prayer, we only got about three days out of each, necessitating more trips to the church. Every evening the tree ended up with more decorations, though, as Laurie recycled the wrappings from our Advent candies.

Our Christmas branch and Advent "wreath."

Because we were leaving for India Monday the 18th, and would be busy getting ready that weekend (especially Cooper and Annie, as they would be flying back to the States from India to apply to graduate programs), we decided to have Christmas Sunday, the 11th. At first it seemed kind of weird, but we all worked hard at acting like it really was, and eventually it really seemed like Christmas. We were limited in size of presents, as anything we got we would have to schlepp back home in our luggage, spend an inordinate amount of money shipping it, or use it before we left. Actually, regular mail was cheap, but I wouldn't send anything I really counted on seeing again. Laurie and I were two out of four on actually receiving incoming packages; Cooper and Annie were doing better at four out of five. So, for presents, Cooper and Annie got a traditional wall hanging made from reeds interwoven with wool thread. Cooper got a t-shirt. Annie got a scarf and a set of those carved nesting dolls that looked like a traditional Kyrgyz man and his wife and son, Jesse got an MP3 player (they were down to about the size of a pack of gum) and a music CD. Laurie got a scarf and some traditional Kyrgyz jewelry, and I got a wool scarf and mittens. Pretty slim pickings all around, but I figured a three-week Indian vacation would ease the sting. Besides, what we lacked in presents, Santa made up for in comestible-loaded stockings. Actually, as none of our socks were big enough, he just left large plastic bags full of goodies sitting on top of our "stockings," which, lacking a chimney, were spread on the dining room table with care.

Opening presents on Christmas morning.

488

Cooper, Annie, and Laurie spent much of the day baking Christmas cookies for their students, the people in their office, the people in my office, and anybody else they could think of. Jesse and I mostly just lazed about, although I did help Laurie shop for and cook Christmas dinner. We splurged and bought a very expensive ham (about twice our usual budget for meat for the week), and had a baked ham dinner with all (well, most of) the trimmings. It had snowed a couple of inches earlier in the week, so all in all, it was a pretty darned nice Christmas

Cooper and Annie making Christmas cookies for students, office workers, and others.

My festive cheer was considerably dampened when, the next morning I opened our apartment door to go to the university, and found two 10-year-old boys sleeping on our steps. They had started coming to our door a couple of times a week during Ramadan, ringing our doorbell and, when we answered the door, singing. We assumed it was some custom followed during Ramadan, and as they seemed to expect some payment, we gave them a few som. After Ramadan was over, however, they kept coming, but quit singing. Instead, they would mumble something in Russian. We asked our students what it was all about, and they told us the boys were trying to take advantage of us because we had been generous during Ramadan. They said we should not keep giving them money, as it was probably just a scam of sorts. Subsequently, when they came around, we just closed the door. We tried not to act mean, but I must admit that I was a bit short with them when they showed up one night at 11:00. My attitude changed dramatically Monday morning when I realized they were homeless, and the few som we had been giving them may have been much of what they had to buy food. Our stairwell was heated (sort of), and as we were on the fourth floor, it wasn't freezing, but I could only imagine how it must have felt to try and sleep on bare concrete steps with only a medium-weight jacket for covers. I was pretty upset that I had been basking in my smug abundance and denying them the pittance that might have kept them from going to bed (such as it was) hungry. I went back into the apartment, put part of a loaf of bread in a plastic bag, and (as they didn't wake up) left it lying on the steps beside them. I can't say it made me feel all that much better, but I couldn't see how we could invite them to come and live with us, so was at a loss for what to do. Laurie and I talked about it, and I talked with some people at the university. They told me there were several shelters for homeless children in Bishkek. We had a note printed in Russian that gave the locations and contact information for those shelters to give the boys. They weren't there Tuesday morning, but were Wednesday. We didn't have the note ready, so I left them half a loaf of bread and two big carrots. When we came home that evening, we found part of the bread and one of the carrots still in the stairwell. That made me feel a little better, as they couldn't have been starving if they felt they could afford to leave food behind. I wasn't able to dig into the goodies in my Christmas stocking, though, without thinking about those boys. There is nothing like being faced repeatedly with the stark reality of others' poverty to make you feel shame at your overabundance and selfishness. One of the faculty told me the boys were just trying to make me feel guilty—well if that was the case, it worked quite well.

A friend had sent us a box of coffee and other goodies from the States on October 3. It included Halloween candy, canned pumpkin for Thanksgiving dinner, and other seasonal goodies. We got it Friday. Oddly, however, the timing was more appropriate than we thought. We picked the box up at the main post office Friday, and that evening our doorbell rang. It was a couple of young Kyrgyz boys, and when we answered the door, they began singing and sprinkling oatmeal on our threshold. When they finished and stood looking expectantly at us, we said, "OK, that was very interesting, now what are we supposed to do?" They couldn't muster enough English to tell us, and we certainly didn't understand their Russian explanation. Then I noticed one of them had a plastic bag half full of Halloween-type treats, so I went and got some of the candy from the goodie box we had just gotten. When I offered it to them, they seemed more relieved that we had gotten the right idea than pleased to have more candy. I asked one of the Kyrgyz faculty about it, and she explained that it was some kind of trick-or-treat-type thing connected with New Year. It actually had a name, the translation of which was "The Old New Year," but I never did understand what that meant, or (more to the point) why it was on December 15.

Chapter 5
End of December and January

I arranged for the university van to take us to the airport to catch our flight to India, and to pick us up when we returned. The driver was to meet us on the street near our apartment at noon on the 19th, for the 40-minute ride to the airport, getting us there the requisite two hours before our 2:40 flight. We got down there, ready to go, at 11:45 and waited…and waited. At 12:10, I hustled the three blocks to the university to find out why the van wasn't there. "Oh, but it has been there for a half hour," they insisted. I told them their "there" must be different than our "there," told them where our "there" was, and headed back for our "there," figuring if he wasn't there by the time I got there, we'd hire the fastest taxi we could get our hands on. As I got to the corner of our street, the van, with Laurie, Jesse, Annie, Cooper, and our luggage pulled up. His "there" had been a block north of ours—just out of sight. After I left the university, they had called the driver on his cell phone, and informed him of that fact, and he had driven the intervening block. He had no trouble sensing that I was not a happy camper, and made up some time on the drive to the airport, arriving only ten minutes late.

Our flight, on Uzbekistan Airlines, made one stop, Tashkent—for seven hours. It seemed what Uzbekistan Airlines did (which somehow figured into their ability to offer really cheap fares) was route all of their flights through Tashkent, where they held everybody until the airport was full to bursting; then arranged all the connecting flights to leave in the span of about an hour—between 11:00 p.m. and midnight, when everyone was at his or her finest. That timing, of course gave no consideration to when passengers would subsequently reach their final destination—Delhi at 3:00 a.m., for example. Given the 4-hour flight, minus a half hour for the mandatory safety instructions, a half hour for drink service, an hour to serve and clean up our 1:00 a.m. lunch, and a half hour for the seats-and-trays-in-their-fully-upright-and-locked-position-ready-to-land bustling about thing, that left a maximum of an hour and a half dozing time. By the time we got through customs and found the Left Luggage Office for the bags Cooper and Annie would be taking back to the States but didn't want to schlep all around India, it was 5:00. We figured we could get to our guesthouse no earlier than 8:00, and it was an hour's drive, so we spent two night-of-the-living-dead hours in Delhi airport's less-than-elegant "transit lounge."

Because we were five significantly-bigger-than-Indian-sized adults, with luggage, we had to take two taxis. The good news was that one of them found the guesthouse. Actually, the other one did too, but not for an additional half hour. Our driver, of course, wanted to leave, having (as he saw it) fulfilled his part of the bargain. I didn't see it that way, and refused to pay him until all of us arrived at the agreed-upon destination. As it turned out, the taxis couldn't actually get us to our guesthouse. Where they did get us was alongside a busy four-lane highway in a pretty seedy-looking part of town (of course "seedy-looking was a relative term, applied to Delhi, but it applied there). The way I chose where we would stay, was to read the descriptions of the possibilities in the "Lonely Planet Guidebook," and chose one that I got a good gut feeling about. I'm not sure how that started, but it had worked surprisingly well in the past. The guidebook's description in this case was of a Tibetan enclave "with an ambience that's delightfully laid-back." The more cognizant I became of our surroundings (for which "delightfully laid-back" as a modifier did not immediately spring to mind), however, the less good my gut feeling was becoming. So before I paid the drivers and let them go, I gathered some of the locals (admittedly more Tibetan- than Indian-looking) and asked if we were, indeed, in the right place. They assured me that we were, but that the taxis couldn't fit in the narrow lanes that wound through the neighborhood. They showed us the nearest entrance to these lanes and assured us that our guesthouse was a short walk away. I paid the drivers and we set off.

After only a few steps, the traffic noise began dying away, and our surroundings underwent a profound change for the better. By the time we reached our guesthouse, my gut was feeling abundantly vindicated. In fact, the house and our rooms were spotlessly clean, the staff were friendly and helpful (even letting us into our rooms hours before the posted check-in time), and the restaurant was the best in the neighborhood—all for about $25 a night for two double rooms with private baths and an extra mattress for Jesse. One of our most pleasant surprises was the fact that we were able to stay in such nice places all over India for $20 to $40 a night for the five of us. In fact, following my final accounting, we spent an average of $100 a day for food, lodging, transportation, admission charges, and incidental expenses. At times, admission charges were our biggest expense of the day—$125 total for the Taj Mahal, for example.

We stayed in Delhi the 20th, 21st, and 22nd. The first thing I did at any new place was make arrangements for transportation to our next stop, and for a place to sleep when we got there. In India, arranging for transportation meant either standing in line for anywhere from 15 minutes to an hour at the train station, or paying either the people at the guesthouse or a travel agent about a dollar a ticket to do it for me. I chose the latter, which meant writing down the possible trains and classes in order of preference and trusting them to get me the best choice available. I found them very dependable in that respect. Reserving rooms in the next town was easier. All over India, people had set up computer-linked phone services. When we picked up the phone, the computer recorded where we called, and for how long. When we hung up, it spit out a ridiculously low bill, and we paid the clerk. For example, when we were in Jaipur, I called four numbers in Udaipur (about 450 km away) to reserve a room for our next stop, and it cost less than 50 cents. That done, Laurie and I generally walked around for a couple of hours, just to get a feel for the neighborhood. I usually chose guesthouses that were either right in the center of the old part of the cities (usually more scenic, easier to get around on foot, and closer to more points of interest, but nosier and more hectic), or ones near the edge of town (usually quieter and more relaxed, but necessary to hire a taxi to get to points of interest). I found either was generally less expensive and more desirable than those in the newer parts of the cities. In Delhi, I had chosen the latter, on the assumption that because Delhi is so huge and crowded, after a day of fighting our way around, we would want to "go home" to a more relaxing situation. It was a good choice. Not only was Wongden House in a quieter part of the city, it was smack in the middle of the Tibetan section, which allowed us to experience food and culture distinct from the rest of India. It was a real kick to sit in the dining room at breakfast, surrounded by orange-robed monks. It reminded me a bit of a diner back home on opening day of deer season.

While in Delhi, we visited the Red Fort, whose massive sandstone walls were two kilometers around. It was built overlooking the river in the mid-1600s, at the height of the Mughals' power. We had been asked by a friend on the AUCA faculty to deliver a package to a friend who worked at the Bahai Temple. We were staying on the far north edge of the city, and it was way on the south side, so we probably would not have gone there had we not committed ourselves to that delivery. As it turned out, we were glad we did, as it was a stunning piece of architecture. Built in 1986, it looked like a huge white lotus blossom, and was, in fact, commonly referred to as the Lotus Temple. We also visited Jama Masjid, the largest mosque in India, in which the central courtyard held 25,000 people. Thank goodness there weren't nearly that many the day we were there (although a pigeon count may have come close).

We regretted paying about $4 apiece to get into the National Museum, as the second floor was closed, and the displays on the first floor were pretty lame. The building itself was very impressive, and the murals on all the courtyard and exterior gallery walls were fascinating. Had we but known, we'd have stayed outside and saved ourselves a few bucks. During the mid-1700s a famous Indian warrior/ruler/astronomer built five incredible observatories, called Jantar Mantar, each comprising several massive, surreal-looking structures designed to measure movements of the stars and planets. We visited two of them: one in Delhi and one in Jaipur.

Jesse perched on one of the massive structures of the Jantar Mantar in Delhi.

We spent a couple of hours at Connaught Place, the very upscale shopping area in the heart of New Delhi, stopping, at Jesse's insistence, for our first McDonalds burger in five months. He was quite disappointed, as, being in India where cows were sacred, there was no beef in the burgers. We're not sure what was, but they bore little resemblance to what he had his mouth set for. The fries, however, could have come straight from any McDonalds counter in the States. We spent some time wandering around the parks and fountains of Rajpath, the wide boulevard bounded at one end by the president's residence, and the other by India Gate, a 150-foot high memorial to 85,000 Indian soldiers who died during World War II. Our favorite, though, was probably the crafts museum. Plunked down smack in the middle of the city, this delightful combination of outdoor and indoor galleries had everything from examples of indigenous peoples houses, to amazing archeological pieces, to stalls where we could watch artisans at work. We figured we'd give it a quick look, and ended up spending half a day, including lunch at their little outdoor café. As it was at the beginning of our trip, we were intent on seeing everything we could, and the relaxed atmosphere of the Tibetan enclave was a welcome respite each evening.

Everybody (except me) knows you can't go to India and not visit the Taj Mahal. I didn't see that it was such a big deal, and was all for giving it a miss, but was soundly outvoted (something in the neighborhood of four to one, if memory serves), so from Delhi, we went 200 km south to Agra. Everything I had read said that in a country geared to taking advantage of foreign tourists, Agra was king, so I prevailed upon the others to make it a day trip. We left on the early train from Delhi, and took the overnight express on to Jaipur. When we exited the train station in Agra, I hired two taxis for the day at less than it would have cost (and with far less hassle) to hire individual taxis each time we wanted to go from one place to another. The trick, I discovered, was, before leaving the station, to ask a couple of people (platform workers were excellent choices) how much we should pay for taxis. Armed with that knowledge, it was easy to convince the drivers that I knew what I should pay, and to avoid being taken advantage of. Most stations had what they called "pre-paid" taxi booths. They were government sanctioned, so most people just assumed that if they went there they would get the best price. Not so. I found I could haggle them down, and often get even lower prices from private drivers outside the stations. In Agra, for example, I bypassed the long line at the pre-paid booth and started walking toward the exit of the parking lot. I was immediately approached by several drivers, who offered their services for 800 rupees (about $20) for the day —more than twice what I was told I should pay. I told them I was willing to pay 350 rupees (about $8) apiece for two cars, and when they protested that was too low I turned to walk away. A couple of them immediately agreed to my offer. In the Indian culture, virtually everything was negotiable, and the haggling sometimes got a bit heated, but once the price was agreed on, it was handshakes and smiles all around. For the 350 rupees, the drivers agreed to take us to the train station on the other side of town (from which we would leave that evening) to drop our bags at the left luggage room (for about a dollar) until we returned that evening to catch our train, to Agra Fort, to a good but inexpensive café for lunch (they all had a few from which they got commissions—and free lunch—for bringing in business), to the Taj, and back to the station in time to catch our train to Jaipur. They agreed that only if we had some extra time—without being hurried—would we let them take us to one of the handicraft factories from which they got a commission if the people they bring buy something, or a small gift if they don't. I always made sure the drivers understood that I was familiar with this practice, and had nothing against them making a bit of extra money through it, but that if they wanted paid, they had better not try to bully us into either going to shops in which we had no interest or rushing through the sites we were visiting just so we'd have enough time to stop at the shops. When the drivers held up their end of the deal (which they almost always did), I gave them a sizable tip at the end. When those guys dropped us off at the station that evening, for example, I gave them 400, instead of the agreed on 350 rupees.

So, what about the Taj Mahal? It was big. It was very white. It looked pretty much like every postcard I'd seen of it, except with way more people. It was impressive, but I wasn't nearly as impressed as I was supposed to be. I'm sure it derived from the same perverse part of my nature that won't allow me to read any book on any best-seller list until at least two years after everybody has stopped talking about it. I truly liked Agra Fort. It was on the wrong side of the river, benefiting from far less hype, far less imposing, far less crowded (that probably had something to do with it), and gracing far fewer postcards. But I was significantly in the minority (about four to one, if memory serves). Judging from their "Oohs" and "Aahs," it pretty much knocked everybody else's socks off. Actually, as it was a holy site, we were required to remove our shoes before entering, and Cooper and Annie, opting for dirty feet over dirty socks, took theirs off voluntarily.

We got into Jaipur at about 10:00 p.m. on the 22nd, and called the people at our guesthouse, who sent a car to pick us up at the station. It was the newest and best kept of any we stayed at during the trip. Exhausted after a full day of Taj and travel, we checked in and went to bed. The next morning, the others slept in while Laurie and I walked the mile or so back to the train station and bought tickets on the overnight express to Udaipur. That afternoon, rather than pay a taxi to take us the eight road kilometers to the Tiger Fort, we had him drop us at the base of a cliff on the north edge of the old city. From there, we walked about two km up a switchback trail carved into the rock, to the fort, which was perched on the cliff overlooking the city. We walked most of the walls, reveling in the variety of beautiful views of the city and surrounding countryside. Lunch was in a small courtyard café on the roof of the central building. We made our way back down the path, where our driver waited to take up to some nearby cenotaphs of the local royals. The six or eight cenotaphs were much like cottage-sized versions of the Taj—less impressive in size, but more impressive, in that they were intricately carved over every square inch of their complex marble structures, including the ceilings. We returned to the hotel fairly early, partly because we needed some down time, and partly because I got angry with the driver, who kept insisting that we needed to stop at his favorite showrooms (the ones from which he would get a commission for delivering us to them). I got tired of arguing with him, and told him if he wanted to get paid to take us to the guesthouse immediately. He got my point, and (sullenly) did so. He left even more sullenly when I informed him that his pushiness had cost him a tip.

After breakfast the next morning, we hired an auto-rickshaw with two sets of seats—one facing front, behind the driver, and the other facing the rear—and set out for a day of sightseeing. Cooper and Annie thought it would be fun to sit in the rear-facing seat, with the unimpeded view, so Laurie, Jesse, and I squeezed into the other. That lasted until the first traffic light, when a huge bus came barreling up behind us, stopping about three feet from their noses. They asked if we would mind switching seats. I had no problem with that, figuring if a huge bus didn't get stopped it wasn't going to much matter which seat we were in, as all of us would be mashed under it somewhere near its transmission. Of everything we did and saw in our three weeks in India, that afternoon riding around Jaipur on the back of that little rickshaw was on the short list of my favorites. Jesse, who had acquired a lip ring, and whose hair and beard were getting long enough to turn heads, was the center of attention. Jaipur was a large city on the tourist track, so the residents had seen plenty of Westerners, but (judging from their obvious interest in him) none quite like Jesse. Cars, trucks, bikes, and motorcycles would stop behind us in traffic, and their bored-looking occupants, on seeing Jesse, would come alive. Their reactions ranged from vain attempts (by the women and older people) to be subtle, to blatant curiosity on the part of children and young men (often accompanied by animated chatter and/or giggles). At first I was concerned that Jesse would be upset or offended, but I need not have worried. He used the opportunity to interact with them: waving, talking to them, and laughing at their reactions. I think he was pleased, as I certainly would have been, to serve as the object of so much delight for so many people.

We stopped at The Palace of the Winds, so named because its 5-story pink sandstone façade was intricately carved to allow for airflow. It was built along the main street of the old city by a Raj to allow the ladies of his court to watch the passersby without being seen themselves. We also spent several hours in the City Palace complex. Inside its walls were a series of beautiful buildings, gardens, and courtyards, some of which were closed to the public, as they still served as quarters for local royalty. Jesse's favorite (mine too) was the former Queen's Apartments, which, when we were there, served as a museum for a huge collection of varied and exotic weaponry. Right next door to the palace (with actual—although very tourist-oriented—snake charmers between) was our second Jantar Mantar. As their builder was from Jaipur, hometown pride made that one the most complex and most impressive. It was restored in 1901, at which time all the instruments were tested and found to be amazingly accurate. Of the ten or so instruments, the most impressive was a sundial that stood almost 100 feet tall, and was supposedly accurate to within a couple of seconds.

We celebrated Christmas Eve with dinner at Pizza Hut. It was delightful, because while we were there, the employees were erecting and trimming their Christmas tree, and were obviously putting extra effort into it just for us. They did fine until they began putting chunks of white cotton "snow" on the branches. As none of them had ever actually seen snow, their efforts (not to put too fine a point on it) were pathetic. Just as we were about to go over and lend a hand (having seen our fair share of snow) the manager (who had been to the States) came out and took over. By the time we left to catch our train, they had, under his guidance, put together a Christmas tree that could have stood proudly in any Pizza Hut in Minnesota.

After an exhausting day, we were glad for the chance to get some sleep on the overnight express to Udaipur. And that's all we got was a chance. It was our first overnight on an Indian train, and I was still in trial-and-error mode. At the time I was buying the tickets, the difference in price between what they called "first class sleeper" and "3-tiered sleeper" didn't seem worth the difference in what you got—blankets, for example. Well everybody knows India is a hot country—who needs blankets? Well, the whole south half is, and while there, we didn't. But we were still firmly ensconced in the north half. We found out later that Delhi had gotten snow for the first time in 15 years. Not to put too fine a point on it, we froze our butts (and everything else, for that matter). By the time we got to Udaipur the next morning, we were wearing almost everything we'd had in our packs. Laurie and I were doings "spoons" on one of the designed-for-a-single-Indian-sized-person bunks and Cooper and Annie were dong the same on another. I felt sorry for Jesse, who was "spoonless." When we got to our guesthouse, we were thrilled to find that it had an inner courtyard in which some eminently sensible person had a fire going. We all gathered around it and ordered breakfast, which they brought to us there. Until the sun came up (which wasn't as soon as we would have liked, as Udaipur is on the west side of a pretty good sized string of hills), we only strayed from its warmth to go to the bathroom.

After settling into our rooms in Udaipur and taking nice hot showers, the lazy-bum contingent took naps, while Laurie and I scouted the neighborhood. We were delighted to find that our guesthouse was right in the center of the old town. Well, actually, Lake Pichola was right in the center, but our guesthouse was on the east shore of the lake, which put it within easy walking (or boating) distance of almost anything worth walking (or boating) to. We had a great view of the lake, including the Lake Palace, from both our rooms and the rooftop dining area. The Lake Palace was one of the primary locations in "Octopussy." Consequently, many of the restaurants offered a free showing of the movie (which we took advantage of our first night) following dinner. Jesse was excited, as that made the third James Bond movie location we had visited. While in Thailand, we snorkeled in the ocean surrounding what is commonly referred to as "James Bond Island," from "The Man with the Golden Gun." While in Bulgaria, we spent our Christmas vacation in Istanbul, and saw them filming the submarine-docking scene from "The World Is Not Enough." Actually, we'd almost certainly been to others as well (in Prague, Rome, Bangkok, Paris, and others), but Jesse didn't count them, because they were just in the same city, rather than identifiable locations. We didn't actually set foot in the Lake Palace, as it had been converted into the Lake Palace Hilton, and the only way for non-guests to visit it for lunch or dinner (which were very expensive) was to pay on the jetty before they would even let us on the hotel launch. We did putt around it at the permissible peon-view distance when we took a boat tour of the lake, which included a stop to tour "the other" lake palace, much smaller and less impressive, but still pretty nice.

Laurie and I went for a walk the next morning, and we realized, when people started greeting us with "Happy Christmas," that it was indeed (both happy and Christmas). There was a different feel about Udaipur. It was a large city, but with a more personal feeling. Many more people smiled and greeted us with no ulterior motives. Oh, business people still urged us to come into their shops "for a cup of tea," but when we told them no thanks, they weren't as pushy as the shopkeepers

*The Lake Palace in Udaipur; one of the primary locations
in the James Bond movie "Octopussy."*

further north, usually responding with, "OK, welcome to our city," or
"No problem, have a nice visit." One specialty of the Udaipur region
was miniature paintings on handmade rice paper, and we encountered
a new ploy in that respect. An "artist" would stop us on the street and
ask where we were from. When we told him the States, he would ask
if we had heard that the students from his workshop were leaving the
next day for an exhibit of their work in (fill in the name of a city—Taos,
New Mexico, was a frequent destination, probably because they'd heard
it had a big artist's community). We, of course, would congratulate him,
and he would invite us to his "workshop" (which, conveniently enough,
was just around the corner) to see the works that would be exhibited.
When we said maybe later, he would respond that it had to be now, as
they were leaving the next day. We said that we'd just have to be the
poorer for having missed the opportunity. It was funny, the second day,
when one of the same "artists" was still going to leave "tomorrow." I
sympathized with him for having missed his plane that morning, and he
realized (with only minor embarrassment) that it wasn't the first time
I'd heard the story from him.

The sting of being excluded from the Lake Palace was assuaged
by the fact that we did spend a half-day in the City Palace—the "real"
one, as the Lake Palace was just the summer palace. They were only
a couple thousand feet apart, so I guess the difference (in addition to
the fact that no self-respecting maharani would have been caught dead
without at least one spare palace), was that, being in the middle of the
lake, as opposed to on the lakeshore, the Lake Palace got breezes from

502

all sides. Anyway, the real palace was absolutely huge, and I kept wondering how long it took them to relearn the layout after a summer in the other one. We had gotten used to the fact that the Indian government (in response to growing tourism) had added to most palace courtyards moneychangers, banks, phone services, cafes, and souvenir shops; but we were bemused to find in the courtyard of the City Palace in Udaipur an office of the World Wide Fund for Nature. Our favorite part of the castle was a courtyard on the roof, complete with trees larger than those many people had growing in their yards. It was hot enough that we had a hard time remembering we had almost succumbed to hypothermia only two nights before, so we sat there in the shade, with a cool breeze blowing off the lake. It was, for me, one of those times, visiting some historical site, when I really could envision how it must have been for the people who lived there.

While Laurie and I were walking around Udaipur, we stumbled on two temples within a block of each other, one Hindu and the other Jain. The Hindu one was huge, taking up pretty much a whole block, made from elaborately carved white marble, with a black stone image of Vishnu in his incarnation as Jagannath (Lord of the Universe) as its central focus. The Jain temple, as virtually all of them, was an architectural dichotomy. On the outside, it was relatively simple (at least compared to the Hindu and Buddhist temples), but inside it was a riot of color, mirrors, and all manner of sparkly stuff. The dichotomy derived from the fact that central to the Jain faith was the need to strip away all worldly accoutrements. In fact, some of the monks went naked, and didn't use any implements made by people, begging food in their cupped hands. The four million adherents in India who weren't monks, however, were generally among the wealthiest class. Consequently, the upkeep of the Jain temples was generally noticeably better than the others.

We spent a couple of hours one afternoon strolling through the Garden of the Maids of Honor. Nobody seemed to know exactly for whom it was named, but it was a very peaceful spot in the center of the city, with beautiful flowers, a very nice lotus pool, a series of impressive carved elephants, and a couple of fountains (which when we entered were significantly unimpressive, but which got noticeably more so when an attendant—who must have decided the number of strollers had reached critical mass—reached into a hole in the ground and turned a handle, about quadrupling the water flow). The really fun part of the garden, however, was a small, poorly maintained science center. The fact that many of the exhibits were in disrepair (many to the point of being non-functional) didn't detract from the enjoyment of the dozens of children rushing from one to the other, laughing and shouting like it was a World's Fair pavilion. That evening we visited Shilpgram, a craft village three km west of the city. As luck would have it, we hit it during a special 3-day festival, during which, we were told, the number of exhibits was much greater than usual, and a virtually continuous series of entertainments representing various cultures from throughout the region were taking place on several stages scattered throughout the grounds. The most important event, though, was that we bought blankets. Actually, they were more like comforters: two layers with light, insulating material quilted between. When he learned that we wanted five of them, the man gave us a great deal. Several times during the remainder of our trip, we remarked that they would have been worth two or three times what we paid for them. They were a bit of a pain to schlep about, but all we had to do was remind each other about the butt freezing we had endured on that train ride between Jaipur and Udaipur to nip any complaints in the bud.

The third night at 10:00 we took an overnight sleeper bus (actually equipped with double and single sleeper compartments, similar to those on some trains) to Ahmedabad, where (at 4:00 in the morning) we caught a train to Jalgaon. There wasn't much in Jalgaon, but it was a convenient place to stay for a day trip to the Ajanta Caves. Basically, if we wanted to visit caves in India (which we did), we needed to stay either in Jalgaon and go to the Ajanta Caves, or in Aurangabad (about 200 km away) and visit the Ellora Caves. I had promised Cooper and Annie that I would get them to a beach on the ocean for their first anniversary on January 1, so we didn't have time to do both. We compared the two: Ellora was a World Heritage site, with 34 caves, some Buddhist, some Hindu, and some Jain, all sculpture, no painting; Ajanta had 30 caves, all Buddhist, both sculpture and paintings. We chose Ajanta because 1) they were more ancient (200 BC to 650 AD, compared to 600 to 1000 AD); 2) they had been abandoned for centuries, until 1819, when they were rediscovered, so were in better shape; 3) they were less accessible and not listed as a World Heritage site, so were not as crowded; and 4) we had already seen a lot of religious sculptures but the paintings were much more unusual.

We were not disappointed. The caves were cut into a sheer rock cliff in a horseshoe shape, following the bend of a river. Aside from the caves, the setting itself was marvelous. All the concessions attendant such a tourist site had been moved several kilometers away, and we were bussed into the site, so we were not bothered by people trying to sell us stuff while we toured the caves. A few crystal hawkers had hiked in illegally, but they couldn't get into the actual cave site, so could only bother us in the surrounding park and lookout sites. Each of the caves was impressive in its own right, but my favorites were the three that had not been completed. In them, it was possible to see the process the monks had used to hew the huge temples out of solid rock. They had no light other than candles, so to provide the illumination necessary for the fine stone carving and painting, they had first carved out the large central hall. Then they flooded it with a couple of inches of water. The caves faced south, so the sun shone in the entrance, reflected off the water on the floor, and gave plenty of light for the monks to work. During the evening, and on cloudy days, they retired to their "bedrooms," tiny cubicles with bunks (complete with stone pillows) carved into the walls, where they would meditate. It was a great experience, but there were a lot of caves, and we agreed that another 34 at Ellora would probably have constituted overkill.

We had gotten from Bishkek to Jalgaon without a hitch, and had three days until Cooper and Annie's anniversary—plenty of time to spend a day at the caves and still get to Kochi, our next stop, in the far south, a romantic tropical setting, complete with wonderful beaches for them to relax on. That's when things started to unravel. What I hadn't planned on was New Years, or more specifically, the fact that every person in India (as well as a significant number who had emigrated, but returned for the holiday) travelled during New Years.

To buy train tickets in India, we first filled out a form that told how many tickets we wanted, of what class, from where, to where, on which train, leaving at what time, from what station, arriving at what time, at what station, for how many males, of what age, and for how many females, of what age. Then we stood in line. Each station had a special window for "unaccompanied women, unaccompanied elders, freedom fighters, members of the press, police officers, and tourists." The lines at these windows were always shorter than those at the other windows, but that was sort of like saying it's better to freeze than burn to death, because it's less painful. The waits were sometimes significant. When we got to the counter, we were faced with a wall of glass, sometimes with a small hole to talk and listen through; sometimes not. If not, we were forced to bend down to counter level and shout or insert our ear, in turn (as there was always an unholy din in the surrounding room) through the slot through which we exchanged money for tickets. The entire communication process was not enhanced by the fact that we didn't speak Hindi, and the first requirement on their job description was obviously not fluency in English. I'm not one who thinks it is the duty of every person on earth, for my convenience, to become fluent in my native tongue. I am simply stating a fact: communication, even without the omnipresent glass barrier would not have been ideal. If there were not enough tickets available on that train, at that time, in that class, we had to fill out another form, either for a different train, a different time, or a different class; then stand in line again.

I had, as usual, gone to the train station as soon as we got settled in at the guesthouse, to reserve tickets on the 30th for our next destination. The problem was there were none. The man at the ticket counter was very helpful, and put us on the waiting list (numbers 15-19), for the 31st, which was the best he could do. He assured me that those were low numbers, and that chances were very good that we would get the tickets we needed. OK, that would be cutting it a bit close, but we would still get into Kochi on the morning of the 1st, and Cooper and Annie could be on the beach by early afternoon. He said I could come back the afternoon of the 30th and pick up the tickets.

So, we had an extra day in Jalgaon, about which the "Lonely Planet" guidebook said: "Jalgaon is on the main railway line from Mumbai to the country's northeast, and is a hub for trains in all directions. For many (us, for example) it's a practical overnight stop en route to the Ajanta Caves." Under the section on "Things to Do,".... Well, actually there was none. It skipped right to "Getting There and Away." Not a good sign. Undaunted, we asked the owner of the guesthouse, and he had a couple of suggestions. The first was an unusual Jain temple on the northeast edge of town, and the second was "a place where they save cows." Laurie, Jesse and I decided to give it a go—at least we'd have a chance to get out and about. Cooper and Annie opted out. We hired a neat old guy with an autorickshaw for the afternoon and set off. The temple really was interesting—unlike any others we saw in India. It was so modern looking that we didn't even realize we were there until the old guy parked and indicated that we were. We entered the gate, and were confronted by what looked more like a classic example of the Prairie School of architecture than a Jain temple. The doors were locked, however, so we had to content ourselves with walking around the exterior and peeking in the windows. As we started to leave, though, our driver indicated that we should hang around, as a service would be starting in a while, so somebody would be coming to open up. He was right: in about five minutes a man came, and not only opened the doors, but welcomed us inside, and showed us a large model on display of what was clearly a temple, but just as clearly not the one we were in, as it was much more traditionally ornate. The further south and the further inland we got, the fewer people spoke any English, and although our Hindi did not diminish, that wasn't very helpful, as it started with none. The result was, that although he tried his best to explain to us what it was a model of, and we tried our best to understand, it just wasn't working. Finally, he took me by the arm, led me to the front gate, and pointed across the street. There stood a structure—either partially built or partially restored—that was obviously the one represented by the model. I spent about a half hour walking around it trying to decide, and finally came to the conclusion that it was being built on the ruins of a former temple, and that it had been many years in construction. I asked the owner of our guesthouse later, and he said that my deduction was correct. He said that it was taking so long because they only worked on it when they had accrued enough in donations to do so, and that they didn't expect to finish it for decades.

The "place where they save cows" was about five km outside town, and turned out to be a sort of combination theme park and dairy farm. It was clearly not on many tourists' agendas, and we were treated like royalty. A man met us at the gate and took us to meet the owner. He greeted us in Hindi; then turned us over to the manager, who greeted us in broken English; then turned us over to one of his assistants who spoke pretty good English; who took us (past a row of cages containing dozens of rabbits and a couple of monkeys) into a sort of lounge, served us tea, and showed us a video that explained what the place was all about. What it was all about was, indeed, saving cows. Most, but not all of the people in India were Hindi, and therefore treated cows as sacred. Some of the non-Hindi contingent, however, not only didn't revere them, but ate them. The farm had been set up to save as many cows as possible from that ignoble fate. After the tea and video, the assistant and another man gave us a tour of the place. They explained that the rabbits and monkeys were sort of an offshoot of their primary objective; that in the process of saving cows, they occasionally had the opportunity to save other animals as well. The hundreds of pigeons we came across later on the tour were another example. They had a couple hundred cows that have been purchased from slaughterhouses; or from farmers who were going to destroy them because they were sick, old, or had otherwise outlived their usefulness. They employed a staff of more than 200, three of which were veterinarians. The cows that were in good shape they took care of, and used the milk and excrement; the ones that weren't, they turned over to the vets to take care of. The milk they used themselves, or sold. Methane converters provided more than half their energy needs with methane derived from the excrement.

A good part of their operating funds, however, was supplied by marketing medicines and other products derived from the cows' urine and dung—products such as vitamins and (my personal favorite) toothpaste. We bought several tubes to take back to the States for our friends and family. The theme park element derived from the fact that they were vehemently pro-vegetarian, if not pro-vegan. One of the buildings, for example, was a sort of museum of pro-vegetarian propaganda—most in the form of hundreds of large full-color posters. They ranged from subtle (movie stars such as Tom Cruise telling why they were vegetarian), to anything but (models with dead, bloody corpses draped on their bodies in place of fur coats). The huge sign over the entrance was similar to the finger-pointing Uncle Sam of WWII recruiting posters, with the slogan "U-Turn." Another building we found fascinating was a sort of pavilion, with a statue of Krishna seated under a palm in the center, surrounded by seven stables with pregnant cows in them. It seemed that if pregnant women came there and petted all seven of the cows, they were virtually guaranteed to have a "strong, healthy, boy baby." We noticed that the woman taking care of the cows was very pregnant, and asked if that meant she would be maximally blessed. They assured us that would indeed be the case.

We watch a parade of some of the two hundred residents at "the place where they save cows."

I went back to the station after we returned from the cow place, and stood in line. The nice man at the counter informed me that we had moved from numbers 15-19 to numbers 5-9 on the waiting list. It was then 5:00, and we were supposed to catch the train the next morning at 3:00. I said it didn't look good, and maybe I'd better cancel and get my money back. He said that, on the contrary, numbers 5-9 were a sure thing. I asked what he really thought the chances were that we would get tickets, and he replied, "100 percent." I said, "Are you sure?" He said, "Absolutely." He said to come back after 7:00 p.m., when the train had left Mumbai, and he would know which seats had not been taken. I came back at 7:15 and stood in line. When I reached the counter at 8:00 he was not there, and the woman who was did not fall anywhere near the "helpful" category. In fact "surly" didn't do her justice. I gave her the form that showed we were on the waiting list for tickets. She said, "No tickets." I said, "But the man who was here before said...." She said, "No tickets." I saw that it was a losing battle, so said OK then, I'd just cancel and take my money back. She said, "We're closed," and walked away.

Well, I had promised I would get Cooper and Annie to a beach for their anniversary on the 1st. We were several hundred kilometers inland, it was 8:00 p.m. on the 30th, and I had just found out that we could not get tickets for the train to Kochi at 3:00 a.m. on the 31st. Time for plan "B," which I didn't have, as I had believed the nice man at the ticket counter when he told me the tickets were a 100 percent sure thing. After extensive research, I found that we could get a 10:00 p.m. bus to Mumbai, where both the owner of our guesthouse and the young man at the bus station assured me we could get plane tickets to Kochi for less than $100 apiece. That would throw us significantly off our $100 a day budget, but would get us to a beach by the afternoon of the 31st. I figured it was worth it to keep my promise to Cooper and Annie. So, I had two hours to get my refund from the train tickets and purchase the bus tickets—no problem, as the stations were only a couple of blocks apart, and the bus station was directly across the street from our guesthouse. I told everybody to get packed and ready to leave at 10:00; then went to the refund office at the train station, where they told me I had to get my refund from the ticket window. I told them the window was closed until the next morning, we were leaving on a 10:00 bus, and what was a "Refund Office" for anyway, if not to give refunds. They said that, as we would have caught the train (if, in fact, we had caught the train at all) at a station about 25 minutes down the line, I would have to go to the refund office there to get my refund. I said there was absolutely no way that I could get to a station 25 minutes away, get my refund, and get back in time to catch the 10:00 bus (especially as a half hour of my two hours had already elapsed). They said OK, it was very unusual, but because of the special circumstances, they would give me a refund from that office. I thanked them very much and relaxed a bit. It wasn't quite that straightforward, however. By the time they had rounded up all the forms they needed; then found all the people who needed to approve the transaction, it was after 10:00, and we hadn't even begun to actually fill out the forms. I told them to forget it; it was too late. They said that if I would go to the ticket window at 8:00 the next morning, it would be very easy: I could just give them the waiting list form and they would give me my money back (minus about $2 per ticket—I assumed as a "non-service charge," given that I hadn't gotten the tickets to begin with). So, we reserved seats on the 1:00 bus to Mumbai for the next afternoon.

The next morning at 8:00 I was waiting when Ms Congeniality opened her window. I handed her my waiting list form and asked for my refund. She said she couldn't give me my refund until they had sold enough tickets to have that much money, so I would have to come back in a couple of hours. I came back at 10:00, stood in line, and handed her my form. She said I needed to go two windows down. I said the people in the Refund Office had told me to come to her window. She said they were wrong; I needed to go two windows down. I asked her why she hadn't told me that at 8:00, and she just looked at me. I took my place at the end of the other line. Fifteen minutes later, when I got to that window, I handed the woman there my form. When she saw me hand over my form, the woman from the first window got up, came over, took it from the other woman's hand, and told me to come back to her window. When we got back to her window, she told me I would have to go the station 25 minutes down the line. I told her the people in the Refund Office had said to come to her. She said they were wrong; I had to go the other station. I really did try to take local customs into consideration when traveling, but that was it—local customs be damned. I snatched the form from her hand, said something that, in retrospect, I was not proud of, and stormed straight to the stationmaster's office. He wasn't in yet, so I went to the assistant stationmaster's office. Although I was doing my best to maintain, they took one look at me and scrambled for their kid gloves. Through gritted teeth, I recounted my ordeal to the assistant stationmaster. Making soothing sounds, he took me to the stationmaster's office, made me some tea, and assured me that the stationmaster would be right with me (I could tell he was thanking

Vishnu—and probably several of the other 329 Hindu gods and goddesses—that the buck didn't have to stop with him). The stationmaster showed up about a half hour later, and it was clear that he had been forewarned. He was very cooperative, and set about immediately to get me my refund. An hour later, I had the necessary paperwork, and more importantly, an official to walk it through with me. He took me back to the woman at the first window. She sent him to another office. We went there. The person there asked us to wait while he went to get someone else. That official came and talked at length with my official; then asked us to wait while he went to get some more forms to fill out. He brought them back. We filled them out. He asked us to wait while he went to get the money. He brought the money back. He counted it twice. He registered it by denomination in a log. He counted it twice more. He gave it to me and asked me to count it. I said that was OK, I had counted it with him the other four times and was confident that it was correct. I thanked him and my official and left. Of course, by then we had long missed the 1:00 bus, so we bought tickets for the overnight bus leaving at 10:00pm. That meant we would catch a plane to Kochi on the morning of the first, but would get there before noon, and Cooper and Annie could still spend the afternoon of their anniversary on the beach.

The bus dropped us off right at the airport, and the others collapsed into some nearby chairs while I set out to find the cheapest tickets to Kochi. All the domestic airlines had counters within 100 feet of each other, and (oddly enough) there were no lines, so it didn't take long to discover that "less than $100" was a conservative estimate. In fact, they were slightly more than $300. I multiplied $300 by five and come up with way more than I could afford—promise or no promise. I certainly didn't have a plan "C," and was pretty much running on fumes by that time. A well-dressed gentleman approached, told me he was a travel agent, and asked if he could help. I told him my situation, and he said he was sure he could get me five cheap tickets. He made some calls on his cell phone, and announced that he had good news: he had found me five tickets to Kochi for only 2600 soms apiece. I divided that by 40 soms to the dollar, and got $290. I told him that I appreciated his help, but a saving of $50 wouldn't do it. He asked me how much I could afford, and I told him $100 apiece. To his credit, he didn't laugh in my face. While he had been making the calls, I had been looking through the guidebook, and had found Ratnagiri: "About 425 km south of Mumbai. The town itself is not hugely alluring...." But, "Just outside the town center are a few lovely strips of sand, including the pretty

Bhatya Beach. Come dusk, it's a perfect place to watch the sun sink." All was not lost. I had promised a beach; not necessarily the beach at Kochi. I asked the travel agent how long it would take to get there by train, and he said we couldn't get there before 8:00pm. He said, however, that he could arrange a car and driver that would get us there by early afternoon for "only" $200. I weighed the cost against how pleased Cooper and Annie would be to spend the afternoon on the beach, and how romantic it would be for them to lie there and watch the sun go down over the ocean. I bit the bullet and took him up on his offer. It was a very comfortable car, and we got there by early afternoon. I had called ahead for reservations at a small hotel, so we checked in and headed for the beach. I had prevailed. Except 1) it was one of those fine black sand beaches that are more like mud bar than sand beach, 2) the tide was (way) out, 3) it had been a while since anybody had collected the trash, and 4) it was New Years Day, so everybody and his or her dog was there. We made the best of it, strolling up and down the beach (Jesse exercised his fascination with sea creatures by exploring all manner of crustaceans—alive and dead), watching the sunset (which wasn't all that great), buying roasted corn from the vendors, and having a delicious seafood dinner at a very nice restaurant overlooking the water. Technically, I guess I had kept my promise, but it was a hollow victory, at best.

At least we were on the main rail line to the south, so there were several trains a day to Kochi. I went to the train station the next morning to book tickets on one of them for the following day. There were no seats available for at least three days. Had we spent three more days there, we could not have made it to the places we wanted to go in the south, and still gotten back to Delhi in time to catch our plane on the eleventh, so I walked back to the hotel in a funk. The man who owned the hotel asked me what the problem was. When I told him, he suggested that we hire a car to Kolhapur, about 100 km (back) inland, where we could catch an overnight bus to Kochi. I asked him if he was sure, so he said he would call someone at Kolhapur and reserve us seats. About a half hour later, he told me he had hired a car and reserved the seats for us. He said our driver knew where to take us to pick up our tickets and catch the bus at 6:00. Kolhapur was on the western edge of the Central Highlands, so the highway climbed up over the Western Ghats in a series of narrow, tortuous switchbacks, seldom bordered by anything vaguely resembling guardrails. The good news was that it was a gorgeous drive, with wild monkeys along much of the way to keep us entertained. We got there just in time to catch our bus. Except that around the central square, there were a dozen places that sold long distance bus tickets. Our driver asked us which one we wanted. I told him the hotel owner had said he would know. He looked at me blankly; then suggested that he call the owner to straighten it out. When he hung up, he said the owner had told him any of the places would do; just pick one and buy tickets. In other words, he hadn't reserved us seats at all. So we started at the nearest one.

After trying them all, we found some that had open seats, but the bus had already left, some that the bus hadn't left but there were no seats available (if only we had contacted them a few hours before, they could have saved us some), and one (the last one we tried) that the bus had not left and he could sell us his last four seats. I said we needed five. He said he only had four, but could give me a good deal on them, as the bus was about to leave. I asked which of my family he suggested I leave behind, and he just shrugged. I decided OK, I'd just go back to the one with the nicest people, and buy five tickets to Kochi for the next evening. We'd be yet another day behind schedule, but there wasn't really anything we could do about it. I went back and told them I'd like to by five tickets to Kochi for the next day, and they said, oh, we don't have a bus to Kochi. I asked them which place did, and they said none; I'd have to buy tickets to Bangalore; then buy tickets there to go on to Kochi. I said what if we get to Bangalore and there are no tickets to Kochi. They said, oh there are always tickets from Bangalore to Kochi. So I bought five tickets to Bangalore for the overnight bus leaving the next evening. Then all we needed was a place to stay in Kolhapur. I checked the guidebook, and found a place called Hotel Sony recommended, but for some reason it gave no address. I told Laurie, and said for them to wait while I found someone who knew where it was. She pointed up. We were standing under a lit sign that said, "Hotel Sony," with an arrow pointing down the walkway behind us. It was less than half a block away. We checked in and went to the restaurant next door for dinner. Back in our room after dinner, I got out the map and started reshuffling places and dates. It was the evening of the second, and it didn't take long for me to realize that if we spent the third in Kolhapur and the fourth in Bangalore, getting to Kochi on the afternoon of the fifth, we would have just about enough time to get comfortably across to Chennai on the east coast in time to catch our train back to Delhi on the eighth. We all discussed the alternatives, and decided to exchange the tickets to Bangalore for ones to Goa, where they had real beaches. I did so the next morning, and we were in Goa in time for dinner on the fourth.

Goa was the smallest state of India, comprising (among a wealth of other attractions), about forty beaches, half of them developed for

513

tourists. Each of them had a personality of its own, attracting primarily one or two types of tourists. The jet-setters and the ex-hippies laid claim to some, but certainly not all of them. The Lonely Planet Guidebook characterized each of them in a sort of chart. We chose Colva, about which it said: "It's much quieter and still has a noticeable fishing industry. There's a mix of package tourists, Indian tourists, and backpackers, but no party scene." Also, the state was divided into North and South Goa, with the south being the less developed. Colva was in the southern part, but only six km from the southern capitol, Margao. That meant we were close to a transportation center, and only about 35 km from Panaji, the population center, and northern capitol; but still within a few hundred yards of a gorgeous, palm-lined beach. The strip between our guesthouse and the beach was lined with shops, cafes, and all manner of tourist traps, but our guesthouse was set back a hundred meters or so from the street, so was very quiet and peaceful.

The first morning there, I went to a place right across the street from our guesthouse to change some dollars for rupees. It was mentioned in the guidebook as a dependable travel agency as well. Throughout the trip, when I could, I avoided standing in line at railroad stations to buy tickets by paying a bit extra for somebody else to do it. At an extra dollar a ticket, I considered it well worth the expense. So, after changing money, I asked the young woman if they had someone who could do that. She said of course they did, and wanted to know how many tickets we wanted, to where, and for what date. Before I had given up on getting to the southern part of India, I had purchased return tickets to Delhi from Chennai in the southeast. That meant we would have to spend a couple of days getting there from Goa, and a couple more days just getting back to Delhi. As it was already the fourth and we had to be in Delhi on the tenth, four days of travel meant we would have only two days in Goa. I asked if it would be possible for her to cancel those tickets and use the money for tickets directly back to Delhi from Goa, essentially converting two days of travel time to beach time. She got on her computer to check the possibilities. She spent the next two days finding out there were no tickets available to Delhi from Goa. Once again, we were stuck. Then she had an idea: take an overnight bus back to Mumbai and fly from there to Delhi. It would take only one day—five beach days/one travel day, instead of four travel/two beach—a far more acceptable ratio, to all our minds. It would cost little more than the 4-day train trip would have, and tickets were available. I reined my enthusiasm short of leaping over her desk and embracing her, but only just. She had spent a lot of time and worked very hard getting us back to Delhi in time to catch our plane, and I think she was almost as pleased as I by her success. We spent the rest of our first day in Goa walking on the beach, sitting on the beach, sipping cold drinks on the beach, eating lunch and dinner in a little open-air restaurant on the beach, and drinking coffee on the beach while watching the sun set over the ocean. If only it could have been three days earlier, it would have made a great first anniversary present.

After lunch, Cooper, Annie, and Jesse opted (no surprise) to spend the afternoon on the beach. Laurie and I walked a bit inland to the nearby village of Colva, to see what things were like on the other side of the highway. It was very different from the highly commercial, tourist-oriented area near the beach. For one thing, we got a much calmer feeling. Everyone seemed to be operating at a slower pace, and we found ourselves responding. Our visit became a leisurely stroll. We lost all sense of time; stopped worrying about schedules and transportation. We seemed to be the only non-residents in a town where most of the residents probably worked across the road, serving people who looked like us in some capacity. Yet virtually everyone smiled and greeted us as friends. It was a heartwarming feeling. Because Goa had been a Portuguese colony many more people were Catholics than in the rest of

One of the creches in the village of Colva in Goa.

India. One result of that fact was that many of the cottages in Colva had homemade creches displayed in their front yard beginning Christmas day. They started with the wise men at the very edge of the scene, moving them closer each each of the twelve days of Christmas, until they arrived at the manger on Epiphany.

The next day Cooper and Annie spent pretty much as they had the day before. Laurie, Jesse, and I took an auto rickshaw into Margao, where we caught a bus into Panaji. The Portuguese maintained Goa as a shipping colony from 1510 until as late as 1961 (more than 15 years after the British had given over the rest of the country), when the Indian government unceremoniously kicked them out. That meant the whole state, but especially the area around the capitol, had a distinctively different feel than the rest of the country. There were more Christian churches than temples or mosques, the architecture was decidedly Mediterranean, and the food was even more varied than elsewhere in India. The city of less than 100,000 was quite compact, nestled between the surrounding hills and the ocean, so it was possible to cover pretty much all the interesting areas on foot in a day—which we did. We started by spending a couple of hours strolling the narrow cobbled streets of the old city; then climbed a seemingly endless series of steps to a hill where we could look out over the city and its harbor. From there, we descended to the Catholic Church of Our Lady of the Immaculate Conception. That huge, ornate, very white edifice was built in 1541, and was still in use, with daily masses in English, Portuguese, and Konkani (the local indigenous language). On the way back to the bus station, we passed a statue of Abbe Faria, a famous Goan hypnotist, who (we assumed) was in the process of hypnotizing his female assistant, but looked for all the world as though he was strangling her. We also walked around the old secretariat building, which was built in the 1500s as a Shah's palace; became the viceroy's residence in 1759; later served as their legislative assembly building; and had fallen on hard times, serving as what seemed to be an office building for minor functionaries. As such, we had to sort of squint to see it in its former grandeur.

We generally tried to avoid organized tours, but the Goa Tourism Development Corporation (a thinly disguised office of the state government) had a couple of deals that we couldn't pass up. One was an all-day bus tour of (mostly) the rural areas of South Goa for about $4.00 apiece; the other an all-day river cruise for about $15.00 apiece. They were the low-end tour packages, so we were in the company of almost all Indian people both days. The foreign tourists generally opted for the classier (and much more expensive) versions of essentially the same experiences. To have covered on our own what we did on those two tours would probably have either cost four times as much for private transportation, or taken four times as long using public transportation. For the river cruise on Friday, we took the early bus into Panaji and walked to the dock, where, with about 40 other people, we boarded an old (it was named the Santa Monica, and the Portuguese had been gone for 45 years) two-tiered river boat, and set off up the Mandovi River. The $4^{1/2}$-hour trip upstream was a mix of wonderfully scenic views along the shore of agricultural land interrupted occasionally by lush stands of mangrove trees, and a series of huge ore boats, ferrying iron ore to the harbor from three mines operating near the river. As we passed the docks where those boats were being loaded, we saw a continuous stream of trucks backing up to the docks and dumping ore into the holds, while two or three boats waited their turn to be loaded. We also got a preview, in the form of the tops of the tallest steeples and watchtowers above the trees, of Old Goa, the ancient capitol, which we would visit on the other tour. After four and a half hours, we pulled into (and I do mean "into," as the pilot hit it hard enough that we weren't sure it would still be there to disembark from) a rickety old wooden dock and climbed off for a 20-minute walk to a spice plantation for lunch and a tour.

As our group was too large for one person to take us all through the plantation, we were divided into two groups. As luck would have it, we got the bad guide. We were close enough to the other group to hear that their guide was giving them significantly more (and significantly more interesting) information. Cooper, Annie, and Jesse gave up and went back to the dining area to relax. Laurie was pretty much into the spice thing, so when we noticed a couple of people drifting away from the other group, we slipped over into it. We were rewarded by extensive and fascinating discussions of the various spices in evidence. We were off-season for harvest on most of them, so had to make do with looking at the plants and explanations of how they produced their various spices. The woman leading our adopted group did a great job, however, so we were happy with the result. After either a great or a terrible lunch (I said "great," as the only non-spicy item was the steamed rice), we headed back to the boat for the 4-hour return trip (the half hour difference a result of the current). We got back to Colva Beach just in time for dinner at what had become our regular beach restaurant. Cooper and I may have gotten our fill of great seafood if we had stayed another two weeks or so.

Jesse, Cooper, and Annie with the owner of our favorite restaurant on the beach at Colva.

Saturday was pretty much a repeat of the first afternoon: hanging around the beach. Sunday morning after breakfast, we walked down to the parking lot near the beach, where we caught the bus for the South Goa tour. Laurie and I were looking forward to the first stop, Ancestral Goa, as it was an open-air museum of the various ethnic histories that went into the cultural mix of the area. We enjoyed that kind of experience, because it gave us a greater understanding of the people and modern customs we encountered. The problem was we enjoyed the experience when we were left to wander at our own pace through the exhibits, spending as much or as little time at each as we liked. The guide was determined that we would all stay together and be herded from one exhibit to the next, spending as much time as it took for him to explain each to us. I discussed the situation with Cooper, Annie, Jesse, and Laurie. They were no more willing to accept those rules than I was, so I told him we didn't want to do that. I explained that it was nothing against him or his tour, but that we just didn't want to experience the exhibits that way. He said we had no choice. I said we didn't want to cause a problem, and that all he had to do was tell us when to be back at the bus, and we would be sure to be there. He said we had to stay with him and the group. I said that if that was our only alternative, we chose to leave the tour completely, and would find our own transportation back to Colva, thank you very much. When he saw how determined we were, he relented. For the rest of the day, he simply told us at each stop what time we should be back and we made sure not to be late. Problem solved, the rest of the tour was great. To our guide's credit, he did take me aside later and apologize, explaining that he just wasn't used to working with people who preferred to experience the sites outside the group, and that, in fact, our family had been no problem at all once we had reached an understanding.

We spent Monday, our last day in Goa, relaxing on the beach. That evening we took a taxi into Margao, where we caught an overnight bus to Mumbai. We got to the airport the next morning in plenty of time, and caught our plane to Delhi without incident. As we were staying at the same guesthouse in the Tibetan quarter, we had no trouble finding the place. I had called from Goa before we left to confirm our reservations: two rooms for one night (Laurie, Jesse, and I were leaving for Bishkek on Wednesday), and one for two nights (Cooper and Annie were leaving for the States on Thursday), so everything was all set. We collapsed into the lobby of our guesthouse after 24 hours in bus, plane, taxis, and airports, and I went to the desk to check in. "But you called and cancelled your reservation," she said, "so we gave your rooms away." All I said was, "You what?" and I really said it very quietly, maybe too quietly, or maybe it was something about my eyes, for she quickly handed me a couple of keys, saying, "Here, why don't you just take these rooms. These people aren't here yet. Maybe they won't show up at all. If they do, we'll figure something out. OK?" "OK," I said (very quietly), took the keys, picked up my bag, and slowly climbed the stairs to our rooms.

The promise I had made to Cooper and Annie to get them to a beach for their first anniversary was one of two promises I had made on the India trip. I had also promised Jesse that if we were in a city where the fourth Harry Potter movie was playing, and if we had time, we would go. We didn't have to be at the airport until Wednesday evening to catch our plane to Bishkek, so Jesse got on the Internet and found two theatres in Delhi at which the Harry Potter movie was playing. He told me, and I leaped at the chance to balance the sort-of-kept promise to Cooper and Annie with a well-and-truly-kept one to Jesse. The movie was playing at 12:45 in one theatre, and 2:00 in the other. It is an especially long movie, so the 2:00 showing would not allow enough time for us to get back to the guesthouse, pick up our bags, check out, and make it to the airport the requisite two hours before our flight time. So we decided to go the theatre with the 12:45 show time. Just to be safe, I went to the taxi stand and asked them how long it would take to get to that theatre. They said half an hour at most. To avoid any possible problem, I arranged for one of the drivers (who assured us that he knew exactly where the theatre was, and who had a van that would hold all five of us comfortably) to meet us at 11:45. I wasn't taking any chances. We had an early lunch and were at the taxi stand right at 11:45. He wasn't.

Nor was he there at 12:00. When another driver offered to take us, I asked him if he would accept the same price as the first driver, if he had a van that would hold us all comfortably, and if he knew for sure how to get to theatre. He said, "Yes," "Yes," and "Yes," so I said, "OK, let's go." He took us to a compact car designed to carry four; not five and a driver. I protested that he had said he had a van that would hold us all comfortably, and he protested that we could all fit in his car. As time was wasting, and as everybody said they didn't mind riding for a half hour in cramped quarters (and as I would be relatively un-cramped in the front seat), I relented, we piled in, and he took off, still with 45 minutes for the half-hour ride. The first time he stopped for directions, I said I thought he had told me he knew how to get there. He assured me that he did, but just wanted to be sure. When he had gotten directions, I asked if he was now sure, and he said, "Oh, sure." By the fourth time he stopped, it was patently obvious that he was lying through his teeth. He never had known how to get there, but wanted the fare, so wasn't about to admit it. By then it was too late to do anything but grind my teeth, mumble under my breath, and hope he would get good enough directions from somebody to get us there on time. After six stops for directions, and numerous wrong turns, we arrived at the theatre—15 minutes late. I felt awful about notching up another sort-of-kept promise, but Jesse assured me it would be fine, as we hadn't missed anything but the previews. It took us a couple of minutes to locate the theatre, on the second floor of the mall, but at least there was no line when we rushed up to the ticket window. I asked if we were in time for "Harry Potter," and if there were tickets left. He said there were tickets, and that we had plenty of time, as the next showing wasn't until 2:00. I wanted so badly not to believe it, that it took me some time to register the fact that the driver had taken us to the wrong theatre. It was probably a good thing the theatre was only on the second floor. I was afraid that if I jumped it wouldn't actually kill me, and I didn't want to spend time in an Indian hospital.

We had arranged for our driver to pick us up in two hours, so we spent the time wandering around the mall. Much of it I spent pouting over an overpriced cup of coffee, in a hushed, but intense conversation with God. I admitted to Him 1) that yes, I sometimes needed to be reminded that I wasn't (nor should I be) the one in control; 2) that yes, I realized (sometimes after being reminded in one way or another) that He was, in fact, better equipped than I to run things; and 3) that yes, given time to reflect on both 1 and 2 above that everyone (myself included) was probably better off given the situation as it was. I did protest vociferously, however, that I saw no need for two such strident reminders following so closely on the heels of one another. I stopped pouting, but I never did get a satisfactory response. One good thing came of the situation: there was a large bookstore in the mall, and there was a Lonely Planet guidebook for Eastern Europe in the bookstore. I bought it, and spent hours using it to plan the trip we would take between the end of school at AUCA and the time we returned to the States. When the driver picked us up, he didn't ask how the movie was, so we didn't tell him—after all, what would have been the point? The ride back to the guesthouse was uneventful—unless you count hitting the cow. It was on a six-lane overpass. There were cars and trucks in the left lane, an auto rickshaw in the center lane, and a cow in the right lane. To Hindus cows were sacred, and they were allowed to roam freely; people considered it an honor to feed and water them; and nobody would think of doing anything (such as hitting them with a car) to injure them. Well, our driver was fast overtaking the much slower auto rickshaw, and decided he would have time to pass it on the right before we got to the (even slower) cow. When he realized he was wrong, he slammed on the brakes, and squealed to a stop about two feet past the rear end of the cow. The result was sort of like when we were kids, and snuck up behind our friend, and bent our knees into the back of his or hers, and quickly straightened up, either catching our friend, or leaving him or her to sit unceremoniously on the ground. The difference was that the cow sat unceremoniously on the hood. She paused, looked noncommittally over her left shoulder at us, and sauntered off the hood and on her way down the right lane of the highway. The driver, realizing she was uninjured, breathed again, checked his mirror, and cautiously passed her in the center lane. I think she glanced casually at him out of the corner of her eye as we went past. Now, I'm sure that God would never do such a thing just to punish a taxi driver for causing a young man to miss a movie that he had his heart set on, and causing that young man's father anguish for failing to keep his promise regarding that movie, but I didn't know enough about Hinduism to say the same for Vishnu. We arrived back at our guesthouse a half hour to the minute after leaving the movie theatre.

We had one more Tibetan meal at the restaurant in the guesthouse, gathered our bags, said goodbye to Cooper and Annie, and left for the airport. We had a 4-hour layover at the airport in Uzbekistan, made longer by an unexplained (as they all are here) 2-hour delay. We were pretty frazzled when we exited the airport in Bishkek, and were not happy to find that the university had not sent a van for us as they had said they would. I was relieved when a man approached us and said, "Taxi?" I said, "How much to the corner of Jibek Jolu and Panfilova?" He said, "How much do you want (instead of twice what it should be)?" I said, "Three hundred and fifty soms (a fair price)." He said, "OK," and we were on our way. He dropped us at our apartment building, I paid him (including a 50-som tip for the hassle he'd saved me), and we lugged our bags up the 63 steps to our apartment and collapsed. We made good use (by using them as little as possible) of the four recuperation days we had allowed before spring semester classes began the next Monday.

Spring semester, Laurie and I were taking part in a role reversal of sorts. When I was teaching at my university in the States, I got up every morning at 6:00, was at work by 7:30, taught my first class at 8:00, and usually got home between 6:00 and 7:30 in the evening. Spring semester, I taught only two classes, with a total of 16 students. I got up about 7:00, got to work about 8:00 Monday, Tuesday, and Friday, when I had 9:30 classes; more like 10:00 Wednesday when I had no classes, and Thursday when my class wasn't until 4:00. I went home any time between 3:00 and 5:30 in the afternoon, depending how I felt. Laurie, on the other hand, who worked part time at an elementary school in the States, had four composition classes Spring semester, with a total of 65 students. She went in about 7:30 every morning, and spent all day teaching, meeting with students, and grading papers. The only time she came home early was when she couldn't get her grading done at school because too many students wanted to meet with her. Lest it sound as though I had nothing to do, one of my classes comprised five seniors who were finishing their theses, and I was advising one senior thesis from another department and a master's thesis from another university. All of those required many hours a week of individual consultation.

Chapter 6
March

I spent March 2 through 6 at a conference in Tbilisi, Georgia. My attendance was "strongly encouraged" by George Soros, the multi-billionaire who spent hundreds of millions a year trying to enhance democracy and education in Eastern Europe and Central Asia. Actually, it was the folks who administered his Open Society Foundation, the organization that sponsored the Academic Fellowship Program—including my presence at AUCA. I wasn't really keen on missing three days of classes to sit in stuffy meeting rooms listening to presentations of questionable interest to me, but as it was their money that payed most of our expenses in Kyrgyzstan, I thought it best that I humor them. As it turned out, some of the sessions really weren't bad—of the ones I attended when I wasn't engaged in academic tourism, that is. I saw enough of the other participants engaged in said tourism, incidentally, that I couldn't help but conclude that was a good part of the objective of the conference.

I had to get up in the wee hours to catch a taxi for the half-hour ride to the airport, arriving the requisite two hours before the 6:00 a.m. flight to Moscow. That is, the drive would have been a half hour if we hadn't been stopped by the police for a 50-som "fine" for some random, and likely made-up infraction of some probably just as made up law. On the other hand, none of the Kyrgyz paid any attention to the requisite 2-hour rule, so I was the first passenger in the terminal that morning, and had no competition for getting my carry-on bag x-rayed, and my person metal-detected. The others wandered in anywhere from an hour to 15 minutes before flight time. As the officials seldom started even loading planes until their scheduled departure time, that made it so the latest checked in and boarded in one smooth operation, handily avoiding the 2-hour-plus wait of some of us. We landed in Moscow, had our baggage x-rayed and our persons metal-detected on the way into the airport. I assumed they wanted to be sure none of their flight attendants had passed us any weapons while enroute. We then walked through the terminal to the gate area for the Georgia flight, had our baggage x-rayed and our persons metal-detected for entry into the gate area, and boarded for the short hop to Tbilisi.

My experience in Georgia was on the far end of the spectrum from our usual traveling mode (ie. five of us throughout much of India for less than $100 a day). A driver was waiting for us at the airport, to take us to the Courtyard Marriott, where we checked into our $150 a night single rooms. I spent the two hours before dinner exploring the downtown area in which the hotel was located. As with Bishkek, much of the downtown was dedicated to parks and walking malls: lots of trees, and flowers, and outdoor cafes. I returned to the Marriott lobby at 6:00 to meet the rest of the group and walk several blocks into the center of the old city. There we stopped at a picturesque (and very swank) old restaurant, where we were treated to an embarrassingly abundant (and obviously expensive) multi-course meal comprising a dozen traditional Georgian dishes (not counting appetizers, of which there were a dozen more). Some of the more notable dishes were, 1) beans in a pot: beans mixed with herbs and boiled in clay pots (one of my favorites); 2) imeruli khachapuri: round, pizza-like bread stuffed with melted cheeses; 3) iki-biri: chunks of lamb tail and fat alternated on a skewer and grilled over charcoal; 4) kharpukhi: beef, lamb, chicken, or sturgeon kebabs wrapped in lavashi (thin, crepe-like dough); 5) satsivi: chicken immersed in a thick walnut and herb paste; and 6) khinkali: large boiled dumplings, filled with a little ground meat, and a lot of broth. The real treat, however, was the wine. Georgian wine was the best in Eastern Europe. It was quite inexpensive ($5-$10 a bottle), and compared favorably with French, in my (and many others') opinion. They were justifiably proud of it, and served us many bottles of many varieties. Needless to say, a good time was had by all, and (to hear them tell it) an even better time was had by the half who went to a disco until 3:00 a.m. Maybe so, but they didn't look as though they were having that great a time during the sessions the next morning. As it happened, that dinner was the first of four equally lavish, in what had to have been the four swankiest restaurants in the city. Each of them also offered traditional music and dance shows as entertainment during and after the meals. The shows were quite impressive, but not nearly as impressive as they were loud. It seemed that residents of the former Soviet countries (for some reason nobody I asked seemed to be able to explain) weren't happy drinking or eating without piercingly, ear-splittingly, head-throbbingly, can't-think loud music blaring at them. I just couldn't take it, and walked back to the hotel (or in the case of the one night when we were more than a couple of miles away, took a taxi) as soon after eating as I could without being completely boorish (or until I just couldn't stand it any more, whichever came first).

The night that I took a taxi, I asked one of the hosts at the restaurant how much I should pay for the trip back to the hotel. He said he would go out with me and make sure I didn't get cheated. There was a taxi

524

conveniently parked outside the front door, so I told the driver where I wanted to go and asked him how much. He told me about twice what I thought it should be. I asked the host, and he quickly agreed that was a good price. I just laughed and started to walk away. They called me back and asked me what was the matter. I told them that just because I was Western didn't mean I was rich, stupid, lazy, or all three; it was only about four km back to the hotel and it was a nice night, so I would pay half what they were asking or walk. The host looked guilty; the driver just grinned and said, "OK." I got in and we took off. We hadn't gone more than a few blocks when he had a flat tire. He got out to change it, and about fell over with surprise when I started to help. With both of us working, it only took a few minutes, and we were on our way again. When he pulled up in front of the hotel, I gave him the agreed on price, plus a healthy tip. He tried to give the tip back, saying (in Georgian and sign language) that it was enough that I had helped him change his tire. I told him (in English and sign language) to use it to get the flat tire fixed. He grinned, shook my hand, and said something that I could tell from his expression was complementary.

Breakfasts and lunches were at the hotel, paid for by the Soros Foundation, and were lavish. I took a peek at their menu to get an idea of the prices. A toasted cheese sandwich was the cheapest thing on it, at $7.50 U.S., followed by mushroom soup, at $8.00 U.S. Our meals weren't from the menu, but were buffet-style, which is not to say we lacked choices. The lunch buffet comprised two kinds of meat, fish, several vegetable choices, at least two kinds of potatoes, and dozens of side dishes. compared to breakfast, however, it was sparse. The first morning, I entered what I thought was the dining room, but was, in fact a separate room just for the breakfast buffet—and it needed a room to itself. It took a lot of willpower to limit myself to yoghurt, fruit, and muesli. I did gain four pounds in four days, but I was able to shed them within a week of returning to Bishkek and a sane eating pattern.

The conference was over Saturday, and my department chair, who had arranged for our plane tickets, had scheduled our return for Monday evening, so I spent all day Sunday and Monday morning sightseeing. I had met a German professor who was serving as a non-resident scholar (meaning he traveled back and forth about four times a year) at a university in one of the former Soviet countries. He was a specialist in network theory, and had (as specialists are wont to do) tried to teach us everything about his discipline in an hour and a half session. He seemed like a very nice fellow, and I got the feeling that there was probably a very interesting topic lurking about there somewhere. He was one of about three other people who were at breakfast when I went down Sunday morning at 8:00, and invited me to join him. He asked what I planned to do that day, and when I told him I'd like to do some sightseeing, he informed me that he had rented a minivan for the morning. He said he and several others were going to Mtskheta, the ancient capital of Georgia, built in the 3rd Century B.C. at the confluence of the country's two main rivers, about 20 km north of Tbilisi, and that I was welcome to join them. Mtskheta was one of the places I had wanted to see, but I hadn't wanted to spend $50 for a car and driver, and although it was accessible by public transportation, it would have taken most of the day just getting there and back. I, therefore, readily accepted his offer. I told him that I'd be happy to help pay the cost, but he said the van was only $20 more than a car would have been, and it was his treat, as he would be happy to have the company—obviously, he was spending Euros at German salary levels; not soms at Kyrgyz salary levels. It turned out that one of those in our group was an art historian specializing in architecture, so it was both an informative and enjoyable trip.

The two highlights of the Mtskheta trip were the Jvari Monistary and the Svetitskhoveli Cathedral. The former was built high on a hill overlooking the ancient city in the 6th Century, when Georgia was summarily converted (by royal edict) to Christianity. It was on the list of World Heritage Sites, and as that fact might suggest, was architecturally impressive. Its name meant "The Cross," because that's what it was shaped like. The latter was built near the center of the city in the 11th Century, primarily as a burial vault for Georgian kings. Its name meant "Life-Giving Pillar." Legend had it that it was constructed on the grave of Saint Sidonia, who (legend also had it) was wrapped in Christ's cape when he was buried. After lunch Wolfgang and I spent all afternoon walking around Tbilisi. The name (aptly) meant "Warm Place," as the city was built in the 4th Century around and near a series of hot sulphur springs. It lived up to its name the first week in March, as we spent the afternoon in our shirtsleeves. We wandered through the beautiful (although a bit seedy) botanical gardens. We climbed the steep path to the Narikala fortress, which towered over and protected the city from the 4th through the 8th Century. We walked around the Turkish Baths, heated naturally (from the smell of them) by one of the aforementioned springs. We visited several churches, a mosque, and a synagogue, all within three blocks of each other, testament to the relative harmony the people of Georgia enjoyed. Mostly, though, we just wound our way through the narrow streets of the older part of the city, past many monuments (of both the uplifting Communist and the post-Soviet variety), and too many architecturally impressive structures to enumerate. One site we didn't visit, but got a good look at from the walls of the fort, was the almost-completed gigantic neo-classical cathedral the city fathers had seen fit to spend millions of dollars building on the highest point in the city. Well, the highest point other than the one already occupied by the fort. I assumed they couldn't see their way clear to providing a spot for what some thought was a monument to self-glorification, by razing that 1600-year-old structure, choosing to raze the dwellings of hundreds of their citizens instead.

The Narikala fortress, which towered over and protected the city of Tbilisi from the 4th through the 8th Century.

Wolfgang left Monday on one of the pre-dawn flights so common to that part of the world. As mine was one of the almost as common flights that left late afternoon and arrived pre-dawn, I spent Monday morning wandering the city by myself. The company wasn't as good, and we had covered the most impressive sights, but it was still a great way to pass a beautiful morning. We took George W. Bush Highway (evidence of how low some governments would stoop to massage the egos of those on whom they thought such action might be accompanied by a loosening of purse strings) to the airport for our 3:00 p.m. (mostly sleepless) flight to Moscow, and subsequently (also mostly sleepless) to Bishkek. I made it home in time to take a shower, shave, change clothes, and make it to my 9:30 class.

We assumed that it must have officially been spring when they turned the heat off in our apartment the second week in March. Actually, that was no problem, as we'd been walking around in our shirtsleeves for a couple of weeks by then.

We spent four days of our spring break in Osh. It was located in the Fergana Valley in the southwest, and with a population of about 300,000, was the second-largest city in Kyrgyzstan. It was an ancient city (5th Century BC), but most of its antiquities had been replaced with what Cooper referred to as "Uplifting Communist Art" during Soviet times. It was still more Soviet than most cities in the former USSR. A huge statue of Lenin graced the park in front of the municipal administration building, and one of the main streets bore his name. Its population was 40 percent Uzbek and heavily Muslim, but we never felt threatened, or even unwelcome. The people were generally less attractive than those in Bishkek, and more openly curious about us. Jesse's lip ring, beard, and long hair drew relatively constant (curious rather than unfriendly) stares. English was much less in evidence than in Bishkek, and at times we felt as though we were auditioning for parts in a mime troupe. We flew down and back, as a very high mountain range (complete with large snow drifts) separated it from Bishkek, and we had no desire to spend our break snowbound—also because it cost only about $80 apiece round trip. Everything in Osh was cheaper than in Bishkek. I was appalled when the manager of the hotel told me we would have to get a separate room for Jesse—until she told me the rooms were 400 soms ($10) each. We treated ourselves to very nice dinners at a couple of the fanciest restaurants in town for less than $15 for the three of us.

The morning we left Bishkek, we went to the airport in our shirtsleeves. We had to talk Jesse into taking even a light jacket "just in case." So of course Osh was cold and rainy for all but the last day—enough so that Jesse 1) admitted he was glad he had listened to us about the jacket, and 2) even deigned to borrow one of my long sleeved shirts to wear under it. Intrepid travelers that we were, we went out when it was sprinkling, holing up in our rooms only the one morning that it rained hard, and we had a great time despite the inclement weather. The first afternoon we found our hotel—no small feat, as it 1) wasn't where it was shown on the map in the guidebook; 2) had nothing identifying it as any hotel, let alone the one we were looking for; and 3) was on the second and third floors, accessed by narrow stairs on the side of the building. It made it a bit easier that we happened to get a taxi driver who took us right there and had us wait in the car while he went up and got the manager to come down and meet us. I tipped him nicely. The hotel was a bit run down, with hard beds, small rooms, and tiny baths; and it was near the intersection of two main streets, so was very noisy; but for people who had learned to sleep in the cities of India, it was a piece of cake. We spent the rest of the afternoon just walking around, getting a feel for the place.

We spent most of the next day exploring the huge Jayma Bazaar, which ran along one side of the river through about half the town. The Lonely Planet guidebook said it was, "one of Central Asia's best markets, teeming with Uzbeks, Kyrgyz, and Tajiks dealing in everything from traditional hats and knives to pirated cassettes, horseshoes, Chinese tea sets, and abundant seasonal fruits and vegetables." I couldn't have said it better myself. We stopped at one of the many little cafes scattered throughout the bazaar for lunch. A couple of tables away two middle-aged (obviously upper-middle class) women were knocking back one shot of vodka after another, and judging by their salubrious demeanor, had been doing so for some time (a common occurrence for men, but quite unusual for women). Eventually (as is often the case when someone has been knocking back one drink of anything after another), one of them got up (then sat back down; then got up again, a bit more slowly) to go to the bathroom. A few minutes later, as she made her way determinedly back past our table, she missed a step and stumbled into Laurie's chair, which she used to maintain her balance. She smiled rather sheepishly and apologized in Russian. Subsequently, the other woman undertook the same excursion. It became quickly apparent that she was in even less suitable condition to do so. She made it as far as our table, where she paused to lean on Laurie and adjust her bearings. Obviously feeling the need to explain the situation to us, she began speaking in animated and rapid-fire Russian, not one word of which I, and only two (but luckily the critical two) of which Laurie understood: "den rojdenia:" "birthday." When she realized that Laurie actually understood that it was her birthday, the woman became (if possible) even more effusive. She asked Laurie something in Russian, and it was obvious from her body language that she wanted a birthday hug. Laurie was happy to oblige, and the woman added a kiss on each cheek for good measure. It was such moments that made any small inconveniences that went with life in a developing country all but meaningless.

After lunch, we again immersed ourselves in the cacophony of the market. I bought dessert: a small bag of sesame seed covered peanuts—delicious. A couple of hours (and several kilometers) later, at the far end of the market, on the edge of the city, we came across several small forges and carpentry shops where men were creating metal pieces and furniture from raw materials with the most rudimentary tools. I could have spent hours watching them, but Laurie and Jesse dragged me away. We wandered along the other side of the river, back to our hotel. After a couple of hours to recuperate, we set out for dinner.

The next day was still drizzly and cool, but we decided to climb to Solomon's Throne anyway. We set off across town, but didn't get far before we came across a couple of young men trying to pull a heavily-loaded two-wheeled cart up a hill to the market. It was the kind of cart meant to be pulled by a donkey, and if that had been the case, they'd have had no problem, but the two of them just weren't the equivalent of one donkey. It wasn't all that big a hill, but it was a very heavy cart. They had gotten it up about a quarter of the way, but it was the least steep quarter, and they were clearly running out of steam. Jesse and I rushed over, grabbed one of the ropes, and gave it all we had. Several other men stopped to watch, and a couple pitched in and pushed from below. It wasn't quick, and it wasn't pretty, but the six of us got it to the top. The two pushers, when they saw we had it, waved and went back down to the street. We were all pretty exhausted, and sat down to rest for a while. After we recuperated, the young men were clearly very grateful for our help, and wanted to give us some of the rice from their load. We didn't want to seem ungrateful for their offer, and it took a lot of pantomime to make them understand that we had no way to get it home with us. After many more enthusiastic "thank you"s, the young men set off for the market, and Jesse, Laurie, and I continued our trip to King Solomon's Throne.

A huge, jagged rock outcropping that towered over the city, it was named for King Solomon, who vied with several others (including Alexander the Great) for credit as the founder of Osh. The site had long been a Muslim holy place, because the Prophet Mohammed supposedly

Jesse and I helping pull a heavy cart up a hill to the market in Osh.

once prayed there. Seven hundred and fifty stone and concrete steps (of greatly varying height) wound around the east face of the rock, depositing us at the top, where we could look out over the entire city (at least as much of it as wasn't obscured by the pall emitted from various smokestacks scattered about). The best view was of a huge Muslim cemetery spread out around the base of the mountain. Perched on the top was Dom Babura (Babur's House), a small, private mosque built in the 15th Century by the 14-year-old king of the region. It had been destroyed and rebuilt several times since, most recently about ten years before. A path of about half a mile (and incorporating another 350 steps—some down; others up) along the south side of the mountain brought us to the most bizarre-looking museum we had ever seen. The Soviets, with a significant dynamite charge, had enlarged the entrance to one of the caves that dotted the side of the mountain, and covered the resulting gaping hole with a sheet metal and glass face that (to say the least) looked a bit out of place in the otherwise pastoral setting. "Funky" fell a bit short of describing the threadbare exhibits inside, but the structure

Dom Babura, a 15th Century mosque, repurposed
by the Soviets as a bizarre-looking museum.

of the cave itself was interesting. Jesse's and my favorite exhibit was a ratty stuffed animal that looked like a cross between a bear and a dachshund. Laurie said she thought there really were bears in existence with stumpy little legs like that, but I remained skeptical.

Our first two evenings, we had been treated to wonderful dinners in two restaurants, so looked forward that evening to another great experience in a third—but it was not to be. Our luck had run out in a big way. We chose a nice looking place, but almost didn't go in when we realized there was a (very loud) wedding reception going on upstairs. One of the waiters saw our hesitation, and (in Russian and sign language) hastened to assure us that the raucous atmosphere would be limited to the floor above, and would not diminish our dining experience. We asked him if he could reduce the volume on the background music in the dining room (as we were the only ones there—maybe that should have served as a warning). He hastened to do so, and we decided to give it a shot. He brought us menus. After much deliberation, made more complicated by the fact that they were in Russian, so our grasp of the details was tenuous, we chose three delicious-sounding (based on our limited comprehension) dishes—none of which were available, he informed us. We chose three more—nyet. OK, then, we asked, what did they have? He showed us three that he assured us were the most delicious they had to offer. We understood that one was chicken, one was beef, and one was something else. They seemed our best bet (I volunteered to take the "something else"), so we said OK. He brought us a basket of stale bread, and warm beer and Coke; then disappeared. Just as we were beginning to wonder if we were, in fact, going to get any dinner, three things happened relatively simultaneously: 1) a DJ entered, turned off all the lights except the lazar reflecting from the revolving crystal ball in the ceiling, turned the music up to a level guaranteed to cause at least moderate hearing loss after 12 seconds of exposure, and began to shout over it into a microphone; 2) the door to a private dining room opened, and the occupants (who had clearly been doing as much drinking as dining) poured out and began laughing, shouting, and dancing; and 3) our food arrived. We told our waiter that either we would take our food to one of the private rooms (which generally cost extra) or we would pay for our warm drinks and stale bread, and leave. He understood that we were not entirely pleased with our dining experience to that point, and hustled us into one of the private dining rooms (which had not been cleaned up following the exit of its former occupants). He moved their clutter to one end of the table, set us up at the other, and left, closing the door—which had no latch, and would not stay closed. He realized that would be a problem, so came back and wedged a folded napkin between the door and the jamb. The result diminished the racket barely enough to make it bearable. We ate in about ten minutes. My something else was awful, Jesse said his beef was pretty bad, and Laurie said her chicken was OK. I tasted it, and thought it fell significantly short of "OK."

The next morning Laurie and I let Jesse sleep in while we had breakfast of meat pies and tea (as we had every morning) at a tiny little place around the corner from the hotel. It consisted of a guy cooking the meat pies under an umbrella on the sidewalk; a dining area about eight feet square; waist-high shelves lining three walls; and low stools to sit on. I looked around while we ate, and counted 11 other diners sharing the space. After breakfast we spent an hour or so walking around the city; then went back to the hotel to take Jesse (as we had every morning) for his breakfast of sweet rolls at a little stand quaintly named (in English) "I Am Baker." After a couple of hours in the Silk Road Museum (nowhere near as impressive as the name implied,) and a late lunch at a nearby café, we returned to the hotel for our bags and took a taxi to the airport. We got on the plane about 6:00, and in an hour were back in Bishkek (as opposed to a 16-hour drive through the mountains—assuming we could have, in fact, gotten through the mountains without being snowed in).

The next week was a busy one, what with Nooruz (Muslim New Year) Tuesday, and the anniversary of last year's "Tulip" Revolution Friday. As nearly as we could tell, the thing to do on Nooruz was eat. All of the streets in the city center, which was mostly parks, walking malls, public squares, museums, and theatres, were blocked off, and literally hundreds of food stands were set up along them. Most of the offerings were: home made ice cream, plov (steamed, seasoned rice with a few vegetables and a teeny bit of meat—usually lamb—mixed in; some also with hard boiled eggs; prepared mostly for holidays), shashlyk (kebabs of lamb, beef, or chicken), manty (steamed dumplings), piroshki (deep fried dough; some filled with meat or mashed potatoes), samsi (meat pies), and samalak (prepared only by the women, and only on special holidays: wheat soaked in water for three days until it sprouted; then ground; mixed with oil, flour, and sugar; and cooked over low heat for 24 hours until it formed a substance sort of like sweet wallpaper paste mixed with mud). The shashlyk was grilled over charcoal fires, and there were so many going downtown Tuesday that in many places it looked like ground fog had settled in. Thank goodness it was a breezy day, which helped disperse the smoke a bit.

In addition to eating, we were treated to many folks dressed in traditional garb—some as costumes, but just as many old folks for whom that was just what they had always worn on holidays. For a few, coming in from the countryside, it was still their everyday dress. Stages were set up with young people singing, playing, and dancing to traditional music. There were numerous athletic contests such as ping-pong, tug-of-war, three-on-three basketball, arm wrestling, rock carrying (as in seeing who could carry a big bolder the farthest), and karate. The entertainment was rounded out (as on any holiday) with occasional areas where three or four young men had chalked out a circle about 20 feet in diameter and placed a 200 som note (about $5) in the center and four 100 som notes around it; all anchored by what looked like bones from

*Making plov on the main square of Bishkek
during the Muslim New Year celebration.*

the backs of cows. Men gathered around the circle, and payed one som
to throw a fist-sized bone and try to knock the bone off one of the bills.
If they did so, they could keep the bill. Theoretically, it sounded good:
the chance to make a 200 percent profit on their money. The problem
was that, although I assumed it was technically possible, we spent a lot
of time during the various holidays watching many men try, and had
never seen anyone actually do it.

The anniversary of last year's "Tulip" Revolution on Friday was pretty much a repeat of Tuesday, only with lots more police and soldiers in evidence, including mounted police and the K-9 unit. Actually, we only assumed they were in evidence, as we saw several horses and German shepherds tied to trees in one of the parks. Rumor had it that we should hunker down in our apartment, as violence was sure to erupt. We paid as much attention to that advice as we had in 1999, when the U. S. Secretary of State virtually forbade Americans overseas to venture out during what she had been assured by the "U.S. intelligence community" would be widespread global violence directed at Americans in celebration of the new millennium. Actually, during New Year of 2000, we spent a couple of weeks in Turkey, whereas Friday we only went downtown, so I suppose we were relatively conservative. At any rate, the rumors (as rumors are wont to be) were completely wrong. Not once, all day, did we get even an inkling that anybody was interested in anything but fun—except maybe when (completely without warning) the army shot off four rounds (blanks, I assumed) from what sounded like 50 mm cannons. Now that got everybody's attention. Jesse said it felt like somebody had poured pop-rocks into his bloodstream. It certainly did make my heart go pitty-pat. A second difference was the parade, com-

The Kyrgyz army making a show of force in Bishkek during the anniversary of the "Tulip" Revolution.

plete with the half of the army that was not dispersed throughout the downtown area. They spent a lot of time with the army band playing stirring martial music to accompany a review of the troops by a couple of high mucky-mucks (probably the president and the commanding general of the army; but we couldn't get close enough to see for sure), and several stirring-sounding speeches interrupted occasionally by loud huzzahs from the assembled troops and perhaps a few significantly less enthusiastic huzzahs from a smattering of assembled onlookers. These festivities were followed by the passing in review of six troop carriers, four trucks pulling wheeled cannons, and two missile launchers. Then three helicopters (with huge flags fluttering beneath them) did a fly-by. We thought that was it, but the best was yet to come. The helicopters came back; that time much higher, and disgorged three skydivers each. The first trio trailed smoke; the second did tricks such as linking up for part of their descent; but the third really impressed everybody when they exploded. Well, they didn't really explode, but it certainly looked like they had at first, when they set of fireworks part way down.

Speaking of fireworks, we were in our apartment late that evening when a tremendous explosion shook the building, rattling the windows, and setting off every car alarm within a half mile. At first we thought the revolutionaries had just waited until dark to attack the parliament building (two blocks away) and the White House (four blocks); but then we realized it was just the opening salvo of what turned out to be one of the most impressive fireworks displays we had ever seen. Coincidentally, another impressive one was over the Blue Mosque in Istanbul in celebration of New Year 2000—the very one we would have missed had we heeded the wishes of our Secretary of State at the time.

Jesse showing off what the Easter Bunny brought him.

Chapter 7
April

Well, once again rumors of impending disaster were greatly overstated. I was working in my office about 4:30 the first Friday afternoon in April, when one of the university security guards opened the door and seemed very concerned that I was there. He told me (some Russian; some English; some sign language) that classes and other events (including an April Fool's celebration scheduled for 4:00) had been cancelled, and everyone was supposed to have left by 4:00. They had it on good authority that a revolution was planned for that evening. As the Parliament building was right next door, and as they generally went home at 5:00, and as it wouldn't make much sense to have a revolution after they had left, and as it was then 4:30, it seemed that doom was, as they say, "impending." So, at his urging, I shut down my computer and closed my office. He hustled me out the back door, and I went home. On the way, I noticed a proliferation of police, and an abundance of army, but a paucity of protesters. The entire downtown area was cordoned off, and rush hour traffic (luckily, there was not really all that much, even on Friday, so the disruption was minimal) was being routed around about a nine-block area. No screaming or gunfire interrupted our sleep, nor when Laurie and I walked around Saturday did we see anything untoward. By Sunday, the police, the army, and their attendant cordons were no longer in evidence. The protesters—revolutionaries, as the government insisted—to the best of our knowledge, never had been. It rained pretty continuously (although certainly not very heavily) all weekend, so that could have quashed their zeal (from what we've seen and heard, it didn't take much quashing). At any rate, it seemed some officials once again got pretty excited over nothing.

The Easter bunny managed to find Jesse. He got an Easter basket—not packed in great abundance, but he seemed happy with it. We attended Maundy Thursday services at the International Church (the only one in town with services in English). We were walking home on that gorgeous spring evening, when Jesse piped up with, "I really miss going to church back home." After all the Sundays we'd had to virtually drag him out of bed, all I could do was gape at him in response. We had heard about this church when we first came to Bishkek, and thought we'd give it a try. A series of circumstances conspired to discourage us, however. First, the woman who told us about it was, shall we say, evangelistic, so we assumed it would be a very conservative congregation. Second, it was part of a seminary operated by Scottish Presbyterians; so again, we expected conservatism beyond that with which we would be comfortable. Third, we walked by to have a look, and found it surrounded by an 8-foot high brick wall, complete with locked solid-steel gates, so that we couldn't even see in, let alone enter. Fourth, we went there at the time we thought the woman had said Sunday services began, and the gate was locked, with nobody around. So, basically, we let it slide. Laurie felt compelled to go to the Maundy Thursday service, however, and we found the pastor and his wife were warm, welcoming folks. The service was low-key and quite ecumenical; anything but conservative. We were really sorry that we hadn't started going when we first arrived.

We had the four young Turkmen women who are Jesse's friends, and two "single" (in that they are there alone) professors over for Easter dinner. At least two of the young women, and one of the professors were vegetarian, so in addition to Swedish meatballs, we had stuffed mushroom caps, cowboy caviar (a salad made from chick peas, two kinds of beans, cold corn, chopped tomatoes, cilantro, and spices), and pasta with black olives and cheese sauce. Not our usual Easter dinner, but it wasn't our usual Easter. After dinner Laurie cleaned up, I washed dishes, and Jesse played host, teaching them the card game "Phase 10." In all, it was a very nice day; we felt blessed.

Near the middle of April it hit us how little time we had left: only a month of school; then two months of travel, and we'd be home. As always, we had mixed feelings—balancing what we'd lose there with what (and especially who) we miss at home.

For a couple of weeks in April, on the days I went in about 8:00, I got to watch the Shoro folks setting up their stands. Shoro was the brand name of a ubiquitous summer drink made from fermented barley. The best I could describe the taste was a mix of buttermilk, tonic water, vinegar, and wheat germ. We tried it, and it ranked second only to fermented mare's milk. It must have been an acquired taste, as the Kyrgyz loved it. The trucks dropped off plastic barrels at virtually every intersection; two at the busy ones—the one nearest our apartment, for example, which adjoined the parliament building, one corner of the busiest city park, a hotel, and an apartment block. Young women (it must not have been considered suitable work for men, as we never saw one doing it) sat on very uncomfortable looking stools all day serving passersby small paper cups full for 3 soms (about seven cents); large ones for five soms (about 12 cents). On hot days, people actually lined up, waiting to be served. Most of the customers were on foot, but occasionally cars stopped—sometimes pulling up onto the sidewalk, so as to not block the street. It seemed to be seasonal work for all but the best looking (and shapeliest) of the women. They seemed to keep their jobs all year, dressed in mini-skirts and skimpy tops (maybe the choice of career apparel discouraged male participation), trolling the crowds at conferences, expos, and department stores with free samples during the off-season.

Much of the food in Kyrgyzstan was very tasty, and we took to it from the beginning. One, however, that neither Laurie nor I were crazy about at first (unlike Jesse, who had never been able to get enough), but it gradually grew on us, was hamburgers. They didn't do "h," so the resulting pronunciation was "gom boo'gur. Even in that permutation, the name was still the most familiar part. Well, actually, that's not true—the bun was pretty much the same. They started by spreading their version of mayonnaise (runnier and blander) on the bun. Next came the meat, which was similar to that in Greek gyros: shaved from a loaf roasting on a vertical spit, but not nearly as much of it—one sandwich contained about a large tablespoonful. They added two slices of cucumber and one of tomato (except for Jesse, who had never considered tomatoes edible), and the equivalent of a couple of tablespoons of coleslaw and one of French fries. That mélange was topped with a generous dollop of ketchup and another slather of mayonnaise. They were available exclusively from street vendors, who (as the ingredients were pretty much the same for all of them), tried to outdo each other in the showmanship they exhibited in constructing their offerings. They served them in small plastic bags—true of just about everything in Bishkek, which fact, coupled with the fact that virtually everyone dropped trash on the ground wherever they happened to be when they deemed it no longer useful, resulted in hundreds of them collecting in the ditches and lee sides of structures. Their version of the hamburger, however, was so messy that without the bag we would probably have gotten more on, than in us.

Laurie, Jesse, and I at the farewell party given by the students in my thesis class.

Chapter 8
May

Following the tried and true Blackwood/Buehler if-you-hear-loud-music-somewhere-follow-it principle, at 10:00 a.m. the first Saturday in May (an absolutely glorious spring morning) we went looking for the music we could hear from our apartment. It sounded as though it were coming from the stairwell of our building, but from experience, we knew that placed it several blocks away. Sure enough, we found a stage set up in Ala-too Square, at the center of the city, four blocks south. Traffic was being routed around the square, a marching band was warming up, and a crowd was gathering (many in matching athletic gear, looking a lot like teams). Various traditional ethnic groups were performing on the stage. Laurie deciphered a couple of words on a banner stretched across one of the buildings fronting the square, and said she thought it had something to do with sports (not a bad guess, given the number of people who looked as though they were waiting to compete in a sporting event). She asked a young woman who looked as though she might be a college student (therefore most likely to speak some English), and she confirmed that we were observing Bishkek Health and Sport Day. We ordered coffee at a nearby outdoor café, and awaited the heating up of festivities, an eventuality, it gradually became clear, that was not approaching with any great alacrity. The marching band did so (for one block), and traditional acts kept appearing on the stage, but little else seemed imminent. At any rate, we allowed as how it was far too nice a day to spend sitting around. Besides, at a very similar celebration the past fall all that had happened was a lot of pretty out-of-shape people looked like they had a lot of fun playing games that looked like they might have been fun to play, but were fun to watch for only about 15 minutes. So we went for a walk. I doubted we missed much, and if we did, we'd probably never know what it was, and besides, we had a great walk.

On the evening of our last day of classes, the seniors from my thesis class threw a party for us at one of the better restaurants in town. Their theses were the most important work they had done as undergraduates, and would probably have an effect on their applications to graduate school in the States. They were, therefore, the students with whom I had spent the most time, and been the strictest. As with any Kyrgyz party, there was much food and drink, much singing and dancing, and much laughter. They presented Jesse and me with traditional felt hats.

A fewof my best students held back after everyone else had left, and gave me a small Kyrgyz sand painting. I thanked them for their thoughtfulness, but had no idea just how thoughtful it was until we got back to the apartment, and I noticed that they had written personal messages on the back. The message from my best student was:

Dr. Blackwood—
     Heartfelt thank you for teaching me that harsh but very useful lesson. To me you are like a strict semi-professor/semi-father figure. May God never leave you.   Synat

Faced with such a heartfelt message, it was difficult not to feel great joy about the year: in what we had given, but far greater, in what we had received.

We flew to Estonia May 20; travelled to Latvia, Lithuania, Poland, Ukraine, Slovakia, Hungary, Croatia, Slovenia, Bosnia Herzegovina, and Serbia Montenegro; flew to Los Angeles from Belgrade on July 13; spent a few days with our daughter, McCall, her husband, Kyle, and Harper, our granddaughter, who was three weeks old by then; drove the 1971 Volkswagen that McCall gave Jesse to Billings, where we spent 10 days with Laurie's family; and drove it on home to Bemidji, Minnesota, where we arrived August 1st.

Afterword

Some thoughts about spending time in other countries: Laurie and I had discussed at great length the possibilities. I had spent considerable time in other cultures, but she hadn't. After we were married, I confined my excursions to no more than a month or two at a time, every couple of years, to avoid gaping holes in our family relationship. I didn't feel satisfied with that, however, because such short visits never get you out of the honeymoon stage of experiencing a culture. Laurie also wanted to try living in another culture for an extended period. I had a sabbatical coming in 1988-89, and Laurie wasn't working outside our home, so we saw it as a good opportunity. After a year of family life in China, we were both able to address the attendant questions more knowledgeably. We decided we wanted—and wanted Cooper and Jesse—to experience other cultures in that depth, but we also didn't want to give up our roots in Bemidji. After a lot of discussion, we decided that one year away and four at home would be the right mix. Although we chose countries where I would have a position teaching at a university, Laurie had the opportunity to teach, as well. In China, she taught English for the Foreign Languages Department at Liaoning University, where I taught Journalism and English Literature. As we could get no child care for Jesse, we juggled our schedules to share that responsibility. She felt a bit disconnected there, however, because she was treated as my spouse, and thus as a second-class citizen. In Thailand, she felt much better. Monday, Wednesday, and Friday, she taught English at the Thai grade school Cooper and Jesse attended, and Tuesday and Thursday she taught English at Bangkok University, a high-class private college. She felt much better, because the teachers at the boys' school went out of their way to include her in things, take her to lunch, buy her gifts, and invite our whole family to outings the teachers of various classes arranged. We also became good friends with a Thai couple who had boys about Cooper's and Jesse's ages, so had close personal contact with much of the Thai culture. In Bulgaria, Laurie became good friends with a Bulgarian woman, and we also became good friends with a Russian woman who had lived in Bulgaria for much of her life. Also, we had lived in other cultures for two years, so were more adaptable. The major problem there was for Jesse. He was 13, a tough age for most boys; made tougher for him because there was no school appropriate for him. In Kyrgyzstan, Laurie and I made no close friends, but we had enough experience in

545

other cultures that it was relatively easy for us to blend in. Cooper and Annie were in their first year of marriage, so were pretty well ensconced in their own private world. Jesse was going to the university there, and made friends with several other students. The dynamics in each of the four experiences were somewhat different, but the joy of experiencing aspects of life with which we would never have come in contact had we not taken the plunge, was life changing.

I have always felt that Westerners, and especially those from the United States, are generally myopic in their view of the world and others in it. They seem to think that in every case, not only is theirs the best way, but the only reasonable way to do things. I have never been able to accept that attitude. Also, I saw our students at BSU existing in a state of parochialism that bordered on xenophobia. They seemed to think that a weekend drunk in Winnipeg constituted a valid international experience. I didn't want my children to be like that, and I didn't want to unconsciously foster that attitude in others through my ignorance, so I spent time experiencing other cultures. I was blessed with a wife and children who were responsive to the experiences. As a result of our experiences, I think we are more sensitive to the needs of those who are different from us—not just of different nationalities, but different in any substantive way. Both Cooper and Jesse are much more comfortable interacting with people who have mental or physical handicaps than are most young people. When new children came into their classes at school or came to our church, both boys seemed more open to accepting them and making friendly overtures—especially if they were of another culture. Numerous international students at BSU told me they experienced prejudice from other students and from faculty, but that I had a reputation for being sensitive to their needs and treating them fairly without coddling them. But the greatest difference is much more selfish. We have seen views, and experienced events that few others have. We have accumulated a store of shared memories that nobody or nothing can ever negate. We have functioned successfully for extended periods in surroundings foreign to us, and as a result, we have become convinced that we are "the masters of our fate." We can act, rather than wait to be acted upon. I had a friend once who's job it was to enlist American faculty for a multidisciplinary roster of professors who wanted to teach in other countries. He told me the easiest thing in the world was to find people who wanted to live and teach overseas; the hardest thing was to find one of them who would actually do it. When the iron hits the fire, people find it's impossible to pull up and move "right at this time." There are always numerous reasons why "now" is impossible—and they're right. Jesse was going into first grade—an impossible time to take him out of school. Cooper was very active in the hockey program, and was at the critical point when the coaches started dividing the boys into teams based on their potential—an impossible time to take Cooper out of the program. Many other situations all made it impossible for us to go "just now." But there would have been others the next year, and the year after. Closing down four lives for a year is a daunting task: finding someone to rent your house, taking care of the car and truck, going without medical and dental insurance for a year, figuring out how to take care of financial obligations, and on, and on. We weren't sure how much a year would cost us, or whether, without borrowing, we'd have money to live on between the time we got back and when I started getting paid again. Our best guess was that we'd be down about $10,000, but our attitude was that we'd rather have that experience than a new car. I had gotten the distinct impression that the attitude of the my university's administration was "enough is enough, already." They talked internationalization, and little bits spread throughout the faculty was fine, but I'd carried it entirely too far. I'd lost sight of what was good for the university, and was seeking personal gain. Consequently, I noticed a cooling in their attitude toward my efforts, and in their willingness to support them—psychologically or financially. Because we wanted the boys to experience other cultures, and meet children from those cultures, we put them in their schools, rather than international schools. Their schools weren't geared to teaching the material the boys needed to pass into their next grades, however, so we needed to home school them, as well. It was hard for them (and us) to look forward to another two or three hours of school after a full day in school. These were not highly developed countries, and consequently we had to make do with much less than we had at home. We got tired sometimes of cold showers. I had to have a root canal done, and would have preferred some novocain. A small canal flowed by one of our apartment buildings that was so polluted I'm sure we could have walked on the "water." We had to buy our drinking water in plastic bottles. I wanted some cheese. I could go on, but I can also say that no more than two days would pass that something didn't happen to make me stop and smile, because I knew I could have lived a lifetime in the States and not had the experience. It was a wonderful feeling.

Roy Blackwood, was raised on a small farm in northwestern Pennsylvania. After graduating from high school, he spent four years in the Marine Corps, one-and-a-half years of that time in Panama. After his release from the military, he spent a year at the University of Alaska, six months as a reporter for the "Daily News" in Anchorage, and eight months traveling in Southeast Asia.

He has a BA from Cleveland State University with majors in theatre and English literature; and an MA in theatre, and a Phd in adult education and communication from Cornell University. He taught at the University of Illinois for four years, and at Bemidji State University for 23 years, retiring in 2005.

In 1982 he served as a United States Agency for International Development consultant on use of audio visual materials to the government of Guyana, South America; in 1987 was one of 16 selected for the first study tour of the Chinese media by U.S. academics; and in 1990 was one of 20 Minnesota State University faculty selected to receive a Fulbright Travel Grant for a six-week study tour of Costa Rica.

He taught journalism at Liaoning University in Shenyang, China, in 1988-89; at Chulalongcorn University, Bangkok, Thailand, in 1993-94; American University in Bulgaria in Blagoevgrad, Bulgaria, in 1999-2000; and American University of Central Asia in Bishkek, Kyrgyzstan, in 2005-06.

Since his retirement in 2005, he has spent about 1800 hours a year doing volunteer work for 12 local organizations. In his spare time, he has restored a 1971 Volkswagen and a 1951 Chevrolet. He is currently working on placing a 1958 Chevrolet pickup body on a 2001 Dodge pickup frame, engine, and running gear.

CPSIA information can be obtained
at www.ICGtesting.com
Printed in the USA
FFHW021805260319
51230503-56731FF